INTERNATIONAL LAW

VOLUME I
THE GENERAL WORKS

INTERNATIONAL LAW

BEING THE COLLECTED PAPERS OF

HERSCH LAUTERPACHT
Q.C., LL.D., F.B.A.

SYSTEMATICALLY ARRANGED AND
EDITED BY
E. LAUTERPACHT, Q.C.

VOLUME I
THE GENERAL WORKS

CAMBRIDGE UNIVERSITY PRESS
CAMBRIDGE
LONDON NEW YORK MELBOURNE

CAMBRIDGE UNIVERSITY PRESS
Cambridge, New York, Melbourne, Madrid, Cape Town, Singapore, São Paulo, Delhi

Cambridge University Press
The Edinburgh Building, Cambridge CB2 8RU, UK

Published in the United States of America by Cambridge University Press, New York

www.cambridge.org
Information on this title: www.cambridge.org/9780521109499

© Elihu Lauterpacht 1970

This publication is in copyright. Subject to statutory exception
and to the provisions of relevant collective licensing agreements,
no reproduction of any part may take place without the written
permission of Cambridge University Press.

First published 1970
Reprinted 1978
This digitally printed version 2009

A catalogue record for this publication is available from the British Library

Library of Congress Catalogue Card Number: 70-92250

ISBN 978-0-521-07643-2 hardback
ISBN 978-0-521-10949-9 paperback

CONTENTS

Sir Hersch Lauterpacht	*frontispiece*
Preface	*page* vii
Table of Cases	xi
Abbreviations	xvii
I INTERNATIONAL LAW—THE GENERAL PART	1
Editor's Note	2
Contents	5
Text	9
II GENERAL RULES OF THE LAW OF PEACE	179
Editor's Note	181
Contents	183
Author's Preface	189
Text	193
III SURVEY OF INTERNATIONAL LAW IN RELATION TO THE WORK OF CODIFICATION OF THE INTERNATIONAL LAW COMMISSION	445
Editor's Note	446
Contents	447
Text	449
Index	531

EDITOR'S PREFACE

Sir Hersch Lauterpacht's academic writings include five major monographs, of which two later appeared in much expanded revisions; four courses of lectures at the Hague Academy of International Law; over sixty articles; and two Reports on the Law of Treaties prepared for the International Law Commission. He prepared four editions of volume I, and three editions of volume II, of Oppenheim's *International Law*. He also edited Part III of the *Manual of Military Law*, containing 'The Law of War on Land'. This list leaves aside book reviews and notes, many of which it is difficult or impossible to trace. In addition, he wrote numerous unpublished memoranda and opinions. Finally, as a Judge of the International Court of Justice, he produced four Separate Opinions, two Dissenting Opinions, and a Declaration.

Although Lauterpacht's writing covered the full range of public international law, he never published a comprehensive treatise of his own. On looking at his work as a whole—and being anxious, in presenting his collected papers, to construct from them something which would serve both as a memorial to their author and as a work of lasting value to other international lawyers—it seemed to me that if the writings were assembled in a systematic form they might well stand as a substitute for the treatise that was never written. Each item has therefore been printed as if it were a chapter or a section of a comprehensive work covering the traditional divisions of international law—peace, disputes, war and neutrality. My hope is that, presented in this way, the whole will be greater than the sum of its parts.

The scheme which I have followed is based upon drafts (found amongst Lauterpacht's papers) of an outline of the textbook which he intended writing—though it has been necessary, of course, to make some adjustments to accommodate the available material. The contents of these volumes are, therefore, now divided into the following principal parts: 'International Law in General', covering the nature, history, sources and subjects of international law, as well as the relationship of international law and municipal law; 'States as Subjects of International Law', comprising recognition, State succession and jurisdiction; 'State Territory'; 'The Individual in International Law'; 'The Law of Treaties'; 'Organs of International Government'; 'The International Court of Justice'; 'Renunciation of Force'; and 'War and Neutrality'.

vii

EDITOR'S PREFACE

However, the collection begins, in this first volume, not with the material falling within the classification just described, but with three more general works—the newly written 'General Part' prepared for a ninth edition of Oppenheim that Lauterpacht never completed, an English text of the 'general' course of lectures delivered in French at the Hague Academy in 1937 and the *Survey of International Law in relation to the Work of Codification of the International Law Commission*, written for the United Nations in 1948. Their publication as the introductory volume of this collection requires no justification. A more detailed editorial note is printed before each of these items.

The contents of these volumes are limited to Lauterpacht's articles, published courses of lectures, reports and judgments. Within these categories, the collection is as complete as I can make it—save for various articles which were subsequently reprinted, almost unchanged in content, in some of his monographs. The subject principally affected is 'Recognition'. Between 1939 and 1945, Lauterpacht published a number of articles on various topics of Recognition which were then incorporated in his book on *Recognition in International Law* published in 1947. The same is true of some, though not all, of his works on human rights. The essential substance of the lectures given at the Hague Academy in 1947 and the Report on the subject presented to the International Law Association in 1948 reappear in the volume entitled *International Law and Human Rights* published in 1950. On the other hand, some of his earlier articles and lectures, for example on the doctrine of non-justiciable disputes, are included, though their content is largely reflected in his work on *The Function of Law in the International Community* (1933).

It has not been easy to reach the decision to exclude the articles mentioned above. The argument in favour of the complete presentation of all Lauterpacht's articles within these volumes is a cogent one. At the same time, the bulk of these Collected Papers already runs large without these articles; and the total size of the publication must be kept within reasonable limits. Moreover, *Recognition in International Law* is likely to be reprinted in the not too distant future with notes and comments bringing it up to date; and *International Law and Human Rights* has already been reprinted.

Also omitted from these volumes are book reviews—principally because, as comments upon the work of others, they do not properly belong in a work which is presented essentially as an exposition of the law. Nor have I been able to include all his occasional papers. Where

viii

EDITOR'S PREFACE

there exists a reasonably polished text, I have used it; but where there exist only rough notes or unrevised drafts, I have felt it best to omit these. Opinions written in a professional capacity have, with rare exceptions, also been excluded, largely because it has not been possible to secure the consent necessary for their publication.

Edited by anyone else than his son, these papers should no doubt have been introduced by some account of Lauterpacht's life and some over-all consideration of his work. But I am not the person to comment upon his work nor yet to write about his life. In any case, both tasks have already been carried out by the most qualified hands. To mention but some, Dr Jenks has written about Lauterpacht's contribution to international law in volumes XXXVI, XXXVII and XXXVIII of the *British Year Book of International Law*, as have Dr Rosenne, Judge Jessup and Professor Baxter in volume LV of the *American Journal of International Law*; while Lord McNair and Sir Gerald Fitzmaurice have written about his life in the *Proceedings of the British Academy*, volume XLVII, p. 371, and in *Graya*, the journal of Gray's Inn.

In planning this collection, I have had the great advantage of being able to turn for general guidance and help to a number of Hersch Lauterpacht's close friends: Lord McNair, Sir Gerald Fitzmaurice, Dr C. W. Jenks and Professor R. Y. Jennings. They are, of course, not responsible for what I have done; nor would they necessarily agree in every detail with my selection of items. But they have approved of the general scheme and have provided me with stimulus and encouragement, for which I am deeply grateful. In the actual execution of the work I have had important assistance from Dr Gillian White, Miss M. MacGlashan, Mrs A. B. Lyons, Mrs C. J. French, Miss A. Munkman, Miss E. Gawler, Mrs E. E. Jansen and Mrs S. Rainbow—to whom I express my warmest thanks. The personnel of the Cambridge University Press have tolerated the numerous delays which have beset the delivery of copy and the return of proofs with a tolerance and patience for which I remain much beholden. And last, but by no means least, I must say a word to acknowledge the loving concern which Hersch Lauterpacht's widow, my mother, Rachel Lauterpacht, has shown at every stage of the evolution of this work.

E. LAUTERPACHT

Trinity College
Cambridge
November 1969

TABLE OF CASES

Abu Dhabi Arbitration: *see under* Petroleum Development Ltd. *v.* Sheikh of Abu Dhabi

Acquisition of Polish Nationality, 246

Administrative Decision No. I (Tripartite Claims Commission—United States, Austria, and Hungary), 144, 292

Administrative Décision No. II (Mixed Claims Commission, U.S.–Germany), 75

Administrative Decision No. V (Mixed Claims Commission, U.S.–Germany), 292

Administrator of German Property *v.* Knoop, 144, 161, 291

Aix-la-Chapelle-Maastricht Railroad Company A. G. *v.* Thewis and Royal Dutch Government, Intervener, 374

Alabama Arbitration, 82, 241

Alsing Trading Co. *v.* The Greek State, 78

Ambatielos Claim, 86, 132

American-Mexican Claims Bureau *v.* Morgenthau, 144

Anglo-Norwegian Fisheries Case, 62, 69, 82

Annapolis, The, 157

Appam, The, 236

Application of the Convention of 1902 Governing the Guardianship of Infants, 40

Arbitration under Article 181 of the Treaty of Neuilly (Forests of Central Rhodope), 398

Arrow River and Tributaries Slide and Boom Co., Ltd., *Re,* 161, 226

Asylum Case, 43, 62, 63, 124

Austria (Emperor) *v.* Day and Kossuth, 45, 156

Bank of Ethiopia *v.* National Bank of Egypt and Liguori, 348

Bank voor Handel en Scheepvaart *v.* Slatford, 162

Barbuit's Case, 155

Bardoff *v.* Belgien, 223

Behring Sea Arbitration, 82, 241, 384, 425, 523

Bellon Case, 401

Berizzi Brothers Co. *v.* Steamship *Pesaro,* 484

Berli, *In re,* 174

Birma *v.* State, 161

Brazilian Loans Case; *see under* Payment in Gold of Brazilian Federal Loans Contracted in France

British Guiana Arbitration, 378

British Homophone Co. *v.* Kunz, 360

British Nylon Spinners Ltd. *v.* Imperial Chemical Industries, Ltd., 45

Brown (Robert E.) Case, 397, 398

Brunswick (Duke) *v.* King of Hanover, 156

Caire (Jean-Baptiste) Case, 401

Canadian Claims for Refund of Duties Case, 387

Canton of Thurgau *v.* Canton of St. Gallen, 356

Carthage, The, 394, 395

Cayuga Indians Claim, 85, 122

Certain German Interests in Polish Upper Silesia, Case concerning, 69, 70, 95, 132, 230, 245, 247, 249, 389, 390, 423

Certain Norwegian Loans, Case concerning, 25

Charming Betsey, The, 170

Chinn (Oscar) Case, 87, 359

Chorzów Factory Case, 69, 95, 137, 245, 292, 342

TABLE OF CASES

Chung Chi Cheung *v.* The King, 166

Civilian War Claimants' Association Ltd. *v.* The King, 144, 291

Clipperton Island Arbitration, 379, 380

Commercial and Estates Co. of Egypt *v.* Board of Trade, 156, 166, 167, 220

Competence of the International Labour Organisation (Regulation of Conditions of Work of Persons Employed in Agriculture), 96, 133

Competence of the International Labour Organisation to Regulate, Incidentally, the Personal Work of the Employer, 96

Contract between the Greek Government and the Société Commerciale de Belgique of 27 August 1925, Case concerning, 290

Cook *v.* United States (*The Mazel Tov*), 170, 343

Corfu Channel Case, 24, 70, 95

Crichton *v.* Samos Navigation Company and Others, 236

Cristina, The, 167, 484

Croft *v.* Dunphy, 157, 228

D., *In re*, 171

Danzig Railway Officials Case: *see under* Jurisdiction of the Courts of Danzig

De Haber *v.* The Queen of Portugal, 156

De Lovio *v.* Boit, 168

De Wutz *v.* Hendricks, 45, 156

Delimitation of the Polish-Czecho-slovakian Frontier (Question of Jaworzina), 69

Deserters at Casablanca Arbitration, 483

Desgranges *v.* International Labour Organisation, 74

Deutsche Celluloid Fabrik *v.* Schmerber, 360

Diaz *v.* Guatemala, 145

Dientz *v.* de la Jara, 171

Dirigo, The, 160

Diversion of Water from the River Meuse, 86, 244, 245, 249, 390

Doeuillet *v.* Randnitz, 360

Duff Development Company, Ltd. *v.* Government of Kelantan, 162

Eastern Carelia Case: *see under* Status of Eastern Carelia

Eastern Extension, Australasia and China Telegraph Co., Ltd. *v.* United States, 96

Eastern Greenland case: *see under* Legal Status of Eastern Greenland

Effect of Awards of Compensation made by the United Nations Administrative Tribunal, 69, 96

El Neptuno, The, 45

Engelke *v.* Musmann, 156

Estades *v.* French Government, 175

Factor *v.* Laubenheimer, 364

Farmer *et Al. v.* Rountree, 171

Fisheries Case: *see under* Anglo-Norwegian Fisheries Case

Forests of Central Rhodope case: *see under* Arbitration under Article 181 of the Treaty of Neuilly

Foster *v.* Driscoll, 44

Foster & Elam *v.* Neilson, 163

Fox, The, 165, 248

Francis *v.* The Queen, 161

Franconia, The (Reg. *v.* Keyn), 155, 156, 219, 221

Free Zones of Upper Savoy and the District of Gex, 69, 86, 235, 342, 356, 357, 385, 423, 425, 426, 509

Genocide Convention Case: *see under* Reservations to the Convention on Genocide

Gentini Case, 70

Georgina, The, 333

German Railway Station at Basle Case, 375

xii

TABLE OF CASES

German Settlers in Poland, 246, 300, 390

Glenroy, The, 165

Godman *v.* Winterton, 139

Goering and Others, *In re*, 148

Goldenberg & Sons *v.* Germany, 75, 244

Gordon (L. B.) Case, 402

Governo Rumeno *v.* Trutta, 484

Green, *In re*, 122

Grisbadarna Case, 132

Gschwind *v.* Swiss Confederation, 144

Guardianship Case: *see under* Application of the Convention of 1902 Governing the Guardianship of Infants

H. *v.* Public Prosecutor, 161

Hart *v.* Gumpach, 45

Heathfield *v.* Chilton, 156, 167

Hellfeld *v.* Russia, 171, 223

High Treason (Treaty of Versailles in Germany) Case, 281

Hilton *v.* Guyot, 45

Hines *v.* Davidowitz, 475

Home Frontier and Foreign Missionary Society of the United Brethren in Christ Case, 400

Hopkins (George W.) Case, 387

I'm Alone, The, 395, 396

Imperial and Royal Austrian Ministry of Finance *v.* Dreyfus, 171

Interest on Indemnities Arbitration, 356

Interhandel Case, 25, 171

International Institute of Agriculture *v.* Profili, 139

International Refugee Organisation *v.* Republic S. S. Corp., 139

International Status of South-West Africa, 142

Interpretation of the Convention of 1919 concerning Employment of Women During the Night, 96

Interpretation of the Greco-Turkish Agreement of December 1, 1926...70, 245

Interpretation of Peace Treaties with Bulgaria, Hungary and Romania, 24, 79

Interpretation of the Statute of the Memel Territory, 343

Interpretation of the Tardieu-Jaspar Agreement of January 12, 1930...76

Interpretation of the Treaty of Lausanne, Article 3, paragraph 2...69, 88, 236, 245, 420–1

Italy (Republic) *v.* Hambro's Bank, 161

Janes Case, 396

Jaworzina Case: *see* Delimitation of the Polish-Czechoslovakian Frontier (Question of Jaworzina)

Johanna Stoll, The, 157

Johnston *v.* Compagnie Générale Transatlantique, 45

Josserand *v.* Leclère, 360

Joyce *v.* Director of Public Prosecutions, 45, 490

Judgments of the Administrative Tribunal of the International Labour Organisation upon Complaints Made against UNESCO, 74, 139

Jurisdiction of the Courts of Danzig, 69, 133, 142, 288, 289, 291, 420

Kling Case, 71

Koninklijke Hollandsche Lloyd *v.* Dampskibsselskabet Torm A/S, 173

Kronprins Gustav Adolph, The, 88, 235

Labrador Boundary Case, 83

Lambert *v.* Jourdain, 173

Lauritzen *v.* Larsen, 170

Lazare Case, 134

Le Louis, The, 157

Legal Status of Eastern Greenland, 234, 338, 342, 343, 379, 492

xiii

TABLE OF CASES

Lena Goldfields Arbitration, 76, 77, 244, 290

Lighthouses in Crete and Samos, 372, 373

Lizzie Thompson, The, 333

Llandovery Castle, The, 285

Lockwood *v.* Coysgarne, 156

Lola, The, 250

Lopez *v.* Burslem, 157

Lotus, The Case of the S.S., 56, 62–3 81, 156, 221, 234, 488

Lusitania Case, 395

Luzon Sugar Refining Co. Case, 388

Macedonian, The, 333

Magdalena Steam Navigation Co. *v.* Martin, 156

Mallén Case, 396

Maria, The, 84, 165, 248

Maria Luz, The, 120

Martini Case, 230

Mavrommatis Palestine Concessions Case, 291, 292, 296

Mazel Tov, The: see under Cook *v.* United States

Mead (E. E.) Case, 400

Mecham (Laura A.) Case, 400

Mexico (Republic) *v.* Hoffman, 163 484

Minerva Automobiles Inc. *v.* United States, 170

Ministère Public *v.* Carillo-Frontello, 175

Minority Schools in Albania, 246

Minquiers and Ecréhos Case, 132, 134

Missouri *v.* Holland, 133, 159, 226, 475

Monetary Gold Removed from Rome in 1943...24

Mortensen *v.* Peters, 157, 165, 167, 220, 228

Mosul Boundary Case: *see under* Interpretation of the Treaty of Lausanne, Article 3, paragraph 2

National Bank of Egypt *v.* Austro-Hungarian Bank, 292

Naulilaa Arbitration (Damages), 395 n.

Navemar, The, 163

Neidecker Case, 365

Nereide, The, 169

Neuilly (Treaty of) Arbitration: *see under* Arbitration under Article 181 of the Treaty of Neuilly

New Jersey *v.* Delaware, 251

New York (State of) and Saratoga Springs Commission *v.* The United States of America, 484

New York, The, 158

North American Dredging Company Case, 144, 292

North Atlantic Coast Fisheries Arbitration, 374, 425, 525

Norwegian Loans Case: *see under* Certain Norwegian Loans, Case concerning

Norwegian Shipowners' Claims, 85

Novello *v.* Toogood, 45

Palmas Island Arbitration, 130, 131, 132, 379, 380

Paquete Habana, The, 170, 250

Parker (William A.) Case, 144, 292

Parlement Belge, The, 44, 45, 161, 226, 239

Payment in Gold of Brazilian Federal Loans Contracted in France, 356

Payment of Various Serbian Loans Contracted in France, 42, 82, 137, 291, 356

Pecuniary Claims of Danzig Railway Officials Transferred to the Polish Service: *see under* Jurisdiction of the Courts of Danzig

Pelletier Case, 134

Peru, *Ex parte,* 163

Pesaro, The: see under Berizzi Brothers *v.* Steamship *Pesaro*

xiv

TABLE OF CASES

Peter Pazmány University v. The State of Czechoslovakia (Appeal), 291, 390

Petroleum Development Ltd. v. Sheikh of Abu Dhabi, 77, 132

Pinson (Georges) Case, 86, 88, 235

Piracy *jure gentium, In re*, 250

Politis v. The Commonwealth, 157

Porter v. Freudenberg, 160, 227

Porto Alexandre, The, 484

Qatar (Ruler of) v. International Marine Oil Co., 78

Railway Traffic between Lithuania and Poland, 346

Receiver in Bankruptcy of the N.V. 'Zeilschip Nest' v. The State of the Netherlands, 144

Recovery, The, 84, 165, 248

Reg. v. Keyn: *see under Franconia, The*

Reparation for Injuries Suffered in the Service of the United Nations, 60, 88, 140, 146

Reparations Levy (Aliens in Germany) Case, 172

Repetti, Estate of, 173

Reservations to the Convention on the Prevention and Punishment of the Crime of Genocide, 54, 62

Respublica v. De Longchamps, 45, 142, 169, 170

Rhineland (German Legislation) Case, 376

Rights of Nationals of the United States of America in Morocco, 63, 132

Rose v. Himely, 163

Roumania (Kingdom of) v. Guaranty Trust Co. of New York, 484

Russian Socialist Federated Soviet Republic v. Cibrario, 45, 239, 327

Ryan v. United States of America, 134

Rylands v. Fletcher, 399

S.R. v. Bayerische Bierbrauerei zum Karlsberg, 360

Sarropoulos v. Bulgarian State, 70, 514

Savarkar, Arrest and Return of, 488, 523

Schooner Adeline, The, 165

Scotia, The, 158, 170

Serbian Loans Case: *see under* Payment of Various Serbian Loans Contracted in France

Sharma v. State of West Bengal and Others, 161

Sison v. The Board of Accountancy and Ferguson, 45

Socobel v. Greek State, 46

Southern Rhodesia, *In re*, 122

South-West Africa Case: *see under* International Status of South-West Africa

Spanish Zone of Morocco Claims, 389

Standard Oil Company Tankers Case, 387

Status of Eastern Carelia, 24, 79

Steevworden v. Société des Auteurs, 172

Steiner and Gross v. Polish State, 146, 289, 290, 291

Suarez, *In re*, 156

Succession in Obligations (Advance Payment of Duty) Case, 131

Syndicate of Co-owners of the Alfred Dehodencq Property Company, *In re*, 175

Talbot v. Three Brigs, 169

Thireaut case, 375

Timor Island Arbitration, 71

Tolten, The, 46

Totus v. United States, 122

Trail Smelter Arbitration, 487, 523

Treatment of Polish Nationals and Other Persons of Polish Origin or Speech in the Danzig Territory, 390

Triquet v. Bath, 155

TABLE OF CASES

Tunis and Morocco Nationality Decrees, 133
United States v. Claus, 170
United States v. Ferris, 343
United States v. Germany (Sources of Decision), 244
United States v. Guy W. Capps, Inc., 171
United States v. Milligan, 365
United States v. Pink, 475
United States v. Smith, 169–70
Verini v. Paoletti, 172
Vigoureux v. Comité des Obligataires Danube-Save-Adriatique, 140
Viveash v. Becker, 45, 156
Waghorn, In re, 69

Wakerville Brewing Co. v. Maynard, 44
Walker v. Baird, 160, 226
West (F. R.) Case, 396
West Rand Central Gold Mining Co. v. The King, 115, 156, 168, 220, 224, 267
Westage v. Harris, 44
Whitney v. Robertson, 170
Williams Case, 70
Wimbledon, The S.S., 385
Wing v. L. G. O., 399
Youmans Case, 401
Z. & F. Assets Realization Corporation *et Al. v.* Hull, 144
Zafiro, The, 401
Zamora, The, 165, 220, 248
Ziemer v. Rumänien, 223

ABBREVIATIONS

OF TITLES OF BOOKS, ETC., QUOTED IN
THIS VOLUME

The books referred to in the bibliographies and notes are, as a rule, quoted with their full titles and the date of their publication. But certain books and periodicals which are often referred to in this volume are quoted in an abbreviated form, as follows:

Accioly	Accioly, *Tratado de Direito internacional público*, 3 vols. (1933–5).
A.J.	*American Journal of International Law.*
Annuaire	*Annuaire de l'Institut de Droit International.*
Annual Digest	*Annual Digest and Reports of Public International Law Cases*: 1919–22, edited by Sir John Fischer Williams and H. Lauterpacht (1932); 1923–4, edited by the same (1933); 1925–6, edited by A. D. McNair and H. Lauterpacht (1929); 1927–8, edited by the same (1931); 1929–30 (1935); 1931–2 (1938); 1933–4 (1940); 1935–7 (1941); 1938–40 (1942); 1941–2 (1945); 1919–42 (supplementary volume) (1947); 1943–5 (1949); 1946 (1951); 1947 (1951); 1948 (1953); 1949 (1955)—all edited by H. Lauterpacht.
Anzilotti	Anzilotti, *Corso di diritto internazionale*, vol. I, 3rd ed. (1928), French translation by Gidel (1929); vol. III, part I (1915).
A.S. Proceedings	*Proceedings of the American Society of International Law.*
Balladore Pallieri	Balladore Pallieri, *Diritto internazionale pubblico* (1937).
Baty	Baty, *The Canons of International Law* (1930).
Bibliotheca Visseriana	*Bibliotheca Visseriana Dissertationum Jus Internationale Illustrantium.*
Bittner	Bittner, *Die Lehre von völkerrechtlichen Urkunden* (1924).
Bluntschli	Bluntschli, *Das moderne Völkerrecht der zivilisierten Staaten als Rechtsbuch dargestellt*, 3rd ed. (1878).
Borchard	Borchard, *The Diplomatic Protection of Citizens Abroad* (1915).
Br. and For. St. Papers	*British and Foreign State Papers* (Hertslet), vol. I (1841), continued up to date.
Brierly	Brierly, *The Law of Nations*, 5th ed. (1955).

ABBREVIATIONS OF TITLES OF BOOKS

Bustamante	Bustamante, *Derecho internacional público*, 3 vols. (1933–5).
B.Y.	*British Year Book of International Law.*
Calvo	Calvo, *Le Droit international théorique et pratique*, 5th ed., 6 vols. (1896).
Cavaglieri	Cavaglieri, *Lezioni di diritto internazionale* (general part, 1925).
Clunet	*Journal du droit international.*
Cruchaga	Cruchaga-Tocornal, *Nociones de Derecho internacional*, 3rd ed., 2 vols. (1923–5).
Dicey	Dicey, *Conflict of Laws*, 4th ed. (1927).
Dickinson, *Cases*	Dickinson, *Cases and Other Materials on International Law* (1950).
Documents	*Documents on Internatinoal Affairs.*
Fauchille	Fauchille, *Traité de droit international public*, 8th ed. of Bonfils' *Manuel de droit international public*, vol. I, part 1 (1922), vol. I, part 2 (1925), vol. I, part 3 (1926), vol. II (1921).
Fenwick	Fenwick, *International Law*, 3rd ed. (1948).
Fiore	Fiore, *Nouveau droit international public*. French translation by Antoine from the 2nd Italian edition, 3 vols. (1885).
Fiore, *Code*	Fiore, *International Law Codified*. Translation by Borchard from the 5th Italian edition (1918).
Fischer Williams, *Chapters*	Fischer Williams, *Chapters on Current International Law and the League of Nations* (1929).
Fontes Juris Gentium	*Fontes Juris Gentium*, edited by V. Bruns.
Garner, *Developments*	Garner, *Recent Developments in International Law* (1925).
Gemma	Gemma, *Appunti di diritto internazionale* (1923).
Genet	Genet, *Traité de diplomatie et de droit diplomatique*, 3 vols. (1931–2).
Gidel	Gidel, *Le droit international public de la mer, le temps de paix*: vol. I, *Introduction—La haute mer* (1932); vol. II, *Les eaux intérieures* (1932); vol. III, *La mer territoriale et la zone contiguë* (1934).
Grotius	Grotius, *De Jure Belli ac Pacis* (1625).
Grotius Annaire	*Grotius Annuaire International.*
Grotius Society	*Transactions of the Grotius Society.*
Guggenheim	Guggenheim, *Lehrbuch des Völkerrechts*, Parts 1 and 2 (1947).
Guggenheim, *Traité*	Guggenheim, *Traité de Droit International Publique*, vol. I (1953); vol. II (1954).
Hackworth	Hackworth, *Digest of International Law*, 7 vols. (1940–3).

xviii

ABBREVIATIONS OF TITLES OF BOOKS

Hague Recueil	*Recueil des Cours, Académie de Droit International de La Haye.*
Hall	Hall, *A Treatise on International Law*, 8th ed. (1924), by A. Pearce Higgins.
Harvard Research	*Research in International Law*. Under the Auspices of the Harvard Law School. Draft Conventions Prepared for the Codification of International Law. Directed by M. O. Hudson: (1929) I. *Nationality* (Reporter: Flournoy); II. *Responsibility of States* (Borchard); III. *Territorial Waters* (G. G. Wilson); (1932) I. *Diplomatic Privileges and Immunities* (Reeves); II *Legal Position and Functions of Consuls* (Quincy Wright); III. *Competence of Courts in regard to Foreign States* (Jessup); IV. *Piracy* (Bingham); V. *A Collection of Piracy Laws of Various Countries* (Morrison); (1935) I. *Extradition* (Burdick); II. *Jurisdiction with respect to Crime* (Dickinson); III. *Treaties* (Garner).
Heffter	Heffter, *Das europäische Völkerrecht der Gegenwart*, 8th ed. by Geffcken (1888).
Heilborn, *System*	Heilborn, *Das System des Völkerrechts entwickelt aus den völkerrechtlichen Begriffen* (1896).
Hertslet's *Commercial Treaties*	Hertslet, *Collection of Treaties and Conventions between Great Britain and Other Powers, so far as they relate to Commerce and Navigation*, vol. 1 (1820), continued to date.
Higgins and Colombos	Higgins and Colombos, *The International Law of the Sea*, 2nd ed. (1951).
H.L.R.	*Harvard Law Review.*
Holland, *Lectures*	Holland, *Lectures on International Law*, edited by T. A. and W. L. Walker (1933).
Holland, *Studies*	Holland, *Studies in International Law* (1898).
Holtzendorff	Holtzendorff, *Handbuch des Völkerrechts*, 4 vols. (1885–9).
Hudson, *Cases*	Hudson, *Cases and Other Materials on International Law*, 3rd ed. (1951).
Hudson, *Legislation*	Hudson, *International Legislation*: vols. I–XI (1931–50).
Hyde	Hyde, *International Law, chiefly as interpreted and applied by the United States*, 2nd ed., 3 vols. (1945).
I.C.J.	*International Court of Justice.*
I.C.L.Q.	*International and Comparative Law Quarterly.*
I.L.R.	*International Law Reports*, being the continuation of *Annual Digest*, edited by H. Lauterpacht until volume 24 and thereafter by E. Lauterpacht.

ABBREVIATIONS OF TITLES OF BOOKS

J.C.L.	*Journal of Comparative Legislation and International Law.*
Keith's Wheaton	*Wheaton's Elements of International Law*, 6th English edition by A. Berriedale Keith, vol. I (1929); vol. II (7th ed., 1944).
Klüber	Klüber, *Europäisches Völkerrecht*, 2nd ed. by Morstadt (1851).
Lapradelle-Politis	Lapradelle-Politis, *Recueil des arbitrages internationaux*, vol. I (1905), vol. II (1924), vol. III (1954).
Lauterpacht, *Analogies*	Lauterpacht, *Private Law Sources and Analogies of International Law* (1927).
Lauterpacht, *The Function of Law*	Lauterpacht, *The Function of Law in the International Community* (1933).
Lawrence	Lawrence, *The Principles of International Law*, 7th ed., revised by P. H. Winfield (1923).
Lindley	Lindley, *The Acquisition and Government of Backward Territory in International Law* (1926).
Liszt	Liszt, *Das Völkerrecht*, 12th ed. by Fleischmann (1925).
L.N.O.J.	*League of Nations, Official Journal*
L.N.T.S.	*League of Nations Treaty Series.* Publication of Treaties and International Engagements registered with the Secretariat of the League of Nations.
Lorimer	Lorimer, *The Institutes of International Law*, 2 vols. (1883–4).
De Louter	De Louter, *Le droit international public positif*, French translation from the Dutch original, 2 vols. (1920).
L.Q.R.	*Law Quarterly Review.*
McNair	McNair, *The Law of Treaties: British Practice and Opinions* (1938).
McNair, *Opinions*	McNair, *International Law Opinions* (1956).
Maine	Maine, *International Law*, 2nd ed. (1894).
Martens	Martens, *Völkerrecht*, German translation from the Russian original, 2 vols. (1883–6).
Martens, G. F.	G. F. Martens, *Précis du droit des gens moderne de l'Europe*, new edition by Vergé, 2 vols. (1858).
Martens, R. Martens, N. R. Martens, N. S. Martens, N. R. G. Martens, N. R. G., 2nd ser. Martens, N. R. G., 3rd ser.	These are the abbreviated quotations of the different parts of Martens, *Recueil de Traités*, which are in common use.
Martens, *Causes célèbres*	Martens, *Causes célèbres du droit des gens*, 2nd ed., 5 vols. (1858–61).

xx

ABBREVIATIONS OF TITLES OF BOOKS

Mérignhac	Mérignhac, *Traité de droit public international*, vol. I (1905), vol. II (1907), vol. III (1912).
Möller	Möller, *International Law in Peace and War*, English translation from the Danish, vol. I (1931), vol. II (1935).
Moore	Moore, *A Digest of International Law*, 8 vols. (1906).
Moore, *International Arbitrations*	Moore, *History and Digest of the International Arbitrations to which the United States has been a Party*, 6 vols. (1898).
Nordisk T.A.	*Nordisk Tidskrift for International Ret. Acta scandinavica juris gentium.*
Nys	Nys, *Le droit international*, 2nd ed., 3 vols. (1912).
Off. J.	*Official Journal of the League of Nations.*
Oppenheim, I, II	Oppenheim, *International Law*, vol. I, 8th ed. (1955), by H. Lauterpacht; vol. II, 7th ed. (1952), by H. Lauterpacht.
O.Z.ö.R.	*Österreichische Zeitschrift für öffentliches Recht.*
P.C.I.J.	*Publications of the Permanent Court of International Justice*:
	Series A: Judgments.
	B: Advisory Opinions.
	A/B: Cumulative Collection of Judgments and Advisory Opinions given since 1931.
	C: Acts and Documents relating to Judgments and Advisory Opinions.
	D: Collection of Texts governing the Jurisdiction of the Court.
	E: Annual Reports.
Perels	Perels, *Das internationale öffentliche Seerecht der Gegenwart*, 2nd ed. (1903).
Phillimore	Phillimore, *Commentaries upon International Law*, 3rd ed., 4 vols. (1879–88).
Praag	Praag, *Juridiction et droit international public* (1915).
Praag, *Supplément*	Supplement to the above (1935).
Pradier-Fodéré	Pradier-Fodéré, *Traité de droit international public*, 8 vols. (1885–1906).
Pufendorf	Pufendorf, *De Jure Naturae et Gentium* (1672).
Ralston	Ralston, *The Law and Procedure of International Tribunals*, revised ed. (1926). Supplement (1936).
Ray, *Commentaire*	Ray, *Commentaire du Pacte* (1930).
Recueil T.A.M.	*Recueil des décisions des tribunaux arbitraux mixtes.*
Reddie, *Researches*	Reddie, *Researches, Historical and Critical, in Maritime International Law*, 2 vols. (1844).
Répertoire	Lapradelle et Niboyet, *Répertoire de droit international.* Founded by Darras in 1929.

xxi

ABBREVIATIONS OF TITLES OF BOOKS

R.G.	*Revue générale de droit international public.*
R.I.	*Revue de droit international et de législation comparée.*
R.I. (Geneva)	*Revue de droit international, de sciences diplomatiques, politiques et sociales.*
R.I. (Paris)	*Revue de droit international.*
R.I.F.	*Revue internationale française du droit des gens.*
Rivier	*Rivier, Principes du droit des gens,* 2 vols. (1896).
Rivista	*Rivista di diritto internazionale.*
Rousseau	Rousseau, *Principes généraux du droit international public,* vol. 1 (1944).
Satow	Satow, *A Guide to Diplomatic Practice,* 3rd ed. by Ritchie (1932).
Scelle	Scelle, *Précis de droit des gens,* vol. 1 (1932), vol. 11 (1934).
Schücking und Wehberg	Schücking und Wehberg, *Die Satzung des Völkerbundes,* 2nd ed. (1924).
Schwarzenberger	Schwarzenberger, *International Law as Applied by International Courts and Tribunals,* vol. 1 (1945).
Scott, *Hague Reports*	Scott, *Hague Court Reports* (1916).
Scott, *Hague Reports* (2nd)	Scott, *Hague Court Reports (Second Series)* (1932).
Sibert	Sibert, *Traité de droit international public,* 2 vols. (1951).
Sirey	*Recueil général des lois et des arrêts* (founded by Sirey).
Smith	Smith, *Great Britain and the Law of Nations, a Selection of Documents,* vol. 1 (1932), vol. 11 (1935).
Spiropoulos	Spiropoulos, *Traité théorique et pratique du droit international public* (1933).
Stowell	Stowell, *International Law. A Restatement of Principles in Conformity with Actual Practice* (1931).
Strupp, *Éléments*	Strupp, *Éléments du droit international public, universel, européen et américain,* 2nd ed., 3 vols. (1930).
Strupp, Wört.	*Wörterbuch des Völkerrechts und der Diplomatie,* ed. by Strupp (begun by Hatschek), 3 vols. (1924–9).
Suarez	Suarez, *Tratado de Derecho internacional público,* 2 vols. (1916).
Temperley	Temperley, *History of the Peace Conference of Paris,* 6 vols. (1920–4).
Testa	Testa, *Le droit public international maritime,* translation from the Portuguese by Boutiron (1886).
Toynbee, *Survey*	Toynbee, *Survey of International Affairs.*
Travers	Travers, *Le droit pénal international,* 5 vols. (1920–2).
Treaty Series	United Kingdom Treaty Series, vol. 1, 1892, and a volume every year.

xxii

ABBREVIATIONS OF TITLES OF BOOKS

Twiss	Twiss, *The Law of Nations*, etc., 2 vols., 2nd ed., vol. I (Peace, 1884), vol. II (War, 1875).
U.N.R.I.A.A.	United Nations, *Reports of International Arbitral Awards*.
U.N.T.S.	*United Nations Treaty Series*.
Vattel	Vattel, *Le droit des gens*, 4 books in 2 vols., new edition (1773).
Verdross	Verdross, *Die Verfassung der Völkerrechtsgemeinschaft* (1926).
Walker	Walker, *A Manual of Public International Law* (1895)
Walker, *History*	Walker, *A History of the Law of Nations*, vol. I (1899).
Walker, *Science*	Walker, *The Science of International Law* (1893).
Westlake	Westlake, *International Law*, 2 vols., 2nd ed. (1910–13).
Westlake, *Chapters*	Westlake, *Chapters on the Principles of International Law* (1894).
Westlake, *Papers*	*The Collected Papers of John Westlake on Public International Law*, ed. by L. Oppenheim (1914).
Wharton	Wharton, *A Digest of the International Law of the United States*, 3 vols. (1886).
Wheaton	Wheaton, *Elements of International Law*, 8th American edition by Dana (1866).
Z.I.	*Zeitschrift für internationales Recht*.
Z.ö.R.	*Zeitschrift für öffentliches Recht*.
Z.ö.V.	*Zeitschrift für ausländisches öffentliches Recht und Völkerrecht*.
Z.V.	*Zeitschrift für Völkerrecht*.

I

INTERNATIONAL LAW—
THE GENERAL PART

EDITOR'S NOTE

In 1933 Lauterpacht became the fourth editor of Oppenheim's treatise on *International Law*. This two-volume work, which for over half a century has been accepted as a standard English work of reference on international law, first appeared in 1905. Oppenheim, who was then Whewell Professor of International Law at Cambridge, produced the first and second editions. In them he established the division of the subject into two parts, 'Peace' and 'Disputes, War and Neutrality', each represented by a separate volume; and within each volume he established a system of classification which has since had considerable influence upon many students of international law. The third edition of the work was produced by R. F. Roxburgh, who subsequently became a judge of the High Court of Chancery. The fourth edition was edited by Dr Arnold (later Lord) McNair. The fifth and subsequent editions were prepared by Lauterpacht.

In his Preface to the eighth edition of Volume One, written in October 1954, he observed '... that there may be objection to the continued publication of a treatise in which the Sections written by its original author comprise only one-third—or less—of the total contents of the work'. He continued:

Even those Sections—or what is left of them—have undergone changes both of substance and of form. I am conscious of the doubts voiced, on that account, by friendly critics and of their exhortations that I should assume full responsibility, under my own name, for a treatise on International Law. I hope in due course and subject to other calls, to comply with those wishes. In the meantime, so long as the demand for 'Oppenheim' continues, I have not felt justified in abandoning a treatise whose usefulness is widely acknowledged.

Thus by 1954, at the latest, he had begun to feel that 'Oppenheim' as such had absorbed too much of his creative effort and that it was time that he should produce a comprehensive text-book of his own. In the period after the publication of the eighth edition he considered a number of ways of going about this. Sometimes he spoke of converting 'Oppenheim' into an up-to-date treatise, which would henceforth be known as 'Lauterpacht–Oppenheim'. He also contemplated the possibility of abandoning Oppenheim's work completely and, instead, of assuming over-all responsibility for the production of an entirely new treatise which he would prepare in

EDITOR'S NOTE

association with a number of other authors possessing recognized specialist qualifications. Thirdly, he considered the alternative of producing a new treatise of his own without the aid of others, but in which he would incorporate much that he had already written in 'Oppenheim'.

Eventually, as an interim measure, he decided to prepare a ninth edition of 'Oppenheim', into which he proposed to introduce a considerable amount of new writing with the intention of using it ultimately for his own work. The material which is here printed for the first time represents the first stage in the implementation of this idea. It consists of 364 typewritten pages, of which he revised some 186 before he died. Although the material taken as a whole is entitled 'International Law—The General Part'—a title which he gave to it intending it to replace the Introduction and some of Part I of 'Oppenheim'—he did not in fact complete all the sections which he had originally intended to incorporate therein. In particular, the original Table of Contents of Chapter IV on 'International Law and the Law of the State' lists two additional sections entitled 'Municipal Law in the International Sphere' and 'The So-Called Monistic and Dualistic Doctrine', of which there exists no manuscript or typescript copy.

I have adopted a somewhat restricted view of my task as Editor, and have felt it better to maintain as far as possible the integrity of the original text. This has meant that I have not brought the references up to date; have not mentioned new materials bearing on the topics here discussed; and have not revised those few sections where, in the light of subsequent developments, the views expressed by Lauterpacht may no longer be fully accurate. My approach has been based on the view that the value of these papers lies as much in their record of what he thought and produced at a given time as in their substantive content.

Because the material was intended for use in a new edition of 'Oppenheim', he made liberal use of the existing footnotes and bibliographies in 'Oppenheim' (most of which he had himself introduced into earlier editions). I have retained these footnotes just as they appear in the typescript, as well as the abbreviations in the 'Oppenheim' manner. The full titles of the works thus referred to can be found in the Table of Abbreviations. He himself marked the typescript in such a way as to indicate that he intended that the bibliographies should, in contrast with the prevailing 'Oppenheim' technique, be placed at the end of the relevant chapter.

INTERNATIONAL LAW—THE GENERAL PART

So far as style is concerned, I have not attempted to revise Lauterpacht's writing in any significant respect. It is a distinctive and dignified, if solid and sometimes complex, style. Only occasionally, where sentences were unusually involved, have I ventured some minor transpositions or simplifications. I have felt freer about doing this in the later part of the text which Lauterpacht himself did not have time to revise thoroughly. Those footnotes and bibliographies which appear in 'Oppenheim' are reprinted here with the permission of Messrs Longmans, Green & Co. Ltd and of Mr Geoffrey Hudson, in whom the 'Oppenheim' copyright is vested.

CONTENTS

page

CHAPTER I. THE DEFINITION AND NATURE OF INTERNATIONAL LAW AND ITS PLACE IN JURISPRUDENCE

9

(1) Definition of international law; (2) International law as 'law'; (3) The elements of law absent from the International Legal System; (4) The absence of a sovereign law-making authority; (5) The absence of a sovereign executive authority enforcing international law; (6) The partial observance of international law; (7) The limitation of the scope of matters regulated by international law; (8) The absence of authority endowed with compulsory jurisdiction to ascertain the law; (9) Indefiniteness of rules of international law; (10) The existence of an international community; (11) The cumulative effect of the shortcomings of international law; (12) International law as a system of law; (13) International public law and international private law; (14) International law and international comity; (15) International law and morality

CHAPTER 2. THE SOURCES OF INTERNATIONAL LAW

51

1 The Sources of International Law in General

51

(16) The basis of the causes of international law; (17) The causes and the sources of international law; (18) The consent of States as a source of international law

2 The Particular Sources of International Law

58

(19) Treaties; (20) International customary law; (21) General principles of law recognized by civilized States; (22) The basis of the validity of general principles of law; (23) Decisions of international tribunals; (24) Decisions of municipal courts; (25) Equity as a source of international law

3 The Hierarchy and the Completeness of the Sources of International Law

86

(26) The hierarchy of the sources of international law; (27) The ultimate source of international law; (28) The problem of the completeness of the sources of international law

5

INTERNATIONAL LAW—THE GENERAL PART

page

4 **Codification of International Law** 98

(29) The meaning of codification; (30) Non-governmental projects and drafts of codification; (31) The work of the First Hague Peace Conference; (32) The work of the Second Hague Peace Conference; (33) Codification in the period after the First World War; (34) Codification under the auspices of the League of Nations; (35) The Hague Codification Conference of 1930; (36) The limits and prospects of the codification of international law; (37) The Codification Conference on the Law of the Sea (1958); (38) Codification and development of international law; (39) International legislation and the revision of international law

5 **The Scope of the Validity of the Sources of International Law** 112

(40) Particular international law; (41) Universal international law; (42) Modern international law as created by Christian States in Western civilization; (43) So-called American international law; (44) The so-called Anglo-American and Continental schools of international law; (45) National conceptions of international law; (46) The element of time in respect of the validity of the sources of international law (so-called inter-temporal international law): (*a*) The element of time in respect of customary international law; (*b*) 'Inter-temporal law' and the interpretation of treaties; (*c*) 'Inter-temporal law' and the law of tortious and criminal responsibility

CHAPTER 3. THE SUBJECTS OF INTERNATIONAL LAW 136

(47) The definition of subjects of international law; (48) The traditional view; (49) Collective bodies other than States; (50) The individual as a subject of international law; (51) The procedural capacity of individuals in the international sphere; (52) The rights and duties of States as rights and duties of man

CHAPTER 4. INTERNATIONAL LAW AND THE LAW OF THE STATE 151

1 **The Practical and the Doctrinal Aspects** 151

(53) The practical aspect; (54) The doctrinal aspect

6

CONTENTS

page

2 International Law before National Courts and Agencies   153

(55) In general; (56) Incorporation of international law by the common law of England. Customary international law; (57) The rule of presumptive conformity with international law; (58) Proof of international law; (59) The principle of incorporation in relation to treaties; (60) The limitations of the practice of incorporation. Executive determination involving questions of international law; (61) The supremacy of Acts of Parliament; (62) The significance of the principle of incorporation; (63) Judicial and doctrinal criticism of the doctrine of incorporation; (64) The principle of adoption in the law of the United States; (65) Customary adoption of the principle of incorporation in other countries; (66) Express adoption of international law in constitutions; (67) Constitutional adoption of particular principles of international law; (68) Constitutional authorization of renunciation of sovereignty

CHAPTER I

THE DEFINITION AND NATURE OF INTERNATIONAL LAW AND ITS PLACE IN JURISPRUDENCE

1. *Definition of international law*

International law is the body of rules of conduct, enforceable by external sanction, which confer rights and impose obligations primarily, though not exclusively, upon sovereign States and which owe their validity both to the consent of States as expressed in custom and treaties and to the fact of the existence of an international community of States and individuals. In that sense international law may be defined, more briefly (though perhaps less usefully), as the law of the international community.[1]

All these elements of the definition of international law are controversial. It is a matter of dispute whether it may properly be described as law in the sense generally accepted in jurisprudence; whether its rules extend to bodies and persons other than States; whether there exists an international community; and whether there is a source of international law other than the consent of sovereign States. Although it is generally agreed that international law is enforceable by physical compulsion, the precariousness and uncertainty of its enforcement have caused many to question, on that account, its claim to be considered as law in the proper sense of that term. There is substance in the doubts thus expressed as to the legal nature of the body of rules and principles currently described as international law. While, as will be shown, these doubts do not, upon examination, prove to be decisive, no useful purpose can be served by claiming for international law as now

---

[1] The above simplified definition of international law approaches closely that given by Westlake: 'International Law, otherwise called the Law of Nations, is the law of the society of states or nations' (*International Law*, Part I (1st ed. 1904), p. 1). With this there may be usefully compared that given by Hall: 'International Law consists in certain rules of conduct which modern civilised States regard as being binding on them in their relations with one another with a force comparable in nature and degree to that binding the conscientious person to obey the laws of the country, and which they also regard as being enforceable by appropriate means in case of infringement' (*International Law* (3rd ed. 1890), p. 1). There may be an advantage in indicating in the definition of a subject such as international law the complexities inherent in it as distinguished from what is no more than a tautological description.

9

INTERNATIONAL LAW—THE GENERAL PART

existing a degree of legal reality which it does not possess. It is more accurate to admit its imperfections when gauged by the notion of law as it is known in civilized societies than, as is often done, to assert its legal nature by reference to a tenuous conception of law derived from a contemplation of conditions said to prevail, or to have prevailed, in primitive communities.[1]

[1] Already after the First World War one of the effects of the cataclysm was to produce among international lawyers widespread dissatisfaction with the inadequacies of existing law and its philosophy and a conviction of the necessity of restating much of the law and finding a new basis for it. Amongst a mass of literature the following may be mentioned: Fauchille, §§ 1711–21; Niemeyer, *Aufgaben künftiger Völkerrechtswissenschaft* (1917); Nippold, *The Development of International Law after the World War* (1917) (trans. by Hershey, 1923); Lammasch, *Das Völkerrecht nach dem Kriege* (1917); Schücking, *Die völkerrechtliche Lehre des Weltkrieges* (1917); Nelson, *Rechtswissenschaft ohne Recht* (1917); Jitta, *The Renovation of International Law* (1919); Van Vollenhoven, *The Three Stages in the Evolution of the Law of Nations* (1918); Zitelmann, *Die Unvollkommenheiten des Völkerrechts* (1919); Woltzendorf, *Die Lüge des Völkerrechts* (1919); Garner, *Developments*, pp. 1–42, 775–818, and in *R.G.* 28 (1921), 413–40; Feilchenfeld, *Völkerrechtspolitik als Wissenschaft* (1922); Burckhardt, *Die Unvollkommenheit des Völkerrechts* (1923); Politis, *Les nouvelles tendances du droit international* (1927), and in *R.I.* (Paris), 1 (1927), 57–75; Fischer Williams, *Chapters*, pp. 68–85; Cavaglieri, *La rinnovazione del diritto internazionale ed i suoi limiti* (1931); Kraus, *Die Krise des zwischenstaatlichen Denkens* (1933); Laun, *Der Wandel der Ideen Staat und Volk* (1933); Scott, *Le progrès du droit des gens* (1934); Van Vollenhoven, *The Law of Peace* (trans. from the Dutch, 1936), pp. 113–261; Griziotti, *Riflessioni di diritto internazionale* (1936); Alvarez, *Le nouveau droit international* (1924), and *La psychologie des peuples et la reconstruction du droit international* (1936); Rolin in *R.G.* 26 (1919), 129–41; De Louter, *ibid.* pp. 76–110; Pound in *Bibliotheca Visseriana*, 1923, i, 73–90; Kunz in *Grotius Society*, 10 (1925), 115–42, and in *Strupp, Wört*, iii, 294–302; Hudson in *A.J.* 22 (1928), 330–50; Dickinson in *West Virginia Law Quarterly*, 32 (1925), 4–32, and in *Michigan Law Review*, 25 (1927), 622–44; Garner in *R.G.* 37 (1930), 225–40, and in *Hague Recueil*, 35 (1931) (i), 609–720; Del Vecchio, *ibid.* 38 (1931) (iv), 545–649; Le Fur, *ibid.* 41 (1932) (iii). 548–98; Scelle in *R.I.* (Paris), 15 (1935), 7–35; Brierly in *Nordisk T.A.* 7 (1936), 3–17. See also the literature in regard to the recent criticism of the conceptions of sovereignty at pp. 35n. and 36n. and in regard to the bases of the Law of Nations at p. 90.

The international crisis which preceded and followed the Second World War, and the fact that organized international society once more proved unable to check frequent and flagrant breaches of the Law of Nations, gave rise both to further criticisms of international law and to attempts to answer them. See, for instance, Fischer Williams, *Aspects of Modern International Law. An Essay* (1939); Niemeyer, *Law Without Force* (1941); Kelsen, *Law and Peace in International Relations* (1942); Brierly, *The Outlook for International Law* (1944), and in *International Affairs*, 22 (1946), 352–60; Dickinson, *Law and Peace* (1951); Corbett, *Law and Society in the Relations of States* (1951), and the same, *Law in Diplomacy* (1959); Ch. de Visscher, *Théories et réalités en droit international public* (1st ed. 1953, trans. by Corbett in 1957); Vedel in *R.G.* 46 (1939), 9–36; Jessup in *Foreign Affairs* (U.S.A.), 18 (1939–1940), 244–53; Keeton in *Grotius Society*, 27 (1941), 31–58; Schwarzenberger in *A.J.* 37 (1943), 460–79; Kunz in *American Political Science Review*, 38 (1944), 354–69; Dickinson in *California Law Review*, 33 (1945), 506–42; Friedmann in *A.J.* 50 (1956), 474–514; Kunz, *ibid.* 51 (1957), 77–83.

It is important to distinguish between criticism of international law and criticism of the science of international law. The latter cannot be held responsible, to any appreciable degree, for the shortcomings of international law, whose growth and authority must depend upon the willingness of States to accept, through progressive limitations of their sovereignty, the normal restraints of law. The science of international law can assist in that development by disclosing the shortcomings of existing law, by examining the possibilities of its improvement, by refraining from generalizing the effects of phenomena

DEFINITION AND NATURE

2. *International law as 'law'*

The question whether international law is law presupposes a definition, commanding general agreement, of what is law. It may be an undue simplification of the issue to expect that that generally agreed definition can differ in every respect from what is usually described as the Austinian conception of law conceived as a body of external rules partaking of the nature of a command set and enforced by a sovereign authority and habitually obeyed by those subject to it. In particular, caution must be exercised in resorting to the argument that the Austinian conception of law is based upon an unjustifiable generalization of the experience of modern States. According to that argument, we are not entitled to restrict ourselves to that limited orbit of legal experience and to disregard the law of primitive communities which know no law-giver, no regular tribunals, and no superior agencies of enforcement. The answer to that view is that a workable conception of law cannot, except for the purposes of abstract speculation, be properly formulated by way of a most comprehensive generalization which takes decisively into account the so-called law of primitive communities. A conception of law which aims at embracing the experience of human society from the very inception of its political existence may result in a notion of law so diluted and so elastic as to render it of little value except for the purposes of anthropological or sociological study.[1] In particular, care must be taken not to exaggerate the so-called specific character of international law as a reason for acquiescing in or justifying solutions departing radically from general principles of law as adopted within the State and from rules of morality as embodied in those principles.[2] We must not, in any case, lose sight of the fact that modern States are not primitive

which may be purely temporary, and by exercising restraint in rationalizing its defects as being inherent in the nature of States and in the impossibility of subjecting their vital interests to the rule of law. See also Briggs, *The Progressive Development of International Law*, and Smith, *The Crisis of the Law of Nations* (both in the form of publications of the Turkish Institute of International Law, 1947); Jessup, *A Modern Law of Nations* (1948), an important work of a general character. And see McDougall in *Hague Recueil*, 82 (1953) (i), 143–226; Corbett, *ibid.* 85 (1954) (ii), 471–540; Kunz, *ibid.* 88 (1955) (ii), 9–100.

[1] For the literature on the so-called sociological approach to international law see Oppenheim, I, 15, n. 1.

[2] See Lauterpacht, *The Function of Law*, p. 406. And see Westlake, *Papers*, p. xxii: 'If we give the name of law to anything which we so discover in a remote state of society before we have fixed in our minds what we mean by that name, we beg the question, and we have no security that our language has any consistent, or therefore useful, meaning.'

communities and that, consequently, any attempt to judge, in reliance upon the law prevailing within and among the latter, the nature of the rules governing the conduct of modern States in their mutual relations is likely to result in a test which is not only artificial but which also constitutes in itself a challenge to progress. Austin's conception of law must therefore be considered as still providing in many respects the accurate starting point for assessing the nature of the rules which govern the relations of States and which States consider binding upon them. However, it is doubtful whether the Austinian conception of law necessarily leads to an unqualified denial of the legal nature of these rules.

3. The elements of law absent from the International Legal System

The weakness of the denial, on the strength of the Austinian definition of law, of the legal nature of international law has been not so much the definition of law which is taken as a starting point as the mistaken insistence on the rigidity of that definition. The legal quality of a rule or of a body of rules is a matter of degree. It is the result of a complex variety of elements. The inadequacy or even the absence of any of the constitutive elements of law need not detract decisively from the legal character of a system of rules of conduct. It is probable that the various shortcomings of international law, in relation to the constituent elements of the Austinian conception of law, are not necessarily destructive of the legal nature of international law so long as they are conceived as associated with a transient stage of immaturity which humanity, under the increasing impact of the interdependence of the modern world, of the growing collective sense of morality and of the realization of the consequences inherent in the absence of an effective international legal order, is destined to overcome by conscious effort.

Even if international law complied with most of the requirements of the Austinian definition as here stated, the strength of its claim to be a system of law might still legitimately be subject to enquiry from the point of view of its compliance with other requirements which are widely considered to be essential to any legal system. Such requirements include the possession of a sufficient degree of uniformity, generality and precision; the effective regulation of matters vitally affecting the life of the community as distinguished from matters of minor and formal importance; and, above all, its conformity with a general sense of right and justice. But although, as will be shown, international law as at present constituted falls

DEFINITION AND NATURE

short of these requirements, it is probable that, in the aggregate, it approaches more the conception of law than any other category of rules of conduct. In particular, it differs fundamentally from ethics inasmuch as in its very essence the latter—operating, as it does, exclusively upon the human conscience—lacks the element of external enforcement. This is so although the essential content of rules of law and those of morality is normally[1] identical. As has been rightly said, law is the maximum of socially obtainable morality.

With these considerations in mind we may now approach the examination of the arguments traditionally adduced against conceiving international law as law, and the answers usually given to these objections.

4. *The absence of a sovereign law-making authority*

There is in the international sphere no superior authority endowed with legal power to impose new rules of law binding upon all States. No State is bound to acquiesce in a change of international law, by way of an addition to its rules or otherwise, which may result in impairing its rights or increasing its obligations. There exist some international organizations in which, by virtue of consent given in advance by their members, the authorities of the organization are empowered to adopt general rules, mostly of a technical nature, binding upon all the members of the organization. However, these apparent exceptions to the general rule tend to emphasize rather than to derogate from the existing position in which international law does not vest in any superior authority the function of overriding and law-creating legislation. It is true that the general rule of unanimity no longer prevents international conferences from adopting, by an agreed majority, new international conventions; but, subject to some important exceptions,[2] these are binding only upon those States which expressly agree to them. According to the Charter of the United Nations, while the validly adopted amendments thereto are not binding upon the permanent members of the Security Council except by their own consent, they are binding upon other members of the United Nations even if they decline to agree to them; but probably the latter members may, in such contingencies, exercise their right of withdrawal from the United Nations.

There is, it must be noted in particular, no international legislation in the accepted sense of the term, i.e. a process of enacting rules

---

[1] See below, p. 46.　　　　[2] See below, pp. 115–16.

13

binding upon all States regardless of whether they have assented thereto. Admittedly, the terms 'legislative treaties' or 'law-making treaties' are often used; such designation of treaties concluded between a large number of States is convenient and useful so long as it is remembered that it is essentially inaccurate. Their generality and, correspondingly, their importance are reminiscent of legislation. But the analogy stops there. 'Law-making' treaties are not binding upon States which are not parties thereto. It may, in the long run, be productive of confusion if for the purposes of discussion and classification terms are used in a connotation different from that which they possess in current legal terminology. Undoubtedly, treaties—other than those usually described as executed treaties (such as treaties providing for cession of territory)—lay down rules of future conduct binding upon the parties. In that sense all treaties are law-making—for law is a rule of future conduct, enforceable by external sanction, for persons bound thereby. The Charter of the United Nations lays down rules of conduct for the parties to the treaty—for the Charter is a treaty—which established the United Nations. So do the Hague Conventions of 1899 and 1907 on the conduct of war on land; the various Geneva Conventions on the treatment of prisoners of war; the Hague Conventions of 1930 codifying parts of the law in the sphere of nationality; and the Geneva Conventions of 1958 relating to the law of the sea. But so also does an ordinary bilateral treaty of commerce between two States. There is, from that point of view, no difference between a treaty between two States providing for extradition, for mutual grant of regulated aerial passage or for the exchange of postal parcels, and a multilateral treaty, often approaching universality, laying down the constitution and principles of an international organization or codifying large segments of the international law of peace or war.

What is the effect, upon the legal nature of international law, of that absence of an overriding legislative authority? It may be said that the existence of a legislative organ is not essential to the legal character of a system of rules of conduct for the reason that legislation does not constitute the only method of creating law. It may be asserted that custom is an equally important method of creating law and that this is so in particular in primitive communities. There is much force in that answer. However, its persuasive force ought not to be exaggerated. In modern society—and it is with the international society of modern States that we are here concerned—custom is one, but only one, of the sources of law. Moreover, in

DEFINITION AND NATURE

modern society custom is a source of law in so far as it is recognized and ascertained as such by courts endowed with compulsory jurisdiction and acting by and under the authority of the State which endows decisions of courts with the force of law. This is not the position in existing international law. It is possible—a somewhat speculative possibility—that in early political societies law may have been created and developed through the exclusive medium of custom. However, the question is not whether law can, in addition to other methods, be created also by custom, but whether, in modern political society, it can be predominantly the creature of custom. The answer to that question must be in the negative. A society which does not provide means for amending and developing customary law by deliberate processes of an overriding law-making authority is the product of speculation rather than actual occurrence. The same considerations apply with even greater cogency in the international sphere. The exigencies of the interdependence of States do not permit exclusive or predominant reliance upon custom as a law-creating agency. For in the relations of States custom is not only slow of growth; in the absence of compulsory jurisdiction of international tribunals both existing and nascent custom are difficult of impartial ascertainment. For that reason, although the principles of international law are, in most of its aspects, covered by custom, its details are often uncertain and controversial. It is not predominantly through custom that the development, or even the normal functioning, of international law is likely or possible in modern conditions.

The existence of an overriding legislative power is thus more than a vital condition of the normal life of a political society. It is both an expression—though not the only expression—of the imperative character of the law and, through the power of interpreting custom, an essential condition of its satisfactory application by tribunals. Moreover, the absence of an international legislature amending and supplementing the existing law has, in turn, frequently provided support for the still valid rule of international law according to which the jurisdiction of international tribunals is, in principle, of a voluntary character. For, it has been argued, in the absence of an international legislature modifying the existing law by reference to special conditions and the needs of international society, international tribunals may often be compelled to render decisions which, though in accordance with the existing law, may be contrary alike to moral justice and to progress.

15

INTERNATIONAL LAW—THE GENERAL PART

While the absence of a legislative power thus constitutes a serious impairment of the legal quality of international law, this does not mean that the latter is on that account altogether deprived of that imperative character which is essential to all law. That imperative character, universally acknowledged by States, applies not only to the binding force of its rules established by custom and treaty. In particular, it manifests itself in the fundamental principle, which forms part of international law, that its rules emanate not only from the consent of States as expressed in customary and conventional rules, but from the paramount fact of the existence of an international community of States bound by an ultimate solidarity of interests transcending any immediate conflict of aims and interests.[1] The full operation of that basic fact is at present still largely limited by the predominantly consensual character of international law, but it is not without profound significance or actual effect.

5. *The absence of a sovereign executive authority enforcing international law*

An essential characteristic of law is that it is enforceable by external sanction—'enforceable' meaning not only general agreement that the law ought to be enforced, but also that it is in fact generally enforced and that there exists an organ, different from and superior to those subject to law, which renders effective the sanction behind the law. These conditions do not normally obtain in the international sphere. It is occasionally maintained that there exist other means, in particular self-help, war and public opinion, which may be regarded as instruments, admittedly imperfect, of enforcement. Care must be taken not to exaggerate the importance of these factors.[2]

It is true that—notionally—enforcement is compatible with self-help, i.e. with the vindication of the violated rule of law by the

---

[1] See below, pp. 28–31.

[2] As to the sanctions of international law see the following: Root in *A.J.* 2 (1908), 451–7; Higgins, *The Binding Force of International Law* (1910); Siotto-Pintor in *Rivista*, 12 (1918), 208–28; Roxburgh in *A.J.* 14 (1920), 26–37; Hyde, 1, §4; Stowell, pp. 11–15; Dupuis in *Hague Recueil* (1924) (i), 407–44; Mitrany, *The Problem of International Sanctions* (1925); Buell and Dewey, *Are Sanctions Necessary to International Organisation* (1932); Brück, *Les sanctions en droit international public* (1933); Morgenthau, *La réalité des normes* (1934), pp. 214–26; the same in *R.I.* 3rd ser. 16 (1935), 474–503, 809–36; Widmer, *Der Zwang im Völkerrecht* (1936); Kelsen, *Law and Peace in International Relations* (1942), pp. 3–26; Brierly in *Grotius Society*, 17 (1931), 67–8; Scott in *A.S. Proceedings*, 1933, pp. 5–33; Hyde, *ibid.* pp. 34–40; Wehberg in *Hague Recueil*, 48 (1934) (ii), 7–132; Scelle, *ibid.* 55 (1936) (i), 156–77, 193–6; Cavaré in *R.G.* 44 (1937), 385–445, and, as to the sanctions under the United Nations Charter, in *Hague Recueil*, 80 (1952) (i), 195–288; Husserl in *University of Chicago Law Review*, 12 (1945), 115–39; Hsu Mo in *Grotius Society*, 35 (1949), 4–15. And see Oppenheim, II, § 52b. See also Oppenheim, I, §§ 156, 528a.

DEFINITION AND NATURE

injured party himself. Yet self-defence, when constituting the only or the main means of enforcement, must necessarily bring the conception of law to its vanishing point. Enforcement of the law by an interested party, who is both judge and the organ executing the law, is a euphemism unrelieved by the suggestion that that is just the kind of enforcement which is prevalent among primitive communities. Enforceability, conceived as a condition of the legal quality of a rule of conduct, means habitual enforcement through the collective and impartial strength and organs of the community. Subject to some recent, and still rudimentary, developments there is no such enforcement·in the international sphere. In a—somewhat paradoxical—sense, the problem of enforcement in existing international law is less acute for the reason that the question of enforcement arises normally in relation to rights ascertained by an impartial tribunal applying rules of law and that there is as yet, in principle, no compulsory jurisdiction of international tribunals.

War and reprisals have been occasionally described as the main sanction of international law and as fulfilling the same function as self-help in primitive society. However, to describe war as a sanction is to strain legal conceptions beyond the accepted and reasonable use of language. This is so not only because a sanction imposed by the interested party cannot properly be described as enforcement of the law. The more important reason for the artificiality of the instrument of war as a sanction is the precariousness and uncertainty of its operation. Unless we abandon ourselves to the Hegelian view that the victorious war is the expression of right, it is clear that wars are not decided by exclusive or preponderant reference to the intrinsic legal or moral merits of the conflict dividing the belligerents. The justice and the legality of the cause for which war is waged may be, and has often been, a factor in determining the result of a contest of physical forces; but it is only one factor. The irresistibility of compulsion wielded by the overwhelming impact of the collective power of the community is of the essence of a legal sanction. There is no such certainty of outcome attaching to the enforcement of the law by means of war waged by the injured State against a wrongdoer.

Moreover, whatever may be the merits of war as a weapon of enforcement wielded by individual States in defence of their interests, war has now ceased to be a means of enforcement, by individual action of States, authorized or permitted by international law. In the General Treaty for the Renunciation of War of 1928—one of the most fundamental and universal international compacts—

INTERNATIONAL LAW—THE GENERAL PART

practically all States renounced and condemned war as an instrument both for enforcing and for changing rights.[1] That Treaty, whose validity is unaffected by its repeated violation, is an integral part of international law. The Charter of the United Nations prohibits recourse to force by members of the United Nations, except in self-defence, whether as a sanction against violations of the law or otherwise. Similar considerations apply to so-called reprisals, conceived as resort to force short of war, as a unilateral sanction against alleged violations of the law. These, too, are now prohibited.[2]

In view of this it is not necessary to elaborate on the artificiality of the view, occasionally propounded in relation to war and reprisals, that international law—being a decentralised system of law—permits the enforcement of the law by individual members of the international society. Any such explanation is probably no more than a figure of speech calculated to conceal the actual and legal situation.

Finally, although instances of disregard by Governments of awards and judgments of international tribunals are exceptional, the fact is that the Charter of the United Nations does not provide for their regular enforcement by the organized international community. The Charter of the United Nations lays down, with regard to the judgments rendered by its principal judicial organ, that if a party to a case before the International Court of Justice fails to give effect to the judgment of the Court, the other party may have recourse to the Security Council, which may, *if it deems necessary*, make *recommendations* or decide upon measures to be taken to give effect to the judgment.[3]

Neither can public opinion be properly regarded as the main means, or one of the means, of enforcing international law. In fact, the frequent reference to public opinion is, in this connection, no more than an example of the absence of a sense of reality which surrounds the discussion on the subject. Public opinion may be a—relatively inadequate—means of enforcement within the State, where community of outlook and tradition endows it with some degree of effectiveness. But within the State the law does not rely on public opinion for the enforcement of its precepts. Reliance on 'public opinion' as a means of enforcing international law amounts to an admission that, to use Austinian terminology, it is not law, but positive morality. It is an admission of its weakness as a system of law. It is true that States are not in the habit of showing avowed

---

[1] See Oppenheim, II, §§ 52*fe et seq.*   [2] See Oppenheim, II, §§ 33 *et seq.*   [3] Article 94.

DEFINITION AND NATURE

contempt for public opinion. Law-breaking Governments have often appealed to it amidst cynical professions of adherence to international law, with the object of gaining the support of public opinion in their own country. However, as experience has shown, the latter is often insensitive to the public opinion of the world and regards outside censure as an affront to national dignity and as a sufficient reason for ranging itself, in a righteous assertion of independence, with the law-breaker. Public opinion of the world enlightened by a long-range process of education divorced from appeal to facile realism, may indeed become a powerful agent in effecting changes in international law in the direction of a true political integration of international society. But its power as a sanction of the law faced with a deliberate challenge to its authority is precarious and, often, to a large extent nominal. In these circumstances appeal to public opinion emphasizes not its strength but its weakness as a means of enforcing international law.

More recent developments have tended to give recognition to a more accurate notion of legal sanction, namely, one conceived as collective enforcement of the law. The provisions in the matter of sanctions embodied in Article 16 of the Covenant of the League of Nations marked the first step in that direction. The apparently more stringent clauses of the Charter of the United Nations[1] established the principle and made provision, as yet nominal, for permanent collective organs of enforcement within the limited sphere of preservation of international peace and security (as distinguished from enforcement of legal rights in general). They fall short of some of the conditions regarded as fundamental in political society under the rule of law—in particular inasmuch as they lay down, in effect, that the relevant Articles of the Charter cannot be enforced against any of the Great Powers who are permanent members of the Security Council; however, they affirm in emphatic terms the principle of collective enforcement of the law. Finally, and most significantly, at the end of the Second World War the principal Powers in an important Treaty, subsequently adhered to by many States and providing for the punishment of major war criminals, accepted the notion of enforcing international law, by way of recognition of criminal responsibility, not only against the State as such but also against its individual agents guilty of acts stigmatized as crimes against peace, the laws of war, and humanity.[2]

[1] See Oppenheim, II, § 25 b–gc.
[2] See Oppenheim, I, § 156 b, on criminal responsibility in international law.

It would thus appear that, once we have reduced to their proper and tenuous proportions self-help, war and public opinion as instruments of enforcement of international law, we are in a position to point to more persuasive and tangible evidence of international law possessing a sanction in the sense ordinarily attaching to that term. But it is a sanction which is as yet in an incipient stage and the further development of which depends upon the continued legal and political integration of international society. On the other hand there is habitual and effective enforcement of rules and principles of international law in so far as these are administered by municipal courts[1] for the purpose of adjudicating upon rights and obligations, under international law, of individuals and occasionally —in matters such as jurisdictional immunities—also in respect of foreign States.[2] That aspect of the enforcement of international law is often ignored. It is nevertheless not without significance.

6. *The partial observance of international law*

The question of the habitual observance of international law is closely connected with the potentialities and realities of its enforcement. In general, the legal quality of a rule is not dependent upon its observance, or enforcement, in any particular case. Unlike a physical law, which would cease to be valid if it could conclusively be shown to have been contradicted even by a single event, a legal rule survives individual or even repeated breaches of the law. Like a rule of ethics or grammar, it is often described as a normative rule indicating not conduct which is actually observed but conduct which ought to be observed. However, it is possible to exaggerate, in relation to law, the difference between a normative rule and one in the field of natural science. A rule of law is not only one which ought to be obeyed; it is also one which is habitually obeyed. It is true that a rule laid down by an Act of Parliament becomes a rule of law *ab initio*, irrespective of the prospects of its observance. But if that rule were to be habitually disregarded with impunity, it would, after a time, cease to be a rule enforced by courts. There are, therefore, limits to the accuracy of the statement that law is a normative system of rules which are valid regardless of their actual observance and enforcement. For facts if persistent, tolerated, and regularly followed, have themselves a normative—a law creating— effect.

[1] See below p. 165.
[2] See Oppenheim, I, §§ 115*a*, 115*ac*, 115*ad*.

DEFINITION AND NATURE

These considerations are relevant to the impact, upon the degree of the legal quality of international law, of the question of its habitual observance. The view frequently advanced in this connection is that there is a tendency to over-emphasize the degree of non-observance of international law; that such over-emphasis is the result of undue concentration on the gross violation of political treaties and, in particular, of the obligations of pacific settlement; and that the daily intercourse of States and the ordinary routine of Governments and of their Foreign Offices show a remarkable and almost uniform adherence to international law.

While there is some force in these and similar arguments, it may be doubted whether the answer thus given is as persuasive as appears at first sight. A system of law in which duties of secondary importance are ordinarily observed while obligations touching substantial or vital interests of States are broken with impunity partakes of a high degree of unreality. There is no reason for impatience on the ground that public opinion concentrates on violations of political treaties and on resort to war in disregard of existing obligations. When viewed against the background of transgressions of that magnitude, the normal observance of other rules of international law can only imperfectly maintain the authority of the system shaken by major exhibitions of lawlessness. Similarly, only limited importance can be attributed to the fact that States recognize the binding force of international law even when in fact they violate it. Only the development of the legal organization of mankind in the direction of providing an effective sanction against violations of international law in matters vitally or substantially affecting the life and independence of States will cause it to approximate more decisively than is as yet the case to the notion of law as generally understood.

7. *The limitation of the scope of matters regulated by international law*

With the question of the observance of international law there is closely connected that of the scope of matters regulated by it. A system of law which does not regulate matters of vital importance to the community and to the maintenance of peace between its members is a system the legal character of which is to that extent nominal. That is a position which international law approaches in some respects. Its weakness lies not only in the fact that that part of it which is normally observed is of minor import in comparison with that which is often violated with impunity. Another source of its weakness lies in the circumstance that it fails to regulate affirmatively the conduct of States in certain important spheres of their mutual relations. From this point of view, international law, even when fully observed, must create an impression of unreality. Substantial portions of it are devoted to rules, often controversial, on such subjects as diplomatic intercourse and privileges and jurisdictional immunities of foreign States, their heads, their ships and their public property. It is concerned to a considerable extent with delimiting the jurisdictional rights of States in various spheres. At the same time, in many spheres traditional—and, to a large extent, existing —international law abdicates any regulative or remedial function. The Charter of the United Nations lays down in a comprehensive manner that so-called matters of domestic jurisdiction are not subject to intervention by the United Nations. With minor exceptions, international law leaves States freedom of action with regard to legislation concerning acquisition and loss of nationality, with the resulting hardships and complications following upon double nationality and statelessness. Subject to recent developments in the international protection of human rights, it sets no limit to the discretion, or arbitrariness, with which a State may treat its subjects —with consequences inimical to the fate and dignity of the individual as the ultimate unit of all law and, often, to international peace itself.

Moreover, that absence of affirmative regulation of matters of importance is coupled with the fact that in some respects, vitally affecting the independence of States and some fundamental obligations of international law, the border-line between law and lawlessness was, until recently, almost completely obliterated.[1] While accepting the sovereignty and the independence of States as its guiding principle, traditional international law by permitting war not only for the purpose of enforcing rights but also for the purpose of challenging legitimate rights (including the right to continued national existence), failed to protect the very life of States. Prior to the General Treaty for the Renunciation of War of 1928,[2] even members of the League of Nations had not fully abandoned that right. By availing itself of the legally unlimited right to wage war a

---

[1] For an instructive discussion of various problems of international law from this point of view see Corbett, *Law in Diplomacy* (1959). The usefulness of some such appreciation of various questions of international law is not impaired by the possible danger of blurring the dividing line between the legal and sociological approach—a possibility which the discerning lawyer will doubtless bear in mind. The same applies to yet another important work in that field of enquiry, namely, Judge Charles de Visscher's *Théories et réalités en droit international public* (1953) (translated into English by Professor Corbett in 1957). [2] See Oppenheim, II, §§ 52 *fe et seq.*

DEFINITION AND NATURE

State could thus, while remaining within the orbit of the law, assail the most vital of all rights which the law set itself to protect, namely, the right to existence. Similarly, according to a widely held view, a State could not only set aside its basic obligation when acting in exercise of the so-called right of self-preservation; it also claimed to remain the sole judge of the question whether the circumstances justified the exercise of the right of self-preservation. Finally, with regard to the recognition of States and Governments, international law as often propounded by writers and Governments exhibited to a considerable extent the same tendency to obliterate the border-line between law and fact, between legality and total absence of restraint. While, according to what is probably the more accurate assessment of the practice of States, recognition is a legal duty whenever there are present the necessary conditions of statehood or of governmental capacity, the fact that the fulfilment of that duty is left to the unfettered individual judgment of States renders that important aspect of statehood a subject of uncertainty and possible abuse of power. The result is that, in this respect, the acquisition and exercise of essential rights of statehood are more a function of politics and power than of law. For, in the absence of recognition, there are—according to a widely held view—no rights attaching to an unrecognized State or Government. According to another view, no legal duty of recognition exists in any circumstances.

It would thus appear that both the exclusion of matters of vital importance to the life of the international community from positive regulation by international law and the obliteration, with regard to others, of the border-line between respect for fundamental rights of States and political action unrelated to law, tend to impair the character of international law conceived as a system of law as generally understood.

8. *The absence of authority endowed with compulsory jurisdiction to ascertain the law*

A legal system in which the ascertainment of disputed rights of the members of the community is left to the individual judgement of the interested parties is a deficient system of law. It may be—and has been—a subject of controversy whether, as a matter of historical fact, the functioning of courts preceded the evolution of a coherent system of law or whether development took place in an inverse order. The basic fact remains that unless the law as promulgated by the legislature or as crystallized in custom is authoritatively ascer-

INTERNATIONAL LAW—THE GENERAL PART

tained by courts, the very existence of the law becomes questionable. Yet in the relations of States the rule still obtains that, unless it has agreed to do so in a particular case or in advance with regard to specified categories of disputes, no sovereign State is under a legal obligation to submit to impartial determination, on the basis of law, its controversies with other States concerning legal rights. The existing jurisdiction of international tribunals, including that of the International Court of Justice, is still, in principle, of a voluntary character. The International Court, and its predecessor which functioned under the League of Nations under the name of the Permanent Court of International Justice, have repeatedly affirmed that, even when established by an undertaking given in advance, their jurisdiction is essentially of a voluntary nature, that it cannot be presumed, and that it must be strictly proved. On occasion, the Court has declined to give a Judgment or to render an Advisory Opinion for the reason that the case before it affected a State which was not a party to the proceedings before the Court.[1]

In the Covenant of the League of Nations, disputes as to any question of international law or as to the interpretation of treaties were designated merely as being 'generally suitable for arbitration' without members of the League undertaking any explicit obligations in this respect. The Charter of the United Nations has not introduced any appreciable change in the matter. There exists a wide network of bilateral and multilateral treaties conferring in advance obligatory jurisdiction upon international tribunals. But these treaties, limited as they are in duration, often subject to termination with or without notice, and frequently qualified by comprehensive reservations destructive of the effectiveness of the obligation said to have been undertaken in them, merely accentuate the absence in

[1] Thus in the Advisory Opinion concerning the *Status of Eastern Carelia* (*P.C.I.J.*, Series B, No. 5 (1923)), the Permanent Court declined to give an Advisory Opinion on the ground that if given it would directly affect a dispute between Finland and Soviet Russia which latter State was not at that time a member of the League and had refused to participate in the proceedings before the Court. See, however, the Advisory Opinions in the case of *Interpretation of the Peace Treaties with Bulgaria, Hungary and Romania* for a substantial modification of that attitude: *I.C.J. Reports* 1950, p. 65 and pp. 227, 228, and comment thereon in Lauterpacht, *The Development of International Law by the International Court* (1958), pp. 352–5. For an emphatic affirmation of the principle of consent see the Judgment of the Court in the case of *Monetary Gold Removed from Rome* (*I.C.J. Reports* 1954, p. 19), where the Court declined jurisdiction for the reason that it could not, in the absence of Albania as a party to the proceedings, adjudicate upon her international responsibility. That Judgment is significant seeing that the gold in question was claimed by the United Kingdom in satisfaction of a Judgment which the Court had previously rendered in the *Corfu Channel Case* between the United Kingdom and Albania (*I.C.J. Reports* 1949, p. 4) and with which Albania had refused to comply.

24

DEFINITION AND NATURE

the international community of a fundamental principle of order generally regarded as essential to the existence of a political society under the rule of law. It is still not considered as incongruous, or devoid of inherent contradiction, for States which profess a strict respect for international law either to decline to recognize altogether the obligatory jurisdiction of international tribunals or, while recognizing it, to do so subject to reservations which often render the undertaking to a large extent nominal, or, after having recognized it in general, to challenge—often successfully—the competence of the court on the ground that it is excluded either by the reservations appended by the State in question or the reservations attached by the opposing party but liable to be legitimately invoked by virtue of reciprocity. On occasions, as in the case of the United States of America, these reservations leave—or assert—for the State in question the right to decide unilaterally whether the reservation applies to any particular case. The resulting situation, in addition to leaving room for considerable doubt as to the validity and meaning of the reservation thus qualified, is open to an interpretation rendering invalid the very acceptance of the jurisdiction of the Court.[1] There is not as yet even an incipient recognition of the principle that the duty to agree to an impartial ascertainment of disputed legal rights is a duty owed to the international community and to the professed respect for law unconditionally and not merely by way of reciprocity. Nearly one half of the judgments rendered by the International Court of Justice have been concerned with pleas to its jurisdiction; the majority of them have been successful.

9. *Indefiniteness of rules of international law*

The combined effect of the absence of an international legislative authority and of tribunals endowed with compulsory jurisdiction accounts for yet another impairment of the legal quality of the body of rules governing the conduct of States. It is an essential requirement of a system of legal rules that they should possess an appreciable degree of certainty and precision. These requirements are met, within the State, by the normal activity of the legislature and, in particular, of courts elucidating, defining and giving concrete expression to the necessarily general rules of law emanating either from the legislature or from the less articulate operation of custom and judicial precedent. These conditions do not obtain in the

---

[1] See the various Dissenting and Separate Opinions in the *Case concerning Certain Norwegian Loans* (*I.C.J. Reports* 1957, p. 9) and the *Interhandel Case* (*ibid.* 1959, p. 6).

international sphere on a comparable scale. In particular, because of the absence of compulsory jurisdiction of judicial and arbitral tribunals, their activity is relatively rare and sporadic and not commensurate with the need for reducing the principles of international law to some degree of precision. Thus, for instance, though the principle of diplomatic immunity is universally recognized, there is no similar measure of agreement on the details of the application of that principle, in particular on such questions as the extent of diplomatic immunity with regard to acts of a private law nature, the immunities of the retinue of the diplomatic representative, the requirements of a valid waiver of immunity, and the like. The same applies to the question of jurisdictional immunities of foreign States or Governments and, in a different sphere, to the law of treaties.[1] While on many—perhaps most—subjects there is a consensus of opinion on broad principle, there is no agreement in relation to specific rules and situations.

Moreover, the lack of certainty surrounding many a rule of international law is, in addition, due to the fact that with regard to a considerable number of subjects there exists an unresolved divergence of practice on account either of a diversity of interests or of a disparity of views grounded in reasons other than conflict of interest. The difference of view on the subject of the limits of territorial waters is an example of the former; the divergence of opinion with regard to jurisdiction over foreign vessels in national ports and waters is an instance of the latter. That absence of precise and agreed rules has shown itself conspicuously in connection with the efforts to codify international law. Prior to the first Hague Codification Conference in 1930, preliminary enquiries addressed to Governments revealed that owing to the disparity of views and practice there were only three subjects in the entire field of international law which, by reference to a provisional ascertainment of the existence of agreement, were considered ripe for codification. The Conference itself produced agreement only with regard to some aspects of one of the three subjects selected as ripe for codification.[2] The International Law Commission set up by the United Nations succeeded, after ten years, in rendering possible the codification, by way of international convention, of the law of the sea with the exception of the most controversial topic, namely, that of the limits of territorial waters. Undoubtedly, in a mature legal system such

---

[1] For an elaboration of this view with regard to treaties and other topics of international law see Lauterpacht in *A.J.* 49 (1955), 16–43.   [2] See below, p. 104.

DEFINITION AND NATURE

gaps in the law, due to divergent practice, uncertainty, or other reasons, provide no decisive obstacle to the normal operation of the law. The gaps are filled through the activity of courts endowed with obligatory jurisdiction and precluded, by virtue of a basic principle of law, from refusing to decide a case on the ground of the absence of an agreed or otherwise binding rule of law.[1] However, no such jurisdiction exists in the international legal system as at present constituted.

While the above limitations of the scope of international law are the result—or an expression—of the existing legal position, views of a doctrinal character have occasionally been expressed pointing to yet another limitation of international law deduced from the very structure of international society. Thus it has been suggested that as the number of States who are members of the international community is distinctly limited in comparison with the numbers of individuals within the State, the content of international law must necessarily be restricted so far as regulation by general rules is concerned. For, it is contended, in international society, where the number of independent States is small and where 'every State is unique', with the result that they have only a few qualities in common, stress must be laid on the features and interests which are particular to them—and these, it is argued, are not capable of regulation by rules of law of a general character.[2] There is no compelling reason for regarding that factor as necessarily conducive to a limitation of the scope of international law. The specific character of situations due to the restricted circle of legal persons to whom they apply, does not render impossible their regulation by way either of particular rules or of regional international law[3] or of general principles suitably formulated. Thus, although it may be true that no two international rivers are the same, and that therefore general principles applicable to all international rivers cannot be established, there are nevertheless general principles of law applicable to all international rivers of whatever description—for instance, the

[1] See below, p. 94.

[2] For an elaboration of that view see Brierly in *Outlook for International Law* (1944), pp. 40 *et seq.* and in *Hague Recueil*, 58 (1936) (iv), 17. That view was previously propounded by Schindler, *ibid.* 46 (1933) (iv), 265. See also Fisher, *Frederic William Maitland* (1910), p. 48, for a letter from Maitland to Henry Sidgwick in which the following passage occurs: 'In my view the great difficulty in obtaining a body of international rules deserving the name of law lies in the extreme fewness of the 'persons' subject to that law and the infrequency and restricted range of the questions which arise between them.' See also Charles de Visscher, *Théories et réalités en droit international public* (2nd ed. 1955), p. 448.   [3] See below, pp. 113, 124.

principle which lays down that rights must be exercised in good faith and that no riparian State is entitled to use the flow of an international river without regard to the interests of other riparian States.[1]

10. *The existence of an international community*

The existence of an international community constitutes—on the face of it—a somewhat obvious part of the definition of international law as given above. For law presupposes a political community— just as the notion of a political community presupposes, or is identical with, the existence of some system of law. *Ubi societas, ibi jus.* Moreover, the question of the existence of an international community is not only a relevant element in the definition of international law. It is directly germane to the question of its sources. For, as will be seen, it is largely from the fact of the existence of an international community that there is derived the authority of those rules and principles of law—whether they are called 'general principles of law' or 'the reason of the thing' or 'the law of nature' or 'the modern law of nature'—which owe their validity to a source of obligation other than the express or implied consent of States.[2] It is, however, necessary to advert to that question for the reason that the existence of a true international society, of sufficient degree and intensity, has often been denied. There are, indeed, various factors which give substance to doubts on the subject. These include the conspicuous conflicts of interests between States; the undeniable factor of diversity of race, religion, language, culture, and economic development; deep ideological diversities of a political and economic character, occasionally of prolonged duration, such as those which have divided the world since the First and Second World Wars; the persistent policies of economic nationalism pursued by Governments and expressed in restrictions upon trade and movement of goods and persons; and the artificial barriers occasionally erected by Governments in the way of communication of ideas between their nationals through the restriction or prohibition not only of personal contact but also of admission of books and newsprint and even of receiving of information and knowledge by wireless.

All these factors constitute a true impediment to the growth of a harmonious and effective international community. However, they do not decisively affect its existence for the essentially limited

---

[1] See Lauterpacht in *B.Y.* 32 (1955–6), 10.
[2] See below, p. 68.

DEFINITION AND NATURE

purpose of providing a basis for a system of external rules of conduct. They are powerless to do away with or to hide the ever-present fact of the economic interdependence of States; their mutual dependence in matters of health, communications and the like; the extensive and growing intercourse, in most spheres, of individuals across national frontiers; the vast variety of international, governmental and private organizations created for the purpose of protecting and developing economic and cultural interests; the widespread and growing sense of the moral unity of mankind transcending the confines of the State; the universality of the basic legal principles—rising sovereign over national, cultural and racial differences—expressive of the unity of moral sentiment inherent in the very nature of man; the corresponding recognition of the dignity and worth of individual human beings as members both of their own State and of the international community in the wider sense; the undeniable recognition by Governments, in their mutual relations, of binding rules of conduct, regardless of whether these are given the name of law or positive morality; and, above all, the objective, and increasingly realized, solidarity of the paramount interest in the preservation of peace as the condition of survival of civilized life. That essential solidarity of interest, transcending the conflicts of interest which are a natural and persistent factor in the relations of States and individuals alike, has been recognized by international institutions—such as the League of Nations and the United Nations—for the formulation and collective enforcement of the duties of pacific settlement and the prohibition of war. This is so although these obligations are imperfect in many ways and although, even when clearly binding, they are not yet of sufficient potency to overcome considerations of immediate national interest.[1]

However, these and the other factors which impair the reality and impede the growth of the international community do not affect its essential existence as outlined above. There is nothing absolute in the notion of a community. It is scientifically questionable to pitch the requirements in this sphere too high[2] and to elevate the often transient conflicts of interest and ideologies among States to

---

[1] In this connection there is an occasional tendency among Governments to assert that, being the trustees of interests of others, they are not at liberty, by fulfilling the obligations of a legal system of collective security, to jeopardize the immediate peace of their State for the sake of the wider and less immediate interests of international peace. See below, p. 48.

[2] For an interesting discussion of the question from this point of view see Stone in *Hague Recueil*, 89 (1956) (i), 125–35, and the same, *Legal Controls of International Conflicts* (1954), pp. xli *et seq.* See also Corbett, *Law and Society in the Relations of States* (1951),

INTERNATIONAL LAW—THE GENERAL PART

an importance which obscures the powerful and overriding reality[1] of an already existing international community.[2] That solidarity of interests is, from the inception of human history, the cause and the expression of the social nature of man which underlies all law. Although not as conspicuous as conflicts of interests—which are prone to focus the attention of the outside observer[3]—it is a more enduring reality and constitutes the true structure of civilization and of its legal fabric.

The international community of interdependence and solidarity which is thus a significant factor adding to the legal character of international law is a community not only of States but also of individuals. This is so although that aspect of the situation has not

pp. 40 *et seq.* and in *Hague Recueil*, 85 (1954), 473. For a much-needed reminder of the modest limits of the notion of community required for the existence of the State or—what is the same—of law, see Kelsen, *Der soziologische und der juristische Staatsbegriff* (1922), pp. 105 *et seq.*—a work of enduring importance. See also Hold-Ferneck, *Lehrbuch des Völkerrechts*, I (1930), 17–26, 84–110; Balladore Pallieri, pp. 3–30; Burckhard, *Die Organisation der Rechtsgemeinschaft* (1927), pp. 374–416; Meinecke, *Weltbürgertum und Nationalstaat* (1928); Knubben, *Die Subjekte des Völkerrechts* (1928), pp. 1 9–20, 351–71; Delos, *La société internationale et les principes du droit public* (1929); Stratton, *Social Psychology of International Conduct* (1929), pp. 293–305; Walz, *Das Wesen des Völkerrechts und Kritik der Völkerrechtsleugner* (1930), pp. 157–62; De la Brière, *La communauté des Puissances* (1932); Laun, *Der Wandel der Ideen Staat und Volk als Äusserung des Weltgewissens* (1933), pp. 327–445; Blühdorn, *Einführung in das angewandte Völkerrecht* (1934), pp. 90–100; Corbu, *Essai sur la notion de règle en droit international* (1935); Scelle in *Hague Recueil*, 46 (1933) (iv), 339–46, and in *R.I.* (*Paris*), 15 (1935), 7–35; Zimmern in *Grotius Society*, 20 (1934), 25–44; Walsh in *Hague Recueil*, 53 (1935) (iii), 101–70; Del Vecchio in *Théorie du Droit*, 10 (1936), 1–13; Schwarzenberger in *Year Book of World Affairs*, 1 (1947), 159–77. On some psychological aspects of international relations see also West, *Conscience and Society* (1942), pp. 176–212, and in *Grotius Society*, 28 (1942), 133–50.

[1] While there may be an excess of euphemism, partly justified by traditional usage, in the *occasional* reference to the 'family of nations', there may also be a disadvantage in attaching conditions of some rigidity to the acceptance of the existence of an international community as an element of the definition of international law and of international obligation. Neither is it conducive to clarity to attach in this connection decisive importance to the distinction between 'community' and 'society' and to assert that there exists an international society but not an international community. These terms do not in themselves connote a higher or lower degree of cohesion. Within the State the existence of a community as a basis of law is not necessarily conditioned by an identity of language, race or religion; nor by an acceptance of common standards of the purpose of the State in terms of desirable political systems or economic bases of society; nor by the absence of actual and deep conflicts of interests between various classes of the population; nor by common historic experience. With regard to the latter it may be maintained, with some cogency, that there exists a common historic experience of mankind pointing in the direction of some minimum degree of order and integration as a condition both of welfare and of survival.

[2] 'Every constant factor which brings any two nations into touch with one another, establishes a positive society': Taparello, *Essai théorique de droit naturel* (1875), III, 40 (as quoted by O'Connell in *Sydney Law Review*, 2 (1957), 256).

[3] It is particularly in the works of so-called realist writers on international relations—such as Carr, Morgenthau and others (see below, p. 49)—that the phenomenon of conflict of interest between nations has been elevated to the importance of a paramount and decisive factor rendering illusory the very notion of an international society.

DEFINITION AND NATURE

yet fully crystallized into a positive rule of law. Yet it is clear that inasmuch as the interests of States are but the interests of the individual human beings of which they are composed,[1] the international community is a community not only of States but also of individuals both as members *generis humani* and, on an increasing scale, as parties to transactions and legal situations transcending the borders of the sovereign State.[2] When we speak of the growing international intercourse of States we speak to a large extent of the growing international intercourse, in its various manifestations, of individual human beings. Moreover, in so far as individuals, who are the ultimate subjects of all laws, are subjects of rights and duties grounded in international law—and they are so to a considerable extent[3]—they are in a distinct sense members of international society. In the sphere of private international law, which has to some degree become the object of regulation by public international law, the recognition and enforcement, across national boundaries, of private rights and status created under foreign law testifies in a different sphere to the existence of an international society.[4]

11. *The cumulative effect of the shortcomings of international law*

What is the cumulative effect of the shortcomings of international law as discussed in the preceding sections, namely, the lack of a sovereign law-making authority, the absence of a sovereign executive authority enforcing the law, the incomplete observance of international law, the limitation of the scope of matters regulated by it, the absence of an authority endowed with compulsory jurisdiction to ascertain the law, and the uncertainty and lack of precision of the rules of international law? The answer to this question is that, while seriously impairing the legal nature of what is described as international law, these shortcomings do not destroy it altogether so long as we do not regard them as permanently associated with it and as inherent in its very nature in the sense that it is a system of law intrinsically different from that obtaining within the State.

Admittedly, in some respects these defects bring international law

---

[1] See below, pp. 48–49.

[2] For an interesting attempt at applying a new concept of 'transnational law' to include 'all law which regulates actions or events that transcend national borders', see Jessup, *Transnational Law* (1956); and see the same, *The Use of International Law* (1959).

[3] See below, p. 141.

[4] Jitta, one of the most distinguished modern writers on the subject, speaks of the 'société internationale des individus' as the basis of private international law: *La méthode du droit international privé* (1916), p. 69. And see below, pp. 36–43.

31

INTERNATIONAL LAW—THE GENERAL PART

to the vanishing point of law. But they do not destroy it altogether. There is probably no single element of law which is so essential to it that its absence is in itself sufficient to deprive a rule of conduct of the quality of law. Yet we are not likely to enhance its authority *qua* law by ignoring that fact or by defending it by arguments such as that the element of enforceability of international law is supplied by war, reprisals and public opinion, or that it is on the whole as well observed as municipal law. While the Austinian conception of law is in many ways formal and incomplete,[1] there is no justification for the complacency with which the sound elements of Austin's definition have been challenged for the sake of the well-meant attempt to vindicate the legal nature of international law. The fact that consent, as distinguished from the overriding will of the legal sovereign, is one of the two principal sources of international law—and that it figures as such in its definition as outlined at the outset of this chapter—is not a sign of its strength as a system of law. However, as is shown below, this is not the only[2] or the necessarily decisive[3] feature of international law.

From one point of view 'consent' falls within the Austinian, the positivist, conception of law inasmuch as it is synonymous with the will of the State irrespective of the merits—the moral content, the social justice and the legal propriety in terms of general conceptions of law—of the rule laid down by the command emanating from the State. Within the State it is the will of the overriding sovereign organ; in the relations of States it is the concurrent will of the 'co-ordinated' sovereign States. In both cases it is the will of the State, the positive law expressly laid down by it (or by them). However, that is only one part of the law. The other part is that flowing from a source wholly different from the will of the State as the basis of the validity of the law. It is law as synonymous with reason, with objective necessity, with justice. As will be seen in the Section on the Sources of International Law, this is the second main source of international law.[4] There is a tendency among writers—and, much less frequently, among judges—to think of 'law as will' and 'law as reason' in terms of opposing and perhaps inherently conflicting conceptions of law. Yet there is no antinomy between the two. Law comprises both those conceptions in proportions varying with historical development and circumstances. There may be a conflict between them as a matter of strict juridical logic,

[1] See below, p. 209. [2] See below, pp. 54, 56
[3] See below, p. 57. [4] See below, p. 76.

DEFINITION AND NATURE

whether appearing as the so-called 'pure theory of law' or in any other form. That logic insists, legitimately from its point of view, on an ultimate source of authority in cases of conflict between law conceived as will and law conceived as reason. Yet, it is a logic the necessity of which is contradicted by experience dating from the very inception of political society. For it is not logic which decides whether judges declare the law or make it. It is not logic which tells us whether courts in applying principles of good faith, reason, public policy, and the like, change the law or give effect to it. However that may be, for reasons which are inherent in the present structure of international society and which narrow the scope of law conceived as command, that second aspect of the law constitutes a substantial part of international law and compensates for its shortcomings as seen from the angle of the positivist, imperative, Austinian conception of law. That second aspect, starting from the much decried but ever inspiring antecedents of the law of nature, has now acquired a less controversial formulation. It is in the light of these considerations that it is necessary to view the undoubted shortcomings of international law.

12. *International law as a system of law*

It has been suggested in the preceding Sections that the cumulative effect of the shortcomings of international law in relation to the normal requirements of the notion of law is not such as to be destructive of the legal character of the body of rules and principles currently described as international law. That is so provided that these shortcomings are conceived not as necessarily and permanently inherent in international law but as temporarily associated with a transient stage of its immaturity which humanity, impelled by the growing interdependence of States and individuals in the modern world, by the realization of the nature of the alternatives to an effective legal ordering between States and by a growing sense of collective morality transcending the borders of the national State, is bound to overcome by conscious effort. So long as that paramount consideration is kept in mind it is proper and convenient to describe the rules of international law as rules of law rather than to choose another designation for them. The fact is that, in many essential respects, they approach the categories of law rather than those of any other system of rules of conduct. Unlike rules of morality, they are external in their nature; their binding force is generally regarded —and must logically be regarded—as grounded primarily in a

INTERNATIONAL LAW—THE GENERAL PART

source superior to the will of States; even if not regularly enforced, they are deemed to be enforceable by external compulsion and are so to some extent. Nor is it irrelevant that they are considered to be and are treated as law by the judicial and political organs of the State.[1]

Above all, while all these factors are clearly germane to the formal content of the notion of law, a great deal of the substance of international law has been developed in association with, and is permeated by rules and principles of law as generally practised and understood, in particular of private law. The law of treaties, of State responsibility and of acquisition of territorial sovereignty are particularly prominent in this connection. That reliance upon rules of private law, largely identical with 'general principles of law as recognized by civilized States',[2] is by no means a feature of the formative period of international law. It is a continuing process explained by the fact that, as will be suggested in the Chapter on the Subjects of International Law,[3] the legal rights and duties of States are essentially the legal rights and duties of individuals who act on their behalf and who, upon final analysis, constitute the political entity of the State. The analogy of States and individuals is a constant factor in the creation and development of international law. This is so not only—and not primarily—because in some respects States are like individuals and because they enter into legal relations and find themselves in legal situations analogous to those of individuals. It is so, primarily, because they act through and are comprised of individuals. States are not only like individuals; they consist of individual human beings.

For these reasons it is more practicable and less inaccurate to describe international law, as generally understood, by that name rather than as positive international morality[4] or the like, and to treat

---

[1] There is a measure of refinement in the suggestion that the definition of rules of conduct as law is a task which can validly be undertaken not by courts or governments but by the jurist. Similarly, there is an excess of simplification in the suggestion that rules of international law are regarded by municipal courts as law only because and in so far as they have been incorporated into domestic law and *pro tanto* endowed with a sanction. Their legal quality is pre-existent to, and a condition of, their recognition as part of the law of the land.   [2] See below, p. 68.

[3] See below, chapter 3, pp. 136 *et seq.*

[4] The following passages from Austin's *Lectures on Jurisprudence* (edition of 1885) may be noted: 'But the greatest logical error of all is that committed by many continental jurists, who include in public law, not only the law of political conditions, of crimes, and of civil and criminal procedure, but also *international* law; which is not positive law at all, but a branch of positive morality (Lecture 44, vol. II, p. 754).

'The law obtaining between nations is not positive law: for every positive law is set by a given sovereign to a person or persons in a state of subjection to its author . . . the law

DEFINITION AND NATURE

it as part of jurisprudence. As suggested above, the use of that terminology is profitable and accurate only so long as it is understood that the acknowledged shortcomings of international law *qua* law are not a quality inherent in it—by virtue of its being a primitive type of law conceived as a 'law of co-ordination' based on agreement and devoid of the imperative element of command—but a transient stage in the rational progression of mankind towards a more effective system of international law between sovereign States.[1] That development, in turn, may be no more than a phase leading to some kind of federal organization of humanity in which the sovereignty of States, inasmuch as it gives the decisive impress to international law, will yield to a conception of interdependence more in accordance with a true legal order among States.

The prospects of any such consummation cannot, as yet, be assessed. The political and ideological divisions of the world in any particular period may combine to make them appear wholly remote. Yet it may not be consistent with moral duty, or with a rational estimate of the conditions of survival of the human race, to view such a consummation as an infinite ideal, or, under the impact of immediate experience, to give to any particular period of stagnation or retrogression the hall-mark of permanency. The view, often voiced, that any such development will mean an end to international law as at present understood is dialectically attractive and, to a substantial extent, true. But there seems to be no reason why international law as at present understood should not be transmuted into an international law which is more in accordance with

obtaining between nations is law (improperly so called) set by general opinion. The duties which it imposes are enforced by moral sanctions' (Lecture 6, vol. 1, pp. 225–226).

In the Index there occurs the following entry: 'International Law...(*see* Positive International Morality).' The most vigorous criticism of the exaggeration of the Austinian conception of law, especially in its relation to international law, has come not from Continental but from English lawyers. For recent powerful criticism of this kind see Allen, *Law in the Making* (6th ed. 1958), p. 151. See also Goodhart in *Grotius Society*, 22 (1936), 32–4; Pollock in *Columbia Law Review*, 2 (1902), 511; Jethro Brown, *The Austinian Theory of Law* (1906), p. 52.

[1] For an account and analysis of these and similar theories of international law, propounded mainly by German writers prior to the two World Wars, see Lauterpacht, *The Function of Law*, pp. 399–423. Their general character is clearly exposed in the following passage of a treatise by a leading Italian writer: 'It is impossible to base, from whatever point of view, the binding force of international law upon the idea of a command emanating from a will, however conceived, superior to that of States. Moreover, such impossibility corresponds to the actual character of international society: a society of States which are sovereign and juridically equal. What remains therefore is to conceive international law as a system of promises between subjects which are coordinated and juridically equal. Recent studies in the field of general jurisprudence have made it clear that a legal rule need not necessarily assume the character of an overriding command but that it can, under certain conditions, have its source in a promise' (Cavaglieri, p. 44).

INTERNATIONAL LAW—THE GENERAL PART

the notion of a system of true law among States and, as such, with the true function of the State.[1]

In the meantime, however, the circumstance that international law, once accepted by States, is binding upon them by way of an external obligation and that many of its precepts are binding upon them even without their concurrence,[2] by virtue of their existence as States and their membership of the international community, ought not to obscure the fact that, in contrast with municipal law, new rules of international law are not, in general, binding upon them except with their consent. To that very substantial extent international law as at present constituted is a 'law of co-ordination' as distinguished from subordination to a law-giving authority. For the reasons stated this is not a characteristic which decisively affects its character as a system of law.

13. *International public law and international private law*

The present treatise is concerned only with public international law as defined above and as distinguished from private international law or, as it is often called, Conflict of Laws. The latter is that branch of the municipal—the national—law of various States which is concerned, primarily, with the rules and principles in accordance with which municipal courts give effect to rights and status originating in a foreign country. These rules and principles have reference, in

---

[1] The literature of international law abounds in examples of radical changes of view, on the part of writers, on this subject. Thus while Oppenheim, in the first edition of his treatise, was emphatic that there 'is not, and never will be, a central authority above the several States', in his analysis, written in 1919, of the Covenant of the League of Nations he advocated such a central authority by urging that 'membership of the League ought to be compulsory and that a recalcitrant member should, if necessary, be coerced by force to submit to the decisions of the League, and to fulfil its duties' (3rd ed. 1919, I, 352). Liszt, a leading German textbook-writer, urged in the tenth edition of his treatise that international law is radically different from municipal law and that it must necessarily lack the element of compulsion. In the eleventh edition, published in 1918, he urged that international law is of the same nature as the law of the State and that recognition of the principle of enforcement is a necessary practical condition of its development as a system of law (at p. 8). Judge Max Huber, one of the most distinguished modern international lawyers, writing in 1910, urged that an organization of an overriding nature embracing all States was a 'political impossibility' ('Beiträge zur Kenntnis der soziologischen Grundlagen des Völkerrechts' in *Jahrbuch des öffentlichen Rechts*, 4 (1910), 133, reprinted in his collected writings under the title 'Gesellschaft und Humanität' (1948), p. 49). Yet, writing in 1958, he said: 'The unity of law and the dependence of all national law on international and supra-national order is not merely a systematic question in the philosophy of law. It is, first and foremost, a question of political life and death . . .'—'On the Place of the Law of Nations in the History of Mankind' in *Symbolae Verzijl* (1958), p. 194. On the compatibility of the maintenance of the idea of the ultimate goal of international organization with the practical requirements of the legal organization of mankind in any given period see Oppenheim, I, §§ 166–7. [2] See below, p. 76.

DEFINITION AND NATURE

particular, to the determination of the system of law to be applied by the local court in cases involving foreign rights and status. Thus, for instance, when a German subject domiciled in Great Britain dies intestate in the United States leaving property, movable or immovable or both, in France, the question arises which law will govern the disposition of his property—in particular whether that law will be determined by the German nationality, the British domicile, or the French *situs* of the property. When two persons, one of Belgian and the other of Dutch nationality, both resident in Great Britain, conclude a contract in France for the delivery in Germany to German nationals of goods manufactured in France, the question arises as to what law an English court shall apply in relation to the contract. Similarly, there is a question of private international law in connection with the choice of law for the determination of the validity, in England, of a marriage concluded in Russia by two German nationals domiciled in Denmark or for the appointment of a guardian of a child of Dutch nationality born in Sweden and permanently residing there.[1]

In all these cases the problem is one of the choice, the determination, of the law to be applied by the court confronted with what is somewhat loosely described as a foreign element. This constitutes the main, but not the only aspect of judicial activity in this sphere. When courts enforce a foreign judgment or when they decide whether to assume jurisdiction in a petition for divorce in a case involving parties domiciled abroad, they are concerned with giving effect, without—strictly speaking—having to proceed to a choice of law, to rights and status originating abroad. These matters must be regarded as constituting the specific province of private international law—although text-books on the subject occasionally, and probably mistakenly, devote attention to such questions as immunity from jurisdiction enjoyed by foreign States, their sovereigns and their diplomatic representatives[2] or even such matters as treatment of aliens, nationality and extradition.[3]

---

[1] See below, p. 41.

[2] There is in these cases no question of a choice of one system of law in preference to another. They are cases of a refusal, on grounds of public international law, to apply affirmatively any system of law whatsoever. It is probably the presence of the 'foreign element' which has led to the inclusion, without persuasive logical reason, of this topic among those of private international law. There is a foreign element present when two foreign nationals conclude an ordinary contract in the United Kingdom but, normally, such contract does not give rise to questions of private international law.

[3] For criticism of the tendency to expand the system of private international law to include these subjects, see Beckett in *B.Y.* 7 (1926), 73–96.

37

It will appear from the examples given above that the sphere of private international law is different from that of public international law. That does not mean that there is no relation whatsoever between these two branches of law. On the contrary, inasmuch as private international law is part of the internal—the municipal—law of States, it stands to that extent in the same relation to public international law as municipal law generally. This means that it ought to be in accordance with any relevant rules of public international law. Undoubtedly, States and their courts are, in principle, free to decide upon the manner in which they will determine the choice of the law to be applied. Thus with regard to personal status and family relations, such as validity of marriage, mutual relations of husband and wife, divorce, legitimation and adoption, some countries—for instance, France—proceed generally on the view that the foreign law applicable is that of the nationality of the parties. Others—for instance, the United Kingdom—attach decisive importance to the domicile of the parties. Both systems have their advantages and disadvantages. Apart from treaty, public international law in no way limits the freedom of action of States in the matter.

However, this does not mean that States enjoy absolute freedom of action in this respect. Although they are free to choose between various foreign laws, they are not, in principle, free to disregard foreign law altogether and to extend indiscriminately the operation of their own law, with regard to persons who are not their nationals or who are not domiciled within their jurisdiction, to rights and relationships created abroad. Thus, if the courts of a State were, in relation to foreign nationals generally or foreign nationals resident abroad, to decide upon the validity of marriages contracted abroad or of property ostensibly acquired abroad by reference to their own law only and exclusively, such conduct would give justifiable ground for complaint. This is so although it may be controversial whether such action is improper because it offends against the recognized principle of respect for acquired rights of aliens; or because, upon analysis, it amounts to a wide claim of extraterritorial jurisdiction over persons and property abroad; or because it is inconsistent with the obligation of recognition of the legislative, administrative or judicial acts of foreign recognized States—an obligation which, within limits prescribed by their own sovereignty and public order, international law imposes upon States. While the grounds of any such complaints may be controversial and not always easy to

DEFINITION AND NATURE

define,[1] the action which gives rise to them may be contrary to public international law inasmuch as it may constitute a violation of the international rights of a State or its nationals.

To suggest, therefore, as is occasionally done, that no direct interest of a foreign State is involved if, say, an English court refuses to apply the law of that State, is to oversimplify the problem. A State is interested in justice being done to its nationals and in the recognition of their rights validly acquired. That can be done by making either the law of nationality or that of domicile the decisive test for the purposes of private international law. It is, as a rule, inconsistent with that purpose to make the *lex fori* the decisive consideration.[2] On the other hand, although national exclusiveness or prejudice have occasionally placed unjustifiable obstacles in the way of the application of foreign law, circumstances may arise in which the application of foreign law may prove wholly obnoxious to national conceptions of justice and legality. Thus, prior to the Second World War the courts of most countries declined to apply certain laws enacted by the National-Socialists in Germany—in

[1] In particular, the obligations of the State are in this respect limited by the requirements of public policy as understood by its courts. As falling under this head there must be considered the various aspects of guardianship, especially in the case of infants.

[2] It is only subject to that general consideration that it can be accurately stated that international law does not, in general, impose upon States the obligation to have a particular kind of private international law, for instance, that their choice of law should be determined by the nationality rather than by the domicile of the parties. However, as stated, if a State were to adopt a system by virtue of which all matters now regulated by reference to either of these two principles should be regulated exclusively by its own substantive law, foreign States would have a just cause of complaint, under international law, in all cases in which such action would have injurious effects upon them or their nationals. Public international law imposes upon States no particular duties with regard to the kind of private international law to be administered by them. It does impose upon them the general duty to administer private international law in a manner consistent with the international obligations of the State.

For a general discussion of the objects of private international law and, in particular, a discussion of the relation of public and private international law see Westlake, *Papers*, pp. 285–311 (an early, important essay on the subject); Cheshire, *Private International Law* (5th ed. 1957), pp. 3–44; Wolff, *Private International Law* (2nd ed. 1950), pp. 1–18; Batiffol, *Traité élémentaire de droit international privé* (2nd ed. 1955), pp. 26–36; Arminjon in *R.I.* 3rd ser. 10 (1929), 680–98; Nussbaum in *Columbia Law Review*, 42 (1942), 189 *et seq.*; Rundstein in *R.I.* 3rd ser. 17 (1936), 314–49; Starke in *L.Q.R.* 52 (1936), 395–401; Niederer in *Annuaire Suisse de Droit International*, 5 (1948), 66–82; Kopelmanas in *Etudes Georges Scelle* (1950), II, 753–804; Stevenson in *Columbia Law Review*, 52 (1952), 561–88; Wortley in *Hague Recueil*, 85 (1954) (i), 243–338; Katzenbach in *Yale Law Journal*, 65 (1956), 1087 *et seq.*; Yntema in *Canadian Law Review*, 35 (1957), 721 *et seq.*; Fitzmaurice in *Hague Recueil*, 92 (1957) (ii), 218–22; Unger in *Grotius Society*, 43 (1957), 87–108; Carswell in *I.C.L.Q.* 8 (1959), 268–88. And see Oppenheim, 1, § 115*b*, on the limits of enforcement of foreign legislation. See also, on the English conception of private international law, Foster in *Hague Recueil*, 65 (1938) (iii), 399 *et seq.*; Llewelyn Davies, *ibid.* 62 (1937) (iv), 427 *et seq.*; Wortley, *ibid.* 71 (1947) (iv), 5 *et seq.* And see Sack, *Conflicts of Laws in the History of the English Law* (reprinted from *Law: a Century of Progress, 1835–1935* (1937)); Nadelmann in *University of Pennsylvania Law Review*, 102 (1954), 323–62.

INTERNATIONAL LAW—THE GENERAL PART

particular the so-called Nuremberg Laws providing for impediments to marriage on racial or religious grounds. To that extent at least the notion of public policy is generally recognized in the law of most countries as having a special place in the sphere of private international law.[1]

Moreover, although the courts and legislatures of States are free to determine the principles of the choice of foreign law, States may by treaty limit their freedom of action in this respect. They have occasionally done so. Thus the Hague Convention of 1902 regulating the validity of marriage provided that all the impediments to marriage under the national law of one of the parties shall be given effect regardless of the place of marriage and that no party shall refuse to recognize such impediments except in cases expressly provided for by the treaty.[2]

By virtue of such treaties private international law enters directly

---

[1] This seems to have been admitted by both parties in the *Guardianship Case* between Netherlands and Sweden, decided by the International Court of Justice in 1958 (*I.C.J. Reports* 1958, p. 55)—although they differed on the question whether particularly stringent conditions for the application of *ordre public* applied when the subject was regulated by treaty. The Court did not decide on this aspect of the question. It held that although the Hague Guardianship Convention of 1902 provided that guardianship shall be determined by reference to the nationality of the minor, a Swedish Law on Protective Upbringing which operated so as to interfere in fact with the functions of the guardian appointed in accordance with the Convention, was not contrary to the Convention for the reason that guardianship and protective upbringing were wholly different institutions. For a different view on the subject, expressed in an Individual Opinion, see *ibid.* pp. 79–87. [This is reprinted in Part VI D 3 of these Collected Papers under the heading 'Interpretation of treaties in practice'.]

[2] That Convention was one of a number of Conventions concluded in 1902 and 1905 at The Hague in connection with a series of conferences of Governments on private international law convened on the initiative of the Dutch Government. The two other Conventions concluded in 1902 related to divorce and separation, and guardianship (see above, n. 1). In 1905 three Conventions were concluded: on the effects of marriage, on interdiction of incapable persons and on civil procedure. The Convention of 1902 on marriage is now binding upon Germany, Italy, Luxembourg, the Netherlands, Poland, Portugal, Romania, Switzerland and Hungary—all countries in which the test of nationality, as distinguished from domicile, is treated as decisive for the purpose of status. The scope of the other Hague Conventions is similarly limited. For a survey of these treaties as well as other treaties on private international law see Wolff, *Private International Law* (2nd ed. 1950), pp. 46–51, and Cheshire, *Private International Law* (5th ed. 1957), pp. 12–16. In 1951 a Treaty was signed establishing the Statute of the Hague Conference on Private International Law. The Treaty, to which also Great Britain is a party, came into force in 1955: Treaty Series No. 65 (1955), Cmd. 9582. The Treaty recognizes the permanent character of the Hague Conference on Private International Law for the purpose of the progressive unification of rules of private international law. It establishes a Bureau entrusted with the function of preparing proposals for the unification of private international law.

In 1930 and 1931 Conventions were concluded in Geneva bearing upon rules of private international law in the matter of bills of exchange and cheques. In 1923 and 1927, Conventions were concluded in Geneva relating to arbitration clauses and the execution of foreign arbitral awards. Practically all European countries, including Great Britain, are parties to these Conventions. In 1931 Sweden, Norway, Denmark, Finland and Iceland concluded, in addition to other treaties signed in that period, a Treaty for

DEFINITION AND NATURE

within the sphere of international law. This becomes especially apparent when treaties contain, as they occasionally do, clauses conferring upon international tribunals jurisdiction in disputes concerning their interpretation or application. Such jurisdiction may also be acquired by virtue of a more general obligation of judicial or arbitral settlement. Thus in 1957 the Netherlands, as a signatory of the Optional Clause of the Statute of the International Court of Justice, brought before that Court a complaint against Sweden based on the allegation that contrary to the Convention on Guardianship of 1902 Sweden prevented the functioning of a guardian duly appointed by the Dutch authorities.[1] It is possible that in so far as uniformity in the standards of private international law is desirable and feasible, it may to some extent be secured through the activity of international tribunals.[2] They are in the

the unification of rules of private international law in the matter of marriage, adoption and guardianship—a Treaty which effects an interesting compromise between the tests of nationality and domicile (see Cheshire, *op. cit.* p. 15). In 1951 a series of treaties on the subject was concluded between the 'Benelux Countries'—Belgium, the Netherlands and Luxembourg. Previously, considerable efforts were made by various Latin-American countries to achieve, by way of treaties, a measure of unity in that sphere. In 1889 there were signed the two Conventions of Montevideo on Civil International Law and Commercial International Law. In 1928 a large number of Latin-American States adopted the detailed Bustamante Code on Private International Law which is now binding on about fifteen States in Central and South America. See, generally, Kosters and Bellemans, *Les Conventions de la Haye sur le droit international privé* (1921); Plaisant, *Les règles de conflit de lois dans les traités* (1946); and, on the interpretation of these treaties by tribunals, Batiffol, *op. cit.* pp. 37 *et seq.* On the codification of private international law generally see Nolde in *Hague Recueil*, 55 (1936) (i), 303–427. For a collection of texts of conventions and statutes see Makarov, *Quellen des internationalen Privatrechts* (1929).

From these treaties, which aim at the unification of municipal law with regard to the choice of law and determination of jurisdiction, there must be distinguished treaties the object of which is to introduce substantive uniformity with regard to the contents of some branches of municipal law, in particular those which have an international aspect. These include the various conventions for the protection of literary and artistic property; for the protection of industrial property in the matter of patents and the like; on some aspects of maritime law, for instance, collisions at sea, assistance and salvage; for a uniform law of bills of exchange and cheques as formulated in conventions concluded in 1930 and 1931—conventions which are partly conventions on private international law and partly conventions on unification of private law; on the law concerning carriage by rail, as in the Berne Convention of 1924; on the international carriage of persons and goods by air, as in the Warsaw Convention of 1929. And see generally, on unification of private law, Matteucci in *Hague Recueil*, 91 (1957) (i), 387–441. See also Schnitzer, *De la diversité et de l'unification du droit* (1946); David, *Traité élémentaire de droit civil comparé* (1950); Lilar, *L'unification internationale du droit maritime* (1955); Zweigert in *Zeitschrift für ausländisches und internationales Privatrecht*, 16 (1951), 387–97; Nadelmann in *University of Pennsylvania Law Review*, 1954; Michaélidès-Nouaros in *Revue Hellénique*, 10 (1957), 40–131. [1] See above, p. 40 n. 1.

[2] On the projected international tribunal on questions of private international law see Carlander in *Nordisk T.A.* 2 (1931), 49–60. For a survey of the decisions of the Permanent Court of International Justice on questions of private international law, see Hammarskjöld in *Revue critique de droit international*, 30 (1934), 315–44. As to the decisions of international tribunals in the matter generally, see Lipstein in *Grotius Society*, 27 (1941), 141–81, and 29 (1943), 51–84.

INTERNATIONAL LAW—THE GENERAL PART

position to do so by way, mainly, of interpreting treaties concerned with questions of private international law. Such interpretation properly includes not only the question whether any particular national enactment is in accordance with the treaty, but also whether it has been applied in accordance with the object and the spirit of the treaty.

However, as mentioned, some of these questions raise issues of public international law and may become subject to international adjudication regardless of treaty in so far as they have a bearing upon the obligation of a State to respect the rights of aliens guaranteed by international law or upon the obligation of States to recognize the legislative and judicial acts of other States legitimately performed within the scope of their competence in a manner not inconsistent with international law. In the case concerning the *Serbian Loans* the Permanent Court of International Justice stated that rules of private international law may also be established by international conventions or custom, in which case they 'may possess the character of true international law governing the relations between States'.[1] The regulation of the details of private international law by international treaty or custom is still the exception rather than the rule. As the relations and situations with which private international law is concerned are transnational[2] in character—i.e. transcending the borders of any single State—they would seem, as such, to provide a proper subject for international regulation so far as the custom of the State and its judicial and other organs is concerned. The occasions for such regulation are bound to multiply in proportion as international law is transformed from a body of rules governing exclusively the traditional aspects of the relations of States and assumes the complexion of an international law of mankind of which sovereign States are the principal but not the exclusive subjects and beneficiaries.[3] However that may be, although the observance of the legal principles which underlie private international law is occasionally—and inaccurately[4]

---

[1] Series A, nos. 20–1, p. 41.

[2] See Jessup, *Transnational Law* (1956), for a wider treatment of the subject from various aspects.

[3] Pillet in *R.I.* 3rd ser. 4 (1923), 345–55, regards private international law not primarily as municipal law, but as a cosmopolitan customary law based on general concurrence —upon which see Pollock's comment in *L.Q.R.* 40 (1924), 271–4. The basic conception underlying the teaching of Jitta, a Dutch international lawyer whose treatise was published in 1916 and who was one of the principal authorities on the subject, is that there is an 'international community of individuals', i.e. of mankind as a whole, which lies at the roots of private international law.

[4] See Cheshire, *Private International Law* (5th ed. 1957), p. 5; Wolff, *Private International Law* (2nd ed. 1950), p. 15; Beckett, *B.Y.* 7 (1926), 85. The criticism of the term 'comity'

DEFINITION AND NATURE

—described as due to, or having its origin in 'comity', it has been suggested above that it is in fact dictated to a large extent by certain overriding considerations of public international law.

14. *International law and international comity*

In connection with the definition of international law it is necessary to distinguish between rules of international law proper and so-called international comity.[1] The latter are rules of practice followed not as a matter of obligation but of courtesy, convenience, and neighbourly accommodation. Thus, for instance, many States which grant to diplomatic representatives of foreign States exemption from customs duties do so as a matter of courtesy, as distinguished from legal obligation.[2] According to some this is also the basis of the immunities granted to diplomatic representatives within the territories of third States while proceeding to or from their mission.[3] Similarly, while as a matter of law some States claim full jurisdiction over foreign merchant vessels in their ports and territorial waters, as a matter of comity and convenience that jurisdiction is exercised only in certain categories of cases.[4] While international custom, conceived as a source of international law, is, according to what is still the authoritative view, evidence of practice followed as law— *opinio necessitatis juris*—or as a matter of obligation generally, this is not the case with international comity. In the *Asylum* case between Colombia and Peru the International Court of Justice declined to concede the character of a legal obligation to certain practices, as between Latin-American States, in the matter of diplomatic asylum; these, it pointed out, were not due to 'constant and uniform usage, accepted as law'; they were due to 'considerations of convenience or simple political expediency'[5] not accompanied by any sentiment of legal obligation. As in the case of chivalry in the sphere of the law of war, so also, on occasions, rules of courtesy have acquired

in private international law is as persistent as it is in judicial decisions. See, e.g. Read, *Recognition and Enforcement of Foreign Judgments* (1938), pp. 52–8; Cohn in *I.C.L.Q.* 7 (1958), 642. As to 'comity' in public international law, see below.

[1] The *New English Dictionary* (Murray) gives the following explanation: 'Apparently misused for the company of nations mutually practising international comity (in some instances erroneous association with L[atin] *comes*, "companion", is to be suspected).'

[2] A view going back to Vattel, Book IV, ch. 7, sec. 105: 'If the sovereign is pleased to exempt him from them, it is a courtesy which the minister cannot claim of right.' The British Foreign Office Regulation of 1904 refers to that exemption as being not 'in the nature of a right' but as springing 'from the courtesy of the Government to which the foreign representative is accredited'. And see Oppenheim, I, § 394; Hall, p. 235.

[3] See Hall, p. 363 (with a detailed note); *sed quaere*: see Oppenheim, I, § 398.

[4] See Oppenheim, I, § 390 c.

[5] *I.C.J. Reports* 1950, p. 266, at pp. 277, 286.

43

INTERNATIONAL LAW—THE GENERAL PART

the complexion of a legal customary rule. This, probably, has been the case with regard to immunity from taxation accorded to diplomatic representatives—an immunity now generally granted as a matter of law.

Although the distinction between international comity (or courtesy) and international law proper is firmly established in the literature of international law and in international practice (including the practice of the Governments of the United Kingdom[1] and the United States), in the judicial practice of some countries—in particular that of Great Britain and, to a lesser degree, of the United States of America—there has been a persistent tendency to refer to 'international comity' with regard to matters clearly governed by international law. This has been the case, in particular, with regard to such questions as the jurisdictional immunities of foreign States, their heads and diplomatic representatives;[2] the obligation to respect[3] or give effect to the legislative and judicial

[1] That the distinction, in that sense, between international law and international comity is not unknown to English lawyers may be seen from an Opinion given in 1896 by Sir Richard Webster and Sir Robert Finlay, as Law Officers of the Crown, on the legality of certain restrictions imposed by the Government of Iceland on British trawlers in the territorial waters of Iceland. They expressed the view that there was no principle of international law imposing upon any State the duty to permit commercial intercourse, but that it would be 'a violation of international comity and of right conduct as between civilized States' to prohibit such intercourse without adequate reason. However, in their opinion the conduct of the Government of Iceland did not, in the circumstances of the case, offend against international comity (McNair, *Opinions*, 1, 343).

[2] See, e.g. *The Parlement Belge* (1880), L.R. 5 P.D. 197, 214, 217, where Brett L.J. referred to the rules relating to the jurisdictional immunities of foreign ambassadors and sovereigns as being the consequence of 'international comity which induces every sovereign State to respect the independence and dignity of every other sovereign State'. Unless 'comity' means 'law' the statement is not intelligible. For it would appear that respect for the independence of other States is a primary duty imposed by international law.

[3] Thus Judges have expressed the view that it 'would be contrary to our obligations of international comity as now understood' to enforce in England a contract made abroad with a view to deriving profit from the commission of a criminal act in a foreign country and that its enforcement would furnish a just cause of complaint on the part of the foreign Government: *Foster* v. *Driscoll*, [1929] 1 K.B. 470, *Annual Digest*, 4 (1927–8), Case no. 10 and Note; *Wakerville Brewing Co.* v. *Maynard* (1928–9), Ontario Law Reports, pp. 5–12, 573; *Westage* v. *Harris* (1929) *ibid.* p. 358. See on these cases Webber in *New York University Law Quarterly Review*, 7 (1929–30), 674, and Marjorie Owen in *Canadian Bar Review*, 81 (1930), 413. An international agreement may impose upon a State a direct obligation to refuse to enforce private contracts violative of foreign laws enacted in conformity with that agreement. Thus the Bretton Woods Agreement of 1945 relating to the International Monetary Fund provided, in Article viii, Section 2(*b*), that 'exchange contracts which involve the currency of any member and which are contrary to the exchange control regulations of that member maintained or imposed consistently with this Agreement shall be unenforceable in the territories of any member'. For a review of numerous judicial decisions on the subject see Gold, *The Fund Agreement in the Courts* (a series of Staff Papers of the International Monetary Fund) and the same in *Zeitschrift für ausländisches und internationales Privatrecht*, 22 (1957), 601–42; Bülck in *Jahrbuch für*

DEFINITION AND NATURE

acts of recognized States and Governments; and the duty, within certain limits, to refrain from assuming jurisdiction over aliens with respect to acts committed abroad.[1]

The use of that terminology, in itself inaccurate in relation to generally accepted usage in international practice, is not free of a measure of obscurity and confusion. At times it is used as synonymous with courtesy; occasionally it is, apparently, used as synonymous with a rule of law, international or municipal, which owes its origin to comity;[2] finally, it is resorted to as denoting a half-way house between comity and law.[3] Although, in relation to public international law, of comparatively recent origin,[4] it is somewhat archaic and there is little doubt that its abandonment, having regard to its studied vagueness, would be conducive to clarity.[5] There may otherwise be some danger that courts may on occasion be inclined

internationales Recht, 5 (1955), 113–23; Mann in *I.C.L.Q.* 5 (1956), 295–301; Schutzer in *International Law Association, Report of 47th Conference* (1956), pp. 299–319; Seidl-Hohenveldern in *Ö.Z̧.ö.R.* 8 (1957), pp. 82–105.

[1] *Joyce* v. *Director of Public Prosecutions*, [1946] A.C. 374, 372; see also, with regard to an alleged claim to extraterritorial jurisdiction in England on the part of an American court, *British Nylon Spinners Ltd.* v. *Imperial Chemical Industries, Ltd.*, [1953] Ch. 19.

[2] See, e.g. *Russian Socialist Federated Soviet Republic* v. *Cibrario, Annual Digest*, 2 (1923–4), Case no. 17, where the New York Court said: 'Comity may be defined as the reciprocal courtesy which one member of the family of nations owes to the others. It presupposes friendship . . . Rules of comity are a portion of the law that they [courts] enforce.' The Court then proceeded: 'A foreign power brings an action in our courts not as a matter of right. Its power to do so is the creature of comity.' In some cases 'comity of nations' has been held to apply as forming part of a public policy (*Hart* v. *Gumpach* (1872) L.R. 4 P.C. 439).

[3] 'Comity, in the legal sense, is neither a matter of absolute obligation, on the one hand, nor of mere courtesy and good will, upon the other. But it is the recognition which one nation allows within its territory to the legislative, executive, or judicial acts of another nation, having regard both to international duty and convenience...' *Hilton* v. *Guyot* (1895) 159 U.S. 113. While the subject-matter of this case had reference to the enforcement of a foreign judgment, the Court treated it as one of international law generally. See, to the same effect, the judgment of the Supreme Court of the Philippines in *Sison* v. *The Board of Accountancy and Ferguson, I.L.R.*, 18 (1951), 14. For an example of a further complication latent in the lax use of the term, see *Johnston* v. *Compagnie Générale Transatlantique* (1926) 242 N.Y. 381, 387, where the Court of Appeals of New York said: 'Comity is not a rule of law, but it is a rule of practice, convenience and expediency. It is something more than mere courtesy.'

[4] In the sphere of public international law that term seems to have gained currency following upon the judgment in *The Parlement Belge* (see above). In earlier English cases there was no hesitation in referring in appropriate cases to the 'law of nations' pure and simple. See *Viveash* v. *Becker* (1814) 3 M. & S. 284; *De Wutz* v. *Hendricks* (1824) S.C., 9 Moore 586, where Best C.J. held that 'it was contrary to the law of nations (which in all cases of international law is adopted into the municipal code of every civilized country)' to raise money in England in support of a rebellion in a foreign country; *Emperor of Austria* v. *Day and Kossuth* (1861) 2 Giff. 628; *Novello* v. *Toogood* (1823) 1 B. and C. Reports 554. The same applies to early American cases: see, e.g. *Respublica* v. *De Longchamps* (1784), 1 Dallas Reports, 111. And see below, p. 154.

[5] In *The El Neptuno*, a case involving jurisdictional immunities of a vessel claimed by two recognized Governments, the Court observed that 'the whole doctrine of immunity from arrest is a matter that rests upon the comity of nations' and exhorted the parties

to treat as a revocable concession what is in fact an established principle of law. It is possible that the persistence in resorting to it is due to some extent to the surviving doubts, under the influence of the Austinian notion of law, as to the legal character of international law. From that point of view 'international comity' seems to supply a solution which, although purely verbal, appears to some to be in the nature of a compromise. This is not necessarily a good reason for its retention. There is questionable merit in reducing the rules of international law to the uncertain level of international comity both in general and in particular among States between whom 'comity' in its ordinary connotation may occasionally be no more than a form of words.[1]

15. *International law and morality*

The main difference—which is both formal and substantial—between law and morality has already been indicated. While law is a command made effective, if necessary, by external compulsion, morality operates within the realm of conscience. The same applies to the relation of international law and morality. However, care must be taken not to exaggerate the importance of the difference thus conceived. That is so quite apart from the fact that, normally, the law is obeyed not because of the threat of external sanction but because of the impact of its moral and social content and the general sentiment of willing obedience to the law. In addition, there are a number of factors which bring to mind the close connection between law and morals in the sphere of international law.

In the first instance, like any other law, international law is to a large extent the expression of dictates of morality. This applies particularly, though not exclusively, to that part of international law which draws its strength from what has in the past been referred to as the law of nature and which is now usually accorded the more

not to strain the obligation of courtesy 'resting as that obligation does upon that slender point' (Lloyd's List Law Reports, 62 (1938) 7; *Annual Digest*, 9 (1938–40), Case No. 91 (Note)). That 'slender point' of comity of nations was described in a later case as a 'paramount rule of law': *The Tolten* [1946] p. 135, at p. 151. For a somewhat inconclusive discussion of the term 'international comity' by a Belgian Court see *Socobel* v. *Greek State, I.L.R.* (1951), 8. And see above, p. 42, n. 4, as to 'comity' in private international law.

[1] See, generally, on international comity and courtesy Störk, *Völkerrecht und Völkercourtoisie* (1908); Heilborn, *Grundbegriffe des Völkerrechts* (1912), pp. 107–110; Praag, § 24; Dimitch, *La courtoisie internationale et le droit des gens* (1930); Walz, *Das Wesen des Völkerrechts und Kritik der Völkerrechtsleugner* (1930), pp. 229–37; Jordan in *Répertoire*, 5, 324–30; Rousseau, pp. 8–11; Lauterpacht in *Cambridge Law Journal*, 9 (1947), 330–2. On some historical origins of the term see Paradisi in *Hague Recueil*, 78 (1951) (i), 329–77.

DEFINITION AND NATURE

modern name of general principles of law.[1] Thus the principle of good faith—an ever-present factor in the interpretation of obligations of treaties and in the application of rights accruing thereunder as well as under international custom in general—is an acknowledged part of international law. To the, now diminishing, extent to which international law is still a primitive system of law permitting unilateral application of force for giving effect to or challenging existing rights through war—with the result, for instance, that in traditional international law duress does not invalidate a treaty—that unity of law and morals is impaired. However, such departures constitute the exception rather than the rule. They tend to disappear in proportion as unilateral resort to force is eliminated as part of the law. In general, as in the sphere of municipal law, whenever on account of considerations of certainty, stability and the fulfilment of legitimate expectations the rigour of the law seems to depart from the equity or fairness of a moral rule, the departure is more apparent than real. For the occasional rigidity of the law, although it may result in hardship in individual cases, is, like law itself, part of the moral order of society.

Secondly, inasmuch as the subjects of the duties imposed by international law are in the last resort individual human beings, the moral content of rules of international law cannot—and does not—to any substantial degree depart from that underlying the rules of municipal law. This is an additional reason why the generally recognized principles of law of civilized States are intrinsically part of international law—and have increasingly been regarded as such. There may be danger, in this connection, in exaggerating the consequences of the distinction between international morality and private morality. It is true that groups of individuals, said to be endowed with a collective reality of their own, often create the impression of acting, or in fact do act, upon standards of morality less exacting than those obtaining between individuals. This is so, it has been asserted, for the reason not only that the moral responsibility of collective units[2] is divided and

---

[1] See below, p. 68.

[2] In modern political thought, largely influenced in this respect by the researches of Gierke and Maitland, the notion of the real personality of groups was due mainly to the desire to stress the rights of associations—such as the church, trade unions, and private organizations generally—as against the omnipotent State. It was not anticipated that the attribution of a real personality to collective units, including unavoidably that of the State itself, may act as a stimulus to the assertion of moral standards different from and inferior to those binding upon what is the true substance of the group, namely, its individual units. This is largely the reason why the insistence on the real personality of groups in relation to the State has tended to diminish the science of politics.

anonymous, but also because persons acting on behalf of collective units deem themselves free of ordinary restraints of morality on the ground that being the trustees of interests entrusted to them they deny themselves the right and the obligation to abide by the restraints of individual morality.

These factors have undoubtedly had an influence upon some aspects of international relations, in particular upon the legal organization of international peace. Thus Governments have occasionally considered themselves unable to abide by obligations, voluntarily undertaken, to enforce peace by collective action on the ground that they are not at liberty to sacrifice the peace of their own country for the sake of the wider and less immediate considerations of an indivisible peace of the international community at large. It is believed that the influence of these and similar considerations must tend to diminish in proportion to the realization that, in a period when the instrumentalities of power at the disposal of the modern State have assumed a complexion of unprecedented magnitude, they may, unless fully subjected to restraints of law and to effective legal safeguards of international peace, endanger the very existence of the national State itself. These factors, combined with the reality of the interdependence of States in many spheres, must progressively bring about a growing realization of the close interconnection, often approaching identity, of the international interest and the national good entrusted to the care of Governments, as well as a corresponding limitation of the impact of the idea of 'reason of State' as justifying the dualism of ethical standards within and outside the State.

Finally, in so far as the ethical content of international law is adversely affected by the duality of moral standards resulting from the idea of 'reason of State' and the omnipotence of the State as against the individual, some recent developments have marked the beginnings of a significant change. Such developments consist in the recognition, by international agreement and otherwise, of fundamental human rights and freedoms. These provide an assurance of the growing effectiveness, even as against the State itself, of the moral sense of the individual in matters affecting international life and the mutual relations of the members of the international community. The resulting addition of moral content to the body of international law cannot but strengthen its legal quality. For, as already stated, the essential and normal, though not exclusive, substance of all law is morality reduced to

DEFINITION AND NATURE

rules and principles of a sufficient degree of clarity, precision and enforceability.[1]

SELECTED BIBLIOGRAPHY ADDITIONAL TO THAT APPEARING IN THIS CHAPTER

Fischer Williams, *Chapters*, pp. 1–27; Lauterpacht, *The Function of Law*, pp. 399–438, and in *Hague Recueil*, 62 (1937) (iv), 100–28; Sibert, pp. 2–21; Higgins, *The Binding Force of International Law* (1910); Oppenheim, *The Future of International Law* (1911) (English translation, 1921); Heilborn, *Grundbegriffe des Völkerrechts* (1912), §§ 1–15; Krabbe, *The Modern Idea of the State* (1917) (English translation, 1921), pp. 233–62; Kelsen, *Das Problem der Souveränität und die Theorie des Völkerrechts* (1920), pp. 102–274, *Allgemeine Staatslehre* (1925), pp. 119–32, *General Theory of Law and State* (1945), pp. 328–54, and *Principles of International Law* (1952), pp. 3–44, 196–201; Verdross, pp. 1–42 and 92–6, *Die Einheit des rechtlichen Weltbildes* (1923), pp. 36–135, and in *Z.I.* 29 (1921), 65–91; Spiropoulos, *Théorie générale du droit international* (1930), pp. 1–83; Blühdorn, *Einführung in das angewandte Völkerrecht* (1934), pp. 1–106; Schiffer, *Die Lehre vom Primat des Völkerrechts in der neueren Literatur* (1937); Ziccardi, *La costituzione dell'ordinamento internazionale* (1943), pp. 19–157; Sperduti, *La fonte suprema dell'ordinamento internazionale* (1946); Constantanopoulos, *Verbindlichkeit und Konstruktion des positiven Völkerrechts* (1948); Giuliano, *La communità internazionale e il diritto* (1950); Ago, *Scienza giuridica e il diritto internazionale* (1950); Corbett, *Law and Society in International Relations* (1951), pp. 36–53; Pollock in *L.Q.R.* 18 (1902), 418–29; Scott in *A.J.* 1 (1907), 831–66, and in *R.I.* (*Paris*), 1 (1927), 637–57; Willoughby and Root in *A.J.* 2 (1908),

[1] On international morality see Sidgwick, *Elements of Politics* (1897), ch. xvii, 'International Law and Morality', and his two lectures on 'Public Morality' and the 'Morality of Strife', reprinted in 1918 from *Practical Ethics*; Hobhouse, *Metaphysical Theory of the State* (1918); Galliard, *La morale des nations* (1920); Bosanquet, *The Philosophical Theory of the State* (4th ed. 1923), pp. 298–311; Meinecke, *Die Idee der Staatsräson* (1924) (3rd ed. 1929); McDougall, *Ethics and Some Modern World Problems* (1924), pp. 1–170; Kraus, *Gedanken über Staatsethos im international Verkehr* (1925); Stratton, *Social Psychology of International Conduct* (1929); Walz, *Das Wesen des Völkerrechts und Kritik der Völkerrechtsleugner* (1930), pp. 220–9; Hocking, *The Spirit of World Politics* (1932), pp. 470–519; Laun, *Der Wandel der Ideen Staat und Volk* (1933), pp. 327–44; Beard, *The Idea of National Interest* (1934), especially pp. 358–406; Mowat, *Public or Private Morality* (1934); Folliet, *Morale internationale* (1935); Carr, *The Twenty Years' Crisis, 1919–1939* (1939), pp. 186–215; Politis, *La morale internationale* (1942); Gooch, *Studies in Diplomacy and Statecraft* (1942), pp. 311–40; Schwarzenberger, *Power Politics* (2nd ed. 1951), pp. 218–31; Benoist in *Hague Recueil*, 9 (1925) (iv), 131–303; Ponsonby in *International Journal of Ethics*, 25 (1915), 143–64; Woolf, *ibid.* 26 (1916), 11–22; Mayer in *Archiv des öffentlichen Rechts*, 28, Part 1, pp. 1–37; Bourgeois in *R.G.* 29 (1922), 5–22; Higgins in *Contemporary Review*, no. 711 (1925), 314–22; Scott in *A.S. Proceedings*, 1932, pp. 10–29; Siotto-Pintor in *Rivista internazionale di filosofia del diritto*, 15 (1935), no. 6, pp. 639–48; Réglade in *Archives de philosophie de droit*, 1936, pp. 176–97; Ginsberg in *Papers of the Aristotelian Society*, 1942; Huber in *Friedenswarte*, 53 (1956), 305–29. See also Ornstein, *Macht, Moral und Recht* (1946); Keeton and Schwarzenberger, *Making International Law Work* (2nd ed. 1946), pp. 49–69; Therre, *La psychologie individuelle et collective dans l'efficacité du droit international public* (1946).

INTERNATIONAL LAW—THE GENERAL PART

357–65 and 451–7; Nys, *ibid.* 6 (1912), 1–29, 279–315; Salvioli in *Rivista*, 3rd ser. 1 (1921–2), 20–80; Cavaglieri, *ibid.* pp. 289–314, 479–506; Brierly in *Hague Recueil*, 23 (1928) (iii), 467–549, and 58 (1936) (iv), 5–34; Bruns in *Z.ö.V.* 1 (1929), 1–56; Spiropoulos in *R.I. (Paris)*, 3 (1929), 97–130; Heydte in *Z.ö.R.* 9 (1931), 526–46; Redslob in *R.I.* 3rd ser. 14 (1933), 488–513, 615–33; Salvioli in *Hague Recueil*, 46 (1933) (iv), 5–17; Schindler, *ibid.* pp. 233–322; Strupp, *ibid.* 47 (1934) (i), 263–300; Rundstein in *R.I.* 3rd ser. 12 (1931), 491–512, 669–89; Le Fur in *Hague Recueil*, 54 (1935) (iv), 5–193; Corbett in *University of Toronto Law Journal*, 1 (1) (1935), 3–16; Jones in *B.Y.* 16 (1935), 5–19; Wengler in *Z.ö.R.* 16 (1936), 322–92; Goodhart in *Grotius Society*, 22 (1936), 31–44; Scrimali in *Z.ö.R.* 21 (1941), 190–216; Hurst in *Grotius Society*, 30 (1944), 119–27; Glanville Williams in *B.Y.* 22 (1945), 146–63; Kelsen in *Ö.Z.ö.R.* 1 (1946), 20–83; Paradisi in *Communicazioni e Studi*, 3 (1950), 55–78; Campbell in *Grotius Society*, 35 (1950), 113–32; Quadri in *Hague Recueil*, 80 (1952) (i), 585–630; Jenks in *B.Y.* 31 (1954), 1–48; Ago in *Hague Recueil*, 90 (1956) (ii), 857–954, and in *A.J.* 51 (1957), 691–733.

CHAPTER 2

THE SOURCES OF
INTERNATIONAL LAW

I. THE SOURCES OF INTERNATIONAL LAW IN GENERAL

16. *The basis and the causes of international law*

The attempt is often made to distinguish between the basis, the causes, the sources, the formal and material sources, and the evidence of sources of international law.[1] These and similar distinctions may be useful, within limits, so long as their importance is not exaggerated and so long as they are not permitted to conceal the essential identity of the subject-matter which they are intended to elucidate. The basis—the primary cause—of international law is the fact of the existence of an international society composed of human beings organized as sovereign States. Its more immediate cause (or, as it is occasionally referred to, its objective source) is the interdependence, in its manifold manifestations, of these sovereign States; the need to safeguard their interests and their independent existence by means of binding rules of law; and the necessity to protect the individual human being who is the ultimate unit of all law, in so far as such protection, both of nationals and aliens, is rendered relevant by reference to the existence of separate sovereign States. The necessity of acting upon these causes by way of legal regulation is the objective source of international law in the sense that disregard of them must, in the long run, entail the disruption of the foundations of civilized life as well as the impairment of the reality of the law already established in pursuance of those needs and interests.

The more direct sources of international law are the agencies, human or other, by means of which it is expressed and rendered binding. As one such agency we may regard, in the first instance, the individual sovereign States which create conventional international law by treaty, or the aggregate body of States which by their uniform conduct, expressive in most cases of a sense of already existing legal obligation, give concrete form to or supply authoritative evidence of customary international law. The evidence of these

[1] For a survey see Corbett in *B.Y.* 6 (1925), 20–30.

51

INTERNATIONAL LAW—THE GENERAL PART

sources is to be found in their concrete records, such as the written instruments of treaties, instructions issued to various organs of the State, opinions of their legal advisers, pronouncements and statements of their Governments in the international and internal spheres, and documents and State papers which show the existence of international custom.

The second main—impersonal—agency through which the objective basis of international law is given legal form and substance are the principles and rules of law which are due not to an ascertained direct expression of the will of States, but to the reason of the thing —which in this context means the existence of the international community—formulated in general principles of law. These are the modern, the less controversial and probably more articulate expression of the law of nature which nurtured the growth of international law and which assisted powerfully in its development.[1]

The two main sources, thus formulated, of international law are in accordance with—in fact, are a restatement of—the part of the definition of international law given above, namely, as owing its validity to the will of States as expressed in custom and treaties and to the fact of the existence of an international community of States and individuals.[2] That formulation of the sources of international law brings to mind the fact that as with regard to the definition of international law so also in the matter of its sources the nature of the problem does not permit of a simple formula or solution. There is no room here for a rigid choice between the so-called positivist view which sees the exclusive source of international law in the will, express or implied, of sovereign States; for that will must be interpreted in the light of and, if need be, supplemented and corrected by the other main source of international law. Neither is there room, in relation to existing international society, for an affirmation of the supremacy of a law of nature, of the reason of the thing, of general principles of law expressive of the widest common acceptance of principles of legal justice; for that source may, in appropriate cases, be modified or overridden by the will of sovereign States. There are thus, in the sphere of international law, particular reasons why the rigid alternative of law conceived as will (whose validity is independent of its ethical content) and law conceived as reason rising sovereign over the sovereignty of the State cannot be regarded as appropriate.[3] The activity of judicial tribunals—national and international—applying international law provides, when viewed

---

[1] See below, p. 68.   [2] See above, p. 9.   [3] See above, p. 32.

52

SOURCES OF INTERNATIONAL LAW

in its entirety, a constant reminder of the insufficiency of exclusive reliance on either of these two main categories of sources of the law.

However, though the limited degree of usefulness of the distinction between the basis, the cause, the sources and the evidence of sources of international law is thus apparent,[1] it is not devoid of value. The notion of the source of law on the analogy of the source of a stream as the first external manifestation of an already existing, though inarticulate, body of law is particularly appropriate in the sphere of international law. It brings to mind the fact that the will of sovereign States, which is often regarded as the exclusive source of international law, is but the expression of an underlying objective reality.

17. *The causes and the sources of international law*

The basic causes of international law—its hidden sources—become a material source directly binding upon States and cognizable by international tribunals mainly in two ways: in the first instance, they become so by being adopted by States as binding rules of conduct. They can be so accepted either by tacit acknowledgment expressed through custom, that is to say, uniform practice followed as a matter of obligation, or by specific consent, i.e., through treaties laying down rules expressly adopted by States. Custom and treaties thus give concrete form and substance to what may be called the causes, the objective sources, of international law. In that sense custom and treaties are declaratory of the impact of the forces which make the international society; they bring these forces to the surface; they constitute a source of the law. Prior to that declaration, these forces, however potent, are not directly and immediately operative as a source of legal obligation and, as such, of decisions of tribunals. To that extent the consent of States as expressed in custom and treaty is the principal and normal source of international law. Unless the law is thus authoritatively declared and evidenced, it must remain largely in the realm of speculation and controversy.

However, although custom and treaty are the normal and, from the point of view of practice, the most important operative sources

[1] Thus, for instance, international custom has been variously described as being the foundation, a source, and the evidence of international law. Persuasive arguments could be adduced in favour of each of these descriptions. As will be suggested later, in many instances the distinction between the sources of law and evidence of these sources is far from being clear or meaningful. See below, p. 65.

53

INTERNATIONAL LAW—THE GENERAL PART

of international law, they are not its only, or most significant, sources. They can—and must—be supplemented, in proper cases, by reference to legal principles derived from the 'reason of the thing' which has not as yet found expression in custom and treaty. The 'reason of the thing' is the existence and the needs of the international society conceived as a community of States under the rule of law. These principles are not in the nature of mere speculation. They are the result of the application of general principles of law— including the acknowledged general principles of international law itself—to the relations of States and, in proper cases, of the individuals who compose them. They do not formally override international law as declared by custom and treaty. They supplement it and, when necessary, supply a beneficent instrument of its interpretation.[1] This they do, however, subject to the ever-present consideration that, so long as international law is an imperfect law and the international society an imperfectly organized society, the general principles of law must occasionally yield to the peculiarities and immaturity, willed by States, of positive international law. Thus, contrary to a general principle of law, duress does not, in traditional international law, vitiate a treaty.[2] On the other hand, custom as well as treaty may have to be interpreted and is often interpreted —to the point of being interpreted away[3]—by reference to general principles of law. It is thus clear that there may be a deceptive element of simplification in the attempts to establish a hierarchical order of priority with regard to these sources.[4] For although 'the reason of the thing', 'the law of nature', 'the general principles of law', cannot override normally positive international law as expressed in custom and treaties, it is against the background of these concepts that positive international law is interpreted.

For these reasons it is not possible to understand accurately the true nature of the sources of international law if we think of them in the exclusive terms of two rival notions—of what may be called the voluntaristic and the objectivistic conceptions of law. For the former, international law is the product of will, of the will of States as expressed in their consent—a view differing only in degree from

---

[1] See below, p. 68. This was the case when the International Court of Justice in its Advisory Opinion on the *Reservations to the Convention on Genocide* referred to genocide as 'contrary to moral law and to the spirit and aims of the United Nations'. It said: 'The first consequence arising from this conception is that the principles underlying the Convention are principles which are recognized by civilized nations as binding upon States, even without any conventional obligation' (*I.C.J. Reports* 1951, p. 15 at p. 23).

[2] See below, p. 352.   [3] See below, p. 88.

[4] See below, p. 86.

54

SOURCES OF INTERNATIONAL LAW

the imperative theory of law within the State according to which the essence of the law is that it is the command of the State. On the other hand, for what may be described as the objectivistic doctrine international law is the inexorable result of an existing social reality. We see thus re-enacted in the wider sphere of international relations the enduring and crucial dilemma of jurisprudence—that of the nature of the law: Is it the will of the sovereign—the Leviathan of Hobbes, the 'general will' of Rousseau, the 'determinate sovereign' of Austin? Or is it law as constituted by its conformity with reason —reason in relation to law conceived as justice and in relation to the State conceived as the recognition of the individual human being as its primary and ultimate unit. It is in that sense that law is often pictured as the manifestation of the reality of social life— Duguit's law of social solidarity, Scelle's law of biological symbiosis and, possibly, the 'initial hypothesis' which caps, or underlies, the pyramid of Kelsen's structure of pure law.[1] As suggested above, law—when viewed from the angle of its actual operation as distinguished from the exclusiveness of logical reasoning—must properly be conceived in terms not of opposition but of a fusion of these elements. Because of the problems and the vicissitudes arising out of the fact of the imperfect integration of the international political community, international law exemplifies in a particularly instructive way this aspect of general jurisprudence.

So far as the sources of international law are concerned the view which seems to be most in accordance with the practice of States and with the attitude of tribunals is that we must consider the objective reality of the international community as the primary source of international law; that sovereign States are the principal organs declaring, with constitutive effect, the rules of international law as a consequence and expression of that reality by means of custom and treaty; and that, in the absence of international law thus created and revealed, the rules and principles derived from the fact of the existence of the international community and formulated with the assistance of general principles of law—of the modern law of nature—must be regarded as one of the primary sources of international law. Article 38 of the Statute of the International Court of Justice gives expression, in part, to that provisional hierarchy of sources of law by laying down that

the Court, whose function is to decide in accordance with international law such disputes as are submitted to it, shall apply:

[1] For references to these writers see below, pp. 90 n., 214, 217.

55

a. international conventions, whether general or particular, establishing rules expressly recognized by the contesting States;

b. international custom, as evidence of a general practice accepted as law;

c. the general principles of law recognized by civilized nations.[1]

That Article of the Statute, while containing an authoritative formulation of the legal position—binding upon the Court and the States parties to the Statute—is essentially of a declaratory character and effect. As such it has occasionally been applied by other international tribunals.[2]

18. *The consent of States as a source of international law*

The fact that there is no international legislature empowered to enact new rules of international law, binding alike upon concurring and upon dissenting States, has brought into prominence the part played by individual States in the creation of international law. The result has been to lend weight, occasionally excessive, to the notion that the will of States is the exclusive source of international law. That view has at times found support in authoritative judicial pronouncements stressing the importance of the consent of States as a source of international law. Thus in the case of *The Lotus* the Permanent Court of International Justice said:

International law governs relations between independent States. The rules of law binding upon States therefore emanate from their own free will as expressed in conventions or by usages of law and established in order to regulate the relations between these co-existing independent communities or with a view to the achievement of common aims. Restrictions upon the independence of States cannot therefore be presumed.[3]

Among writers the same view has found expression in the positivist[4] and cognate doctrines such as the doctrine that international law owes its existence and binding force to a voluntary self-limitation of States[5] or to mutual promises, as distinguished from a command of a superior authority, of co-ordinated sovereign States.[6]

None of these doctrines can be accepted as accurate except to the extent that, apart from the distinctly limited possibilities inherent in the activity of judicial tribunals,[7] new rules of international law become binding upon sovereign States only with their consent. It is

---

[1] As to subsidiary sources see below, p. 78.
[2] See below, p. 75.
[3] *P.C.I.J.* Series A, no. 10, p. 18.
[4] See below, p. 209.
[5] See below, p. 208.
[6] See above, pp. 35–36, and below, p. 208.
[7] See below, p. 78.

SOURCES OF INTERNATIONAL LAW

clear, in the first instance, that the will of States cannot—in itself—provide an explanation of the binding force of international law. The binding force of treaties and of custom must necessarily be sought outside custom and treaty. No State is entitled to adduce its will as a decisive reason for liberating itself from the obligations of customary or conventional rules of international law. Secondly, the will of States is not a relevant factor so far as new States entering the international community are concerned. Such States are not in the position to pick and choose among existing rules of customary international law and to decide for themselves which to accept and which to reject as a future rule of conduct.[1] They are bound by all universally or generally recognized rules of international customary law. It is occasionally said that in applying for, or by receiving without reservations, the recognition of its statehood, a new State by implication agrees to be bound by the existing rules of international law. To assume such implied consent is, in effect, to say that consent is irrelevant. Thirdly, a State is bound by generally recognized rules of international law even if its consent to such rules cannot be proved in any particular instance. It is sufficient if the rule is so generally recognized that it is difficult to imagine that a civilized State would refuse its assent to it[2] or if the rule has been acted upon by the States most likely to find themselves in the position to apply it. Thus, for instance, in the sphere of the law of the sea a rule uniformly acted upon by the principal maritime States assumes the character of a binding rule of customary international law.[3] Finally, the recognition in Article 38 of the Statute of the International Court of Justice of 'general principles of law' as a source of international law, as distinguished from custom and treaty, is not only an authoritative consecration of a practice evidenced by a long series of treaties in which States have defined in that sense the sources of law applicable by international tribunals. It is something more. It is a recognition of the fact that while the will of States, in its two typical manifestations of custom and treaty, constitutes one of the two primary sources of international law, the absence of specific regulation by custom or treaty leaves no gap which could justifiably prevent an international tribunal from adjudicating upon a dispute before it.[4]

It would seem, therefore, that to regard the will of States as the

---

[1] But see Tunkin, 'Co-existence and International Law', in *Hague Recueil*, 95 (1958) (iii), 61, for a distinction in this respect—so far as the Soviet view is concerned—between 'reactionary' and 'democratic' principles of international law.

[2] See below, p. 115.   [3] See below, pp. 66, 238.   [4] See below, p. 94.

57

INTERNATIONAL LAW—THE GENERAL PART

exclusive source of the validity of international law is to confuse the creation, by treaty or custom, of new law—for which, in general, the consent of States is required—with, in the wider sense, the establishment and the binding force of international law as a whole. These are grounded in a factor superior to and independent of the will of States—a factor which gives validity to the law created by the will of States. That superior source is the objective fact of the existence of an interdependent community of States. It is also a source which, in appropriate cases and subject to the very wide freedom of action which international law leaves to States,[1] gives rise to legal rights and duties independently of the will of States. It is that source which supplies the answer—so far as a juridical answer can be given at all—to the question why treaties and custom are binding. It is occasionally said that treaties are binding because there is a customary rule to that effect. There still remains the question why custom is binding. The answer, beyond which it is in law not possible to go, is that it is the will of the international community that international law, in its various manifestations, shall be binding. It is an answer which corresponds to the obtainable maximum of reality in the relations of States. However deficient in its political and legal organization, there does exist an international community of transcending reality.[2] The constituent members of that community recognize international law as binding. Its binding force imposes itself as a necessary condition of the existence of that indispensable and interdependent community. That ultimate assumption of international law[3]—the assumption of the will of the international community that international law shall be obeyed—is therefore not a fiction. It combines the two essential, and inseparable, elements of law—the law conceived as reason and the law conceived as will imposing itself upon the subjects, however independent, of the community.

2. THE PARTICULAR SOURCES OF INTERNATIONAL LAW

19. *Treaties*

Treaties are agreements between States analogous in nature to contracts between private individuals.[4] Like contracts, they fulfil a large variety of purposes. They lay down the rules of law to be followed by the parties as a matter of legal obligation. Having regard

---

[1] See below, p. 95.   [2] See above, p. 28.   [3] See below, p. 92.
[4] [On the law of treaties, see Part VI of these Collected Papers.]

58

SOURCES OF INTERNATIONAL LAW

to the absence, in the present state of international organization, of legislative machinery in the proper sense of that term, treaties fulfil in many respects a function similar to that performed by the national legislature within the State. This applies in particular to general treaties which bind a substantial number of States. Some of these treaties—for example, the Charter of the United Nations, the General Treaty for the Renunciation of War, or the International Postal Convention—bind practically all the members of the international community. There is for this reason a tendency to refer to multilateral treaties, especially those approaching universality, as 'legislative' and as constituting international legislation. These expressions may be convenient inasmuch as they point to the fact that such treaties are often concluded for the regulation of general and permanent interests as distinguished from treaties registering what is no more than a mere bargain or those providing for cession of territory or payment of an indemnity. But that terminology may be misleading if it is intended to imply that such treaties—often referred to as law-making treaties—are governed by different rules in the matter of their conclusion, their validity, and their termination, or that they constitute anything in the nature of legislation as ordinarily conceived, namely, the authoritative imposition of rules of conduct of universal validity regardless of the dissent of the minority. There is no such legislation in the international sphere—though it must be regarded as a proper object of rational endeavour.[1]

In the enumeration of the sources of law in the Statute of the International Court of Justice[2] treaties appear in the first place. There are various reasons which justify that order. In the first instance, there is room for the view that treaties constitute the most important part of international law. In comparison with international custom, which has now crystallized to a large extent and which in any case is slow of growth and difficult of ascertainment, treaties constitute the bulk of international law as a growing body of rules. While, in many matters, custom provides the general structure of the law, treaties represent its actual and expanding substance. The

---

[1] See above, p. 13. See, on the use of the term 'international legislation', McNair in *Iowa Law Review*, 19 (1933–4), 177–89; Hudson, *Legislation*, 5, viii. See also Brierly in *Problems of Peace*, 5th ser. (1930), pp. 205–29; Gihl, *International Legislation* (1937); Jenks in *B.Y.* 29 (1952), 107–10; and, on the concept of legislation in general, Akzin in *Iowa Law Review*, 21 (1936), 713–50. It is of interest to note that Scelle, who seems to attach importance to the distinction between law-making and other treaties, admits in effect that practically all treaties are 'law-making' (*La théorie juridique de la révision des traités* (1936), p. 41).   [2] See above, p. 55.

INTERNATIONAL LAW—THE GENERAL PART

great majority of cases decided by the International Court of Justice have been concerned with the interpretation of treaties. Secondly, States may—within very wide limits[1]—by treaty modify, *inter se*, the rules of customary international law. *Modus et conventio vincunt legem.* Thus States may by treaty renounce the jurisdictional immunities which by international custom their public vessels enjoy before foreign courts; or they may agree by treaty to a foreign State exercising on the high seas jurisdiction over their vessels in derogation of the customary principle of the freedom of the seas. For this reason it is natural for an international tribunal confronted with a dispute between two States to direct its attention in the first instance to the question whether and to what extent the subject of the dispute is covered by a treaty—in the same manner as a municipal court will enquire, in the first instance, whether and to what extent the subject matter of the dispute is covered by a contract between the parties.

Finally, the importance of treaties as a source of international law is emphasized by the fact that in some cases they may become so not only as between the parties but in general *erga omnes*. This may happen in cases in which a series of treaties concluded at different times between various States show such a marked uniformity as to amount, in their cumulative effect, to the creation of a customary rule of international law. Thus a uniform series of treaties in which the parties recognize, or act upon, the principle that a State acquiring territory by cession is under a duty to take over certain liabilities of the predecessor State may provide evidence of a customary rule, created by those very treaties, of international law in the matter. This is so although it may be open in proper cases to assert that the treaties in question, or some of them, were concluded not by way of recognition of a legal obligation (which requirement is normally a condition of the creation of custom) but rather by way of a special concession or act of accommodation negativing the existence of a legal duty.[2] Moreover, it would seem to follow from an Opinion of the International Court of Justice that in some cases treaties of a universal character, such as the Charter of the United Nations, may create rights and obligations for States not parties thereto.[3] The above factors explain the importance of

---

[1] See below, pp. 87, 113–114, 234.

[2] See E. Lauterpacht, 'Freedom of Transit in International Law', *Grotius Society*, 44 (1959), at p. 322.

[3] See Advisory Opinion on *Reparation for Injuries Suffered in the Service of the United Nations: I.C.J. Reports* 1949, p. 185. And see below, p. 88.

SOURCES OF INTERNATIONAL LAW

treaties as a source of international law and their place in the Statute of the International Court. However, as will be suggested presently, they do not necessarily signify the absolute priority of treaties over the other sources of international law.

20. *International customary law*

The Statute of the International Court of Justice lays down, in Article 38, that the Court shall apply, *inter alia*, 'international custom as evidence of a general practice accepted as law'. International custom signifies constant and uniform practice followed by States as a matter of obligation. Substantial portions of international law—such as the law of diplomatic and other jurisdictional immunities of foreign States, the principle of the freedom of the seas, and most rules of warfare—owe their validity, in the first instance, to that source. 'In the first instance', for ultimately the binding force of custom itself is grounded in a higher rule of law.

The importance of custom in the international sphere is considerable not only because it embodies a substantial—and most ancient and fundamental—portion of international law but also because, although it may be modified or replaced by treaties between the States directly interested, it constitutes that fixed body of rules and principles against the background of which and by reference to which treaties must be interpreted in case of doubt. Moreover, it may be said that the validity of the third main source of international law—namely, 'general principles of law'—is, to some extent, due to a customary rule of international law.[1] The factors which tend to diminish the importance of custom will be referred to below.

As stated, two elements are decisive for the ascertainment of international custom: the first is constancy and uniformity of practice; the second is that that practice must be followed under the impulse of a sense of obligation, *opinione necessitatis*. These requirements must, unavoidably, be considered at some length for the reason that they raise issues of considerable complexity.

Constancy and uniformity of practice are a matter of degree. There is no rule of thumb which renders it possible to predict with any degree of assurance what amount of precedent will cause an international tribunal to assume in any given case that the degree of accumulation of precedent qualifies as custom. Moreover, when there is a question of a general customary rule, the problem arises whether an occasional departure, by a single State or a small

[1] See below, p. 76.

61

number of States, from the general practice excludes the assumption of a general customary rule. It is clear that if absolute and universal uniformity were to be required, only very few rules could rank as general customary rules of international law. Nevertheless, it appears that, because of the underlying requirement of consent, the condition of constancy and uniformity is liable on occasion to be interpreted with some rigidity when there is a question of ascertaining a customary rule of general validity. Thus in the *Fisheries* case between the United Kingdom and Norway[1] the International Court of Justice declined to treat as obligatory rules of customary international law those rules which the United Kingdom invoked, as having been generally followed, in the matter of the methods of delimiting the baseline of territorial waters and bays. It did so on the ground that some States had in the past adopted a different rule. For the same reason, in the Advisory Opinion in the case of *Reservations to the Convention on Genocide*,[2] the Court refused to treat as generally binding the rule requiring the unanimous consent of all signatories of a treaty to a reservation appended by a State desirous of becoming a party thereto. In the *Asylum* case,[3] it declined, on the ground of absence of constancy and uniformity, to accede to the contention that there existed a customary rule of international law which permitted the diplomatic agent of a foreign State to determine unilaterally whether there existed the necessary conditions for granting diplomatic asylum.[4]

Similarly, there has been a tendency to attach an exacting interpretation to the second constituent element of custom, namely, *opinio necessitatis*. The International Court of Justice and its predecessor did so on a number of occasions. Thus in *The Lotus* case the Permanent Court held that the rarity of judicial decisions by municipal courts in the matter of assumption of jurisdiction over aliens for offences committed abroad was merely an indication of the fact of abstention from instituting judicial proceedings, but not of any recognition of the obligation to refrain from exercising such

---

[1] *I.C.J. Reports* 1951, p. 116.   [2] *I.C.J. Reports* 1951, p. 15.
[3] *I.C.J. Reports* 1950, p. 266.
[4] The Court said: 'The facts brought to the knowledge of the Court disclose so much uncertainty and contradiction, so much fluctuation and discrepancy in the exercise of diplomatic asylum and in the official views expressed on various occasions, there has been so much inconsistency in the rapid succession of conventions on asylum, ratified by some States and rejected by others, and the practice has been so much influenced by considerations of political expediency in the various cases, that it is not possible to discern in all this any constant and uniform usage, accepted as law, with regard to the alleged rule of unilateral and definitive qualification of the offence' (*I.C.J. Reports* 1950, at p. 277).

SOURCES OF INTERNATIONAL LAW

jurisdiction; 'for only if such abstention were based on their being conscious of having a duty to abstain would it be possible to speak of an international custom'.[1] In the *Asylum* case the Court referred to the fact that State practice had been influenced by considerations of political expediency rather than of law.[2] The Court said:

> The Party which relies on a custom . . . must prove that this custom is established in such a manner that it has become binding on the other Party. . . . that the rule invoked . . . is in accordance with a constant and uniform usage practised by the States in question, and that this usage is the expression of a right appertaining to the State granting asylum and a duty incumbent on the territorial State.[3]

The above instances, referring to the necessity for a sense of legal obligation as an essential condition of custom, serve primarily to emphasize the distinction between international custom and international courtesy. The first is followed as a matter of pre-existing obligation (for there is no other meaning that can usefully be attached to *opinio necessitatis*); the second is followed on the express understanding that the course adopted is one devoid of any element of duty. However, put in that way the definition of custom—such, for instance, as is given in the Statute of the International Court of Justice—raises questions of some difficulty. If custom is no more than practice followed as a matter of an already existing *legal* obligation, then it is not a source of law but merely evidence of a pre-existing legal rule. There is substance in the question thus raised inasmuch as it emphasizes both the relative value of the distinction between a source of law and the evidence thereof and the difficulties surrounding the definition, however valid, of the conception of custom as given above. These difficulties may be surmounted by a flexible interpretation of the notion of *opinio necessitatis* in the sense that a course of conduct, pursued uniformly and constantly, may become the basis of custom provided that, in contrast with the case of international comity,[4] there is no clear intention to deny to it the element of obligation—though not necessarily legal obligation.[5] In that sense a course of action,

---

[1] *P.C.I.J.* Series A, no. 10 (1927), p. 28.

[2] *I.C.J. Reports* 1950, p. 276. See also the case concerning *Rights of Nationals of the United States of America in Morocco, I.C.J. Reports* 1952, p. 200.

[3] *I.C.J. Reports* 1950, at p. 276. On the application of customary international law by the International Court generally, see Sørensen, *Les sources du droit international* (1946), pp. 84–112, and Lauterpacht, *The Development of International Law by the International Court* (1958), pp. 368–93.   [4] See above, p. 43.

[5] It is not believed that the use, in this connection, of the term 'usage' as connoting something less than custom is helpful. Thus it is often maintained that usage is conduct

63

INTERNATIONAL LAW—THE GENERAL PART

constantly pursued and believed to be dictated by duties of neighbourliness, reasonableness and accommodation, may, in the interest of international stability and good faith, assume the complexion of binding international custom.

This, for instance, may have been the case with regard to the recent developments in the matter of the rule of international law relating to jurisdictional immunities of States before tribunals of foreign countries. The increasing acquiescence of States in a limitation of their customary jurisdictional immunities, so as to exclude from the purview of immunity acts of a private-law nature—for instance, those in the field of commerce—may provide a basis for a new customary rule in the matter;[1] this is so although it is not clear that such acquiescence has been dictated by a feeling of a legal duty of acquiescence. Again, when after the Second World War a large number of States proclaimed the so-called doctrine of the Continental Shelf, that practice, accompanied by absence of protest or reservation on the part of other States, became in itself the basis of a customary rule.[2] It is not certain that that acquiescence stemmed from a consciousness of a clear legal duty—as distinguished from a recognition of the reasonableness of the claim made—to treat the proclamation of the Continental Shelf as creating or declaring a valid legal right. Similarly, the general acquiescence in the exercise, by the littoral State, of protective functions in a contiguous zone outside the recognized limit of territorial waters has resulted in a customary rule of international law in that sphere.

It would thus appear that the accurate approach to the question of international custom in this respect is neither insistence on the element of legal obligation nor abandonment of the requirement of any element whatsoever of obligation accompanying the practice in question.[3] There must be some sentiment of obligation—not necessarily and not primarily of a legal nature and not necessarily accompanied by an apprehension of sanction in case of non-compliance.[4] In this respect the conditions for the creation of custom

which has not yet hardened into custom, namely, into conduct pursued as a legal obligation. To assert that is, to a large extent, to identify usage with 'comity' (see above, p. 43). For an example of the use of these terms in the opposite sense see Hall, § 139, where he says: 'this custom has since hardened into a definite usage.'

[1] [See 'The Problem of Jurisdictional Immunities of Foreign States', reprinted in a later volume of these Collected Papers.]

[2] [See 'Sovereignty over Submarine Areas', reprinted in a later volume of these Collected Papers.]

[3] See, e.g., for the latter view, Guggenheim, I (1947), 46, and Kopelmanas in *B.T.* 18 (1937), 135–8.   [4] But see Brierly, p. 60.

64

SOURCES OF INTERNATIONAL LAW

as a binding law in the international sphere do not differ substantially from those required within the State.

As within the State so also in the relations of States the emergence of custom as binding law does not lend itself to exact logical and historical analysis. Although the definition of custom as given in Article 38 of the Statute of the Court—namely, as being 'evidence of a general practice accepted as law'—has occasionally been subject to criticism, it is not certain that any other definition would be less open to objection. Conduct which is originally followed spontaneously as a matter of social habit, convenience, reasonableness, accommodation or necessity acquires the complexion of some kind of obligation; the conduct thus followed as a matter of inarticulate obligation gives substance and confirmation to its legal character. It is only in that way that it is possible to overcome the logical dilemma involved in the question: What is the nature of the thing of which custom is merely the evidence? For—as the words of Article 38 would seem to indicate—if custom is a source of law, then that thing cannot itself be law. On the other hand, if we say that custom is identical with—or what is substantially the same, evidence of—conduct pursued on the basis of the conviction of legal obligation, that is to say that the legal obligation is the *cause*, the condition, of custom, then we cannot say—as is normally said—that the customary rule is the unconscious *effect* of conduct pursued as a law. For in logic a thing cannot be both cause and effect. However, as in other matters, we cannot be sure that the difficulty must or can necessarily be solved by logic. The practical answer to the dilemma is that it is the common conviction of the binding nature—not necessarily legally binding nature—of the conduct as habitually followed which is the source of the customary rule. The question at what particular point or moment that common conviction assumes, the complexion of a clearly binding source of law, or of a source of clearly binding law, is not capable of a precise legal answer. It is probably advisable not even to attempt to formulate it. What, however, is essential is that when a tribunal, or any other agency, in a considered pronouncement either sanctions the existence of a customary rule or declines to recognize it, such pronouncement should be accompanied by an exacting examination of the underlying facts.

The assumption of the common conviction as the source of the customary rule makes it possible—and permissible—to conceive of the binding force of international custom as being grounded in the implied consent, in the *consensus intentium*, of the members of the community—a view which goes back to Roman jurists. As Ulpian put it: 'Mores sunt tacitus consensus populi longa consuetudine inveteratus.'[1] The fact that it is not necessary—or possible—to prove the consent of every member of the community is irrelevant in this connection. Thus in the sphere of international law it is not necessary—or, normally, possible—to show that a rule, asserted to represent a customary rule, has been followed (i.e. consented to) by all States. The element of consent is satisfactorily met by the circumstance that a rule has been generally followed, that it has been generally consented to. The fact that universal consent is not required for the creation of custom and that general consent is sufficient, is not a factor pointing to the irrelevance of consent in the creation of custom; it is merely a factor pointing to the irrelevance of the consent of every single State. It is a fact showing that the will of States, of every single State, is not an absolute condition of the creation of a rule of international law. To require general consent, as distinguished from universal consent, is not to admit that consent is a mere fiction. It is a requirement of substance—though it does not go to the length of exacting articulate consent to participate in the creation of a rule of law. It is a requirement of substance inasmuch that, although it is not necessary to prove the consent of every State, express dissent in the formative stage of a customary rule will negative the existence of custom at least in relation to the dissenting State. For that reason there is no impropriety or undue artificiality in conceiving of custom as based on consent. This does not necessarily mean that consent is the final reason for the binding force of custom. The question why custom—whether conceived as consent or otherwise—is binding is considered elsewhere in this Section.[2]

The flexible approach,[3] as here suggested, to international custom

---

[1] *Reg.* par. 4; or see the reference, in the *Digest*, to custom as 'velut tacita civium conventio': D.1.3.35 (Hermogeniam).

[2] See below, p. 91. Professor Kelsen, who rejects the notion of the binding force of custom as based on consent, is content to base it on the 'fundamental rule' that 'states ought to behave as they have customarily behaved' (*General Principles of Law* (1952), p. 418). If that be so, then the 'fundamental rule' does not apply to the State which has not participated in the creation of the customary rule in question, for that State has not followed a course of habitual behaviour in relation to that rule.

[3] That flexible approach must create some impression of inconclusiveness. However, without such flexibility the notion of custom as the creation by conduct, by way of conscious consent, of an already existing rule—for this is the meaning of the requirement *opinione necessitatis juris*—is not comprehensible and brings to mind the image of someone attempting to stand on his own shoulders. The more satisfactory solution of the problem —some of the intricacies of which are brought out by Professor Kunz in *A.J.* 47 (1953), 662–9, and Dr MacGibbon in *B.Y.* 33 (1957), 115–45—can probably be attempted on the basis of the realization that while *opinio necessitatis* and consent must continue to be

SOURCES OF INTERNATIONAL LAW

also explains why avoidance of rigidity is indicated in designating the agencies which may be deemed to act *opinione necessitatis* or in exacting any deliberate degree of formality in the conduct amounting to creation of custom. The agencies in question are the individuals and the organs which act on behalf of the State. Unlike treaties, participation in the creation of custom is not dependent upon any formal and express will to enter into a reciprocal legal obligation. Accordingly, custom is created by—and evidence of custom is to be found in—acts and instruments which, while expressing the attitude of the organs of a State, are not necessarily addressed to any other State or group of States. Thus uniform legislation of a considerable number of States on a particular subject may properly be regarded as 'evidence of a general practice followed as law'—i.e. of customary international law. The same applies to decisions, partaking of a sufficient degree of uniformity, of municipal courts of States adjudicating on matters of concern for international law.[1]

While, for reasons stated, the importance of custom in the international sphere is still considerable, the part which it can play in à dynamic society of modern States is necessarily limited. The exigencies of international relations call for law-creating methods which are more articulate and more expeditious. Moreover, it would appear that rules and principles which have evolved under the aegis of custom in the formative period of international law cannot, through the instrumentality of custom itself, adapt themselves easily to changing conditions. This, for instance, would seem to apply to the customary rule of international law exempting States and their agencies from the jurisdiction of foreign courts—a rule which is no longer in keeping with modern developments, in particular those which have brought about an increase in the economic activities of the State and, in many instances, have led to the assumption by the State of the activities of an ordinary trader.[2] However, as pointed out above, that very example shows that also

regarded as the constituent conditions of custom, it is not feasible, or accurate, to view these conditions with exacting rigour.

[1] See below, p. 80. From such participation in the creation of custom or acquiescence in or confirmation of custom already established there must be distinguished the question to what extent a State is bound by views expressed by its Government on any specific matter of international law before its own legislative bodies, at international conferences, in proceedings before international tribunals and on various other occasions in circumstances not intended as or amounting to an express acceptance of an international obligation or to a deliberate inducement, acted upon by another State, to alter the position of that State for the worse—a typical case of estoppel. See below, p. 70.

[2] See Lauterpacht in *B.Y.* 28 (1951), p. 220 [reprinted in a later volume of these Collected Papers].

67

INTERNATIONAL LAW—THE GENERAL PART

in this respect custom may, through gradual and uniform acquiescence, assist in effecting a change in existing customary rules.[1]

21. *General principles of law recognized by civilized States*[2]

The fact that, on the face of it, there are no provisions of a treaty or of customary international law directly applicable to a given situation does not necessarily mean that there exists a gap in the law and that there is, therefore, no room for the application of international law. In many cases it is likely, in view of the wide scope of freedom of action in matters of domestic jurisdiction which international law leaves to States, that the apparent gap is merely a specific affirmation of that general rule of international law. On the other hand, when the situation is not obviously covered by that comprehensive principle of presumptive freedom of action and when there might, as the result, appear to exist a clear gap in the law as laid down by custom or treaty, international practice recognizes, and the very existence of the international community necessitates, a residuary source of law on which States are entitled to act and by reference to which international courts are bound to render decisions.[3] That residuary source is, in the language of

---

[1] As to customary international law see Gianni, *La coutume en droit international* (1931); Gouet, *La coutume en droit constititionnel interne et en droit constitutionnel international* (1932); Küntzel, *Ungeschriebenes Völkerrecht* (1935); Haemmerlé, *La coutume en droit des gens d'après la jurisprudence de la Cour Permanente de Justice Internationale* (1936); Balladore Pallieri in *Rivista*, 20 (1928), 338–74; Ziccardi, *La costituzione dell'ordinamento internazionale* (1943), pp. 317–70; Barile, *La rilevazione e l'integrazione del diritto internazionale non scritto e la liberta di apprezamento del giudize* (1953); Bourquin in *Hague Recueil*, 35 (1931) (i), 61–75; Raestad in *Nordisk T.A.*, 4 (1933), 61–384, 128–46; Séfériadès in *R.G.* 43 (1936), 129–96; Kopelmanas in *B.Y.* 18 (1937), 127–51; Rousseau, pp. 815–38; Guggenheim in *Etudes Georges Scelle* (1950), 1, 275–84; Barile in *Comunicazioni e Studi*, 5 (1953), 141–229, and in *Rivista*, 37 (1954), 168–202; Ch. De Visscher in *R.G.* 59 (1955), 353–69; MacGibbon in *B.Y.* 33 (1957), 115–45; Ago in *A.J.* 51 (1957), 691–733; Kunz, *ibid.* 47 (1953), 662–9, and 52 (1958), 85–91. And see below, pp. 70, 238, on acquiescence and estoppel.

[2] For the literature on the subject see Oppenheim, II, 69, n. 1. And see Grapin, *Valeur internationale des principes généraux du droit* (1934); Korte, *Grundfragen der völkerrechtlichen Rechtsfähigkeit* (1934), pp. 70–84; Blühdorn, *Die Einführung in das angewandte Völkerrecht* (1934), pp. 142–57; Ziccardi, *La costituzione dell'ordinamento internazionale* (1943), pp. 399–412; Stuyt, *The General Principles of Law as Applied by International Tribunals to Disputes on Attribution and Exercise of State Jurisdiction* (1946); Gutteridge, *Comparative Law* (2nd ed. 1949), chapter v; Cheng, *General Principles of Law as Applied by International Courts and Tribunals* (1953); Petraschek in *Archiv für Rechts und Sozialphilosophie*, 28 (1935), 61–88; Heydte in *Z.ö.R.* 11 (1931), 526–46; Verdross in *Hague Recueil*, 52 (1935) (ii), 195–250, and in *R.G.* 45 (1938), 44–52; Cosentini in *R.I.* (Geneva), 13 (1935), 102–18; Kopelmanas in *R.G.* 43 (1936), 285–308, and 45 (1938), 44–52; Giuliano in *Rivista*, 33 (1941), 69–121; Cheng in *Current Legal Problems*, 4 (1951), 35–53; Pau in *Comunicazioni e Studi*, 6 (1954), 99–178; Schlesinger in *A.J.* 51 (1957), 734–53; McNair in *B.Y.* 33 (1957), 1–19; Mann, *ibid.* pp. 20–51 (with special reference to what the author describes as the commercial law of nations). See also Sereni, *Principi generali di diritto e processo internazionale* (1955).

[3] It has been suggested by Professor Kelsen (*Principles of International Law* (1952), p. 305), that it is logically impossible to envisage a situation in which neither conventional

68

SOURCES OF INTERNATIONAL LAW

Article 38 of the Statute of the Court, the body of 'general principles of law recognized by civilized nations'.

What is the meaning of that expression? These 'general principles' are not, as such, principles of moral justice as distinguished from law; they are not rules of 'equity' in the ethical sense; nor are they a speculative law conceived by way of deductive reasoning from legal and moral principles. They are, in the first instance, those principles of law, private and public,[1] which contemplation of the legal experience of civilized[2] nations leads one to regard as obvious maxims of jurisprudence of a general and fundamental character— such as the principle that no one can be judge in his own cause, that a breach of a legal duty entails the obligation of restitution, that a person cannot invoke his own wrong as a reason for release from a legal obligation, that the law will not countenance the abuse of a right, that legal obligations must be fulfilled and rights must be exercised in good faith, and the like. The International Court of Justice[3] and its predecessor have occasionally acted on

nor customary international law is applicable to a concrete case. The statement is unobjectionable on the assumption that 'general principles of law' are part of conventional and customary international law—an assumption which is only partly acceptable (see below, p. 76).

[1] See Lauterpacht, *Analogies, passim*; Blühdorn, *Die Einfuhrung in das angerwandt Völkerrecht* (1934), pp. 142–6; Laun, *Der Wandel der Ideen Staat und Volk* (1933), pp. 70–85; Knubben in *Z.V.* 16 (1931–2), 146–59, 300–13; Ripert in *Hague Recueil*, 44 (1933) (ii), 569–660; Scheuner, *ibid.* 68 (1939) (ii), 99–199. And see the literature cited above, p. 68 n. 2, as to 'general principles of law'. On the application of 'general principles of law' by international administrative tribunals adjudicating upon disputes between international organizations and their officials see Bastid in *Hague Recueil*, 92 (1957) (ii), 478–87. The Administrative Tribunal of the International Labour Organisation applies general principles of law as a matter of course. See, e.g., *In re Waghorn, I.L.R.* 24 (1957), 748.

[2] There is probably no need to introduce an additional element of complication by attaching undue importance to the word 'civilized' and to embark upon the uncertain path of enquiring as to the meaning of that word. See below, pp. 113–117, on the universality of international law.

[3] See, in particular: Advisory Opinion No. 12 on the *Interpretation of the Treaty of Lausanne (P.C.I.J.* Series B, no. 12, pp. 29 *et seq.*) for an affirmation of the principle that no one can be judge in his own cause, and the direct and indirect references to the principles relating to abuse of rights in the *Case concerning Certain German Interests in Polish Upper Silesia (P.C.I.J.* Series A, no. 7, p. 30), in the *Free Zones* case *(P.C.I.J.* Series A, no. 24, p. 12, and Series A/B, no. 46, p. 167) and in the *Anglo-Norwegian Fisheries* case *(I.C.J. Reports* 1951, p. 142). For the principle that a breach of an engagement involves an obligation to make reparation see *Chorzów Factory* case *(P.C.I.J.* Series A, no. 17, p. 29). For the principle of authentic interpretation by the author of the instrument see the *Jaworzina* case *(P.C.I.J.* Series B, no. 8, p. 37); for the principle of *res judicata* see the Advisory Opinion on the *Effect of Awards of Compensation made by the United Nations Administrative Tribunal (I.C.J. Reports* 1954, p. 53); for the principle that a party cannot rely on its own wrongful conduct as a reason for the non-fulfilment of an obligation, see *Chorzów Factory case (P.C.I.J.* Series A, no. 9, p. 31) and *Danzig Railway Officials* case *(P.C.I.J.* Series B, no. 15, p. 27); for the principle of so-called litispendency (namely, that a dispute should not be subject to two simultaneous judicial proceedings) see the

INTERNATIONAL LAW—THE GENERAL PART

these and other general principles of law. So have international tribunals generally.[1]

However, the recourse to and the utility of general principles of law are not confined to fundamental, or abstract, maxims of jurisprudence of a general character. 'General principles of law' are, and have been, a legitimate source of judicial decision and State action in regard to specific rules and situations. Thus, to mention some examples, international tribunals have acted, expressly or by implication, upon general principles of law when they applied the rules of prescription, on account of lapse of time, with regard both to acquisition of territorial title and to loss of the right to advance a claim;[2] of estoppel—a principle of law of an apparently technical complexion but recognized, under various designations, in most legal systems as precluding a person from relying, to the detriment of another, upon his own contradictory conduct;[3] of particular rules of interpretation of treaties;[4] and in many other cases.

case of *German Interests in Polish Upper Silesia (P.C.I.J.* Series A, no. 6, p. 20); for limitations on the right of outside independent action by members of a corporate body see *Interpretation of the Greco-Turkish Agreement of December 1, 1926* (Series B, no. 16, p. 25). For other examples, in particular of resort by the Court to 'general principles of law' without mentioning them *eo nomine*, in particular with regard to estoppel and 'subsequent conduct' as an element of interpretation of treaties, see Lauterpacht, *The Development of International Law by the International Court* (1958), pp. 167 *et seq.* And see *ibid.* p. 167, n. 20 for references to Separate and Dissenting Opinions of Judges on the subject. As to the principle of respect for vested rights as applied by the Court and other international tribunals see McNair in *B.Y.* 33 (1957), 16–18. It is probable that these 'general principles of law' include the 'elementary considerations of humanity, even more exacting in peace than in war' which the International Court of Justice, in the *Corfu Channel* case, adduced as one of the grounds of the responsibility of Albania for the failure to give warning of the existence of minefields in her waters (*I.C.J. Reports* 1949, p. 22). See also *Corfu Channel* case (*ibid.* p. 18) on circumstantial evidence as being admitted in all systems of law. See Grapin, *Valeur Internationale des Principes généraux du Droit* (1934), pp. 49–168; Hudson, *The Permanent Court of International Justice, 1920–1942* (1943), pp. 610–12; Rousseau, pp. 890–930; Guggenheim, pp. 139–47, and Sørensen, *Les sources de droit international* (1946), pp. 123–52.

[1] See Lauterpacht, *Analogies, passim*, and, in particular, p. 67; the same, *The Function of Law*, pp. 115–18; Cheng, *General Principles of Law as Applied by International Courts and Tribunals* (1953).

[2] See, e.g., *Sarropoulos* v. *Bulgarian State*, decided in 1927 by the Greco-Bulgarian Mixed Arbitral (*Annual Digest*, 4 (1927–8), Case no. 173), where the Tribunal said: 'Positive international law has not established any precise and generally adopted rule either as to the principle of prescription as such or as to its duration. Neither do arbitral decisions or opinions of writers yield any agreed solution. However, prescription appears to constitute a positive legal rule in almost all systems of law. It is an expression of a great principle of peace which is at the basis of common law and of all civilised systems of jurisprudence . . . Prescription being an integral and necessary part of every system of law must be admitted in international law.' For a similar affirmation, in terms of general principles of law, of the doctrine of prescription see the *Williams* case, decided in 1885 by the United States–Venezuelan Claims Commission (Moore, *International Arbitrations*, IV, 4181 *et seq.*) and the *Gentini* case (*Venezuelan Arbitrations*, Ralston's Report (1904), pp. 724–30), and others in Lauterpacht, *Analogies*, pp. 273 *et seq.*

70

SOURCES OF INTERNATIONAL LAW

Moreover, prior judicial or arbitral authority is not a condition of valid recourse to general principles of law. Whenever a question arises which is not governed by an existing rule of international law imposing an obligation upon a State or, in the absence of such a rule, acknowledging by implication its freedom from obligation,[1] or in which the existing rule requires elucidation or development, the rich repository of 'general principles' may be legitimately resorted to by a tribunal, a Government, or the scholar grappling with a novel or difficult situation. Such instruction is available not automatically but only as the result of a search which may be exacting and, possibly, unrewarding. That enquiry consists in ascertaining what, in the absence of a rule of international law, is the way in which the law of States representing the main systems of jurisprudence regulates the problem in the situations in question. That method has often been adopted by tribunals and writers. It is a method combining the processes of comparison of the law of various countries in the sphere of the various branches of private and public law, of deduction from such comparison, and of application of the results thus achieved to the special conditions of international law and international society.[2] There is no question here of what, under

---

[3] See McNair in *B.Y.* 5 (1924), 31–7; Lauterpacht, *Analogies*, §§ 87–9; Friede in *Z.ö.R.* 5 (1935), 517–45; Cheng in *Current Legal Problems* (1951), 141–9. See Cheng, *op. cit.* (n. 1, p. 70) as to the burden of proof. See, by way of example, the statement in the *Kling* case before the United States–Mexican Claims Commission, in 1930, that 'with respect to matters of evidence they [international tribunals] must give effect to common sense principles underlying rules of evidence in domestic law' (*U.N.*, *R.I.A.A.* IV, 575 at p. 582).

[4] See the statement by the Arbitrator, quoting a passage from Rivier, in the *Island of Timor* case, decided in 1914 by the Permanent Court of Arbitration: 'Principles of treaty interpretation are, by and large, and *mutatis mutandis*, those of the interpretation of agreements between individuals, principles of common sense and experience, already formulated by the Prudents of Rome' (Scott, *Hague Court Reports*, p. 365). He then quoted the relevant articles in the French, German and Swiss Codes.

[1] See above, p. 58, and below, p. 95.

[2] An example in the sphere of the law of treaties will illustrate this aspect of the operation of general principles of law. The question has occasionally arisen whether a treaty between two parties which, to the knowledge of one or both of them, conflicts with a provision of a previous treaty binding upon them, is valid and enforceable (see below, p. 395). The practice of States on the subject affords little guidance; the same applies to the infrequent international judicial decisions on the subject. It is legitimate in the circumstances—and instructive—to ascertain what solution is offered in the matter in the various municipal laws, such as Articles 1131, 1133 and 1382 of the French *Code Civil* and the judicial decisions interpreting these provisions; Articles 138 and 826 of the German Civil Code; and a series of English decisions in the field of the law of contract and tort (inasmuch as there arises in some of these cases the question of the consequences of tortiously inducing a breach of contract). For an attempt at an answer to that question on the basis of comparative law see Lauterpacht in *L.Q.R.* (1936), pp. 494–529. The same method can be applied—and ought properly to be applied—to such questions as whether the breach or invalidity of one of the several provisions of a treaty entails the lapse or invalidity of the treaty as a whole; or to what extent the non-fulfilment by one

71

INTERNATIONAL LAW—THE GENERAL PART

the influence of repetitive warnings to caution, has occasionally been described as uncritical application of conceptions of private law to relations between States. The proper task of courts and writers in this sphere is not to disdain the search for general legal principles on the ground that the relations of States are wholly different; their task is, in case of need, to ascertain the general principle in question and then to relate it to the specific character, if any, of international relations or of the particular international relation. While comparative law has for a long time ·been a fruitful object of study for purposes of its own widely acknowledged in the past, the importance of the part which it can play in the elucidation and application of general principles of law as a source of international law is being increasingly recognized.[1]

On occasions, the search for a general principle of law may fail to offer direct assistance for the reason that national systems of law differ with regard to the particular subject. Even in such cases the negative result may not be altogether without usefulness inasmuch as it may throw light on the intricacies of the problem involved. However, experience shows that in the vast majority of cases such differences are limited to questions of form and procedure and that behind national differences of technique and approach there asserts itself an essential uniformity of the law[2]—a reminder that the increasingly frequent description of general principles of law as the modern law of nature is no mere form of words.

Finally, in the rapidly expanding field of relations between Governments which are substantially indistinguishable from that of ordinary commercial relations between private persons, circumstances call, on that account, for the application of general principles of law approximating to general principles of private law in the restricted sense. Thus, there has been a growing number of treaties between Governments providing for the sale or exchange of goods, the grant or opening of a credit, the loan of money or guarantee of a debt, the lease of property of an ordinary private law character,

party of a treaty obligation entitles the other party to abstain or refuse the fulfilment on its part of some or all of the obligations of the treaty; and the various rules, actual or alleged, of interpretation of treaties, such as those relating to restrictive interpretation or the *contra proferentem* rule. As to the two latter rules, by reference to their treatment in the law of contract, see Lauterpacht in *B.Y.* 26 (1949), 56–7 [reprinted in a later volume of these Collected Papers]. And see the same, *The Function of Law*, pp. 272–6 and 292–5, on the doctrines, received as general principles of law, of *rebus sic stantibus* and abuse of rights.

[1] See Gutteridge, *Comparative Law* (2nd ed. 1949), pp. 61–71; Mann in *B.Y.* 33 (1957), 48–51; Schlesinger in *A.J.* 51 (1957), 734–54.

[2] See below, p. 125. And see Lauterpacht in *B.Y.* 12 (1931), 31–62.

SOURCES OF INTERNATIONAL LAW

and the like.[1] It is possible that in the case of some of these treaties the legal relations in question may be governed by rules determined by private international law, namely, in general, the rules of private law of one of the contracting parties. However, the circumstances of these transactions do not as a rule point to an intention of the parties to submit to the law of the other party. In view of this the

[1] Some examples, selected from treaties concluded in the period following the Second World War, will illustrate this aspect of international conventional law. An Agreement of 23 March 1948, between the United States of America and the United Nations, provided for a loan to the latter without interest of a sum not exceeding $65,000,000 for the construction and furnishing of the permanent headquarters of the United Nations. It provided that while any indebtedness under the Agreement is outstanding and unpaid the United Nations shall not 'create any mortgage, lien or encumbrance on or against any of its real property in the headquarters district'. (*U.N.T.S.* 19, 44). An Agreement of 28 June 1950, between the Governments of the United Kingdom, Australia, India, Pakistan and Ceylon on the one hand and the Government of Burma on the other hand, provided for a loan, and the modalities of its payment, to be made to the latter by the five Commonwealth Governments (*ibid.* 87, 154). While in this and similar cases the lending of money or the opening of a credit (Agreement of 1 July 1946 between Yugoslavia and Albania concerning a credit to be extended to the latter (*ibid.* 111, 83)) have been the exclusive objects of the transaction, in others they have been attached to a particular object, such as the purchase of goods in the country providing the loan or credit. Thus the Financial Agreement of 5 February 1946 between Canada and the Netherlands provided for a loan to the latter of an amount not exceeding one hundred and twenty-five million dollars to enable her to pay the cost of Canadian-produced goods (*ibid.* 43, 4). Similar Financial Agreements were concluded with China, France, Norway and Czechoslovakia (*ibid.* pp. 23, 43, 67, 81). See also Exchange of Notes between the United Kingdom and Yugoslavia of 28 December 1950, granting a credit of £3,000,000 to Yugoslavia for the purchase of consumer goods, foodstuffs, etc. (*ibid.* 88, 330).

A considerable number of treaties have been concluded for the sale and purchase of goods—a phenomenon not unnatural in a period characterized by the growing direct management (as distinguished from regulation) by the State of the economic life of the nation. (See Economic Agreement of 17 September 1946, between the United Kingdom and Argentina in which, apart from the regulation of questions relating to railways and payments, the United Kingdom agreed to purchase the exportable surplus of meat at prices laid down in the Agreement (*ibid.* 88, 40).) In 1946 the United States concluded a series of agreements for purchasing natural rubber: see Agreement of 28 January 1946 with France (*ibid.* 3, 239); with the Netherlands (*ibid.* p. 247); with the United Kingdom (*ibid.* p. 293). A detailed Agreement—occupying an entire volume of the *U.N.T.S.* (114) —of 24 July 1947, between Yugoslavia and Hungary, provided for the purchase in Hungary over a period of five years of complete plants, mechanical equipment, machines and materials to be paid for from the proceeds of specified exports from Yugoslavia.

In some cases it has been found necessary to regulate by contractual agreement the conditions of what has been no more than an outright gift (see, e.g., Exchange of Notes between Australia and Hungary of 28 June 1948, concerning a gift of wool to Hungary (*U.N.T.S.* 22, 3)). In a different sphere, contractual arrangements relying upon the use of private law notions have been concluded for regulating what is in essence a gift made in the interest of neighbourly relations. Thus the Agreement of 6 April 1951 between Belgium and the United Kingdom provided for the grant of a lease to the former of a site in the port of Dar-es-Salaam to facilitate Belgian traffic through the territories of East Africa through the construction of a deep-water berth in that port. The rental was fixed at one franc per annum (*ibid.* 110, 4). To the same category, though in a different sphere, belong arrangements such as the Agreement of 11 June 1946 between the United Nations and the Swiss Confederation on the Ariana site providing that the land on which the United Nations buildings are situated shall be subject to a transferable and exclusive

73

INTERNATIONAL LAW—THE GENERAL PART

relations in question—although they do not aim primarily at achieving financial gain—are more properly governed by what has been described as the commercial law of nations,[1] namely, general principles of private law applicable to the transaction in question.

The same may apply to agreements, especially in the sphere of private law, between one public international organization (i.e. an organization whose membership is confined exclusively or predominantly to States) and another, between public international organizations and States[2] and, probably, between public international organizations and private individuals. The relations between public international organizations and their officials—an expanding field of international administrative law—call for the application of 'general principles of law' in that particular sphere.[3]

The preceding considerations explain the nature of 'general principles of law'. They are principles arrived at by way of a comparison,[4] generalization and synthesis of rules of law in its various branches—private and public, constitutional, administrative, and procedural—common to various systems of national law. They are the modern *jus gentium* in its wider sense. In the sense here suggested, they are no more than a modern formulation of the law of nature which played a decisive part in the formative period of international law and which underlay much of its subsequent

real right of user of the surface—*un droit réel de superficie cessible et exclusif*—to continue as long as the buildings themselves; that the same shall apply to certain roads leading to or connecting the buildings; and that the United Nations 'shall enjoy a *servitude personelle* of non-transferable and exclusive user' over certain other plots of land (*ibid.* 1, 154).

Finally, reference may be made to contractual agreements between Governments for the joint construction and operation of works and installations of common interest. Thus in the Treaty of 14 November 1944 between the United States of America and Mexico the two Governments agreed to construct jointly various works in the main channel of the Rio Grande, the cost of the construction to be divided between them in proportion to the benefits which the respective countries receive therefrom, as determined by the Commission set up by the Treaty (Article 5) (*ibid.* 3, 32). For the Exchange of Notes of 20 July 1925 between Colombia and Venezuela concerning the construction of an international bridge on the river Tachira, see *L.N.T.S.* 39, 15–24. For a further enumeration see Mann in *B.Y.* 33 (1957), 23–6.

[1] See Mann in *B.Y.* 33 (1957), 20 *et seq.*

[2] On agreements concluded between and by public international organizations see Jenks, *The Common Law of Mankind* (1958), pp. 201–4, who suggests that rules of private international law may be developed for governing relations of this kind.

[3] See the Advisory Opinion of the International Court of Justice in the case of *Judgments of the Administrative Tribunal of the International Labour Organization upon Complaints Made against the United Nations Educational, Scientific and Cultural Organization* (*I.C.J. Reports* 1956, p. 77, and *Pleadings* etc. in that case, pp. 138 *et seq.* and 199 *et seq.*). And see *Desgranges v. International Labour Organization* (*I.L.R.* 20 (1953), 523, at p. 529).

[4] From this point of view there is a meaningful and important connection between comparative law and public international law. See Gutteridge, *Comparative Law* (2nd ed. 1949), pp. 61–71, and Mann, 'The Commercial Law of Nations', in *B.Y.* 33 (1957), 48–51.

SOURCES OF INTERNATIONAL LAW

development. For there is no warrant for the view that that law of nature was mere speculation which gave a legal form to deductive thinking on theology and ethics. It was primarily a generalization of the legal experience of mankind. The gradual secularization, in that sense, of the law of nature, although usually linked with Grotius, the founder of modern international law, was part and parcel of legal thought in the centuries which preceded him.[1]

. The importance of that source of law does not consist in any frequency of its express application. As stated, normally the customary and conventional rules of international law supply a sufficient basis for determining the conduct of States or the judicial or arbitral decisions. Yet the explicit affirmation, in the Statute of the International Court, of that particular source of law is nevertheless of considerable significance. It definitely removes the possibility, asserted by the extreme positivist school of writers, that international tribunals may have to decline to give a decision because of the apparent absence of an applicable rule of law—a contingency unknown to the internal law of the State.[2] It successfully challenges the mistaken view that the will of sovereign States is the only source of international law. Finally, it gives express legal sanction and encouragement to the continued enrichment of international law from the accumulated experience of the legal development of the nations of the world.

22. *The basis of the validity of general principles of law*

The basis of the validity of 'general principles of law' as a source of international law is of a threefold character.

(*a*) In the first instance, it is a valid and authoritative source of law in so far as it is laid down in a practically universal international instrument, namely, the Statute of the International Court of Justice—an instrument of even wider universality than the Charter of the United Nations.[3] Moreover, although the provisions of Article 38 of the Statute are binding only on the Court, they have —because of their inherent authority—been acted upon by other international tribunals.[4]

---

[1] See Lauterpacht, 'The Grotian Tradition in International Law', in *B.Y.* 23 (1946), 53 n. 1.　　　[2] See below, p. 94.

[3] The Statute of the Court is an integral part of the Charter and binding upon all Members of the United Nations. In addition, it has been adhered to by some States which are not members of the United Nations.

[4] See, e.g., *Administrative Decision No. II* by Judge Parker, Mixed Claims Commission between the United States and Germany, 1 November 1923 (*Annual Digest*, 2 (1923–4), Case no. 205); *Goldenberg & Sons* v. *Germany*, Special Arbitral Tribunal between Romania

INTERNATIONAL LAW—THE GENERAL PART

(*b*) Secondly, the authority of 'general principles of law' as a source of international law is grounded in international custom itself. International tribunals, as well as the International Court of Justice acting in accordance with its Statute, have applied general principles of law from the very inception of modern arbitration. Treaties laying down the basis of decision of arbitral tribunals have frequently and expressly authorized them to act in that way.[1] Above all, the actual development of international law, as a body of practice pursued by Governments, has taken place under the impact of constant recourse to general principles of law—mainly of private law.[2] Thus viewed, the provision of Article 38 of the Statute of the Court in the matter of 'general principles of law' is essentially declaratory of international customary law. Even if the Statute of the Court or the relevant provision of Article 38 were to cease to be binding, the authority of 'general principles of international law' as a source of decision would remain substantially undiminished.

(*c*) Thirdly, the authority of 'general principles of law' as a source of law independent of both treaty and custom stems from what is often described as the reason of the thing, namely, from the twin circumstances that there exists an international community both as a matter of paramount fact[3] and as a society of States claimed and recognized by them to be a society under the rule of law.

As stated, the 'general principles of law' conceived as a source of international law are in many ways indistinguishable from the law of nature as often applied in the past in that sphere. There is no occasion for treating it, for that reason, with suspicion or embarrassment. The part of the law of nature in legal history—including the history of international law—is more enduring and more beneficent than that of positivism, which either identifies the law with, or considers it the result of, the mere will of the State and its agencies. Natural law may occasionally have impaired what some consider to be the purity of law conceived as a science of systematization of rules and principles deduced by logical analysis and deduction from the 'basic rule'[4] which in effect is no more than a reflection of the reality of the physical power of the legal order actually in operation.

and Germany, 27 September 1928 (*ibid.* 4 (1927–8), Case no. 369); *Lena Goldfields Arbitration*, 2 September 1930 (*ibid.* 5 (1929–30), Case no. 1). See also the Award given in 1937 in the case between France and Belgium (*Interpretation of the Tardieu-Jaspar Agreement of January 12, 1930*), reciting the rules of decision provided for in the arbitration agreement (*ibid.* 8 (1935–7), Case no. 223).

[1] See Lauterpacht, *Analogies*, pp. 60–2. See also *United Nations, Systematic Survey of Treaties for the Pacific Settlement of International Disputes, 1928–1948* (1948), pp. 117–19.

[2] See above, p. 68.   [3] See above, p. 28.   [4] See below, p. 90.

SOURCES OF INTERNATIONAL LAW

Natural law may at times have acted as a vehicle for the interpretation of the law in accordance with vested political interests inimical to law and progress. However, exclusive adherence to logical deduction and analysis is not an acceptable hall-mark of law as a science. Nor can it be denied that, in the wider perspective, natural law has acted as a lever of justice, progress and reason rather than as an instrument of oppression and injustice. This being so, there can be no objection to or cause for concern in describing the 'general principles of law' as the modern law of nature. At the same time the formulation of Article 38 of the Statute—in referring to 'general principles of law recognized by civilized States'—emphasizes their pragmatic and inductive character inasmuch as they are derived from systems of law actually in operation as distinguished from the speculative and philosophical aspects of the classical law of nature. For that reason the language of Article 38 is believed to represent a more satisfactory formulation than that of 'the law of nature' of what may fairly be regarded as both the fundamental and the residuary source of international law.[1] However that may be, both treaties and custom, which recognize 'general principles of law' as a source of international law, are merely declaratory of a situation in international relations in which, owing to the existing imperfections of the law-creating process in the international sphere, it is not possible to dispense with reliance on that basic source supplementing and, in some exceptional cases,[2] modifying the law as expressly laid down by treaty and as tacitly accepted by custom. It is in that sense that the definition of international law as given at the outset of this treatise refers to international law as the body of rules of conduct owing their validity both to the will of States as expressed in custom and treaties and to the fact of the existence of an international community of States and individuals. In that latter sense—as referring to an international society composed not exclusively of States—'general principles of law' are applicable and have been applied by non-national tribunals to disputes between sovereign States and private companies and individuals.[3]

---

[1] For a powerful vindication of the law of nature as the main formal source of international law see Sir Gerald Fitzmaurice in *Symbolae Verzijl* (1958), pp. 153–76.

[2] See above, p. 54, and below, p. 88.

[3] See, e.g., the *Lena Goldfields Arbitration* (*Annual Digest*, 5 (1929–30), Case no. 1). See also the valuable Award of Lord Asquith, given in 1951, in the dispute between *Petroleum Development Ltd.* v. *Sheikh of Abu Dhabi* (*I.L.R.* 18 (1951), Case no. 37) and the reference therein to 'the application of principles rooted in the good sense and common practice of the generality of civilized nations—a sort of "modern law of nature"' (at p. 149). For

INTERNATIONAL LAW—THE GENERAL PART

23. *Decisions of international tribunals*

Among the sources of law to be applied by the International Court of Justice its Statute enumerates judicial decisions 'as subsidiary means for the determination of rules of law'.[1] That term covers judicial decisions of both municipal and international courts. Decisions of international courts include those of the International Court of Justice itself (and of its predecessor, namely, the Permanent Court of International Justice) as well as of other international tribunals, in particular international arbitral tribunals conceived as bodies rendering decisions on the basis of law.[2]

International judicial decisions, in the language of the Statute of the Court, are only a subsidiary source of law. In the first instance, the common law doctrine of judicial precedent as an independent source of law has no place in the international sphere. This is so mainly for the reason that in the international sphere tribunals do not occupy the same position as within the State, namely, as organs normally endowed with compulsory jurisdiction. The jurisdiction of international courts and tribunals is, in principle, of a voluntary character.[3] Moreover, if States were to concede the authority of a source of law to the decisions of international tribunals they would be endowing them, to some extent (having regard to the always latent possibilities of judicial legislation), with a competence approaching that of the legislature within the State—a limitation of sovereignty in which States have so far been unwilling to acquiesce.

On the other hand, although the function of judicial tribunals is

an application of principles of 'common law springing from Roman Law' see the Award given in 1954 by the President of the Swiss Federal Court in the case of *Alsing Trading Co.* v. *The Greek State* (*ibid.* 23 (1956), 633). And see *ibid.* 20 (1953), 534, for the Award by Sir Alfred Bucknill in the case of *Ruler of Qatar* v. *International Marine Oil Co.* Some concessionary contracts between private companies and Governments contain arbitration clauses referring, as the source of decision, to 'general principles of Law'. See, e.g., Article 46 of the Agreement of 1954 between Iran, the National Iranian Oil Company, and certain non-Iranian corporations (the Consortium Agreement), which provided as follows: 'In view of the diverse nationality of the parties to this Agreement it shall be governed by and interpreted and applied in accordance with the principles of law common to Iran and the several nations in which the parties to this Agreement are incorporated, and in the absence of such common principles then by and in accordance with principles of law recognized by civilized nations in general, including such of those principles as may have been applied by international tribunals.' For a discussion of this provision see Farmanfarma in *Texas Law Review*, 34 (1955), 259 *et seq.* And see generally Lord McNair in *B.Y.* 33 (1957), 1–19. See also Jessup, *Transnational Law* (1956), pp. 1–16; Domke, 'Arbitration of State-Trading Relations', in *Law and Contemporary Problems* (1959).   [1] Article 38 (1) (*d*).

[2] The main difference between international judicial settlement by the International Court and international arbitration is one of machinery; both adjudicate according to law. See Oppenheim, II, § 15.   [3] See above, p. 23.

78

SOURCES OF INTERNATIONAL LAW

to apply the law and not to make it, experience shows that the effects of judicial precedent—even if not formally recognized as a source of law—cannot always be distinguished from the creation of law. Accordingly, while decisions of international courts and tribunals are, in the language of the Statute of the Court, merely a subsidiary source of law, that circumstance is only a partial indication of their true importance. For these decisions constitute persuasive and, within limits,[1] authoritative evidence of international law. Such evidence is particularly weighty having regard to the relative rarity of the occasions on which controversial questions of international law can be impartially ascertained and clarified. And as the distinction between a source of law and the evidence of law is to a large extent one of terminology[2]—a source of law is often described as the evidence, the manifestation, of the hitherto inarticulate substance of the law—the importance of the distinction is relative.

For this reason, while Article 59 of its Statute lays down that the decisions of the International Court have no authority outside the case in which they were given, and while Article 38 is expressly qualified by reference to Article 59, as a matter of actual practice the Court has repeatedly invoked and relied on its own decisions.[3] In fact, one of the reasons which prompted the establishment of the Court was the widely felt necessity of creating an institution which, by the continuity of its jurisprudence, might itself become an organ of importance in developing international law. For, as stated, decisions of tribunals, even if not binding, are of persuasive authority. It is reasonable to assume that in practice a decision—or series of decisions—which contains persuasive evidence of accepted law will be treated as particularly weighty.[4] At the same time experience teaches that decisions which have ceased to be persuasive will be 'distinguished' and in fact disregarded.[5]

The Court has also referred occasionally, in a somewhat general fashion, to awards of international arbitral bodies. There is room

[1] For emphasis on these limits see Tunkin in *Hague Recueil*, 95 (1958) (iii), 28.
[2] See above, p. 51.
[3] For a survey of that practice see Lauterpacht, *The Development of International Law by the International Court* (1958), pp. 5–15.
[4] See the observations on the subject by Sir Gerald Fitzmaurice in *Symbolae Verzijl* (1958), pp. 168–75, who suggests that decisions of international tribunals approximate to a formal source of law.
[5] See, for instance, the manner in which the Court, in its Advisory Opinion on the *Interpretation of Peace Treaties with Bulgaria, Hungary and Romania (First Phase)* (*I.C.J. Reports* 1950, p. 65), distinguished the issue before it as being 'profoundly different' from that in the *Status of Eastern Carelia* case before the Permanent Court in 1923 (Series B, no. 5).

INTERNATIONAL LAW—THE GENERAL PART

for expansion of that practice.[1] Numerous awards of arbitration tribunals and of single arbitrators have achieved distinction equalling in authority and elaboration that of judicial decisions in the strict sense of the word.[2]

24. *Decisions of municipal courts*

Decisions of municipal courts bearing upon matters of international law are one of its subsidiary sources.[3] Article 38 of the Statute of the International Court of Justice enumerates 'judicial decisions'

[1] See Lauterpacht, *The Development of International Law by the International Court* (1958), pp. 15–18, for an account of that aspect of the practice of the Court. On the authority in English courts of the decisions of the International Court see Jenks in *B.T.* 20 (1939), 1–36.

[2] Of the digests and collections of decisions of national and international courts and tribunals the following ought to be mentioned: *Annual Digest and Reports of Public International Law Cases*, continued as *International Law Reports* (for details see List of Abbreviations, above, p. xvii); *Fontes Juris Gentium* (ed. by Bruns): Series A, Part I, vols. I and 3, Digest of the Decisions of the Permanent Court of International Justice, 1922–1930 (1931) and 1931–1934 (1935); Series A, Part I, vol. 2, Digest of the Decisions of the Permanent Court of Arbitration, 1902–1928 (1931); Series A, Part II; Decisions of the German Supreme Court relating to International Law, 1879–1929 (1931); *Decisions of German Superior Courts, 1945–1949* (1956), ed. by Bilfinger; Moore, *History and Digest of International Arbitrations to which the United States has been a Party*, 6 vols. (1898), and *International Adjudications, Ancient and Modern* (six volumes of this series were published between 1929 and 1933; they contain a detailed account and analysis mainly of the awards of the British–American Mixed Commissions in the first part of the nineteenth century); Lapradelle et Politis, *Recueil des arbitrages internationaux*, I (1798–1855) (1905); II (1856–1872) (1924); III (1872–1875) (1954). A valuable earlier collection is that by Lafontaine, *Pasicrisie internationale* (1902); Publications of the Permanent Court of International Justice: Series A, nos. 1–24, Judgments (1923–1930); Series B, nos. 1–18, Advisory Opinions (1922–1930); Series A/B, nos. 40 *et seq.*; Judgments, Orders, and Advisory Opinions from 1931; Series E, nos. 1 *et seq.*, Annual Reports from 1925. The Judgments, Advisory Opinions and Orders of the International Court of Justice are published in a separate series since 1947, and in another series there appear the Pleadings, Oral Arguments and Documents. For an analytical digest of the jurisprudence of the Court see Hambro, *The Case Law of the International Court* (1952 and 1959). See also United Nations, *Reports of International Arbitral Awards*.

Of the case books, which include decisions of both national and international tribunals, the following may be mentioned: Pitt Cobbett, *Leading Cases and Opinions on International Law* (vol. I, 6th ed. 1947; vol. II, 5th ed. 1937, by Walker); Hudson, *Cases and Other Materials on International Law* (3rd ed. 1951); Dickinson, *Cases on International Law* (1950); Fenwick, *Cases on International Law* (2nd ed. 1951); Briggs, *The Law of Nations* (2nd ed. 1952); MacKenzie and Laing, *Canada and the Law of Nations* (1938); Green, *International Law through the Cases* (2nd ed. 1960); Bishop, *International Law, Cases and Materials* (1953); Orfield and Re, *Cases and Materials on International Law* (1953). For critical comment on some case books see Hudson in *A.J.* 32 (1938), 447–56. And see, in particular, the comprehensive treatise of Schwarzenberger, *International Law*, I. *International Law as Applied by International Courts and Tribunals* (3rd ed. 1957).

[3] See Lauterpacht in *B.T.* 10 (1929), 65–95, for a detailed discussion of the subject; Finch in *Hague Recueil*, 53 (1935) (iii), 605–27. See also De Louter, I, 56, 57; Fauchille, nos. 55–7; Westlake, *Papers*, p. 83; Rivier, I, 35; Brierly, p. 52; Triepel, *Völkerrecht und Landesrecht* (1899), pp. 28–32, 99–101, 127; Anzilotti, *La Teoria generale della responsabilità dello Stato nel diritto internazionale* (1902), pp. 30 *et seq.* and see below, pp. 247–249. On the interpretation of municipal law by the Permanent Court see Jenks in *B.T.* 19 (1938), pp. 67–103.

SOURCES OF INTERNATIONAL LAW

among the 'subsidiary means for the determination of rules of law'. This must be deemed to include decisions of municipal courts.[1] They cover, in addition to prize law (which is concerned largely with the application of the law concerning blockade and contraband), most branches of international law, in particular those relating to: diplomatic immunities; the jurisdictional immunities of foreign States; the effects of recognition of States, Governments and belligerency; extradition; State succession; various aspects of the jurisdiction of the State on the high seas, in its territorial waters, and in the air; the treatment of aliens and their property; the interpretation and application of treaties; and many questions of the law of war including, but not limited to, the punishment of war crimes. There is hardly a question of international law which is not covered by a decision or a series of decisions of municipal courts. Having regard to the voluntary character, and the resulting infrequency, of adjudication by international courts and tribunals, decisions of municipal courts are at present the principal instrument for judicial interpretation and application of international law. There are two additional factors operating in the same direction. In the first instance, rights and obligations of private persons which normally call for a decision by a municipal court are often determined by a rule or principle of international law binding upon States and laid down in international custom or a treaty. Secondly, as will be shown later, international law on occasions confers rights directly upon individuals and imposes upon them obligations cognizable before municipal courts.[2]

The significance of decisions of municipal courts as a source of international law and as a means for its clarification and development was for a time obscured under the influence of the so-called positivist doctrine. In the first instance, the latter insisted, with regard to international custom, that the consent of States must be given formally through organs specially authorized to declare it and by way of declarations of will intended to create international obligations. In the nature of things, neither of these conditions can be fulfilled in the case of judgments given by municipal courts. Secondly, according to the positivist doctrine as then understood,

---

[1] In view of this, it may be difficult to follow the passage in the Judgment in *The Lotus* case which was prefaced by the following statement: 'Without pausing to consider the value to be attributed to the judgments of municipal courts in connection with the establishment of rules of international law' (*P.C.I.J.* Series A, no. 10, p. 28). However, it is submitted in the text above that decisions of municipal courts, in so far as they supply evidence of practice followed as a matter of obligation, constitute one of the principal sources of international law, namely, international custom.   [2] See below, p. 141.

INTERNATIONAL LAW—THE GENERAL PART

international and municipal law are wholly disparate systems of law, whose subjects and subject matter are different, with the result that a decision of a municipal court can never become a source of international law.[1] That phase in the doctrine of international law is now a matter of the past.[2] The recognition of the place of decisions of municipal courts is not limited to the Statute of the International Court. They have become a conspicuous feature of the exposition of international law in treatises and textbooks. Naturally, their authority as evidence of the existing law must depend on the intrinsic merits of any individual decision and the standing of the tribunal which renders them.

While no single decision of a municipal court irrevocably binds a State in relation to other States, in one respect its probative value is higher than that of pronouncements of other organs of the State. Although decisions of municipal courts are often coloured by the particular interests and approach of their State[3] (quite apart from the fact that, as a rule, they are bound to apply national legislation even if it is contrary to international law),[4] being judicial organs they naturally exhibit a higher degree of impartiality and independence.[5] Moreover, a Government may on occasions disclaim, as no longer being in accordance with its views, an opinion previously expressed by its representative in Parliament, at an international conference or before an international tribunal.[6] No comparably wide

---

[1] The consistent positivist view on the subject was expressed with lucidity by Anzilotti, *Il diritto internazionale nei giudizi interni* (1906), pp. 143–96. It is instructive, as showing the drastic change in international law on the subject in the last fifty years, to quote the relevant passage in that essay: 'A rule of international law is by its very nature absolutely unable to bind individuals, i.e. to confer upon them rights and duties. It is created by the collective will of states with the view to regulating their mutual relations . . . If several states were to attempt to create rules directly regulating private relations, such an attempt, by the very nature of things, would not be a rule of international law, but a rule of uniform municipal law common to several states. It is only by such rules that the private duty, as willed by international law, can be given effect' (at p. 197). With this passage there may be compared the pronouncement of the Permanent Court of International Justice in the *Serbian Loans* case (see above, p. 42).

[2] As stated above (at p. 67), contrary to the case of treaties, it is not necessary for the creation of international custom that there should be on the part of the acting organs of the State an intention to incur mutually binding obligations; it is enough if the conduct in question is dictated by a sense of obligation in the sphere of international law. For the same reason uniform municipal legislation constitutes in a substantial sense evidence of international custom (see, to the same effect, Gianni, *La coutume en droit international* (1931), p. 129). [3] See below, pp. 84, 248. [4] See below, pp. 84, 241. [5] See below, pp. 84 163.

[6] For an example of an admission of 'vacillation in Great Britain's statements' as being 'no doubt evidence of inconsistency' in the matter of the width of bays see the *Reply* of the United Kingdom in the *Fisheries* case before the International Court of Justice: *Pleadings* etc. II, 479. On the question of damages for loss of profits, the attitude of Great Britain in the *Behring Sea Arbitration* was wholly opposed to that previously assumed by that country in the *Alabama Arbitration* (see Lauterpacht, *Analogies*, p. 220). And see Lauterpacht in *B.Y.* 10 (1929), 83 [reprinted in later volume], for other examples.

SOURCES OF INTERNATIONAL LAW

freedom of action obtains with regard to the previous pronouncements of its municipal courts.

There is a further consideration which adds to the importance of municipal decisions as a source of international law. In some countries possessing a Federal constitution the higher municipal tribunals have been endowed with jurisdiction to decide disputes, on the basis of international law, between members of the Federation (which are occasionally described, as in the United States of America, as sovereign States). In that capacity these national tribunals have decided on such questions as the utilization of the flow of international rivers, sovereignty over territorial waters and adjacent areas, the interpretation and termination of treaties, and the doctrines of discovery and of the watershed in relation to acquisition of territory.[1]

Decisions of municipal courts provide evidence of international law in two ways: In the first instance, as courts are organs of the State the decisions given by them may, when sufficiently uniform, be treated as supplying evidence of international law as understood by the State in question in the sense that, in general, that State is precluded from denying the validity of a rule or principle traditionally acted upon by its own courts in the sphere of international custom. This applies not only to general but also to particular customary international law. Thus, for instance, if the courts of a country have acted in the past on the view that the territorial waters of a State extend to three miles, that State would be precluded from asserting, as a matter of legal claim, a wider limit. Similar considerations apply to the interpretation, by its courts, of treaties binding upon a State. Secondly, in cases in which decisions of municipal courts of a number of States on a specific subject show a marked degree of uniformity, they are evidence of international practice followed as a matter of obligation. As such they may accurately be regarded as part of customary international law. In that sense they are not only a subsidiary but also a principal source of international law.

Pending the wider adoption of the principle of obligatory jurisdiction of international tribunals, municipal courts are thus the main instrument for the judicial determination of international law. They are an important means for the clarification and development

[1] See the *Labrador Boundary* case, decided in 1927 by the Judicial Committee of the Privy Council, between Canada and Newfoundland (43 T.L.R. at p. 294, and *Annual Digest*, 4 (1927–8), Case no. 81).

INTERNATIONAL LAW—THE GENERAL PART

of its rules. Undoubtedly, municipal tribunals are organs of the State and they must apply its law—even if inconsistent with international law—both as laid down by the legislature and, often, as determined by statements of the Executive.[1] Thus, to a degree varying in different countries, municipal courts regard as conclusive the determination made by the Executive on such matters as the existence of diplomatic status and the right to diplomatic immunities, divers questions connected with recognition—and its effects—of foreign States and Governments, the existence of a state of war, and many others.[2] In some countries, like France, courts consider the interpretation of treaties to be within the province of the Executive department.[3] On some questions, such as the obligation of the successor State to take over the obligations of its predecessor, municipal courts have occasionally been subject to the tendency to provide an interpretation of international law favourable to the financial interests of their countries, or to hold that such questions fall within the category of 'Act of State' removed from the orbit of judicial decision.[4] However, in general, municipal tribunals have been conscious of their function as judicial bodies administering international law. In that capacity they act as the organs of the international community.

Unavoidably, the contribution of municipal tribunals is, in this respect, adversely affected by the circumstance that the decisions of tribunals of various countries do in many cases exhibit a considerable degree of divergence. It is possible that the usefulness and authority of decisions of municipal courts could be enhanced if States were to adopt an international agreement, amending the Statute of the International Court, so as to permit the highest municipal courts in various countries to apply, through their Governments or otherwise, for advisory determination by the International Court of

---

[1] See below, p. 162. Prize courts, acting as they do in time or under the influence of war, may not always be in a position to preserve an attitude of detached impartiality. See the judgment of Lord Stowell in *The Maria*, 1 Chris. Rob. 350, for an affirmation of the universality and impartiality of the law administered by the British Prize Court. But see Lauterpacht in *B.Y.* 10 (1929), 65 n. 1, as to the circumstances bearing upon that aspect of Lord Stowell's judgment. In *The Recovery*, Lord Stowell referred to his court as being a 'Court of the Law of Nations, though sitting here under the authority of the King of Britain', as belonging 'to other nations as to our own', a court in which aliens have 'a right to demand . . . the administration of the Law of Nations simply, and exclusively of the introduction of principles borrowed from our municipal jurisprudence' (6 Chris. Rob. 349). As to the character of prize courts see Oppenheim, II, §434. And see Walker, *Science*, p. 49, for an expression of the hope that in the future 'municipal courts may become the trusted mouthpieces of International Law as local divisions of the great High Court of Nations'.   [2] See below, p. 162.

[3] See below, p. 174.   [4] See below, p. 163 n.1.

84

SOURCES OF INTERNATIONAL LAW

difficult and controversial questions of international law. The importance of municipal decisions as a source of international law is now being increasingly recognized and, in addition to the *International Law Reports*, the publication of these decisions has become a regular feature of many periodicals of international law.[1]

25. *Equity as a source of international law*

Equity, in its wider sense as connoting ideas of fairness, good faith and moral justice, is a source of international law to the not inconsiderable extent to which it may be regarded as forming part of general principles of law recognized by civilized States.[2] It is so also to the extent to which some relief must be regarded as part of international law.[3] While the securing of moral justice is an essential object of the law, that object cannot always be achieved. It must yield, in particular cases, to requirements of certainty, stability and fulfilment of legitimate expectations—all of which are directly related to moral justice. It is in that sense that there must be understood the various treaties providing for arbitral settlement of disputes between States on the basis of 'law and equity' or 'international law and equity'.[4] The fact that an asserted rule of law is

---

[1] See Anzilotti, *Il diritto internazionale nei giudizi interni* (1906), for the suggestion that within the State special tribunals should be created to adjudicate upon questions of international law—a suggestion which does not meet the difficulty referred to in the text above. See also Dickinson in *Hague Recueil*, 40 (1932) (ii), 372–92, for a critical survey of the contribution of English and American courts; Pergler, *Judicial Interpretation of International Law in the United States* (1928); Hyde in *B.Y.* 18 (1937), 1–16. And see Challine, *Le droit international public dans la jurisprudence française de 1789 à 1848* (1934). As to the interpretation and application of treaties by English courts see McNair in *Hague Recueil*, 43 (1933) (i), 251–302. As to Germany, see *Fontes Juris Gentium*, Series A, Section II(1), for digests of decisions of the German Supreme Court from 1879 to 1929. See also above, p. 80, for a list of collections of decisions of courts. And see generally, on the application of international law by municipal tribunals, Mosler in *Hague Recueil*, 91 (1957) (i), 625–709; Morgenstern in *B.Y.* 27 (1950), 42–92; Kraus in *Festschrift für Rudolf Laun* (1953), pp. 223 *et seq.*; and see below, p. 153.

[2] See above, p. 69.   [3] See above, p. 69.

[4] Thus, for instance, the Convention of 18 August 1910 between Great Britain and the United States provided that the Arbitral Tribunal set up by the Treaty shall render its awards in accordance 'with treaty rights and with the principles of international law and equity'. The Tribunal consistently interpreted this provision as precluding it from departing from rules of international law—although in cases in which it considered that the strict application of international law might be conducive to hardship it recommended, for consideration by the successful party, a course of action calculated to alleviate any hardship resulting from the award. For a survey of these cases see Lauterpacht, *The Function of Law*, pp. 311–13, and in *Symbolae Verzijl* (1958), pp. 213–61. For an account of some of the relevant arbitration treaties see Lauterpacht, *Analogies*, pp. 65–7, and in *Annuaire*, 40 (1937), 271. And see the *Cayuga Indians Claims* case, decided by the above Tribunal (*A.J.* 20 (1926), 581–6) for a detailed analysis of the term 'international law and equity'. See also *Annual Digest*, 3 (1925–6), 399. In the Award of the Arbitration Tribunal in the *Norwegian Shipowners' Claim* the Tribunal considered that the phrase 'law

INTERNATIONAL LAW—THE GENERAL PART

productive of hardship and, in that sense, inequitable in its operation does not in itself—unless reliance upon it is contrary to the over-riding principle of good faith—deprive it of its character as a legal rule. This applies equally to international law.

However, States may agree that in a particular case their rights shall be determined not only by existing law but also by other considerations which, in all the circumstances, ought to underlie a new legal relation. The constitution of an international court may enable it to give decisions on that basis. Thus the Statute of the International Court of Justice, after enumerating in the first paragraph of Article 38 the sources of the law to be applied by it, lays down in the second paragraph that it is open to the Court 'to decide a case *ex aequo et bono*, if the parties agree thereto'. That exceptional power, which constitutes a departure from the normal judicial function, ought to be interpreted restrictively. It ought not to be assumed unless the treaty unequivocally confers upon the tribunal a power to that effect.[1] On the other hand, no special authority is required to enable a judicial tribunal, after it has determined the legal position, to make to the parties recommendations—which are not binding—with a view to a voluntary modification of their legal rights in accordance with moral justice, equity, and convenience.[2]

3. THE HIERARCHY AND THE COMPLETENESS OF THE SOURCES OF INTERNATIONAL LAW

26. The hierarchy of the sources of international law

The order in which the sources of international law are enumerated in the Statute of the International Court of Justice is, essentially, in accordance both with correct legal principle and with the character of international law as a body of rules based on consent to a degree higher than is law within the State. The rights and duties of States

and equity' used in the Special Agreement did not empower it to depart from the terms of a legal instrument or its consequences: 'The majority of international lawyers seem to agree that these words are to be understood to mean general principles of justice as distinguished from any particular system of jurisprudence or the municipal law of any State' (*Annual Digest*, 1 (1919–22), Case no. 261). See also the *Georges Pinson* case, decided in 1928 by the Mexican–French Claims Commission (*Annual Digest*, 4 (1927–8), Case no. 318); the Individual Opinion of Judge Hudson in the case of *Diversion of Waters from the Meuse* (*P.C.I.J.*, Series A/B, no. 70 (1937), p. 77); and the Award in the *Ambatielos Claim* (*I.L.R.* 26 (1956), p. 306). And see, for the literature on the meaning of 'equity' in arbitration treaties, Oppenheim, II, § 15 n. 5.

[1] See the case of *Free Zones of Upper Savoy and the District of Gex* (*P.C.I.J.* Series A, no. 24, p. 10).

[2] See Lauterpacht, *The Function of Law*, pp. 312, 313; *The Development of International Law by the International Court* (1958), pp. 213–17; and in *Symbolae Verzijl* (1958), pp. 210–20.

SOURCES OF INTERNATIONAL LAW

are determined, in the first instance, by their agreement as expressed in treaties—just as in the case of individuals their rights are specifically determined by any contract which is binding upon them. When a controversy arises between two or more States with regard to a matter regulated by a treaty, it is natural that the parties should invoke and that the adjudicating agency should apply, in the first instance, the provisions of the treaty in question. Like a contract between individuals, a treaty between States constitutes the law between them. *Modus et conventio vincunt legem.* Within these limits—which may be substantial[1]—a treaty overrides international customary law and even general principles of law; it may also, subject to some obvious limitations,[2] depart from a general treaty binding upon the parties. Thus the parties may agree, as between themselves, to modify some particular aspect of the customary law relating to diplomatic immunities; they may, for instance, agree that the diplomatic immunities reciprocally to be granted in the future shall be limited to the heads of missions or that their diplomatic representatives shall not enjoy immunity in matters of taxation. In the above sense, treaties must be considered as ranking first in the hierarchical order of the sources of international law.

It is only when there are no provisions of a treaty applicable to the situation that international customary law is, next in hierarchical order, properly resorted to. Although its importance as an instrument of developing the law may tend to diminish,[3] custom still represents the firm core of international law. It is, though in a less articulate form than a treaty, expressive of the consent of States. As such, custom may, again within certain limits, derogate from an otherwise obvious general principle of law. Thus, at a time when international law imposed no restriction upon the resort to war, the general principle of law according to which duress vitiates an agreement did not obtain in customary international law; peace treaties imposed by force enjoyed full validity. It is only when neither customary nor conventional international law as formulated by treaty provides an answer that recourse may—and must—be had to the third, the residuary, source of international law, namely,

[1] As examples of treaties which may exceed the relevant limits, consider treaties providing for encroachments on the freedom of the high seas, or immoral treaties, or treaties which, to the knowledge of both parties, are inconsistent with a treaty previously concluded by both or one of them. See McNair, p. 113, and the Individual Opinion of Judge Schücking in the *Oscar Chinn* case (*P.C.I.J.* Series A/B, no. 63, p. 150).

[2] Such as that the particular treaty must not affect adversely the rights of the parties to a general treaty or their legal interest in the continued fulfilment of the purpose of a general treaty. [3] See above, p. 67.

87

INTERNATIONAL LAW—THE GENERAL PART

'general principles of law as recognized by civilized States'. Thus viewed, the order of enumeration adopted in the Statute of the International Court of Justice provides a workable and accurate starting point for the application of the law.

However, the order of the sources of international law as thus indicated cannot be applied in a mechanical way. Nor does it fully express their relative importance. Undoubtedly, the rights and duties of States must be determined in the first instance by reference to applicable treaties. Yet, while it is true that international customary law applies only in the absence of available provisions of treaties, and that 'general principles of law' are merely a residuary source of law in cases in which there is no applicable treaty or custom, treaties, in turn, must be interpreted in the light of customary international law[1]—just as the latter, as well as treaties, must be interpreted against the background of general principles of law. When the meaning of a treaty is not clear, it must be assumed that the parties intended it to be in conformity with general, customary, international law—and it is then that customary international law becomes relevant and decisive, notwithstanding any hierarchical order establishing the priority of a treaty. Thus, in the Advisory Opinion on the *Frontier between Turkey and Iraq* the Permanent Court of International Justice interpreted the rule of unanimity— which was a rule both of the Covenant of the League of Nations in the matter of decisions of its Council and of customary international law in relation to decisions of international bodies generally—in the light of the general principle of law that no one can be judge in his own cause.[2] In the result, the Court interpreted away the customary rule of unanimity. In an even more drastic manner, in the Advisory Opinion on *Reparation for Injuries Suffered in the Service of the United Nations* the Court, by reference to a general principle derived from the needs of the international community, modified the customary rule according to which treaties cannot affect the rights and obligations of States which are not parties thereto.[3] A treaty may be rendered obsolete or inoperative, wholly or in part, by custom—as has been the case with regard to the provisions of the Treaty of Vienna of 1815 classifying the categories of diplomatic agents.

In view of this, while the hierarchy of sources of international

---

[1] For an affirmation of that principle see the decision of the French–Mexican Claims Commission in the *Georges Pinson* case (Verzijl, President) (*Annual Digest*, 4 (1927–8), Case no. 292) and of the Permanent Court of Arbitration (Borel, Arbitrator) in the case of *The Kronprins Gustav Adolph* (*A.J.* 26 (1932), 839).

[2] Series B, no. 12, p. 31.   [3] *I.C.J. Reports* 1949, p. 174.

SOURCES OF INTERNATIONAL LAW

law, as indicated in the Statute of the International Court, provides an authoritative initial basis for the application of international law, it does so subject to the fact that these sources are mutually, and intimately, interrelated. They cannot properly be derived one from the other. Thus, it cannot be accurately said, by way of a reversal of the order indicated in the Statute of the Court, that the binding force of treaties must be deduced from a customary rule of international law laying down that treaties must be observed. Apart from the fact that international practice has not, unfortunately, been uniform on that subject, the principle that a treaty—like any other compact —is binding must be deemed to have been associated with the notion of treaties from its very inception independently of any custom. In fact, the binding force of a treaty is inherent in the very conception of a treaty. If it is considered necessary to look for a higher source of the validity of treaties, it may be more accurate to deduce their binding force—as, indeed, that of customary international law itself—from general principles of law. It is a general principle of law that compacts must be kept and that persons—and States—ought to observe custom, namely, that they ought to conduct themselves as they have customarily agreed to conduct themselves. There would still remain the question of the legal authority of general principles of law in the sphere of international law. That question cannot be answered with finality—though it can be answered provisionally by the statement that it is a principle of customary international law that general principles of law form part of international law. Yet this is a statement which, upon analysis, causes the enquiry to turn in a circle. The ultimate foundation of the binding force of any particular legal order—which means of the principal sources of its validity—must itself be in the nature of an assumption, a postulate, of a non-legal character. That fundamental assumption, if it is not to be artificial and if it is to carry conviction, must make the validity of the legal order correspond to, or be derived from, an existing obtainable maximum of social and political reality. The latter statement, which is not entirely self-explanatory, may usefully be elaborated in connection with the consideration, in the Section which follows, of what may be described as the ultimate source of international law.

27. *The ultimate source of international law*

There is a recurrent tendency in the science of law to deduce the validity of any legal rule from one which is superior to it in

89

INTERNATIONAL LAW—THE GENERAL PART

hierarchical order. This is dictated by considerations which appear to be of a doctrinal rather than a practical nature.[1] Thus the validity of treaties as a source of international law has occasionally been

[1] While the notion of the 'fundamental norm' has received particular attention from Continental lawyers—see references below—it is by no means of Continental origin. It was developed with some clarity in Salmond's *Jurisprudence* (1st ed. 1902), where he said, in § 48, in a Section entitled 'Ultimate Legal Principles': 'It is requisite that the law should postulate one or more first causes, whose operation is ultimate, and whose authority is undenied. In other words there must be found in every legal system certain ultimate principles, from which all others are derived, but which are themselves self-existent.' He then elaborated the subject in some detail. See also Hall's statement that 'the ultimate foundation of international law is an assumption that states possess rights and are subject to duties corresponding to the facts of their postulated nature' (*A Treatise on International Law*, 3rd ed. (1890), § 7). He said in § 1: 'It is postulated of those independent states which are dealt with by international law that they have a moral nature identical with that of individuals.' And see, more recently, Sir Gerald Fitzmaurice in *Modern Law Review*, 19 (1956), 1–13. Generally on the subject of the 'initial hypothesis' see Kelsen, *Das Problem der Souveränität und die Theorie des Völkerrechts* (1920), *passim*; *Die philosophischen Grundlagen der Naturrechtslehre und des Rechtspositivismus* (1928); *Reine Rechtslehre* (1934), pp. 129–54; and in *Hague Recueil*, 14 (1926) (iv), 231–329 and 42 (1932) (iv), 121–351. See also Lauterpacht, *The Function of Law*, pp. 420–3; Brierly in *Hague Recueil*, 23 (1928) (iii), 467–549; Cavaglieri, *ibid.* 26 (1929) (i), 362; Bourquin, *ibid.* 35 (1931) (i), 76–80; Métall in *Ž.ö.R.* 11 (1931), 416–28; Le Fur in *Hague Recueil*, 54 (1935) (iv), 146–66; Giuliano, *La comunità internazionale e il diritto* (1950). And see Oppenheim, 1, § 493, on the binding force of treaties. The doctrine of the initial hypothesis as the basis of international law has been clearly formulated by Kelsen, the originator of what has become known as the Vienna School, in a series of writings referred to above. As to the influence of Kelsen and of the Vienna School on international law, see Lauterpacht in *Modern Theories of Law* (1933), pp. 125–9; Kunz, *Völkerrechtswissenschaft und reine Rechtslehre* (1923), and in *New York University Law Quarterly Review*, 11 (1933–4), 370–421; Schiffer, *Die Lehre vom Primat des Völkerrechts in der neueren Literatur* (1937); Man, *L'école de Vienne et le développement du droit des gens* (1938); Akzin in *R.I.* (*Paris*), 1 (1927), 342–72; Balladore Pallieri in *Rivista*, 27 (1935), 24–8; J. M. Jones in *B.Y.* 16 (1935), 42–55; Starke, *ibid.* 17 (1936), 66–81; Stern in *American Political Science Review*, 30 (1936), 736–41. That influence has extended in particular to such matters as the relation of the systems of international and municipal law, State sovereignty, the subjects of international law, personification of the State, etc. On these questions there is a striking similarity of view between the Vienna School and the views of the French writer Duguit and his followers. Duguit's principal works in this connection are *Traité du droit constitutionnel*, 3 vols. (2nd ed. 1921), and *Le droit social et le droit individuel et la transformation de l'Etat* (3rd ed. 1922). On Duguit's contribution to international law see Le Fur in *Archives de philosophie du droit*, 1932, pp. 175–212, and in *Hague Recueil*, 54 (1935) (iv), 72–94; Guggenheim in *R.G.* 63 (1959), no. 4; and, in particular, Reglade, *ibid.* 37 (1930), 381–419. See also Bonnard in *Théorie du droit*, 1 (1926), 18–40, and 3 (1928), 55–70; Kunz, *ibid.* 1 (1926), 140–52 and 204–21. The doctrines of Duguit have been amplified and applied to international law in a creative manner on a biological basis by Scelle in his *Précis de droit des gens*, 1 (1932) and 11 (1934). See also the same, *La théorie juridique de la révision des traités* (1936). And see Segal in *Théorie du droit*, 9 (1935), 186–94. According to Scelle there exists over and above the legal order a natural order conceived as the sum total of biological laws whose observance imposes itself upon the legislator with absolute necessity; his task is to translate these laws into legal rules; the concordance of the legal and biological law is the intrinsic basis of the validity of the law. It may be of some interest to compare Scelle's sociological and biological foundation of international law with Westlake's attempt to base it on 'the social nature of man and his material and moral surroundings': *Papers*, p. 81. See also Reeves in *Hague Recueil*, 3 (1924) (ii), 5–94. And see Chklaver, *Le droit international dans ses rapports avec la philosophie du droit* (1929); Alvarez, *Le nouveau droit international* (1924); the same, *La philosophie des peuples et la reconstruction du droit international*

SOURCES OF INTERNATIONAL LAW

deduced from customary international law[1]—a proceeding which, as pointed out above, is possibly open to some doubt. For, after the validity of treaties has thus been deduced from the allegedly higher rule of customary law, there arises necessarily the question of the source of the validity of that superior rule. Eventually the point is reached at which no legal answer can be given to the question thus put. Thus, in a different sphere, in Great Britain the authority of any particular source of law may be derived from the will of Parliament. What is the legal authority of the will of Parliament? It may be said that the authority of Acts of Parliament is legally grounded in the basic unwritten law of the Constitution. What is the legal source of the binding force of the Constitution? A point must be reached when the answer cannot be given in terms of a legal obligation derived from a higher legal rule. The highest rule must be assumed; and it must be assumed to exist as a rule which is not itself of a legal nature.

Thus with regard to the question of the source of the validity of customary international law the solution adopted by some is that the binding force of customary international law is based on the 'fundamental rule', which is itself of a non-legal character, namely, that States must behave as they have customarily behaved. There are objections of some cogency to the fundamental norm thus expressed. In particular, it does not take into account 'the general principles of law recognized by civilized nations'—an important source of law[2] which though recognized to a large extent by the practice of States is essentially independent of it and owes its validity to the very existence of the international community. Secondly, the fundamental rule thus formulated is open to the objection that it gives customary law a complexion of sanctity and immutability which may not be in accordance with the progressive development of international law. It appears to leave no room for changing international law by treaty or by contrary custom. Thirdly, it attaches to custom an importance which is not in keeping with its necessarily diminishing part in a dynamic international society. Most of existing international law is composed of and is developed through treaties. For these reasons it is preferable and, indeed,

(1936), and *Le droit international nouveau* (1959). See also Djuvara in *Hague Recueil*, 64 (1938) (ii), 485–616; Rousseau, pp. 55–105; Ziccardi, *La costituzione dell'ordinamento internazionale* (1943), pp. 19–157.

[1] See e.g. Kelsen, *General Theory of Law and State* (English translation, 1945), p. 369, and *Principles of International Law* (1952), p. 416. See also Guggenheim, *Traité*, 1, 6–8.

[2] So important that Verdross (*Völkerrecht* (3rd ed. 1955), pp. 18–25) regards it as *the* fundamental norm.

INTERNATIONAL LAW—THE GENERAL PART

inevitable—in so far as the formulation of the 'fundamental rule' is a matter of practical significance—to derive it from a fact other than the existence of international custom and its habitual observance. That fact is the existence of the international community whose general will as expressed in treaties, custom and general principles of law, must be obeyed.[1] The choice of that basic fact and the initial deduction therefrom are, in a sense, discretionary and any excess of dogmatism bestowed upon that question may be out of place.

However, although the choice of the ultimate basis of the law is a discretionary process inasmuch as it is not determined by legal considerations, it is not an arbitrary process. For it is determined by reference to a political and social reality actually in operation. From that point of view the 'ultimate foundation' constitutes a bridge between what is usually described as the purely normative character of law (whose validity, unlike that of a physical law, is not affected by any breaches that may occur) and its necessarily factual basis. Thus, the 'ultimate assumption', in relation to the law of England, that Parliament must be obeyed is based on the fact that, as a matter of actual social and political occurrence, the will of Parliament is—by consent and by necessity—supreme. The same considerations apply to the ultimate source of international law. That ultimate source is the assumption that the impersonal will of the international community—as formulated by treaties voluntarily concluded by its members, by custom created by their implied consent, and by general principles of law expressive of the fact that the international legal community is a community under law—must be obeyed. It has been shown that, notwithstanding contrary appearances, facts and tendencies, the international community constitutes a powerful and overriding reality[2]—a reality which includes the general recognition, by States and Governments, of the legally binding force of international law. Thus understood, the ultimate source of international law as here formulated, far from being arbitrary, represents the obtainable maximum of approximation as between law and reality. The attempt at such approximation in the choice of the fundamental source, namely, the general will of the international community, does not amount to a recognition of a mere fact—a mere naked might constituted by any predominant power, or balance or alliance of powers—as a starting point of legal

---

[1] See, for the formulation of the 'fundamental principle' in that form, Lauterpacht, *The Function of Law*, pp. 420–3.   [2] See above, p. 28.

92

SOURCES OF INTERNATIONAL LAW

obligation. For the actual emergence of the latter, in the international sphere, is in every case related to a particular source of law as expressed in consent, through treaty or custom, or by general principles of law. All these in turn give expression in different ways to the main substantive requirements of all law conceived both as the emanation of human will and as products of conformity with reason and justice.[1]

In the sphere of international law, in which the element of will necessarily tends to assume the complexion of consent of independent States rather than of a command imposed upon them, the basic legal assumption as here expressed seems particularly appropriate. The 'will of the international community' is not a dictate of a ruler. It is an expression of the paramount and—in a wider sense—coercive reality, in its various manifestations, of the international community.[2] It is no impairment of that reality to acknowledge its operation and manifestation not only through 'general principles of law' but also through the consent, express or implied, of its members. The fact that a rule is sanctioned by or brought into operation through consent, is not inconsistent with its essential quality as evidencing the general will of the international community of which the

---

[1] As already stated (see above, pp. 32, 52), it is probably deceptive to think of law in the exclusive terms of either will (whether expressed through command or consent) or the inherent qualities of the law which may be summed up as reason (or justice, or the reason of the thing, or the law of nature). Similarly, there may be an excess of simplification in defining positive law exclusively as a command of a superior authority, or as an act of human will and of deliberate creation (whether by command or agreement), or as the body of rules which, independently of having been 'laid down', are actually in operation and upon which the quality of law is conferred (or recognized) by legal science and legal thinking in accordance with their notions as to the proper content of the law —a view which seems, in effect, to substitute the will of writers for the will of the other human law-creating agencies. For a scholarly survey of the various approaches to the notion of positive law in the international sphere see Ago in *A.J.* 51 (1957), 691–733, who is inclined to regard as positive all 'law in force' in the legal system in any existing human society. It is not certain that that solution answers the question as to what rules can claim to be the 'law in force' in any society.

[2] From this point of view also, the difference between law conceived in terms of reason and law conceived as will, whether imposed or expressing agreement, is less fundamental than is often assumed. This is so in particular in the international sphere. That fact explains—and justifies—the reluctance of writers to jettison altogether the element of will from their definition of law. See, e.g., Giuliano, 'Considerazioni sulla costruzione dell'ordinamento internazionale', in *Comunicazioni e Studi*, 2 (1946), 201, and the other authorities referred to by Ago in *A.J.* 51 (1957), 723–7. It is desirable not to replace the excesses of positivism, for which the will of the State is the exclusive constituent element of law, by the exaggerations of an amorphous conception of law divorced from the articulate reality of the historical processes of its creation; these processes include authoritative formulation of the law through acts of will by way of command or express agreement. Accordingly, there is merit—and no mere cumulation of tests—in Professor Rousseau's formulation of positive international law both as that which is actually followed by Governments and tribunals and that which is effectively laid down by competent agencies (Rousseau, pp. 38, 42).

INTERNATIONAL LAW—THE GENERAL PART

consenting States are members. Thus it must be considered to be the general will of the international community that its members should regulate their legal relations through treaties constituting a source of binding legal obligations.[1] The same applies to consent given by way of custom. Thus viewed, the consideration of the 'ultimate principle' of international law, far from constituting a mere doctrinal exercise, affords assistance in comprehending the true foundations of international law.

While the 'ultimate principle' as here formulated is reduced to the aggregate element of the will of the international community, it would be equally possible—though less satisfactory—to formulate it by reference to its three specific manifestations, namely, treaty, custom and general principles of law, and to regard the binding force of each of them as one of the three ultimate assumptions of international law. There is no compelling reason why the legal system should be derived only from one basic principle. On the other hand, there is an advantage in identifying the 'ultimate assumption' with what, far from being a mere assumption, is in fact a substantial reality, namely, the reality of the international community asserting itself against the disruptive factors menacing the development of the civilized life of nations and of the individual. Thus viewed, the ultimate assumption, conceived as the first source of international law, is far from being a doctrinal exercise.

28. *The problem of the completeness of the sources of international law*

Like any other system of law, so also the international legal system must be regarded as complete in the sense that an international judicial or arbitral tribunal, when endowed with requisite jurisdiction, is bound and able to decide every dispute submitted to it by allowing or dismissing the claim advanced by the plaintiff State. It is not at liberty to pronounce a so-called *non liquet*, namely, to decline to give judgment on the ground of insufficiency or obscurity of the law. Nor can it proceed in that way on the ground that the case before it is novel and raises an issue of an unprecedented character. In the absence of a clear rule of law directly applicable to the case before it an international tribunal must decide the dispute—or,

---

[1] It is important that consent in the international sphere justifies and calls for the attribution to it of a place as an integral part of the 'ultimate principle'. From that point of view treaties may properly be regarded as a general category of sources of law, a 'formal' source of law—and not merely as a material source of obligations. But see Fitzmaurice in *Symbolae Verzijl* (1958), pp. 157–60. There may be a disadvantage in reducing the authority of the most important operative source of law in the relations of States.

SOURCES OF INTERNATIONAL LAW

in the case of advisory jurisdiction, give its opinion—by reference to or by way of analogy with a wider legal principle derived, in the first instance, from existing international law. One of these principles —which is a principle of general application—is that, in the absence of a clear rule imposing upon a State a duty of action or abstention, a State is entitled, subject to the obligation to act in good faith, to proceed according to discretion and that a claim which is not based on any such rule must be dismissed. In such cases there is no question of a gap in the law; the situation is governed by the residuary rule that the State possesses freedom of action.[1] Thus, for instance, the fact that there is no rule of public international law which imposes upon a State the duty to regulate certain questions of private international law according to either the nationality or the domicile of the parties or the persons involved, does not signify that there is a gap in the law on the subject; it merely means that the State is entitled to freedom of action in the matter.

Secondly, the fact that international law comprises general principles of law recognized by civilized States[2] confirms, for most —if not all—practical purposes the notion of the completeness of international law. The activity of international judicial and arbitral tribunals has amply revealed the potentialities of that source of law.[3] Thirdly, with regard to that part of international law which is laid down in treaties, there has been applied on a large scale the principle that, frequently, the *lacuna* is only apparent and provisional in the sense that it may legitimately be filled, consistently with the intentions of the parties, by reference to the principle that treaties must be interpreted so as to be effective in accordance with the maxim *ut res magis valeat quam pereat.* Thus the Permanent Court of International Justice held that a provision of a treaty which conferred upon it jurisdiction to decide whether there had taken place a violation of a treaty implied its jurisdiction to decide as to the compensation due for the breach of the treaty; otherwise, the jurisdiction conferred upon it 'instead of settling a dispute once and for all would leave open the possibility of further disputes'.[4] By

---

[1] It is of interest to note that the members of the Committee of Jurists who drafted the Statute of the Court, in the course of the discussion on that part of Article 38 which refers to 'general principles of law', considered that the principle that 'that which is not forbidden is allowed ... is one of the general principles of law which the Court shall have to apply' (statement by Ricci-Busatti, *Minutes of the Committee*, II, 314. Lord Phillimore spoke to the same effect: *ibid.* at pp. 315, 316).

[2] See above, p. 68.   [3] See above, pp. 69–70.

[4] Case of *Certain German Interests in Polish Upper Silesia* (Series A, no. 9 (1927), p. 23). See also, to the same effect, the *Corfu Channel* case (*I.C.J. Reports* 1949, p. 26).

95

INTERNATIONAL LAW—THE GENERAL PART

reference to the same principle the Court held that the competence of the International Labour Organisation, although limited to the regulation of conditions of work in 'industry', did in fact and in law include agriculture.[1] It also held that, although no express power to that effect had been conferred upon the United Nations in its Charter, the United Nations, notwithstanding an apparent gap in its Charter, had the power to establish an Administrative Tribunal to decide disputes between the United Nations and members of its staff; for 'under international law, the Organisation must be deemed to have those powers which, though not expressly provided in the Charter, are conferred upon it by necessary implication as being essential to the performance of its duties'.[2]

The principle of the completeness of the international l gal order is a general principle of law. It is one of the most fundamental legal principles.[3] As such, as well as by virtue of the practice of international tribunals, it must be regarded as part of positive international law as administered by international tribunals.[4] The principle in question has been lucidly expressed in a well-known arbitral award:

International law, as well as domestic law, may not contain, and generally does not contain, express rules decisive of particular cases; but the function of jurisprudence is to resolve the conflict of opposing rights and interests by applying, in default of any specific provision of law, the corollaries of general principles, and so to find—exactly as in the mathematical sciences—the solution of the problem. This is the method of jurisprudence; it is the method by which the law has been gradually evolved in every country, resulting in the definition and settlement of legal relations as well between States as between private individuals.[5]

[1] Advisory Opinion concerning the *Competence of the International Labour Organisation (Regulation of Conditions of Work of Persons Employed in Agriculture)* (*P.C.I.J.* Series B, no. 2 (1922), p. 25). See also the Advisory Opinion concerning the *Competence of the International Labour Organisation to Regulate, Incidentally, the Personal Work of the Employer* (*ibid.* no. 13 (1926), p. 18), and the Advisory Opinion concerning the *Interpretation of the Convention on the Employment of Women During the Night* (Series A/B, no. 50 (1932), p. 374).

[2] *I.C.J. Reports* 1954, p. 57.

[3] Thus Sir Frederick Pollock says in a note in Maine's *Ancient Law* (1930 ed. p. 48): 'The [judges] are bound to find a decision for every case, however novel it may be . . . Perhaps this is the first and greatest rule of our customary law; that, failing a specific rule already ascertained and fitting the case in hand, the King's judges must find and apply the most reasonable rule they can, so that it be not inconsistent with any established principle.'

[4] For a full discussion of the subject and a survey of judicial and arbitral practice see Lauterpacht, *The Function of Law*, pp. 60–135, and in *Symbolae Verzijl* (1958), pp. 196–210. See, however, for a different assessment, Stone, *Legal Controls of International Conflict* (1954), pp. 154–64.

[5] *Eastern Extension, Australasia and China Telegraph Co. Ltd.*, decided in 1923 by the British–American Claims Arbitral Tribunal (*Annual Digest*, 2 (1923–4), Case no. 225).

SOURCES OF INTERNATIONAL LAW

The completeness of international law from the point of view of the right of States to freedom of action—unless circumscribed by a rule of international law in accordance with one or more of its sources as described above[1]—or of the capacity and duty of international tribunals to decide all disputes submitted to them for decision on the basis of law does not signify that the particular source of international law is in every respect satisfactory.[2] In fact, the uncertainty and insufficiency due to lack of precedent, divergencies of practice arising out of actual or assumed conflicts of interests or mere peculiarities of national practice, absence of effective international legislation amending and supplementing the existing law, and other reasons, may rightly be considered as one of the causes of the weakness of international law as a system of law.[3] Thus while in various branches of international law—such as the law of treaties, or jurisdictional, diplomatic and other immunities—there is general agreement as to the broad principle applicable, there is no such consensus of opinion as to the details of its application.[4] The resulting situation is necessarily productive of uncertainty and controversy in the intercourse of Governments. Moreover, while unable to prevent international judicial tribunals from deciding disputes submitted to them, it adds to the difficulties and the responsibilities of their normal functioning by enlarging the element of judicial discretion. The corresponding impairment of the element

---

[1] See above, p. 68.

[2] Neither, contrary to the view reiterated by some writers, can it properly be interpreted as intended to signify that the international judicial process is the best instrument for resolving all conflicts between States—for, clearly, if a State admits in advance that its attitude is at variance with law and that it claims a change in the law, there is no point in having recourse to a judicial tribunal. What the principle of completeness of the international legal order does signify in this connection is that there is no substance in the distinction, for the purpose of treaties of obligatory judicial settlement, between legal and political disputes in the sense that owing to the material insufficiency of international law cases may occur in which there is no law by reference to which the tribunal can decide a dispute. But see Charles De Visscher, *Théorie et réalités en droit international public* (1953), p. 397 n. 2. One of the reasons for the recurrent criticism of the notion of the completeness of international law is the view that having regard to the unsatisfactory state of some branches of international law and the absence of an international legislature amending and supplementing the law, international tribunals may be compelled to render decisions which, although strictly in accordance with the existing law, are open to objection by reference to the needs of a developing international community and, generally, by reference to international peace and justice. While that view is entitled to respect, it is impossible to admit that the remedy lies, in such cases, in a refusal of a tribunal to render a decision. An international tribunal possesses no such right. Nor does a rational solution consist in the denial, on that account, of the principle of obligatory settlement of disputes on the basis of law. For some alternative solutions see Lauterpacht in *Symbolae Verzijl* (1958), pp. 217–21 and *The Function of Law*, pp. 310–18.

[3] See above, p. 31.

[4] See, for some examples, Lauterpacht, 'Codification and Development of International Law', in *A.J.* 49 (1955), 17–23.

of certainty in the administration of international justice has been considered by some as constituting one of the factors influencing adversely the attitude of Governments with regard to submission in advance to obligations of compulsory judicial settlement. It is for that reason that the Commission of Jurists who in 1920 drafted the Statute of the Permanent Court of International Justice proposed that the Council of the League of Nations should take the initiative in the matter of codification of international law. In view of the close connection of this subject with the question of the sources of international law it is convenient to give in the present chapter an account of the problem and of the progress of codification in international law.

4. CODIFICATION OF INTERNATIONAL LAW

29. *The meaning of codification*

As within the State, so also in the international sphere, codification presents a double aspect. In the first instance, it may signify the task of clothing in the garb of a code a body of non-controversial rules of acknowledged validity. This is what is occasionally described as consolidating codification.[1] However, more frequently, the process of codification aims both at a measure of reform or development of the law and at removing its inconsistencies, obscurities and uncertainties. Thus the Conference for the codification of the law of the sea, which took place under the auspices of the United Nations in 1958, had a double aspect in the sense here described. While two of the Conventions adopted by it—the Convention on the Territorial Sea and the Contiguous Zone and the Convention on the High Seas—in the main give expression to existing law, the Convention on Fishing and Conservation of the Living Resources of the High Seas introduced an essentially new system of rights and obligations. The fourth Convention—that on the Continental Shelf—exhibited equally a distinct complexion of novelty although, as is suggested elsewhere in this treatise, the practice in the matter of the Continental Shelf was to some extent declaratory of existing rights of States and although in the decade preceding the Convention its conformity with the law was generally acknowledged.[2]

The second major distinction is that between total codification and codification concerning particular branches of the law or even individual topics. Thus a treaty concerned with the treatment of

[1] See Brierly in *B.Y.* 12 (1931), 1–6.
[2] See above, p. 64.

SOURCES OF INTERNATIONAL LAW

sick and wounded members of the armed forces constitutes a codification of that subject—which, without affecting the character of the treaty as a piece of codification, may be, as in fact it has been, sub-divided into treatment of sick and wounded in armies in the field and at sea. Indeed, any convention regulating in a general way a particular subject, however limited, may be described as a codification thereof. It is not essential that such codification should aim at universality. It has often been expressly confined to a number of States limited by geographical propinquity. Thus in 1938 the Scandinavian States agreed among themselves on uniform rules of neutrality to be issued separately by each of them.[1] By treaty they adopted common rules on some questions of private international law.[2] The efforts at codification in Latin America are surveyed below.[3]

30. *Non-governmental projects and drafts of codification*

The conviction that the authority of international law as a body of clear and ascertainable rules, the necessities of orderly international intercourse, and the requirements of international judicial settlement require the progressive codification of international law has prompted impartial efforts by private writers and organizations in that field from the beginning of the nineteenth century. In England Jeremy Bentham put forward a detailed scheme with that object in view.[4] In 1795 the Abbé Grégoire, a member of the French Convention, proposed at its request a Declaration, of twenty-one articles, of the Rights of Nations as a pendant to the Declaration of the Rights of Mankind; in the end the project was abandoned.[5] The second half of the nineteenth, and the beginning of the twentieth century, witnessed a series of private efforts in that field by individual scholars and learned societies, in particular the Institute of International Law.[6] The most notable effort at private codification undertaken in the twentieth century was that which, over a series of years prior to the Second World War, took place under the

---

[1] See Oppenheim, II, 712.   [2] See above, p. 40, n. 2.   [3] See below, p. 123.
[4] See Bentham's *Works*, ed. by Bowring, VIII, 537; Nys in *L.Q.R.* 1 (1885), 226–31. See also Schwarzenberger, *Jeremy Bentham and the Law* (1948), pp. 152–84 (a valuable assessment of Bentham's contribution to international law).
[5] The full text of these twenty-one articles is printed in Rivier, I, 40.
[6] An Austrian jurist, Alfons von Domin-Petruschévecz, published in 1861 a *Précis d'un code de droit international*. In 1863 Professor Francis Lieber, of Columbia College, New York, drafted the Laws of War in a body of rules which the United States published during the Civil War for the guidance of her army (see Oppenheim, II, § 68(4); and see Scott in *R.I. (Paris)*, 4 (1929), 393–408). In 1868 Bluntschli, the celebrated Swiss writer, published *Das moderne Völkerrecht der civilizierten Staaten als Rechtsbuch dargestellt*. This draft code has been translated into the French, Greek, Spanish, and Russian languages. In

INTERNATIONAL LAW—THE GENERAL PART

auspices of the Harvard Law School under the guidance of Professor (subsequently Judge) Manley Hudson.[1] It provided impressive evidence of the usefulness—according to some, of the urgency—of the efforts undertaken by non-governmental bodies to codify the entirety of parts of international law. Such efforts, when undertaken on a sufficiently large scale, may obviate some of the drawbacks, referred to below, of official codification accomplished through the conclusion of binding conventions.[2] Although it is of potentially great scientific value and although it may provide considerable assistance in connection with codification of treaties, private codification is not a substitute for it.[3]

1872 the great Italian politician and jurist Mancini proposed codification of the Law of Nations in his essay, *Vocazione del nostro secolo per la riforma e codificazione del diritto delle genti.* Likewise in 1872 appeared at New York David Dudley Field's *Draft Outlines of an International Code.* In 1873 the Institute of International Law was founded at Ghent in Belgium. That association of international lawyers meets periodically, and has produced a number of drafts concerning various aspects of international law, public and private. In 1874 the Emperor Alexander II of Russia took the initiative in assembling an international conference at Brussels for the purpose of discussing a draft code of the Law of Nations concerning land warfare. This conference agreed upon a body of sixty Articles under the name of the Declaration of Brussels. These Articles have never been ratified. In 1880 the Institute of International Law published its *Manuel des lois de la guerre sur terre.* In 1887 Leone Levi published his *International Law with Materials for a Code of International Law.* In 1890 the Italian jurist Fiore published his *Il diritto internazionale codificato e la sua sanzione giuridica,* of which a fifth edition appeared in 1915. An English translation of the fifth edition appeared in 1916. In 1906 E. Duplessix published his *La loi des nations.* In 1911 Jerome Internoscia published his *New Code of International Law* in English, French, and Italian. In the same year Pessoa published his *Projecto de codigo le direito internacional publico.* In 1913 the Institute of International Law published its *Manuel de la guerre maritime.* In general, the Institute of International Law confines itself to formulating, by way of Resolutions, general principles governing specific questions of international law. A collection of these Resolutions was published, in the French language, in 1957. Various resolutions and drafts have also been adopted from time to time by the International Law Association—a body founded in 1873 and widely open to lawyers of various countries, including those interested particularly in maritime and commercial law. See also Alvarez, *Exposé de motifs et Déclaration des grands principes du Droit international moderne* (1936), and for comment thereon Redslob, *Les principes du droit des gens moderne* (1937), *passim,* and Le Fur in *Hague Recueil,* 54 (1935) (iv), 132, 133.

[1] The reports produced by the Harvard Research cover most topics of international law. They are scholarly and detailed studies, in the form of codes, the articles of which are accompanied by comment and rich documentation. In addition to their value as a contribution to the task of codification, they constitute an important contribution to the literature of international law. [2] See below, p. 106.

[3] See below, p. 107. There may be an excess of simplification in the view that, unlike codification by treaty, private codification is free of national bias and thus able to achieve a higher degree of objectivity. Experience does not confirm the view that private bodies, whether national or international, are impervious to considerations of national interest. Moreover, there is no reason for divorcing the work of codification from considerations of national interest. Its object is to reconcile conflicts of interests by reference to wider considerations of justice and the needs of the international community. For an emphasis on private codification see Sir Cecil Hurst in *Grotius Society,* 32 (1946), 135–53; the report of a Committee of the International Law Association in 1946, *Reports,* 42 (1947), 64–121; and Stone in *Columbia Law Review,* 57 (1957), 16–51.

SOURCES OF INTERNATIONAL LAW

31. *The work of the First Hague Peace Conference*

At the end of the nineteenth century, in 1899, the so-called Peace Conference at The Hague, convened on the initiative of Emperor Nicholas II of Russia, revealed the potentialities of partial codification of the Law of Nations.[1] In addition to three declarations of limited scope, and the convention concerning the adaptation of the Geneva Convention to naval warfare, this Conference succeeded in producing two important conventions of partial codification— namely, first, the 'Convention for the Pacific Settlement of International Disputes' and, secondly, the 'Convention with respect to the Laws and Customs of War on Land'. The first-named Convention, in particular that part of it which is concerned with arbitral procedure, is of practical importance, as is demonstrated by the various tribunals acting as the Permanent Court of Arbitration which have given awards in a number of cases.[2] Although the second-named Convention contains many gaps, even in the amended form given to it by the Second Hague Peace Conference of 1907, it represents a model the existence of which showed persuasively the potentialities of practical codification of the Law of Nations. The First Hague Peace Conference thus marked an epoch in the history of codification of international law.[3]

32. *The work of the Second Hague Peace Conference*

The Second Hague Peace Conference of 1907[4] produced no less than thirteen conventions,[5] some of which are codifications of parts of maritime law. Three of the thirteen conventions, namely, that for the pacific settlement of international disputes, that concerning the laws and customs of war on land, and that concerning the adaptation of the principles of the Geneva Convention to maritime war, took the place of three corresponding conventions of the First Hague Peace Conference. But the other ten conventions were entirely new.

---

[1] As to the conventions codifying private international law see above, p. 40.

[2] See Oppenheim, II, § 25 *aa*.

[3] For a general account of the work of the Hague Conferences see Wehberg in *Hague Recueil*, 37 (1931) (iii), 533–664.

[4] Shortly after the Hague Peace Conference of 1899, the United States of America took action with regard to sea warfare similar to that taken by her in 1863 with regard to land warfare (see above, p. 99 n. 6). She published on 27 June 1900 a body of rules for the use of her Navy under the title *The Laws and Usages of War at Sea*—the so-called *United States Naval War Code*—which was drafted by Captain Charles H. Stockton of the United States Navy. Although withdrawn in 1904, it provided the starting-point of a movement for the codification of maritime international law.

[5] For an enumeration of these Conventions see Oppenheim, II, § 68.

101

INTERNATIONAL LAW—THE GENERAL PART

Apart from the conventions on the limitation of the employment of force for the recovery of contract debts and on the opening of hostilities,[1] they were devoted to the regulation of rules of warfare and neutrality in war on land and at sea.[2]

33. *Codification in the period after the First World War*

In the domain of the law of war the period after the First World War produced in 1929 general conventions on the treatment of prisoners of war[3] and sick and wounded[4] and, in 1925, on the use of poisonous and asphyxiating gases.[5] In the field of the law of peace that period produced important pieces of partial codification through general instruments like the Covenant of the League of Nations, the Statute of the Permanent Court of International Justice,[6] the General Act for the Pacific Settlement of International Disputes of 1928,[7] the General Treaty for the Renunciation of War,[8] conventions concerning air navigation[9] and inland[10] and maritime navigation,[11] and a great number of conventions of a scientific, economic, and humanitarian[12] character, including the imposing series of conventions concluded under the aegis of the International Labour Organisation.[13] These conventions were concerned with specific matters and could only in a distant sense be described as constituting codification. It was left to the League of Nations to approach in a systematic manner the problem of codification properly so called.

34. *Codification under the auspices of the League of Nations*

The Committee of Jurists, which in 1920 drafted the Statute of the Permanent Court of International Justice, adopted a resolution urging the calling of an international conference charged with reconciling divergent views on particular topics of international law and the consideration of those which were not adequately regulated.[14] In 1924 the Council of the League of Nations appointed a committee of sixteen jurists to report on the codification of international law. The Committee was not instructed to prepare codes, but to report to the Council on the questions which it regarded as ripe for codification, and also as to how their codification could best be

[1] See Oppenheim, II, § 94.
[2] *Ibid.* § 68.
[3] *Ibid.* §§ 126–32.
[4] *Ibid.* §§ 119–24 a.
[5] *Ibid.* § 113.
[6] *Ibid.* § 25 ae.
[7] *Ibid.* § 25 aj.
[8] *Ibid.* § 52 i.
[9] See Oppenheim, I, § 197 c.
[10] See *ibid.* § 178 b.
[11] See *ibid.* § 265.
[12] See generally, on the part played by so-called law-making conventions, Hudson, *Legislation*, I (1931), xvii and xviii, and v (1936), viii–x; and the same in *A.J.* 22 (1928), 330–49, and *ibid.* Suppl. pp. 90–108.
[13] See Oppenheim, I, § 340 *fg.*
[14] *Procès-Verbaux* of the Meetings of the Committee, p. 747.

102

SOURCES OF INTERNATIONAL LAW

achieved. The Committee then considered a number of reports prepared by its sub-committees on various topics; it examined the replies of the Governments on these reports; and in April 1927 it reported to the Council that the following seven topics were ripe for codification: (i) Nationality; (ii) Territorial Waters; (iii) Responsibility of States for Damage Done in their Territory to the Person or Property of Foreigners; (iv) Diplomatic Privileges and Immunities; (v) Procedure of International Conferences and Procedure for the Conclusion and Drafting of Treaties; (vi) Piracy; and (vii) Exploitation of the Products of the Sea.[1]

In 1927 the Assembly took into consideration the Committee's Report to the Council and the Council's observations thereon and decided that a conference should be held at The Hague for the purpose of codifying the subjects mentioned under (i), (ii), and (iii). The Council then instructed a preparatory committee to consider and recommend to the Council what action it should take in execution of the Assembly's Resolution. The Committee examined the replies made by the Governments to the various questions covering the principal topics of the three proposed subjects of codification and drew up bases of discussion for the use of the Conference. (The replies of the Governments, the bases of discussion and the Committee's final report are printed in three separate volumes which are an authoritative and invaluable source of information.[2])

[1] For the Report of the Committee see Doc. C.196.M.70.1927.V. As to topics (v) and (vii), the Committee recommended a procedure more technical than an international conference. In June 1928 the Committee reported two more topics as being ripe for codification, namely, the Legal Position and Functions of Consuls and the Competence of Courts in regard to Foreign States.

The Committee, after examining reports upon (i) Nationality of Commercial Corporations and their Diplomatic Protection, and (ii) the Recognition of the Legal Personality of Foreign Commercial Corporations, reported to the Council that these topics were ripe for regulation by international agreement, and might usefully be left to a Conference upon Private International Law.

The Committee examined and reported as not being ripe for international regulation the following topics: (i) Criminal Competence of States in respect of Offences Committed Outside their Territory; (ii) Extradition; (iii) Interpretation of the Most-Favoured-Nation Clause. (The Committee also studied, and considered to be ripe for international regulation, the 'Legal Status of Government Ships Employed in Commerce'; but, in view of the conferences which had already been held under the direction of the International Maritime Committee and the Convention prepared by that body, recommended the Council to take no further action at that time.)

[2] They are: vol. I, Nationality: C.73.M.38.1929.V.; vol. II, Territorial Waters: C.74.M.39.1929.V.; vol. III, Responsibility of States, etc.: C.75.M.69.1929.V. For an account of the preparatory work of the Conference up to 1930 see Hudson in *A.J.* 20 (1926), 656–69; Wickersham in *A.S. Proceedings*, 1926, pp. 121–35; Reeves in *A.J.* 21 (1927), 659–67, and 24 (1930), pp. 52–7; McNair in *Grotius Society*, 13 (1928), 129–40.

INTERNATIONAL LAW—THE GENERAL PART

35. *The Hague Codification Conference of* 1930

The first Conference on the Progressive Codification of International Law was held at The Hague from 13 March to 12 April 1930. It resolved itself into three Committees, one for each of the three topics for the consideration of which the Conference had been convened. As the result of the work of the First Committee the Conference adopted: (*a*) a Convention concerning Certain Questions relating to the Conflict of Nationality Laws; (*b*) a Protocol relating to Military Obligations in Certain Cases of Double Nationality; (*c*) a Protocol relating to a Certain Case of Statelessness; and (*d*) a Special Protocol concerning Statelessness. These Conventions, although falling short of a comprehensive codification of international aspects of nationality, covered important questions and have subsequently been ratified by a number of States, including Great Britain.[1] With regard to Territorial Waters, the Conference was unable to adopt a convention as no agreement could be reached on the question of the extent of territorial waters and the problem of a 'contiguous zone' adjacent thereto. There was, however, some measure of agreement on such questions as the legal status of territorial waters, including the right of innocent passage, and the baseline for measuring the territorial waters. The views of the Conference on these matters were embodied in a Report submitted by the Second Committee of the Conference.[2] With regard to State responsibility, the Conference disclosed complete disagreement on the question, *inter alia*, of responsibility for the treatment of aliens in cases in which there is no discrimination against the aliens as compared with the nationals of the State.[3]

---

[1] The Convention and the three Protocols came into force in 1937, following upon the receipt of the tenth ratification.   [2] See *A.J.* 24 (1930), Suppl. p. 234.

[3] On the various aspects of the Hague Codification Conference of 1930 see Alvarez, *Les résultats de la Ière Conférence de codification de droit international* (1931); Reeves in *A.J.* 24 (1930), 52–7, 486–99; Hudson, *ibid.* pp. 447–66; Flournoy, *ibid.* pp. 467–85; Hackworth, *ibid.* pp. 500–16; Borchard, *ibid.* pp. 517–40; Hunter Miller, *ibid.* pp. 674–93; Guerrero in *R.I.* (*Paris*), 5 (1930), 478–91; Niemeyer in *Z.I.* 42 (1930), 1–26; Rolin in *R.I.* (*Paris*), 3rd ser. 11 (1930), 581–99; Hunter Miller in *A.S. Proc.* 1930, pp. 213–21; Borchard, *ibid.* pp. 221–9; Hudson, *ibid.* pp. 229–34; Rauchberg in *Z.ö.R.* 10 (1931), 481–522. For the texts of the Final Act, the Convention on Nationality, the three Protocols adopted by the Conference and the Reports of the Committee on Nationality and Territorial Waters see *A.J.* 24 (1930), Suppl. pp. 169–258. See also Hudson, *Legislation*, v, 359–94; League Doc. A. 19.1931.V.; C.351.M.145.1930.V. (the Final Act).

The most important aspect of partial codification is regional codification, for instance, on the American continent. As long ago as the Panama Congress of 1826 the movement for the codification of international law among the States of the New World became prominent. In 1906 the Pan-American Conference at Rio de Janeiro (at which the United States of America was represented) decided to establish a commission of jurists

104

SOURCES OF INTERNATIONAL LAW

36. *The limits and prospects of the codification of international law*
Those participating in the Hague Conference of 1930 apparently assumed that it was to be the first of a series of conferences for pursuing the work of codificaton under the auspices of the League. For the Conference adopted detailed recommendations concerning the methods of preparation and summoning of future conferences.[1] In 1930, the Eleventh Assembly reaffirmed the great interest of the

for the purpose of preparing codes both of public and of private international law for submission to a future conference. After the interruption caused by the First World War the task was actively resumed, with the close co-operation of the new American Institute of International Law founded in 1912; and in 1925 that Institute transmitted to the Pan-American Union the texts of thirty projects of conventions for a code of public international law (printed in *A.J.* Special Suppl. October 1926). These projects were considered at a meeting of an International Commission of American Jurists in Rio de Janeiro in April and May 1927, and twelve of them were adopted and recommended for consideration by a Sixth Pan-American Conference, which was held in January and February 1928. For the twelve projects referred to see *A.J.* 22 (1928), Special Suppl. January 1928. The Conference adopted, on 20 February 1928, the following seven codifying conventions: (1) On the Status of Aliens; (2) On Treaties; (3) On Diplomatic Officers; (4) On Consular Agents; (5) On Maritime Neutrality; (6) On Asylum; (7) On Duties and Rights of States in the Event of Civil Strife. For the texts of these conventions see *A.J.* 22 (1928), Suppl. pp. 124 *et seq.*; Hudson, *Legislation*, IV, 2374–2419. The Seventh Pan-American Conference adopted on 26 December 1933 the following conventions: (1) On the Nationality of Women; (2) On Nationality; (3) On Extradition; (4) On Political Asylum; (5) On Rights and Duties of States. For the texts of these conventions see *A.J.* 28 (1934), Suppl. pp. 61 *et seq.* The Conference also passed a resolution on methods of codification to be pursued in the future (*ibid.* p. 55). The resolution proposed, *inter alia* (*a*) the establishment of a permanent commission whose members were to serve both as experts and as official representatives of their Governments with full powers to sign conventions, and (*b*) the elimination of codification from the agenda of future Pan-American conferences. For comment on the resolution see Reeves in *A.J.* 28 (1934), 319–21. See also Borchard in *A.J.* 31 (1937), 471–3, and 33 (1939), 268–82, on the work of the Committee of Experts created by the resolution of 1933. For the various conventions codifying, to some extent, the previous conventions as to pacific settlement and adopted by that Conference see *International Conciliation* (Pamphlet No. 238), March 1937. See Alvarez, *La Codification du droit international* (1912, a work which was considered in some detail by the Codification Commission of American Jurists in that year), *La codificacion del derecho internacional en América* (1923), *Le nouveau droit international et sa codification en Amérique* (1924), and in *R.G.* (1913), pp. 24–52 and 725–47; Rauchhaupt, *Völkerrechtliche Eigenthümlichkeiten Amerikas* (1924); Scott in *A.S. Proc.* 1925, pp. 14–48, in *A.J.* 19 (1925), 333–7, 20 (1926), Suppl. no. 2, pp. 284–95, and 21 (1927), 417–50; *Revista de Derecho Internacional*, March 1925, special number; Brierly in *B.T.* 7 (1926), 14–23. On American efforts to codify international law see Léger, *La codification du droit des gens et les conférences des juristes américains* (1929); Urrutia in *Hague Recueil*, 22 (1928) (ii), 85–230. The Conference of American States at Lima adopted, on 21 December 1938, a Resolution concerning the methods for the gradual and progressive codification of international law through a number of agencies: see *A.J.* 34 (1940), Suppl. p. 194, and *The International Conferences of American States. First Supplement*, 1933–1940 (1940), p. 246. The Conference of 1954 adopted conventions on Diplomatic Asylum and Territorial Asylum. See also literature cited below, p. 122, on 'American International Law'. See also the successive volumes of the *Inter-American Juridical Year Book* published by the Pan-American Union.

[1] See the Final Act of the Conference: Doc. C.351.M.145.1930.V., p. 138; *A.J.* 24 (1930), Suppl. p. 257.

105

League in the work of codification and invited the observations of member-States concerning the recommendations of the Conference.[1] These observations were on the whole not unfavourable[2] to continuing the task of codification. The Twelfth Assembly, while deciding in principle to continue that work, laid down elaborate details governing the future procedure in the matter.[3] Their main effect was to transfer the formal initiative from the League and its organs to the members of the League and thus to lessen the chances of codification in the near future.

In any case the experience and results of the Hague Conference of 1930 made it possible to assess the desirability and the prospects of codification, In the first instance, that Conference revealed clearly the difference between codification conceived as a systematization and unification of agreed principles and codification regarded as agreement on hitherto divergent views and practices. Its progress and results showed that different methods may be required for the achievement of these two different purposes and that, in particular, the securing of agreement on existing differences is primarily a matter of policy and cannot well be settled by conferences of legal experts. Secondly, there was revealed the danger that, given the cautious attitude of Governments, attempts at codification may in many cases reveal and emphasize differences in cases where agreement was hitherto supposed to exist. Thirdly, it appeared that, in so far as codification implies uniform regulation, its scope must necessarily be limited for the reason that in many cases the diversity of interests and conditions amongst States renders uniformity difficult or undesirable. Fourthly, the Conference showed that even with regard to generally non-controversial matters, the work of codification requires lengthy preparation and discussion which cannot always usefully take place in the hurried atmosphere of an international conference. The programme of the Hague Conference in 1930 was probably too ambitious inasmuch as it attempted within the space of one month to codify three important branches of international law.

On the other hand, the results of the Conference showed that it would be a mistake to regard these obstacles as a sufficient reason for abandoning the task of introducing, through general conventions, uniformity and certainty in those branches of international law which are sufficiently developed for that purpose. The danger of failure, or

---

[1] *L.N.O.J.* Special Suppl. no. 83, p. 9.

[2] See Docs A. 12. 1931 . V., A. 12(*a*) . 1931 . V., and A. 12(*b*) . 1931 . V.

[3] *L.N.O.J.* Special Suppl. no. 92, p. 9. For comment see Hudson in *A.J.* 26 (1932), 137–43. And see Brierly in *B.Y.* 12 (1931), 1–12.

SOURCES OF INTERNATIONAL LAW

even of retrogression, in consequence of the operation of the unanimity rule, may be circumvented by the adoption of conventions by the majority of the States represented at the Conference. The scope of conventions thus adopted is likely to become enlarged as the result of subsequent accessions. The very fact of their continued validity among large groups of States cannot fail to exercise considerable influence. While therefore the mere re-statement by authoritative official or private bodies—a course occasionally urged on account of the dangers and drawbacks of formal codification—would be of considerable usefulness, formal codification incorporating its results as part of positive international law must be regarded as a proper and legitimate object of endeavour on the part of the organized international community. It is probably in this sense that the Charter of the United Nations lays down, in Article 13, that the General Assembly shall initiate studies and make recommendations for the purpose, *inter alia*, 'of encouraging the progressive development of international law and its codification'.[1] The Second General Assembly decided, in 1947, to set up an International Law Commission charged with the task of codifying and developing international law.[2] At the same time the General Assembly adopted a statute of the Commission, defining its functions and regulating the periodic election of its members by the General Assembly. The Statute provides that the Commission shall consist of fifteen members who shall be persons of recognized competence in international law; it also lays down that there shall be assured in the Commission as a whole the 'representation of the main forms of civilisation and of the principal legal systems'. The combination of these two tests must necessarily prove a source of difficulty. The Commission, which was first elected in 1948 for three years, meets yearly for periods of eight to ten weeks. It possesses no permanent organs of its own—apart from having at its disposal the services of the Secretariat of

---

[1] See Jessup in *A.J.* 39 (1945), 755–7. For the recommendations of the Inter-American Juridical Committee of October 1944 on the reorganization of agencies engaged in the codification of international law see *A.J.* 39 (1945), Suppl. pp. 231–45.

[2] The decision was adopted in pursuance of the recommendations of a committee composed of representatives of Governments, which sat in June 1947. See Finch in *A.J.* 41 (1947), 611–16. See also the Resolutions of the International Law Association of 1947 based on the Report of a Committee of the Association under the chairmanship of Judge McNair, and emphasizing the importance of a restatement—not amounting to official codification in the form of conventions—of selected portions of international law (*Report* of the Session of the International Law Association held in Prague in 1947). For a useful survey, prepared by the Division of Development and Codification of International Law of the United Nations, of the development and codification of international law by international conferences see *A.J.* 41 (1947), Suppl. pp. 29–147.

107

INTERNATIONAL LAW—THE GENERAL PART

the United Nations through its Division for the Codification and Development of International Law.[1] In 1957 its membership was enlarged from fifteen to twenty-one. Owing to the political condition of the world during the period following the Second World War and the preoccupation of the United Nations and its Members with problems affecting international peace, the Commission has not been able to fulfil its task on the scale probably intended by the Charter and as required by the needs of international law. Its authority as a system of rules partaking of a sufficient degree of clarity and certainty; orderly intercourse between Governments; and considerations of the growth of judicial and arbitral settlement all combine to constitute codification of international law through conventions accepted by Governments a proper and urgent object of endeavour. The risks of codification thus conceived have been noted above. They are not believed to be decisive. While the process of codification may tend to emphasize and bring to light disagreements, it may also tend, in the long run, to bring about a compromise between and reconciliation of conflicting interests. Agreement thus reached and embodied in conventions, such as those adopted at the Geneva Conference of 1958 on the Law of the Sea, may—even if not accompanied by early ratification by a large number of States—provide a legal standard of regulation available for future acceptance in the light of the experience of its actual working. An account of the results of that Conference is given in the section which follows.

37. *The Codification Conference on the Law of the Sea* (1958)

The United Nations Conference on the Law of the Sea, which met at Geneva between 24 February and 27 April 1958, and which was attended by eighty-six States (in addition to observers from certain

---

[1] The work of the Commission is surveyed in the annual reports of the Commission submitted to the General Assembly. See also the following publications of the Secretariat of the United Nations: *Preparatory Study concerning a Draft Declaration on the Rights and Duties of States* (1948); *Survey of International Law in Relation to the Work of Codification of the International Law Commission* (1949) [reprinted at p. 445, below]; *Ways and Means of Making the Evidence of Customary International Law more readily available* (1949); *Historical Survey of the Question of International Criminal Jurisdiction* (1949); *The Charter and the Judgment of the Nuremberg Tribunal* (1949). See also the United Nations Legislative Series, published by the Division for the Development and Codification of International Law and including the following volumes: *Laws and Practices concerning the Conclusion of Treaties* (1952); *Laws and Regulations on the Régime of the High Seas* (2 vols. 1952); *Nationality Laws* (1954); *Laws Concerning the Nationality of Ships* (1956); *Laws and Regulations on the Régime of the Territorial Sea* (1957); *Laws and Regulations regarding Diplomatic and Consular Privileges and Immunities* (1958). On some aspects of the work of the Commission see Marx in *Archiv des Völkerrechts*, 1 (1948–9), 279 *et seq.*; Parry in *B.Y.* 26 (1949), 508–28; Cheng in *Current Legal Problems*, 5 (1952), 251–73; Hertz in *Friedenswarte*, 52 (1953), 19–47; Lauterpacht in *A.J.* 49 (1955), 16–43; Stone in *Columbia Law Review*, 57 (1957), 16–51.

SOURCES OF INTERNATIONAL LAW

Specialized Agencies[1] and inter-governmental organizations[2]) showed clearly the close connection between these two aspects of codification. Although the Conference failed to produce the necessary measure of agreement with regard to the most controversial topic which divided the participating States, namely, the question of the breadth of territorial waters, it produced results of value. It adopted four Conventions: on the territorial sea and the contiguous zone; on the high seas; on fishing and conservation of the living resources of the high seas; and on the Continental Shelf.[3]

The Conference adopted at the outset rules of procedure which laid down that its decisions on all matters of substance should be taken by a two-thirds majority of the representatives present and voting[3] and that decisions on matters of procedure should be taken by a majority. Thus, although considerable efforts at compromise were necessary to obtain a majority of two-thirds and although the principles of equality of voting power imparted some element of artificiality to the process of taking decisions, the immediate impact of the problem of unanimity was considerably reduced. For the 'decisions', for which a majority of two-thirds was required, included also those relating to the adoption of Conventions. Admittedly, these decisions also were in a distinct sense procedural in character. The adoption of a Convention by the Conference meant no more than that a text was established open for signature (which was, moreover, subject to ratification) or accession by all Members of the United Nations or by any other State invited by the General Assembly to become a Party to the Convention. However, considerable importance must be attached to the Conventions thus adopted by the Conference—usually by very substantial majorities approaching unanimity. They signify an impressive consensus of opinion which, without being formally binding, is of considerable authority; and they provide the concrete basis for the formal acceptance of the obligations of the Conventions by States so minded.

[1] These were: Food and Agriculture Organization; International Civil Aviation Organization; International Labour Organisation; International Telecommunication Union; United Nations Educational, Scientific and Cultural Organization; World Health Organization; World Meteorological Organization.

[2] These were: Conseil Général de Pêches pour la Méditerranée; Indo-Pacific Fisheries Council; Inter-American Tropical Tuna Commission; Inter-Governmental Committee for European Migration; International Council for the Exploration of the Sea; International Institute for the Codification of Private Law; League of Arab States; Organization of American States; Permanent Conference for the Exploration and Conservation of the Montana Resources of the South Pacific.

[3] See Ferron, *Le droit international de la mer*, I (1958).

38. Codification and development of international law

The distinction between codification and development of international law has been adopted both in the Charter of the United Nations and in the Statute of the International Law Commission. In the latter the expression 'progressive development of International Law' is used—for convenience—for 'the formulation of draft conventions on subjects which have not yet been regulated by International Law or in regard to which the law has not yet been sufficiently developed in the practice of States'. The expression 'codification of International Law' is used—similarly 'for convenience'—as meaning 'the more precise formulation and systematization of International Law in fields where there already has been extensive State practice, precedent and doctrine.'[1] It is probable that such usefulness as can be attributed to that distinction depends upon the realization that its theoretical value is limited and its practical application insignificant. The Statute of the Commission provides for different procedures for these two kinds of activity, but such differentiation of procedure has proved unworkable and has been altogether disregarded in practice. Subjects—such as the limit of territorial waters—on which there is 'extensive State practice', precedent and doctrine are often so controversial that nothing but a legislative innovation, by way of a formulation of new rules, can meet the exigencies of the case. Moreover, it may happen that with regard to the subjects, which are of some rarity, where there is full agreement in existing practice and doctrine, the requirements of international progress may call for a modification of the existing rule. Conversely, principles relating to topics of distinct novelty—such as the régime of the Continental Shelf—can be formulated by way of 'development' only by taking into account, and to that extent 'codifying', an established principle of international law. Thus the régime of the Continental Shelf, as formulated by the Commission and adopted by the Geneva Conference of 1958, is based on the full recognition and preservation, subject to reasonable modifications, of the principle of the freedom of the seas. In fact, the usefulness and justification of the entire process of codification, in its wider sense, must, as a rule, depend upon the combination, in relation to the same subject, of the processes of restatement of existing principles with the formulation of new law.

[1] Article 15 of the Statute of the Commission.

SOURCES OF INTERNATIONAL LAW

39. *International legislation and the revision of international law*

From the codification and development of international law as envisaged by the Charter and the Statute of the Commission there must be distinguished the deliberate revision and change of territorial settlements and analogous situations—such as those relating to sovereignty over the air or the exclusive competence of States to regulate tariffs or migration—with a view to adapting them to changed conditions and removing causes of international friction. There is at present no machinery of international legislation[1] for effecting changes of this nature against the dissent of a minority of interested States.[2] The establishment of such machinery would amount, to a substantial degree, to setting up an international legislature.[3] That development, while possible in itself and while fully consistent with the nature and objects of international law, is not one which Governments are at present prepared to accept. Its realization must be a matter of gradual transition from the existing principle of unanimity to a process of international legislation which, in turn, is conditioned by the adoption of far-reaching changes in the matter of equality of voting and representation. Article 19 of the Covenant of the League of Nations, which authorized the Assembly to recommend the consideration of treaties and international situations in accordance with changed conditions, could well have provided the starting point for a development of that nature.[4] Although no corresponding provision has been adopted in the Charter of the United Nations, the wide powers of discussion and recommendation which Article 11 of the Charter confers upon the General Assembly may properly be used for the same purpose.

SUPPLEMENTARY BIBLIOGRAPHY ON THE CODIFICATION OF INTERNATIONAL LAW

Fauchille, §§ 153 (5)–153 (22); Nys, 1, 174–93; Rivier, 1, §§ 124–7; Cavaglieri, pp. 74–81; Guggenheim, pp. 152–9; Holland, *Studies*, pp. 79–95; Scelle, 11, 526–43; Rousseau, pp. 862–85; Bustamante, pp. 81–113;

[1] On the metaphorical use of that term see above, and pp. 13–14 and 59 n.

[2] On the existing and possible substitutes for international legislation see Lauterpacht, *The Function of Law*, pp. 245–347.

[3] This is not always realized by those who speak of the necessity of providing effective institutions of peaceful change as a condition of progress in other fields of international organization.

[4] See Kunz in *A.J.* 33 (1939), 33–55; Bourquin, *Dynamism and the Machinery of International Institutions* (1940); Gihl, *International Legislation* (1937); Brierly, *The Outlook for International Law* (1944), pp. 95–108.

INTERNATIONAL LAW—THE GENERAL PART

Répertoire, II, 520–61; Bergbohm, *Staatsverträge und Gesetz als Quellen des Völkerrechts* (1877), pp. 44–77; Bulmerincq, *Praxis, Theorie und Codification des Völkerrechts* (1874), pp. 167–92; Alvarez, *La codification du droit international* (1912), *Méthodes de la codification du droit international public* (1947), and in *R.G.* 20 (1913), 24–52, 725–47; Politis, *Les nouvelles tendances du droit international* (1927), pp. 193–229; Maresh, *La codification du droit international* (1932); Cavalcanti in *R.G.* 21 (1914), 183–204; *A.S. Proc.* 4 (1910), 208–27; 5 (1911), 256–337; 10 (1916), 149–67; 17 (1923), 55–61; 20 (1926), 27–57, 108–21; Nys in *A.J.* 5 (1911), 871–900; Crocker, *ibid.* 18 (1924), 38–55; Scott, *ibid.* pp. 260–80; Baker in *B.Y.* 5 (1924), 38–65; De Visscher in *Hague Recueil* 6 (1925) (i), 329–452; Garner, *Developments*, pp. 708–74, and in *A.J.* 19 (1925), 327–33; Root, *ibid.* pp. 675–84; Hudson, *ibid.* 20 (1926), pp. 655–69; Niemeyer in *Z.I.* 37 (1926), 1–10; Alvarez in *Annuaire*, 35 (i) (1929), 1–113; Brierly in *B.Y.* 12 (1931), 1–12; Garner in *Hague Recueil*, 35 (1931) (i), 676–93; Cosentini in *R.G.* 42 (1935), 411–30; Hurst in *Grotius Society*, 32 (1946), 135–53; Jennings in *B.Y.* 24 (1947), 301–29; Liang in *A.J.* 42 (1948), 66–97, and in *Hague Recueil*, 73 (1948) (ii), 411–527; *International Law Association Report*, 47 (1950), 64–121; Lauterpacht in *A.J.* 49 (1955), 16–43; Stone in *Columbia Law Review*, 57 (1957), 16–51.

5. THE SCOPE OF THE VALIDITY OF THE SOURCES OF INTERNATIONAL LAW

40. *Particular international law*

Like all law, international law is, in principle, of a general and universal character; it is intended to operate in relation to all its subjects—in particular, its typical subjects, namely, independent and sovereign States. However, within the orbit of its general and universal operation it leaves room for adaptation, variation and detailed regulation—by custom or treaty—between individual States or groups of States; it leaves room for particular international law. In some respects the position is not dissimilar to that obtaining within the State where, under the shelter and within the framework of the general body of law, a vast mass of rights and obligations governing the relations of individuals is determined by contractual arrangements—that is to say, by particular rules of law as agreed by them and as endowed by general law with binding character.

In the international sphere, the part of particular law is of special importance for the reason that international legislation in its proper sense,[1] namely, as a source of rules of general application binding upon all and, for that reason, approaching universality, is still in a

---

[1] See above, p. 13.

112

SOURCES OF INTERNATIONAL LAW

rudimentary stage. From that point of view particular international law, so long as it does not assume the complexion of a denial of the wider and universal international law, fulfils a useful function. Thus in the field of custom it gives expression to regional characteristics and traditions, as, for instance, in the case of diplomatic asylum in the countries of Latin-America. The Charter of the United Nations recognizes (in Article 52), as did previously the Covenant of the League of Nations, the existence of regional arrangements for the maintenance of international peace.

There is the further twin factor of the smallness of the number of States composing the international community and the wide differences of geography, culture, economics and political systems between them. While, as suggested elsewhere,[1] this factor does not in itself provide an obstacle to the legal regulation of the relations between States, it adds to the justification and usefulness of adjustments through regional and particular international law. However, the latter presupposes the existence, and must be interpreted in the light, of principles of international law binding on all States.

The force of particular international law, which may be grounded either in custom or in treaty, may vary considerably. It may be binding upon two States; or it may embrace a number of signatories so vast as to become general to the point of universality.[2] Yet it is in universal international law that lie the roots and the binding force of particular international law and it is only by reference to the notion of an international law of universal validity that particular international law achieves its proper significance and authority.

41. *Universal international law*

The notion of international law itself and of an international community under the rule of law is based on the assumption—which, upon analysis, is a statement of fact—that there exist rules and principles of international law of universal validity binding upon all subjects of international law, whether States or not, regardless of their race, religion, geographical situation, political creed or degree of civilization. Most of these rules and principles of universal international law are liable to be changed by express agreement or custom. Some of them, inasmuch as they embody overriding

[1] See above, p. 27.

[2] There is occasionally a threefold distinction made between particular, general, and universal international law—general international law being understood as particular international law embracing a large number of States, while universal international law is said to correspond to general international law of unusually wide scope. Thus conceived the distinction is a matter of degree.

INTERNATIONAL LAW—THE GENERAL PART

principles of morality or of paramount international interest, are binding in all circumstances.

These universal rules and principles of international law stem, by and large, from four causes.

Universal international law represents, in the first instance, that aspect of international law which has been described as grounded in the existence of a society of States.[1] The very notion of international law, it has been suggested, is based on the assumption that there exists an international community embracing of necessity all political communities organized as independent States and, in a wider sense, all human beings. These rules and principles of universal international law supplement that based on express or implied consent; they give it validity; they supply the constant element of its interpretation. They are not an eternal law of nature of the society of States. But they have a sufficient degree of permanence and immutability to supply an enduring standard for the criticism and evaluation of that international law, general and particular, which is the result of consent. Thus conceived, universal international law does not loom large in daily practice and in proceedings before international tribunals. But it is constantly in the background of the application of international law in its capacity as 'the reason of the thing' expressive of the necessity of securing the co-existence and peaceful intercourse of States and of safeguarding, as yet to an imperfect degree, the fundamental rights of the individual who is the ultimate subject of all law.

Secondly, the universality of a substantial body of international law is due to the fact that it is based to a large, although not conspicuous extent upon 'general principles of law recognized by civilized nations'.[2] These general principles are in themselves, by definition, of a universal character. The reference to 'civilized nations' does not, in this connection, imply any general or specific test of degree of culture or civilization—though probably it implies a minimum of it.[3] Neither is it connected with the frequent emphasis

---

[1] See above, pp. 28, 51.   [2] See above, p. 68.

[3] See, e.g. the insistence on the obligation to comply with a minimum standard of civilization in the matter of treatment of aliens. See on this subject Jennings in *B.Y.* 34 (1958), 352, quoting Westlake *Papers* (1914), p. 143. The subject is not free from difficulty. It may not be sufficient to say that for the purposes of international law the test of civilization is the existence of a Government possessing sufficient stability and orderliness to enable it to maintain normal relations with other States and to afford protection to foreigners. For such protection must, in turn, be in accordance with a certain minimum standard of civilization. The solution of the difficulty lies probably in agreeing that the minimum standard of civilization should not be determined by exclusive reliance upon any particular political or economic system.

SOURCES OF INTERNATIONAL LAW

upon Christian civilization and religion as constituting the basis and origin of modern international law.

Thirdly, certain principles of customary international law—such as those relating to immunities of diplomatic representatives, or the freedom of the high seas, or the obligation to spare the life of prisoners of war who surrender at discretion—have secured such wide and unchallenged acceptance that their universal validity must be assumed. Thus, when in *West Rand Central Gold Mining Co. v. The King*[1] the Court described as binding upon English courts rules of international law to which Great Britain had given her assent or which were so generally accepted that it was inconceivable that a civilized State should refuse its consent to them, it was referring to universal international law in the sense here indicated.

Finally, there are certain treaties of a general character, approaching or described as international legislation,[2] which, while in strict law binding only upon the parties thereto and while subject to denunciation, are so widely accepted that, for some purposes, they may be considered to constitute universal international law. To mention a conspicuous example, to this category belong the Geneva Conventions of 1949 relating to the treatment of prisoners of war, of sick and wounded armies in the field and at sea, and of the civilian population in time of war. This is so, not only because of the large number of States effectively bound by these Conventions or because many of the provisions of these Conventions, following as they do from compelling considerations of humanity, are declaratory of universally binding international custom. It is so also for the additional reason that numerous articles of the Conventions make express provision for the universality of their acceptance and application. The Conventions are open to accession by any State without limitation; they bind the parties even in relation to a non-contracting party if the latter, after the outbreak of hostilities, accepts and applies the provisions thereof; they apply not only to the case of war but also to any other armed conflict, even if a state of war is not recognized by one of the parties to the conflict (which means, in effect, that the Conventions cover civil wars—a significant indication that they apply also to entities not recognized as States).

Moreover, some of these very widely adopted treaties which approach universality in terms of the numbers of signatories thereto partake also of the character of universality for the reason that in

---

[1] [1905] 2 K.B. 391. And see below, pp. 156, 168.
[2] See above, p. 59.

115

some respects they are expressed to confer rights and impose obligations upon States which are not signatories and, albeit in an imperfect way, upon entities other than States. Thus the Charter of the United Nations binds its Members to observe certain principles in relation to non-member States, in particular with regard to respect for their independence and territorial integrity. Conversely, in effect, the Charter imposes obligations upon non-member States. For instance, Article 2(6) of the Charter lays down that 'the Organization shall ensure that States which are not Members of the United Nations act in accordance with these Principles so far as may be necessary for the maintenance of international peace and security.' The International Court of Justice has held, in a different sphere, that the Charter may impose obligations upon non-member States.[1] There is authority for the view that treaties of a so-called legislative character which, having regard to the number of their signatories, approach universality—for instance, the Treaty of 1928 for the Renunciation of War—survive changes of territorial sovereignty and apply by way of succession to new States which have not expressly acceded to them.

It will thus be seen that the affirmation of the universality of international law is of significance from various points of view. In the first instance, it records, as a statement of fact, the existence of a substantial portion of international law—whether created by custom or treaty—which has been adopted by all or practically all States. Secondly, it recalls that in many cases the general acceptance, approaching universality, of a rule of international law raises the presumption, which cannot be rebutted, that it has been adopted by and is binding upon all States. Thirdly, it is an expression of the fact that, independently of any express adoption, there is a body of international law which is of universal validity inasmuch as it is the result of 'the reason of the thing' determined by the existence of the international community of States and individuals. Fourthly, it records the fact that inasmuch as that international body of States of diverse systems of law is in itself a community under law, international law is to a substantial degree governed by general principles of law which by definition are of universal application. Fifthly, and to some extent negatively, it provides a warning against any excessive identification of international law with or its dependence upon any particular system of religion, civilization, or economic or political creed.[2]

[1] See above, p. 60, and below, p. 140. See also Jenks in *B.Y.* 29 (1952), 105–44.
[2] For a recent important and comprehensive treatment of this subject see a series of

SOURCES OF INTERNATIONAL LAW

The significance, or the very existence, of universal international law, in the sense here described, has been obscured by the prominence given to the fact that the States which between the sixteenth and nineteenth centuries almost exclusively participated in and shaped the development of modern international law were States of Christian religion and Western civilization, as it has been also by the excessive emphasis on the various aspects of particular international law. That emphasis has included the exaggeration of so-called American international law, the weight given to the asserted fundamental differences between the so-called Anglo-American and Continental schools of international law, and the importance attributed—out of.proportion to any accurate claim to a lasting and intrinsic permanence in the relations of States—to various national conceptions of international law. All these factors will now be considered. It is not necessary to examine in the present context that cause of the denial of universal international law which stems from the rigid—and diminishing—adherence to the positivist doctrine.[1] That doctrine, which is discussed elsewhere[2] in this volume, sees in the express will of States the only source of obligation in the sphere of international law—a view which is incompatible with the conception of universal international law as grounded in the very existence of the international community independently of any express or implied manifestation of the will of its members.

42. *Modern international law as created by Christian States in Western civilization*

Modern international law is to a large extent the product of the practice of European States since the sixteenth century[3] as well as of the United States of America and the Latin-American States since the achievement of their independence in the last decades of the eighteenth and the first decades of the nineteenth centuries. Its doctrinal foundations were largely laid down by Catholic Spanish

lectures delivered by Dr Jenks in 1957 at the Geneva Graduate Institute of International Studies and reproduced in his book, *The Common Law of Mankind* (1958), pp. 62–172. And see *ibid.* pp. 409–18.

[1] See, e.g., Blühdorn, *Einführung in das angewandte Völkerrecht* (1934), pp. 95, 96; Anzilotti, 1, 89; Strupp in *Hague Recueil*, 47 (1934) (i), 317–24. See also Fedozzi, *Trattato di diritto internazionale* (2nd ed. 1933), pp. 69 *et seq.* But see Bustamante, 1, 33, 34; Verdross, p. 92; Scott, 'L'universalité du droit des gens', in *Le progrès du droit des gens* (1931), 1, 151 *et seq.*, in *Annuaire*, 33 (1927), 61, 62, and in *A.S. Proc.* 1929, pp. 48–54.

[2] See above, pp. 32, 52, 54, and below, p. 207.

[3] See Holdsworth, *Some Makers of English Law* (1938), p. 218, quoting the statement of Sir Leoline Jenkins, Admiralty Judge under Charles II: 'By the law of nations I do not mean Civil Imperial Law, but the generally received customs among the European Governments which are most renowned for their justice, valour, and civility.'

INTERNATIONAL LAW—THE GENERAL PART

writers[1] in the sixteenth and Protestant writers in the seventeenth centuries. It is therefore not surprising that there has been a tendency to refer to modern international law as being the product of Christian and, particularly, Western civilization and as being limited in its operation, at least till the middle of the nineteenth century, to the mutual relations of Christian States. Some importance was attached to the fact that it was not until 1856 that Turkey was formally admitted, by Article 7 of the Treaty of Paris, to participation 'in the advantages of public law and the Concert of Europe'— though it is usually conceded that such express admission was in the nature of a formality.[2] Hall gave expression to the current view on the subject:

It is scarcely necessary to point out that as international law is a product of the special civilization of modern Europe, and forms a highly artificial system of which the principles cannot be supposed to be understood or recognized by countries differently civilized, such states only can be presumed to be subject to it as are inheritors of that civilization.[3]

The view that, with respect both to practice and doctrine, the contribution of States of Christian—and, in particular, of Western —civilization has been almost exclusive and decisive for the rise and development of modern international law in the seventeenth, eighteenth and nineteenth centuries is, by and large, an accurate statement of historical fact. It is not seriously affected by the circumstance that there were during that period occasional contacts—by way of treaties, diplomatic intercourse[4] and otherwise[5]—between

---

[1] See Eppstein, *The Catholic Tradition of the Law of Nations* (1935); Wright, *Medieval Internationalism* (1930); and Bentwich, *The Religious Foundations of Internationalism* (1933), pp. 83–158. For an exposition of international law from the Catholic point of view see Pasquazi, *Jus internationale publicum*, 1 (1935).

[2] See Hall, § 6, who, however, in the same paragraph notes that 'states outside European civilization must formally enter into the circle of law-governed countries'. And see, on the effect of the Treaty of Paris on Turkey's status in international law, McKinnon Wood in *A.J.* 37 (1943), 262–74, and generally, as to non-Christian States, Smith, 1, 14–18, 34–7.   [3] See Hall, § 6.

[4] See, e.g., *Br. and For. St. Papers*, 12, 994, for a Declaration of the Bey of Algiers granting diplomatic privileges to the British Representative.

[5] See, for instance, Smith, 1, 281–98, relating to the observance of the attitude of neutrality by Great Britain during the Greek war of independence. It is of interest to note that in the early volumes of Martens' *Recueil des Traités* there are included agreements concluded with Indian States and potentates by the Dutch East India Company (1773; Martens, R. 5 (1799), 58) and the British East India Company (1787; *ibid.* 4 (1799), p. 268). See also Aitchison, *Collection of Treaties, Engagements and Sanads relating to India and Neighbouring States*, 13 vols. (1909–30). And see, for example, a treaty concluded in 1631 between the King of Persia and the States General of the United Provinces of the Netherlands, reproduced in Dumont, *Corps Universel Diplomatique du Droit des Gens* (1731), and referred to by Alexandrowicz in *The Indian Year Book of International Affairs*, 7 (1958), 201–6.

SOURCES OF INTERNATIONAL LAW

Christian States and others. Until the middle of the nineteenth century these contacts were sporadic. Oriental States such as China and Japan[1] showed reluctance to enter into normal relations with the European Powers. The latter considered, in turn, that in many ways the state of civilization and the administration of justice within the Oriental and African nations and communities did not permit the application to them of rules of international law—especially those relating to the protection of the rights of their nationals in those countries. Such nationals were for a long time protected by the régime of capitulations, which—providing as it did for the exemption of foreign nationals from the jurisdiction of local courts and occasionally from the local law—was not in keeping either with the ordinary rules of international law or with the sovereignty of those States. Moreover, neither the scope nor the character of the international intercourse between non-Christian communities *inter se* was such as to permit an accurate statement that they were governed by rules of international law as currently understood.

It will thus be seen that to the extent here outlined the statement that modern international law is the product of Western and Christian civilization is not open to objection. It is a statement of historical fact. On the other hand, it is important not to exaggerate either its scope or its implications.

In the first instance, since the end of the nineteenth and the commencement of the twentieth century the membership of the international community has increasingly become universal in character. The notion that it is *a priori* limited to States of Christian religion or civilization and that with regard to other States there is required some formal act of admission to what was described as the Christian family of nations is now a patent anachronism. Although prior to the First World War some of the non-European States— such as China and Persia—continued to be bound by the régime of capitulations, their participation in international intercourse on a footing of equality with other States was not open to doubt. China,

---

[1] Thus it was not until 1856 that Japan signed a treaty with a Western Power, namely, the United States of America. The nature of the Japanese reluctance to enter into relations with the Western Powers may be gauged from the following passage in a letter from the President of the United States to the Emperor of Japan, delivered by Commodore Perry who arrived in 1853 in the Japanese port of Uruga in command of four warships: 'These are the only objects for which I have sent Commodore Perry, with a powerful squadron, to pay a visit to your Imperial Majesty's renowned city of Yedo: friendship, commerce, a supply of coal and provisions, protection for our shipwrecked people' (as reproduced by Ohira, 'Japan's Reception of the Law of Nations', *Annals of the Hitotsubashi Academy*, 4 (1953), 55–66).

119

INTERNATIONAL LAW—THE GENERAL PART

Japan,[1] Persia and Siam took part in the first Hague Peace Conference in 1899. In addition to these and other States, including India, a number of non-Christian States became members of the League of Nations. Numerous non-Christian States—such as Egypt, Iraq, Saudi Arabia, Lebanon and Syria—participated in the Conference of San Francisco for the establishment of the United Nations. At present more than a quarter of the Members of the United Nations are non-Christian States;[2] the European States constituting only one quarter, or less, of the total membership of the United Nations. With regard to a number of States in which the formal separation of religion from the State has been accompanied by a radical secularization of their culture and civilization in relation to large sections of their peoples, the test of religion as a relevant standard of membership of the international community has become somewhat artificial. Religion and the controversial test of degree of civilization have ceased to be, as such, a condition of recognition of States. In general, the question of membership of the Family of Nations, as based on membership of the Christian community of Western States, is now a matter of purely historical interest.

Secondly, even at the time when the predominance, or exclusiveness, of the Western and Christian contribution to international law was a fact, there was a wide measure of recognition of the inherent tendency to universality, conceived as an expression of the essential unity of mankind, as the principal condition of the rational existence and development of international law. The Catholic precursors of Grotius, such as Vitoria and Suarez, based international law on the immutable and universal law of nature. Gentili, an Italian who wrote in England as a Protestant refugee from the persecution of the Inquisition, insisted, in relation to various aspects of international law, that it applied to all independent States irrespective of

---

[1] After the Russo-Japanese war in 1904 Japan gradually acquired the status of a Great Power and was so treated when she became one of the permanent members of the Council of the League of Nations. See Matsudaira, *Le droit conventionnel international du Japon* (1931). And see Lapradelle-Politis, III, 582 *et seq.* for an account of an arbitration, in 1875, between Japan and Peru arising out of a decision given in 1872 by a Japanese court in the case of *The Maria Luz* and purporting to be based, in part, on international law. See also Ohira, *loc. cit.* When in 1872 the Japanese Government discontinued the lunar calendar and adopted the solar system, it stated that the measure taken would accord with the Law of Nations (*ibid.* p. 66).

[2] Since 1945 a large number of Moslem communities in Asia and Africa have become independent States and Members of the United Nations. They include Pakistan, Indonesia, Tunis, Morocco, Sudan, Jordan, Yemen, Ghana, Libya. Among other Asiatic Members of the United Nations are Burma, Ceylon, Malaya, Nepal, Cambodia, Laos, Vietnam.

SOURCES OF INTERNATIONAL LAW

religion.[1] Grotius himself, in many ways the founder of the modern doctrine of international law, approached it not only as part of a general system of jurisprudence, with the secularized law of nature as its pivot, but also as part of a universal moral code.[2] In fact, in so far as, as a matter of both doctrine and practice, international law is based on the law of nature whether in its traditional or its modern garb,[3] its universality follows of necessity from that very source. That doctrinal recognition of the universality of international law received a decisive accession of strength from the obvious fact of its growing universality in the persons of the political communities willingly and necessarily subjected to its sway. It found expression in such instruments as the Statutes of the International Court of Justice and of the International Law Commission, which directed the electors of these bodies to bear in mind the representation of the main forms of civilization and of the principal legal systems of the world. Moreover, the various factors—in the domain of politics, economics, communications and science—which have tended to endow the conception of an international community with a new and tangible measure of reality,[4] have given new substance to the notion of the universality of international law.

Thirdly, in so far as the origins of modern international law are accurately stated to lie in the contribution of States of Western civilization, it must be borne in mind that the latter embodies, in turn, to a large extent a heritage of the ancient Greek, Roman and Jewish civilizations.[5] An account of the contribution of these latter to international law in its entirety is given later on in this treatise. Moreover, the picture is not complete without a due appreciation of the legal aspects of international relations as understood and practised by Islamic communities and other States of Asia,[6] as well as the Oriental–Byzantine civilization.[7]

---

[1] See in particular *De Legationibus, Libri tres* (1581), English translation by Laing (1924), pp. 90, 92.

[2] See Lauterpacht in *B.Y.* 23 (1946), p. 51 [reprinted in a later volume of these Collected Papers].   [3] See above, pp. 76–77.

[4] See above, p. 28. As to the position of non-Christian States and peoples at different stages of the development of international law see Westlake, I, 40; Phillimore, I, §§ 27–33; Bluntschli, §§ 1–16; Heffter, § 7; Rivier, I, 13–18; Fauchille, §§ 40–4(1); Martens, § 41; Nys, I, 126–37; Westlake, *Papers*, pp. 141–3; Lindley, pp. 10–47 and *passim*; Smith, I, 14–33; Plantet, *Les Consuls de France à Alger avant la Conquête*, 1579–1830 (1930); Irwin, *The Diplomatic Relations of the United States with the Barbary Powers*, 1776–1816 (1931); Scott, *The Spanish Origin of International Law. Francisco de Vitoria and his Law of Nations* (1934).   [5] See Rosenne in *Netherlands International Law Review*, 1958, p. 122.

[6] As to the Islamic contribution to international law see Armanazi, *Les principes islamiques et les rapports internationaux en temps de paix et de guerre* (1929); Bentwich, *The Religious Foundations of Internationalism* (1933), pp. 159–80; Hamidullah, *The Muslim*

INTERNATIONAL LAW—THE GENERAL PART

All these factors inevitably tend to qualify, without altogether denying its validity as a statement of historical fact, the view that modern international law owes its origin to a large extent to States of the Western and, in particular, of Christian civilization. However, as stated, the problem is now essentially of no other than historical interest. The same applies to the question of the treatment of communities, not forming part of recognized States, which have not acquired a requisite degree of civilization and cohesion approaching a condition of statehood as normally understood.[1] There was general agreement that they ought to be treated in accordance with the principles of morality and humanity.[2] The United States of America applied, in some respects, the rules of international law to their relations with the Red Indians.[3]

43. So-called American international law

The historic circumstances accompanying the rise of the various American Republics as independent States caused them to stress certain principles such as self-determination, the right to independence, freedom from intervention on the part of European States, freedom of expatriation and migration, and so on. Some of these doctrines were subsequently taken over by European nations and played a prominent part in the history of Europe; others, like freedom of immigration, have now been abandoned, at least

Conduct of State (revised ed. 1945); Kruse, *Islamische Völkerrechtslehre* (1953); Khadduri and Liebesny (ed.), *Law in the Middle East*, 1 (1955), 348–72; Khadduri, *The Law of War and Peace in Islam* (1955), and in *A.J.* 50 (1956), 358–92; Rechid in *Hague Recueil*, 60 (1937) (ii), 375–502. As to the contribution of ancient India see Chacko in *Hague Recueil*, 93 (1958) (i), 121–42; Bandyopadhyay, *International Law and Custom in Ancient India* (1920); Viswanatha, *International Law in India* (1925). As to China see Sui Tchoan-Pao, *Le droit des gens et la Chine antique* (1924); Escarra, *La Chine et le droit international* (1931); Yung, *China and Some Phases of International Law* (1940); Chow, *La doctrine de droit international chez Confucius* (1940); Martin in *R.I.* 14 (1882), 227–42; Britton in *A.J.* 29 (1935), 616–35, with a detailed bibliography; Chen, *ibid.* 35 (1941), 641–50.

[7] See de Taube in *Hague Recueil*, 11 (1926)(i), 345–535, and, in particular, as to the Byzantine contribution, *ibid.* 67 (1939), 237–9. And see Papaligouras, *Théorie de la Société Internationale* (1941).

[1] See above, p. 114, n. 3.

[2] As to the application of the laws of war to non-civilized States and savage tribes, see Wright in *A.J.* 20 (1926), 265–8, and Colby, *ibid.* 21 (1927), 279–88. See also McNair, *Opinions*, 1, 65.

[3] See Rice in *J.C.L.* 3rd ser. 16 (1934), 78–95. For a discussion of the rights of aboriginal tribes in lands inhabited by them, see *In re Southern Rhodesia* [1919] A.C. 211. See also generally Snow, *The Question of Aborigines in the Law and Practice of Nations* (1921); Octavio, 'Les sauvages américains devant le droit', in *Hague Recueil*, 31 (1920) (i), 181–289; Scott, cited above, p. 121, and the Award of the British-American Arbitral Tribunal in the case of the *Cayuga Indians Claims, A.J.* 20 (1926), 574–94. See also *Totus v. United States (Annual Digest,* 10 (1941–2), Case no. 1) and *Ex parte Green (ibid.* Case no. 128).

SOURCES OF INTERNATIONAL LAW

temporarily, by most of the American States. In addition, the States of the American Continent, with the exception of Canada, have created a permanent organ of non-political co-operation in the form of the Pan-American Union and periodical Pan-American Conferences. They have also adopted, subject to numerous reservations, a series of general conventions codifying *inter se* various topics of public and private international law.[1] The principles underlying these conventions do not, in so far as they have secured the general consent of all American States, differ appreciably from those binding on States in other parts of the world. It is possible that the special problems of the American Continent may necessitate in the future a clear departure from some of the rules and principles obtaining elsewhere. However, up till now, American international law, although looming large in discussions of writers, does not seem to have developed any distinctive features of a general character of its own.[2] Geographical propinquity may serve as a basis for more developed forms of international co-operation and mutual political assistance in the preservation of peace than is possible between all States at large; it may also necessitate the adoption of special rules of international law with regard to particular interests and situations. But the controversy surrounding the question of the existence of an American international law shows that it is important not to magnify either the extent or the significance of such regional peculiarities.[3]

[1] See above, p. 41 n.

[2] Many writers refer to the doctrine of *uti possidetis* as an example of American international law, but this is often the only example given. See, e.g., Urrutia, *Le continent américain et le droit international* (1928), p. 199.

[3] The existence of an American international law has been asserted in particular by Alvarez in a series of able writings beginning with his *Le droit international américain* (1909); in *A.J.* 3 (1909), pp. 269–353, and in *R.G.* 20 (1913), 48–52; *La reconstruction du droit international et sa codification en Amérique* (1928); and the works referred to above, p. 112 n. 0. However, it appears that that distinguished writer, far from denying the existence of universal rules of international law, merely stressed 'the existence of particular rules relating to special American problems with regard to matters which have not yet been regulated by general international law': Institut Américain de Droit International, *Historique, Notes, Opinions* (1916), p. 111. See also his *Le droit international nouveau dans ses rapports avec la vie actuelle des peuples* (1959), pp. 143–59.

The term 'American international law' was adopted in the Draft Code of American International Law which was presented by the Pan-American Union to the Governments of all the American States. In Project 2 of this Code (*A.J.* 20 (1926), Suppl. 2, p. 302), American international law was defined as 'all of the institutions, principles, rules, doctrines, conventions, customs, and practices which, in the domain of international relations, are proper to the Republics of the New World', thus giving a very wide significance to the term *law*, and comprising apparently principles of policy such as the Monroe Doctrine, which is not a rule of law. This Project was not amongst those adopted by the International Law Commission of American Jurists at Rio de Janeiro in April–May 1927 (see Scott in *A.J.* 21 (1927), at p. 437).

See also, in support of the thesis that there exists an American international law:

123

INTERNATIONAL LAW—THE GENERAL PART

On the other hand, account may properly be taken of local and regional traditions which have resulted in the adoption of rules and customs not clearly incompatible with cogent principles of general international law. In the *Asylum* case between Colombia and Peru, the International Court of Justice showed no disposition to attach decisive importance to some of the apparent consequences of the institution of asylum which, because of the relative frequency of internal commotions, acquired a certain prominence in Latin-American countries. The Court preferred to base its Judgment upon general principles of international law—including the pro-hibition of intervention which, it held, required a restrictive inter-pretation of the right of foreign missions to shelter in their legations fugitives from the justice of the receiving country and to determine unilaterally the justification of such action. The Judgment met with criticism in some Latin-American countries, and a Convention was subsequently adopted affirming the right of unilateral qualifica-tion by the State granting asylum.[1]

44. *The so-called Anglo-American and Continental schools of international law*

The differences in the notions and methods of various systems of municipal law have equally given rise to an attitude questioning, in a different sphere, the universal character of international law. Thus it has been maintained that there exist fundamental differences on essential questions of international law between the so-called Anglo-American and Continental schools.[2] In fact, there are at

Urrutia, *Le continent américain et le droit international* (1928); Yepes, *La contribution de l'Amérique Latine au développement du droit international public et privé* (1931), and in *Hague Recueil*, 32 (1930) (ii), 697–792, and *ibid.* 47 (1934) (i), 5–137; Baak in *R.I.* 3rd ser. 13 (1932), 367–97. See, on the other hand, Vianna, *De la non-existence d'un droit international américain* (1912); Leger, *La codification du droit des gens et les conférences des juristes américains* (1929), pp. 88 *et seq.*; Guerrero, *La codification du droit international* (1930), p. 12. See also Lamas, *La crise de la codification et la doctrine argentine du droit international* (1931); Fauchille, §§ 44(2)–44(12); Cereti, *Panamericanismo e diritto internazionale* (1939); Savelberg, *Le problème du droit international américain* (1946); Yepes, *Philosophie du Panaméricanisme et organisation de la paix* (1945); Cok Arango, *Derecho internacional Americano* (1948); Puig, *Principios de derecho internacional publico americano* (1952), and *Les principes du droit inter-national public américain* (1954); Jacobini, *A Study of the Philosophy of International Law as Seen in Works of Latin-American Writers* (1954); Dupuy, *Le nouveau panaméricanisme* (1956); Langrod in *Revue Hellénique*, 10 (1957), 132–230. As to American international law in relation to the law of the sea, see Yepes in *R.G.* 60 (1956), 10–79. And see above, p. 41n, on the numerous attempts at regional codification of parts of international law on the American continent.

[1] But it will be noted in mitigation of any such criticism that the very notion of non-intervention, relied upon by the Court, has been frequently referred to in Latin America as being a product of 'American international law'.

[2] See, e.g., Keith's Wheaton, I, 34; Fischer Williams, *Chapters*, p. 58; Pearce Higgins, *International Law and Relations* (1928), pp. 30, 31; Lord Hailsham, then Lord Chancellor, in the House of Lords on 1 May 1929: *House of Lords Debates*, 74, cols. 303, 304.

SOURCES OF INTERNATIONAL LAW

present no such divergencies in either the law of peace or the law of war.[1] With regard to supposed differences in basic notions and methods of approach, international practice has, with regard to the few relevant matters, resulted in an assimilation and mutual approximation of apparently opposed conceptions of the Anglo-American and Continental systems of jurisprudence. This is shown, for instance, in the manner in which the practice of the Permanent Court of International Justice and its successor have combined formal disregard of the doctrine of judicial precedent with constant and fruitful regard for their previous decisions.[2]

Admittedly, notions of private law have exercised a beneficent influence upon the development of international law. But any manifest influence of a particular system of private law has made itself felt only in so far as it represents a 'general principle of law recognized by civilized nations'.[3] These general notions exhibit, as a rule, an essential uniformity notwithstanding terminological and technical differences resulting from dissimilarity of language and procedure and from historical peculiarities. This may be seen from the comparative study of subjects such as abuse of rights,[4] unjustified enrichment,[5] termination of contracts as the result of supervening impossibility of performance,[6] and others—studies which, when applied to corresponding situations in the field of international law, disclose the affinity of disparate legal systems notwithstanding national peculiarities. When put to the test of practice, vague suggestions of fundamental differences occasionally reveal themselves as due largely to an absence of familiarity with other systems of law.[7] This applies in particular to the view that, in contrast with the Anglo-American notion of law, the Continental conception—as expressed in the terms *Recht, droit, diritto*—confuses law and ethics.

[1] With regard to the law of war, the undoubted divergence between the Anglo-American and Continental views as to the subjects of the relation of war (see Oppenheim, II, § 57) has probably been rendered obsolete by the changes in the character and scope of modern warfare. See Lauterpacht in *B.Y.* 12 (1931), 31–62, for a discussion of the whole question [reprinted in a later volume of these Collected Papers].

[2] See Lauterpacht, *The Development of International Law by the International Court* (1958), pp. 6–23. There is no pronouncement of the International Court referring to any difference between the two schools of thought in international law.

[3] See above, p. 68.　　　[4] See Lauterpacht, *The Function of Law*, pp. 292–300.

[5] See O'Connell, *The Law of State Succession* (1956), pp. 103 *et seq.* And see the comparative studies of Friedmann in *Canadian Bar Review*, 16 (1938), pp. 243–72, 365–86, and Dewson, *Unjust Enrichment* (1951); see also Lord Wright in *University of Pennsylvania Law Review*, 100 (1952), 612–28.　　　[6] See Lauterpacht, *The Function of Law*, pp. 272–6.

[7] See the judicious observations of Dr Jenks on 'certain elements of initial strangeness' in the approach to foreign systems of law: *The Common Law of Mankind* (1958), pp. 89–92. See also *ibid.* pp. 109–14, 120 *et seq.* on the interaction of various systems of law. And see above, p. 72.

INTERNATIONAL LAW—THE GENERAL PART

In so far as substantive differences exist between various systems of law they affect areas of conduct lying specifically within the field of municipal law and are not, therefore, of a nature likely to render impossible or difficult a uniform development and administration of international law.[1]

45. *National conceptions of international law*

Finally, the universality of international law has been assailed by a variety of national conceptions of international law evolved in the abnormal period following the First World War. Thus writers in Soviet Russia denied for a time the possibility of a permanent and general international law;[2] they spoke of an international law of transition, based largely on particular or general agreements as distinguished from customary or municipal international law, pending the extension of the Russian system to other countries. Subsequently, that and similar doctrines underwent considerable changes, often at the hands of their originators, as the result of internal vicissitudes and external developments. Thus Krylov, a Judge of the International Court of Justice, writing in 1947, stated that on many questions there is no universal international law; but he admitted that 'in many spheres there exists a common, general, international law'.[3] He defined international law as 'the aggregate of rules which govern the relations of States in their rivalry, their struggle, and

[1] There has probably been in recent years a weakening of the tendency to assume the existence of differences between the Anglo-American and Continental schools as a ready explanation of difficulties or as a reason for questioning the desirability of submitting to the jurisdiction of tribunals said to be composed, in the majority of their members, of representatives of the 'Continental' school of thought. On the contribution of Great Britain and the United States to international law see Dickinson in *Hague Recueil*, 40 (1932) (ii), 309–93. But it is probably not inconsistent with the view of the learned author to point out that that contribution is not, in most matters there referred to, exclusively confined to Anglo-American countries and that it is not connected with the peculiarities of the Common Law as distinguished from Continental law.

[2] See Korovin, *Das Völkerrecht der Übergangszeit* (translated from the Russian, 1929), pp. 7, 24. And see, generally, on the relation of Soviet Russia to international law, Hrabar in *Z.V.* 14 (1927–8), 188–214; Mirkine-Guetzévitch in *R.I.* (*Paris*), 2 (1928), 1012–1049; Alexeiew and Zaitzeff in *Z.V.* 16 (1931–2), 72–99; Hazard in *A.J.* 32 (1938), 244–52; Florin in *Revue internationale de la théorie du droit*, 12 (1938), 97–115.
See also Taracouzio, *The Soviet Union and International Law* (1935), and in *A.S. Proc.*, 1934, pp. 105–20; the same, *War and Peace in Soviet Diplomacy* (1940); Stoupnitzky, *Statut international de l'U.R.S.S. Etat commerçant* (1936); Hazard, *Law and Social Change in the U.S.S.R.* (1953), pp. 274–300; Lapenna, *Conceptions soviétiques de droit international public* (1954); Calvez, *Droit international et souveraineté en U.R.S.S.* (1953); Schlesinger, 'Soviet Theories of International Law', in *Soviet Studies*, (iv) (3) (1953), 334 *et seq.*; Kelsen, *The Communist Theory of Law* (1955), pp. 148–92; Corbett, *Law in Diplomacy* (1959), pp. 83–109 and, as to the practice of Soviet Russia generally, *passim*; Kulski in *A.J.* 49 (1955), 518–34; Schulz in *Jahrbuch für internationales Recht*, 5 (1955), 78–92.

[3] Krylov in *Hague Recueil*, 70 (1947) (i), 422.

SOURCES OF INTERNATIONAL LAW

their co-operation, which reflect the will of the ruling classes in those States, and which provide for enforcement exercised by States separately or collectively'.[1] At the same time, there have been features of both practice and doctrine in Soviet Russia which have exhibited a certain complexion of constancy. These include the rigid insistence on the view that only States are subjects of international law and that individuals have no rights directly conferred and supervised or enforced by international law;[2] and that the sovereignty of States, being one of the most essential principles of international law, is not amenable to restriction (by reference to a concept of implied consent)[3] by decisions of political bodies unless rendered unanimously with the participation of all the States concerned or by judicial tribunals endowed with obligatory jurisdiction—which latter competence Soviet Russia has so far been unwilling, apart from isolated exceptions,[4] to accept. In both these respects the attitude of some other States, wedded to a different political and economic system, has not always, in its results, been drastically dissimilar to that of Soviet Russia—without, however, receiving doctrinal support on the part of writers. There is no compelling reason for endowing these features of the doctrine of international law in Soviet Russia —as, indeed, the very conception of Soviet Russian international law—with any inevitable character of permanency.

Similarly, with the advent of the new political régime in Germany in 1933, some German writers stressed the idea of an 'inter-corporative international law of co-ordination' of States built on the principle of racial consanguinity.[5] Animated by the desire to assist

[1] *Ibid.* p. 420—a definition textually adopted by Vishinsky, a leading Soviet lawyer and statesman (quoted by Snyder and Bracht in *I.C.L.Q.* 7 (1958), 70).

[2] This feature explains and seeks to justify the opposition to international recognition and enforcement of fundamental human rights and freedoms as enshrined in the Charter of the United Nations. Soviet Russia and some States associated with her abstained from voting for the Universal Declaration of Human Rights adopted by the General Assembly in 1948.

[3] This explains the importance—occasionally exclusive—attached by writers in Soviet Russia to treaties as distinguished from custom in so far as it is identical with implied consent.

[4] As, for instance, with regard to the interpretation of the Constitution of the International Labour Organisation—a competence which admits of no reservations or exceptions.

[5] The following selection from the literature on the German National-Socialist conception of international law may be of historical interest: Guerke, *Volk und Völkerrecht* (1935); Wolgast in *Z.V.* 18 (1934), 129–32, and the same, *Völkerrecht* (1934), § 545; Rühland in *Z.V.* 18 (1934), 133–44; Walz, *ibid.* pp. 145–54; Török, *ibid.* pp. 249–94; Preuss in *R.G.* 41 (1934), 661–74, *ibid.* 42 (1935), 668–77, in *American Political Science Review*, 29 (1935), pp. 596–609, and in *J.C.L.* 3rd ser. 16 (1934), 268–80; Tartatin-Turnheyden in *Archiv für Rechts- und Sozialphilosophie*, 29 (1936), 295–319; Gott in *A.J.* 32 (1938), 704–18; Bristler, *Die Völkerrechtslehre des Nationalsozialismus* (1938); Fournier, *La conception national-socialiste du droit des gens* (1939); Bonnard, *Le droit et l'Etat dans la*

INTERNATIONAL LAW—THE GENERAL PART

in the termination of the remaining elements of political inequality resulting from the Treaty of Versailles, they elevated the notion of equality of States to the level of a basic principle of international law[1]—an emphasis soon to be superseded by the contrary doctrines of *Grossraumordnung* (legal order of vast territorial units).

These and similar intrusions of national policies into the sphere of international law are essentially transient.[2] On the other hand, in so far as the internal legal system and the international practice of some States are based on notions radically and militantly opposed to conceptions prevailing in the large majority of States, a situation is unavoidably created in which the society of States is for the time being deprived of that community of political, juridical and ethical outlook which is the necessary condition of both the normal functioning and the full development of international law. However, while in such periods the growth of international law is necessarily impeded, its principal function of regularizing intercourse and maintaining and enforcing peace continues to be capable of fulfilment and, indeed, gains in practical importance and urgency.

It must be added that there is no assertion of a national conception of international law in the sense described above in cases in which writers present a general picture of international law as applied by their own country. Treatises such as Hyde's *International Law. Chiefly as Interpreted and Applied by the United States*,[3] Guggenheim's *Traité de*

doctrine national-socialiste (2nd ed. 1939); Schmitt, *Völkerrechtliche Grossraumordnung* (1939); Janssens, *Le droit des gens d'après le national-socialisme* (1940); Walz in *Z.V.* 23 (1939), 129–64. As to Fascism, see Baak in *Z.ö.R.* 9 (1929), 1–31, and Sereni, *The Italian Conception of International Law* (1943), pp. 269–78.

[1] See Bruns, *Deutschlands Gleichberechtigung als Rechtsproblem* (1934), and in *Z.ö.R.* 5 (1935), 326 *et seq.*; Keller in *Z.V.* 17 (1933), 342–72; Bilfinger in *Z.ö.V.* 4 (1934), 485. Walz (*op. cit.* p. 153) insisted that the duty of courts to interpret municipal law in accordance with international law did not apply to the provisions of the Treaty of Versailles imposed upon Germany in derogation of her equality among States.

[2] As to the change of the Russian attitude in connection with her entry into the League of Nations see Mannzen, *Sowjetunion und Völkerrecht* (1932); Davis, *The Soviet Union and the League of Nations* (*Geneva Special Studies*, 5, no. 1, 1934); Kleist, *Die völkerrechtliche Anerkennung Sowjetrusslands* (1934); Miliokov, *La politique extérieure des Soviets* (1936); Hartlieb, *Das politische Vertragssystem der Sowjetunion, 1920–1935* (1936); Makarov in *Z.ö.V.* 5 (1935), 34–60 (with a bibliography), and 6 (1936), 479–95; Maurach in *Z.V.* 21 (1937), 19–45; and Beckhoff, *Völkerrecht gegen Bolschewismus* (1937). See also Prince in *A.J.* 36 (1942), 425–45 (on the participation of Soviet Russia in international organization), and *ibid.* 39 (1945), 450–85; Hazard in *Yale Law Journal,* 55 (1946), 1016–1035; Krylov in *Hague Recueil,* 70 (1947) (i), 407–74.

On the question of universality of international law in relation to the tension between Communist States and what are described as 'Western' States see Schwarzenberger in *Grotius Society,* 36 (1950), 229–69; Wilk in *A.J.* 45 (1951), 468; Berlia in *Clunet,* 79 (1952), 26; Kunz in *A.J.* 49 (1955), 370–6; Snyder and Bracht in *I.C.L.Q.* 7 (1958), 54–71. See also Northrop in *Yale Law Journal,* 61 (1952), 636; and McDougal and Laswell in *A.J.* 53 (1959), 1–29.   [3] 2nd revised edition, 3 vols. (1945).

SOURCES OF INTERNATIONAL LAW

droit international public (avec mention de la pratique internationale et suisse),[1] or, in a different sphere, Lord McNair's *International Law Opinions*[2] (which surveys the British practice as illustrated by the Opinions of the Law Officers of the Crown), perform the useful function of supplying evidence of the practice of individual States without claiming for it an authority other than that grounded in general international law. Their contents provide an instructive illustration of the instances and the manner of the application of international law. Thus conceived, they add to the authority and the understanding of international law in general without in any way questioning its character as an autonomous body of rules ultimately independent of the law of the State.

46. *The element of time in respect of the validity of the sources of international law (so-called inter-temporal international law)*

The question of the scope of the validity of the sources of international law arises not only in relation to their territorial application as determined by the degree of civilization or the religion of any political community. It arises also by reference to the element of time. The span of life of States is longer than that of individuals. Accordingly, in the relations of States there arises more prominently than in the case of individuals the question of the continuing validity and the interpretation at any given time of legal rights arising or created in what may be the distant past. If a State purports to have acquired territory in the sixteenth century, by what legal rules shall its title be decided in case of a dispute arising in the twentieth century? By what standards and rules shall an international tribunal interpret the terms of a treaty concluded two hundred years before a dispute has arisen? If a State claims from another State reparation for an injury done to itself or its nationals, is that claim governed by rules of law as they existed at the time of the alleged injury or by the law, customary or conventional, as it may have developed in the meantime? For the reasons stated, these questions of so-called inter-temporal law[3] are of special importance in the relations of

---

[1] Translation from the German, 2 vols. (1953).   [2] 3 vols. (1956).

[3] That expression has acquired some currency mainly on the Continent of Europe, in the literature of private international law—largely in connection with the question of the recognition of foreign legislation claiming retroactive effect. See Affolter, *Geschichte des intertemporalen Privatrechts* (1902); Roubier, *Les conflits des lois dans le temps* (2nd ed. 1960). For more detailed references see Niederer, *Einführung in die allgemeinen Lehren des internationalen Privatrechts* (1954), pp. 399–400; and Baade in *Jahrbuch für internationales Recht*, 7 (1928), 230 n. 3. See also Wolff, *Private International Law* (2nd ed. 1950), p. 2; Mann, 'Time Element in the Conflict of Laws' in *B.Y.* 31 (1954), 216 *et seq.*; and

INTERNATIONAL LAW—THE GENERAL PART

States. It is convenient to examine them separately in connection with customary law, the law of treaties and the law of State responsibility in its tortious and criminal aspects.[1]

(a) *The element of time in respect of customary international law.* In general, the validity of a title acquired by virtue of customary international law must be judged in the light of the law which obtained at the time of the acquisition or purported acquisition of title. However, there may be difficulty in determining the extent to which the exercise or even the continuation of the right thus acquired may have been influenced by subsequent developments in international custom. The difficulty is illustrated by the arbitral award rendered by Judge Huber in 1928 in the *Island of Palmas* case between the United States of America and the Netherlands.[2] In that case the United States, as successor of Spain,[3] claimed sovereignty over the island in question by reference to the title acquired by Spain through discovery in the first half of the sixteenth century at a time when mere discovery, not necessarily followed by effective exercise of sovereignty, was deemed to confer territorial title. The initial act of the Spanish discovery was not followed by effective occupation. In the seventeenth and eighteenth centuries the Dutch East India Company—whose acts the Arbitrator held to be assimilated to those of the Netherlands State—concluded a series of treaties with native chiefs; by virtue of these treaties the Company was considered by the Arbitrator to have exercised over the island acts corresponding to those of sovereignty. Subsequently, various measures of administration were taken by the Netherlands itself. The Arbitrator awarded the island to the Netherlands. He considered that although, by the standards of international law as recognized in the sixteenth century, Spain might have acquired sovereignty over the island, the continuation of her title must be judged by reference to the rules which governed the subject in the nineteenth and twentieth centuries and which required effective occupation as a condition of title. He held therefore that as no effective Spanish

---

Woodhouse in *Grotius Society*, 41 (1955), 69–89. In the sphere of public international law that term has gained currency in consequence of the award in the *Island of Palmas* arbitration: Scott, *Hague Court Reports* (2nd Series) (1932), p. 84.

[1] For a valuable and detailed treatment of the subject see Baade, *loc. cit.* pp. 229–56. See also Lauterpacht, *The Function of Law*, pp. 283–5; Schwarzenberger, pp. 20–4; Waldock in *B.Y.* 25 (1948), 320, 337; Fitzmaurice, *ibid.* 30 (1953), 5 *et seq.*; 32 (1955–6), 69, 70; 33 (1957), 225–7.   [2] See above, p. 131, n. 1.

[3] Who ceded the island to the United States in the Treaty of Paris of 1898 at the end of the Cuban war.

130

SOURCES OF INTERNATIONAL LAW

administration of the island had ever taken place and as there had been acts of sovereignty performed by or attributable to the Netherlands, sovereignty rested with the latter. He said:

As regards the question which of different legal systems prevailing at successive periods is to be applied in a particular case (the so-called inter-temporal law), a distinction must be made between the creation of rights and the existence of rights. The same principle which subjects the act creative of a right to the law in force at the time the right arises, demands that the existence of the right, in other words its continued manifestation, should follow the conditions required by the evolution of the law.[1]

The Award, which had some appearance of novelty,[2] is of value provided that it is not interpreted as meaning that developing international custom is given retroactive effect so as to render void a title validly recognized—a rule which would be open to objection on general grounds as being inconsistent with the principle, generally recognized, of respect for acquired rights. In making the distinction between the creation of rights and their continuance, the Award goes no further than to lay down in the first instance that a title once validly acquired cannot be annulled by subsequent changes in the law. Thus, for instance, the fact that recent international law has now come to prohibit war, and conquest resulting therefrom, as an instrument of national policy does not mean that title acquired by conquest prior to these changes in the law is extinguished. On the other hand, and this is the second principle emerging from the Award, title—however acquired—is subject to the operation of the changing and developing body of the law. Thus, if the law, as changed, lays down that a State forfeits its title to territory—whether such title is acquired by conquest, cession by treaty, or discovery—if for prolonged periods it fails to maintain over that territory a minimum of effective administration, the change in the law does not retroactively affect the validity of the original title.[3] But it does

---

[1] *A.J.* 22 (1928), 883; *U.N., R.I.A.A.* II, 845; *Annual Digest*, 4 (1927–8), Cases no. 1, 68, 70, 72, 75.

[2] For an expression of views different from those underlying the award see Heimburger, *Der Erwerb der Gebietshoheit* (1888), I, 139; Westlake, I, 114; Strupp in Schücking, *Das Werk von Haag*, Part II (1917), pp. 114 *et seq.* See also F. de Visscher in *R.I.* 3rd ser. 10 (1929), 735–62; and Bleiber, *Die Entdeckung im Völkerrecht* (1933), pp. 67–73, who considers the principle of inter-temporal law as adopted in the award to be fraught with danger to international stability.

[3] The defect, if any, of the Award in the *Island of Palmas* case lies in the fact that the implications of that distinction are not brought out with sufficient clarity. See Jessup in *A.J.* 22 (1928), 739–45. In particular, it is not clear whether according to the Award the continuous display of sovereignty as a condition of preservation of title applies only to title acquired by discovery or to territorial title generally. There would be a distinct

INTERNATIONAL LAW—THE GENERAL PART

affect its continuation. Thus interpreted, the principle, as stated above, of 'inter-temporal international law' in the sphere of custom is not open to objection and provides a desirable instrument of change in an international society in which the machinery of change through legislative processes binding upon all[1] is still in a rudimentary stage. In the *Minquiers and Ecréhos* case between the United Kingdom and France, the International Court of Justice declined to attach decisive importance to an original French feudal title alleged to have been acquired in the thirteenth century but not accompanied by subsequent effective possession.[2]

(b) '*Inter-temporal law*' and the interpretation of treaties. It follows from the principle as stated above that the provisions of a treaty ought to be interpreted in the light of the law and usage existing at the time of the conclusion of the treaty.[3] In general, only such inter-

degree of novelty in the suggestion that, except in case of a clear intention of abandonment, a State which acquired territory by peaceful cession or which has held it from time immemorial should be deemed to have lost title to it by failure to display sovereignty over it for a prolonged period of time. There is no such customary rule of international law—quite apart from the fact that, in the light of judicial and arbitral decisions on the subject, the requirement of continuous display of sovereignty is elastic to the point of being, on occasions, nominal. [See 'Sovereignty over Submarine Areas', reprinted in a later volume of these Collected Papers.] On the other hand, if the ruling of the Award is of limited scope—as may appear from some of its passages—in the sense that it applies only to not fully established sovereignty resulting from symbolic discovery and that even in the sixteenth century the latter conferred merely inchoate title, to be perfected by effective occupation, then there is hardly room for any question of inter-temporal law. For in that case the award would be based on the law as it existed in the sixteenth century.

[1] See above, p. 13.

[2] *I.C.J. Reports* 1953, pp. 56, 57. Both parties seem to have been in agreement as to the principle laid down in the *Island of Palmas* case, although they differed as to its application (see *Pleadings*, II, 53, 206, 275). See also the *Grisbadarna* case, decided in 1909 between Sweden and Norway, in which the Tribunal determined the boundary by reference to principles of division current in the seventeenth century (the general direction of the coast of which the maritime territory formed an appurtenance) and not according to the more modern principle of the *thalweg*: Scott, *Hague Court Reports* (1916), p. 492. In the award in the *Abu Dhabi* arbitration rendered in 1951 by Lord Asquith in a dispute between the Sheikh of Abu Dhabi and the Petroleum Development Company, the Arbitrator held that even if the doctrine of the Continental Shelf [see 'Sovereignty over Submarine Areas'] had become by 1951 part of international law—an assumption which he denied—it was not so in 1939 when the concession was granted. He therefore decided the issue by reference to the law as it existed in 1939: *I.L.R.* 18 (1951), Case no. 37; *I.C.L.Q.* I, 4th series (1952), p. 247.

[3] See, for a clear statement of that rule, the case concerning *Rights of Nationals of the United States of America in Morocco* (*I.C.J. Reports* 1952, p. 189). And see the Judgment of the Permanent Court in the case concerning *Certain German Interests in Polish Upper Silesia* (*Merits*), stating that Article 256 of the Treaty of Versailles must be construed 'in the light of the law in force at the time the transfer of sovereignty took place' (Series A, no. 7, p. 41). See also the award rendered in 1956 by the Anglo-Greek Commission of Arbitration in the *Ambatielos* case (*I.L.R.* 23 (1956), 306). Speaking of certain treaties concluded in the seventeenth century, the Commission said: 'Naturally their wording was influenced by the customs of the period, and they must obviously be interpreted in the light of this fact' (at p. 321).

132

SOURCES OF INTERNATIONAL LAW

pretation will correspond to the intention of the parties. At the same time it must be borne in mind, in particular in relation to treaties of a constitutional and legislative character, that the true intention of the parties may on occasions be frustrated if exclusive importance is attached to the meaning of words divorced from the social and legal changes which have intervened in the long period following upon the conclusion of those treaties.[1] Moreover, the parties to a treaty may by their subsequent conduct put upon the treaty an interpretation which, having regard to changed conditions, may depart from the meaning of words obtaining at the time of its signature.[2]

(c) *'Inter-temporal law' and the law of tortious and criminal responsibility.* It is clear that in these spheres a State cannot properly be made accountable for acts and omissions which at the time of the alleged injury were not prohibited by international law. The same applies to cases in which international law imposes direct responsibility upon individuals as, for instance, in the matter of the observance of the laws of war.[3] While it cannot be accurately maintained that the prohibition of retroactive operation of the law constitutes a principle of law of universal and unqualified validity, its general application in the sphere of tortious and criminal responsibility is dictated by cogent considerations of justice.[4] Various arbitration agreements in connection with claims for damages provide expressly that the award shall be given in accordance with the rules of international

---

[1] Reference may be made in this connection to the Advisory Opinion of the Permanent Court in the case of the *Tunis and Morocco Nationality Decrees* where the Court, in interpreting the expression 'solely within the jurisdiction of a party' as appearing in Article 15(8) of the Covenant of the League of Nations, pointed out that 'the question whether a certain matter is or is not solely within the jurisdiction of a State is essentially a relative question' which 'depends upon the development of international relations' (Series B, no. 4, p. 24)—which means that that expression is not confined to matters exclusively within domestic jurisdiction as determined by international law at the time of the adoption of the Covenant.

[2] See, e.g., Advisory Opinion on *Competence of the International Labour Organisation to Regulate Conditions of Work of Persons Employed in Agriculture* (*P.C.I.J.* Series B, nos. 2 and 3, p. 41); Advisory Opinion on the *Jurisdiction of the Courts of Danzig* (*ibid.* no. 15, p. 17). And see the passage in the Opinion of Justice Holmes in *Missouri* v. *Holland* (252 U.S. 416, 433 (1919))—a case of some international implications (see below, p. 159): '... when we are dealing with words that also are a constituent act, like the Constitution of the United States, we must realize that they have called into life a being the development of which could not have been foreseen completely by the most gifted of its begetters'.

[3] See below, pp. 141, 284.

[4] It has been suggested that in a claim for damages arising out of interference with slave traffic at a time when it was not regarded as contrary to international law, a tribunal would be entitled to base its decision on the law as existing at the time of the award (Lammasch, *Schiedsgerichtsbarkeit* (1914), p. 179). *Sed quaere.*

133

INTERNATIONAL LAW—THE GENERAL PART

law obtaining at the time of the events complained of.[1] In Article 6 of the Treaty of Washington of 1871 between Great Britain and the United States of America, which provided for the submission to arbitration of the Alabama claims in accordance with the rules defining certain duties of neutral States,[2] the British Government recorded its refusal to recognize that the rules as laid down in the Treaty constituted principles of international law in force at the time of the acts which gave rise to the claim; it agreed to them as the basis of the award 'in order to evince its desire of strengthening the friendly relations between the two countries, and of making satisfactory provision for the future'.[3] Cases may occur—and the conduct of National-Socialist Germany during the Second World War confirmed that possibility—where the degree of transgression against the laws of humanity, which in any case are part of international law,[4] is such as to call, as a compelling dictate of justice, for punishment, if necessary with retroactive effect, of crimes and atrocities.[5]

It would thus appear that the problems arising from the operation of the element of time—whether these problems are referred to by the somewhat technical term of inter-temporal law or otherwise—are capable of solution not so much by way of a precise rule as by way of a judicious combination of considerations of justice, stability and change.[6]

---

[1] See, e.g., the arbitration agreements between the United States of America and Haiti in the cases of *Pelletier* and *Lazare* (Moore, II, 1750), and between the United States of America and Russia in the case of the *Cape Horn Pigeon* and others (Lafontaine, *Pasicrisie internationale* (1902), p. 618). See also the award of Judge Hutcheson rendered in 1937 in the case of *Ryan* v. *United States of America* (*U.N., R.I.A.A.*, III, pp. 1768, 1771), stating that the Prize Court proceedings which formed the subject of the complaint must be examined and interpreted in the light of the applicable principles of international law, as that law existed in 1915 when the acts complained of took place and the claim arose.   [2] See Oppenheim, II, § 335.   [3] Moore, VII, § 1330.   [4] See above, pp. 19, 70 n.

[5] Subsequent to the Second World War and the prosecution of German war criminals in pursuance of the Agreement for the Prosecution and Punishment of Major War Criminals before the International Military Tribunal at Nuremberg and other tribunals, there were allegations to the effect that the Agreement and the resulting trials constituted a serious departure from the principle of non-retroactivity of criminal law. See Oppenheim, II, § 257, which shows that, with minor exceptions, there was no basis for these allegations. See also *ibid.* §§ 253 and 253a, in respect of the plea of superior orders as a ground for avoidance or mitigation of punishment.

[6] See the observations of Professor André Gros in the case of the *Minquiers and Ecréhos* (*I.C.J., Pleadings, Oral Arguments, Documents*, II (1953), p. 375) on the reconciliation, in this respect, of the possibly conflicting considerations of legal security and adaptation of the law to changed conditions.

SOURCES OF INTERNATIONAL LAW

SUPPLEMENTARY BIBLIOGRAPHY ON THE SOURCES OF INTERNATIONAL LAW GENERALLY

Cavaglieri, *La consuetudine giuridica internazionale* (1907); the same in *R.G.* 18 (1911), 259–92, and in *Rivista*, 14 (1921), 149–87, 289–314, 479–506; Heilborn, *Grundbegriffe des Völkerrechts* (1912), §§ 6–9, and in *Hague Recueil*, 11 (1926) (i), 5–60; Lauterpacht in *Hague Recueil*, 62 (1937) (iv), 149–87 [reprinted at p. 179 below]; Blühdorn, *Die Einführung in das angewandte Völkerrecht* (1934), pp. 112–85; Borchard in *Recueil d'Études Gény*, 3 (1934), 328–61; Ziccardi, *La costituzione dell'ordinamento internazionale* (1943), pp. 161–449; Sereni, *Diritto internazionale* (1956), pp. 111–90; Siorat, *Le problème des lacunes en droit international* (1959); Oppenheim in *Z.I.* 25 (1915), 1–13; Perassi, *ibid.* 6 (1917), 195–223, 285–314; Reeves in *A.J.* 15 (1921), 361–74; Verdross in *Hague Recueil*, 30 (1929) (v), 275–305; Bourquin, *ibid.* 35 (1931) (i), 48–80; Hostie, *ibid.* 40 (1932) (ii), 476–87; Morelli in *Rivista*, 24 (1932), 388–404, 483–506; Gihl in *Nordisk T.A.* 3 (1932), 38–64; Castberg in *Hague Recueil*, 43 (1933) (i), 313–81; Strupp, *ibid.* 47 (1934) (i), 301–88; Le Fur, *ibid.* 55 (1935) (iv), 192–213; Kaufmann, *ibid.* 55 (1935) (iv), 491–524; Basdevant, *ibid.* 58 (1936) (iv), 497–522; Wengler in *Z.ö.R.* 16 (1936), 333–92; Kopelmanas in *R.I.* 3rd series, 18 (1937), 88–143, and in *R.I.* (*Paris*), 21 (1938), 101–50; Maranini in *Annuario di diritto internazionale*, 2 (1939), 144–71; Barile in *Comunicazione e Studi*, 5 (1953), 141–229; Morelli in *Hague Recueil*, 89 (1956) (i), 450–471; Vallindas in *Festschrift Spiropoulos* (1957), pp. 425–31.

SUPPLEMENTARY BIBLIOGRAPHY ON THE SCOPE OF THE VALIDITY OF THE SOURCES OF INTERNATIONAL LAW

Phillimore, 1, §§ 27–33; Bluntschli, §§ 1–16; Nys, 1, 121–37; Fauchille, §§ 40–4(15); Schwarzenberger, pp. 79–86; Smith, 1, 14–36; Sibert, 1, 21–30; Jenks, *The Common Law of Mankind* (1958), pp. 62–172; Heilborn, *Grundbegriffe des Völkerrechts* (1912), §§ 10–12; Decevla, *Concetti di 'Civiltà' e di 'Nazioni Civili' nel diritto internazionale* (1937); Cavaglieri in *R.G.* 18 (1911), 259–92; Wright in *A.J.* 20 (1926), 265–8; Kunz in *Z.ö.R.* 7 (1927), 86–99, and the same, *Staatenverbindungen* (1929), pp. 258–73; Kelsen in *Hague Recueil*, 42 (1932) (iv), 178–81; Basdevant, *ibid.* 58 (1936) (iv), 484–96; Lauterpacht, *ibid.* 62 (1937) (iv), 188–206; Wilk in *A.J.* 45 (1951), 648–70; Fitzmaurice in *Hague Recueil*, 92 (1957) (ii), 95–108; Jennings in *B.Y.* 34 (1958), 350–4.

CHAPTER 3

THE SUBJECTS
OF INTERNATIONAL LAW

47. *The definition of subjects of international law*

As in any other legal system, so also in the international sphere the subjects of law are the persons, national and juridical, upon whom the law confers rights and imposes duties. In international law these persons are normally States; but they are not so exclusively. Organizations of States, having a different juridical personality from the States composing them, may and have become subjects of international law. This is hardly startling seeing that it is difficult to deny to States acting in association the unchallenged legal personality which they possess when acting in isolation. Individuals possess in a limited sphere international legal personality, not always accompanied by corresponding procedural capacity, accorded to them expressly or by implication. For these reasons the relevant part of the definition of international law given above[1] speaks of international law as a body of rules 'which confer rights and impose obligations primarily, though not exclusively, upon sovereign States'. However, the view that entities other than States can be subjects of international law has been denied by many; and although opposition to it has receded under the impact of modern developments it cannot, as yet, be said that it has been generally accepted. Its effects linger, in some ways, in existing international law.

48. *The traditional view*

According to what may be described as the traditional view in the matter, States only and exclusively are the subjects of international law. In particular, on that view, individuals are not the subjects of international law; they are its objects in the sense that by customary and conventional law States may be bound to observe certain rules of conduct in relation to individuals. Thus, while they may be bound to accord privileged treatment to foreign diplomatic representatives, the latter are not on that account subjects of international law; the right to privileged treatment is the right of their own State.

[1] See above, p. 9.

136

SUBJECTS OF INTERNATIONAL LAW

Similarly, although aliens residing in the territory of a foreign State are entitled to be treated by it in conformity with rules of international law, according to the traditional view the resulting rights are not the rights of the alien but of his State.[1] Although in concessionary or similar contracts made with a foreign State the individual alien may agree not to have recourse to protection by his own State until he has exhausted the local remedies available to him, he cannot effectively renounce the protection of his own State if the rights recognized for his benefit by international law have been violated; for these are not his rights but those of his State. Further, it would seem to follow from the view stated above that a treaty cannot directly confer rights upon individuals and, generally, that international law cannot do so unless these rights are incorporated as part of municipal law. The rigid exclusion of bodies other than States and of individuals from exercising any procedural capacity before international tribunals would appear to be yet another consequence of the traditional doctrine. As will be shown in this chapter, there are other equally far-reaching consequences of that view as here outlined.

In its main aspects the doctrine stated above gives an accurate picture of the existing position in international law. However, it is important to qualify it; to note the numerous exceptions to its operation; and, above all, to bear in mind that the range of subjects of international law is not rigidly and immutably circumscribed by any definition of the nature of international law but is capable of modification and development in accordance with the will of States. and the requirements of international intercourse. These propositions will now be considered in relation: (*a*) to collective bodies other than States; (*b*) to individuals.

49. *Collective bodies other than States*

International practice has recognized that bodies other than States may on occasions be endowed by international law with rights and made subject to its duties. This may occur, for instance, in the case of persons engaged in hostilities against their lawful Government

---

[1] For an authoritative statement of this principle see the following passage of the Judgment of the Permanent Court of International Justice in the case of the *Serbian Loans*: 'reference should be made to what the Court has said on several occasions, and in particular in Judgments No. 2 and 13, namely, that by taking up a case on behalf of its nationals before an international tribunal, a State is asserting its own right—that is to say, its right to ensure, in the person of its subjects, respect for the rules of international law' (Series A, nos. 20/21, p. 17). See also the *Chorzów Factory case* (*Merits*) (*ibid.* no. 17, pp. 27, 28).

137

and recognized as belligerents by other States. Such belligerents, without having been recognized as a State, become entitled to exercise as against neutrals certain rights of war. They also become subject to the obligations of the law of war. The same, on a more limited scale, applies to persons recognized as insurgents. In a different sphere, political units not as yet endowed with full statehood have been treated as subjects of international law. This was the case of the Holy See between its extinction as a State in 1870 and the restoration of its temporal sovereignty in the Lateran Treaty of 1929 in the international sphere. In the intervening period the Holy See, although not a State in international law, concluded treaties and sent and received diplomatic representatives—it was a subject of international law. The British Dominions, prior to their achieving full statehood in the sphere of international relations, acted and were treated for various purposes—for instance, in the matter of conclusion of treaties and diplomatic intercourse—as fully sovereign States.

Moreover, it is now generally recognized, in a variety of treaties and otherwise, that international public bodies composed of States possess an international personality and as such are subjects of international law. This applies, in particular, to the so-called specialized agencies of the United Nations such as the International Labour Organisation, the International Civil Aviation Organization, the Food and Agriculture Organization, the United Nations Educational and Cultural Organization, and others. The constitutions of these bodies provide for a measure of separate personality in respect of each of them. Thus the constitution of the Food and Agriculture Organization lays down that 'the Organization shall have the capacity of a legal person to perform any legal act appropriate to its purpose which is not beyond the powers granted to it by this Constitution'.[1] The Treaty of 1952 constituting the European Coal and Steel Community provides not only generally that the Community shall have juridical personality but also specifically that in its international relationships the Community shall enjoy the juridical capacity necessary for the exercise of its functions and the attainment of its ends.[2] The capacity of public international organizations to conclude treaties is recognized in their constitutions

[1] Article xv(1) of the Constitution. The constitutions of other specialized agencies and other international organizations confine themselves to laying down that the organization shall enjoy in the territory of each of its members such legal capacity as may be necessary for the exercise of its functions and the fulfilment of its objectives.
[2] Article 6 of the Treaty: *A.J.* 46 (1952), Suppl. p. 109.

SUBJECTS OF INTERNATIONAL LAW

and frequently acted upon in practice. They have concluded agreements with one another, with the United Nations, and with individual States, and these have been registered like 'every treaty and every international agreement' under Article 102 of the Charter. Thus, for instance, the International Labour Organisation concluded, in 1946, an agreement with Switzerland concerning the privileges and immunities of the Organisation in that country.[1] The Treaty of 1957 establishing the European Atomic Energy Community provides expressly that, within the limits of the powers conferred upon it, the Community may enter into agreements or conventions with an outside State or an international organization.[2] The specialized agencies possess a degree of procedural capacity before the International Court of Justice as a result of having been granted, in Article 96 of the Charter of the United Nations, the right to ask, subject to authorization by the General Assembly, for an Advisory Opinion of the Court. That authorization has invariably been granted in general terms[3] and has been used.[4] Previously the international personality of public international organizations had been recognized in various ways by decisions of various courts.[5] The international personality of numerous other bodies—such as the Reparation Commission,[6] the international river commissions or the Cape Spartel Lighthouse Commission[7]—has often been asserted, probably with justification.[8]

---

[1] *U.N.T.S.* 15, 378.   [2] Article 101 of the Treaty: *A.J.* 51 (1957), Suppl. p. 984.

[3] For details see Lauterpacht, *International Law and Human Rights* (1950), p. 16. See also the same in *Grotius Society*, 32 (1946), 1–41.

[4] See Advisory Opinion of 23 October 1956, in the case of the *Judgments of the Administrative Tribunal of the International Labour Organization upon Complaints made against UNESCO* (*I.C.J. Reports* 1956, p. 77).

[5] In 1931 the Italian Court of Cassation held in the case of *International Institute of Agriculture* v. *Profili* (*Annual Digest*, 5 (1929–30), Case no. 254) that the International Institute of Agriculture was an 'international person . . . free . . . from interference by the sovereign power of the States composing the Union [i.e., the Institute of Agriculture]'. The Court overruled the Court of Appeal of Rome which had held that the Institute was not a subject of international law seeing that it did not exercise sovereignty over a fixed territory and a population. See also *Godman* v. *Winterton*, decided in 1940 by the English Court of Appeal (*Annual Digest*, 11 (1919–42), Case no. 111), where it was held that the members of the Intergovernmental Committee for Refugees were entitled to jurisdictional immunity seeing that it was a Committee of sovereign States—a line of reasoning which may be regarded as in accordance with the view, suggested in the text above, that the international personality of public international bodies and their quality as subjects of international rights and duties follows from the fact that they are associations of States of which each is a subject of law. See also *International Refugee Organisation* v. *Republic S.S. Corp.* decided by the United States Court of Appeals (*I.L.R.* 18 (1951), Case no. 140).

[6] See Fischer Williams in *B.Y.* 13 (1932), 33–5, and in *A.J.* 24 (1930), 665.

[7] For a bibliography on the international personality of these bodies see Jenks in *B.Y.* 22 (1945), 267 n. 1. See also Morelli in *Hague Recueil*, 89 (1956) (i), 557–84, and in

INTERNATIONAL LAW—THE GENERAL PART

The question of the position of the League of Nations as a subject of international law was widely discussed but never judicially determined. On the other hand, in the Advisory Opinion in the case concerning *Reparation for Injuries Suffered in the Service of the United Nations* the International Court of Justice rejected the view that only States can be subjects of international law and affirmed the international personality of the United Nations as being indispensable to the fulfilment of the purposes for which it was created. The Court pointed out, with regard to the more general question of subjects of international law, that 'throughout its history, the development of international law has been influenced by the requirements of international life' and that 'the progressive increase in the collective activities of States has already given rise to instances of action upon the international plane by certain entities which are not States'.[1] 'Such new subjects of international law', the Court explained, 'need not necessarily be States or possess the rights and obligations of statehood.' For 'the subjects of law in any legal system are not necessarily identical in their nature or in the extent of their rights, and their nature depends upon the needs of the community'.[2] As already stated, the question of the international legal personality

Rivista, 40 (1957), 3–25; Zemanek in *Ö.Z.ö.R.* 7 (1956), 335–72. As to the contractual capacity of international unions see Capotorti in *Comunicazioni e Studi*, 7 (1955), 145–98.

[2] From public international organizations—which are organizations composed of States—there must be distinguished international organizations of individuals and private associations, of which there is a very considerable number. A French tribunal has held that a Committee of debenture holders of the Danube-Adriatic Railway Company, a Committee empowered by the Treaty of Trianon of 1919 to represent the interests of the holders, was 'necessarily and validly endowed . . . with legal personality in international law' which enabled it to sue in French courts: see *Vigoureux v. Comité des Obligataires Danube-Save-Adriatique (I.L.R.* 18 (1951), Case no. 1). On the consultative status of private international organizations by virtue of Article 71 of the Charter authorizing the Economic and Social Council to make 'suitable arrangements for consultation with non-governmental organizations which are concerned with matters within its competence' as well as by virtue of the constitutions of the various specialized agencies see Lauterpacht, *International Law and Human Rights* (1950), pp. 23–6. Also, as to the access of non-governmental organizations to the Headquarters of the United Nations for consultative purposes, see Liang in *A.J.* 48 (1954), 434–50.

[1] *I.C.J. Reports* 1949, p. 174.

[2] *Ibid.* at p. 178. As international personality is not limited to States, the latter are bound to fulfil international duties—i.e. duties prescribed by general international law —not only in relation to other States but, in proper cases, to international persons generally. This explains why in the *Reparation for Injuries* case the International Court of Justice held that the United Nations was entitled to bring a claim even against a non-member State, although in the same case the Court held that the basis of the claim by the United Nations was a breach of a duty to it. For, once the Court found that the United Nations was endowed by the Charter with international personality not only in relation to its Members but *erga omnes* (*ibid.* at p. 185), it followed that all States—whether Members of the United Nations or not—owed it duties as prescribed by general international law. *Sed quaere.* See Fitzmaurice in *B.Y.* 29 (1952), 21.

SUBJECTS OF INTERNATIONAL LAW

of an association of States each of which is indisputably a subject of international law ought not to give rise to difficulty. However, that Advisory Opinion must be regarded as one of the most important pronouncements of the Court inasmuch as it provided a much-needed qualification of the doctrine that only sovereign States are the subjects of international law.

It may also be noted that international practice recognizes in the contractual field a measure of international personality of territorial units, such as colonies and dependencies, which are not States but which nevertheless are admitted to participation in their own name in public organizations of States such as the Universal Postal Union or the World Health Organization.

50. *The individual as a subject of international law*

As a matter of moral principle, individuals have no independent position in international law and any rights which they may possess and any duties to which they may be subject in consequence of international law are rights and duties prescribed by the municipal law of the State. However, that principle is not absolute, and it is necessary to bear in mind the numerous exceptions which the practice of States has already engrafted upon it. These exceptions cover both rights and duties created by international custom and treaty. With regard to duties, the most important example of direct subjection of individuals to international law is the operation of the law of war. It is an established principle that individual members of the armed forces of a belligerent are bound as such by the law of war and that the belligerent into whose hands they may fall is entitled to punish them for violations of that law—even if, at least in the case of ruthless and inhuman crimes against the law of war, they acted in obedience to superior orders. It was by reference mainly to violations of the law of war that the International Tribunal for the Trial of Major War Criminals rejected, in 1946, the view that, as States only are subjects of international law, there could be no individual responsibility for the violation of the laws of war. It is often contended, without apparent exaggeration, that piracy *jure gentium* is no mere formula and that it constitutes a direct imposition upon individuals of the duty, under international law, not to commit piracy—although there is room for the view that States exercise jurisdiction over aliens in the matter of piracy by virtue of a customary rule according to which States concede to each other the right to exercise jurisdiction over their subjects for the commission of piracy rendered criminal by municipal law. Moreover, the municipal law of many States penalizes in other spheres what are termed violations of the law of nations, for instance, offences against foreign diplomatic representatives. In an early case, *Respublica* v. *De Longchamps*, decided in 1784 by a Pennsylvania Court, the accused—who had insulted the French ambassador—was found guilty of a 'violation of the law of nations'.[1] In a distinct sense, in countries in which international law is, by legislation or otherwise,[2] incorporated as part of the law of the land, it may be considered that the duties—as well as rights—of international law are directly operative in relation to individuals; this is so although such direct effect of international law is due to a general act of incorporation. The constitutions of some countries provide expressly that international law directly creates rights and duties for the inhabitants of the State.[3] Moreover, treaties may impose duties directly upon individuals. This is probably the effect of the Convention of 1948 for the Prevention and Punishment of the Crime of Genocide.

Similarly, both customary and conventional international law may confer rights directly upon individuals. In the Advisory Opinion concerning the *Jurisdiction of the Courts of Danzig*, the Permanent Court held that although in principle a treaty cannot, as such, create direct rights and obligations for private individuals, 'the very object of an international agreement, according to the intention of the contracting parties, may be the adoption by the parties of some definite rules creating individual rights and obligations and enforceable by national courts'.[4] The Court rejected the view that as the provisions of a treaty adopted in favour of Danzig railway officials had not been incorporated in Polish law, those officials had no enforceable right of action. As will be indicated presently, the contracting States may agree to create in favour of individuals rights enforceable directly not only before national but also before international tribunals. To the extent to which the Charter of the United Nations established the legal obligation of its members to respect human rights and fundamental freedoms (though there are

---

[1] 1 Dallas Reports 111. [2] See below, p. 154.

[3] See, e.g., Article 25 of the Constitution of the Federal Republic of Germany of 1949.

[4] Series B, no. 15, p. 17. In the Advisory Opinion, given in 1950, on the *International Status of South-West Africa*, the International Court of Justice assumed, without elaborating the point, that as the result of certain resolutions adopted in 1923 by the Council of the League of Nations in the matter of petitions from the inhabitants of mandated territories, these inhabitants acquired a corresponding right—a right under international law —and that right was subsequently maintained by Article 80 of the Charter of the United Nations: *I.C.J. Reports* 1950, p. 133.

SUBJECTS OF INTERNATIONAL LAW

many who deny the provisions in question the character of a legal obligation), it conferred upon individuals a corresponding right not dependent for its international validity upon national legislation, and even though unaccompanied by effective provisions for its enforcement. To that extent the Charter constituted the individual a subject of international law. Similarly, though more indirectly, this is also the effect, in one important respect, of the Agreement of 8 August 1945 between the four Principal Powers establishing an International Military Tribunal for the Punishment of the Major War Criminals. That Agreement provided, *inter alia*, for the punishment of crimes against humanity. These were acts deemed to be violative of the sanctity of human personality to such a degree as to make it irrelevant whether or not they were committed in obedience to the law of the State. The inclusion of crimes against humanity in an international instrument reflected the acknowledgement of fundamental human rights of the individual recognized by international law and grounded in considerations superior to the law of the State. To that extent, again, the instrument in question recognized the individual as a subject of a fundamental international right.[1]

51. *The procedural capacity of individuals in the international sphere*

The significance of the status of individuals as direct beneficiaries of rights conferred by treaty or customary international law—and, in consequence thereof, as subjects of international law—has been somewhat obscured by the fact that, in the present state of the law, their procedural capacity is severely limited. In particular, apart· from exceptional cases they have no right to appear as parties before international tribunals. Article 34 of the Statute of the International Court, the drafting of which was influenced by the predominant view of the exclusiveness of States as subjects of international law, lays down expressly that 'Only States may be parties in cases before the Court'.[2] Various treaties providing for the settlement of claims arising out of injuries to individuals clearly provide that the claims shall be presented by Governments; that agents and counsel shall be appointed by Governments;[3] and that

[1] See Lauterpacht, *International Law and Human Rights* (1950), pp. 35–8, and Schwelb in *B.T.* 23 (1946), 178–226.

[2] See Oppenheim, II, 54. And see, as to the position of individuals in connection with the advisory jurisdiction of the Court, Gross in *A.J.* 52 (1958), 16–40.

[3] See, e.g., the provisions of the Treaty of 8 September 1923 between the United States of America and Mexico, setting up a General Claims Commission. For the text of the Convention see Feller, *The Mexican Claims Commission*, 1923–1934 (1935), p. 321. And see *ibid.* pp. 83–90, for an account of the position of the individual claimants before the Commission.

143

INTERNATIONAL LAW—THE GENERAL PART

the latter shall retain decisive control over the claim and its prosecution.[1] However, although this is, in general, the existing legal position, some qualifying considerations must be kept in mind.

In the first instance, a person or organization may be a subject of international law—i.e. directly endowed by international law with rights and charged with duties—without at the same time enjoying full procedural capacity by way of being able to claim before international tribunals and agencies any rights thus granted. Thus if the Charter of the United Nations were to impose unequivocally upon its Members the legal obligation to respect human rights and fundamental freedoms,[2] and if the faculty to invoke these obligations were confined to the United Nations as such or its Member States, without conferring upon the individual an independent status before the organs of the United Nations for that purpose, the individual could still properly be considered a subject of international law in that sphere. In the European Convention for the Protection of Human Rights and Fundamental Freedoms, 1950, provision was made not only for securing human rights as there defined but also for the implementation of those provisions by the action both of the signatory States and, as soon as a requisite number of States have agreed thereto, by private individuals themselves. The resulting rights are vested in the individual inhabitants of the States concerned, independently of whether they have been made part of the law of the signatory States. Individuals are subjects of the rights in question by virtue of the provisions of the Convention even before their right to petition the Commission has been recognized. There are treaties which contain clauses providing

---

[1] For an emphatic instance of the affirmation of the full control of the State over claims adjudicated before an international tribunal see *Z. & F. Assets Realization Corporation et Al.* v. *Hull, Secretary of State, et Al.* (*Annual Digest*, 10 (1941–2), Case no. 134). See, however, for some qualifications of this rule *American-Mexican Claims Bureau* v. *Morgenthau* (*ibid.* 9 (1938–40), Case no. 106); *Administrative Decision No. 1* in the Tripartite Claims Commission, 1927 (*ibid.* 4 (1927–8), Case no. 172); *William A. Parker* case, decided by the Mexican-United States General Claims Commission (*ibid.* 3 (1925–6), Case no. 178) and, by the same Commission, the *North American Dredging Company* case (*ibid.* Case no. 179). On the other hand, as laying down the principle that in concluding treaties the Crown does not act as trustee of the subject and that therefore the latter has no legal right to any compensation provided for in a treaty, see *Civilian War Claimants' Association Ltd.* v. *The King* [1932] A.C. 14; 46 T.L.R. 581; 47 T.L.R. 102; *Administrator of German Property* v. *Knoop* [1933] Ch. 439; *Gschwind* v. *Swiss Confederation*, decided by the Swiss Federal Court in 1932 (*Annual Digest*, 6 (1931–2), Case no. 120); *Receiver in Bankruptcy of the N.V. 'Zeilschip Nest'* v. *The State of the Netherlands*, decided by the Hague Court of Appeal on 14 January 1937 (*ibid.* 8 (1935–7), Case no. 117). And see *B.Y.* 13 (1932), 163, 164.

[2] As stated above, p. 142, it is controversial whether the provisions of the Charter in the matter amount to a clear legal obligation on the part of the Members of the United Nations.

144

for the treatment of individuals who possess no nationality and whose rights cannot therefore be protected by a State of which they are nationals; those rights can only be protected by the various States signatories of the treaty. The Minorities Treaties as well as the treaty provisions in the matter of mandated and trust territories make it possible for the parties thereto to invoke the jurisdiction of the International Court concerning the interpretation and application of these provisions with regard to the interests both of their nationals and of persons who are not their nationals. The rule as to the 'nationality of claims' cannot be invoked in cases such as these. The treaties in question offer examples of rights which are created by international law and whose international existence—and the attribution to the individual of the quality of a subject of international law resulting from them—is independent either of any incorporation of such rights into the municipal law of any State or of the formal procedural capacity of individuals to assert the rights in question in their own name.

Secondly, there are instances in which such procedural capacity has been created, wholly or in part, in favour of individuals. In the Statute of the proposed—and eventually unratified—International Prize Court adopted at the Second Hague Peace Conference of 1907, private claimants were given the right to appeal to that Court against judgments of national prize courts.[1] In the Treaty which, in 1907, established the Central American Court of Justice between the five Central American Republics, individuals were given the right of direct access to the Court.[2] In the Treaty of Versailles the nationals of the Allied Powers were accorded the right to advance against Germany claims in their own name and, if so desired, without the assistance of agents appointed by their Governments.[3] The Upper Silesian Convention of 1922 between

---

[1] See Oppenheim, II, 485.

[2] For an account of the case of *Diaz* v. *Guatemala*, brought under that Treaty and involving a claim for false arrest, imprisonment and expulsion, see Hudson, *The Permanent Court of International Justice, 1920–1942* (1943), p. 54.

[3] But see Anzilotti, p. 136, for a different view. See also, generally, as to the Mixed Arbitral Tribunals, Blühdorn in *Hague Recueil*, 41 (1932) (iii), 174–6. And see generally on the access of individuals to international tribunals: Fleury, *Un nouveau progrès de la justice internationale: L'accès des particuliers aux Tribunaux internationaux* (1932); Schulé, *Le droit d'accès des particuliers aux juridictions internationales* (1934); *Annuaire*, 33 (1927) (ii), 601–26; Rundstein in *R.I.* 3rd ser. 10 (1929), 431–53; 763–83; Borchard in *A.J.* 24 (1930), 359–65; Ténékidès in *R.I.* 3rd ser. 13 (1932), 89–111; Baumgarten, *ibid.* pp. 742–99; Séfériadès in *Hague Recueil*, 51 (1935) (i), 5–120; Kaufmann, *ibid.* 54 (1935) (iv), 420–7; Idelson in *Grotius Society*, 30 (1944), 50–66. As to the access of individuals to international authorities by way of petition see Richard, *Le droit de pétition* (1932); and Feinberg in *Hague Recueil*, 40 (1932) (ii); 529–640.

INTERNATIONAL LAW—THE GENERAL PART

Germany and Poland not only established a tribunal open to the nationals of both parties; it also gave it jurisdiction to entertain actions brought by nationals of either party against their own State, notwithstanding the contention of Poland that under international law an individual cannot invoke the aid of an international authority against his own State.[1] In the same case the Tribunal held that a national of a third State, which was not a party to the treaty in question, could exercise rights enforceable before the Tribunal.[2]

In fact, apart from the somewhat unreal emanations of the doctrine that only States—as the exclusive subjects of international law—possess procedural capacity in the international sphere, there is no true obstacle to further developments in that direction. Undoubtedly, so long as the principle of obligatory jurisdiction of international tribunals as between States has not been adopted, it would be premature to urge that individuals should be in the position to bring Governments against their will before an international jurisdiction. However, there is no reason why international tribunals should not, with the agreement of Governments, adjudicate with regard to claims advanced by and made against individuals, including those in the sphere of criminal responsibility. International practice contains instances of proceedings of this nature.[3] As stated, no such power to entertain claims advanced by private bodies or individuals, or even public bodies other than States,[4] is vested in the International Court of Justice; Article 36 of its Statute limits its jurisdiction to disputes between States.[5] There is no intrinsic

[1] See *Steiner and Gross* v. *Polish State*: *Annual Digest*, 4 (1927–8), Case no. 188.

[2] *Ibid.* Case no. 287.

[3] As to criminal responsibility see above, p. 133. For an example of a special arbitral tribunal created by agreement between a Government and a private party, and deciding . on the basis not of municipal law but of international law or general principles of law, see above, p. 77.

[4] This situation may appear somewhat anomalous in view of the Advisory Opinion given by the Court in 1949 in the *Reparation for Injuries* case, where it held that the United Nations has the capacity for certain purposes to bring an international claim (see above, p. 140). This means, presumably, a claim before an international tribunal—but not, at present, before the international tribunal which is the principal judicial organ of the United Nations.

[5] A possible line of development in this sphere might consist in enlarging the present scope of Article 36 so as to give the Court jurisdiction not only in disputes between States but also in disputes between States and private or public bodies or private individuals in cases in which States have consented, in advance or by special agreement, to appear as defendants before the Court. An extended jurisdiction of this nature, if invoked with some frequency, might necessitate consequential changes in the Statute or the Rules of the Court, for instance, by enabling the Court to sit in divisions. The existing Statute authorizes the Court to create special chambers. It will be noted that, in effect, the vast majority of cases decided by the Court have involved claims arising from actual or alleged injuries to private persons.

SUBJECTS OF INTERNATIONAL LAW

necessity, in the light of the definition presented earlier,[1] to confine international law—and its adjudicatory agencies—to relations between States. International law can properly be comprehended as regulating the rights and duties of States in the international sphere and, as the result of international custom and agreement, also in relation to entities other than States. It must also be noted that international practice recognizes a distinct measure of procedural capacity of individuals before international organs. That has included, in varying degrees, the right of petition before such bodies as the Mandates Commission, the Minorities Commission, the Trusteeship Council and the European Commission of Human Rights.

The quality of a subject of international law—i.e. the capacity of being a subject of rights created or recognized by international law—does not, as already stated, depend upon the capacity to claim or enforce such rights in the beneficiary's own name. Nor does it depend upon whether the persons or body concerned are a contracting party in relation to the instrument creating such rights. It is sufficient if such rights are created in their favour and are effectively vested in them.[2] Moreover, although the contractual capacity of individuals in relation to States and with effect in the sphere of international law is not as yet recognized in international practice—with the effect, for instance, that such agreements are not capable of registration as 'international treaties and agreements' under Article 102 of the Charter—it is not certain that they cannot be so recognized at all. International law is not exclusively a law governing the relations between sovereign States. It is wide enough, especially having regard to the applicability of general principles of law as one of its sources, to include agreements made by States with persons other than States and not expressly or by implication made subject to the municipal law of such States.

52. *The rights and duties of States as rights and duties of man*

It has been shown that although the question as to who are the subjects of international law is to some extent of a doctrinal character,

---

[1] See above, p. 9.

[2] For a different view see the valuable contribution by Sperduti, 'L'individu et le droit international', in *Hague Recueil*, 90 (1956) (ii), 824, who suggests that as individuals are not persons in relation to whom States undertake direct contractual engagements, they are not, for that reason, invested by international law with subjective legal rights proper. However, he admits that individuals possess in international law the legal powers for putting into effect the engagements contracted for their benefit and that therefore they are 'titulaires d'intérêts internationaux légitimes' (*ibid.*).

it has important practical implications. The answer to that question has influenced considerably the existing law relating to access of individuals—and, generally, of bodies other than States—to international tribunals and agencies. However, its importance goes much further and explains the occasional emphasis of the discussion with which it has been surrounded. This is so in particular in the field of duties imposed by international law. Individuals are subjects of international law in the sense that—in Westlake's phrase[1]—the duties and rights of States are the duties and rights of men who comprise them. The composite personality of the State is not a sufficient reason for disregarding the fact either that the State is not an irresponsible instrumentality of power but primarily an expression of the legal order operating within a defined territory or that its conduct is imputable to the individual persons acting on its behalf and, in a wider sense, to the individuals comprising the State. Thus viewed, individuals are the subjects of international law. Unless the obligations of international law are directed to individual human beings, they are directed to no one. It is in that sense that the International Military Tribunal of Nuremberg, in rejecting, in 1946, the submission that violations of international law could not be attributed to individuals, said: 'Crimes against international law are committed by men, not by abstract entities, and only by punishing individuals who commit such crimes can the provisions of international law be enforced.'[2]

The realization that, in the matter of observance of the obligations of international law, individuals are the true subjects of international law must entail two main results of practical significance. First, it must tend to limit the consequences of the personification of the State inasmuch as these tend to foster the assertion of two standards of morality—one to be observed by the individual and the other by the personified State. While the ethical shortcomings of the international conduct of States have often been exaggerated, there is no doubt that the notion of the personified State as the only and true subject of international law, distinct from the individuals who compose it and act on its behalf, has not been without influence. Secondly, as appears from the passage in the Nuremberg Judgment just quoted, the effectiveness of international law is bound to suffer unless the notion gains ground that the true subjects of the duties

---

[1] *Papers*, p. 78. See also to the same effect Krabbe, *The Modern Idea of the State* (English transl. 1922), p. 240; Duguit, *Traité de droit constitutionnel* (1927), 1, 560; Kelsen, *Das Problem der Souveränität* (1920), pp. 130–4, 162–7. [2] *Annual Digest*, 13 (1946), at p. 221.

SUBJECTS OF INTERNATIONAL LAW

imposed by international law are not the metaphysical entities of the State but individual human beings.

Further, the principle that the rights and duties of States are but the rights and duties of man is of importance inasmuch as it lends emphasis to the idea—with which is bound up the progress of international law—that the individual human being is the ultimate unit and end of all law, national and international, and that the effective recognition and protection of 'the dignity and worth of the human person' and the development of human personality is the final object of law. In a different sphere, the recognition of the inalienable rights of the individual in relation to the State signifies the recognition of a legal authority, however impersonal, superior to the State itself—a notion which is congenial to the view that international law as a legal system can be understood only by reference to the principle that the State is subordinated to the international legal order. It signifies the establishment of a direct relationship between the individual and international law similar to the manner in which within a Federation the individual benefits directly from and is subject to federal law. To that extent it constitutes an essential stage in the progression of the international community towards the goal of federal integration.

Finally, such recognition of the individual as a subject of international law—a recognition based on the assumption of some fundamental and inalienable rights of man—in turn sets a limit, both legal and moral, to any omnipotence of the organized international community destructive of the freedom alike of the individual and of the national State. The notion of the subject of international law thus conceived, of which the essence is the denial of any basic difference between the subjects of international and municipal law, gains strength from the fact that in a large and growing number of States international law has been recognized, by judicial practice or express enactment, as forming an integral part of the law of the State. This is the essence of what may be described as the doctrine of incorporation, an account of which is given in the next chapter.

SUPPLEMENTARY BIBLIOGRAPHY ON SUBJECTS OF INTERNATIONAL LAW

The following is a selection of the vast literature on the question of subjects of international law: Kaufmann, *Die Rechtskraft des internationales Rechts* (1899); Westlake, *Papers*, p. 78; Kelsen, *Das Problem der Souveränität*

INTERNATIONAL LAW—THE GENERAL PART

und die Theorie des Völkerrechts (1920), pp. 124–34; the same in *Hague Recueil*, 42 (1932) (iv), 141–72, and *Principles of International Law* (1952), pp. 94–147; Krabbe, *The Modern Idea of the State* (English transl. 1921), pp. 240–5; Duguit, *Traité de droit constitutionnel* (1923), i, 551–60; Politis, *Les nouvelles tendances du droit international* (1927), pp. 59–93; Lauterpacht, *Analogies*, pp. 73–82; the same in *Hague Recueil*, 62 (1937) (iv), 207–43, in *L.Q.R.* 63 (1947), 438–60, and 64 (1948), 97–119, and *International Law and Human Rights* (1950), pp. 3–72; Knubben, *Die Subjekte des Völkerrechts* (1928); Spiropoulos, *L'individu en droit international* (1928); Segal, *L'individu en droit international* (1928); Ténékidès, *L'individu en droit international* (1928); Jessup, *A Modern Law of Nations* (1948), pp. 15–42; Sperduti, *L'individuo nel diritto internazionale* (1950), and in *Hague Recueil*, 90 (1956) (ii), pp. 733–846; Corbett, *Law and Society in International Relations* (1951); Anzilotti, pp. 121–36; Balladore Pallieri, pp. 167–72; Scelle, i, 167–72; Diena in *R.G.* 16 (1909), 57–76; Cavaglieri in *Rivista*, 17 (1925), 18–32, 168–87; Hamburger in *Z.I.* 36 (1926), 117–48; Akzin in *R.I.* (*Paris*), 4 (1929), 451–89; Bourquin in *Hague Recueil*, 35 (1931) (i), 33–47; Fischer Williams in *B.Y.* 13 (1932), 33–45; Hostie in *Hague Recueil*, 40 (1932) (ii), 488–509; Siotto-Pintor, *ibid.* 41 (1932) (iii), 251–357; Scelle, *ibid.* 46 (1933) (iv), 363–73; Strupp, *ibid.* 47 (1934) (i), 418–22, 463–8; Geöcze in *R.I.* (*Geneva*), 12 (1934), 119–34; E. Kaufmann in *Hague Recueil*, 54 (1935) (iv), 402–27; Herz in *Théorie du droit*, 10 (1936), 100–11; Schoen in *Z.V.* 23 (1939), 411–48; Preuss in *R.I.F.* 8 (1939), 160–74; Aufricht in *American Political Science Review*, 37 (1943), 217–43; Bourquin in *Études Georges Scelle* (1950), i, 37–54; De Soto, *ibid.* ii, 687–716; Wengler in *Lann Festschrift* (1953), pp. 341–65; McDougal in *Hague Recueil*, 82 (1953) (i), 227–56; Eustathiades, *ibid.* 84 (1953) (iii), 405–20; Morelli, *ibid.* 89 (1956) (i), 505–11.

CHAPTER 4

INTERNATIONAL LAW AND
THE LAW OF THE STATE

I. THE PRACTICAL AND THE DOCTRINAL ASPECTS

53. *The practical aspect*

The question of the relation of international law to the law of the State—to municipal law—is often referred to as being primarily a question of the application of international law, both customary and conventional, by municipal, i.e. national, courts and other organs of the State concerned with the administration of international law. It involves, in particular, the following issues: Are rules of international law applicable as such by courts and other organs of the State—that is to say, is international law directly binding upon them and upon individuals within the jurisdiction of the State, or must its rules be incorporated—'transformed'—as part of municipal law expressly or by implication? If so transformed by an express or implied act of incorporation, do the rules of international law lose their character as such and, when applied by the organs of the State, have they to be regarded as rules of municipal law pure and simple? When incorporated, generally or specifically, as part of the law of the State, can the rules thus incorporated be subsequently changed by an act of the national legislature with the result that municipal courts and agencies can no longer apply such rules and that the courts must henceforth apply municipal law even if inconsistent with international law? The preceding questions bear upon the position of international law before courts and other agencies administering the law within the State. The second main aspect of the mutual relations of international law and the law of the State is concerned with the position of the municipal law of States in the field of international law and before the organs administering it. Here the problem can be put in the form of a single question: To what extent, if any, is a State entitled to invoke its municipal law as an explanation of or excuse for its failure to comply with an obligation of international law? To put it differently, does municipal law override international law in the sense that the international obligations of a State are dependent upon and sub-

151

INTERNATIONAL LAW—THE GENERAL PART

ordinated to its municipal law, or does the fact that the latter does not measure up, in its content or application, to the international obligations of a State involve its international responsibility of a contractual, tortious or even criminal nature? This may be so although—and because—its courts are bound to apply municipal law even when it is inconsistent with international law.

54. *The doctrinal aspect*

Upon the above two questions, which are of practical importance for the administration of the law and which will be mainly considered in the present chapter, there have been engrafted a number of problems which are predominantly of a doctrinal character. They comprise the question of the primacy—the supremacy—of international law over municipal law or the reverse of that position; also, in view of their alleged total disparity and independence of one another, the question of co-ordination—of coexistence—of the two systems of law without involving the supremacy of one over the other. They comprise also the question whether international law is derived from and sanctioned by municipal law or whether the converse is true. Finally, these questions include that of the opposition between the so-called monistic and pluralistic theories of the relation between international and national law. According to one version of the monistic view there is only one universal legal order—the international—of which the national systems of law are subordinated and delegated branches. This is so, it is contended, largely because it is international law which determines the territorial and personal spheres of validity of the national systems of law and thus makes their coexistence legally comprehensible. This is not the only meaning of 'monism'. It is equally arguable that the rival doctrine, by virtue of which international law is derived by delegation—by recognition—from municipal law, is equally logical and 'monistic' at least from the point of view of each State concerned—for the result in that case also is that there exists logically only one system of law, namely, that based on municipal law. However, the latter approach has currently been described as dualistic or, rather, pluralistic inasmuch as it has been said to result, on analysis, in the existence of as many independent systems and conceptions of international law as there are States. In practice, that conception of the relation of international and municipal law has been 'dualistic' in a different sense. According to it, international law and municipal law are separate, independent, and wholly

INTERNATIONAL LAW AND THE LAW OF THE STATE

different legal orders which regulate different matters, which have different sources, which operate in relation to different subjects and which, as the result, lie in altogether different fields. The consequence of that disparity and independence of the international and national legal systems is that rules of international law cannot operate directly in the sphere of municipal law either in whole or in part. In order to be applicable by municipal courts, international law must have been incorporated by custom or statute as part of municipal law. Moreover, in view of the essential disparity of the two systems of law operating in notionally different fields, there can be no question of any conflict between them whatsoever.

It will be suggested that the doctrinal controversy outlined above, which has grown round the problem of the relation between international and municipal law, is to a large extent unreal and that, in fact, no practical consequences of importance follow from any of the solutions adopted—though in the course of the controversy doctrines have been propounded, in support of one or the other solution, which either did not, or no longer, correspond to existing law and which are essentially retrogressive. However, it is first necessary to examine the relation of international and municipal law with regard to those aspects which alone are of practical importance in the administration of justice and in the intercourse of States generally.

2. INTERNATIONAL LAW BEFORE NATIONAL COURTS AND AGENCIES

55. *In general*

The question of the extent, if any, to which as a matter of municipal law the organs of the State—i.e. courts and other agencies administering the law—apply international law is clearly a question of municipal law. As international law is largely implemented by the organs of the State—whether courts[1] or other agencies called upon to apply it—that question is of paramount importance. It is in practice independent of any doctrinal assumptions. It is a matter of ascertaining what is the position adopted in that matter by the municipal law of any particular country.

At the same time, the practice adopted in the matter by most States is of direct interest to international law not only because, as mentioned, it is through the judicial and other organs of the State acting within its territory that effect is normally given to much of

---

[1] See above, p. 80, on the place of decisions of municipal courts as a source of international law.

153

INTERNATIONAL LAW—THE GENERAL PART

international law but also because the constant and general practice of most States of treating international law as part of their domestic law may in itself amount to the creation of a customary rule of international law, expressive of a legal conviction of States, to that effect. That practice is the consequence of a voluntary and revocable decision of the State—whether express or implied, whether legislative or customary. It is nevertheless a fact. In the present context, it is not necessary to consider whether international law thus applied preserves its quality as such or whether as the result of its adoption as part of municipal law it is henceforth applied as municipal law. Nor is it necessary here to enquire whether such adoption is constitutive of a new legal principle or whether it is declaratory of the efficacy, within the State, of a body of rules the validity of which imposes itself irresistibly upon every civilized State. Our object in the present context is more limited. It is to ascertain the scope of and the degree to which the principle of adoption of international law as part of domestic law has become part of the practice of modern States, as well as the history of that practice, the limits of its application, its significance for international law as a whole, and the possibilities of its further development. An examination of these questions can most suitably be attempted by reference to the history and the existing practice of the doctrine of adoption in England— the country which first gave it articulate expression and to the impetus of which there must be traced, to a considerable extent, the spread of the principle of adoption throughout the world.

56. *Incorporation of international law by the common law of England. Customary international law*[1]

In 1765, Blackstone first formulated the principle of adoption in clear and solemn language:

the law of nations (whenever any question arises which is properly the object of its jurisdiction) is here adopted in its full extent by the common law of the land. And those acts of parliament, which have from time to time been made to enforce this universal law, or to facilitate the execution of its decisions, are not to be considered as introductive of any new rule, but merely as declaratory of the old fundamental constitutions of the kingdom; without which it must cease to be a part of the civilized world.[2]

---

[1] See, generally, as to the position in England, Westlake in *L.Q.R.* 22 (1906), 14–26 (reprinted in *Papers*, pp. 498–518); Picciotto, *The Relation of International Law to the Law of England and the United States of America* (1915); Lauterpacht in *Grotius Society*, 25 (1939), 51–88; McNair, *ibid.* 30 (1944), 11–21; Lefébure in *Z.ö.V.* 17 (1957), 568–612.

[2] *Commentaries on the Law of England*, bk. IV, ch. 5. In connection with the last words of the passage cited, reference may be made to the observation, which is open to question,

154

INTERNATIONAL LAW AND THE LAW OF THE STATE

It is of interest to note that in 1764 Blackstone had been counsel in the case of *Triquet* v. *Bath*,[1] in which Lord Mansfield, one of the greatest of English judges, laid down in emphatic terms the principle of adoption of international law 'to its full extent' as 'part of the law of England'.

The historic circumstances and causes, which cannot be elaborated here, of the doctrine of incorporation thus formulated are largely connected with the origins of international law as grounded in natural law and as expressive, together with the law merchant and maritime law, of a universal law of mankind[2] which of necessity must form part of the law of the land. It is sufficient to state that, subject to one apparent exception an account of which will be given presently,[3] and subject also to its doctrinal qualifications both by judges and writers,[4] and to the overriding supremacy of Acts of Parliament,[5] the doctrine of incorporation must, so far as customary international law is concerned, be regarded as forming part of English law. It has been so applied for two centuries in a manifold variety of cases.[6] Admittedly, novel cases have been decided by

in Maine's *International Law* (2nd ed. 1894), p. 38, to the effect that as the result of the judgment in the *Franconia* case (*Reg.* v. *Keyn*, referred to in n. 6 below)—a case directly germane to the subject here discussed—Great Britain by disclaiming the authority of international law may have placed herself 'outside the circle of civilised nations'.

[1] 3 Burr. 1478. Previously, in *Barbuit's Case* (Cas. t. Talb. 281), decided in 1735 and in which Lord Mansfield (then Mr William Murray) acted as counsel, Lord Talbot had affirmed that principle in similar language.

[2] For a concise and lucid account of these circumstances see Dickinson in *University of Pennsylvania Law Review*, 101 (1952), 26–34. See also Holdsworth, *A History of English Law*, 1 (1903), 300–37, and *Select Essays in Anglo-American Legal History*, 1 (1907), 289–331.

[3] See *Reg.* v. *Keyn*, below, n. 6.   [4] See below, p. 166.   [5] See below, p. 163.

[6] Reference must be made here to the case of *The Franconia* (*Reg.* v. *Keyn* (1876) 2 Ex.D. 63) which is regarded by some as being in the nature of a drastic departure from English practice on the subject (see the observation of Sir Henry Maine, cited at p. 154 n. 2 above). In that case a bare majority of the Court for Crown Cases Reserved held that, in the absence of a clear rule of English law to that effect, English courts had no jurisdiction to try an alien for an offence committed in British territorial waters. The decision might have signified a departure from the traditional practice if there had in fact existed at that time a rule of international law authorizing the jurisdiction of a State with regard to criminal offences committed by aliens within its territorial waters. In fact no such rule of international law had definitely crystallized at that time; the issue was controversial. It was largely on that issue that the Court was divided—though some of the judges insisted that even if there had been a clear rule of international law to that effect legislation expressly authorizing it would have been necessary. There is perhaps room for the view—which, however, is not quite consistent with the principle of incorporation —that in the case of a permissive rule of international law authorizing jurisdiction, municipal legislation giving effect to such authorization is necessary and that the need for such legislation is not obviously inconsistent with the principle of the direct operation of international law. The Territorial Waters Jurisdiction Act of 1878 declared that 'the rightful jurisdiction' of Her Majesty had 'always extended' without limitation over her coastal waters, and expressly provided for the application of criminal law to all offences therein committed. For an examination of the case of *The Franconia* see Lauterpacht,

155

INTERNATIONAL LAW—THE GENERAL PART

reference to international law as properly meeting a deficiency in municipal law. The law of jurisdictional immunities of States has largely been shaped in reliance upon international law as forming part of the law of the land.[1] Remedies hitherto unknown have been accorded on the ground that they followed clearly from international law. Thus, in the case of *Emperor of Austria* v. *Kossuth* the Court issued an injunction restraining the defendant, a leader of the revolutionary Government of Hungary, from printing currency in derogation of the rights of the Emperor, and said: 'A public right, recognised by the law of nations, is a legal right; because the law of nations is part of the common law of England.'[2] In the case of *Duke of Brunswick* v. *King of Hanover*, apparently the first case which raised the issue of the immunity of a foreigner from civil suit, the Court, in granting immunity, said: 'There is no English law applicable to the present subject, unless it can be derived from the law of nations, which, when ascertained, is to be deemed part of the common law of England.'[3] This prolonged practice permits the statement that in Great Britain customary international law is part of the municipal law, that it confers rights and imposes duties upon private persons, and that it is applied by courts as such without the necessity of proving any specific act of transformation. For reasons which will be indicated later, the position is different with regard to conventional law, i.e. international law established by treaty.

Analogies, p. 76 n., and in *Grotius Society*, 25 (1939), 10–12 [reprinted in vol. II of these Collected Papers]. See also Phillimore, I, § 198b; Maine, pp. 39–45; Stephen, *History of the Criminal Law of England* (1883), II, 29–42.

[1] See, e.g., the early cases decided by Lord Mansfield holding that the Statute of 7 Ann. c. 12 relating to diplomatic immunities was merely declaratory of the law of nations which in any case forms part of the law of the land; *Lockwood* v. *Coysgarne* (1765) 3 Burr. 1676; *Heathfield* v. *Chilton* (1767) 4 Burr. 2015. See also *Viveash* v. *Becker* (1814) 3 M. & S. 284, relating to consular immunities.

[2] (1861) 2 Giff. 628. And see *De Wutz* v. *Hendricks* (1824) S.C. 9 Moore 586; 2 Bing. 314, relating to the legality of loans in support of foreign revolutions.

[3] (1844) 6 Beav. 1. See also *De Haber* v. *The Queen of Portugal* (1851) 17 Q.B. 170, 208; *Magdalena Steam Navigation Co.* v. *Martin* (1859) 2 E. and E. 94; *West Rand Central Gold Mining Co.* v. *The King* [1905] 2 K.B. 391 (see above, p. 115); *In re Suarez* [1918] 1 Ch. 176, 192; *Engelke* v. *Musmann* [1928] A.C. 433, 449; *Commercial and Estates Co. of Egypt* v. *Board of Trade* [1925] 1 K.B. 271 (see below, p. 167). In his Dissenting Opinion in *The Lotus* case Lord Finlay said: 'International law, wherever applicable, is considered as part of the law of England, and our judges must apply it accordingly' (*P.C.I.J.* Series A, no. 10, p. 54). And see *ibid.* p. 75, for the reference by Judge Moore to 'the majestic stream of the common law, united with international law' which, after the passing of the Territorial Waters Jurisdiction Act of 1878, resumed 'its even and accustomed flow' which had been disturbed by the observations of some of the judges in the case of *The Franconia* (see above, p. 155, n. 6).

156

INTERNATIONAL LAW AND THE LAW OF THE STATE

57. *The rule of presumptive conformity with international law*

The substantive rule of incorporation of international law as part of municipal law has resulted in two rules of adjective law—one of which is a rule of interpretation and the other a rule of evidence. The rule of interpretation is that, while Acts of Parliament must be given effect even if contrary to international law,[1] they must, so far as possible, be interpreted so as not to imply any conflict with international law. That rule of interpretation is firmly embedded in the practice of British courts. However, the principle of the absolute superiority of Acts of Parliament, emphatically affirmed in numerous decisions[2] bearing upon the subject, has been accompanied by an equally emphatic judicial insistence that courts must do their utmost to interpret a statute so as not to impute to the legislature the intention to violate international law. The presumption that Parliament does not intend to act in a manner inconsistent with international law has been acted upon with a determination which on occasions has come near to a denial of the omnipotence of the legislature in matters affecting international law.[3] There is probably no case on record in which an English court has applied an Act of Parliament considered to be in violation of international law,[4] though there are such instances in other countries. Thus in *Politis* v. *The Commonwealth*[5] the High Court of Australia, in reliance upon the principle of the overriding supremacy of the legislature, upheld the legality of Regulations issued under an Act of Parliament which, in so far as it authorized Regulations imposing the duty of military.

---

[1] See below, p. 163.

[2] See, e.g., the observations of Dr Lushington in *The Annapolis*; *The Johanna Stoll*, Lush. 295; and of Lord Stowell in *Le Louis*, 2 Dods. 210, 251, 254. And see the clear statement by Lord Macmillan in *Croft* v. *Dunphy* [1933] A.C. 156; *Annual Digest*, 6 (1931–2), Case no. 82: 'Legislation of the Imperial Parliament, even in contravention of generally acknowledged principles of international law, is binding upon and must be enforced by the Courts of this country, for in these Courts the legislation of the Imperial Parliament cannot be challenged as *ultra vires*' (at p. 158).

[3] See, e.g., Lord Stowell in *Le Louis*, 2 Dods. 210, 251, 254: '. . . no nation can privilege itself to commit a crime against the law of nations by a mere municipal regulation of its own . . . the Legislature must be understood to have contemplated all that was within its power, and no more.' And see Lord Campbell in *Lopez* v. *Burslem* (1843) 4 Moore 300, 305 (while affirming at the same time the ultimately binding force of an Act of Parliament): 'the British Parliament certainly has no general power to legislate for foreigners out of the dominions and beyond the jurisdiction of the British Crown'.

[4] *Mortensen* v. *Peters* (1906) 14 S.L.T. 227, 43 S.L.R. 872—a Scottish case referred to below at p. 165—is occasionally cited as an instance of the application of an Act of Parliament which the Court itself held to be contrary to international law. *Sed quaere* whether the Court went to the length of any such clear admission. See below, p. 228.

[5] (1945) 70 C.L.R. 60; *Annual Digest* 12 (1943–5), Case no. 61.

157

service upon aliens, was in the view of the Court contrary to an established rule of international law.

58. *Proof of international law*

The second consequence of the accepted practice of incorporation is that the substance of international law, in contrast with the content of foreign law (which must be proved as a fact—usually by experts), is treated as a proper subject for judicial notice, suitably aided by legal argument on behalf of the parties, in the same way as Acts of Parliament or any branch of the common law.[1]

59. *The principle of incorporation in relation to treaties*

For reasons connected with British constitutional practice, treaties which affect private rights of persons subject to English law and which, having been ratified by Great Britain are internationally binding upon her, are nevertheless not enforceable by British courts unless an enabling Act of Parliament has been passed to render such enforcement possible. A treaty may affect private rights in a variety of ways. Thus, for instance, a treaty extending the jurisdictional immunities of foreign States or their diplomatic representatives to that extent deprives other persons of their ordinary remedies before British courts. A treaty of extradition authorizing the surrender to a foreign State of a person accused in that State of a criminal offence affects the right of a person to rely upon the constitutional remedy of habeas corpus. To state the rule in broader language, an enabling Act of Parliament is necessary, apart from certain exceptions,[2] to render possible the application by a British court of the provisions of a treaty which requires for its implementation a change in the existing law[3] and which, having been ratified by the Crown, is part of international law binding upon Great Britain.

To that extent the rule applicable to customary international law

[1] While there is no English judicial formulation of this view, it is believed to be in accordance with practice. The rule is clearly formulated in a number of American cases. See, e.g., *The Scotia* (1875) 14 Wall. 170, 187; *The New York* (1899) 175 U.S. 187. For a view contrary to that expressed in the text above see Picciotto (*op. cit.* below, p. 168), at pp. 103–5. [2] See below, p. 160.

[3] For an authoritative treatment of the subject see McNair, *The Law of Treaties* (1938), pp. 7–37. See also Carter in *I.L.Q.* 3 (1950), 413; Preuss in *Michigan Law Review*, 51 (1953), 1122–24. There are other treaties which require parliamentary sanction by way of an enabling Act, for instance, treaties in which Great Britain undertakes to guarantee a foreign loan—such as the Trade Facilities and Loans Guarantees Act, 1922, Section 2, in which Great Britain undertook to guarantee a proportion of the Austrian Loan—or treaties involving cession of British territory. However, such treaties do not in general raise the question of application of international law by British courts and are not therefore germane to the subject here discussed.

INTERNATIONAL LAW AND THE LAW OF THE STATE

—namely, that international law is part of the law of the land directly enforceable by the courts—does not apply in respect of treaties. Enabling legislation is necessary even if Parliament has previously expressed approval (by a resolution or motion falling short of legislation) of the terms of a treaty to be ratified by the Executive (a practice which although not clearly defined has been increasingly approaching the status of a constitutional convention). The reason for the departure, in respect of treaties, from the general rule that international law is directly operative as part of the law of the land, lies in the fact that in Great Britain the function of conclusion and ratification of treaties is within the prerogative of the Executive. Accordingly, but for the existing rule requiring an enabling Act of Parliament, the Executive would be in the position to affect the private rights of the citizen and generally alter the law of the land by the device of concluding and ratifying a treaty. That possibility does not exist in countries in which the action of the Legislature, or part of it, is necessary as a condition of ratification. In those countries implementation of a treaty by enabling legislation is not required except when the treaty itself, directly or by implication, renders such action necessary. This, for instance, is the case in the United States of America where the concurrent action of the Senate is necessary as a condition of ratification. There is thus, as a rule,[1] no

---

[1] For an interesting example of the treaty-making power being used, in effect, for (legislative) action which might otherwise be impossible under the Constitution see the American case of *State of Missouri* v. *Holland, United States Game Warden* (1920) 252 U.S. 416; Dickinson, *Cases*, p. 1037; *Annual Digest,* 1 (1919–22), Case no. 1 (with further references). And see Black in *Illinois Law Review,* 25 (1930, 1931), 911–28, for criticism of the decision, in which the Court held that the United States Migratory Birds Act of 1918 was valid, although dealing with a subject matter otherwise reserved by the Constitution for the legislation of the individual States, in view of the fact that a treaty had been concluded on the subject in 1916 and that by the Constitution treaties are declared the supreme law of the land—alongside of the Constitution and laws of the United States made in pursuance thereof. It was by reference to possibilities deemed to have arisen from decisions such as *State of Missouri* v. *Holland* that proposals have been made in the United States for constitutional amendment expressly eliminating these possibilities. Thus it was proposed in the abortive amendment introduced in 1952 by Senator Bricker that a treaty should become effective as internal law in the United States only through legislation *which would be valid in the absence of a treaty*. But see the statement, made in 1957 by Senator Bricker, that the amendment was not in opposition to the decision in *Missouri* v. *Holland*, and comment thereon by Oliver in *A.J.* 51 (1957), 606–8. For a discussion of the amendment see Whitton and Fowler in *A.J.* 48 (1954), 23–56; Finch, *ibid.* pp. 57–82; Sutherland in *H.L.R.* 67 (1953), 281–93; Alagia in *Georgetown Law Journal,* 42 (1954), 262–89. See also, as to the action taken thereon by the Senate, *ibid.* p. 494. See also—for a decision similar to that in *State of Missouri* v. *Holland* —*R.* v. *Burgess, ex. p. Henry*, decided in 1936 by the High Court of Australia: (1936), 55 C.L.R. 608, *Annual Digest,* 8 (1935–7), Case no. 19. With these judgments may be contrasted the important decision of the Judicial Committee of the Privy Council in *Attorney-General for Canada* v. *Attorney-General for Ontario* [1937] A.C. 326, *Annual Digest,* 8 (1935–7), Case no. 17. For comment thereon see a symposium in *Canadian Bar Review,*

INTERNATIONAL LAW—THE GENERAL PART

possibility of the treaty-making power being used as an instrument of internal legislation.

The requirement of enabling legislation is said to be qualified by exceptions—most of which are controversial or probably obsolete. Thus, for instance, it has been contended that the requirement does not apply to treaties of peace. In *Walker* v. *Baird*[1] it was contended on behalf of the Crown that a Treaty between Great Britain and France concerning the protection of lobster fisheries on and off the coasts of Newfoundland did not require enabling legislation for the reason that, although not a treaty of peace, it was analogous to one inasmuch as its object was to prevent friction which might lead to war. The Court, without denying—or affirming—the validity of the major proposition relating to treaties of peace, confined itself to stating that the case before it did not come within that category. It would appear that that exception is of doubtful validity. The same applies to the alleged exception of treaties conferring diplomatic or consular immunities. In particular, with regard to treaties of peace, recent practice has been to enact enabling legislation. Thus after the First World War the Treaty of Peace Act, 1919, relating to the Treaty of Versailles, provided that 'His Majesty may make such appointments, establish such offices, make such Orders in Council, and do such things as appear to him necessary for carrying out the said Treaty, and for giving effect to any of the provisions of the said Treaty.' The same procedure was adopted in respect of the Treaty of Peace with Italy in 1947. There is almost uniform authority for the proposition that treaties relating to the exercise of the belligerent rights of the Crown are enforceable without enabling legislation— apparently as a corollary to the theory that the waging of war is in the prerogative of the Crown.[2] Generally, however, the principle of enabling legislation with regard to rights sought to be enforced

15 (1937), 393–507, and in particular the articles by Mackenzie, pp. 436–54; Jennings, pp. 455–63; and Jenks, pp. 464–77. See also Stewart in *A.J.* 32 (1938), 36–62. The effect of the decision was to deny the legislative competence of the Dominion Parliament to give effect to certain International Labour Conventions assented to and ratified by the Dominion Legislature.   [1] L.R. [1892] A.C. 491.

[2] See, e.g., *Porter* v. *Freudenberg* [1915] 1 K.B. 857, where it was apparently assumed that Article 23(h) of the Hague Regulations respecting the Laws and Customs of War on Land was enforceable by British courts although that Convention has never received express legislative assent. See also *The Dirigo* [1919] P. 204 and earlier cases, referred to in McNair, p. 19. But it will be noted that enabling legislation has been passed to give effect to the various Red Cross Conventions of 1907, 1929 and 1949 (see e.g., Oppenheim, II, § 123, as to the 'distinctive emblem'). However, although, for instance, the Geneva Conventions Act, 1957, is entitled 'An Act to enable effect to be given to certain international conventions done at Geneva', it is arguable—it cannot be put higher than that—that the true object of the Act was to provide for the details and the machinery of implementation of those Conventions.

160

INTERNATIONAL LAW AND THE LAW OF THE STATE

before a court is well established in the United Kingdom.[1] It has been acted upon by other countries, in particular the members of the British Commonwealth of Nations,[2] in which the constitutional practice in the matter of ratification of treaties is the same as in the United Kingdom.

It is clear that the refusal—or inability—of English courts to apply the provisions of an internationally valid treaty which has not been previously incorporated as part of municipal law does not absolve the United Kingdom of any resulting international responsibility so far as the interests of foreign States or their nationals are concerned. Nor is any international remedy available to British subjects unable to obtain redress under a treaty to which the United Kingdom is validly a party. That anomalous situation, which is out of keeping with the general practice acknowledging the unity of international and municipal law, may to a large extent be avoided through the device of enacting the necessary enabling legislation prior to ratification of or accession to the treaty. In fact, that has increasingly become the practice of the United Kingdom. Thus the Geneva Conventions Act, 1957, passed to enable effect to be given to the four humanitarian international conventions concluded at Geneva in 1949 in the sphere of the conduct of war—the Red Cross conventions—became law on 31 July 1957; the Conventions themselves were ratified on 23 September 1957. Similarly, after the Second World War the enabling legislation with regard to the Treaties of Peace with Italy, Bulgaria, Finland, Hungary and Romania was passed on 29 April 1947 and the ratifications of those treaties were deposited on 15 September 1947. The growing practice of submitting treaties to parliamentary approval prior to ratification[3]—which is different from enabling legislation—may assist in promoting development in the direction of avoiding, or rendering unlikely, situations in which a treaty approved by Parliament cannot be given effect for the reason that Parliament has failed to pass the requisite enabling legislation.

---

[1] See *The Parlement Belge* (1879) 4 P.D. 129—the leading case on the subject. See also *Administrator of German Property* v. *Knoop* [1933] Ch. 439; *Annual Digest*, 6 (1931–2), Case no. 119; *Republic of Italy* v. *Hambro's Bank* [1950] Ch. 314; and see in this connection E. Lauterpacht in *I.C.L.Q.* 8 (1959), 188–90.

[2] See, e.g., the following Indian cases: *Birma* v. *State*, *I.L.R.* 17 (1950), Case no. 5; *Sharma* v. *State of West Bengal and Others* (a decision of the High Court of Calcutta) (*ibid.* 21 (1954), p. 272); and the following Canadian cases: *Re Arrow River Tributaries Slide & Boom Co.* [1932] 2 D.L.R. 250; *Annual Digest*, 6 (1931–2), Case no. 2; and *Francis* v. *The Queen* [1955] 4 D.L.R. 760; *I.L.R.* 22 (1955), p. 591. See also the decision of a Luxembourg Court in *H.* v. *Public Prosecutor* (*ibid.* 18 (1951), Case no. 6).

[3] See Lauterpacht, *Analogies*, p. 77 n., for references to the practice combining, in effect, the procedure of approval with that of enabling legislation.

INTERNATIONAL LAW—THE GENERAL PART

60. The limitations of the practice of incorporation. Executive determination involving questions of international law

The principle of recognition of international law as part of the law of the land seems, to some extent, to be limited by the fact that on certain issues of international law, or questions of fact germane to international law, courts accept as conclusive information or statements from the Executive department. In the United Kingdom this is known as the principle of the conclusiveness of statements of the Crown in matters relating to foreign affairs. They include such questions as the status of a foreign country or of its sovereign or whether a state of war exists between two foreign countries. Upon examination, these cases do not, as a rule, signify an exclusion of international law or its subjection to municipal law. Their true explanation is rather that on certain questions the agency which administers international law is not a court of law but the executive organ of government charged with the conduct of foreign affairs. Some of these questions which come before courts in this connection are essentially questions of fact; for instance, whether a State or person claiming diplomatic immunity is a person whose status as such has been recognized by the proper executive authority and whether he is on the list of persons accepted by them as enjoying diplomatic status. On the other hand, the extent of the immunity— or the very existence of immunity—to which that person is entitled in the circumstances of the case, for instance, having regard to the question whether the acts in respect of which immunity is claimed are of a public or private law nature, is a question of international law cognizable by courts.

In these cases reliance upon the opinion of the Executive, as being binding, which is deemed to be particularly qualified to obtain information and form an opinion on questions of fact is not inconsistent with the principle of the application of international law as part of the law of the land. The position is rendered more difficult and controversial when judicial submission to executive determination is due to a desire, expressed or inarticulate, not to embarrass the Executive or to make all organs of the State speak with one voice—a desire which has been judicially described as representing a maxim of policy rather than of law.[1]

---

[1] Lord Sumner in *Duff Development Company, Ltd.* v. *Government of Kelantan* [1924] A.C. 797 at p. 824. It will be noted that in other spheres the desire not to embarrass the Executive has not been a feature of judicial activity. See *Bank voor Handel en Scheepvaart* v. *Slatford* [1953] 1 Q.B. 248, at p. 266, *per* Devlin J.

INTERNATIONAL LAW AND THE LAW OF THE STATE

In some countries, it must be noted, the self-imposed limitations of the functions of courts goes much further. Thus in the United States of America the courts accept as conclusive the statement—the 'suggestion'—of the executive department as to whether immunity ought to be accorded having regard to the character of the acts or transaction in question or to other factors claimed.[1] In France, it has been customary for courts to decline to interpret treaties —even when they involve private rights—and to regard as conclusive the interpretation given by the Government. However, even in these cases—assuming the determination of the executive authorities to observe the treaty—there is no question of a refusal to treat international law laid down by treaty as part of municipal law. The difference, which is of a substantial character and which may have a bearing upon both the competence and the impartiality of the administration of international law, is primarily one of the nature of the organ applying it.

Mention may also be made in this connection of the practice, still widely—though by no means uniformly—adopted, according to which the courts of some countries in reliance upon a purported rule of international law give effect to so-called foreign acts of State which themselves are contrary to international law.

61. *The supremacy of Acts of Parliament*

While, according to the law of England, international law is part of the law of the land—voluntarily adopted as such whether in recognition of inherent necessity and conformity with reason or for other causes—it is not superior to the law of the land. This means that in

---

[1] For a scholarly discussion of the attitude of the courts of the United States on the subject see Dickinson in *University of Pennsylvania Law Review*, 104 (1956), 451–93. In most cases the practice of American courts to avoid a judicial pronouncement in matters of this description—often described as 'political'—has been due to considerations connected with the relevant principles of separation of powers. That consideration was given expression in the leading case of *Foster & Elam* v. *Neilson*, decided in 1829 by Chief Justice Marshall (27 U.S. (2 Pet.) 253): 'A question like this respecting the boundaries of nations . . . is more a political than a legal question; and, in its discussion, the courts of every country must respect the pronounced will of the legislature.' He had expressed the same view, with regard to the exclusive competence of the Government in the matter of recognition, in *Rose* v. *Himely*, 8 U.S. (4 Cranch) 241 (1808). In a series of cases relating to jurisdictional immunities of foreign States American courts have taken the view that they are bound to give effect to the recognition, by the American Government, of a claim to immunity: *The Navemar*, 303 U.S. 68 (1938), at p. 74; *Ex parte Peru*, 318 (U.S.) 578 (1943); *Republic of Mexico* v. *Hoffman*, 324 U.S. 30 (1945)—for an outspoken criticism of which see Jessup in *A.J.* 40 (1946), 168, describing the decision in the last-mentioned case as an abdication of the function of the court. See also Jessup (Cooley Lectures, 1959) and, in particular, Jaffe, *Judicial Aspects of Foreign Relations* (1933). And see generally the important articles of Mann in *L.Q.R.* 59 (1943), 55, 155, and 70 (1954), 181–202.

INTERNATIONAL LAW—THE GENERAL PART

those cases—normally the product of doctrinal speculation rather than of actual occurrence—in which an Act of Parliament expressly, without reasonably leaving room for any alternative interpretation, is in breach of international law, courts must apply the Act of Parliament. This is so for the obvious reason that municipal courts are organs of the State and must apply the law as laid down by its legislative organ—unless, as is the position in some countries, they are specifically required by the Constitution to disregard laws which are in violation of customary international law or treaty. Even in those countries, it may be added, the relevant constitutional provisions are liable to change by appropriate processes. Moreover, in those countries the question whether a statute is in violation of international law is decided by the judicial organs—generally the highest judicial organs—of the State in question. Accordingly, even in countries which give expression, by constitutional provision, to the principle of incorporation in a way apparently amounting to subordinating the law of the State to international law, the supremacy of international law cannot be regarded as complete unless a further series of conditions is fulfilled. These include: (*a*) A possibility of review, through an international judicial authority, of decisions of municipal courts ascertaining the conformity of national law with the international obligations of the State; (*b*) some guarantees, in the nature of international obligations, of compliance with the decisions of the international judicial authority of review; (*c*) in so far as the constitution acknowledges the superiority of international obligations as applied by the judicial organs of the State, an international undertaking by the State not to amend this aspect of its constitution unilaterally.

These are stringent conditions. Normally, and in the absence of express and effective constitutional provisions to the contrary, the supremacy of Acts of Parliament, even if inconsistent with the obligations of international law, follows inevitably from the fact that courts are organs of the State and that as such they must administer the law as decreed by its Legislature. This in any case is the position in the United Kingdom. However, contrary to the view occasionally expressed, that fact has no bearing upon the validity of the principle that international law is part of the law of England. It is so—provided that an Act of Parliament has not deliberately, in a manner which admits of no other possible interpretation,[1] violated international law. So long as that has not occurred international law provides a

---

[1] See above, p. 157.

INTERNATIONAL LAW AND THE LAW OF THE STATE

valid external standard for the administration of the law of the land.[1] In that sense the undoubted supremacy of the Legislature is fully consistent with the principle of incorporation of international law as part of the law of England.[2]

62. *The significance of the principle of incorporation*

While the purpose of the preceding sections has been to indicate the extent of the operation of the principle of adoption in judicial practice, it is important to bear in mind its significance as a factor in securing the authority, the effectiveness and the progress of international law. In the first instance, in so far as the possibilities of judicial determination of questions of international law are limited, having regard to the still voluntary character of international adjudication,[3] the normal application of rules of international law by municipal tribunals provides some guarantee, though within a distinctly limited sphere, of its effectiveness.

[1] To that extent it is not possible to regard as legally accurate the frequently quoted *dictum* in *Mortensen* v. *Peters* (see below, p. 167) stating that 'there is no such thing as a standard of international law extraneous to the domestic law of a kingdom, to which appeal may be made'.

[2] The practice of British prize courts provides an instructive illustration of the situation. While other British courts administer international law only when occasion arises, prize courts do it as the normal and almost exclusive object of their activity. In that sense they are courts of an international character and their character as such has been repeatedly affirmed. Thus in *The Recovery* Lord Stowell said in 1807: 'This is a Court of the Law of Nations, though sitting here under the authority of the King of Great Britain. It belongs to other nations as well as to our own' (6 C.Rob. 341, 348). See also *The Maria*, 3 C.Rob. 350; *The Fox*, 1 C. Rob. 312. And, for an even more emphatic affirmation of that view in relation to American prize courts, see Justice Story's statement in *The Schooner Adeline*, 9 Cr. 244, 284 (1815). Nevertheless, in their capacity as organs of the State, they are bound to give effect to the will of the national legislature even if the latter is contrary to international law. The principle involved was stated with lucidity in the leading case of *The Zamora*. There the Court said: 'the Prize Court, like any other Court, is bound by the legislative enactments of its sovereign State. A British Prize Court would certainly be bound by Acts of the Imperial Legislature. But it is none the less true that if the Imperial Legislature passed an Act the provisions of which were inconsistent with the law of nations, the Prize Court in giving effect to such provisions would no longer be administering international law. It would in the field covered by such provisions be deprived of its proper function as a Prize Court' ([1916] 2 A.C. 77, 93). However, while asserting their subjection to Acts of Parliament even if the latter were inconsistent with international law, prize courts have stressed their international character by drawing a line which, although its logic is not wholly apparent, has been adhered to with some rigidity. Thus, although Orders-in-Council find their legal basis in Acts of Parliament, Orders-in-Council which are not in conformity with international law have been judicially declared not to be binding upon British prize courts unless they amount to a mitigation of the rights of the Crown in favour of the enemy or a neutral, or unless they provide for reprisals which are justified by the circumstances of the case and do not entail upon neutrals an unreasonable degree of inconvenience. See Oppenheim, II, § 434, for further details. Reference may be made here to the observation of Lord Merriman in *The Glenroy* [1943] Ll.P.C. (2nd) 135 at 139 suggesting that the prize court may not necessarily be bound by decisions of other English courts. [3] See above, p. 23.

165

INTERNATIONAL LAW—THE GENERAL PART

Secondly, the principle of adoption of international law as being directly and *per se* part of the law of the land signifies that, for a variety of purposes, the quality of a subject of international law is not limited to States but extends also to individual human beings—a result which must be regarded both as being in accordance with actual recent developments in international law and as securing, from yet another point of view, a measure of effectiveness of its observance.[1]

Thirdly, the principle that international law as applied by municipal courts operates directly not only in relation to the State but also to individuals amounts to a refutation of the view, which is believed to be inaccurate, that international law and municipal law are wholly disparate and fundamentally different legal systems.

Finally, the principle of adoption of international law as being *per se* part of the law of the land signifies the voluntary submission of the State to the authority of international law—a submission which, as suggested above, is not affected by the circumstance that the authority of national legislation, even if contrary to international law, is supreme. That supremacy is limited to the confines of the State and may be only provisional. In general, the acknowledgment by the State—through the principle of adoption—of the direct operation of international law within the municipal sphere provides a significant accession to the authority of international law as the universal law of mankind. As already stated, such acknowledgment is not inconsistent with the legal doctrine of the supremacy of Parliament and of the sovereignty of the national State.

63. *Judicial and doctrinal criticism of the doctrine of incorporation*

In view of what has been stated in the preceding section, literal importance need not be attached to occasional judicial statements criticizing or qualifying the principle of adoption of international law as part of the law of the land.[2] In so far as they imply that any

---

[1] See above, pp. 148–149. It is of interest to note in this connection the passage in Blackstone's *Commentaries*, bk. IV, ch. 5, in which, in referring to offences against the law of nations which 'are principally incident to whole states or nations', he insisted that the relevant rules of the law of nations may also be binding directly upon individuals and that it is the duty of States to penalize their infraction.

[2] See, for instance, the following observation by Lord Atkin in *Chung Chi Cheung v. The King* [1939] A.C. 160, at pp. 167, 168: 'It must be always remembered that, so far, at any rate, as the Courts of this country are concerned, International Law has no validity save in so far as its principles are accepted by our own domestic law. There is no external power that imposes its rules on our own code of substantive law and procedure.' And see, for a similar statement by Atkin L. J. (as he then was), *Commercial and Estates Co. of Egypt v. The Board of Trade* [1925] 1 K.B. 271, at p. 295.

166

INTERNATIONAL LAW AND THE LAW OF THE STATE

particular rule or principle of international law must have received prior statutory or judicial assent before it can be acted on by courts, they are clearly contrary to general practice. It is of the essence of the doctrine of adoption as uniformly acted upon that no specific prior consent to any particular rule of international law is required. In so far as that criticism or qualification asserts that the principle of adoption is not in the nature of a command imposed by an external power, it is of a somewhat doctrinal character. It enunciates a proposition which is wholly uncontroversial. Actually, in practically all cases in which the principle of adoption has been exposed to judicial questioning it has in fact been fully acted upon.[1]

Doctrinal criticism, in the second part of the nineteenth century and the first decades of the twentieth, of the principle of incorporation of international law as part of municipal law, has been due to some extent to the historic association of that concept with the law of nature—an association which was apt to be viewed with disfavour at a time of the ascendancy of positivist tendencies which saw in the express will of the State not only the main but also the exclusive source of the law. In fact, there are passages in some of Lord Mansfield's judgments which vividly recall the origins of that association. These passages go to the length of asserting that the law of nations, like the law of nature, is so much an integral part of the law of the land that it could not be changed even by an Act of Parliament.[2] In a sense, like the law merchant and maritime law, so also inter-

---

[1] See, e.g., *Commercial and Estates Co. of Egypt* v. *The Board of Trade* (above, p. 166, n. 2)—a case *primae impressionis* involving the right of angary—where Atkin L. J., after noting that the right of angary was 'well recognized by the conventions of civilized nations which constitute the body of International Law', stated: 'The right of angary therefore is a right recognized by English law.' And see, in the same line of thought, the observations of Lord Wright in *The Cristina* [1938] A.C. 485, at p. 502, where, after quoting with approval the frequently cited passage in *Mortensen* v. *Peters* (see above, p. 165), he proceeded to decide the issue of immunity of foreign public ships by reference to standards of international law and the developments which had taken place there.

[2] In *Heathfield* v. *Chilton*, 4 Burr. 2015, he said: 'The Act of Parliament of 7 Ann. c. 12 did not intend to alter, nor can alter the law of nations.' No such assertion seems to have been advanced by Blackstone, who said: 'But if the parliament will positively enact a thing to be done which is unreasonable, I know of no power that can control it' (*Commentaries*, I, 91). For a criticism of Lord Mansfield's observation that international law is part of English law as being historically inaccurate in relation to the seventeenth and eighteenth centuries, see Adair, *The Exterritoriality of Ambassadors in the Sixteenth and Seventeenth Centuries* (1929), pp. 238–43. *Sed quaere*. That the principle involved was deeply rooted in English philosophical and religious thought may be seen from the following passage in Richard Hooker's *Laws of Ecclesiastical Polity* (bk. I, §§ 10, 12 and 13) written nearly two centuries before: 'The strength and virtue of that law [the law of nations] is such, that no particular nation can lawfully prejudice the same by any their several laws and ordinances, more than a man by his private resolutions, the law of the whole common wealth or state wherein he liveth.' See also Holdsworth, *History of English Law*, IV (1924), 214.

167

INTERNATIONAL LAW—THE GENERAL PART

national law was treated, both in Great Britain and in the United States,[1] as part of the universal law, common to all mankind and of equal validity at all times and in all political communities.[2] However, in the course of its practical application the principle of adoption of international law, whatever may have been its origin, was combined with the recognition of the legitimate part of the State in the formation of and assent—express or implied—to the rules and doctrines of international law thus incorporated.[3] From that point of view the principle of incorporation is not necessarily incompatible with the tenets of the positivist doctrine.

The more articulate reason for the current criticism of the principle of adoption and of the denial of its reality is that international law and municipal law, being fundamentally different systems, one cannot *per se* be part of the other. This is the attitude of what may be called the dualist school of thought.[4] However, this is a case in which the doctrine, itself of doubtful validity,[5] of the duality of the international and municipal legal order is confronted with the reality of the practice of the adoption of international law as being *per se* part of the law of the land. This being so, any remaining controversy is reduced to somewhat dialectical questions such as whether international law *having been adopted* can be regarded as being *ipso facto* part of the law of the land;[6] whether the rules of international law thus incorporated are applied as rules of international or of municipal law; and whether, although not being strictly speaking part of English law, they are a source of it.[7] It is

[1] See below, p. 169.

[2] See the reference by Mr Justice Story to 'this great system of maritime law [of which] it may be truly said, "Non erit alia lex Romae, alia Athenis, alia nunc, alia posthac; sed et omnes gentes, et omni tempore, una lex, et sempiterna et immortalis, continebit"' (*De Lovio* v. *Boit*, 7 Federal Cases 418 and 443).

[3] See above, p. 115, for the statement in *West Rand Central Gold Mining Co.* v. *The King* of the necessity for such express or implied consent—implied consent covering a rule of international law which is 'of such a nature, and has been so widely and generally accepted, that it can hardly be supposed that any civilized State would repudiate it'.

[4] See above, p. 152, and below, p. 216.   [5] See below, pp. 218, 227.

[6] Oppenheim, who in the original version of his treatise denied—on the ground of the purported fundamental differences of the two systems—the possibility of international law being *per se* part of English law, subsequently modified his view. In his Introduction to Picciotto, *The Relation of International Law to the Law of England and of the United States of America* (1915), p. 10, he said: 'If *per se* means that international law is applicable by municipal courts by virtue of a rule of international law superior to the will of the State, then the doctrine of adoption is not a rule of existing law. If, on the other hand, the expression *per se* means that international law as a whole has been incorporated by the law of the State so that its rules and principles are applicable as such without any specific act of transformation, then that expression is properly used in this context.'

[7] The distinction between a 'source' of law and 'part' of the law may be as artificial as that between formal and material sources (see above, p. 51) or between the sources

168

INTERNATIONAL LAW AND THE LAW OF THE STATE

not necessary to pursue these questions here. The denial of the principle of adoption on account of the ultimate supremacy of Acts of Parliament is discussed elsewhere in this chapter.[1]

64. *The principle of adoption in the law of the United States*

The principle of the English common law according to which international law is part of the law of the land was fully taken over by the United States when it achieved independence. For reasons connected with considerations of the national dignity of a community claiming full stature as an independent State within the international community,[2] of the necessities of its Federal structure, as well as of considerations bearing upon the development of the law merchant and maritime law—to which the law of nations was deemed to be allied[3]—the principle of adoption found emphatic expression in early American judicial practice[4] and, with regard to treaties, in the Constitution of the United States.[5] Customary international law

and the evidence of law (see above, pp. 51–53). See, for a discussion of this aspect of the question, Lauterpacht in *Grotius Society*, 25 (1939), 67–73 and 84–8. And see McDougal in *South Dakota Law Review*, 4 (1959), 71.   [1] See above, p. 164.

[2] In *Talbot* v. *Three Brigs*, 1 Dall. 95, Dickenson, President, said in 1784: 'Are we then, because in England they call the admiralty court a prize court when it acts in a cause of prize, and it then proceeds in a different manner, with an appeal to commissioners of the Privy Council, to reject the "universal and immemorial" compact of mankind? There was a time—when we listened to the language of her Senates and her courts, with a partiality of veneration, as to oracle. It is past—we have assumed our station among the powers of the earth, and must attend to the voice of nations—the sentiments of the society into which we have entered.' See also the following passage in an Opinion of Attorney General Randolph to the Secretary of State, 26 June 1792 (*Opinions of the Attorney General*, 1, 27) in the matter of the arrest of the domestic servant of a public minister: 'The law of nations, although not specially adopted by the constitution or any municipal act, is essentially a part of the law of the land. Its obligation commences and runs with the existence of a nation, subject to modifications on some points of indifference. Indeed a people may regulate it so as to be binding upon the departments of their own government, in any form whatever; but with regard to foreigners, every change is at the peril of the nation which makes it.'

[3] For a lucid exposition of these factors see Dickinson in *University of Pennsylvania Law Review*, 101 (1952), 26–56, and 101 (1953), 792–833.

[4] In 1784, in *Respublica* v. *De Longchamps* (1 Dall. 111), M'Kean, Chief Justice of Pennsylvania, pronounced sentence upon the accused, who had insulted and assaulted the Minister of France, for not only 'an infraction of the Law of Nations' which 'in its full extent is part of the law of this State', but also, in more emphatic language, for 'a crime against the State and all other nations'. The case is an early instance of municipal courts punishing acts committed by individuals and considered contrary to international law.

[5] See Wright, *The Enforcement of International Law through Municipal Law in the United States* (1916) and in *A.J.* 11 (1917), 1–21; Scott, *ibid.* 1 (1907), 852–66; Potter, *ibid.* 19 (1925), 315–26; Sprout, *ibid.* 26 (1932), 280–95; Wright in *A.S. Proc.* (1952), 71–85; Dickinson, *ibid.* pp. 239–60, and in *Hague Recueil*, 40 (1932) (ii), 328–49, who—rightly, it is believed—arrives at the conclusion that the doctrine is not only fully valid, but that it has had an influence which is far-reaching and beneficent; Hackworth, 1, 24–39; Hyde in *B.Y.* 25 (1937), 1–16. And see *The Nereide* (1815) 9 Cranch 388; *United States* v. *Smith*

169

INTERNATIONAL LAW—THE GENERAL PART

is, subject to any clearly conflicting Act of Congress, part of the law of the land. By virtue of Article VI of the Constitution treaties made under the authority of the United States, along with the Constitution and together with the laws of the United States made in pursuance of the treaty, are declared to be the supreme law of the land. They override any Act of Congress or the legislation of the States of the Union in so far as those are inconsistent with the treaty. And, seeing that the Legislature participates in and thus gives consent to treaties prior to their ratification by the Executive, no enabling Act of Congress is necessary to make them enforceable before American courts except in the case of treaties which by their express terms or necessary implication require further legislative action.

On the other hand, as—and because—both customary and conventional international law are placed in the same position as any other part of municipal law, they may be overridden by an Act of Congress clearly intended to derogate from international law—an intention which may be assumed only in cases where no other construction is possible.[1] In this and other respects the law of the United States approximates to that of Great Britain, for instance, with regard to the conclusiveness of statements of the Executive in

(1820) 5 Wheaton 153; *The Scotia* (1871) 14 Wallace 170; *The Paquete Habana* (1899) 175 U.S. 677; *Respublica* v. *De Longchamps*, 1 Dall. 111. It seems to follow that the residuary power of a final and authoritative interpretation of international law is within the jurisdiction of the supreme legislative and judicial organs of the Union as distinguished from those of the States. See also Jessup in *A.J.* 33 (1939), 740–3. It is in the application of that principle that lies to some extent the explanation of the occasional refusal of the courts of the United States to exercise jurisdiction following upon seizure or arrest contrary to international law. See *The Mazel Tov*, reported as *Cook* v. *The United States* (1933) 288 U.S. 102. And see, for comment thereon, Dickinson in *A.J.* 27 (1933), 305–10, and *ibid.* 28 (1934), 231–45. As to the position in the American Republics see Moore and Wilson in *A.S. Proc.* (1916), 11–30.

[1] A principle enunciated in clear terms by Chief Justice Marshall in 1804 in *The Charming Betsey*, 6 U.S. (2 Cranch) 64, 118: 'An act of Congress ought never to be construed to violate the law of nations, if any other possible construction remains.' For an affirmation of the rule that in the United States a subsequent statute overrides the provisions of a treaty see *United States* v. *Claus*, 63 F.Supp. 433; *Annual Digest*, 13 (1946), Case no. 83. For a strong affirmation see the decision of the Supreme Court in *Lauritzen* v. *Larsen*: 345 U.S. 571; *I.L.R.* 20 (1953), 197. As to the effects of the President's proclamation of a treaty see Reiff in *A.J.* 30 (1936), 63–79. For a clear restatement of the principle that a subsequent treaty supersedes a prior conflicting statute and that a treaty will not be deemed to have been abrogated or modified by a later statute unless the Legislature clearly expressed itself to that effect see *Cook* v. *The United States* (1933) 288 U.S. 102; *A.J.* 27 (1933), 559–69. See also, to the same effect, *Whitney* v. *Robertson* (1888) 124 U.S. 190, 194; *Minerva Automobiles Inc.* v. *United States*, decided in 1938 by the United States Court of Customs and Patent Appeals (*Annual Digest*, 9 (1938–40), Case no. 196). On the problems raised in the United States by a conflict between a treaty and the provisions of the Constitution see Cowles, *Treaties and Constitutional Law: Property Interferences and Due Process of Law* (1941). And see generally on conflicts between treaties and municipal law Kopelmanas in *R.I.* 3rd ser. 17 (1937), 83–143, 310–61.

170

INTERNATIONAL LAW AND THE LAW OF THE STATE

matters relating to foreign affairs.[1] On the other hand, the nature of the distribution of legislative powers between the Union and the States[2] and the peculiar, and in some secondary respects not fully clarified, status of so-called executive agreements[3] have given rise to problems of their own. As in Great Britain, the principle of adoption of international law as part of the law of the land has been generally regarded as opening avenues of progress in the development of international law and as one of the guarantees of its effectiveness.[4]

65. *Customary adoption of the principle of incorporation in other countries*

While in Great Britain and in the United States the principle of adoption of international law as part of the law of the land has been followed in reliance upon an articulate judicial doctrine, in a considerable number of other States a similar practice has been followed in fact. In these countries courts have repeatedly rejected the view that prior express adoption, by the State concerned or its courts, of a particular rule of international law is a condition of its application by courts.[5]

---

[1] See above, p. 162. As stated there, it would appear that the self-imposed limitation upon the judicial function in matters bearing upon foreign relations and the desire not to embarrass the Executive in that sphere have perhaps gone somewhat further than in Great Britain—although in the great majority of the relevant cases established principles of separation of powers and the very text of the international instruments invoked might have been sufficient for the purpose. See, e.g., *Farmer et Al.* v. *Rountree*, decided in 1956 by the United States District Court in Tennessee, where the plaintiff claimed to be relieved from taxation on the alleged ground that the United States had been pursuing a policy of world domination contrary to international law (149 F.Supp. 327; *I.L.R.* 23 (1956), 1).   [2] See above, p. 170.

[3] For the apparent statement that the principle of priority of treaties over Acts of Congress does not apply to executive agreements, see *United States* v. *Guy W. Capps, Inc.* (*I.L.R.* 20 (1953), 412). And see the observation of the International Court of Justice in the *Interhandel* case (*I.C.J. Reports* 1959, p. 28), where it was contended on behalf of Switzerland that as the instrument upon which she relied was an executive agreement American courts would not be in the position to give effect to it.

[4] Reference may also be made to the frequent application by the Supreme Court of the United States of rules of international law for determining disputes between the States members of the Union. See Scott, *Judicial Settlement of Controversies between States of the American Union* (2 vols. 1918), and the same, *Sovereign States and Suits* (1925). For a short account see Smith, *The American Supreme Court as an International Tribunal* (1920). See also Lauterpacht, *The Function of Law*, pp. 439–45.

[5] See, for instance, the German case of *Hellfeld* v. *Russia*, involving jurisdictional immunity, in which the Court declined to accept the view that international law is applicable only in so far as it has been adopted by German customary law: for the text of the decision see *A.J.* 5 (1911), 514. As to France see *Dientz* v. *de la Jara*, decided in 1878 by the Civil Tribunal of the Seine (*Clunet*, 5 (1878), p. 500); see also *ibid.* 43 (1916), 164, for the decision *In re D.* holding that the members of the Belgian Government-in-exile in France were entitled to the rights of jurisdictional immunity 'without there having been a necessity to embody them in a French statute or decree'. In Switzerland the practice has been even more pronounced in that direction. See, e.g., *Imperial and Royal Austrian Ministry of Finance* v. *Dreyfus*, *Entscheidungen des Bundesgerichts*, 44 (1918) (i), 49, where the Court stated that 'the rule of international law in the matter of jurisdiction is to be

INTERNATIONAL LAW—THE GENERAL PART

66. *Express adoption of international law in constitutions*

In an increasing number of countries the principle of adoption has been incorporated as part of the national Constitution and partakes of the safeguards—and the measure of rigidity—congenial to written constitutions. While in many of these countries these constitutional provisions were, to a considerable extent, declaratory of pre-existing practice, their object has been mainly twofold: In some cases the purpose of the constitutional act of incorporation has been the intention—prompted by the experience of the country concerned—to manifest attachment to international law as a rule of its future conduct. Thus Article 4 of the German Weimar Constitution of 1919 provided that 'the universally recognised rules of international law are valid as binding constituent parts of German Federal Law'.[1]

In other cases, the constitutional act of incorporation was intended not only to recognize the direct operation of international law within

regarded in Switzerland as Federal law, since, by its very nature, it has a claim to general validity in the municipal sphere, and must, therefore, be placed upon an equal plane with municipal law as a whole'. For a clear affirmation, by reference to judicial practice, of the principle of incorporation in Switzerland with regard to both customary and conventional international law see Guggenheim, i, 35–7, and the same, with particular reference to treaties, in *Studi in Onore di Tomaso Perassi*, ii (1958), 501–13, where he expounds the primacy of treaties with regard not only to ordinary legislation but also to provisions of the Constitution. See also, for a detailed analysis of the position in Switzerland, Rice in *A.J.* 46 (1952), 641–66. And see *Verini* v. *Paoletti*, *I.L.R.* 21 (1954), 264, in which the Swiss Federal Tribunal held that the provisions of a treaty must be applied even if in conflict with the Federal Constitution. On the other hand, see a prior decision, in the contrary sense, in *Steenworden* v. *Société des Auteurs* (*Annual Digest*, 8 (1935–7), Case no. 4), where the Swiss Federal Court seems to have held that it would be bound by a subsequent statute derogating from a treaty; but see Kopelmanas in *Revue critique de droit international*, 33 (1938), p. 252, and in *R.I.* 3rd ser. 18 (1937), 95, 96. As to Norway see Raestad in *Grotius Society*, 30 (1944), 34–47; as to Greece see Ténékidès in *R.I.* 3rd ser. 9 (1928), 338–45. And see for a general survey Ruth Masters, *International Law in National Courts* (1932).

[1] See Wenzel, *Juristische Grundbegriffe* (1920); Walz, *op. cit.* (in bibliography, p. 177 below); Stier-Somlo, *Die Verfassung des deutschen Reichs* (1920), pp. 95 *et seq*. In the *Reparations Levy* (*Aliens in Germany*) case the German *Reichsgericht* held in August 1928 that, notwithstanding Article 4 of the Constitution, it was bound to act on the principle *lex posterior derogat priori* and to apply a statute which was contrary to the provisions of the Treaty of Versailles (*Annual Digest*, 4 (1927–8), Case no. 225). During the National-Socialist régime there was a tendency to give a restricted interpretation to that Article in the sense of making it apply to such rules only as had received the specific consent of Germany: see, e.g., Walz in *Z.V.* 18 (1934), 150, 151. See also Mohr, *Die Transformation des Völkerrechts ins deutsche Reichsrecht* (1934), and Schüle in *Z.ö.V.* 6 (1936), 269–85. See also, to the same effect, Article 8 of the Austrian Constitution of 1934, re-enacting Article 9 of the Constitution of 1920. See Verdross, *Die Einheit des rechtlichen Weltbildes* (1923), pp. 111–18; Wittmayer in *Z.V.* 13 (1926), 1–5; Métall, *ibid.* 14 (1927), 161–87; Steiner in *A.J.* 29 (1935), 125–9; Seidl-Hohenveldern, *ibid.* 49 (1955), 451–76. Article 9 of the Spanish Constitution of 1931 was to a similar effect. See Strupp in *Friedenswarte*, 32 (1932), 264, 265; Perassi in *Rivista*, 24 (1932), 453–6; Morelli, *ibid.* 25 (1933), 3–23; Mirkine-Guetzévitch in *Théorie du droit*, 7 (1932–3), 115–32; Lacambra in *R.I.* (*Paris*), 15 (1935), 72–89.

INTERNATIONAL LAW AND THE LAW OF THE STATE

the municipal sphere but also to safeguard its effectiveness by subordinating future statutory law—though not any future changes in the Constitution itself—to the obligations of international law. Thus Article 26 of the French Constitution of 1946 provided as follows: 'Diplomatic treaties duly ratified and published shall have the force of law even when they are contrary to internal French legislation; they shall require for their application no legislative acts other than those necessary to ensure ratification'[1]—a provision which probably covers legislation enacted both before and after the conclusion of the treaty. This marks a clear departure from the position in other countries, such as the United States of America, where a statute which is enacted subsequently to a treaty and which is inconsistent with it will be enforced by the courts. While the provision of the French Constitution still leaves some doubt on the subject,[2] there is no such doubt in the relevant Article 66 of the Dutch Constitution as revised in 1956. That Article provides expressly that Dutch legislation shall not apply in so far as it is inconsistent with treaties concluded prior or subsequent to such legislation. It may be noted that according to the Constitution treaties are binding 'upon all persons'—a direct intimation of the direct operation of treaties without any further act of legislative transformation.[3]

In some cases the act of incorporation has been combined with an almost doctrinal profession of adherence to some of the consequences, as outlined above, following from the direct operation of international law within the municipal sphere. Thus Article 25 of the Constitution of the German Federal Republic of 1949 provided not only that generally recognized rules of international law form part of Federal

---

[1] See Preuss in *A.J.* 44 (1950), 641–69. See also Rousseau in *Études Georges Scelle* (1950), II, 565–81, and Luchaire, *ibid.* pp. 815–60; Bial in *A.J.* 49 (1955), 347–55 (a detailed review of French decisions). For examples of a clear declaration, by reference to the Constitution, of the superiority of a treaty over municipal legislation see the decisions of the Court of Appeal of Paris in *Lambert* v. *Jourdain* (*Annual Digest*, 15 (1948), Case no. 111) and the Civil Tribunal of the Seine in *Estate of Repetti* (*I.L.R.* 18 (1951), Case no. 120). As to the position in Luxembourg see Pescatore in *Journal des Tribunaux*, 68 (1953), 645.

[2] But only slight doubt. For Article 28 lays down that 'diplomatic treaties duly ratified and published have authority superior to that of French internal legislation' and that accordingly their provisions shall not be abrogated, modified, or suspended without previous formal denunciation through diplomatic channels. Article 44 of the Constitution of 1958 is to the same effect except that the supremacy of treaties over legislation is made subject to the condition of their being applied by the other party.

[3] For an application of this provision in relation to the Brussels Convention of 1910 in the matter of Collisions between Vessels, see the judgment of the District Court of Rotterdam in the case of *Koninklijke Hollandsche Lloyd* v. *Dampskibsselskabet Torm A/S.* (*I.L.R.* 22 (1955), p. 634.)

INTERNATIONAL LAW—THE GENERAL PART

law and have precedence over the laws, but also that they create rights and obligations directly for the inhabitants of Federal territory. These constitutional provisions are of significance. There is no reason to underestimate their importance on the ground that their effectiveness is limited for various reasons or that in some cases they are expressed as being no more than declarations of intention to abide by international law in relation to other States—a form of words which may be construed, perhaps not very cogently, to imply that it does not extend to the application of international law within the State.[1]

There are, nevertheless, some limitations upon the efficacy of the constitutional acceptance of the principle of incorporation. Thus although the Constitution may put a check upon ordinary legislation conflicting with international law, it cannot, except through the requirement of an exacting majority necessary for constitutional changes, prevent constitutional amendments abrogating such checks or otherwise of a character inconsistent with international law. Again, unless provision is made for ultimate judicial review by an international authority, the question whether a statute is contrary to international law is left to the decision of the national court, even if that be the highest national court.[2] Moreover, in some countries—in particular France—courts as a rule deem themselves precluded from interpreting treaties, a function which they consider to be within the province of the Executive. In France

[1] Thus, for instance, the Constitution of Ireland of 1937 provides, in Article 29, that 'Ireland accepts the generally recognized principles of international law as its rule of conduct in its relations with other States'. Article 211 of the Burmese Constitution of 1947 is similarly worded. It would seem that the phraseology of these provisions has no reference to observance of international law within those States—as distinguished from their conduct of international relations. There is no compelling necessity for giving them that restrictive interpretation. A State which is intent upon observing international law directly in its relations with other States must also observe it within its own territory in matters affecting its relations with other States. Moreover, occasions may arise, as in the case of State succession, when the observance of international law may become relevant in relation to a State's own subjects. The Spanish Constitution of 1931 avoided these ambiguities by providing, in Article 7, that 'Spain will observe the universal rules of international law by incorporating them in her national law'. Similarly, the Italian Constitution of 1948 provides that 'the Italian juridical order shall conform with generally recognized rules of international law' (Article 10). For an example of the application of this provision see *In re Berli*, decided in 1949 by the Supreme Court of Cassation (*Annual Digest*, 16 (1949), Case no. 3). The Preamble to the French Constitution of 1946 is more general in providing that the Republic, 'faithful to her traditions, abides by the rules of international law'.

[2] As is provided, for instance, in the German Federal Constitution of 1949 which lays down, in Article 100 (2), that if in a case before a court there is doubt whether a rule of international law is part of Federal law and whether, in accordance with Article 25 of the Constitution (see above, p. 173), it creates directly rights and obligations for the individual, the court is bound to obtain a decision of the Federal Constitutional Court.

174

INTERNATIONAL LAW AND THE LAW OF THE STATE

courts decline to interpret treaties involving relations with foreign States as distinguished from treaties concerned with private interests —a distinction of considerable elasticity.[1]

However, these problems, real as they are, are not typical of the normal and potentially beneficent operation of the constitutional incorporation of international law as part of the law of the land. Such deliberate and solemn adoption of international law as a body of rules ordinarily administered by municipal tribunals in relation to individuals without any specific act of transformation reveals the serious, and probably insurmountable, difficulty in the way of the view according to which international and municipal law are fundamentally disparate systems of law operating in different fields and in relation to different subjects. The position is essentially the same in countries in which the principle of adoption is the result of judicial practice irrespective of any constitutional provision.[2] It has already been noted that in most cases such constitutional provisions are declaratory of existing practice.[3]

67. *Constitutional adoption of particular principles of international law*

From the general incorporation, in the written national constitutions, of international law as part of the law of the land there must be distinguished the adoption of particular rules and principles thereof and of international conduct generally. Thus some Constitutions contain a prohibition against engaging in wars of conquest.[4] The German Federal Constitution lays down, in Article 26(1), that

[1] This is the reason why the reality of the change introduced by Article 26 of the French Constitution in the matter of treaties (see above, p. 173) is somewhat impaired. See *Estades* v. *French Government* (decided by the Court of Cassation, *I.L.R.* 21 (1954), p. 277); *Ministère Public* v. *Carillo-Frontello* (decided by the Court of Appeal of Paris: *ibid.* p. 281); and numerous similar cases reported in practically every volume of the *International Law Reports*. On the other hand, there is no reason for assuming that such governmental interpretation must invariably result in a restrictive construction of international obligations. See, e.g., the decision of the Court of Cassation in *In re Syndicate of Co-owners of the Alfred Delwodencq Property Company (I.L.R.* 21 (1954), p. 279).

[2] See, e.g., as to the law of Israel, greatly influenced in this respect by the English common law doctrine of incorporation, Lapidoth in *Scripta Hierosolymitana* (1958), pp. 132–76.

[3] See generally on the development of the constitutional law of various countries in that direc. on Mirkine–Guetzévitch in *R.G.* 52 (1948), 375–86; Morgenstern in *B.Y.* 27 (1950), 86–90; Lipartiti in *R.I.* 32 (1954), 149–60, 373–88; Verdross, *ibid.* pp. 3–14; Deener in *Cornell Law Quarterly*, 36 (1951), 523–6; Preuss in *Michigan Law Review*, 51 (1953), 1117–42; Paul de Visscher, 'Les tendances internationales des constitutions modernes', in *Hague Recueil*, 80 (1952) (i), 515–76; Yves L. Auguste, *L'Internationalisation des Constitutions* (1952); Mangoldt in *Jahrbuch für Internationales Recht*, 3 (1954), 11–25; McDougal in *South Dakota Law Review*, 4 (1959), 73–7.

[4] See, e.g., the Preamble to the French Constitution of 1946 and Article 11 of the Italian Constitution of 1947. Article 6 of the Spanish Constitution of 1931 provides for the renunciation of war as an instrument of national policy.

175

INTERNATIONAL LAW—THE GENERAL PART

activities which tend to disturb, or are undertaken with the intention of disturbing, peaceful relations with foreign States, and especially preparing for aggressive war, shall be deemed unconstitutional and made subject to punishment. Some provide for legislative consent to a declaration of war.[1] The Italian Constitution of 1947 provides for treatment of aliens in accordance with international law (Article 10(1)). The very first Article of the Federal German Constitution of 1949 lays down that the dignity of man shall be inviolable and that 'the German people acknowledge inviolable and inalienable human rights as the basis of every human community, of peace and justice in the world'. Some Constitutions provide expressly for the right of asylum from political prosecution.[2] While these and similar provisions do not represent rules of international law, they give in some cases expression to incipient and, it may be added, desirable developments. This applies, for instance, to the provision of the German Federal Constitution of 1949 which lays down, in Article 16, that German nationality must not be withdrawn and that the loss of German nationality may take place by virtue of a law and contrary to the wish of the person concerned only on condition that such withdrawal does not result in statelessness.

68. *Constitutional authorization of renunciation of sovereignty*

Finally, there must be noted constitutional provisions which, in effect, incorporate in advance as part of municipal law provisions of treaties in which the State in question delegates part of its sovereignty, in matters as yet unascertained, to international authorities. These were intended to apply, in particular, to the series of treaties covering the activities of the European Economic Community, the authorities of which are granted, within limits laid down by the treaty, powers of legislation binding upon all the members of the Community. Such legislation may involve the necessity for changes in municipal law, as well as limitations of sovereignty which may amount to a change in the Constitution of the State concerned. In view of this it has been deemed necessary in some countries to provide in the Constitution itself for an authoriza-

---

[1] E.g. Article 66(2) of the Brazilian Constitution of 1946 or Article 28(3) of the Irish Constitution of 1937.

[2] See, e.g., the Preamble to the French Constitution of 1946 and Article 10 of the Italian Constitution of 1947.

In the French Constitution of 1946 the principle of self-determination of peoples is recognized to some extent in Article 27, which lays down that 'no cession, no exchange, and no addition of territory shall be valid without the consent of the populations concerned'.

INTERNATIONAL LAW AND THE LAW OF THE STATE

tion to enter into treaty obligations of that nature. Thus the Constitution of the Netherlands of 1956 lays down that legislative, administrative and jurisdictional powers may be conferred by treaty upon international organizations and that if so required by the development of the international juridical order a treaty may derogate from the provisions of the Constitution—in which case the treaty must be approved by a majority of two-thirds of both Chambers of the States-General. Article 24 of the Federal German Constitution of 1949 lays down that the Federation may, by way of legislation, transfer rights of sovereignty to international institutions. The Preamble to the French Constitution of 1946 provides that 'on condition of reciprocity, France consents to limitations of sovereignty necessary for the organization and the defence of peace'.[1]

SELECT BIBLIOGRAPHY ON INTERNATIONAL LAW AND THE LAW OF THE STATE

Hyde, 1, § 5; Praag, §§ 17–22, 276–81; Scelle, 1, 27–42; Accioly, 1, 40–50; Guggenheim, 1, 21–44; Kaufmann, *Die Rechtskraft des internationalen Rechts* (1899); Triepel, *Völkerrecht und Landesrecht* (1899) (translated by Brunet, *Droit international et droit interne*, 1920), and in *Hague Recueil*, 1 (1923), 77–121; Anzilotti, *Il Diritto internazionale nei Giudizi interni* (1905), pp. 49–65; Picciotto, *The Relation of International Law to the Law of England and the United States* (1915); Wenzel, *Juristische Grundprobleme* (1920), pp. 359–421, 444–59; Wright, *The Enforcement of International Law through Municipal Law in the United States* (1916); the same in *A.J.* 11 (1917), 1–21, and 17 (1923), 234–44; Verdross in *Hague Recueil*, 16 (1927) (i), 262–75, and 30 (1929) (v), 301–11; Kelsen, *Das Problem der Souveränität und die Theorie des Völkerrechts* (1920), pp. 102–241, *General Theory of Law and State* (1945), pp. 363–80, in *Hague Recueil*, 15 (1926) (iv), 231–6, *ibid.* 84 (1953) (iii), 182–200, *Principles of International Law* (1952), pp. 190–6, 401–50, in *Z̆.ö.R.* 4 (1924), 207–22, and in *R.G.* 43 (1936), 5–49; Kosters in *Bibliotheca Visseriana*, 4 (1925), 261–73; Walz, *Die Abänderung völkerrechtsgemässen Landesrechts* (1927), and the same, *Völkerrecht und staatliches Recht* (1933) (a comprehensive treatise); Strisower in *Z̆.ö.R.* 4 (1924), 272–98; Spiropoulos, *Théorie générale du droit international* (1930), pp. 71–83; Monaco, *L'ordinamento internazionale in rapporti all'ordinamento statuale* (1932); Masters, *International Law in National Courts* (1932) (a useful study); Grassetti, *Diritto interno e diritto internazionale nell'ordinamento giuridico anglo-americano* (1934); Chailley, *Le problème de la nature juridique des traités internationaux* (1932), pp. 283–327; Laun, *Der*

---

[1] Article 11 of the Italian Constitution of 1948 is to a similar effect. For a lucid analysis of the international and constitutional problems involved see Paul de Visscher in *Hague Recueil*, 80 (1952) (i), 545–54.

INTERNATIONAL LAW—THE GENERAL PART

Wandel der Ideen Staat und Volk (1933), pp. 3–62; Sereni, *Diritto internazionale* 1 (1956), 191–232; Potter in *A.J.* 19 (1925), 315–26; Baumgarten in *Z.ö.V.* 2(1) (1930), 305–34; Mirkine–Guetzévitch in *Hague Recueil*, 38 (1931) (iv), 311–25; Blondeau in *R.I.* (*Paris*), 9 (1932), 579–616; Dickinson in *A.J.* 26 (1932), 239–60, and in *Hague Recueil*, 40 (1932) (ii), 328–49; Sprout in *A.J.* 26 (1932), 280–95; Salvioli in *Hague Recueil*, 46 (1933) (iv), 30–7; Decencière–Ferrandière in *R.G.* 40 (1933), 45–70; Svoboda in *Z.ö.R.* 14 (1934), 487–531; Strupp in *Hague Recueil*, 47 (1934) (i), 389–418; Kaufmann, *ibid.* 54 (1935) (iv), 436–61; Guggenheim in *Théorie du droit*, 9 (1935), 90–100; Balladore Pallieri in *Rivista*, 27 (1935), 24–82; Chiron, *ibid.* 30 (1938), 3–55; Lauterpacht in *Grotius Society*, 25 (1939), 51–88, and in *Hague Recueil*, 62 (1937) (iv), 129–48; Ténékidès in *Friedenswarte*, 41 (1941), 1–23; Holdsworth in *Minnesota Law Review*, 26 (1942), 141–52; McNair in *Grotius Society*, 30 (1944), 11–21; Morgenstern in *B.Y.* 27 (1950), 42–92; Preuss in *A. S. Proc.* (1951), pp. 82–100; Dickinson in *University of Pennsylvania Law Review*, 101 (1952), 26–56, 101 (1953), 792–833, 104 (1956), 451–93; Verdross in *R.I.* 32 (1954), 219–30; Sperduti in *Rivista*, 37 (1954), 82–91; Barile, *ibid.* 39 (1956), 449–507, 40 (1957), 26–102; Morelli in *Hague Recueil*, 89 (1956) (i), 479–98; Mosler, *ibid.* 91 (1957) (i), 626–765; Kelsen in *Z.ö.V.* 19 (1958), 234–48; McDougal in *South Dakota Law Review*, 4 (1959), 25–92.

II

GENERAL RULES OF THE
LAW OF PEACE

EDITOR'S NOTE

In 1937 Lauterpacht gave the so-called 'General Course' at the Hague Academy of International Law, the French text of which appears in the *Recueil des Cours de l'Académie de Droit International*, vol. 62 (1937) (iv), 99–419. Although these lectures were delivered and printed in French, they were originally written in English and were translated into French by Maître Allemès. About five-sixths of the original English text have been found amongst Lauterpacht's papers and are included in what is printed below. In addition, the final one-sixth, comprising the chapters on 'The Organization of Peace and the Revision of the Status Quo', has been re-translated from the printed French text into English. This has been done largely by Miss Maureen Mac-Glashan.

Where the original English text has been used, I have found that it is not always identical with the printed French text. Occasionally, sentences or footnotes which appear in the English text have been omitted from the French. At other times, passages which appear in the body of the English text are transposed into footnotes in the French translation. Although it may be felt that the French version, being the only printed one, is the more likely to represent Lauterpacht's polished views, I have nonetheless thought that it would be inappropriate to interfere with the English text simply for the purpose of making it the same as the French.

CONTENTS

	page
PREFACE	189

PART I. THE FOUNDATIONS OF INTERNATIONAL LAW — 191

CHAPTER 1. THE PLACE OF INTERNATIONAL LAW IN JURISPRUDENCE — 193

(1) The essential elements of the concept of international law; (2) The concept of law in jurisprudence; (3) International law and the fundamental elements of law: (a) Creation of law; (b) The binding force of law; (c) The ascertainment of the law; (d) Enforcement of the law; (4) The legal character of international law; (5) International law and the general concept of law; (6) The extent of the incorporation of general principles of law into international law; (7) General principles of law and the moral basis of international law; (8) The function of law between individuals and States. Spinoza; (9) The theory of the necessarily and permanently weak character of international law; (10) International law as a law of co-ordination; (11) The theoretical and practical consequences of the 'law of co-ordination'; (12) Monism (qualified by dualism) as the basis of international law

CHAPTER 2. INTERNATIONAL LAW AND MUNICIPAL LAW — 216

(13) The monist and dualist theories; (14) The English doctrine of the direct application of customary international law; (15) The bearing of the English doctrine; (16) Continental countries and the direct application of customary international law; (17) The theory of incorporation and the progress of the Law of Nations; (18) English doctrine and the transformation of conventional international law; (19) The theory of incorporation and the primacy of the Law of Nations; (20) Possibilities of development in the future

CHAPTER 3. THE SOURCES OF INTERNATIONAL LAW — 231

A. The Theory of Sources — 231

(21) The theory of sources and the basis of international law

183

GENERAL RULES OF THE LAW OF PEACE

page

B. Treaties as a Source of International Law   234

(22) (*a*) Relation of treaties to other sources; (23) (*b*) The legislative effect of treaties

C. (24) Custom as a Source and as Evidence of International Law   237

D. General Principles of Law   241

(25) The general principles of law in Article 38 and the science of international law; (26) The general principles of law and legal positivism; (27) The general principles of law outside the Statute of the Court; (28) Article 38(3) in the practice of the Permanent Court

E. Judicial Decisions   246

(29) Decisions of international tribunals; (30) Decisions of municipal tribunals

F. The Teachings of the Most Highly Qualified Publicists   249

(31) The teachings of publicists as evidence of the Law of Nations; (32) The impartiality of the teachings of publicists; (33) The task and the problems of publicists

G. Equity   256

(34) Meanings of the term 'equity' in international law

H. Codification of International Law   258

(35) The place of codification in contemporary international law

CHAPTER 4. THE INTERNATIONAL COMMUNITY AND THE UNIVERSALITY OF INTERNATIONAL LAW   261

A. The International Community   261

(36) The essential elements of the international community; (37) The bases of the international community and collective security

B. The Universality of International Law   267

(38) The concept of a universal international law; (39) So-called American international law; (40) National concepts of international law; (41) The supposed differences between the Anglo-American and the Continental schools

184

CONTENTS

page

PART II. THE SUBJECTS OF THE LAW OF NATIONS   277

    CHAPTER 5. THE SUBJECTS OF
    INTERNATIONAL LAW   279
    (42) States and individuals as subjects of international law

A. The Subjects of International Duties   280

(43) The predominant doctrine and the effectiveness of international duties; (44) The reality of the personality of the State and the subjects of international law

B. Individuals as Subjects of International Rights   285

(i) *In the field of municipal law*: (45) The doctrine of transformation; (ii) *In the field of international law*: (46) The international procedural capacity of individuals; (47) The international capacity of the individual as a function of the will of States; (48) The rights of individuals as rights of their States; (49) The possibility of direct enforcement of private claims

C. The Fundamental Rights of the Individual   295

(50) The fundamental rights of the individual in positive international law; (51) The international protection of the international rights of individuals; (52) The international protection of the rights of stateless persons; (53) The rights of individuals and humanitarian intervention

D. The Subjects of International Law and the Creation of Rules of International Law   304

(54) The International Labour Organisation. The Vatican City

CHAPTER 6. RECOGNITION OF STATES   308

(55) The function of recognition in international law; (56) The constitutive theory of the recognition of States; (57) The practice of States. The 'delictual' aspect of recognition; (58) Governmental pronouncements; (59) The existence of a State as a question of fact; (60) The criteria of recognition; (61) The rôle of recognition; (62) Recognition as an international function; (63) Possible developments towards recognition as a collective act

185

GENERAL RULES OF THE LAW OF PEACE

page

CHAPTER 7. RECOGNITION OF GOVERNMENTS AND OF BELLIGERENCY 323

(64) The nature of the function of recognition of Governments; (65) The criteria of recognition. The principle of legitimacy; (66) Other extrinsic criteria of recognition; (67) Recognition of Governments and the principle of effectiveness; (68) Recognition of belligerency. The legal and political concepts; (69) The practice of States. Belligerency as a question of fact; (70) The right to recognition as belligerents; (71) The recognition of insurgents

CHAPTER 8. RECOGNITION OF NEW TERRITORIAL TITLES AND INTERNATIONAL SITUATIONS 337

(72) The practice of States before 1932; (73) The doctrine of non-recognition formulated in 1932; (74) Criticisms of the doctrine of non-recognition; (75) The legal effect of the doctrine of non-recognition; (76) Illegality as a source of rights; (77) Methods of validating illegality; (78) The effect of the declaration of the United States—the so-called Stimson Doctrine; (79) The effect of the Declaration of the League Assembly of 1932 and the American Treaty of 1933; (80) The rôle of the doctrine of non-recognition in international law

PART III. SUBSTANTIVE LAW AND ITS CHANGE 349

CHAPTER 9. CONTRACTUAL RELATIONS BETWEEN STATES. TREATIES 351

(81) Treaties and contracts. General principles of law; (82) The effect of duress; (83) The doctrine of *rebus sic stantibus*; (84) The validity of immoral obligations; (85) Treaties incompatible with the obligations of a previous treaty; (86) Interpretation of treaties. Technical rules of interpretation and various categories of treaties; (87) Preparatory work in the interpretation of treaties; (88) The rules of strict and liberal interpretation

CHAPTER 10. PROPERTY RELATIONS BETWEEN STATES. STATE TERRITORY 367

(89) Territory as subject to a proprietary right of the State; (90) The consequences of the 'object' theory; (91) Divisibility of territorial sovereignty. *Condominium*; (92) Sovereignty and

186

CONTENTS

page

the exercise of sovereignty. Leases and grants in perpetuity; (93) Mandates; (94) International servitudes; (95) Territorial waters and the contiguous zone; (96) Acquisition of territorial title. Prescription; (97) Occupation and effectiveness of possession; (98) Conquest; (99) High seas and air space

CHAPTER II. DELICTUAL RELATIONS BETWEEN STATES. STATE RESPONSIBILITY

383

(100) The principal problems of State responsibility; (101) The limitation of the sources of State responsibility. The prohibition of abuse of rights; (102) State sovereignty and the exceptions to responsibility. The plea of non-discrimination in the treatment of aliens; (103) The property of aliens and the plea of non-discrimination; (104) Limitations of the consequences of liability. Punishment of States; (105) The practice of tribunals; (106) Restrictions upon the admissibility of claims. Exhaustion of local remedies; (107) Requirements of international liability. The requirement of fault; (108) Absolute liability; (109) Limitations upon responsibility for the acts of individuals. Subversive propaganda against foreign States; (110) International boycott

CHAPTER 12. THE ORGANIZATION OF PEACE AND THE REVISION OF THE 'STATUS QUO'

408

(111) Revision of the *status quo* as a general problem of the international society; (112) The meaning of peaceful change as a legal institution; (113) Peaceful change by agreement: (*a*) The obligation to negotiate; (*b*) Conciliation commissions; (*c*) Conciliation by the League of Nations; (114) The effectiveness of peaceful change by agreement; (115) International tribunals and peaceful change. Consideration of changed conditions as an element of the judicial function: (*a*) Jurisprudence and judicial legislation; (*b*) The doctrine of *rebus sic stantibus*; (*c*) The prohibition of abuse of rights; (116) Grant of legislative powers to judicial tribunals: (*a*) Grant of legislative powers for a given dispute; (*b*) Grant of legislative powers in general

CHAPTER 13. THE ORGANIZATION OF PEACE AND THE REVISION OF THE 'STATUS QUO' (*concluded*)

428

(117) Article 19 of the Covenant and international legislation; (118) The possibilities of Article 19; (119) Peaceful change.

GENERAL RULES OF THE LAW OF PEACE

International legislation and the World State; (120) The competence of an international legislature; (121) Gradual development towards an international legislature. The principle of unanimity; (122) The doctrine of State equality; (123) An international legislature and international realism; (124) An international legislature and the sovereignty of States

PREFACE

This course of lectures does not attempt to cover the whole of the law of peace. Thus, for example, questions of jurisdiction, of diplomatic and consular relations, of nationality and of extradition, are not here treated individually. Originally, I also had the intention of studying in some detail the procedure of international relations, the question of the place which law and force occupy respectively in the regulation of conflicts, and the creation of a legal organization of the peace; but lack of space has obliged me to abandon them. On these subjects I would refer the reader to my book, *The Function of Law in the International Community* (1933), and my more limited monograph, *The Development of International Law by the Permanent Court of International Justice* (1934). However, I have examined with particular attention certain problems to which international lawyers have attached special importance during recent years. These include, in particular, the problems of the position of the individual in international law, recognition and peaceful change.

PART I

THE FOUNDATIONS OF INTERNATIONAL LAW

CHAPTER I

THE PLACE OF INTERNATIONAL LAW IN JURISPRUDENCE

1. *The essential elements of the concept of international law*

International law is the law of the individual and collective units composing the international society, particularly and predominantly as organized in the form of independent States. The international society is the totality of human beings inhabiting the earth. This definition is based on two assumptions, both of which are controversial. One is that the body of rules called international law is really law in the established meaning of the word. The other is that States are not the only subjects of international law. This second aspect of the matter will be considered in detail in the lecture devoted to a discussion of the subjects of international law.[1] At present it is proposed to consider it only in so far as it touches upon the general question indicated in the title of the present lecture.

Subjects of law are persons, physical or juristic, upon whom positive law confers rights and upon whom it imposes duties. In existing international law States, and not other units, are normally and predominantly the subjects of the law endowed with full procedural capacity; other units are subjects of international law without procedural capacity. They possess the latter only by way of exception, which must in each case be traced to an express or tacit agreement of States.

These somewhat dogmatic submissions are, in turn, based on two views: one is that legal relations among States are conceivable only with the help of the assumption that human beings inhabiting this earth are under the sway of an international legal order, of which States are the autonomous, independent and, at least at present, indispensable instruments. The other is the assumption that the final purpose of that international legal order is to secure the well-being of its ultimate units, namely, of individuals. This applies to all law, and it is only if we realize that fundamental truth that we can claim for international law a place in jurisprudence. That purpose is normally secured through the instrumentality of the independent State which, in this sense, is the necessary trustee of

[1] See Chapter 5, p. 279 below.

the international order. It thus happens that the State becomes the principal and normal subject of international law; that international law is devoted almost exclusively to regulating the mutual relations of States; and that, although being fundamentally a *jus gentium*, it is in practice largely a *jus inter gentes*. Even the international intercourse of individuals, in so far as it raises the question of conflict and choice of municipal law, is entrusted to the State. This is the reason why, subject to certain fundamental principles, the State is entrusted with laying down, either unilaterally or in agreement with other States, the rules of private international law.

However, although owing to this assignment of function individuals retire into the background as subjects of international law, they do not disappear from it altogether. They remain in the background as the ultimate recipients of its benefits and the ultimate bearers of its burdens. They reappear, as a matter of juridical postulate, as soon as the trusteeship of the State breaks down and as soon as that trusteeship is abused. We say 'as a matter of juridical postulate' for the reason that, apart from the controversial phenomenon of humanitarian intervention, this is not at present the actual legal position. In so far as that legal position falls short of the juridical postulate, international law is a weak law falling short of its primary function and ultimate purpose as a law of the individual and collective members of the international society. Secondly, as will be shown, the individual reappears endowed with a measure of procedural status in the international sphere whenever States deem this to be necessary for the protection and enforcement of his international rights. All these questions will be considered in the lecture on 'The Subjects of International Law'.[1] They have been referred to as explaining the first assumption on which is based the definition here suggested of international law.

The second, no less controversial, assumption is that international law is law. This assumption is accepted here for the reason that, in general, international law as a system complies with a workable definition of law. According to that definition, law is a body of external and imperative rules of conduct which, by general agreement or acquiescence, are set, ascertained and enforced independently of the will of the individual members of the community. This definition, especially in its emphasis on the external character of the rules of conduct, clearly sets law apart from morality. And whatever objections may be raised against straining international law to

---

[1] See below, p. 279.

square with this definition of law, it must be agreed that the difficulties would be much larger and, in fact, insurmountable, if we attempted to construe international law as a species of morality. We shall attempt presently to consider how far international law complies with the suggested definition of law.

2. *The concept of law in jurisprudence*

But before we do this it is necessary to answer one possible and obvious objection: what is there to justify us in adopting this, and not, say, another definition of law? Is not this definition, like any other definition, an altogether arbitrary proceeding? And if this is so, what value is there in trying to elucidate whether international law complies with it? This is to some extent true. As the definition of law, independent of any particular existing system, cannot well be laid down authoritatively by any legislative or judicial organ, it is incumbent upon jurisprudence to undertake that task. To that extent it is true to say that law is what jurisprudence, or any single exponent of it, says is law. But that does not mean that such definition is necessarily arbitrary. It need not be. And it is not arbitrary if it is based on a consideration and generalization of the creation and operation of law in existing civilized communities. It is believed that this applies to the definition of law as suggested here.

On the other hand, this is not a definition of law based on the attempt to generalize legal experience from the inception of the political organization of States. It is not a definition attempting to include law as practised and developed in primitive and savage communities. The consideration of such law is of importance for the legal philosopher, the historian, the anthropologist. But it is of little use for construing a conception of law applied to the facts and needs of modern society. It is highly dangerous if so used; it dilutes the conception of law and renders it unreal. Law may be a historical category, but that does not mean that the idea and conception of law in a backward period of history can legitimately enter as a constituent element of law in a more advanced stage of development. The only arbitrary element in the proposed definition of law is therefore that it is based on the law of modern States; it deliberately excludes the manifestation of law in primitive communities.

3. *International law and the fundamental elements of law*

We may now enquire how far does international law correspond with the requirements of law as outlined above. How far is there an international community whose general agreement or acquiescence constitutes the basis of the actual operation of legal rules? This latter question will be dealt with separately,[1] but it may be pointed out here that that requirement is not as rigid as some tend to believe. What is more important is the answer to the question how far it is created, maintained in its validity, ascertained and enforced independently of the will of States.

(a) *Creation of law.* To say that international law in its entirety is created by the will of States, as distinguished from a source external to them, is to deny an essential element in the legal structure of international law. But there are many who maintain that authoritative creation of the law is by no means essential to its existence. Some point to primitive law, which is made by custom; others deny that law must be a command and assert that, being a law of 'co-ordination', it may consist exclusively of promises. These views cannot be accepted. It will be shown, in connection with the sources of international law, that in actual practice States are bound, and regard themselves as bound, by rules of law arising independently of their express or even tacit acquiescence. But the external character of the source of obligation is largely confined to the existing customary rules of international law and to general principles of law inherent in the fact that States form a legal community. As to the express creation of new rules of international law the fact is that, apart from exceptional cases of minor importance, no State can be bound without its own consent. International legislation, in its ordinary and proper meaning, is non-existent.[2] To that extent international law lacks an important element which is essential for the development and, in the long run, for the very existence of law.

(b) *The binding force of law.* In this respect, more perhaps than in any other, international law satisfies the requirements of the generally accepted conception of law. Once accepted, it is regarded and professed to be treated as binding by States independently of their will. Even those who attribute to the will of States a paramount and decisive place in the creation of rules of law, agree that the binding force of that will, once expressed, is based on a principle of legal obligation which is external and superior to the will of States. However, even in this respect international law exhibits a serious weakness. This is the highly formal nature of the binding force of

---

[1] See below, p. 261. [2] See below, p. 236.

some of its principal obligations to the point of obliteration of the borderline between law and legality. Thus the obligations concerning respect for the existence and the sovereignty of States are regarded as fundamental; but, in orthodox theory and practice, they lose any legal significance whenever a State elects to avail itself of its legal right to go to war and to annihilate the independence of other members of the community; they become meaningless if, according to the widely held doctrine, the granting and withdrawal of recognition of States and Governments, with all the legal consequences flowing therefrom, are a matter not of legal principle but of political discretion exercised by reference to the political interests of the recognizing State;[1] they become devoid of value if, according to a widely held view, international law authorizes or permits the breach of its obligations on the ground of self-preservation and if every State is the sole judge of the circumstances justifying recourse to action in self-preservation; and, with regard to treaty obligations, their value becomes purely nominal if, as many consider, they are subject to the operation of the half-legal and half-political doctrine *rebus sic stantibus* interpreted with finality by the State invoking it. It will be an important task of these lectures to show that in this particular aspect the defect is due in some cases not so much to the practice of States as to legal and political theories of writers.[2]

(*c*) *The ascertainment of the law.* In this respect existing international law totally lacks what is believed to be an essential element in the conception of law. The rule, which is not seriously challenged by anyone, is that, in the absence of express agreement to the contrary, States are not bound to submit disputes with other States to judicial determination; on the contrary, each State is entitled to determine with finality, so far as it is concerned, the legal merits of a dispute with another State. *Omnis judex in re sua.* That rule is, upon analysis, inconsistent with the independence and sovereignty of the other State, but still it is a rule of international law. And yet, while the existence of a sufficient body of clear rules of conduct is not essential for describing a system of rules of conduct as a system of legal rules, it is essential for the rule of law that there should exist agencies bearing evidence and giving effect to the imperative nature of the law. The law's external nature may express itself either in the fact that it is a precept created independently of the will of the subjects of the law, or that it is valid and continues to exist in respect of the

---

[1] See below, p. 308. [2] See below, p. 355.

GENERAL RULES OF THE LAW OF PEACE

subjects of the law independently of their will. Of these two aspects of the external character of law, the second is the more conspicuous and, accordingly, more important in practice. The fact that the source of law is in its creation external to those bound by it may both in primitive and in modern society be effectively concealed behind the phenomenon of customary law; for the latter is beyond the control of the individual members of a community more as a matter of legal analysis than of political and sociological fact. But there is no ambiguity possible about the external nature of the law as ascertained and enforced by courts. In international society there is lacking to a large extent that feature of the external character of law which consists in its being created regardless of the will of those who are subject to it. That shortcoming must probably remain as long as there is no international legislature in existence—a development practically identical with the establishment of what is usually called a super-State. The other manifestation of the legal nature of international law, namely, the objective ascertainment of rights by courts, is one which could be effected within the frame of the existing practice and doctrine of international law. To acquiesce in the permanent absence also of that aspect of international law is to strain its legal character to the breaking-point.

(d) *Enforcement of the law.* The external enforceability of the law is the principal feature distinguishing it from morality. That international law is enforceable by external action is generally admitted. Reprisals, self-help, and (subject to the fundamental change introduced by the General Treaty for the Renunciation of War) war are usually referred to as the weapons of such enforcement. It is true that most writers have never quite made up their minds whether to choose between the enforceability of international law and the cherished principle that sovereign States cannot be punished. Frequently they maintain both at the same time. However, the principal flaw in the enforceability of international law is that (subject to the imperfect obligations of Article 16 of the Covenant) it is not *external* in the true sense of the word. It does not emanate from an objective authority giving effect to the law; it emanates from the interested party. And although it is possible to maintain that the interested party applying force acts as an organ of international law and that this is in fact the situation in primitive society, the solution of the difficulty is purely nominal. It is for this reason that writers on international law have attached so much

INTERNATIONAL LAW AND JURISPRUDENCE

importance to the ineffective weapon of public opinion. It is only when force is external to the interested parties that it may be regarded as an organ of the law. This is the case when force is used collectively or for a collectively declared purpose. This is the most important aspect of the innovation introduced as the result of Article 16 of the Covenant. But the effectiveness of that article is limited from the point of view both of the extent of the obligation to apply it and of the machinery devised for that purpose.

4. *The legal character of international law*

It thus appears that there is lacking in international law one vital requirement of law, namely, impartial ascertainment, and that the other three requirements—creation, binding force, and enforcement—of international law exist in a highly deficient degree. It is usual to defend the legal nature of international law by the attempt to prove that these shortcomings are not so serious as appears at first sight, seeing that they are defects common to primitive communities at a rudimentary stage of legal development and that some of them may even be found in modern society. These defences of the legal nature of international law are open to three objections:

(i) The first is that whatever may be their weight, the cumulative effect of these shortcomings is to reduce international law to the vanishing point of law. It is possible to conceive of an otherwise strong system of law in which any of the elements described as essential exist in a rudimentary form only: it is then possible to accept the explanation of any particular defect. But a system of rules of conduct in which none of these requirements can be found in a satisfactory manner cannot be rationally defended as a system of law so long as it is maintained that the defects are inherent in its nature.

(ii) The second objection is that the drawing of deductions from the stage of legal development obtaining in primitive communities is inappropriate as a legal principle. Modern States are modern, not primitive, communities. And as international law regulates the conduct of the same human beings, it is impossible, as long as we apply the term 'law' to both spheres, to maintain the existence of different standards in each of them.

(iii) The third objection is that it is equally inappropriate to draw consequences from exceptional occurrences and anomalies in the law within the State as explaining or justifying the normal and fundamental defects of international law. It is, for instance, mis-

199

GENERAL RULES OF THE LAW OF PEACE

leading to adduce, as some have done, the fact that a few countries tolerate duelling in exceptional circumstances, as a reason for maintaining that the institution of war is not inconsistent with law. It is misleading to adduce the exceptional admissibility of self-help in municipal law as a reason for maintaining that self-help as a normal institution of enforcement is consistent with law. It is misleading to invoke the fact that within the State decisions of courts or decrees of the Legislature have on occasions given rise to civil strife instead of promoting peace, as a reason for denying the necessity for these institutions as a condition of the functioning of international law as a system of law.

5. *International law and the general concept of law*

The legal nature of international law can only be vindicated by putting it within the frame of the general conception of law based on the legal experience of the modern States which constitute the membership of the international community, and by the admission that it is a weak law in a stage of transition to a developed law as it exists within the State. This and no other is the place of international law in jurisprudence. This and no other is the relation of jurisprudence to international law. The future development of international law is conditioned by its incorporation into the body of general principles and into the conception of law as evolved by civilized communities without regard to the 'state of nature' existing among States. The more international law approaches the standards of internal law, the more it approximates to those standards of morals and order which are the ultimate foundation of all law. It is more scientific to regard international law as incomplete and in a state of transition to a true society of States under the organized and binding rule of law, as generally recognized and practised by civilized communities within their borders, than that, as the result of the well-meant desire to raise its authority as law, it should be treated as a species of wider conception of law so diluted and deprived of its imperative essence that it is not law at all. It is unscientific to let primitive law, if we can call it law, overshadow developed law as the decisive factor in determining the conception of law. We flout both science and progress if in order to give authority and permanence to the authority of international law we create *ad hoc* a conception of law so wide as to be meaningless.

200

INTERNATIONAL LAW AND JURISPRUDENCE

6. The extent of the incorporation of general principles of law into international law

The study of international law shows that, more than in its approximation to any of the formal requirements of law—for the degree of that approximation is, as has been shown, slender—the vindication of its legal character lies in the fact that as a matter of positive international law most of its branches are framed by analogy with municipal, and especially private, law. With regard to State territory its use is more than a lingering echo of the patrimonial conception of the State. This applies to the question of the nature, acquisition and loss of territorial sovereignty. In the science of international law the 'object theory' of State territory, which regards the relation of the State to its territory as identical with or analogous to proprietory relations in private law, is successfully asserting itself against rival theories which visualize that relation in abstract terms of mystical and sacrosanct power. It is corroborated by the modern practice of showing, in cases of exchange, purchase and lease of territory, that territory may suitably be regarded as the object of the State's right. The private law principle of effectiveness of possession as an element of acquisition and maintenance of territorial sovereignty has rendered useful service and, while modified in cases in which there is no rival claim to possession, still holds the field. The same principle was the main legal argument in the development of the conception of the freedom of the sea and of the law of territorial waters. It has not, with regard to either of these, been rendered obsolete by the developments in science and communications. The principle of effectiveness is likely to supply a regulative principle of high practical value in the domain of the law of the air. Prescription, both acquisitive and extinctive, is now generally recognized as forming part of international law; in particular, acquisitive prescription with regard to State territory has supplied, and is bound to supply in the future, a reasonable compromise between the immutability—save by consent of the owner—of territorial sovereignty and the claim to immediate law-creating effect of any change in possession. The conception and practice of servitudes, which undoubtedly has formed part of international law in the past, is bound to play an even more prominent part in the future as supplying a solution of difficulties in cases in which outright cessions of territory are undesirable. The only serious departure from the general principle of private law with regard to acquisition of

201

GENERAL RULES OF THE LAW OF PEACE

territory, namely, the admissibility of conquest, must in law be regarded as doomed to disappear.[1]

In the field of State succession, the analogy of the corresponding conceptions of private law has now, subject to reasonable exceptions, definitely asserted itself against the view which denies the continuity of legal rights and obligations in cases of change of sovereignty. In the field of State responsibility, consistent arbitral practice and the conventional practice of States have shown that the analogy of the private law conception of fault as distinguished from the exceptional application of the doctrine of absolute responsibility is the best method of approach; the same practice has shown that most of the practical difficulties in the day-to-day problems of State responsibility can best be solved by the application of principles governing the relationship of master and servant. In the doctrine of the prohibition of abuse of rights, which notwithstanding terminological differences is common to practically all modern systems of private law, the theory and, to an increasing extent, the practice of State responsibility have found a legal instrument of considerable potential effectiveness. With regard to the consequences of State responsibility the unmistakable tendency has been to approximate to the principles of private law with regard to the award of interest and the measure of damages as including compensation for direct and indirect, although not speculative, losses. Thus with regard to both interest and measure of damages international law has rejected the view that, having regard to the sovereignty of States, the consequences of State responsibility ought to be reduced as far as possible. This view is still predominant with regard to the liability of States to punishment as distinguished from compensation, but even here conventional and arbitral law, although rejecting in theory the principle of vindictive damages, are gradually returning to the general principles of municipal jurisprudence. The purported right of States to determine, on important questions like action in self-defence and self-preservation, the fact and degree of their responsibility is now slowly yielding to the principle, generally recognized in jurisprudence, that such action can be comprehended in terms of law only when the ultimate determination of its legality is within the jurisdiction of an impartial agency.

Equally considerable is the influence of private law on the subject of treaties. Even those who insist on the distinction, which is probably untenable,[2] between law-making and ordinary treaties, do not in

---

[1] See below, p. 380.   [2] See below, p. 236.

INTERNATIONAL LAW AND JURISPRUDENCE

practice refuse to apply the notion and the rules of contract in private law to the conclusion, termination and interpretation of treaties. No other approach to the subject of treaties is possible if due regard is had to convenience and to the practice of States. Even the notorious doctrine *rebus sic stantibus*, which has been used by some as a pliable instrument for denying the binding force of international law, contains a juridical principle common to most principles of private law, and in that capacity it may still render useful service as a means for adapting treaty obligations to changed conditions consistently with the intention of the parties. In elucidating the intention of the parties as a matter of interpretation of treaties, the practice of States and tribunals is increasingly reverting to broad principles of private law which, in its determination to disclose the real intention of the 'contracting parties, refuses to be bound by rigid rules of interpretation. In international law this danger is particularly great in view of the temptation to use State sovereignty or, as in the matter of *travaux préparatoires*, the alleged fundamental differences between the Continental and Anglo-American schools of thought as a reason for adopting artificial and restrictive rules. The principle generally adopted in private law, and postulating the invalidity of contractual obligations inconsistent with former obligations, has not yet been clearly received in international practice, but there are signs of its gradual acceptance.[1] Disregard of the vitiating influence of duress in the conclusion of treaties has, it is true, formed part of international practice and theory. To that extent the analogy between treaties and contracts has broken down; but this important exception, far from expressing an essential difference between treaties and contracts, has been merely a manifestation of the defective legal development of the international community. Moreover, just as in the case of conquest so also in this particular matter the missing link is being restored by the new developments which, in forbidding and rendering illegal war as an instrument of national policy, have removed the basis of the rule according to which treaties concluded under physical compulsion exercised against a State are nevertheless valid.[2]

Finally, rules of private law, even of a technical and formal nature, when embodying a rule of justice and common sense, are recognized in practice as applicable in international law. This is illustrated by the fact that notions like estoppel or *res judicata* are now clearly incorporated in international arbitral practice.

[1] See below, p. 359.   [2] See below, p. 352.

GENERAL RULES OF THE LAW OF PEACE

This cursory survey shows how deep and incisive is the influence of private law on the most fundamental aspects of international law. Article 38, paragraph 3, of the Statute of the Permanent Court of International Justice expressly incorporates that practice as part of international law. As will be suggested later, paragraph 3 of Article 38, which has reference primarily to generally recognized rules of private law, gave to a large extent formal approval to an already existent practice. And yet it is only recently that the scope and the beneficent influence of private law have become recognized by the science of international law. Until recently, under the influence of the positivist doctrine, it was regarded as a sign of unscientific method to have recourse to an analogy of private law, just as it was regarded as an effective argument to describe a view as savouring of natural law. The disparagement of private law went so far as to deny recognition even to those conventional provisions in treaties in which the contracting parties availed themselves *expressis verbis* of a conception of private law, for instance, in the case of international leases and mandates. It is only recently that the view has gained ground that wherever in a treaty use is made of a general conception of private law, the interpretation of the treaty must, unless the contrary is stipulated in the treaty, follow the principles generally recognized as implied in that particular term. These are: first, that in the great majority of cases the measure of approach to standards or to analogy of private law is co-extensive with the strengthening of the element of law, as against the absence of law, within the body of rules governing the conduct of States. Secondly, that the approximation to corresponding general principles of private law is, as a rule, tantamount to the realization of a principle of justice and equity hitherto obscured by the part which force plays in international relations. Thirdly, that such a reception of private law by the practice of States and by international tribunals has taken place to an extent much larger than the current positivist attitude made it appear, and that, this being so, the uncritical rejection of private law created an artificial and unnecessary obstacle in grasping the legal relations of international life, past and present. Finally, that the work of international tribunals would be greatly facilitated by an impartial study of this problem, especially in view of their having to apply 'generally recognized principles of law' supplementing international law proper.

INTERNATIONAL LAW AND JURISPRUDENCE

7. *General principles of law and the moral basis of international law*

If we accept the view here suggested of the place of international law in general jurisprudence, then that essential analogy of rules of law in the national and international sphere applies unavoidably to the field of morality. Law, as has repeatedly been stated, is the minimum of socially obtainable morality. The trite assertion that the standards of international morality not only are but also must be permanently different and, partly, opposed to those of national morality is as false as the corresponding assertion with regard to the analogy of law. This aspect of the matter will be discussed in some detail later.[1] Here it is sufficient to repeat that in proportion as the standards and conceptions of national law become part of international law, the standards and conceptions of national morality must play a part in the international sphere. It is largely due to the misleading personification of the State that the perpetuation of the dualism of national and international morality has become almost an axiom.

This fundamental analogy between the State and the individual applies not because the personality of the State is as real as that of the individual—in fact there are serious objections to the personification of the State—but because the State is composed of individuals and because it is in the long run impossible to apply to them different canons of reason, law, morality, foresight and even generosity according to whether they act in isolation or in their capacity as members of a State. The same applies to the question of enforcement of the law and punishment following its breach. Any doctrine or practice which grants to individuals organized in the framework of a State an immunity from repression and retribution which they do not possess when acting in isolation must in the long run be destructive both of law and of morals.

8. *The function of law between individuals and States. Spinoza*

And the same is the case with regard to the ultimate problem of the political organization of mankind. The necessity which impels the individual to submit to the rule of law within the State exists, if the fundamental analogy applies, in the relations of States. But its application has been denied by many. Spinoza's treatment of the subject supplies an interesting illustration of that method. In general, he is at pains to treat the relations of States as analogous

---

[1] See below, p. 216.

205

to those of individuals—assuming both to be in the state of nature.[1] Thus, for instance, his views on the validity of treaties and the doctrine *rebus sic stantibus* are almost a literal repetition of his views on the binding force of contracts in the state of nature. But then the analogy breaks down. Among individuals, he says, the natural right, which is identical with *potentia*, prohibits nothing except what no one desires or no one can obtain, but it does not prohibit hatred and strife. But reason, the rational principle of human welfare, abhors them; its supreme command is peace. And Spinoza is emphatic that only that man is free who lives according to reason, but not according to the right of nature. However, all this is thrown overboard when he comes to deal with States. A fatalistic determinism takes the place of the reliance upon the power of reason. He gives no truly satisfactory answer to the question: Why should not the same motives which prompt men to live under the reign of law apply to nations? Why must States remain typical specimens of units living in a state of nature? The answer which he gives is astonishingly inadequate. He points out that the State is able to guard itself from oppression by its neighbours, which men in the state of nature cannot do, weighed down as they are daily by sleep, suffering from disease and old age, and liable to other natural troubles from which the State remains immune. Having thus answered the most embarrassing question, he is not slow to draw the consequences. States, being in a state of nature and retaining all the rights of a state of nature, are mutual enemies. Hence the unlimited right of war and conquest. This reasoning, based on the self-sufficiency of the State, is, of course, grossly naïve. The possible range of physical irregularity is incomparably greater between States than between individuals, where intellectual superiority may counterbalance physical valour. The inducement to leave the state of lawlessness is, in the case of States, not smaller than in the case of individuals.

Equally in the case of international organization proper he comes very near to what is believed to be the rational solution. He admits that in the state of nature the natural right of man can be realized and maintained only through a combination of powers. 'If two come together', he says, 'and unite their strength, they have jointly more power, and consequently more right, over nature than both of them have separately, and the more there are that have so joined in an alliance, the more right they will collectively possess.'[2] He was, it seems, prepared to apply the same principle to States. 'We cannot

---

[1] *Tractatus politicus*, III, 2; III, 11, 14, 17; VI, 35; IX, 13; XI, 3.   [2] *Op. cit.* VI, 13.

INTERNATIONAL LAW AND JURISPRUDENCE

at all doubt that if two States are willing to offer each other mutual help, both together are more powerful, and therefore have more right than either alone.'[1] However, in the last resort he fails to draw the almost unavoidable conclusion. Considerations of a different order appear and dominate the field, and he finally rejects the suggested confederation of States. For such an alliance, he says, makes the State less *sui juris* because more dependent on others for the preservation of its rights; it diminishes its faculty to go to war; it binds it to submit to the joint will of the confederation. Here the hesitating argument ends. It has been reproduced here, at some length, as showing the type of philosophy which, throughout the ages, has influenced the question of analogy between States and individuals in this most vital of all matters.[2]

9. *The theory of the necessarily and permanently weak character of international law*

If the view here submitted of the nature of international law and its place in jurisprudence is accepted, then there is no option but to reject the two opposing theories bearing on this subject. The first, while admitting that international law is a deficient and weak law, maintains that it is necessarily and permanently weak and that the removal of its shortcomings would be tantamount to its assertion as a separate system of law. This view was given clear expression by Holland in his *Elements of Jurisprudence*.[3] 'International Law', he says, 'is the vanishing point of jurisprudence ... since in proportion as it tends to become assimilated to true law by the aggregation of States into a larger society, it ceases to be itself, and is transmuted into the public law of a Federal Government.' De Louter, in his *Le droit international public positif*, repeats the same idea. He says:

Le droit international n'a pas de législateur, et, qui plus est, n'en aura jamais ... Dès que le droit international cesse d'être un droit entre les États souverains, pour devenir le droit d'un pouvoir qui leur est supérieur et auquel tous sont soumis, les États perdent leur souveraineté et le droit international se métamorphose en droit public d'un État mondial.[4]

In the earlier editions of Oppenheim's *International Law* the student will find the repeated assertion that there is not and never will be a central authority above the States. It is convenient to discuss elsewhere some of the aspects of this question, in particular the relevance of the assertion that the full development of international law would

---

[1] *Ibid.* III, 12; III, 16.
[2] See Lauterpacht, 'Spinoza and International Law', in *B.Y.* 8 (1927), 88.
[3] 6th ed. (1893), p. 339.   [4] I, 39.

207

GENERAL RULES OF THE LAW OF PEACE

mean its cessation.[1] The main answer to this doctrine follows from what we believe to be the true relation of international law to jurisprudence. International law can form part of jurisprudence only when its present imperfections are regarded as transient. These imperfections are fundamental, and it is only because they are deemed to be provisional that it is possible to treat international law as part of jurisprudence. Once they are regarded as permanent, international law vanishes completely from the horizon of jurisprudence.

10. *International law as a law of co-ordination*

The other view is that international law is not a weak law at all; that it is weak only when measured by the standards of the law obtaining within the State, which is the law of command, the law of subordination; that it is not a weak law when viewed as a specific law, i.e. a law of co-ordination based on promises voluntarily given and not on a command; that it is not permissible to judge international law by standards reached by way of generalization from one limited sphere of law as it exists within the State; that, on the contrary, it must be judged by the standards of a notion of law reached by way of a synthesis of a law of command and a law of co-ordination; and that, judged by these standards, international law does not exhibit any fundamental defect.

This view is based on two premises, each of which must be rejected. The first is that international law, in its present stage, can legitimately form a constituent element in the general conception of law embracing both international and municipal law. In fact it cannot do so, for the reason that in so far as international law is 'specific', as commonly understood, it is not law. Just as it is not permissible to emaciate the conception of law at any given period by incorporating in it the characteristics of a low and rudimentary stage of legal development, so it is not permissible to introduce into it an element of disintegration by infusing in it the elements of a contemporary but abnormal and obviously deficient system of legal regulation whose imperfections are in themselves transient and foreign to its true purpose.

The other assumption that must be rejected is that law can, in the last analysis, be anything but a command. Undoubtedly, legal

---

[1] It is of interest to note that according to some writers the legal defects of international law, far from making it an inferior type of law render it in fact, because of the absence of compulsive force, a superior type from the social and moral point of view having regard to its exclusive appeal to the sense of solidarity and moral obligations.

208

INTERNATIONAL LAW AND JURISPRUDENCE

obligations may be created as the result of agreements. The bulk of obligations by which the individual is bound within the State are due directly to promises voluntarily undertaken. From this point of view the Austinian formula that law is always set by a sovereign authority requires some modification. This contractual nature of legal duties is even more conspicuous in the relations of States where contract, in the form of treaty, fulfils some of the functions which overriding legislation fulfils within the State. But once we have admitted this, there is no escape from the fact that the binding force of obligations voluntarily undertaken is ultimately grounded in a legal command, i.e. in a general rule of law of which the contractual obligation is a concrete expression; or, as some have it, a legal condition. The imperative nature of the law is of its very essence. The insistence on the specific character of international law as a law of co-ordination is either an insistence on a formal point of technique or a denial of the legal nature of international law. The so-called law of co-ordination in so far as it is consistent and denies altogether an external source of obligation is therefore nothing else than a denial of the legal nature of international law; in so far as it has confined itself to stressing the technical peculiarity consisting in the preponderance of the contractual aspect of international law, the resulting mischief is limited to a somewhat exaggerated emphasis on positivism with the consequent tendency to place the practice of States in the procrustean bed of a theory whose insufficiency has now been abundantly proved. Thus the law of co-ordination of writers like Triepel, Anzilotti and Cavaglieri leads them merely into the cul-de-sac of a kind of positivism which, if we may say this respectfully, has at times prevented them from living up to the positivist promise of giving an adequate picture of the practice of States; the law of co-ordination of Jellinek, E. Kaufmann, Hold-Ferneck, of the writers of Soviet Russia and of Germany after 1933 (who call it an inter-corporative law of co-ordination) leads them to nothing short of a denial of international law.

Thus Triepel finds the obligatory force of international law in the common will of States which by means of an agreement (*Verein-barung*—as distinguished from contract) constitutes a common will which henceforth constitutes a binding rule of law for the reason that the common will of States cannot without a violation of the law be changed by a single State.[1] But he admits that the theory of

---

[1] *Hague Recueil*, 1 (1923), 77–118, a very lucid summary of his views, expressed in 1899 in his *Völkerrecht und Landesrecht*.

the *Vereinbarung* amounts to the creation of a legal power over States and that the law of co-ordination means simply that parts of international law owe their *origin* to an agreement and not to an imposed law. Cavaglieri, who equally rejects the view that the binding force of international law rests on an external command and who describes international law as 'a system of promises between co-ordinated and juridically equal subjects',[1] formulates the juridical basis of the binding force of the common will by reference to the principle *pacta sunt servanda* as developed by Kelsen. But the positivistic habit causes him to regard the rule *pacta sunt servanda* as grounded in the practice of States. The vicious circle is thus complete. Anzilotti, whose exposition of international law also rests on the concept of the law of co-ordinates, does not hesitate to regard the rule *pacta sunt servanda* as an external principle independent of the will of States or, what is the same, as an *a priori* assumption of the international legal system which itself cannot be proved juridically.[2] There is still, with all these positivist writers, a reluctance to assume the existence of the consent of States unless there is clear and unequivocal proof to that effect, and there is a tendency to base certain aspects of international law on agreement (presumed or express) as distinguished from the very existence of the international society as a source of legal obligation, but apart from this there is no denial of the binding force of international law to the extent to which it is admitted.

The position is different with other protagonists of the theory of the law of co-ordination. Thus Jellinek, an adherent of that theory, considered the State to be entitled to disengage itself at any time from an obligation deemed to be inconsistent with the interests of the State.[3] He was the author of the obvious but elastic saying that international law exists for States and not States for international law. Although Jellinek defended, by reference to psychological and social factors, the legal nature of an international law thus emaciated, he cherished no doubts as to its true nature. He admitted that 'the community of States is of a purely anarchical nature' and that 'international law, originating from an unorganized authority and possessing accordingly no overriding authority may properly be described as an anarchical law'. That great lawyer probably realized that anarchical law is as difficult to conceive of as immoral

---

[1] *Lezioni di diritto internazionale, Parte generale* (1925), pp. 44 *et seq.*
[2] *Corso di diritto internazionale* (French transl. 1929), p. 46.
[3] *Die rechtliche Natur der Staatenverträge*, pp. 46–9.

INTERNATIONAL LAW AND JURISPRUDENCE

morality. He had no illusions as to the true nature of that anarchical law, and regarded war not only as a necessary factor but also as an element of progress within the frame of that anarchical law.

11. *The theoretical and practical consequences of the 'law of co-ordination'*

The consequences of the law of co-ordination were elaborated, with a welcome wealth of detail, by Professor Kaufmann in 1911 in his book entitled *Das Wesen des Völkerrechts und die clausula rebus sic stantibus*, and in 1935 at The Hague in an interesting exposition of the general principles of the international law of peace.[1] In the first-mentioned work Kaufmann put forward an additional reason why international law, unlike the law within the State, cannot be a law of subordination. The essence of the State, he pointed out, was self-preservation and self-development in history in a world of competing physical forces represented by other States; that function can be fulfilled only by enlisting all the moral and physical forces of the members of the community; and this can be done only by an over-riding law of subordination in the nature of a command. The community of States so far as it exists possesses no such overriding purpose or ideal. Universal peace cannot be such an ideal; for peace is a negative conception correlated to war. Moreover, war is a necessary instrument in a law of co-ordination. It is the tangible instrument of the guiding distributive maxim of the law of co-ordination, which is 'Who can, may'. Accordingly, victorious war is the vehicle both of law and of justice in a society governed by a law of co-ordination. There is no international obligation perma-nently overriding the interests of the State. The State may legally abrogate a treaty whenever circumstances change so that the treaty cannot be kept without disadvantage to the interests of the State. There is, in a law of co-ordination, nothing higher than the interests of *each* of the parties. In the presence of a conflict of those interests and in the absence of agreement, war is the only standard of decision.

These views were repeated by the learned writer in 1935 in substantially the same form, but without express reference to war as the social ideal of the international community. There is in the Hague lectures of 1935 the same emphasis on the assertion that the State only and not the international community 'a la possibilité d'être totalitaire' (p. 349); that the State only is in a position to establish clear standards of distributive justice, whereas the inter-

---

[1] *Hague Recueil*, 54 (1935) (iv), 313–615.

national community cannot 'invoquer avec la même évidence inéluctable les intérêts généraux de la communauté' (p. 466); that even if such standards were possible there is no 'pouvoir concentré et fortifié pour les imposer, sauf dans le cas d'une victoire militaire qui aurait brisé la volonté des vaincus' (*ibid.*); that, accordingly, 'l'Histoire est une tragédie toujours renouvelée, qui exige une attitude héroique de la part des acteurs et de ceux qui l'étudient' (p. 557); that 'd'après les lois éternelles de la vie, il y aura toujours à côté de nations qui remplissent leur espace vital, d'autres, dont l'espace vital laisse encore une sphère à remplir dans l'avenir, et d'autres encore, dont l'espace vital est trop étroit' (p. 558); that in the absence of the distributive principle 'la guerre, le phénomène-limite de la vie internationale, est un rapport social et moral' (p. 560); and, somewhat surprisingly, that its legal admissibility shows that the international community 'remplit les conditions requises pour l'existence objective et la réalité d'un esprit collectif' (*ibid.*). In view of this it is not surprising that much of the learned author's exposition is devoted to proving that international collective action calculated to maintain peace is impracticable and undesirable (pp. 559, 609–12); that this applies in particular to the Covenant of the League, which has 'abandonné la distinction classique entre guerre juste et injuste pour lui substituer celle de guerres légales et illégales' (p. 597),[1] although it is 'impossible d'éliminer de la liberté de la guerre, l'élément de la justice de sa cause' (p. 598); that even the idea of the moratorium laid down in the Covenant is chimerical for 'l'idée de canaliser et de réglementer par des délais les éruptions passionnées que toute guerre entre nations modernes présuppose paraît paradoxale' (p. 597).[2]

Finally, in regard to the binding force of treaties, Professor Kaufmann maintains his previous view modified by a considerable infusion of arguments drawn from the domain of ethics. He insists that 'il faut considérer les Etats comme autorisés à se prévaloir extra-judiciairement des principes généraux dont on interdit au juge l'application'. (This is not easy to follow seeing that Article 38(3) of the Statute of the Permanent Court of International Justice

---

[1] It will be noted that most writers are of the view that the Covenant has in fact restored the classical distinction between just and unjust wars.

[2] The learned author, it may be noted, is torn between his disapproval of the wide obligations of the Covenant (pp. 597, 603) and his inclination to show that the Covenant does not really impose legal obligations and that it is only 'un document du droit politique international ... qui ne donne qu'une série d'autorisations'. On occasions he compromises by describing it as 'un système de droits d'exercer des influences mutuelles et d'obligations de les subir' (p. 609).

contains no limitation on the general principles of law which the Court ought to apply.) He then invokes justice and—eternal but not actual—law at the same time: 'Les États sont liés aux idées éternelles du Droit et de la Justice: il ne le sont pas au contenu temporal du droit: ils sont des entités qui comprennent et représentent les générations passées et futures; c'est ce qui leur impose des responsabilités particulières' (p. 520). These considerations form legitimate 'titres de droit super—et extra—légaux' which (*sic*) 'les autres Membres de la communauté internationale sont obligés, en droit, de reconnaître' (*ibid.*). Some may perhaps find it difficult to understand what are extra-legal rules of law which others are legally bound to recognize. Possibly also some will prefer the simpler, although not substantially different, language of Jellinek or of Professor Kaufmann in 1911.

No apology is necessary for this somewhat detailed account of the views of an adherent of a conception of international law as a law of co-ordination. In view of the *a priori* character of the definition of law it may not be sufficient to discuss that conception from a purely analytical point of view; it is useful to show the results to which it leads. The law of co-ordination, if consistent, is a negation of international law. It is not the business of science to condemn that conception; but it is its business to reveal its true implications.

12. *Monism (qualified by dualism) as the basis of international law*

From what has been said so far it is possible to indicate in general the lines on which the exposition of the general principles of international law in these lectures will approach the various subjects. It is a deliberately monistic approach by means of which, we believe, most of the actual practice can be best understood and the development of international law to a true system of law can be best promoted. It is monistic inasmuch as it conceives of international law as the superior and comprehensive legal order of which the systems of national jurisprudence are in a real sense delegated systems of law; it is monistic inasmuch as, conceiving of individuals as the ultimate subjects of international rights and duties, it regards the principles of law in the corresponding spheres of municipal and especially private law as applicable to the relations of States; it is monistic in so far as it considers the legally relevant principles of morality to be applicable to the relations of States in accordance with standards not essentially different from those applicable to the relations of individuals. In proportion as international law measures

213

up to the ideal of unity in these various aspects, it approximates to the true conception of law as generally accepted in jurisprudence. In its results, the monistic conception represented in these lectures approaches that which, foreshadowed by Verdross, has now been finally established by Kelsen by means of a juristic analysis of lasting value for international law and jurisprudence alike and which Professor Scelle has now developed in an uncompromising fashion on both a sociological and an *a priori* basis. The method here pursued may be different; for it is an attempt to deduce the monistic view from the actual practice of States and judicial tribunals. For this very reason this attempt will appear to some at times not altogether consistent. This is so because the function of States is not consistent or free from contradictions. But we believe that it is a critical and realistic monism, fully alive to the inconsistencies and anomalies of the realities of international life, which must underlie a scientific treatment of international law. Just as international law is at present an imperfect law in a stage of transition to true law, so its monistic structure is not absolute and thoroughgoing. It is a monism qualified by dualistic exceptions and contradictions. This statement may appear paradoxical seeing that in pure juridical logic there is no transition between monism and dualism. But the very imperfection of international law implies that, if we are to give a true picture of its present position, we cannot treat it as a logical system. It is therefore necessary to admit that, so far as positive law is concerned, monism, while providing a working instrument of scientific knowledge for international law as a whole and while providing an adequate and the only possible basis for its development to true law, often breaks down and yields to reality of a dualistic nature. Positive municipal law may be in conflict with international law, and municipal courts have as a rule to enforce such municipal law. The theoretical unity of international and municipal law is not always recognized within the State as implying the primacy of international law. The current theoretical view of the relation of delegation between international and municipal law is not one which forms part of the legal or political consciousness of nations. The unity of fundamental legal conceptions often yields in the international sphere to the law-creating influence of facts and force—an influence which is here more immediate and less governed by principle than within the State. The essential unity of the subjects of law is obscured by the existing technique of international law and by the exalted and exclusive position occupied by sovereign States. It is unscientific,

INTERNATIONAL LAW AND JURISPRUDENCE

and in the long run injurious to progress, to deny these intrusions of dualism. But, it must be repeated, the monistic construction is both the starting point and the framework of international law. It is only by virtue of that construction, critical but unifying, that positive law with all its shortcomings and contradictions can be comprehended as a system of law worthy of that name.

CHAPTER 2

INTERNATIONAL LAW AND
MUNICIPAL LAW

13. *The monist and dualist theories*

The question of the relation of international law to municipal law raises not one but several issues which lead us into the very heart of the nature of international law. From the point of view of what takes place *within* the State, the two principal questions are as follows. There is, first, the question whether rules of international law can become *per se* part of municipal law, i.e. whether they can have a direct legal effect at all on individuals and courts within the State without it being necessary to transform them into municipal law. The second question is whether, even assuming that such direct operation is possible, rules of international law automatically override any conflicting rule of municipal law or, in other words, whether the primacy of international law is a rule of positive law within the State. It will be seen that these are not necessarily two aspects of the same problem. But they are both intimately connected with the larger question of the relative merits of the monistic and dualistic views of international law. These views may be shortly stated as follows.

According to the dualistic view, international and municipal law differ so radically in the matter of the subjects of the law, its sources and its substance, that a rule of international law can never *per se* become part of the law of the land; it must be made so by the express or implied authority of the State. Thus conceived, the dualistic view is merely a manifestation of the traditional positivist attitude. In the international and municipal sphere alike, it makes the will of the State the decisive and exclusive source of obligation. It is not a mere coincidence that positivist writers are as a rule dualists, and vice versa. This applies in particular to the principal protagonists of the dualist doctrine, namely, Triepel, Strupp, Anzilotti and Cavaglieri.

The monistic theory denies the validity of all the premises on which the dualistic doctrine is built. It denies, in the first instance, that the subjects of the two spheres of law are essentially different

216

INTERNATIONAL LAW AND MUNICIPAL LAW

and maintains that in both it is ultimately the conduct of the individuals which is regulated by law, the only difference being that in the international sphere the consequences of such conduct are attributed to the State. Secondly, it asserts that in both spheres law is essentially a command binding upon the subjects of the law independently of their will. Thirdly, it maintains that international law and municipal law, far from being essentially different, must be regarded as manifestations of a single conception of law. This is so not only for the terminological reason that it would be improper to give the same designation of law to two fundamentally different sets of rules governing the same conduct. The main reason for the essential identity of the two spheres of law is, it is maintained, that some of the fundamental notions of international law cannot be comprehended without the assumption of a superior legal order from which the various systems of municipal law are, in a sense, derived by way of delegation. It is international law which determines the jurisdictional limits of the personal and territorial competence of States. Similarly, it is only by reference to a higher legal rule in relation to which they are all equal, that the equality and independence of a number of sovereign States can be conceived. Failing that superior legal order, the science of law would be confronted with the spectacle of some sixty sovereign States each of which would be claiming to be the absolutely highest and underived authority.[1] In the writings of Kelsen there will be found the most authoritative and powerful exposition of that view, which has since been developed from a different angle by Verdross and Scelle.

The dualists have a ready answer to most of these objections. They point out that as a matter of political and psychological fact, States do not regard themselves as units deriving their authority from a more comprehensive legal order; that, as a matter of positive law within the State, that law is clearly superior to any conflicting rule of international law; that in those cases in which international law seems to be applied directly in the municipal sphere without express adoption, it has been adopted tacitly; and finally, that even in those cases in which international law as a whole is accepted as applying *per se* within the State, it is so applied because it is *recognized* by the State as operating in that manner.

---

[1] This seems also to be the principal objection to the theory which, while being monistic, asserts the supremacy not of international law but of municipal law. See e.g. Zorn, *Grundzüge des Völkerrechts* (1903), pp. 7, 151; Wenzel, *Juristische Grundbegriffe* (1920), p. 387; Decencière-Ferrandière in *R.G.* 40 (1933), 45–70; and, for trenchant criticism, Kelsen, *Souveränität*, pp. 151–204.

217

GENERAL RULES OF THE LAW OF PEACE

14. *The English doctrine of the direct application of customary international law*
But here we reach a point at which it is profitable to abandon doctrinal argument and counter-argument and to enquire what is the actual position as expressed in positive rules of municipal and international law. With regard to municipal law the principal question is: Does it recognize the operation *per se* of international law within the State without a special transforming act of municipal legislation? If it does, then monism and not dualism is conclusively shown to be in accordance with legal reality. It will be seen that this actually is the answer after an enquiry into existing law. In this matter the common law doctrine of England—fully adopted in the United States—has impressed itself deeply on international law. That doctrine is that the law of nations forms part of the law of the land. It was enunciated by Blackstone in his *Commentaries on the Laws of England* in a passage which merits quotation:

The Law of Nations [he says] (whenever any question arises which is properly the object of its jurisdiction) is here adopted to its full extent by the common law, and is held to be part of the law of the land. And those Acts of Parliament which have from time to time been made to enforce this universal law, or to facilitate the execution of its decisions, are not to be considered to be introductive of any new rule, but merely as declaratory of the old fundamental constitutions of the kingdom, without which it must cease to be part of the civilised world.[1]

It was enunciated judicially about the middle of the eighteenth century in *Barbuit's* case (in 1736)[2] and other decisions to the effect that the law of nations 'in its fullest extent ... formed part of the law of England'. It was then fully adopted, even more emphatically, in the United States of America. It still forms part of the law of England and of the United States. As will be shown, the view that owing to the fundamental differences between Anglo-American and Continental law there exist in international law on many subjects two schools of thought—the Anglo-American and the Continental —is nothing more than a myth. But it is a fact that on some subjects Great Britain and the United States have made contributions of lasting value to international law. The practice of arbitration, as will be seen, is one of them. The doctrine that international law is part of the law of the land is another. With one exception, which is more apparent than real, that doctrine has been consistently acted upon and applied *eo nomine* in an imposing number of cases in

[1] Bk. IV, section 67 (1876).   [2] (1737) Cas. t. Talbot 281.

INTERNATIONAL LAW AND MUNICIPAL LAW

various situations with regard to which the ordinary law of the land was silent. The apparent exception is the well-known case of *R. v. Keyn* (*The Franconia*),[1] as the result of which the established doctrine seemed to have suffered a temporary eclipse. This well-known case has been so extensively used by Triepel and others who attempted to show that the English doctrine does not mean what it says, that it is necessary to refer to it in some detail. In that case the majority of a special and authoritative English tribunal decided that English courts had no jurisdiction to try a foreigner for manslaughter committed in English territorial waters. But the main issue in that controversy was not the question whether international law is part of the law of the land in the sense that it can be enforced without an Act of Parliament authorizing its enforcement. The real issue was the existence and the content of a rule of international law in the matter of territorial waters. The majority judges based their judgment on the ground that 'by the principles of international law the power of a nation over the sea within three miles of its coast is only for certain limited purposes; and that Parliament could not, consistently with these principles, apply English criminal law within those limits'. Even those judges who contended for the necessity of special legislation did so not because they maintained that international law could never be enforced without an Act of Parliament but merely on the ground that international law on this matter was not settled. There is a significant passage in the main judgment given in that case, namely, that of Cockburn C.J. After stating the divergent views of writers on the question of jurisdiction within territorial waters, the learned Judge proceeded as follows:

Looking to this, we may properly ask those who contend for the application of the existing law to the littoral sea independently of legislation, to tell us the extent to which we are to go in applying it. Are we to limit it to three miles, or to extend it to six? Are we to treat the whole body of the criminal law as applicable to it, or only so much as relates to 'police and safety' . . .? What is there in these conflicting views to guide us, in the total absence of precedent or legal sanction, as to the extent to which we may subject foreigners to our law?

It is clear therefore that the insistence on the necessity for an Act of Parliament was due not to the desire to challenge the established doctrine enunciated by Blackstone, but to the uncertainty of international law on the subject.

Whatever may have been the merits of the *Franconia* controversy,

[1] (1876) 2 Ex.D. 63.

219

GENERAL RULES OF THE LAW OF PEACE

the case of *West Rand Central Gold Mining Co*. v. *The King*[1] showed once more the vitality of the established doctrine. In that case the Court left no doubt that if the contention of the petitioners as to the position in international law in the matter of State succession was correct, the Court would be bound to apply it. The Court said:

It is quite true that whatever has received the common consent of civilized nations must have received the assent of our country, and that to which we have assented along with other nations in general may properly be called international law, and as such will be acknowledged and applied by our municipal tribunals when legitimate occasion arises for those tribunals to decide questions to which doctrines of international law may be relevant.

The *West Rand Central Gold Mining Co*. case was expressly followed in 1924 in *Commercial and Estates Company of Egypt* v. *Board of Trade*,[2] where Bankes L.J. held that the rules of international law relating to angary constituted part of the law of the land.[3] He quoted with approval the passage in Lord Parker's judgment in *The Zamora*,[4] also in relation to angary, where the learned Lord said:

It would be anomalous if the international law by which all nations are bound could only be ascertained by an inquiry into the municipal law which prevails in each. It would be a still greater anomaly if in times of war a belligerent could, by altering his municipal law in this respect, affect the rights of other nations or their subjects. The authorities point to the conclusion that international usage has in this respect developed a law of its own, and has not recognised the right of each nation to apply its own municipal law.

These are persuasive statements. In two isolated *dicta* that doctrine seems to have been doubted by judges,[5] but there is no reason to assume that its authority in English or American law is diminished.

---

[1] [1905] 2 K.B. 391. [2] [1925] 1 K.B. 271.

[3] In Atkin L.J.'s judgment in the case there will be found the following disturbing but significant passage: 'International Law as such can confer no rights cognizable in the municipal courts. It is only in so far as the rules of international law are recognized as included in the rules of the municipal law that they are allowed in the municipal courts to give rise to rights or obligations' (at p. 295). After having committed himself to this iconoclastic view the learned Lord said, in the sentence following immediately upon those quoted: 'The right of angary *therefore* is a right recognized by English Law.' If we are to understand these passages we can do so only by assuming that the learned Lord thought that the rules of international law relating to angary become *ipso facto* part of the law of England, but that having once become so they are applied as rules of municipal and not international law. It is difficult to see the practical importance of that distinction. In fact, the judgment of Lord Atkin is based on the view that international law recognizes the right of angary only subject to the duty to pay compensation, and this being so 'it would be wrong, unless no other construction is possible, to construe general words in domestic legislation' in a way inconsistent with international law (at pp. 293, 294). [4] [1916] 2 A.C. 77, 100.

[5] See *Mortensen* v. *Peters* (below, p. 228) and *Commercial and Estates Company of Egypt* v. *Board of Trade* (above, n. 2).

INTERNATIONAL LAW AND MUNICIPAL LAW

Judge Moore's reference, in *The Lotus* case,[1] to the 'even and accustomed flow' of 'the common law, united with international law' (p. 75), still expresses the actual legal position. In the same case we find Lord Finlay stating emphatically that 'International law, wherever applicable, is considered as part of the law of England, and our judges must apply it accordingly' (at p. 54). Reasons will be suggested presently why that doctrine, which constitutes a beneficent and progressive heritage of the common law, ought not lightly to be abandoned. It is, of course, well known that English Prize Courts, which regard themselves as municipal tribunals, consider themselves as applying international and not municipal law; and this is yet another example of the direct operation of international law in the field of municipal law.

15. *The bearing of the English doctrine*

The common law doctrine that the law of nations is part of the law of the land is still as much part of the law of England as it was in the eighteenth century. It was not in fact seriously challenged in England until the Continental dualistic opposition to it found its way to England largely through the writings of Oppenheim. The reasons why the dualistic theory was anxious to explain away the common law on the matter are clear. The common law doctrine shows the dualist theory to be inconsistent with existing law.

The second line of attack, in addition to the much used and abused *Franconia* case, was to point out that, according to English law, courts are bound to apply municipal law even if it conflicts with international law. This is certainly so. But it is a rule which has no relation at all to the question of the direct operation of international law in the sphere of municipal law. It merely means that there are limits to the direct operation of international law; it merely means that municipal law can, within the State, at any time assert its overriding force and command judges to act as organs of the State and not as organs of international law; it means that within the State the primacy of international law is subject to overriding State legislation. But, in so far as municipal law does not actively and unequivocally interfere, the direct operation of international law is a fact.[2]

[1] *P.C.I.J.* Series A, no. 10.
[2] Attention may be drawn here to the English rule of evidence according to which judges are bound to take judicial notice of international law in the same way as they are bound to with regard to English law in general. Foreign law, on the other hand, must be proved like any other fact.

GENERAL RULES OF THE LAW OF PEACE

Thirdly, it is argued that even if the whole of international law is deemed to be part of municipal law, this is so only because it has thus been, as a body, incorporated in municipal law by the express or implied authority of the State, and that this fact itself shows that international law does not *per se* become part of the law of the land. Here we reach a point at which the discussion becomes highly dialectical. It is undoubtedly by virtue of municipal law that international law is deemed to have a direct effect; it is undoubtedly by virtue of a rule of municipal law that the unity of the two systems is established. But this does not alter the fact either of that unity or of the *per se* operation of international law. Nor is it a case of one system of law incorporating another by way of voluntary reception. Some dualists point to the above-quoted passage in Blackstone in which he states that the law of nations is *recognized* as forming part of the law of the land and emphasize the voluntary nature of the act of reception implied in that recognition. But it appears clearly from Blackstone (see above, p. 218) and from contemporary judicial pronouncements that such recognition is declaratory, and that it is done in pursuance of inescapable political necessity and legal duty. The law of England, as Blackstone said, would otherwise cease to be the law of a civilized country; it would cease to be what it professes to be. The reception of international law is an obligation prescribed by international law, which declines to regard the absence of adequate provisions of municipal law as a good defence in matters involving State responsibility. Any express act of reception, whether *en bloc* or in detail, is declaratory of an existing duty. There is therefore no reason to apprehend, as does, for instance, Professor Scelle, that incorporation amounts to giving international law a precarious status of inferiority as against municipal law.[1] Just as the binding force of international law as a whole obtains in the last resort independently of the will of States, so does its declaratory incorporation as part of the law of the land. It is not a voluntary reception of an external branch of law; it is, upon analysis, a declaratory act of submission to an objective and comprehensive legal order.

16. *Continental countries and the direct application of customary international law*

It is a mistake to assume, as some do, that the direct operation of international law in the municipal sphere is confined to Great

---

[1] II (1934), 354. It is, in fact, difficult to see what else States could do to affirm their submission to international law. Even an express declaration on their part that they recognize their municipal law to be part of the overriding system of international law would be open to the argument that that incorporation rests on the will of the State.

INTERNATIONAL LAW AND MUNICIPAL LAW

Britain and the United States. It is true that to the common law of England belongs the merit of having given legal expression to the unity of international and municipal law. But the courts of many other countries, without adopting the phraseology of English common law, have actually treated rules of customary international law as directly applicable within the State. Two instructive German cases may be referred to in this connection. Thus in *Ziemer* v. *Rumänien*, decided in January 1882 by the Prussian Kompetenzgerichtshof, the Court said: 'The rule of international law, recognized by all the other great civilized States, that the property of foreign States may not be attached, is operative on Prussian courts, although this rule is not expressed in any Prussian statute or in any treaty concluded by Prussia.'[1] The Court was even more emphatic in answering the objection that this rule of customary international law conflicted with Article 24 of the German Code of Civil Procedure. It said: 'The legislature of the German Reich did not and *could not* intend any violation of generally recognized rules of international law, when enacting Article 24 of the Code of Civil Procedure.' Even more emphatic and bearing directly upon the question here discussed is *Hellfeld* v. *Russland*, decided in 1910 by the same Court. In this case, in which the point at issue was the question of exemption from jurisdiction of foreign States, the plaintiff maintained that as this principle had never received recognition in Prussia it could not be applied seeing that 'there ought not to be a direct recourse to the law of nations, except in so far as there has been formed a German customary law'. The Court rejected that contention. It said:

The contention of the creditor that international law is applicable only insofar as it has been adopted by German customary law, lacks foundation in law. Such a legal maxim would, moreover, if generally applied, lead to the untenable result that in the intercourse of nations with one another, there would obtain not a uniform system—international law— but a series of more or less diverse municipal laws.[2]

These pronouncements have been referred to in some detail as they come from the courts of a country in which the dualistic view was especially outspoken. The position is the same in most Continental countries, like France, Belgium and Switzerland.[3] It is often

---

[1] Quoted by Ruth Masters, *International Law in National Courts* (1932), p. 40.

[2] *A.J.* 5 (1911), 513. See also the decision of the Reichsgericht of December 1905 in *Bardoff* v. *Belgien* (another case of jurisdictional immunities of foreign States), in which the Court laid down that as the matter was not governed either by treaties or by German statutes the rules of international law must be applied (*R.G.Z.* 62, 165).

[3] For a survey of the decisions of courts of these countries see Ruth Masters, *International Law in National Courts* (1932), who, after having—correctly, it is believed—shown that in

GENERAL RULES OF THE LAW OF PEACE

obscured by a peculiar interpretation of the judicial statement that courts apply rules of international law *as part of municipal law*. It has been maintained that this shows conclusively that these rules are not applied as rules of international law, but as rules of municipal law. But, apart from the fact that a rule of international law does not lose its quality as such by being applied as part of the municipal system, that interpretation is ingenious to the point of being misleading. The fact is that in all these cases the rule actually applied has not hitherto formed part of municipal law and it is for that very reason that the occasion arises for having recourse to a rule not to be found in municipal law. The decisive point is that, in the absence of municipal regulation, recourse is had directly to international law; it is a matter of trifling argumentative value whether the rule once thus adopted ranks as a rule of international or of municipal law.

After the First World War a number of countries—like Germany, Austria, Estonia and Spain—anxious to give formal expression to their intention to identify themselves with a progressive doctrine in international law, formally adhered to the English common law doctrine. Thus Article 4 of the German Constitution (which it is believed is still binding in Germany notwithstanding the changes which have taken place since 1933[1]) provided that 'the universally recognised rules of international law are valid as binding constituent parts of the German Federal Law'. These and similar provisions in other Constitutions are in a true sense declaratory of the proper juristic relation between international and municipal law. In so far as their effect is more than declaratory, they may be interpreted as implying an undertaking not to enact municipal legislation interfering with that postulated unity between the two systems of law. While declaratory of an existing duty, it is constitutive in the sense of an implied promise to make practice accord with that obligation.

these countries courts apply directly customary international law, states, somewhat surprisingly, that the result is in harmony with the theories of Triepel and Anzilotti. In fact, it constitutes a clear refutation of those theories.

[1] There has recently been a tendency in Germany to interpret that Article restrictively, namely, as referring only to such rules as have received the specific consent of Germany (see Walz in *Z.V.* 18 (1934), 150, 151). Compare with this Lord Alverstone's statement in *West Rand Central Gold Mining Co.* v. *The King*, [1905] 2 K.B. 391, that 'the international law to be applied must, like anything else, be proved by satisfactory evidence, which must show either that the particular proposition put forward has been recognised and acted upon by our country, or that it is of such a nature, and has been so widely and generally accepted, that it can hardly be supposed that any civilised State could repudiate it.' See also Walz, *loc. cit.*, for the suggestion that the duty to interpret municipal law so as not to bring it into conflict with international law does not apply to the interpretation of the Treaty of Versailles which was imposed upon Germany by force.

INTERNATIONAL LAW AND MUNICIPAL LAW

17. *The theory of incorporation and the progress of the Law of Nations*

That the express adhesion to the principle of the unity of international and municipal law as embodied in the doctrine of incorporation signifies an adherence to a progressive principle there ought to be no doubt. It helps, in the first instance, to reveal the fact that the rights and duties of States are the rights and duties of men, with resulting beneficent consequences with regard to the reality of these obligations and their approximation to the standards of law and morality obtaining among individuals.[1] It adds authority to the rules of international law in a world in which, in the domain of external relations of States, these rules are often only imperfectly observed.[2] It broadens the basis of interpretation of international law by authorizing courts to rely on sources other than purely national jurisprudence. And by making international law part and parcel of municipal law it at the same time weaves the latter into the comprehensive structure of international law.[3] This being so, it must be a matter for regret that, owing to the joint dualistic and positivist onslaught, the doctrine of the unity of international and municipal law has lost some of its authority in the country of its origin. An attempt has been made here to show that there is really no reason why this should be so.

18. *English doctrine and the transformation of conventional international law*

There has been one factor which has lent some support to the dualistic view, and that is the rule that some or all conventional international law does not form part of the law of the land until it has been expressly incorporated into municipal law. There is a rule of British constitutional law to the effect that treaties affecting private rights will not be enforced unless they have received the assent of the Legislature through an enabling Act of Parliament. The precise limits of that rule are not quite clear and they have never

---

[1] See below, p. 280. When in 1919 the authors of the German Constitution discussed Article 4 they stated that one of its implications was the rejection of the view that international law binds only States and not individuals. See the observation of Dr Preuss and Dr Simson (Minutes of the Constitutional Committee, 3rd meeting, p. 7).

[2] One is reminded here of the caustic passage in Blackstone's *Commentaries* (II, 25) where, referring to the legal basis of the clergy's right to one-tenth of the produce of the land, he says: 'Considering the degenerate state of the world in general, it may be more beneficial to the English clergy to found their title on the law of the land, than upon any divine right whatsoever, unacknowledged and unsupported by temporal sanctions.'

[3] See Dickinson in *Hague Recueil*, 40 (1932) (ii), 309–95, who describes the influence of the doctrine of incorporation as 'far-reaching and beneficent'.

been authoritatively laid down by a court of law.[1] But the principle has not recently been challenged. It was seized upon by Triepel and his followers as yet another ground for maintaining that the doctrine that the law of nations is part of the law of England is a mere form of words. If a treaty, ratified and internationally valid, is without force within the State unless supplemented by legislative action, then, clearly, the international law embodied in that treaty is not part of the law of the land. This is entirely true. The rule is obviously in the nature of an exception to the principle of incorporation. But the reasons for it lie not in any subtle intention of the law to take away with one hand what it gives with the other, but only and exclusively in the exigencies of constitutional law and the division of powers within the State. It is a rule of British constitutional law that the conclusion and ratification of treaties are a prerogative of the Executive. In other countries, such as the United States, the concurrence of the Legislature, or of a part thereof, is necessary for the valid ratification of a treaty. This is not so in Great Britain. A treaty becomes binding in this country as soon as it has been finally ratified by the Crown. This being so, it might be possible for the Crown to impose burdens upon the subject, and legislate for him, without the concurrence of Parliament, indirectly by means of concluding a treaty.[2] The existing rule which requires in such cases a special enabling Act of Parliament removes that possibility. It may be added that the possibility of courts having to refuse to enforce a valid treaty because of the absence of an enabling Act is of a highly theoretical nature because of the practice of passing the enabling act *prior* to ratification of the treaty. Thus the Treaty of Versailles was signed on 28 June 1919; the enabling Act was passed on 31

[1] In fact, as shown in the cases of *Walker* v. *Baird* [1892] A.C. 491 and *Le Parlement Belge* (1880) 5 P.D. 191, courts are reluctant to lay down in precise language the limits of the rule. But see *Re Arrow River and Tributaries Slide and Boom Co., Ltd.*, decided by the Supreme Court of Canada (1932) 2 Dom. L.R. 250.

[2] The case of *State of Missouri* v. *Holland, United States Game Warden*, decided in 1920 by the Supreme Court of the United States, is an interesting example of a Government arming itself, by means of a treaty, with powers which it did not apparently otherwise possess. In 1915 the Congress of the United States passed an Act concerning the protection of migratory birds. That Act was declared unconstitutional on the ground that it interfered with the rights reserved to the member States. Thereupon the United States concluded a treaty with Great Britain for the protection of migratory birds. The Supreme Court held that a statute providing for the enforcement of that Treaty was constitutional (*Annual Digest*, 1 (1919–22), Case no. 1). The decision of the Judicial Committee of the Privy Council of 28 January 1937, in *Attorney-General for Canada* v. *Attorney-General for Ontario and Others*, 53 T.L.R. 325, is also of interest in this connection. The question was essentially: How far can the Federation in Canada enact labour legislation, in pursuance of international labour conventions, in matters reserved by the Constitution to the Provinces?

July 1919; the formal act of ratification by the King took place on 10 October 1919; the ratifications were exchanged and the Treaty entered into force on 10 January 1920. This practice of passing the enabling Act before the ratification of the treaty has now become the normal practice. Moreover, it appears that, even apart from that practice, in certain not clearly defined matters ratified treaties are binding upon courts and subjects without an enabling Act having been passed.[1] Thus it is established that treaties modifying the belligerent rights of the Crown with regard to maritime warfare will be acted upon by British courts without legislation. In the case of *Porter* v. *Freudenberg*,[2] decided during the First World War, it was apparently assumed that Article 23(*h*) of Hague Convention No. IV respecting the Laws and Customs 'of War on Land was enforceable by British courts although that Convention had never received express legislative assent. These are the reasons why the common law doctrine that international law is part of the law of the land cannot be regarded as seriously shaken by the requirement of a municipal act of transformation in the case of treaties affecting the private rights of the subject.

19. *The theory of incorporation and the primacy of the Law of Nations*

However, while there is hardly any basis for the usual dualistic and positivist attitude on the genuineness of the doctrine of incorporation, there still remains the question of the primacy of international law within the municipal sphere. While it is clear that international law may and does act directly within the State, it is equally clear that as a rule that direct operation of international law is within the State subject to the overriding authority of municipal law. Courts must apply statutes even if they conflict with international law. The supremacy of international law lasts, *pro foro interno*, only so long as the State does not expressly and unequivocally derogate from it. When it thus prescribes a departure from international law, conventional or customary, judges are confronted with a conflict of international law and municipal law and, being organs appointed by the State, they are compelled to apply the latter. Whether they personally are confronted with a conflict of duties may be a matter of nice controversy into which it is not necessary to go here. But that a conflict of legal rules exists in such cases there is no doubt. It may be possible to argue that in law there is no such conflict since the municipal rule, being contrary to the higher rule of international

---

[1] See, for a lucid survey, McNair in *B.T.* 9 (1928), 59–68.   [2] [1915] 1 K.B. 857.

GENERAL RULES OF THE LAW OF PEACE

law, is simply invalid and legally non-existent. But this obviously would be a dogmatic view. Within the State the primacy of international law is not a fact; breaches of international law, when willed by the State, are implemented by courts. This is clearly illogical from the monistic point of view of the conception of delegation. It is a case in which the delegated power, i.e. the State, disregards the terms of the delegation of power without its author being able to assert its authority. Such conflict, when examined from the point of view of international law, cannot be conceived in terms of juridical logic; it is a break in the unity of law; it can be understood only as a manifestation of the political weakness of international law. But it exists all the same as a rule of positive municipal law. It constitutes an intrusion of dualism into the sphere of the monistic construction of the relation of international to municipal law. But it is a fact which ought not to be denied.

Its practical importance is undoubtedly smaller than may appear at first sight. In the first instance, it is as exceptional for a State to enact municipal law which is admittedly contrary to international law, as it is exceptional for courts to give judgments whose substance they expressly declare to be contrary to international law. Before doing that they will go a long way either in interpreting the municipal enactment out of recognition or in interpreting international law so as not to create the appearance of a conflict. Thus in *Mortensen* v. *Peters*[1] the Court, after observing dryly that 'it is a trite observation that there is no such thing as a standard of international law extraneous to the domestic law of a kingdom, to which appeal may be made', took pains to prove that international law recognized the right of the State to legislate for landlocked or land-embraced waters although beyond the three-mile limit. Secondly, it is a well-established and frequently applied canon of interpretation of statutes in most countries that the presumption is against any intention to violate international law. A survey of the numerous cases in which that rule of interpretation has been applied would show that courts have often in this way put themselves in the position of guardian of the permanent interests of international law against the less permanent interest of the national Legislature.

20. *Possibilities of development in the future*

Although weakened by these presumptions, the formal supremacy of municipal law within the State is still a principle of positive law.

---

[1] (1906) 14 Sc.L.T. 227. See also *Croft* v. *Dunphy* [1933] A.C. 156.

INTERNATIONAL LAW AND MUNICIPAL LAW

In its actual operation it interferes little with the observance of international law; it confers a correspondingly small advantage upon the State. But in its formal rigidity it is nothing short of a denial of the authority of international law. It may therefore be worth while to consider, when history has once more entered upon a stage of consciously strengthening international law, whether civilized States should not only adopt international law as part of their Constitutions but should also deprive themselves of the power to enact legislation, even by way of constitutional emendment, which is contrary to the fundamental constitutional provision making international law an integral part of their system. They could also, in order to remove that part of the original Constitution from the vicissitudes of internal changes, bind themselves reciprocally by treaty not to change it except by common consent. They would thus make international law supreme within their borders and immeasurably enhance its authority; they would be doing so, at the same time, without sacrificing any vital interest. But it would be a change implying a limitation upon the legislative power and conferring upon courts the competence to invalidate legislation contrary to international law on the analogy of the Supreme Court of the United States declaring invalid legislation contrary to the Constitution of the Union. As such, it would signify a radical innovation in the constitutional law of most countries in which judicial review of legislation is unknown.[1]

[1] A further and more ambitious advance would lie in subjecting to judicial review not only legislative acts, but political acts of the Executive in the domain of foreign affairs, e.g. in the matter of recognition of States, Governments and belligerency. If, as is shown below, recognition is a matter governed by legal principle, then there would be nothing strange in any such development. The same would apply to most questions in the domain of foreign affairs which, e.g. in English law, are matters within the domain of executive decision and which are governed by the principle of the conclusiveness of statements of the Crown, for instance, the extent of British territory, status of foreign States and sovereigns, diplomatic status of foreign representatives. The position would be more difficult in the principal matter of high policy of the State, namely, the declaration of war in relation to its compatibility with the obligations of the General Treaty for the Renunciation of War. Have courts at present the competence to pass upon the legality of a declaration of war in relation to that Treaty? If, to confine these observations to Great Britain, that Treaty had been expressly made part of the law of England—and it has not—the problem would still remain, how far courts can pass on the question seeing that the declaration of war is within the prerogative of the Crown. It could, of course, be argued that by the incorporation of the Treaty as part of municipal law, the Royal prerogative has been abolished in this matter. However that may be, whether in Great Britain or in any other country, it would appear that the question of the legality of a declaration of war is, with regard to the members of the League of Nations, more properly a matter for an international decision. However, the Permanent Court of International Justice as at present constituted does not always enable the Council or Assembly to render an effective decision of that nature.

229

GENERAL RULES OF THE LAW OF PEACE

These improvements in the law may be far off. But in the meantime it is important to bear in mind that the assertion of conflicting municipal law over international law is merely a rule of municipal law; its operation is confined to the territory of the State; it is in the true sense provisional. From the point of view of international law it constitutes an illegality and gives rise to State responsibility. Municipal courts may be compelled to give judgments contrary to international law because of the absence of adequate municipal legislation or because of the existence of legislation positively violative of international law. But it is well established that these circumstances afford no good defence before an international tribunal; that the judgments in question constitute a breach of international law entailing the duty of compensation; and that, apart from such consequences in the domain of liability, they are, on the international plane, to be of no effect whatsoever.[1] They are, as the Permanent Court has said, mere facts.[2] That purely provisional character of judgments of municipal courts inconsistent with international law is obscured by the fact that, owing to the absence of compulsory jurisdiction of international tribunals and to the absence of remedy so far as the State's own nationals are concerned, it is not always possible to obtain an authoritative declaration of the responsibility of the State concerned and of the invalidity of the judgment in question. But this is a procedural difficulty. From the point of view of international law the conflict exists legally only as a breach of the law; the unity of the two systems as expressed in the subordination of municipal law to the law of nations is complete and undoubted. From the point of view of municipal law that unity must be judged not from the angle of the exceptional phenomenon of possible conflicts but from the point of view of the more typical and normal phenomenon of the direct, *per se* operation of the rules of customary international law.

[1] In the *Martini* case between Italy and Venezuela, decided on 3 May 1930, the Tribunal, after having found that a judgment of a Venezuelan court was contrary to international law, expressly annulled the relevant part of that judgment. It said: 'the Arbitral Tribunal emphasizes that an illegal act has been committed and applies the principle that the consequences of the illegal act must be effaced' (*Annual Digest*, 5 (1929–30), Case no. 93, VIII).

[2] *P.C.I.J.* Series A, no. 7, p. 19 (*Case concerning Certain German Interests in Polish Upper Silesia (Merits)*).

CHAPTER 3

THE SOURCES OF INTERNATIONAL LAW

A. THE THEORY OF SOURCES

21. *The theory of sources and the basis of international law*

The dispute concerning the sources of international law has now, seventeen years after the establishment of the Permanent Court of International Justice, assumed a character less controversial than it exhibited before that event. Article 38 of the Statute of the Court, containing as it does an authoritative definition of the sources of international law, has done much to deprive the controversy of most of its practical interest. And the Court's jurisprudence, showing as it has that that Article is a workable instrument covering a great variety of contingencies, has further contributed to smoothing the edges of controversy and rendering it almost a matter of the past. The sharp knife of policy, as expressed in an almost universal treaty, cut more deeply into the body of positivism than the renascence of national law, the shattering of the dogma of State sovereignty, and other advances in jurisprudence. This being so, it is not proposed to embark here upon a general discussion of the theory of the sources of international law. Neither is it intended—or, indeed, necessary—to expend energy on terminological distinctions between the causes, the basis, the sources, and evidence of sources of international law. The object is rather to draw attention to some salient points.

The conception of sources of international law follows largely from the notion of international law on which these lectures are based. In the last resort, the source of legal obligation is external to States. It is formally external inasmuch as it is ultimately based on a command, not on agreement. It is substantively external inasmuch as it is imposed upon States by the fact—or the postulated fact—of the existence of an international community. The cause, or basis, or source of international law is not the desire of States to be bound by rules. This they cannot help without abandoning—which they cannot do—that society in which they are placed by inescapable necessity. The existence of that society is not merely a sociological

231

source. It is a legal source both as the formal ultimate source of all other obligations under international law and as a substantive source in the form of 'the reason of the thing' or of 'general principles of law'. This is the meaning of Hall's statement that the 'ultimate foundation of international law is an *assumption* that States possess rights and are subject to duties corresponding to the facts of their postulated nature'.[1] This is, in the last resort, the meaning of Duguit's or Scelle's '*droit objectif*' as the basis of international law.

We have said that upon final analysis law is external to the subjects of law. This does not mean that every concrete legal obligation is, in its origin, independent of the will of the subject of the law; the great majority of obligations binding upon the individual within the State have their immediate source in agreement, i.e. in contract, including the contract of marriage. Ultimately, the binding force of these obligations voluntarily undertaken rests on an objective rule of law which lays down that contracts must be kept. All this applies fully to international law. However, apart from obligations voluntarily undertaken—although ultimately grounded in an external rule of law—international law, like any other law, recognizes a source of obligation external to the will of States not only with regard to their continued validity but also in regard to their origin. That source, as we have seen, is the existence of the international society and all the consequences flowing therefrom. The principal, but not fundamental, difference between the international and national society is the result of the absence in the former of a legislative power properly so called. Thus international law differs from municipal law in two respects. On the one hand, it differs by reason of the fact that many a source of obligation which, within the State, is due to legislation imposed upon the individual, is in the international society regulated by treaty. This is so for the simple reason that there is no process of legislation in the international society. Similarly, and for the same reason, many a principle which within the State is regulated by legislation or custom, must in the relations of States be regarded as following from the objective fact of the existence of the international community.

It is this absence of a legislative authority among States which has increased the practical importance of finding a juridical foundation for the ultimate source of obligation from which the formal validity of all other obligations is deduced. This is the function of the so-called initial hypothesis, *la norme fondamentale*. So long as its

[1] Hall, p. 50.

SOURCES OF INTERNATIONAL LAW

purpose is realized it does not perhaps matter much which formula is chosen. Kelsen has clothed his initial hypothesis in the form of the maxim *pacta sunt servanda*. But this form of the fundamental norm is possibly subject to the objection that it covers only obligations grounded in agreement while, as pointed out, there are duties binding upon States without any agreement on their part intervening as a condition bringing the fundamental norm into operation; but possibly Kelsen could answer—one has almost to apologize for the presumption of suggesting to Kelsen a way out of a difficulty—that these other obligations arise out of an implied agreement to enter or to continue membership in the international community.[1] Verdross has put the fundamental hypothesis on a broader basis. Taking paragraph 3 of Article 38 of the Statute of the Permanent Court as his inspiration, he suggests that the duty to respect the general principles of law is sufficient for that purpose. Probably it is. But it is advisable to express even more clearly in the fundamental norm itself both its external, imperative, character and the fact of the existence of the international society. For this reason I have ventured elsewhere[2] to suggest the formula *voluntas civitatis maximae est servanda* as best expressing the rational and ethical postulate of an international community of interests and functions.[3] But, as said, it matters little what formula we give to the 'fundamental assumption' so long as we realize the scientific and social necessity of finding for international law a basis other than the will of States.

We may now approach the consideration of the three principal sources of international law as laid down in Article 38 of the Statute. That Article, it may be recalled, provides in its first three paragraphs as follows:

The Court shall apply:

1. International conventions, whether general or particular, establishing rules expressly recognized by the contesting States;

2. International custom, as evidence of a general practice accepted as law;

3. The general principles of law recognized by civilized nations.

---

[1] An irreverent and irrelevant critic might also be tempted to suggest that at a time when international agreements are honoured more in their breach than in their observance the norm *pacta sunt servanda* is somewhat incongruous; especially in a scientific system in which the fundamental norm is described as based on a maximum of social reality.

[2] *Gesellschaft, Staat und Recht. Festschrift für Kelsen* (1931), p. 362.

[3] *The Function of Law*, p. 422.

B. TREATIES AS A SOURCE OF INTERNATIONAL LAW

22. (a) *Relation of treaties to other sources*

It may be a nice point of discussion whether the order in which the sources of law are enumerated in Article 38 establishes an order of precedence and hierarchy. No simple answer can be given to this question. Treaties clearly constitute the bulk of obligations by which States are bound. A survey of the Judgments and Advisory Opinions given by the Permanent Court of International Justice shows that, with the partial exception of the case of *Eastern Greenland* and one or two less significant cases, all of them were questions of treaty interpretation. Even decisions which are generally regarded as concerned exclusively with a general question of customary international law have actually been concerned with the interpretation of treaties. Thus, to give one example, the principal issue in *The Lotus* case[1] involved the interpretation of the Convention of Lausanne of July 1923, namely, the question whether Turkey, in assuming jurisdiction over an offence committed by an alien on the high seas, acted contrary to Article 15 of that Convention, which provided that all questions of jurisdiction shall, as between the contracting Parties, be decided in accordance with the principles of international law. While custom constitutes the general structure of international law, treaties constitute its actual substance. Moreover, treaties may change custom. It is a recognized principle in jurisprudence that parties may, within legally permissible limits, change, modify or supersede the general law. *Modus et conventio vincunt legem.* They may limit, as between themselves, the normal operation of custom with regard to the extent of territorial waters, the freedom of the sea, the extent of diplomatic immunities, etc. The specific overrides the general. But there are limits to the omnipotence of treaties.

(1) In the first instance, there are rules of general customary law which treaties cannot change. They cannot stipulate, with legal effect, for obligations which are contrary to morality,[2] e.g. an obligation of mutual support in a deliberately planned unprovoked attack against another State. They cannot impose duties upon third States. States cannot, with legal effect, conclude treaties which both contracting parties know to be inconsistent with former treaty obligations binding upon one or both of them.[3]

(2) The second limitation is that treaties, as soon as their meaning becomes disputed, must be interpreted against the background of

---

[1] *P.C.I.J.* Series A, no. 10.   [2] See below, p. 357.   [3] See below, p. 359.

SOURCES OF INTERNATIONAL LAW

customary law. This means that often it is custom that will vitally affect the treaty, and not conversely. This explains why, although the Permanent Court of International Justice, in almost all the cases which have come before it, has been concerned with interpreting treaties, it had actually in those cases to decide on questions bearing on customary international law. Thus, although in the *Free Zones* case it was called upon to interpret the provisions of the Treaties of 1815, of Article 435 of the Treaty of Versailles and of the arbitration agreement itself, in fact its judgment was based on answers to general questions like the effect of treaties on third parties, the doctrine *rebus sic stantibus*, the right of a judicial tribunal to decide *ex aequo et bono*, the binding force of declarations made in the course of proceedings before the Court, the admissibility of *travaux préparatoires*, etc. This method is not confined to the Permanent Court of International Justice. Other international tribunals have not only acted on that principle but have given clear expression to it. Thus in the case of *The Kronprins Gustav Adolf* decided on 18 July 1932 between the United States and Sweden, M. Borel, Arbitrator, was confronted with the contention of the United States that the function of the Arbitrator was confined to the examination of the compatibility of the action of the United States with the treaties in question and that he was not therefore expected to base his decision on principles of international law as such. The Arbitrator dealt with that contention as follows:

However just in itself, this observation must not be allowed to lead to a misapprehension. The decision to be given is undoubtedly to be governed by the treaties, and the Arbitrator is not asked to look for other rules in the field of international law. On the other hand, it is clear that the treaties themselves are part of the international law as accepted by both contracting powers and it may be safely assumed that, when the said treaties were concluded, both parties considered them as being agreed upon as special provisions to be enforced between them in what may be called the atmosphere and spirit of international law as recognized by both of them.[1]

In the *Georges Pinson* case, decided on 19 October 1928 by the French–Mexican Mixed Claims Commission, Verzijl, President of the Commission, laid down—among other rules of interpretation—that 'every international convention must be deemed tacitly to refer to general principles of international law for all questions which it does not resolve in express terms and in a different way'.[2]

---

[1] *A.J.* 26 (1932), 839.   [2] *Annual Digest*, 4 (1927–8), Case no. 292.

GENERAL RULES OF THE LAW OF PEACE

(3) Similarly, there is no doubt as to the precedence of treaties over 'general principles of law' recognized by civilized States. In fact, in so far as these 'general principles of law' are identified with what is usually given the name of the law of nature—and they are to a large extent so identified—modern international law does not assert their superiority over express manifestations of the will of the State. For although international law is not 'positivist', it is also not 'naturalist'. States may abandon or change general principles of law so as to suit their special needs. But, as in the case of customary international law, that autonomy of the parties is circumscribed in two respects. It cannot disregard those principles of ethics and fair dealing which the practice of mankind has incorporated in the 'general principles of law'. Secondly, as is pointed out below, doubtful or controversial treaty provisions must be and are interpreted in the light not only of custom but also of general principles of law. When in the Twelfth Advisory Opinion concerning the Boundary dispute between Turkey and Iraq the Court interpreted the provisions of the Covenant of the League concerning unanimity by reference to the principle *nemo judex in re sua*,[1] it availed itself, without calling it by that name, of a general principle of law in a striking and significant manner.

23. (b) The legislative effect of treaties

Treaties are enumerated as the first source of the law to be applied by the Court. They make law between the parties. All treaties are in this sense law-making. But no treaty is law-making in the sense in which the Legislature within the State is law-making. No treaty can impose an obligation upon a party which has not consented to it, unless it is a treaty which a court can fairly regard as being declaratory of custom.[2] In a metaphorical way certain treaties may be described as law-making or legislative inasmuch as they are binding between a considerable number of signatories and lay down rules of conduct of a certain degree of generality. But the difference between these and other treaties is only one of degree. There is a difference of degree only between a treaty in which two States renounce war as an instrument of national policy and a treaty in

---

[1] *P.C.I.J.* Series B, no. 12, pp. 29–33.

[2] The case of *Crichton* v. *Samos Navigation Company*, decided in 1926 by the Mixed Tribunal of Port Said, seems to go beyond that. There the Tribunal held that although Egypt was not a party to the Brussels Convention of 1910 relating to salvage, it was nevertheless applicable as a rule of international law in Egypt (*Annual Digest*, 3 (1925–6), Case no. 1). See also *The Appam* (1917), 243 U.S. 124.

SOURCES OF INTERNATIONAL LAW

which that obligation is accepted by forty or fifty States. There is a difference of degree only between a treaty providing for the exchange of postal parcels between two or between twenty States. As within the State so also in international relations, an act of legislation is the authoritative imposition of rules binding the subjects of the law regardless of their consent; the uniformity and generality of the legislative act is its typical, but by no means invariable or essential, feature. It is conducive to confusion of thought if we use words in the international sphere in a connotation different from or opposed to that of ordinary legal terminology.

On the other hand, treaties may be law-making in the true sense of the word in their cumulative effect. A long series of treaties of a uniform content between a considerable number of States is evidence of custom. A considerable series of treaties between a considerable number of States recognizing certain duties of States in the matter of State succession is evidence of a customary rule of which these treaties must be deemed to be declaratory. The possible objection that these treaties, far from declaring the existing law, provide for exceptions from a customary rule is easily answered. A rule for which it has been found necessary to lay down constantly a uniform series of exceptions ceases to be a rule, and the uniform exceptions take its place.

C. CUSTOM AS A SOURCE AND AS EVIDENCE OF INTERNATIONAL LAW

24. The order in which custom appears in the list of sources enumerated in Article 38 of the Statute is by no means fully expressive of its place in the hierarchy of sources. It stands discreetly behind the agreed law; but it is there in the background to prevent its abuse, to clear up its obscurities, to interpret it—in extreme cases to the point of interpreting it out of existence. And it is there, in particular, to guide the judge when there is no conventional provision available at all. It is in a way the expression of the necessarily objective international law existing independently of the will of States. Now if this latter statement is true, then it is impossible to accept the positivist view that custom is tacit, implied consent, as distinguished from express consent as given in a treaty. The inaccuracy of that view is shown by a number of cogent considerations. The first is that in certain circumstances custom becomes a source of law even for those States which have not participated in it. This

GENERAL RULES OF THE LAW OF PEACE

is admitted even by positivist writers. Thus we find Oppenheim saying:

A rule is also then a rule of general international customary law, if all States which have had occasion to apply this rule have recognised it by custom, and when the number and importance of these States is so great that one may assume that cogent interests of the international community are in the background of this rule.[1]

Secondly, it is generally admitted that States who are newcomers to the international society are bound by customary rules although naturally they had no opportunity to participate in their creation or to agree to them—unless one resorts to the positivist fiction that membership in the international community is due to a constitutive act of recognition in the form of a mutual agreement to accept and abide by existing rules of international law. In both cases the consent is implied; it is assumed by law; which, as may be said of much implied consent, means that it is not existent in fact. (It is interesting to see, it may be said in parentheses, how often positivism in order to find consent is driven to its practical negation, namely, implied acquiescence.)

On general considerations it is difficult to see how the theory of custom as implied consent creating the law could ever have been widely adopted. Custom is actual practice in pursuance of or in obedience to what is *already* law. It is enough to recall once more the terms of Article 38: 'international custom, as evidence of a general practice accepted as law'. Custom is the cumulative action of the members of the community followed *opinione necessitatis juris*. Practice, however uniform, cannot become a rule of law if it is obnoxious to general notions of law—unless, by admission, the system of law in question falls short of a system of law as generally understood. The admissibility of duress in the conclusion of treaties can be and is regarded as a rule of law only because in this respect international law falls short of standards generally recognized as indispensable to the conception of law. But even so it is a constant duty of the science of international law not to succumb to the fetishism of actual practice. *Communis error facit jus*, but it is doubtful whether *commune crimen facit jus*. In fact, it is in this *opinio necessitatis juris* that lies the distinguishing feature of custom as contrasted with usage and comity. These, too, consist of uniform rules of conduct, but that uniformity is not due to the

[1] In *Z.I.* 25 (1915), 8.

SOURCES OF INTERNATIONAL LAW

conviction of acting in accordance with a legal obligation.[1] Thus conceived and qualified, custom itself is merely evidence of an objective rule existing independently of the will of those who follow it. When we say that uniform action over a long period creates custom, we do not, if we think clearly, mean that such action creates a new rule of law; we mean that it creates valuable and as a rule decisive evidence of the existence of an otherwise indefinite and unascertained rule of law.[2]

Important consequences follow from this deserved relegation of custom from a source of law to evidence of the existing law. One of these is that the State action in question need not necessarily emanate from the organs of the State specifically called upon to express the will of the State in the external sphere. It may be given by any organ of the State called upon to adjudicate upon or deal with matters affecting international law. Neither is it necessary that such acts be performed with the express intention of subjecting the State to international obligations in consideration of mutual obligations undertaken by other States. Custom is created by conduct of the organs of the State giving evidence of what in the opinion of those organs is in accordance with the obligations of the State, or with the necessities of international intercourse, or with general convenience and good faith. For that reason custom is constituted not only by formal uniform conduct in the international sphere proper but also by uniform legislation and uniform decisions of municipal courts, in which States, through their organs, give evidence of their consensus to regard certain rules of international law as binding. A consideration of the place of decisions of municipal courts as a source of international law will illustrate this aspect of the matter. Article 38(4) of the Statute of the Court provides that, 'subject to

---

[1] This being so, it is important to keep apart the terms 'international usage' and 'comity' on the one side and 'international custom' on the other. British judges and writers unfortunately do not always make that distinction. See, e.g., Brett L.J. in *The Parlement Belge*, L.R. 5 P.D. 197, at pp. 214 and 217, who refers to the rules concerning the jurisdictional immunities of foreign ambassadors and sovereigns as being the consequence of 'international comity'. In *Russian Socialist Federated Soviet Republics v. Cibrario*, 235 N.Y. 255, 139 N.E. 259, the Court said: 'Comity may be defined as that reciprocal courtesy which one member of the family of nations owes to the other ... Rules of comity are a portion of the law that they [the courts] enforce.'

[2] This relegation of custom from an independent source of law to—to use once more the language of the Statute of the Court—'evidence of a general practice accepted as law' will be found by some to be too drastic. But this is so only if one attaches undue importance to the distinction between the sources of law and the evidence of these sources. A source of law divorced from its evidence is a hollow phrase; in a very substantial sense international custom on any given topic of international law is nothing else than the sum total of various acts showing a recognition of the legal rule in question.

GENERAL RULES OF THE LAW OF PEACE

the provisions of Article 59', the Court will apply 'judicial decisions ... as subsidiary means for the determination of rules of law'. These judicial decisions include decisions of municipal courts. It will be submitted here that the actual *sedes materiae* of municipal case law in the scheme of sources of international law is to be found not in the passage just quoted, but in that portion of Article 38 which designates as a direct source of international law 'international custom, as evidence of a general practice accepted as law'. The possibility of regarding municipal decisions as a direct source of customary international law has been denied by positivist writers not only on the general ground of the dualistic conception which refuses to recognize the international order as a direct source of municipal rights and vice versa. It has been denied by reference to the formal requirements of custom as a law-creating act. Thus Cavaglieri has pointed out that it is not sufficient for the creation of rules of international law that the manifestations of the will of States should be of identical content. These manifestations must be reciprocal, i.e. deliberately made by the competent organs to correspond to each other with a view to creating mutual obligations.[1] It was yet another characteristic of the positivist doctrine that it not only attached decisive and exclusive importance to the will of States as a source of international law, but that it was most cautious in assuming such will—except when it operated with the help of the fiction of implied consent.

If manifestations of custom were as directly law-creating as the exercise of the treaty-making power, then the formal requirements as formulated by Cavaglieri would have to be regarded as not lacking in justification. But, as has been said, manifestations of custom are but evidence of the existing law. This being so, it is difficult to see why, in relation to custom as evidenced by judicial decisions, to quote Cavaglieri, 'it is necessary that the uniform acts should be reciprocal, that is, intended to meet and to merge into the corresponding acts of other States'.[2] Judicial decisions are not political acts intended to produce new international law; their object is to pronounce judgment *opinione juris*, i.e. in accordance with existing law.[3] *Opinio juris* is the central requirement of custom, and

---

[1] *Lezioni di diritto internazionale, Parte generale* (1925), p. 56.

[2] *Ibid.* See also Anzilotti, *Il diritto internazionale nei giudizi interni* (1905), pp. 143–6, 197, 198.

[3] In my article published in *B.T.* 10 (1929), 65–95, on 'Municipal Decisions as a Source of International Law', I arrived at results largely identical with those put forward here. But I was then still inclined to treat custom as a law-creating phenomenon based on consent, and had to reach that result in a somewhat roundabout way.

240

SOURCES OF INTERNATIONAL LAW

it is in judicial decisions that that condition can be fulfilled in a spirit of detachment and impartiality free from considerations of immediate interests of States. From this point of view judicial decisions are of greater value as evidence of custom than the frequently contradictory or inconsistent attitudes of Governments.[1]

Just as the various acts constituting evidence of custom need not comply with any rigid requirements of form or competence, so also the manifestations of cessation of custom need not bear the impress of a formal act. A rule of customary international law may, of course, be expressly changed by treaty. Thus, to mention the most important example, the General Treaty for the Renunciation of War abolished the customary rule of international law permitting war as an instrument of national policy. How far has that Treaty, in consequence, abolished other rules of customary international law whose *raison d'être* lay in the admissibility of war as a legal process—rules like the principle of absolute impartiality in neutrality, recognition of conquest as conferring a title, disregard of the vitiating influence of duress in the conclusion of treaties? It cannot properly be maintained that, as a rule, a formal and express treaty is necessary to abolish those customary rules whose foundation has been destroyed as the result of the conclusion of a treaty. On the other hand, it may happen that States do not wish to draw all the logical consequences, in the field of custom, flowing from the conclusion of a treaty. This happens, for instance, when they draw only some of these consequences, and thus leave implicitly intact the remaining aspects of the customary rule. It is proposed to consider this question in more detail in the discussion of the effects of the General Treaty for the Renunciation of War. In the meantime, it is enough to state that customary rules when conceived as static and immutable are as much to be deplored as permanent international treaties impervious to social changes and international progress.

D. GENERAL PRINCIPLES OF LAW

25. *The general principles of law in Article 38, and the science of international law*

The centre of gravity of Article 38, paragraph 3, of the Statute of the Court as well as of the doctrine of the sources of international law is the part played by the 'general principles of law recognized

---

[1] Thus, e.g., the attitude of Great Britain and the United States in the *Behring Sea* Arbitration on the question of admissibility in international law of damages for loss of profits was diametrically opposed to the attitude of those countries in the *Alabama* Arbitration.

GENERAL RULES OF THE LAW OF PEACE

by civilized nations'. That Article is, essentially, purely declaratory; and yet it is not often that the express recognition of an existing social or legal fact has played a more pronounced part or has had a more revolutionary effect than paragraph 3 of Article 38. It is declaratory because, prior to the Statute of the Court, arbitral practice and arbitration agreements laying down the rules of decision recognized these principles as a source of decision. The evidence for that statement is abundant.[1] But, apart from that evidence, paragraph 3 of Article 38 must be regarded as declaratory because 'general principles of law' expresses that vast residuum of social necessity—over and above conventional agreements, and over and above customary law, which is often incomplete, controversial and lagging behind developments—that social and legal necessity without which law, international and other, is inconceivable. And yet it is difficult to exaggerate the salutary effect which that provision has had.

It constitutes, when studied by itself, an authoritative pronouncement that international law is part of the general conception of law (not, please note, of the law of primitive communities, but of civilized States); it is an express assertion of the fundamental analogy of individuals and States, with the resulting approximation of the moral standards underlying both; it is a clear affirmation of the binding force of sources of obligation other than the will of States.[2]

26. The 'general principles of law' and legal positivism

So far as the science of international law is concerned Article 38(3) has dealt the death blow to positivism in its most important manifestation, namely, in its theory of the sources of judicial decision. It denies the fundamental tenet of positivism that custom and treaty are the only sources upon which the judge is entitled to draw. It denies, in particular, the doctrine that there exist gaps in international law and that as a result international tribunals are at

[1] I attempted to collect that evidence ten years ago in my book, *The Private Law Sources and Analogies of International Law*, when the results of that enquiry led me to the conclusion that there is a customary rule of international law to the effect that rules of law otherwise independent of custom and treaty are to be regarded as binding in individual cases.

[2] The strictly positivist logician may insist that, after all, it is owing to the express provisions of a treaty—i.e. the international document incorporating the Statute of the Court—that 'general principles of law' are embodied in international law. This is a dialectical point which it may be tedious to discuss. On that reasoning no one—except writers on international law—is competent to affirm the existence of a source of law higher than the will of States. In logic States cannot do it. However, it has already been pointed out that that Article is declaratory of custom as expressed in a long series of conventions and arbitral decisions.

SOURCES OF INTERNATIONAL LAW

liberty, nay, are under an obligation, to pronounce a *non liquet* when the point at issue is not covered by either custom or treaty. It is in this theory of *non liquet*—a theory consistently refuted by long arbitral practice—that this aspect of positivism has had an influence which has been far from beneficial to the rule of law in international society. It was first responsible for the adoption of the unscientific and false distinction between legal and political disputes—a distinction based on the view that owing to the material insufficiency of international law there are classes of international disputes which cannot be a proper subject of judicial settlement and which therefore must be excluded from the purview of compulsory arbitration. This particular basis of the distinction between legal and political disputes has now been abandoned—not least under the influence of Article 38 of the Statute—but it has played its sad part and has paved the way for other distinctions not less unscientific and destructive of the professed object of treaties of arbitration and judicial settlement. Moreover, in affirming the existence of gaps, international positivism departed radically from its prototype in the municipal sphere. In municipal jurisprudence it is of the essence of positivism that it denies the existence of gaps in the law; only thus is positivism in a position to deny the necessity or justification of free judicial activity going beyond strict application of the existing law. In the international sphere positivism has asserted the existence of gaps as a reason for excluding the judicial function in matters said not to be covered by the law. In general jurisprudence, positivism is largely a theory of the nature of the judicial activity; in international law, it has resulted in the negation of the rule of law in a vast and indefinite sphere of relations. Article 38(3), by throwing open to the judge the unbounded field of the legal experience of mankind, in substance removes altogether the possibility of the absence of an applicable rule of law; at the same time it formally achieves the same end for the simple reason that the prohibition of *non liquet* is in itself a general principle of law recognized by civilized States.

Article 38(3) has not disposed of all sources of disagreement between the positivist and rival doctrines. It does not, for instance, affect the controversy as to the nature and function of recognition.[1] But by formally dethroning the will of States as the sole source of international law it cannot, in the long run, remain without effect on other disputed questions.

At the same time, it must be kept in mind that Article 38(3) has

---

[1] See below, pp. 308 *et seq.*

243

GENERAL RULES OF THE LAW OF PEACE

certainly not done away with the conception of the will of sovereign States as expressed in treaties and, in so far as it is based on consent, in custom—far from it. It has assigned to them, in a very true sense, the first place in the hierarchy of sources. It is the first duty of the judge to give effect, if only he can, to the clearly expressed will of the parties. But if that order of precedence is not to prove deceptive it must not be taken too literally. For just as customary international law, although coming second in the enumeration of sources, towers in a sense over treaties because it is against the background of custom that treaties must be interpreted, so it is against the background of general principles of law that those two sources, appearing first on the list, have to be interpreted.

27. *The general principles of law outside the Statute of the Court*

These considerations show the radical character of the innovation introduced by Article 38(3). Little wonder that it was not received favourably and that the most distinguished exponent of positivism referred to that Article as *quest'infelicissimo articolo* and was at pains to point out that these provisions of the Statute constitute mere general and not universal international law, with the effect that tribunals other than the Permanent Court are not at liberty to have recourse to that source of law. But actually in a number of cases decided after the establishment of the Court international tribunals fully adopted Article 38, including its third paragraph, as a correct statement of the law. Thus in laying down, in November 1923, the basic principles governing the decision of all cases submitted to the Mixed Claims Commission between the United States and Germany, Parker, Umpire, fully adopted Article 38(3) as a source of decision.[1] This was also the view of the Special Arbitral Tribunal between Roumania and Germany in the case of *Goldenberg* v. *Germany*, decided in September 1928,[2] as well as of the Arbitrators in the *Lena Goldfields* Arbitration in September 1930.[3]

28. *Article 38(3) in the practice of the Permanent Court*

It is of interest to note that in the last case decided by the Permanent Court of International Justice before these lectures began—the case of the *Diversion of Water from the Meuse*, decided on 28 June 1937[4]— Judge Anzilotti, the distinguished opponent of Article 38, and especially of its third paragraph, invoked the latter in his Dissenting

[1] *Annual Digest*, 2 (1923–4), Case no. 205. [2] *Ibid.* 4 (1927–8), Case no. 369.
[3] *Ibid.* 5 (1929–30), Case no. 1. [4] *P.C.I.J.* Series A/B, no. 70.

244

SOURCES OF INTERNATIONAL LAW

Opinion in support of the Belgian contention that, as Holland herself had constructed certain works contrary to the terms of the Treaty of 1863, she forfeited the right to invoke that Treaty against Belgium. The principle invoked by Belgium was *inadimplenti non est adimplendum*. The learned Judge thought that principle 'so just, so equitable, so universally recognised, that it must be applied in international relations also'.[1] And he added: 'In any case, it is one of these "general principles of law recognized by civilized nations" which the Court applies in virtue of Article 38 of its Statute.' In fact, the history of the Court has disproved the fear that Article 38(3) might act as a disintegrating factor in the application of the law by the Court. On no occasion has the Court expressly referred *ipsis verbis* to Article 38(3), although it has from time to time professed to apply a general principle of law or jurisprudence. Thus in the *Chorzów Factory* case (decision on the merits) the Court observed that 'it is a principle of international law, and even a general conception of law, that any breach of an engagement involves an obligation to make reparation'.[2] In a previous phase of the same case it referred to 'the principles generally accepted in regard to *litispendance*'.[3] In the Advisory Opinion on the *Interpretation of the Greco-Turkish Agreement of December 1, 1926*, it denied the right of members of a corporate body to take 'action of any kind outside the sphere of proceedings within that organization' and spoke of this as 'an accepted principle of law'.[4] On other occasions it actually applied a general principle of law without referring to it as such. This happened, for instance, when in the above-mentioned *Chorzów Factory* case it deduced the extent of reparation from 'the essential principle contained in the actual notion of an illegal act',[5] or when in Advisory Opinion no. 12 on the *Interpretation of the Treaty of Lausanne (Article 3(2))* it based a vital part of its decision on 'the well-known rule that no one can be judge in his own suit'.[6]

While Article 38(3) has not loomed large in the practice of the Court, it would be a mistake to judge its importance by the frequency of the Court's references to it either *expressis verbis* or by the frequency of its reliance on general notions of law not involving an express mention of general principles of law. Its principal function has been that of a safety-valve; of an insurance against the presumed but never actually real danger of the Court finding itself without a legal

---

[1] *Ibid.* at p. 50. [2] *P.C.I.J.* Series A, no. 17, p. 29. [3] *P.C.I.J.* Series A, no. 6, p. 20.
[4] *P.C.I.J.* Series B, no. 16, p. 25. And see for other examples Verdross in *Hague Recueil*, 30 (1929) (v), 301–3. [5] *P.C.I.J.* Series A, no. 17, p. 47.
[6] *P.C.I.J.* Series B, no. 12, p. 32.

245

GENERAL RULES OF THE LAW OF PEACE

rule to decide a controversy before it. Article 38(3) has banished the spectre of *non liquet*, and this has been its principal function. There is—it may be said in conclusion what ought to have been said at the beginning—nothing of legal relevance that is not contained in that significant provision. Probably it can best be described as a general principle of jurisprudence arrived at by way of generalization and synthesis of the rules of law in their various branches—in particular that of private law—common to all civilized nations. It is the *jus gentium* in its widest sense; or, if some prefer it, the modern law of nature. Curiously enough there does not exist any modern detailed and systematic exposition of these general principles of law on a comparative basis. Probably such exposition, if attempted, would not materially differ from large parts of the codified or otherwise actually practised law of any modern State.

E. JUDICIAL DECISIONS

29. *Decisions of international tribunals*

Article 38 lays down that the Court shall apply '(d) subject to the provisions of Article 59, judicial decisions . . . as subsidiary means for the determination of rules of law'. It is convenient to discuss separately decisions of international and municipal tribunals, beginning with the first.

It is perhaps permissible to doubt whether the distinction between principal and subsidiary sources is actually as clear as may appear at first sight. It is well known that the subsidiary source of judicial decisions has been most extensively used by the Court so far as its own decisions are concerned. The constant reference to its previous decisions has been one of the principal characteristics of the work of the Court. The Court, without describing itself as formally bound by its decisions, is often anxious to establish a clear line of continuity in them. Witness, for instance, how in the case of the *Minority Schools in Albania*,[1] decided in April 1935, the Court is at pains to refer,[2] on the question of Minorities Treaties, to what it said on the same subject in Advisory Opinion no. 7 (*Acquisition of Polish Nationality*)[3] in which Opinion it referred, in turn, to Advisory Opinion no. 6 (*German Settlers in Poland*).[4] It is true that Article 59 provides: 'The decision of the Court has no binding force except between the parties and in respect of that particular case', and it is

[1] *P.C.I.J.* Series A/B, no. 64, p. 18. [2] *Ibid.* at p. 20.
[3] *P.C.I.J.* Series B, no. 7. [4] *P.C.I.J.* Series B, no. 6.

SOURCES OF INTERNATIONAL LAW

true that the Court pointed to that article as aiming 'simply to prevent legal principles accepted by the Court in a particular case from being binding upon other States or in other disputes'.[1] But the fact that they are constantly referred to does not mean that the decisions of the Court are binding upon *States*. Neither are they *binding* upon the Court. But having once been given, they help in the future 'to determine rules of law'. No written provision can prevent a judicial pronouncement from having a persuasive value as authoritative evidence of what the law is. That evidence is authoritative because of its impartiality and competence; it is indispensable evidence because of the rarity of the occasions on which controversial parts of international law can be ascertained judicially. Decisions given by a Court show what in all probability the Court will in the future treat as law; and for those for whom the science of law is not mere speculation but a practical art of predicting the future conduct of judges—which is for many the test of science—this is the decisive consideration. We are here once more confronted with the relative nature of the difference between the source of law and its evidence. We are reminded here of the acute, but unreal, controversy between English lawyers on the question whether judges make the law or whether the expression 'judge-made law' is a misnomer concealing the fact that they merely reveal the rule hidden *in gremio legis*. And, as they disdain logic, English lawyers are quite ready to compromise and to admit that judges are at the same time the servants of the past and the masters of the future. It is in the last resort a question of the inherent value and authority of the decision. Witness, for example, the frequency with which the decisions of the Permanent Court of International Justice have been invoked by other international tribunals since the World War.

30. *Decisions of municipal tribunals*

The place of decisions of municipal courts as an element of customary international law has already been discussed.[2] When originating from the courts of a large number of States they constitute, in so far as they are concordant, evidence of the practice of States accepted as law. They are part of customary international law. In so far as they are concordant they have also the beneficent result of showing the inaccuracy of the widely adopted view of fundamental differences of conceptions of international law owing to divergencies in munici-

---

[1] *P.C.I.J.* Series A, no. 7, p. 19.   [2] See above, p. 239.

247

pal jurisprudence. In view of the comparative infrequency of international judicial activity, they have special importance as instruments for developing international law. In fact, in many of its branches—to mention only the law of diplomatic immunities, jurisdiction of courts over foreign States and their property, or extradition—international law has developed largely by means of decisions of municipal courts. For this reason, even when these decisions are divergent they are not altogether deprived of value. By revealing divergencies and by reducing them to their true proportions they indirectly further the development of international law. A uniform series of decisions given by the Courts of a State may be relied upon by others as reflecting the view of the State in question on any particular matter and prevent it, effectively if not formally, from throwing overboard a considered and detached view of its own judicial authorities in deference to the shifting requirements of national policy. From that point of view such decisions may be regarded as a source of particular international law.

The principal danger besetting their authority as an expression of international law is not so much the fact that, being organs of the State, municipal courts must apply its legislation even if expressly contrary to international law. Such contingencies, as we have seen, are rare.[1] The principal danger is that, without being compelled to act as the servants of their States, they may feel inclined, consciously or subconsciously, to favour the special interests of the State of which they are an organ. This must, almost unavoidably, happen in time of war.[2] But experience has shown that even in time of peace, in such matters as State succession or extent of territory and of territorial waters, municipal courts are at times inclined to prefer a view not unfavourable to their own State. There is no institutional remedy for that anomaly. As is pointed out below,[3] it is not practicable to grant to individuals, nationals or aliens, the right of appeal to

---

[1] See above, p. 228.

[2] This applies particularly to prize courts professing to administer international law. In *The Maria* (1 Chr. Rob. 350), *The Recovery* (6 Chr. Rob. 348) and *The Fox* (1 Chr. Rob. 312), Lord Stowell affirmed in eloquent language the impartiality and the universality of the law administered by British prize courts. The judgment in *The Maria* was given in June 1799. But it is of interest to note that these pronouncements of impartiality were made at a time when, in the course of the proceedings of the British-American Mixed Commission, the question of the impartiality and finality of decisions of British prize courts had become one of the main issues. See Moore, *International Arbitrations*, 1, 324 *et seq.* and 2, 361 *et seq.* Similarly, the affirmation in 1916 in *The Zamora* [1916] 2 A.C. 77 of the independent position of the British Prize Court coincided with a discussion with the United States on the question of the remedies open to United States citizens with regard to the decisions of the British Prize Court.   [3] See below, p. 293.

SOURCES OF INTERNATIONAL LAW

international tribunals against decisions of municipal courts involving questions of international law. A more practicable course might be the conferment upon municipal tribunals of the power to ask the Permanent Court of International Justice or a branch of it for an opinion on disputed questions of international law which involve at the same time the political or financial interests of their country. Having regard to the authority of the Permanent Court it might be necessary to combine requests of this nature with an undertaking, implied or express, to follow the Opinion once given. There is, of course, no provision at present in the Statute of the Court for the exercise of any such function. In the absence of such institutional reforms the main hope must lie in the appreciation by municipal courts of the fact that, by the law of their own country, they are bound to administer rules of international law wherever applicable, regardless of transient considerations of national interest. When that attitude becomes general, decisions of municipal courts will play a part even more useful than at present as a source of international law and as an instrument of its development.

F. THE TEACHINGS OF THE MOST HIGHLY QUALIFIED PUBLICISTS

31. *The teachings of publicists as evidence of the Law of Nations*

Article 38 of the Statute lays down that the Court 'shall apply . . . 4 . . . the teachings of the most highly qualified publicists of the various nations, as subsidiary means for the determination of rules of law'. There does not appear to have been a single instance in which the Court as such has invoked the authority of an individual writer on international law.[1] This is in contrast with other international and municipal tribunals in which even nowadays views of writers on international law are cited more frequently than those on other branches of law. Probably international law writers have never been treated as *recepta auctoritas* comparable to that of the Roman authors of the *responsa*, but they have been frequently relied upon in diplomatic correspondence and they are often relied upon today in oral and written argument before international tribunals,

---

[1] There is a passing reference to the 'teachings of legal authorities' on the question of litispendence in Judgment no. 6 (*P.C.I.J.* Series A, no. 6, p. 20) and to the 'doctrine constante' (a phrase not occurring in the English translation) in Advisory Opinion no. 8 (p. 37). But individual writers are referred to from time to time in Dissenting Opinions: see, e.g., the Dissenting Opinion of Judge Hudson in the recent *Diversion of Water from the Meuse* case (*P.C.I.J.* Series A/B, no. 70).

249

GENERAL RULES OF THE LAW OF PEACE

including the Permanent Court of International Justice.[1] Before courts, municipal or international, they have never had any formal authority *per se*. It has been repeatedly stated by courts that the authority of writers is that of evidence of the practice of States. This character of their function was lucidly defined by Mr Justice Gray in *The Paquete Habana and The Lola*.[2] He said:

> Where there is no treaty, and no controlling executive or legislative act or judicial decision, resort must be had to the customs and usage of civilized nations; and as evidence of these, to the works of jurists and commentators, who by years of labor, research and experience, have made themselves peculiarly well acquainted with the subjects of which they treat. Such writers are resorted to by judicial tribunals, not for the speculations of their authors concerning what the law ought to be, but for trustworthy evidence of what the law really is.

Occasionally greater weight has been claimed for them,[3] but on the whole their authority has been one of useful secondary evidence of the practice of States. It does not, for instance, go so far as Article 1 of the Swiss Civil Code which, in case of gaps in the law, authorizes the judge to act as legislator and to be guided by tradition and by recognized legal authority. But the usefulness of writings of publicists as evidence of the law naturally tends to diminish at a time when official and unofficial collections of diplomatic correspondence, of treaties and of judicial decisions have become abundant—perhaps too abundant. Also, their function as evidence of the existing law must suffer in importance before international tribunals which are composed of experts in international law and which possess immediate access to libraries of international law and to other source material.

When jurisprudential consideration, as distinguished from actual practice, plays a part in the decision, the writings of jurists are still recognized as offering some guidance. This will be so particularly in cases in which there is admittedly a dearth of practice. *Re Piracy jure gentium*, decided in July 1934 by the Judicial Committee of the Privy Council, offers an instructive example of this type of case.[4] The Committee had to answer the question, 'whether actual robbery is an essential element of the crime of piracy *jure gentium* or whether a frustrated attempt to commit a piratical robbery is not equally

---

[1] Their works are generally accessible, and no lawyer would be likely now to find himself in the position of Patrick Henry, an American lawyer, who before pleading in a case in Richmond in 1790 before the United States Circuit Court had to send his grandson sixty miles on horseback to fetch a copy of Vattel's treatise.   [2] 175 U.S. 677.

[3] See, e.g., the *Commentaries* of Chancellor Kent, 1, 18.   [4] [1934] A.C. 586.

250

SOURCES OF INTERNATIONAL LAW

piracy *jure gentium*'. Confronted with an almost total absence of judicial authority, their Lordships felt constrained to observe that 'speaking generally, in embarking upon international law their Lordships are to a great extent in the realm of opinion' and that international law 'is a process of inductive reasoning'. In the view of their Lordships, 'the sources from which international law is derived include treaties between various States, State papers, municipal Acts of Parliament and the decisions of municipal courts and last, but not least, opinions of jurisconsults or text-book writers'. Similarly, in the case of *New Jersey* v. *Delaware*,[1] decided in 1934 by the Supreme Court of the United States, Judge Cardozo in claiming for the court the competence to fill what appeared to be a gap in the law governing the boundary between the two States had resort freely to jurisprudential considerations developed by writers with regard to the nature of judicial activity.

32. *The impartiality of the teachings of publicists*

But these are exceptional cases. As a rule tribunals are supplied with sufficient evidence of the practice of States in its various aspects. It is probably this availability of evidence as well as the more developed state of substantive law, and not any other cause, that has reduced the frequency of reference to the writings of publicists. It is a moot question how far that decrease in the authority of writers is due to the increase in the spirit of national partisanship as compared with the impartiality which, it would seem, distinguished writers in the formative period of international law. There may be something in that view. The national State had at that time a less firm hold on its subjects, including writers on international law. Many of them were in a true sense citizens of Europe and not only of their country. They taught at universities other than those of their own country; as diplomatists they often served sovereigns other than those of their own country. But, lest we push generalizations too far, it must not be forgotten that it was as a Dutchman and not as a citizen of the world that Grotius defended the freedom of the sea from the encroachments of England and Spain. His *De Jure Praedae Commentarius*, which grew out of his argument as an advocate of the Dutch East India Company, was the foundation to a large extent of his epoch-making treatise on the *Law of Peace and War*. On the other hand, it must be admitted that his advocacy of national interests was exceptional, not typical. There has undoubtedly disappeared among

[1] (1934) 291 U.S. 361.

GENERAL RULES OF THE LAW OF PEACE

writers on international law—and not only among them—that source of detachment and impartiality which was grounded in the universality of the Latin tongue, in the still effective solidarity of Christendom, whether Catholic or Protestant, and in the still powerful sway of Roman law, the *ratio scripta* common to all men. All this does not, of course, mean that the usefulness and dignity of the science of international law are bound to diminish. The very contrary is the case. The science of international law has real and urgent tasks to fulfil—in a sense more real and more urgent than those confronting the jurist within the State.

33. *The task and the problems of publicists*

In the first instance, the international lawyer must constantly keep in mind that the branch of law with which he is concerned is one which has not yet attained maturity. His principal object is, of course, to give a systematic account of the existing rules as deduced from practice. But at the same time his function must necessarily be more independent and creative. He has to a considerable extent to formulate rules by reference to the sources of international law not based on explicit practice; he has to present and contrast the existing rules in the light of generally accepted notions of law.

Secondly, it lies within his province to reveal the inconsistencies and mutual incompatibility of certain existing rules of international law. The right, in traditional international law, to extinguish another State as the result of a successful aggressive war is utterly inconsistent with the fundamental right to existence and independence. The right to refuse to another State the benefit of judicial settlement and to constitute oneself judge in a dispute with that State is utterly incompatible with the fundamental principle of equality before the law. These glaring inconsistencies may be part of the law, but they do not because of that cease to be contradictions whose recognition as such is essential to the development of the law.

Thirdly, it is the duty of the science of international law to examine critically the reality of international treaty obligations from the point of view of their professed object. In international intercourse treaties are often used to confirm rather than to limit the freedom of action of States; they are often diplomatic documents in which the language used tends rather to conceal than to reveal the real intention of the parties. Political treaties and, in particular, treaties of judicial and, generally, pacific settlement, are typical examples of that misuse of language calculated both to placate public opinion

SOURCES OF INTERNATIONAL LAW

and to reserve for the State full freedom of action. Thus, for instance, the majority of treaties of arbitration and judicial settlement, accompanied as they are by wide and elastic reservations, fail in law to accomplish what is declared to constitute the purpose of the treaty. In such cases the international lawyer is placed in a position of extreme difficulty resulting from the clash of two apparently conflicting canons of interpretation. One is that the treaty is to be interpreted so as to be effective rather than ineffective; the other, and even more fundamental, is that it is to be interpreted so as to give effect to the intention of the parties. But what is the position if the intention of the parties was clearly that the professed purpose of the treaty should not be achieved and if in fact they have used words which upon legal analysis, as distinguished from popular *prima facie* impression, show the absence of obligation? In such cases the usefulness of the science of international law obviously depends on not claiming for such parts of international law a legal effect which, having regard to the intention of the parties, they do not in law possess.

Fourthly, and this is partly a necessary qualification of what has been said before, once the language used is consistent with a clear assumption of obligation and a corresponding change in international law, it is within the province of the science of international law to draw the necessary consequences from the progress thus achieved and, if necessary, to adapt the traditional notions of international law to the changes effected by positive law. It is the business of international lawyers to prevent the new substance from being mutilated in the procrustean bed of old notions. The machinery of international treaties is slow and cumbrous, and it cannot be expected that States accomplishing a change by treaty in one direction will find it necessary to enact other changes following from that expressly accepted. But this does not mean that such changes have not been actually accomplished. How far, for instance, has the agreed prohibition of war as an instrument of national policy affected the right of conquest or the validity of treaties imposed by force on a defeated State? The rules of established international law in this matter followed from the fact that war was admissible as a legally recognized process of enforcing or changing existing rights. It was impossible to admit war without at the same time admitting its consequences. Can it now be maintained that the prohibition of war, although destroying the basis of existing rules, has not affected these rules at all? It is submitted that it is the business of the science

GENERAL RULES OF THE LAW OF PEACE

of international law to ascertain the consequences of these changes in the law and not to tolerate that the law should lag behind its developments in other fields. In the examples referred to it is legitimate for and incumbent upon the science of international law to state that conquest and treaties imposed by the victor upon the vanquished after a war undertaken by the former in violation of the obligations of the Convenant of the League and of the General Treaty for the Renunciation of War do not confer upon it a legal right. The science of international law has not so far shown that, to quote Professor Kaufmann, 'le travail scientifique a la tendance d'exagérer les nouveaux éléments et le caractère absorptif de la nouvelle réglementation vis-à-vis des conceptions acquises et traditionnelles'.[1] The tendency has so far been in the opposite direction.[2]

Fifthly, it is the duty of the science of international law to assert the continuity and validity of the law and its institutions against the exigencies and vicissitudes of political reality or of what some regard as political reality. It is not the duty of the science of international law to translate political reality into terms of law; neither is it its duty to elevate breaches of the law, however frequent, into a law-creating factor. It is a false pursuit for the science of international law to try to be realistic in the sense of making the law fit the political realities; in effect this may result in generalizing illegality. The law, so long as it is not changed, must be superior to political setbacks. Law and its institutions embody accumulated social experience. They thus help to keep alive the continuity, otherwise not very pronounced, of the collective mind in matters affecting international relations. They thus help to protect social experience from the effects of opportunism and passive acquiescence in retrogression. In particular, with regard to the interpretation of

---

[1] *Hague Recueil*, 54 (1935) (iv), 589.

[2] On the other hand, the competence of the science of international law to ascertain the consequences of new developments is limited in cases in which it appears, even indirectly, that it was clearly the intention of Governments to leave intact the parallel branches of the law. This will happen, for instance, when Governments in making a treaty expressly refrain from making changes which they adopted in making another treaty on the same matter. Thus the Covenant of the League provides for fundamental changes in the existing law of neutrality in cases in which a member of the League resorts to war contrary to the provisions of the Covenant; this the Covenant does through the institution of sanctions under Article 16. On the other hand the General Treaty for the Renunciation of War provides for no such sanctions. Although, therefore, the natural inference would be that by removing the historical basis of the law of neutrality it has changed the law of neutrality as such, such inference is probably not permissible seeing that indirectly a contrary and negative inference must be deduced from the terms and the circumstances of the Treaty. The same applies to the question of non-recognition (see below, pp. 337 *et seq.*) and the prohibition of resort to force as distinguished from resort to war.

254

SOURCES OF INTERNATIONAL LAW

the Covenant of the League, experience has shown how essential it is for the science of international law not to generalize events and conditions of any particular period of relapse, but to interpret the fundamental charter of the international community in the light of the intentions of its framers as determined by the experience not only of the World War but also of the period of international anarchy which preceded it.

In general, the science of international law must be conscious of the fact that, while the practice of States is to a very substantial degree the basis of international law, not every manifestation—or succession of manifestations—of the practice of States is a source of international law. Some of them must be disregarded, as contrary either to existing and still valid law or to the general purpose of international law. The function of the science of international law must not be limited to the collection and exposition of the practice of States. It must be a critical science. In this connection attention may suitably be drawn to the threat to the philosophical and critical function of international law by what may be best described as the idolatry of documentation. Undoubtedly it is one of the principal tasks of international law to collect and systematize existing law, but it is not its only task. A page of practice may be more useful than a volume of philosophical disquisition. But a collection of frequently contradictory facts, correspondence, treaties, and even decisions, if unilluminated by scientific criticism relating them to the law as a whole, may be bewildering and devoid of usefulness.

Sixthly, while it must be the constant duty of international lawyers to keep the *lex lata* rigidly apart from the *lex ferenda*, it is within their province to act, in appropriate circumstances, as legal philosophers suggesting what is the rational development *de lege ferenda*. They are well qualified to do this by their knowledge of the existing law; in proportion as that law is imperfect it is their duty to do it. In thus acting they are not judges applying existing law; they are aids to legislation. As exponents of the existing law they must not be influenced by what ought to be the law; conversely, in propounding the *lex ferenda* they must not attach undue importance to the imperfect *lex lata*. They must start from the existing law only in the sense that they know its content; but they must not be realistic in the sense of claiming for it a place in the future scheme of things. It is unnecessary to elaborate the reasons why the need for such activity is of special significance in the sphere of international law.

Finally, it is consistent with the science of international law to

GENERAL RULES OF THE LAW OF PEACE

regard peace and the collective organization of peace not only as a moral and political ideal, but also as a legal postulate. The idea of peace may be morally indifferent inasmuch as it may necessitate the sacrifice of justice on the altar of stability and security. But inasmuch as law is essentially a social institution of order, pacifism conceived as a system of obligations for maintaining and collectively enforcing peace is pre-eminently a legal postulate. Without it the science of international law must remain a descriptive discipline of unrelated and often contradictory phenomena.

G. EQUITY

34. *Meanings of the term 'equity' in international law*

In considering the role of equity as a source of international law it is necessary to distinguish three meanings of the term.

(1) There is, in the first instance, equity in the meaning of '*ex aequo et bono*' settlement, as used in the last paragraph of Article 38 of the Statute which lays down that if the parties expressly agree the Court may settle a dispute *ex aequo et bono*. '*Ex aequo et bono*' in this context has little, if anything, in common with equity conceived as a legally recognized qualification and modification of the law by considerations of morality and fairness. Settlement *ex aequo et bono* is a legislative settlement which consciously departs from the existing law. It is not a source of existing law; it is the basis of future law. There is nothing to prevent courts from acting in that capacity, except that should that function be conferred upon them frequently, there may be a danger of obliterating the borderline between application of existing law and the creation of new law, that is to say, between the judicial and legislative functions.[1]

(2) The second meaning of equity is that peculiar to English law, i.e. the branch of law now administered by the Chancery Division of the High Court in such matters as trusts, legacies, mortgages, company law, partnership, suretyship, wardship, married women, etc. These rules of equity originated in the jurisdiction of the Chancellor aiming at adapting the rigidity of the law to the requirements of good conscience, good faith, and morality generally. These equitable principles have now become rules of law proper, governing the various subjects referred to above. They are, in many cases, as rigid as any other rules of law, although in substance most of them naturally embody those ethical considerations in which they

[1] See below, p. 419.

256

SOURCES OF INTERNATIONAL LAW

originated. But it is not in connection with English 'equity' that we think of equity as a source of international law.

(3) In what sense, then, does equity form part, if it does at all, of international law? It forms part of it to the same degree to which considerations of morality, good conscience and good faith have been generally adopted as part of the municipal systems of various States. Some of these principles have obviously found their way into English equity in the restricted meaning of the term; others have found a place in the English common law proper just as they have found a place in the Codes of France, Germany, or Switzerland. The provisions of the Codes of these and other countries enjoining the interpretation and execution of contracts in accordance with good faith as distinguished from the letter of the contract, are examples of the infusion of equitable principles into a legal code. The same applies to Article 826 of the German Civil Code, which lays down that a person who wilfully causes damage to another in a manner *contra bonos mores* is bound to compensate him for the damage; or the similar Article 1382 of the French Civil Code—that rich fountain of what may be called the French law of tort; or Article 2 of the Swiss Civil Code which provides: 'Every person is bound to exercise his rights and fulfil his obligations according to the principles of good faith. The law does not sanction evident abuse of a person's rights.' The equitable principles are included in the general principles of law which the Court is bound to apply by virtue of Article 38(3) of the Statute. When the Permanent Court of International Justice applied the principle of estoppel or the principle that no one can benefit from his own wrong, it applied an equitable principle which has become a general principle of law recognized by civilized States. This is the meaning of the expression 'principles of law and equity' frequently used in arbitration agreements. Probably the expression 'and equity' is redundant. Equitable principles embodied in general principles of law are applicable in any case. But, as mentioned, they must be clearly distinguished, both from 'equity' in the technical meaning of English law and from settlement *ex aequo et bono* as envisaged in the third paragraph of Article 38 of the Statute. It may be possible for a judge to attempt the latter under the guise of the application of equitable principles. This would be an abuse of the judicial power with results detrimental, if not fatal, to the administration of international justice.

GENERAL RULES OF THE LAW OF PEACE

H. CODIFICATION OF INTERNATIONAL LAW

35. *The place of codification in contemporary international law*

With the question of the sources of international law to be applied
by international tribunals there is closely connected that of codification of international law. For reasons of space the question can be
treated here in a summary way only. Apart from reasons of space it
is probable that it hardly merits nowadays the amount of attention
which has only recently been devoted to it. Codification of international law, conceived as the laying down of relatively detailed
rules and principles in various branches of international law in
general conventions binding upon a considerable number of States
on the analogy of codes within the State, is certainly useful. There
ought to be no doubt that its advantages of certainty and clarity
abundantly outweigh the related disadvantages of rigidity and
premature crystallization. But although codification is useful, it is
not as useful or as urgent as the discussions immediately before or
after the World War have made it appear. In fact, when compared
with the truly urgent problems of international peace and organization it must appear almost in the nature of a luxury. This is particularly so when we consider that much of the benefits expected from
codification can be and have been achieved through the less conspicuous activity of judicial organs, and especially of the Permanent
Court of International Justice. The Committee of Jurists who
drafted the Statute of the Court in 1920 adopted a resolution urging
the necessity of codification with a view to reconciling existing
divergencies and the consideration of topics not yet regulated. This,
of course, implied a legislative task going beyond the systematization
and clarification of existing law. It was then hardly realized to
what wide extent the activity of the Permanent Court of International Justice itself, aided by the rich source of Article 38(3),
might be in a position to accomplish these tasks. There are problems
on which divergencies are so pronounced that nothing short of
either an unusual degree of accommodation or a majority decision
of a legislative body can bring about a solution. One may think in
this connection of such problems as the plea of non-discrimination
in the treatment of aliens or the extent of territorial waters—both
subjects on which the Hague Codification Conference of 1930
revealed total and, it seems, irreconcilable disagreement. But a
court confronted with a dispute arising out of these questions would
not be at liberty to confine itself to registering a disagreement. It

258

SOURCES OF INTERNATIONAL LAW

would have to give a decision based on the analogy of rules already recognized, on general principles of law, and on a due consideration of conflicting claims from the point of view of justice and the interests of the international community. The reasons for a decision thus given would in themselves constitute an important factor in any future attempt to regulate the matter by agreement.

It is certain that there are dangers in the attempts to codify international law through the existing system of conferences labouring under the triple difficulty of the doctrines of sovereignty, unanimity and equality. The combination of the requirement of unanimity and the desire to reach an agreement in the form of codified rules may result in retarding rather than advancing the progress of international law, seeing that the agreed rules will often be determined by the attitude of the most persistent and least progressive States. Even before the Hague Conference of 1930 had met, the Preparatory Committee sounded a warning to that effect.[1] Also, in view of the cautious attitude of Governments there is a danger that the attempts at codification may often have the result of revealing and emphasizing discrepancies where agreement was hitherto supposed to exist.

Obviously, the dangers inherent in attempts at codification would disappear if the States taking part in the work of codification agreed beforehand to be bound by a legislative decision of a majority of three-fourths or four-fifths. But of this there is at present no prospect. It is still possible, even at present, for the majority—as it is possible for the minority—to adopt a convention *inter se* and to trust to future adhesions. This has indeed been represented as one of the advantages of codification under the present system. However, the advantage is a doubtful one. There is hardly an advance in international law if after disagreement has been ascertained the bare majority adopts a convention. A convention of this nature perpetuates and accentuates the disagreement, especially if accompanied by a rival convention of the minority. It does not possess the attractive power of a practically universal agreement. There may be incidental advantages in the work of codification, for instance, the impetus given to scientific activity. One has only to think of the official replies to the various questionnaires of the *Bases of Discussion*, and the excellent volumes prepared under the auspices of the Harvard

---

[1] It said in its second report submitted to the Council: 'The Preparatory Committee would desire merely to state here that the work of codification involves the risk of a setback in international law if the content of the codification instrument is less advanced than the actually existing law.'

GENERAL RULES OF THE LAW OF PEACE

Law School. Also, it may be possible to remove minor anomalies connected with the subject which it is attempted to codify. We think in this connection of the various instruments on nationality adopted by Hague Conventions. They include: (*a*) A Convention concerning Certain Questions relating to the Conflict of Nationality Laws; (*b*) A Protocol relating to Military Obligations in Certain Cases of Double Nationality; (*c*) A Protocol relating to a Certain Case of Statelessness; and (*d*) A Special Protocol concerning Statelessness. But—and this is yet another instance of the difficulty of the problem —although only ten ratifications are required to cause these instruments to enter into force, a sufficient number of ratifications has not yet been received.

In view of these small advantages of codification, at the present stage, as compared with its disadvantages, there arises the question whether we are justified in giving to it an appearance of urgency at a time when vital problems of international peace and progress still await solution. It may be undesirable to yield to the natural inclination to attempt easy and somewhat artificial tasks as a cloak for the inability or unwillingness to come to grips with essential problems of international life.

CHAPTER 4

THE INTERNATIONAL COMMUNITY AND THE UNIVERSALITY OF INTERNATIONAL LAW

A. THE INTERNATIONAL COMMUNITY

36. *The essential elements of the international community*

One of the principal questions in any discussion of the bases of international law is whether the existence of an international community is a necessary element in the conception of international law and, if this is so, whether there is in fact an international community to an extent and degree sufficient to satisfy the requirements of an essential element in the notion of international law. Opinion on the matter is sharply divided. There are some, and their number seems to grow, who are of the view that there is nothing in reality corresponding to the notion of an international community, and that this being so, international law as a body of general rules binding on all States is in itself unreal. It is largely owing to this denial of the existence of the international community that many refuse to acknowledge universal as distinguished from particular international law based on consent. There is, on the other hand, a considerable body of opinion holding the view that the international community is not only a fact, but that it is a fact which is becoming daily more obvious and tangible.

The question is undoubtedly of the greatest importance, and this being so it is our duty to think clearly and to beware of generalizations. We have to be clear as to what we understand by the term 'community'. There are at least three questions to be considered. In the first instance, does 'international community' mean an objective solidarity of interests or does it refer to a solidarity of sentiment? It is obvious that either of these two may exist without the other. Secondly, even when we assume provisionally, although not accurately, that the community of interests and sentiments tend to merge one into the other, what kind of community do we have in mind? Is it the community of the law personified in the State? Or is it the psychological community of tradition, fate, culture, language? Or is the community one of economic interests? Or is

GENERAL RULES OF THE LAW OF PEACE

the political community grounded in the necessity of mutual assistance against external danger? It is obvious that any of these types may exist without the others. Thirdly and lastly, when we speak of an international community of interests (and even of sentiment) do we mean the community of interests (and sentiment) which exists rationally as the result of natural and objective tendencies as determined by economic and scientific interdependence, by the common humanity of man and the innate sense of right and wrong common to all, or do we mean that community of interests (and sentiment) which actually operates having regard to the existence of sovereign States and the constant challenge to reason inherent in the fact of international anarchy?

These questions show how superficial it is to answer the problem of the existence of an international community by a facile generalizing statement. No detailed analysis of these questions can be attempted here, but it may be useful to illustrate some of them and in particular the last one.

It has become almost a truism to postulate the existence of the international community by pointing to the growing interdependence and contacts in most fields of human endeavour. Exchange of commodities is a necessity even for States wedded to the doctrine of self-sufficiency. There can really be no self-sufficing State able to live in isolation. International commerce has become indissolubly part and parcel of modern life as well as a recognition of the rational principle of division of labour among States. Even in the period of economic nationalism international bureaux and unions devoted to economic purposes and to facilitating international intercourse have grown in number and scope. Interdependence and contact have become signs of modern civilization. The invention of wireless has signified a conquest of national boundaries to which even sovereign States must submit (except that they may make it a criminal offence to listen in to broadcasts from certain countries). All these are facts. But although they are facts they do not entirely represent the reality of international life. For there is another undeniable fact and that is that between that rational postulate of interdependence grounded in objective reality there has interposed itself the sovereign State as the guardian of national interests in an isolationist and disorganized world. In the matter of exchange of goods, of movement of persons, and even to a lesser extent with regard to interchange of works of art and literature, the actual reality is a denial of interdependence and a triumphant assertion of its opposite. Undoubtedly, as is

262

COMMUNITY AND UNIVERSALITY

shown by the growing number of new technical unions and the maintenance of the old ones, States co-operate even now in matters of economic, scientific and humanitarian interest. But State co-operation is overshadowed by the fostering of isolation and self-sufficiency. This being so is it possible to give a clear answer to the question whether there exists an international community in the economic field? It exists as a fact of reason and of the natural tendency of economics and science and of the social spirit of man transcending national boundaries, but the reality opposing that tendency is also a fact. We are not at liberty to ignore either. But unless our answer to the question is to be partial and inconclusive, it must be based on a choice between fundamental and rational factors and those which reason prompts us to regard as transient.

But we are here only at the beginning of the problem. For even assuming that there exists a real and working—although temporarily subdued—community of economic and material interests, there emerges the further question: Is a community thus conceived sufficient? Or is the decisive test a community of outlook—moral, political and humanitarian? The correct answer is probably that this is not an essential requirement for the existence of a community for the purposes of a legal order. It may be difficult to maintain that any such community, in the full sense of the word, exists within the State. It is possible to maintain without being misleading that it is the State or, what is the same, the law of the State which creates the community. The effective establishment of international law with an international executive and legislature would in a true sense create an international community. From the point of view of pure legal analysis the community is not the condition but the effect of the law. Legal history will probably substantiate that view. States have as a rule grown on the basis of the rule of law imposed from outside and from above, without reference to organic growth within the society in question; once established, the law has fostered a deeper and more lasting community of history, tradition, culture and institutions. It is the degree of cohesion of that community based on the rule of law which has subsequently determined the growth and the development of the law itself. Both historically and analytically it is, in the first instance, the law as expressed by the State which creates the community. It is on that basis that the community is given the possibility of normal development and, in turn, of influencing the law.

GENERAL RULES OF THE LAW OF PEACE

These considerations supply a workable answer to the problem of the relation of the international community to international law. International law conceived as a body of rules ordering peace (or, what is the same, forbidding violence) and regularizing intercourse is independent of the existence of a deep community of interests and outlook between the nations of the world. Not much more than a primitive degree of community is required for the primary function of ordering peace. But international law conceived as a body of rules for furthering the common interests of States and developing and protecting through international action the interests of human personality as the ultimate purpose of the international society— such international law requires a deeper community of moral and political outlook. Fundamental ideological differences like those between democracy and dictatorship or radical capitalism and radical socialism, as soon as they become translated into State action, do not indeed render international law impossible. On the contrary, they render it more necessary because of the danger to peace involved in the phenomenon of militant ideologies. But they prevent it from fulfilling the wider function which the law fulfils within the State. An international law which does not fulfil these functions is not impossible, but it is a rudimentary and emaciated international law.

37. The bases of the international community and collective security

It is not claimed for this analysis that it goes very far in the direction of giving a substantive and not merely a formal answer to the question of the existence of an international community. For within the State there is not only an ordering of peace and a prohibition of violence; there is enforcement of the peace and suppression of violence by State action. In the international society there is at present no unfailing and overriding enforcement of that fundamental aspect of the law by a superior body; such enforcement is dependent upon the collective action of the community not organized as a State. Does there exist among and within States a sufficient consciousness of a political community of interests so as to supply a basis for the collective enforcement of the peace? Or, to put it in terms to which we are now accustomed, is there a sufficient consciousness of a political community of interests so as to supply a basis for collective security? This is perhaps one of the most important aspects of the question of the existence of an international community.

Now, the term collective security has, of course, become a subject

264

COMMUNITY AND UNIVERSALITY

of political discussion. But essentially it is a legal term; it is perhaps the most fundamental legal term. Isolated from the controversies of the day, collective security is the expression of the reign of law among States; its absence is the measure of the deficiency of international law as a system of law. Law within the State is, in its original and primary meaning, a system of collective security. It is by reference to the necessity for collective security that writers discuss the necessity for an international law. Spinoza, as we have seen, denied the former; it was for that reason that he denied the latter. Grotius arrived at a different conclusion.

> There is no state [he said] so powerful that it may not some time need the help of others outside itself, either for the purposes of trade, or even to ward off the forces of many foreign nations united against it. In consequence we see that even the most powerful peoples and sovereigns seek alliances, which are quite devoid of significance according to the point of view of those who confine the law within the boundaries of states. (*Proleg.* 22.)

Unless war, aggression and conquest are regarded as inherent in an international law worthy of that name or as compatible with the progress of the human race—and they cannot be so regarded on any rational or analytical view—there exists an international community of *interests* in the maintenance and enforcement of collective security. That community of interests is formally given expression in legal instruments of collective security providing for the limitation or prohibition of the right of war coupled with the duty of enforcing such limitation or prohibition. The Council of the League of Nations is such an instrument. But this still does not answer the question whether there exists an international community of sentiment and consciousness in support of collective security thus conceived. It still does not answer the question whether the consciousness of the interdependence of States has reached the stage where nations are prepared to admit by their conduct a direct connection between their own welfare and aggression against others wherever committed. It is difficult to give a simple answer to this question at the time when these lectures are given. This is so for the reason that this period must be regarded as transient and any generalization of its conditions as dangerous and misleading. There are nations like the United States—perhaps the United States is the only representative of this group—which possess such a pronounced sense of their own security from the geographical and political point of view that any participation in a scheme of collective security must be regarded as

GENERAL RULES OF THE LAW OF PEACE

an inadmissible altruism. There are other nations which attach so much importance to the ideological differences between various philosophies of life as embodied in political systems that they find it inconceivable that they might be called upon to enforce the law in favour of nations of which they disapprove. Apart from these groups it is probably true to say that the feeling of political interdependence has become part and parcel of national consciousness among advanced peoples. But that collective consciousness is not continuous. Collective security when brought to the direct test of implementing its obligations by sacrificing life and treasure 'in the quarrels of others' is likely to appeal decisively to the masses of the people only in time of crisis when their Governments make themselves deliberately responsible for proclaiming the cause of collective security as identified in every respect with the national cause proper. The collective memory—which, if it existed to any substantial degree, would be a sure foundation of collective security—is short. Through their laws and institutions peoples gain the advantages of continuity enabling them to profit from the lessons of experience. In the sphere of security from war these laws assume the form of international obligations. But Governments, entrusted with the duty of fulfilling these obligations, are fully exposed to the dualism of public and private morality. They are not only guided by the desire to preserve peace today rather than avoid the danger of war tomorrow. Their action is motivated by the conviction that, being trustees of vital interests, they are not at liberty to show a degree of loyalty and of sacrifice of immediate interests which they would be willing to show if their individual interest were concerned. They do not deem themselves free to assist in maintaining the law at the expense of the immediate interests of those who entrusted them with the protection of the common good. The result is that, in the field of mutual insurance against external danger, the current dualism of public and private morality tends to reduce to impotence the conscious community of the international interest in maintaining and enforcing the rule of law.

These considerations show once more how misleading at the present stage of international relations must be any attempt to give a cut-and-dried answer to the question whether there exists an international community as the necessary basis of international law. It exists in the field of economics and science not only as a postulate but as a fact; but it is a fact severely limited in its operation by the exigencies of national policy in an unorganized and anta-

COMMUNITY AND UNIVERSALITY

gonistic world. It exists among the great majority of peoples in the sphere of collective maintenance of the rule of law; but it does not exist in sufficient strength and continuity to assert itself in time of trial regardless of the attitude of Governments guided by considerations of immediate interests. Neither does there exist at present a sufficient community of moral and political outlook to render possible the achievement of tasks which the law of civilized societies attempts over and above the function of preserving the peace. These defects of the international community necessarily constitute a defect of international law. Like other shortcomings of international law, they must be regarded as temporary and not permanent. They are not the result of the normal growth of human society; they are manifestations of the abnormal.

B. THE UNIVERSALITY OF INTERNATIONAL LAW

38. *The concept of a universal international law*

The last but not the least important question which arises in this connection is whether there exists an international society of sufficient cohesion and community of interests to warrant the view that there exists a universal, as distinguished from general or particular, international law. It is on the whole agreed that general international law means rules binding, as the result of agreement, upon a considerable number of States, and that particular international law refers to rules, similarly grounded in agreement, binding upon a small group of States. There is no clear definition of universal international law. On the face of it it seems to mean international law binding upon all or practically all States. But there is more in it than a mere matter of arithmetic. Properly understood, it is international law which is binding on all States regardless of their consent; most of them may have consented to it, and this is probably the way in which the bulk of conventional international law has come into existence. However, such consent is not essential. When in *West Rand Central Gold Mining Co.* v. *The King*,[1] Lord Alverston declared as binding upon English courts rules of international law to which the United Kingdom has given its assent or which are so generally accepted that it is inconceivable that a civilized State should refuse its consent to them, he was referring to universal international law. But universal international law has also another

[1] [1905] 2 K.B. 391.

267

connotation. It means those rules of international law which, when discussing the sources of the Law of Nations, we describe as grounded in the very existence of a society of States and in the very assumption of the existence of international law. They supplement agreed international law; they tower over it; they are in the background. They are not immutable and fixed for all time; they are not an eternal law of nature of the society of States; but they have a sufficient degree of permanence and immutability to treat with indifference and even with disapproval temporary lapses into retrogression from which the collective life of nations is not immune. The 'general principles of law as recognized by civilized nations' are one example of that universal international law; the rules of morality and good faith which customary international law has adopted as an element of validity and interpretation of treaties are another; 'the reason of the thing' as expressive of the necessity of respecting the existence and securing normal intercourse between States independent one of the other, is yet another.

It appears thus that universal international law is of two kinds. It is, first, general international law based on practice so widespread that its universal validity is presumed. The principle of diplomatic privilege or the immunity of non-combatants from direct attack may be mentioned as examples. It is, secondly, an indefinite but real body of principles necessarily assumed in the existence and purpose of international law. In daily practice and in proceedings before international tribunals that universal international law does not loom large in the picture; governed as we are by the concrete manifestations of agreement and practice, we are not conscious of it. But it is there—an essential and indispensable factor; the very framework and the basis of international law. We are not, in our physical existence, permanently conscious of the process of breathing or of the circulation of the blood. But these processes are of the very essence of life.

This being so, it would not be necessary to discuss this subject in detail but for the fact that the existence of universal international law has been questioned in at least four quarters. In the first instance it has, naturally, been denied by those who see in concrete agreement the only source of legal obligation for sovereign States. For them, i.e. for the positivist doctrine, universal international law is likely to be anathema. So in fact it is. But we have already said enough about the positivist doctrine.

COMMUNITY AND UNIVERSALITY

39. *So-called American international law*

Secondly, the existence of universal international law has been questioned, or at least obscured, by adherents of so-called regional international law, and in particular by those who stress the existence of so-called American international law. There is, of course, in principle no contradiction between the existence of universal and general or particular international law. It is natural and desirable that the special needs of States bound by special ties of geographical propinquity or other interests should find expression in particular agreements; it may be equally natural and desirable that the States in question should adopt *inter se* rules of general international law different from those obtaining between other groups of States or on other continents. There is no special merit in uniformity. On the other hand, the emphasis on regional international law becomes retrogressive and misleading when it is coupled with a deficient appreciation of universal international law or a denial of its ultimate superiority. For it is only by reference to universal international law that regional international law can be comprehended. Even if regional international law were so complete as to cover all branches of international law, there would still be an imperative need for a universal international law to bring unity and adjustment between various systems of regional international law. But, and this is notorious, regional international law is not complete. The exaggerated emphasis on it makes writers forget that it is often a mere programme, not a reality. This applies in particular to so-called American international law. It is extremely difficult to induce any adherent of that particular aspect of regionalism to state in detail what are the specific doctrines of American international law. They mention the doctrine *uti possidetis*, but this is a technical principle of delimitation of the frontiers of the States which succeeded to the Spanish Empire in America. They refer to arbitration as the principle of settling territorial disputes, but this surely is not an ideal more observed by or more peculiar to American States than to other nations. They mention freedom of expatriation and immigration; but here again these principles have, in part, been adopted by non-American States and, in part, they have been abandoned by American States themselves. It is not surprising therefore, that while that doctrine is being ably sponsored by some writers, it is vigorously opposed by others of no smaller authority. It is true that a number of general conventions in the nature of codification have been concluded by American States. But these conventions, which cover only a small part of international law and acceptance of which is counterbalanced in many cases by sweeping reservations, do not signify the adoption of principles strikingly different from those in force on other continents. For these reasons it is to be hoped that the adherents of this and other aspects of regionalism will not impair the value of those developments by an exaggeration of results already achieved or by the propagation of any doctrine tending to jeopardize the unifying influence of universal international law.

40. *National concepts of international law*

Less important, because essentially transient, is the denial of the universality of international law due to the exaggerations of national conceptions of international law. In times of national emotion, following upon revolutionary upheavals, there is a tendency to give to the ideological zeal an outlet transcending the borders of the State. Revolutions have missionary inclinations. They are impatient with international law as they find it, especially when it is regarded as inimical to national interests. In these circumstances it is not surprising that they tend to advocate an international law of their own. The French Convention of 1792 did it to some extent. After the Russian revolution in 1917 international law writers in that country, regarding that particular period of history as one of transition from one economic and political system to another, refused to accept a universal international law based on fixed principles. They emphasized the contractual nature of international law (subject to the operation of the *clausula rebus sic stantibus*) which they interpreted in a way not inconsistent with the political conceptions of the political régime of the time. That interpretation amounted to a large extent to a denial of the binding force of international law and of the possibility of international co-operation for other than purely temporary or formal matters. With the supervening change in the political constellation of the world that Soviet conception of international law became a matter of the past. Similarly, following upon the political changes in Germany in 1931, a number of German writers put forward the theory of a National-Socialist conception of international law. That conception of an inter-corporative law of co-ordination based on racial consanguinity amounts probably, so far as the 'law of co-ordination' is

COMMUNITY AND UNIVERSALITY

concerned, to a denial of international law.[1] In its other aspects it must, as in the analogous case of its predecessors, be regarded as temporary. This is clearly shown by reference to that feature of the new conception of international law which regarded equality (*Gleichberechtigung*) as the fundamental principle of international law. This was at a time when the restrictions of the Treaty of Versailles still weighed on Germany. With their disappearance, partly by agreement and partly by Germany's own efforts, that principle has now lost its practical value and is gradually disappearing. In fact it is difficult to accept as logical any national conceptions of international law. The conception of international law is in its essence international.

41. *The supposed differences between the Anglo-American and the Continental schools*

The fourth factor which has acted in a way likely to weaken the conception of a univeral international law has been the notion that there exist not only on particular subjects but also in the entire method of approach two fundamentally different schools of thought —the Anglo-American and the Continental. That notion is equally dear to the hearts of Continental and Anglo-American lawyers. But there is no substance in it, and it is desirable that it should vanish from the dictionary of international lawyers. It is probably true to say that the process of its disappearance has already set in. But there is no doubt as to the mischief for which it has been responsible already. By supplying a facile generalization it has hindered the serious study of many a subject in international law; in the domain of practice it has, among other things, been an impediment in the way of acceptance of the duties of obligatory arbitration. In Great Britain particularly, the argument has been widely used that it is unsafe to entrust the decision in future disputes to a body of judges who are in their majority wedded to the Continental as distinguished from the Anglo-American school of thought. It may be noted here at the outset that so far as the work of the Permanent Court of International Justice is concerned there has not been a single occasion on which the issue turned on a choice between the two doctrines.

It is convenient to survey this question from two points of view: from that of the differences, if any, with regard to particular subjects; and, secondly, from that of the fundamental differences, if any, in

[1] See above, pp. 208 *et seq.*

GENERAL RULES OF THE LAW OF PEACE

approach and outlook. With regard to the first, an examination of the law of peace fails to reveal a single instance in which the Anglo-American practice is opposed to that of the Continent and other countries. To mention one or two apparent exceptions, it is usual to speak of the Anglo-American as contrasted with the so-called French rule with regard to the jurisdiction of States over foreign vessels in their ports. Actually, the difference is largely one of emphasis; the actual practice is the same except that in France the limitations of jurisdiction are said to be due to a rule of international law, whereas in England and the United States they are self-imposed as a matter of international comity. The general refusal of Anglo-American countries to claim jurisdiction over aliens for crimes committed abroad—a solution represented by some to be distinctly Anglo-American—is common also to Germany, Spain, France and Holland. The alleged difference in the matter of the admissibility of *travaux préparatoires* is essentially non-existent so far as the interpretation of treaties is concerned. In general, with regard to rules of evidence international tribunals have refused to be guided by strict rules evolved in any particular system of jurisprudence.

With regard to the law of war these differences were for a time more substantial (but even there, on the one hand, the Anglo-American practice was shared in many matters by other countries; while, on the other hand, in some matters, such as the capture of private property, the English practice was diametrically opposed to that of the United States). In some of the details of the law of blockade and contraband—like the question of notification of blockade or the consequences of breach of blockade and carriage of contraband—a common Anglo-American (but not wholly Anglo-American) practice has developed. What now remains of these differences and, indeed, what now remains of pre-war prize law, may be a matter for discussion. Their importance cannot be considerable. The same applies with much greater force to the more fundamental difference with regard to the subjects of the relation of war. Great Britain certainly adhered during the World War to her traditional principle that the relation of war is not restricted to States as such. But France and other Continental countries did not —and in fact could not—act on what has been called the Continental doctrine rigidly separating the State from the individuals composing it. The character of modern warfare is not such as to tolerate that distinction—at least so far as interference with property rights is

272

COMMUNITY AND UNIVERSALITY

concerned. And the advent of the totalitarian State, with its conception of *Totaler Krieg*, tends to complete that development. This approximation and merger of the two doctrines found expression during the World War in the obliteration of secondary differences between the Anglo-American and Continental doctrines, for instance, in the matter of the test of enemy character. While Great Britain formally adhered to the test of domicile, she in fact adopted also the test of nationality; she went even beyond that by conferring in practice enemy character upon neutral owners in a neutral country if enemy association could be proved. France completed the development in the other direction. Private enemy property on land was in fact as little respected in one group of countries as it was in the other. It may safely be said that while with regard to the law of peace the difference between the 'two schools of thought' has always been nothing more than a myth, with regard to the law of war it has now lost all practical importance.

But if there are no differences between these 'two schools of thought' on questions of detail, how far is it true to say that the substantive differences of these two systems of law—the common law system and systems based on Roman law—create differences of approach which must have an effect on some or most of the answers given to controversial questions of international law? So far as substantive differences in the various branches of these two systems are concerned, they are on the whole irrelevant in the field of international law for the simple reason that international tribunals do not as a rule decide questions of municipal law. It is true that many branches of international law have been influenced constantly and beneficently by notions of private law. But they have been so influenced not by any particular system, but by general conceptions of private law common to most systems of jurisprudence. These general notions exhibit a surprising degree of uniformity notwithstanding terminological and technical differences due to dissimilarity of language and historical peculiarities. This may be seen from comparative studies on subjects like abuse of rights, unjustified enrichment, termination of contracts as the result of supervening impossibility of performance, and so on. The only relevant differences that exist are of a psychological nature, and these in turn are due to insufficient acquaintance with the legal systems in question.

Thus among English lawyers—and to some extent even among Continental lawyers—it has become widely accepted that the two systems differ in only two vital aspects likely to influence any question which comes up for decision. In the first instance, it is widely believed that the Continental conception of '*droit*', '*Recht*', '*diritto*', is less rigid than the English term 'law'. It is believed that these corresponding Continental conceptions contain a large infusion of ethics, and that they constitute a mixture of what the law is and what the law ought to be. This, of course, is not true. It is difficult to ascertain from what source English lawyers have gained that conception of the Continental definition of law unless, indeed, they have relied on Ulpian's definition of jurisprudence as *rerum divinarum atque humanarum notitia, justi atque injusti scientia*, or on Celsius' definition of law as *ars boni et aequi*.[1] There is nothing to warrant the view that the Continental lawyer, for the reason, for instance, that in the German language the term '*Recht*' may have both an ethical and a legal connotation, does not distinguish between law and justice, as there is nothing to justify the same reproach levelled against English jurisprudence for the reason that the terms 'wrong' and 'right' express both legal and moral conceptions.

Similarly, there is much less substance than is generally assumed in the view which sees a profound difference in the two systems in the supposed fact that judicial precedent plays a decisive part in the common law whereas it has no place at all in the Continental system. It is true that in English law judicial precedent enjoys a formal authority which it does not possess on the Continent. But what English lawyer will commit himself to the view that precedent is all-powerful and that judges are absolutely powerless to disregard it—by the use of the subtle device of 'distinguishing'—if they deem it unreasonable or inconsistent with justice? And what Continental lawyer will deny that judicial precedent actually, although not by virtue of a binding rule of law, plays a conspicuous part in the jurisprudence of his country? Judicial precedent owes its inescapable authority not to any formal legal provision but to its inherent value and to the necessities of the administration of justice. The work of the Permanent Court of International Justice has shown how powerfully, in face of a formal limitation, judicial precedent can influence the development and the application of the law.

It will thus be seen how inaccurate is this aspect also of the theory of the fundamental differences of the 'two schools of thought'. It is to be hoped that it will not be long before it disappears altogether

---

[1] In my article, 'The So-Called Anglo-American and Continental Schools of Thought in International Law', in *B.Y.* 12 (1931), 31–62, this question is examined in some detail.

274

COMMUNITY AND UNIVERSALITY

from the language and arguments of international lawyers. It is inaccurate in itself; it is a denial of that unity of juridical sentiment which is an important condition of the common administration of international justice; it is a constant inducement to the substitution of general phrases for analytical study and thinking. There is no reason why it should be perpetuated. Undoubtedly, various nations or groups of nations have made their contributions to the common stock of international law. Probably, because of their cohesion, historical continuity and other favourable circumstances, the contribution of Great Britain and the United States is particularly conspicuous. We have, for example, referred already to the beneficent doctrine that international law is part of the law of the land. There is also no doubt that the practice of these two States had a decisive effect on the development of international arbitration. This was so because the community of law, language and, to some extent, tradition favoured the judicial settlement of disputes between these two countries. But there is all the difference between pointing to the contribution which various States have made to international law as a whole and the assertion of a fundamental and permanent cleavage of practice and principles. It is undesirable that the unity and the universality of international law should be obscured and endangered by the inaccuracies or exaggerations of regionalism, of transient national conceptions, or of alleged fundamental differences in juristic thought and principle.

PART II

THE SUBJECTS OF THE
LAW OF NATIONS

CHAPTER 5

THE SUBJECTS OF
INTERNATIONAL LAW

42. *States and individuals as subjects of international law*

The question of the subjects of international law has as a rule been discussed in the literature of international law, not without good reason, as the question of the relative position of the State and the individual in international law. The predominant theory is clear and emphatic. International law is a law of States only and exclusively. Individuals are only the objects of international law. International law does not impose duties upon them; neither does it grant to them directly any rights. Such internationally relevant rights as they possess are rights granted by municipal law in accordance with international law. It is obviously a theory which sees in the sovereign State the ultimate unit and maker of international law, with all the consequences attaching thereto. It is for that reason that in the decade after the World War, when there was a tendency to question the doctrine of sovereignty as the foundation of international law and, generally, to find a basis corresponding to what was believed to be a new structure of the political organization of mankind, the question of the subjects of international law once more came up for discussion. Attention was drawn to the increased concern of conventional international law for the regulation of various interests of the individual as distinguished from State interests proper, and the resulting development was described as the emancipation of the individual in the international sphere. At the same time, the established doctrine was attacked as contrary to correct juridical principle and as inimical to the observance and development of international law.

Upon analysis, the question of the subjects of international law and the position of the individual in the international sphere resolves itself into at least five separate issues.

(1) There is, in the first instance, the question, which at first sight is of a theoretical nature: upon whom does international law impose duties—upon individual human beings or upon the impersonal entity of the State?

279

GENERAL RULES OF THE LAW OF PEACE

(2) With this is connected the question of the enforcement of international law in the municipal sphere: how far is it true to say that international law can in the domain of municipal law bind individuals, confer rights upon them and, in general, be enforceable by courts *per se* without having been made expressly part of the law of the land?

(3) Thirdly, there is the question how far do individuals, in the international sphere, possess rights directly conferred by international law and how can they enforce them in their own name before international judicial, arbitral and other organs?

(4) In this connection there arises the question of so-called fundamental rights of the individual as the ultimate unit of the international society, and the protection of those rights by international action if necessary.

(5) There is, fifthly, the question as to the position of individuals in the process of creation of international law.

These various aspects of the question will now be considered in turn.

A. THE SUBJECTS OF INTERNATIONAL DUTIES

43. *The predominant doctrine and the effectiveness of international duties*

Much of the opposition to the predominant doctrine with regard to the subjects of international law is undoubtedly due to such reasons as the reaction against the recognition of sovereign States as the only authors of international law, or to the desire to vindicate the rights of man in the international sphere. But it is an apparently theoretical motive which has supplied much of the driving force of that opposition. That motive is the realization that the predominant doctrine is an obstacle to the proper understanding and effectiveness of international duties. Who is the subject of international duties? Is it the abstract, metaphysical personality of the State, or is it the individual human being in his capacity either as the representative of the State or as the ultimate unit of the international community? To say that the State—and the State only—is the subject of international duties is to say, in the last resort, that international duties bind no one; it is to interpose a screen of irresponsibility between the rule of international law and the agency expected to give effect to it. This consequence of the traditional doctrine that States only are subjects of international law has been clearly recognized and elaborated by Kelsen.

But the interposition of the metaphysical entity of the State

SUBJECTS OF INTERNATIONAL LAW

between the rule of international law and the individual agent thereof has another consequence. It results indirectly in a diminished or qualified application in the sphere of international law of general principles of law as adopted among civilized communities and, in particular, of generally accepted standards of ethics. It is the theoretical and practical foundation of the phenomenon of double morality: one valid for individuals acting within the State; the other for individuals acting on behalf of and through the collective organization of the State. The overcoming of that dualism of standards—and it is a dualism not confined to the principles of ethics proper, but to those qualities of loyalty, courage, foresight and generosity which are of the essence of social intercourse—the overcoming of that dualism of standards is an abiding and fundamental problem of international law. It is not an easy problem. For its solution implies not only a change of what is undeniably the practice, but also a revision of some current notions in the science of politics and morals. The historian of political thought will note with some interest that the idealistic school of philosophy, as represented by the Hegelians, which regarded the State as justified in its existence by virtue of its function as an instrument of moral perfection, found it impossible to advocate an entirely different standard of law and morals in relations between States.[1] This point is put with clarity by Meinecke, a distinguished German historian, who says in his *Die Idee der Staatsräson in der neueren Geschichte*:[2]

The most terrible and most perplexing fact in the history of the world is that it has proved impossible to effect a radical moral improvement in that very community [i.e. the international community] which protects all other communities, which disposes of the richest and most varied possibilities of culture and which therefore ought, by the purity of its own nature, to set an example to other communities.

But the predominant view in the literature is still one of generalization of the present practice into a permanent and unavoidable phenomenon of international life. There is still a tendency to maintain that 'le contenu des prescriptions morales revêt une forme spéciale lorsque leur destinataire participe aux relations internationales'.[3] In this as in many other matters, progress is

---

[1] See, e.g., Bosanquet, *The Philosophical Theory of the State* (4th ed. 1923), p. 303; and, for a criticism of this attitude, Hobhouse, *The Metaphysical Theory of the State* (1918).

[2] 2nd ed. (1925), p. 15.

[3] Kraus in *Hague Recueil*, 16 (1927) (i), 433. An interesting example of judicial approval of this dualism of moral standards will be found in the judgment of the German Reichsgericht of 14 March 1928 (*Annual Digest*, 4 (1927–8), Case no. 5). In this case, which was a prosecution for high treason, the accused was charged with publishing details as to

GENERAL RULES OF THE LAW OF PEACE

dependent on the return to Grotius, who stigmatized as an error the view of those who hold 'that the standard of justice, which they insist upon in the case of individuals within the state is inapplicable to a nation or the ruler of a nation'[1] (*Proleg.* 21). But such progress is, in turn, dependent upon the wider acceptance of the view that the ultimate subjects of international duties are individual human beings.

The present period of history is witnessing an unparalleled increase in the powers of the State and in its standing in the political and spiritual life of the individual. That development is deliberately fostered in some States as a matter of political ideological dogma; it is unwillingly followed by others. But in both cases it is a fact. And in so far as the abandonment or modification of the phenomenon of double morality depends on whether we succeed in divesting individuals organized as States of the sanctity of an absolute value which only Deity can claim, the hopes of any progress in the immediate future may be slender. But this does not alter the essential nature of the ultimate problem confronting international law.

44. *The reality of the personality of the State and the subjects of international law*

The solution of that problem, when its chances become more tangible than at present, will depend to a large extent on the modification of the tendency, so pronounced in recent political theory, to stress the real personality of groups and associations within the State. The well-meant object of these tendencies has been to assert the rights of groups as against the omnipotent Leviathan of the

certain plans of the Reichswehr which, if true, would have constituted a violation of the Treaty of Versailles. The accused contended that the Treaty, which had become part of German federal law, rendered inoperative the relevant provision of the German Criminal Code. The Court upheld the conviction of the accused. It rejected the view that to convict the accused would violate the rule of international law which lays down that treaties ought to be fulfilled in good faith. For this rule, the Court said, binds only the contracting parties, not individuals. 'The citizen has to keep faith with his own country. It is his primary duty to promote the interest of his own State regardless of the interests of another country.'

[1] It is not a far-fetched view to maintain that the absence of adequate moral standards in international relations may in the long run have an effect on the ethical standards within the State. In his Instructions to the American Delegation to the First Hague Conference, Secretary of State Hay said: 'Nothing can secure for human government and for the authority of the law which it represents so deep a respect and so firm a loyalty as the spectacle of sovereign and independent States, whose duty it is to prescribe the rules of justice and to impose penalties upon the lawless, bowing with reverence before the august supremacy of those principles of right which give to law its eternal foundation' (Scott, *The Hague Peace Conferences of 1899 and 1907* (1909), II, Documents, p. 8).

SUBJECTS OF INTERNATIONAL LAW

State. Whatever may be the merits of that tendency, it has had the indirect effect of giving substance to the conception of the real personality of the State itself. The great danger latent in that conception is that it conceals the actual subjects of international duties and facilitates the adoption of a different standard of ethics and law for the personified State. It is this very real problem which lurks behind the niceties of the doctrinal discussion on the subjects of international law. It is the same problem that underlies the current view—a view which is inconsistent with legal principle and not wholly in accordance with practice—that the consequences of State liability are limited to reparation, and do not extend to punishment proper; and, in particular, that such punishment must not aim directly at the individual members of the State.[1] It is the same doctrine which underlay the rigid but in the long run untenable distinction, stressed especially on the continent of Europe but now disappearing even there, between the belligerent State and its citizens to the extent of exempting their property from interference and their persons from inconvenience at a time when the life of the combatants was fair game for the enemy.[2] It is, finally, the same doctrine which, in a different form, lent its support to the distinction between compulsion exercised against the State and that exercised against the representatives of the State in connection with the conclusion of treaties.[3]

Does not the view, which is stressed in these lectures, of the essential analogy of rules of private and international law lend colour to the assertion of the real personality of the State? We do not believe that it does. The analogy, it has already been stated, is here urged not because the personality of the State is as real as that of the individual; the analogy is not between two organic entities. The analogy applies for the simple reason that in both cases it is

---

[1] See below, pp. 390 et seq.

[2] Westlake, who was one of the first to stress the fact that individuals are the ultimate units of international law, criticized the artificial distinction between the State and the individual in time of war in words meriting quotation. He said: 'The men who form a state are not allowed to disclaim their part in the offences alleged against it, whether those on account of which the war was begun or those charged as having been committed by it in the course of the war, or therefore to claim that hostile action shall not be directed against their state through them in their respective measures. And this is just. Whatever is done or committed by a state is done or committed by the men who are grouped in it, or at least the deed or the commission is sanctioned by them. The state is not a self-acting machine. And if we look more closely at the facts, we shall probably find that in the foreign affairs of a state the rulers more often act under the impulse of a mass than by its tacit permission, and that tacit permission is seldom conceded by the mass except to those who embody and represent the national character' (*Papers*, p. 269).

[3] See below, p. 352.

283

GENERAL RULES OF THE LAW OF PEACE

the conduct of individual human beings which is the subject of legal regulation.

It may also be noted, for the sake of completeness, that individuals are the real subjects of international duties not only when they act on behalf of the State. They are the subjects of international duties in all cases in which international law regulates directly the conduct of individuals as such. This applies, for instance, with regard to piracy. Individuals engaged in piracy break a rule of international law prohibiting piracy. They would not, but for the rule of international law, be subject to the jurisdiction of any foreign State into whose hands they fall. The position is analogous in cases in which in numerous anti-slavery and similar treaties the injunction is addressed directly to individuals or in which the contracting parties grant one another the right to punish offenders who are nationals of the other party.[1] Probably this is also the position with regard to persons carrying contraband or breaking a blockade. They do not violate a legal prohibition of their own State; they cannot be punished for violating a prohibition of the municipal law of the belligerent to which they are not subject. It is international law which authorizes the belligerent to assume jurisdiction; in doing this international law constitutes the belligerent an organ of international law inasmuch as it renders unlawful the giving of assistance to belligerents through carriage of contraband or breach of blockade. International law could not authorize the belligerent to treat as unlawful conduct which international law as such does not regard as unlawful.

It is only by dint of some such construction that we can understand the repeated emphasis of British and American courts on the fact that they administer international and not municipal law. Finally, individual members of the armed forces of a belligerent are directly subjects of the international law of war. If they commit war crimes they are liable to punishment by the opposing belligerent if they fall into his hands. They may on occasion put forward successfully the plea of superior orders. But that plea will be of no avail if the crime is one against an obvious and generally recognized rule of international law. This principle was formulated with great

---

[1] See, e.g., Article 11 of the Treaty of 25 January 1825 between Great Britain and Sweden–Norway in which the two high contracting parties declare that 'les vaisseaux appartenant à leurs sujets respectifs, qui . . . seraient trouvés employés dans ce trafic défendu, auront, par ce seul fait, perdu tout droit de réclamer la protection de leur pavillon; et elles consentent mutuellement à ce que les vaisseaux de leurs marines royales . . . pourront visiter les navires marchands . . .' (Martens, N.R. 6 (ii), 618). For other examples see Wild, *Sanctions and Treaty Enforcement* (1934), pp. 180–95.

284

SUBJECTS OF INTERNATIONAL LAW

clarity in 1921 by the German Reichsgericht in the case of *The Llandovery Castle*, where the Court found that persons who fired on a boat containing shipwrecked members of the crew of a British hospital ship sunk by a German submarine were guilty of a war crime.[1]

It may now be submitted, by way of summary, that these examples show that there is nothing in the existing international law which makes it impossible for individuals to be directly subjects of international duties imposed upon them as such. The question is one of technique and procedure which at present tends to impose upon the State as such the direct responsibility for the fulfilment of the object of a treaty. Secondly, reasons have been given why even in those cases in which States are formally made subjects of international duties, the actual centre of legal and moral responsibility is in the individual and not in the metaphysical personality of the State. Decisive reasons of progress of international law and morality seem to favour that construction.

B. INDIVIDUALS AS SUBJECTS OF INTERNATIONAL RIGHTS

(i) *In the field of municipal law*

45. *The doctrine of transformation*

The second consequence of the predominant view in the matter of subjects of international law is the doctrine of transformation, according to which, in view of the duality of the subjects of municipal and international law, no rule of international law can have a direct effect upon individuals—as a matter either of right or of duty— unless it has been incorporated as part of the municipal law of the State to which the individual belongs. It has been suggested in the preceding section that this view cannot be wholly accepted so far as international duties are concerned. The same aspect of the matter was discussed generally in connection with both rights and duties in the chapter on the relation between international and municipal law. It was shown there that the doctrine of transformation is not in accordance with positive law. The direct operation of international law is, in the vast field of conventional international law, prevented

---

[1] *Annual Digest*, 2 (1923–4), Case no. 235. The Court said: 'The ambiguity of many rules of international law, as well as the actual circumstances of the case, must be borne in mind, because in war time decisions of great importance have frequently to be made on very insufficient material. This consideration, however, cannot be applied to the case at present before the Court. The rule of international law, which is here involved, is simple and is universally known. No possible doubt can exist with regard to the question of its applicability.'

285

GENERAL RULES OF THE LAW OF PEACE

as the result of express constitutional provisions of municipal law requiring a municipal act of transformation. But this, as has been pointed out, is due not to the inability of international law to act in a direct way in relation to individuals, but to the exigencies of the division of powers within the State. Similarly, the fact that international law must, before municipal tribunals, yield to conflicting municipal law is an expression of the fact that international law is not, within the limited sphere of the State, superior to municipal law. This is an expression of the weakness of international law, but not of any lacking potentiality of its direct operation. In so far, therefore, as the doctrine of the fundamental difference in the subjects of international and municipal law draws its support from the necessity of transformation, it must be regarded as devoid of scientific basis. In so far as the doctrine of transformation is grounded in the conviction of the absolute difference between subjects of municipal and international law, it is based on a doctrine which is shown in these lectures to be inaccurate. This mutual support which inaccurate theories lend one to the other is not a rare phenomenon in science.

(ii) *In the field of international law*

46. *The international procedural capacity of individuals*

The question whether individuals can possess rights in the international sphere is usually discussed and answered by reference to what is really another question, namely, that of the enforceability before international tribunals and international organs generally of such rights as the individual may enjoy by virtue of international law. The traditional theory is that not only can the individual have no rights directly conferred by international law, but that he is incapable of enforcing directly before international tribunals even such international rights as he is supposed to possess in pursuance of the municipal law of his own or of a foreign country, or from any other source. This rule has found authoritative expression in Article 34 of the Statute of the Permanent Court of International Justice, which lays down that only States members of the League of Nations may be parties to actions before the Court.

It is useful not to exaggerate the importance of what is, in the last resort, a procedural rule. The faculty to enforce rights is not identical with the quality of a subject of law or of a beneficiary of its provisions. A person may be in possession of a plenitude of rights without at the same time being able to enforce them in his own

SUBJECTS OF INTERNATIONAL LAW

name. This is a matter of procedural capacity. Infants and lunatics have rights; they are subjects of law. This is so although their procedural capacity is reduced to a minimum. Secondly, the rule preventing individuals from enforcing their rights before international tribunals is a piece of international machinery adopted for reasons of convenience. It is not a fundamental principle. There is nothing to prevent Governments, if they so wish, from altering that rule. They have done it or attempted to do it on a number of occasions. The abortive Hague Convention of 1907 instituting an international prize court provided for direct access to it of enemy or neutral individuals either by way of appeal from judgments of national courts (other than those of the State of the claimant) or by way of original action in cases in which the national court had failed to give judgment within two years of the date of capture. The Convention of 1908 for the Establishment of a Central American Court of Justice (now no longer in existence) provided for the jurisdiction of that Court in suits between a Government and foreign nationals in cases of an international character or arising out of violations of treaties. In the Mixed Arbitral Tribunals instituted by virtue of the various Peace Treaties, individuals were granted the right of access on a large scale. This applied not only to such questions as pre-war debts between individuals, but to actions against former enemy Governments for damage suffered as the result of violations of the rules of warfare. It also included appeals against certain decisions of municipal courts alleged to be contrary to the Peace Treaties. These provisions may have been due to the exceptional circumstances of the Peace Settlement of 1919, but they show that there is nothing immutable or fundamental about the denial of direct enforceability of claims by individuals. It is true that, with regard to the Mixed Arbitral Tribunals, the treaties in question were the creation of Governments and that the relevant provisions could be and eventually were terminated by States, but so long as they existed an individual could enforce his right independently of his Government and only an abuse of the judicial procedure could, to a limited extent, induce his State to interfere. Such right of interference was provided for in the Convention for the establishment of an international prize court, where it was laid down that a neutral State may forbid its subjects to bring an appeal against the judgment of a court of a belligerent or that the neutral State as such may start proceedings on behalf of its nationals. But the examples referred to above are sufficient to show that there is nothing in the

287

GENERAL RULES OF THE LAW OF PEACE

existing structure of international law to prevent individuals from appearing as parties before international tribunals provided that States expressly agree to grant them procedural capacity to that extent.

47. *The international capacity of the individual as a function of the will of States*

How much the position depends in each case on the will of States has been shown clearly in a decision of the Permanent Court of International Justice whose importance has not yet been sufficiently recognized but which is bound to grow in stature. This is the well-known Advisory Opinion of the Permanent Court of International Justice concerning the *Jurisdiction of the Courts of Danzig* in the matter of pecuniary claims of Danzig railway officials who had passed into the Polish service.[1] Poland contended that the agreement between herself and Danzig regulating the conditions of service of the Danzig officials conferred no right of action upon them. She maintained that as the agreement was an international treaty which had not been incorporated into Polish municipal law, it created rights and obligations only between the contracting parties and that, accordingly, any failure on her part to comply with those obligations did not confer any right of action on the officials concerned. The Court rejected this contention in what must be regarded as a decision of outstanding importance. It admitted that, 'according to a well established principle of international law', the agreement in question, 'being an international agreement, cannot, as such, create direct rights and obligations for private individuals'.[2] But having thus receded, *pour mieux sauter*, it insisted that its decision must depend on the intention of the parties; it refused to regard that 'well established principle' as being so fundamental as to serve as an indispensable basis for interpreting the intention of the parties. It said: 'But it cannot be disputed that the very object of an international agreement, according to the intention of the contracting Parties, may be the adoption by the Parties of some definite rules creating individual rights and obligations and enforceable by the national courts'. The Court found that this was in fact the intention of the parties. The decision amounts to a clear denial of the view that individuals can acquire rights only through the instrumentality of municipal legislation; it denies the exclusiveness of States as beneficiaries of international rights. And yet the Court was so

[1] *P.C.I.J.* Series B, no. 15.   [2] *Ibid.* p. 17.

SUBJECTS OF INTERNATIONAL LAW

ingeniously restrained in the manner in which it gave the decision that some have regarded it not as a far-reaching modification, but as an affirmation, of the established doctrine.

The case of the Danzig officials is not really an example of direct enforceability, in the *international sphere*, of individual rights. It has been given here as showing not only the possibility of direct conferment upon the individual of international rights enforceable before municipal tribunals. It has been adduced here as demonstrating that the existing practice in the matter of the position of the individual in the international sphere is not one flowing with inescapable necessity from a fundamental and unalterable principle of international law, but a rule of convenience yielding, when necessary, to the intention of the parties and to considerations of justice. Moreover, the direct enforceability of individual rights grounded in international law may go to the full logical length of making the claim enforceable against the individual's own State. The Convention concerning the establishment of an international prize court still followed the orthodox lines. It provided expressly that appeals could not be brought by individuals against their own State. But recent practice has shown that the enforcement by the individual of his international rights need not stop short of claims against his own State. The case of *Steiner and Gross* v. *Polish State*, decided on 30 March 1928 by the Upper Silesian Arbitral Tribunal, may be referred to as an interesting example.[1] The claimant, a Polish subject, asked for compensation from the Polish State on the ground that, as a result of the introduction of the tobacco monopoly in Poland, he suffered damage contrary to the provisions of the Upper Silesian Convention providing for respect for private rights and the maintenance of the economic unity of Upper Silesia. Article 5 of that Convention provided: 'La question de savoir si et dans quelle mesure une indemnité pour la suppression ou la diminution de droits acquis doit être payée par l'Etat, sera directement tranchée par le Tribunal arbitral sur plainte de l'ayant droit.' Poland maintained that the expression '*l'ayant droit*' could not be interpreted as meaning that a Polish national had a right of action against his own State, and that the interpretation of the Convention in that sense would be contrary to a general principle of international law. The Tribunal rejected the Polish contention; it refused to attach to the clear wording of the Treaty a qualification not found in its terms. It declined to be impressed by the Polish contention that the contrary

[1] *Annual Digest*, 4 (1927–8), Case no. 188.

GENERAL RULES OF THE LAW OF PEACE

interpretation would place Poland in a position worse than that of countries under a régime of capitulations.[1]

In this connection there must be mentioned other cases in which individuals or groups of individuals possess the right of redress, or of initiating redress, against their own State on account of a violation of rights secured to them by treaties. These cases include the 'representations' which an industrial association of employers or workers may make, under Articles 409 and 410 of the Treaty of Versailles, to the International Labour Office to the effect that a member of the Organisation has failed to secure the observance of a convention which it has ratified. On the other hand, it is now clearly established that the petitions of minorities in pursuance of Minorities Treaties are merely informative and have not the legal effect of putting the matter before the Council and requesting it to intervene. The Minorities Treaties did not transform the minorities into legal entities with international personality. A similar, but probably somewhat wider, effect must be attributed to petitions from inhabitants of a mandated territory; these must be submitted through the Mandatory, who appends comments before sending the petition to the Mandates Commission.

Finally, there must be mentioned instances, which have not yet received adequate treatment in the literature of international law, of special tribunals of an international character being created between States and private individuals of foreign nationality, e.g., as provided by an Agreement of 14 November 1925 between the Lena Goldfields Company and the Government of Soviet Russia. Such tribunals have recourse to international law wherever applicable. Thus, for instance, the Tribunal in the *Lena Goldfields* case relied on Article 38(3) of the Statute of the Permanent Court of International Justice as a reason for applying the doctrine of unjustifiable enrichment.[2] The position is analogous in those numerous cases in which the contract between the Government and the foreign individual or corporation provides for arbitration, the umpire to be chosen, if necessary, by the Permanent Court of International Justice or its President.[3]

---

[1] Moreover, it may be possible for an individual to enjoy and to enforce in his own name international rights created by a Treaty between States of which he is not a national. This was clearly shown in the case of *Steiner and Gross* v. *Polish State*, referred to above, in which it was held that a Czechoslovak subject could invoke the jurisdiction of a Tribunal established in a Treaty between Poland and Germany.

[2] *Annual Digest*, 5 (1929–30), Case no. 1.

[3] See, e.g., the case concerning the contract between the Greek Government and the Société Commerciale de Belgique of 27 August 1925 (*P.C.I.J.* Series E, no. 9, p. 85); the

SUBJECTS OF INTERNATIONAL LAW

48. *The rights of individuals as rights of their States*

The developments as foreshadowed in the Advisory Opinion concerning the *Danzig Officials* and in the case of *Steiner and Gross* v. *Polish State* are still exceptional. They are discussed here not as typical of the existing legal position, but as contradicting the view that individuals can never, by reason of the structure of international law, be direct beneficiaries of international rights. It must also be noted that the enforceability of international rights by individuals in their own name has a direct bearing not only on the question of the procedural status of individuals, but also on the nature of these rights. They cannot be municipal rights if they are directly enforceable by international action. The dogmatic assertion that all individual rights in the international sphere are in the last resort rights under municipal law can thus no longer be upheld. The normal rule is still that the international rights of the individual are not enforceable except through State action. The State must make the individual claim its own before it can become the subject of an international claim; it then becomes a State claim; the State controls it from beginning to end; the compensation is granted to the State; and it is the State which disposes of the claim.[1] This is the orthodox doctrine, which still expresses correctly the existing legal position. The Permanent Court of International Justice has affirmed it on a number of occasions in various connections.[2] But, it must be noted, it has done so almost exclusively in order to rebut an objection to its jurisdiction based on the plea that the dispute originated in a private claim and was not therefore of an international character. The only other case in which the Court affirmed the doctrine of the international character of a claim before it was

Agreement of 12 June 1931 between the Government of Iran and a Czechoslovak company (*ibid.* no. 11, p. 70); and the Agreement of 29 April 1933 between the Government of Iran and the Anglo-Persian Oil Company (*ibid.* no. 10, p. 66).

[1] With regard to compensation granted by treaty in order to cover losses suffered by the national see, for an affirmation of the established view, *Civilian War Claimants' Association* v. *The King*, [1932] A.C. 14 (followed in *Administrator of German Property* v. *Knoop*, [1933] 1 Ch. 439), where the petitioners claimed compensation on behalf of civilians who had suffered losses inflicted by German forces during the War. They alleged that the Crown had invited them to submit their losses to the Reparation Claims Department, which had included the amounts stated in the sum total of reparations which Germany agreed to pay under Article 232 of the Treaty of Versailles. The House of Lords held that the Crown, when acting in this way, had not constituted itself an agent or trustee of the petitioners in respect of any money received from Germany on account of reparations.

[2] See, e.g., *P.C.I.J.* Series A, no. 2 (*Mavrommatis Palestine Concessions*), p. 13; Series A, no. 20 (*Serbian Loans*), p. 17; Series A/B, no. 6 (*Peter Pazmány University*), p. 221.

GENERAL RULES OF THE LAW OF PEACE

when it penetrated behind its artificiality in order to repeat the well-established rule that normally the reparation of the wrong consists in an indemnity corresponding to the damage suffered by the national on whose behalf the claim was brought.[1]

It is important to realize the element of unreality in the established doctrine, as well as the fact that there is a limit to the results to which it may lead.[2] Some conventions disregard in their phrasing the technicalities of the doctrine. Thus the United States–Mexican General Claims Commission of 1923 was given jurisdiction over claims 'against Mexico of citizens of the United States' and over claims 'against the United States of America by citizens of Mexico'. While affirming the full control of the Government over the claim, arbitrators have on occasion emphasized that 'the private nature of such claim continues to inhere in it and the claim only in a very restricted sense becomes a national claim' with the effect that 'the act of espousal does not vest in the nation the title to the claim',[3] or that, in regard to the right of disposal over the sum awarded,

where a demand is made on behalf of a designated national, and an award and payment is made on that specific demand, the fund so paid is not a national fund in the sense that the title vests in the nation receiving it entirely free from any obligation to account to the private claimant, on whose behalf the claim was asserted and paid and who is the real owner thereof.[4]

49. *The possibility of direct enforcement of private claims*

These awards have not been adduced here in order to question seriously the existing rule about the national character of private

---

[1] *P.C.I.J.* Series A, no. 17, p. 27 (*Chorzów Factory (Merits)*). Nor is it without interest to note how, in the *Mavrommatis Palestine Concessions* case, the Court disregarded the fact that the negotiations required as a condition of the Court's jurisdiction were conducted not by the two Governments concerned, but by the representatives of the private parties.

[2] For an interesting survey of the resulting difficulties, see Feller, *The Mexican Claims Commission, 1923–1934* (1935), pp. 82–92. See also Kiesselbach, *Problems of the German–American Claims Commission* (1930), pp. 16–23.

[3] Parker, Umpire, Tripartite Claims Commission (United States, Austria, Hungary), 25 May 1927 (*Annual Digest*, 4 (1927–8), Case no. 172). See also, to the same effect, the *William A. Parker* case before the United States and Mexico General Claims Commission (*ibid.* 3 (1925–6), Case no. 178), and the *North American Dredging Company* case before the same Commission (*ibid.* Case no. 179).

[4] Parker, Umpire, in the United States and Germany Mixed Claims Commission: *Administrative Decision No. V* (*Annual Digest*, 2 (1923–4), Case no. 100). See also *National Bank of Egypt* v. *Austro-Hungarian Bank*, decided in July 1923 by the Anglo-Austrian Mixed Arbitral Tribunal (*ibid.* Case no. 10), where it was held that the termination in 1922 of the British Protectorate over Egypt did not have the effect of depriving Egyptian nationals of their rights as British '*ressortissants*' under the Treaty of Versailles: 'very clear language would, in any case, be necessary to justify a conclusion involving the deprivation of private individuals of their legal rights by a unilateral disposition of the British Government'.

SUBJECTS OF INTERNATIONAL LAW

claims consequent upon the procedural incapacity of individuals in the international sphere. But they are useful as a reminder of the limits and, to some extent, of the highly technical character of the doctrine involved. Moreover, so long as the existing rule denying to individuals the right of independent enforcement of their claims is not generalized and used as an argument on the position of the individual in international law in general, it is difficult to maintain that it is in the present state of international organization an unreasonable doctrine. There are undoubtedly weighty objections to the existing rule. In particular, it is true that the necessity of private claims being taken up by the State imparts a political and controversial aspect to otherwise innocuous and simple claims; that it prevents small or weak States from putting forward otherwise meritorious claims for no other reason than the desire not to incur the displeasure of a powerful neighbour; that it may be, and often has been, used as a means of extortion and unjustifiable pressure, dangerously approaching intervention; that it operates as a rule in favour of strong States which have at their disposal various means of pressure[1] or States unwilling to undertake the commitments of general arbitration treaties or even of *ad hoc* arbitration; and that, by leaving the decision as to the sponsoring of a claim with the authorities of the executive department concerned with foreign affairs, the private rights of the individual are left to an administrative decision not subject to judicial review and influenced not only by general considerations of foreign policy but also by less praiseworthy reasons of departmental convenience. These are weighty objections.

However, it is controversial whether any radical reform of this procedural aspect—for it is no more than that—is practicable at the present stage of international organization. To confer upon an international court obligatory jurisdiction to entertain claims of individuals against foreign States in the matter of the violation of their rights, contractual and other, as aliens, would amount to conferring upon it compulsory jurisdiction with regard to most international disputes. As a matter of experience, the overwhelming

---

[1] This is probably a factor explaining in some degree the existing rule as to the nationality of claims—the rule that an international tribunal has no jurisdiction with regard to a claim of private origin unless the individual concerned was a national of the plaintiff State at the time of the injury, of the arbitration agreement, and of the award. The reason for that rule is the same as in the Middle Ages prompted the prohibition of the *cessio in potentiorem*, i.e. the assignment of a debt to a more powerful creditor. In the absence of the rule as to nationality of claims, these could be transferred to nationals of powerful States or the injured individual might be tempted to change his nationality so as to secure the protection of a more powerful State.

293

majority of cases with which international tribunals are confronted originate in injuries to private individuals. To confer upon international tribunals compulsory jurisdiction in these matters would mean the abandonment, to a substantial extent, of the existing rule of the essentially voluntary jurisdiction of international tribunals—a rule which States have been unwilling to abandon except for limited periods and subject to comprehensive reservations. This, of course, is not an argument against the innovation; it merely shows the practical difficulties which it is likely to encounter. On the other hand, it is possible that if progress is to be made in the matter of obligatory jurisdiction of international tribunals it may be wise to attempt such progress by means of the apparently non-political jurisdiction in the matter of private claims.

The other possible objection to the proposed reform is that it is essentially one-sided. It is not entirely consistent with justice to confer upon individuals the right of directly enforcing, through international tribunals, their claims against foreign States without conferring upon those States the corresponding right in regard to foreign nationals. A foreign national may injure a State, when outside its jurisdiction, in a variety of ways. He may disseminate false information about it; he may plot against its safety; he may organize hostile expeditions against it. But unless the principle be recognized that the individual is the subject not only of international rights but also of international duties, the injured State has no remedy except to rely upon the municipal law or governmental action of the State to which the individual concerned belongs. The opposition to the establishment of an International Criminal Court— one of whose objects would necessarily be the enforcement of international law directly against individuals—shows the difficulties of direct international enforcement of international law against individuals.[1]

The prospects of the conferment upon individuals of the right of direct access to international tribunals are at present slender. The matter does not, it must be admitted, constitute a problem of overwhelming urgency in international organization. Although claims of private origin constitute by far the greater part of claims which come before international tribunals, they are certainly not the most

---

[1] It will also be noted that to grant to aliens the right of independent international action would lead to the result of placing them in a position better than that enjoyed by the nationals of the State within which they reside. However, the fact that nationals of the State possess at present no right of international redress does not mean that it is undesirable to grant such redress to aliens.

294

SUBJECTS OF INTERNATIONAL LAW

important. Exaggerated emphasis on this aspect of the question is to some extent artificial and likely to conceal more urgent problems of international law. Some of the inconveniences and dangers inherent in the present situation might be removed by giving to individuals within the State some judicial or quasi-judicial remedy against the decision of the competent department of the Foreign Office declining to put forward a diplomatic claim. There is no ground for assuming that the foreign departments of Governments refuse intercession without good reasons, but a reform of this nature would have the merit of removing from purely administrative discretion what is in the last resort a legal claim. At the same time it might lessen any probable embarrassment of the political department by shifting some part of the responsibility on to the judicial organ.

C. THE FUNDAMENTAL RIGHTS OF THE INDIVIDUAL

50. *The fundamental rights of the individual in positive international law*

The fourth, and by no means least important, consequence of the established doctrine on the position of the individual in the international sphere is the denial of the existence of so-called fundamental rights of the individual in his capacity as a subject of the law of nations as distinguished from his capacity as a subject of his State. What are these fundamental rights? It is convenient to take as an example the authoritative resolution adopted on this matter by the Institute of International Law in October 1929. The provisions of that resolution, bearing the title 'Declaration of the Rights of Man', are given in the following principal excerpts:

Article 1. It is the duty of every State to recognise the equal right of every individual to life, liberty and property and to accord to all on its territory the full and entire protection of this right without distinction of nationality, sex, race, language or religion . . .

Article 4. No reason derived directly or indirectly from differences of sex, race, language or religion shall authorise States to refuse to any of their nationals the enjoyment of public or private rights, particularly admission to public institutions of learning and the exercise of different economic activities, professions and industries.[1]

We have referred to that resolution as 'authoritative' in view of the considerable persuasive force which attaches to the pronounce-

---

[1] See *Annuaire*, 35 (2) (1929), 298–300. See also Wehberg in *Friedenswarte*, 29 (1929), 354–7, and 33 (1933), 263–6; Steichele, *ibid.* pp. 41–4.

GENERAL RULES OF THE LAW OF PEACE

ments of that body. The resolution was adopted by a majority, and not without some discussion. There are many who are of the opinion that in adopting it the Institute came dangerously near to obliterating the line between *lex ferenda* and *lex lata*. In fact, it had become *de rigueur* to deny the existence of fundamental rights of the individual as a matter of positive international law. Individuals, so runs the predominant doctrine, cannot, as such, possess any rights, fundamental or other.

It is proposed here to enquire how far that negative view is really in accordance with existing law. When we say that there are no fundamental rights of the individual, are we referring to the substantive or procedural aspect of the matter? Do we mean that these rights do not exist, or do we mean that they cannot be enforced by the individual, or, finally, do we mean that States are under no legal duty to repress their violation by other States?

It is necessary, in order to answer these questions, to recall certain generally recognized principles of international law. The most important of these is that international law recognizes rights of a fundamental character belonging to individuals in so far as they are aliens resident in a foreign State. The exact scope of these rights may be a matter of dispute. It may be controversial how far the property of aliens is removed from interference by the receiving State; it may be controversial how far the alien is affected by legislation of a political character. But it is almost generally admitted that his property and person enjoy a certain measure of protection, in accordance with a minimum standard of civilization, irrespective of the treatment accorded to nationals. And there is general agreement that aliens are entitled to the respect of such fundamental rights as are accorded to nationals. However, the general view, frequently and authoritatively stated, is that these are not international rights of the alien, but the rights of his State. As the Permanent Court of International Justice said in the *Mavrommatis Palestine Concessions* case, 'By taking up the case of one of its subjects and by resorting to diplomatic action or international judicial proceedings on his behalf, a State is in reality asserting its own rights—its right to ensure, in the person of its subjects, respect for the rules of international law'.[1] It would be unfortunate if the authority of the institution from which this statement emanates were to prevent a critical examination of its somewhat abstract content.

---

[1] *P.C.I.J.* Series A, no. 2, p. 12.

SUBJECTS OF INTERNATIONAL LAW

What is the meaning of the view that the rights in question are not rights of the State but of the individual? Does it amount to anything more than saying that they are rights enforceable not by the individual but by his State? The current phraseology on this matter has become so generally accepted that there has been no attempt to answer these questions critically. And yet, it is submitted, the expression is meaningless unless we confine it to certain limited purposes like the assertion of the international character of claims put forward by States on behalf of the individual. That phraseology may also be useful as a limitation on the scope of the Calvo Clause in the sense that it prevents rash commitments in contracts with foreign Governments so as to sign away the right to diplomatic protection even in cases in which there is a clear breach of international law. But in general there is little logical substance in the formula that the rights in question are rights of the State and not of the individual. The State could not demand that its nationals should be treated in a certain way if they were not themselves entitled, according to international law, to be so treated. They are entitled as aliens to treatment in accordance with international law even if their own State disregards within its borders the fundamental rights of the individual. If these were truly the rights of the State in the person of its nationals, there would arise the incongruous situation of a State asserting internationally as its own, rights which it denies and condemns within its borders with regard to the same individuals. The dogmatic assertion that the rights in question are the rights of the State and not of the individual is nothing else than a re-statement in a generalized form of the existing position with regard to the procedural disability of the individual in the international sphere. The proper view, it is submitted, is that international law grants these rights to the individual as such—be he an alien, a national, or a stateless person. With regard to aliens these rights are in theory enforceable by their own State; this is the reason why they have become firmly established in international law. There is no agency—national or international—to enforce or protect these rights in the case of stateless persons or in the case of nationals with regard to their own State. But this important procedural difference clearly cannot have an effect on these rights as such; these are fundamental rights of the individual in the international sphere, irrespective of nationality, although some of them may for the time being exist as imperfect rights because of the absence of legal machinery to enforce them. It is pathetic to see writers elaborating in detail the

297

GENERAL RULES OF THE LAW OF PEACE

fundamental rights of the individual in his capacity as an alien while remaining oblivious to these rights when that individual happens to be within his own State.[1] It is only by the assumption that the difference is one between a perfect and an imperfect right that we can escape the somewhat absurd phenomenon of the individual suffering a *capitis diminutio*, from the point of view of the protection of the fundamental rights of his personality, as soon as he ceases to be an alien residing in a foreign State and assumes residence in his home State.

51. *The international protection of the international rights of individuals*

As has been pointed out in the introductory lecture to this course, the individual is a unit not only of international duties, but also of international rights. In no other matter does the monistic ideal express itself more strongly than in the postulate that the ultimate object of the international order must be the protection of the individual human being. The national State is at present the principal, although not the only, trustee of that purpose; but the power of the international community to make it account for the fulfilment of that purpose is only *in posse*, not *in esse*. To that extent the monistic purpose and structure of international law are weakened by the intrusion of the dualistic element embodied in the personified State. It serves no useful purpose to deny that existing procedural international law is in this respect still under the sway of that dualism. On the other hand, the extent and significance of that procedural phenomenon must not be exaggerated; it constitutes a departure from, and not the fulfilment of, the purpose of international law. For that reason it is undesirable to erect it into a dogma manifesting the absolute impossiblity of individuals enjoying international rights protected or enforceable by agencies other than their own State.

It has already been shown that, although this is not the typical case, positive law definitely admits the possibility of the individual possessing and enforcing judicially before international or municipal courts rights granted by international law, irrespective of the municipal law of any single State. Moreover, positive international law denies in another sense the assertion that individual rights granted in pursuance of international law can be protected and

[1] See, e.g., Professor Kaufmann's detailed examination of the alien's right to life, liberty, honour, property, religious freedom, and access to courts, in *Hague Recueil*, 54 (1935) (iv), 427–33.

298

SUBJECTS OF INTERNATIONAL LAW

enforced only by the State of the individual concerned. Some examples will illustrate this possibility. Under the Minorities Treaties any member of the Council of the League may protect and, through the means of the compulsory jurisdiction of the Permanent Court of International Justice, judicially enforce the rights of the minority in question. With the exception of the obligatory jurisdiction of the Court, the same right is granted to other members of the League seeing that the stipulations of the Minorities Treaties are described as constituting obligations of an international character. Under the various Mandates, members of the League have the right to invoke the obligatory jurisdiction of the Permanent Court of International Justice with regard to any disagreement with the Mandatory concerning the interpretation or application of the provisions of the Mandate. This right to invoke the jurisdiction of the Court covers cases involving breaches of the Mandate injurious not only to the inhabitants of the mandated territory or the nationals of the complaining State, but probably also to nationals of other members of the League. A foreign State is thus placed in the position of being able to protect rights of persons other than its own subjects; it need not prove any interest other than its general interest in the maintenance of the Mandates or minorities provisions in question; it need not prove any other interest than its general interest in the protection and enforcement of rights of the individuals protected by these Treaties.

Once this is clearly grasped, there is no reason to confine the operation of this principle to the type of treaties mentioned. It applies to any treaty having for its object the protection, in the common interest, of the rights of human personality. It applies to the numerous international labour conventions. The real nature of the situation is not concealed by the fact that in these cases States are primarily and in theory enforcing their own contractual rights violated by the treatment of the individuals in question. In fact it is the right of the individuals which is enforced, and there is nothing in international law which obliges the claimant State to prove any damage other than the actual injury to the individuals affected. These individuals may, and often will, be subjects of the State against which proceedings are taken or subjects of a third State. The rule as to nationality of claims operates here to only a limited extent. It prevents foreign States from formally putting forward claims for damages on behalf of the individuals in regard to injuries which have actually taken place; it does not prevent them from exacting the cessation of injurious conduct in the future; and, probably, there is nothing to prevent them from demanding that the responsibility of the State concerned should take the form of damages or compensation to the individuals injured by acts contrary to the Treaty. Just as a State may have a legal interest in preventing future violations of a treaty, so it may have a legal interest in restoring the legal position as it existed before the treaty was violated. Thus, e.g., in the dispute concerning the *German Settlers in Poland* and decided in substance by Advisory Opinion no. 6 of the Permanent Court of International Justice,[1] it was open to any member of the Council to bring the matter before the Court for judgment and to ask either for a *restitutio in integrum* or for compensation for the settlers. The same applies to any other treaty providing for the compulsory jurisdiction of an international organ. These will appear to some to be bold deductions. But it is probable that these deductions will gain increased recognition as adequately expressing the existing legal position, hitherto obscured by the technicalities of the rule as to nationality of claims and by the dogmatic denial of international rights of the individual.

52. *The international protection of the rights of stateless persons*

This is shown even more clearly in the case of stateless persons. As will be shown presently, their position has recently been regulated in various aspects in a number of international conventions. If the rules as to nationality of claims were to apply fully in this case, it would mean that these conventions are not enforceable at all. Probably there is nothing to prevent a State which is a party to the treaties in question from taking up the case of a stateless person whose rights, as laid down in the convention, have been disregarded.

The regulation of the position of stateless persons through general international conventions is a comparatively recent development. International law recognizes and permits the condition of statelessness. It does not forbid States to possess legislation or to do acts which bring about statelessness. It does not, for instance, forbid denationalization—except, possibly, subject to certain limited duties of re-admission—of nationals resident in foreign countries at the time of denationalization.[2] This tacit authorization of statelessness constitutes a serious contradiction in the sphere of international law. If, according to the predominant doctrine and practice, nationality is the only link between the individual and the benefits of international law, then international law must charge itself with

---

[1] *P.C.I.J.* Series B, no. 6.   [2] See below, p. 301.

300

SUBJECTS OF INTERNATIONAL LAW

securing to the individual *some* nationality. For whatever may be the theory about the subjects of international law, there ought to be no doubt that the individual human being must be the ultimate object of protection of all law, national or international. The accepted doctrine does not deny this. It only renders the State the instrument of that protection. By permitting statelessness it deprives the stateless individual not only of the protection, but also of the enjoyment, of a series of important rights, like unrestricted access to courts, which according to the legislation of many countries is made dependent upon reciprocity—a condition which the stateless person naturally cannot fulfil. The gap is now being filled by the conclusion of conventions aiming either at reducing the possibilities of statelessness or at rendering the position of stateless persons less difficult by making them the direct object of international, as distinguished from national, protection. Thus the Hague Codification Conference of 1930[1] adopted a number of provisions calculated to reduce the possibility of statelessness. The Convention on Certain Questions relating to the Conflict of Nationality Laws provided that an expatriation permit issued by a State shall not entail the loss of the nationality of that State unless the person to whom it is issued possesses or acquires another nationality. Detailed rules were adopted in that Convention for preventing statelessness as the result of marriage. With regard to the nationality of children, the same Convention provided that if children do not acquire the nationality of their parents as a result of the naturalization of the latter, they shall retain their existing nationality (Article 13), or that a child whose parents are unknown or who have no nationality, or whose nationality is unknown, shall have the nationality of the country of birth. Finally, in a special Protocol concerning Statelessness provision was made for the case of persons rendered stateless as the result of being deprived of their nationality after they entered a foreign country. It was there laid down that the State of origin is bound to admit such a person at the request of the State in whose territory he is if he is permanently indigent, or if he has been sentenced to not less than one month's imprisonment.[2]

---

[1] The Conference adopted a unanimous recommendation to the effect that it is desirable that, in regulating questions of nationality, States should make every effort to reduce cases of statelessness so far as possible.

[2] It will be noted that the Convention does not go to the length of imposing a general duty of re-admission. As the persons in question are as a rule refugees from the political régime, the duty of re-admission and the consequent use of the right of deportation from the foreign State would fly in the face of the principles which, for instance, the law of extradition has evolved with regard to political offenders. For this reason even the

GENERAL RULES OF THE LAW OF PEACE

At the same time attempts have been made in some cases to mitigate the lot of particular categories of stateless persons. Thus in the Convention of 28 October 1933 relating to the International Status of Refugees, the contracting parties undertook definite obligations with regard to the treatment of Russian, Armenian and assimilated refugees as defined in previous Agreements concluded in 1926 and 1928. They agreed to grant to these persons so-called Nansen passports; not to expel, except for reasons of public order and safety, refugees regularly residing in the State concerned; and to grant to them free access to the courts and exemption from the requirement of reciprocity applying in some cases to aliens. A similar arrangement was concluded on 4 July 1936 concerning the Status of Refugees from Germany.[1] As said, notwithstanding the rules as to the nationality of claims, any of the contracting parties may now have recourse to international remedies in case of a breach of these Conventions to the detriment of a stateless person.

53. The rights of individuals and humanitarian intervention

The preceding discussion of individual rights established by treaty has shown the possibility of rights for the benefit of the individual being established by treaty and being enforceable by agencies other than the State whose nationality the injured person possesses and which takes up his claim as 'its own right'. That discussion was necessary in order to show the possibility of the existence of internationally enforceable international rights of the individual having their source in international as distinguished from municipal law. We have thus answered the first, formal, objection to the existence of fundamental rights of the individual. The second question, to which an answer must also be sought in what has already been said, is whether customary as distinguished from conventional international law recognizes rights inherent in human personality and entitled to international protection. We have seen that international law recognizes such rights with regard to aliens. We have seen that, save for express conventional regulation with regard to stateless persons and a State's own nationals within its own territory,

cautious provisions of the Protocol are not entirely beyond criticism. Writers have been so much concerned with the inconvenience caused to the State where the denationalized person is resident, that they have lost sight of the inconvenience to which he might be exposed at the hands of the authorities of his own country.

[1] Treaty Series, no. 33 (1936), Cmd. 5388. In September 1933 the Fourteenth Assembly of the League decided, on the proposal of the Dutch Government, that the problem of the German refugees should be dealt with by international co-operation. See as to this Convention Tager in *Clunet*, 63 (1936), 1136–67.

302

SUBJECTS OF INTERNATIONAL LAW

their non-recognition is not one of substance; it is a procedural and political obstacle. There do exist rights which customary international law recognizes to belong to the individual. In the case of aliens these rights are enforceable; in the case of others they are not as a rule. The difference is procedural, not substantive; and, to a large extent, it is one of politics, not of law.

These considerations contain, implicitly, an answer to the question of so-called humanitarian intervention, i.e. intervention undertaken for the purpose of preventing a State from treating its own nationals in a cruel and barbarous fashion. There has been no such intervention since the time before the World War when European Powers intervened in Turkey in order to prevent the maltreatment of certain of her subjects. But can it be said with assurance that such intervention, if resorted to, would be contrary to international law? The independent and sovereign State is by international law given full autonomy with regard to the treatment of its nationals; it is typically a question of domestic jurisdiction. But this exclusive right may be abused. It ceases then to be a right, and the competence of international law to protect the individual is fully restored. The establishment of effective international organs giving objective and disinterested expression to that competence would remove one of the principal objections to humanitarian intervention, namely, the danger of its being abused for selfish purposes. If the fundamental rights of human personality, however indefinite, controversial and imperfect from the point of view of their enforceability—if these rights are part of the international system and if their protection is the ultimate object of international law, then humanitarian intervention is both a legal and a political principle of the international society.

The existing international practice is far removed from asserting that right of intervention. It is unnecessary here to approve or to regret that fact. Probably it is true to say that the matter is under the influence of the general decline of the standards of international law after the World War. The times are not propitious for asserting the fundamental rights of the individual in the international sphere at a period when in many countries these rights have been abolished by positive law. It is a period in which the State has reduced the authority and independence of the individual not only in his capacity as a citizen of the State, but also in the international sphere. Thus, for instance, his freedom of migration and commercial intercourse have been restricted in a way which would appear intolerable within the State.

Yet if the individual is the ultimate unit of law, then that very

303

GENERAL RULES OF THE LAW OF PEACE

retrogression is a warning against any generalization of the existing situation. The more pronounced the subjection of the individual to the omnipotent power of the State, the more pronounced is the part of international law in protecting him. The measure of that protection depends on the political conditions of the world and the authority of international law. A large and overriding measure of protection, far from being incompatible with international law, is of the essence of its function as a *jus gentium* contrasted with international law as the law between sovereign States. An international law which does not fulfil that function is certainly not inconceivable. In fact this is the position in which it finds itself today—although even today it is called upon to remedy, by special conventional agreements, some internationally obnoxious consequences of the suppression of individual rights and the resulting incidents of statelessness, denationalization, migration, etc.

But it is not unscientific to look into the future and hold before our minds the ultimate rational development in the political organization of nations and of mankind. That must consist in the elimination not only of international but also of civil war in a way comparable to the suppression of civil war within the territories of the member States of a Federal Union as the result of the guarantee in the Federal Constitution of the fundamental rights of the individual. The ultimate political organization of mankind will signify the incorporation of these rights as an organic part of the constitution of the international commonwealth. In so far as civil war is due to a suppression or falsification of these rights, it would be eliminated by the international constitution enforced by judicial review and executive action. However, it is not essential to conjure that final superstructure of the international edifice in order to get a grasp of an essential, although now largely dormant and unenforceable, element embodied in the fundamental rights of the individual. An attempt has been made here to show that the negation of these rights as part of international law is not consistent either with the larger purpose of international law or with its actual developments as expressed both by treaties and by custom.

D. THE SUBJECTS OF INTERNATIONAL LAW AND THE CREATION OF RULES OF INTERNATIONAL LAW

54. *The International Labour Organisation. The Vatican City*

The question of the relative position of the State and the individual in international law can be considered not only from the point of

SUBJECTS OF INTERNATIONAL LAW

view of fundamental and other rights of the individual, but also from the angle of their respective places in the law-creating function. States are generally recognized as exclusively fulfilling that function. Even those who contend for some kind of independent status for the individual in international law agree that the creation of rules of international law is a matter for the State only. This is not only a rule of positive law, but also an obvious and rational principle *de lege ferenda*. States are at present the essential instrument for the execution of international law, and their formal responsibility for the conclusion and enforcement of treaties must remain an essential element of the situation. On the other hand, that principle need not necessarily be pushed to the length of asserting the exclusive participation of Governments in the process of creating rules of international law. A great number, perhaps the large majority, of international conventions relate to matters which are intended to regulate and which are of direct interest not to the State at large, but to definite categories of its population. Reasons of convenience point to the desirability of associating the representatives of the interested categories of the population in the preparation and negotiation of conventions of this nature. Such vocational or similar representation may facilitate and improve the process of international law-making by removing it from the field of merely political consideration and basing it on the expert knowledge of those directly and vitally concerned. The Constitution of the International Labour Organization contains a significant innovation of this nature. It secures to representatives of employers and employees participation not only in the executive but also in the law-making organs of that institution. These representatives are chosen by Governments, but they must be chosen in accordance with rules laid down in the Treaty; once chosen, they enjoy complete freedom from their Governments in the expression of opinion and in voting. Numerically their representation is equal to that of the Governments. But while the ratification of the various conventions is a matter for the competent authorities of the member States, the influence of the vocational representations on the drafting and contents of the conventions is considerable in law and in fact.

The Constitution of the International Labour Organisation is thus the beginning of an entirely new development in the matter of the position of individuals in the international sphere. It signifies their direct participation in the international law-creating process. Secondly, it reveals the possibilities of international co-operation,

GENERAL RULES OF THE LAW OF PEACE

within the sphere of international law, based not on what may be called the vertical division of humanity into political units represented by territorial States, but on the horizontal division of vocational, professional or similar interests. A stage is thus reached in which international law has ceased, even from the point of view of procedure, to be a law exclusively confined to or created by territorial States.

From a different angle and in a different way the restoration of the temporal power of the Holy See signifies a development in the same direction. We say 'restoration of the temporal power', but these words are used here in a formal sense. The temporal power of the Holy See before 1870 was a matter of substance; since 1929 it is a symbol. The head of the Italian Government is reported to have said that the Lateran Treaty, far from resuscitating the temporal power of the Papacy, effectively buried it. This may be a metaphor, but the fact remains that the territorial sovereignty of the Holy See since 1929 is more a symbol than a reality. The Vatican City has a population and territory in comparison with which, as has been said, Andorra and San Marino constitute veritable empires. The degree of its independence, either of Italy or, much more, of the Holy See whose purposes it has been declared to serve, has been the subject of much discussion. Just as its citizenship, it has been said, is in fact nothing else than a neutralization of the effects of citizenship of other countries, so its independence has been said to be merely a kind of neutralization in relation to other sovereignties in a way comparable to the special position of the State of Washington in the District of Columbia effected with a view to securing to the seat of the Government an independent position in relation to the States of the Union.

Be that as it may, it is clear that the Vatican City is, according to the accepted canons, on the very borderline of statehood. But its right to the enjoyment of the normal attributes of statehood has not been seriously controverted; its neutralization and abstention from participation in international conferences are a self-imposed ordinance. We are thus confronted with the phenomenon of a spiritual purpose, utterly different from that normally represented by States in the international arena, clothing itself with the formal attributes of statehood and recognized as such by the other members of the international community. The formal requirements of statehood still constitute a condition of representation of that new type of interest. But it is a condition reduced to a formality. Should any

SUBJECTS OF INTERNATIONAL LAW

other church, or religious denomination, or economic, humanitarian or cultural interest transcending that of a single State deem it necessary to endow itself with these formal paraphernalia of membership of the international community, it might find in the Lateran Treaty an instructive example. The International Labour Organisation, on the one hand, and the Vatican City, on the other, thus suggest possible developments by virtue of which interests other than those normally represented by territorial sovereign States may be admitted to some of the benefits of normal international intercourse and, in turn, may infuse into international relations a humanizing and civilizing element raising them above the level of assertion and protection of sovereign power.

CHAPTER 6

RECOGNITION OF STATES

55. *The function of recognition in international law*

International law is a weak system of law. This is generally admitted, and nothing but good can come from such an admission so long as it is not maintained that the shortcomings of international law are permanent and inherent in its very nature. Among the factors generally recognized as the weak links in the Law of Nations there are some which undoubtedly exist as a matter of positive law. Thus, prior to the Covenant of the League and the General Treaty for the Renunciation of War, the admissibility of war was such a defect. In time of peace a State was bound by minute and exacting duties to respect the existence, the independence, the equality and the dignity of other States. Even in an abnormal time of controversy, recourse to reprisals was—and is—regulated by principles laying down when and to what extent they may be resorted to. But it was sufficient for a State to avail itself of its practically unlimited right to declare war in order to gain freedom from these restraints and in order to be entitled to treat its neighbours as a veritable *caput lupinum* to the point of legally permissible annihilation in the shape of annexation and conquest. The legal admissibility of war showed how unreal is the borderline between law and lawlessness; between the duty to let live and the right to extinguish. It showed that law obtained only so long as the State was willing to tolerate it. It bound the State to details, but it left it free to divest itself of all the restraints by one legally permissible act.

A parallel phenomenon can be witnessed in the matter of recognition of States, Governments, and belligerency—if we assume that the predominant doctrine in the matter gives an accurate statement of the existing practice. The State is bound by minute rules to respect the sovereignty and independence of other States. But just as it is left to its free discretion to terminate the existence of other States as the result of a successful war, so, according to the predominant doctrine, it is free to decide, according to discretion and by consulting its own interests only, whether a foreign community should begin to enjoy those rights of sovereignty and independence. By the simple device of refusing recognition a State is legally entitled,

308

according to a widely adopted doctrine, to deny the right to live to a political community apparently fulfilling the conditions of statehood.

The position is the same with regard to recognition of Governments. A State participates in the benefits of international law largely through the medium of its Government. To refuse to recognize the Government of a State is to refuse, to a substantial degree, to recognize the State and to grant it what is its due in the international sphere. It implies a refusal to admit it to normal international intercourse; it means its exclusion from the jurisdictional immunities and privileges enjoyed by a State; it results in ignoring the legislative, judicial and administrative acts of the State with an unrecognized Government. To say therefore that the granting of recognition to a new Government is a matter of discretion unfettered by legal rule or principle is to maintain that also in this matter the line dividing law and freedom from legal restraint is not more real in the case of recognition than in the matter of war.

However, it will be submitted here that while with regard to war the defect in the structure of international law is one of historical fact and positive law, in the matter of recognition it is largely the creation of writers wedded to the doctrine of consent as the only source of obligation in the international sphere. It will be submitted here that as a matter of legal principle and of weight of practice, recognition is not a question of the arbitrary will of States but of international law, of which the States are organs. This applies to all kinds of recognition—of States, Governments, and belligerency. They are all governed by the same principle. With regard to all of them the matter is governed by the same question: Is recognition a matter of law or politics, of rule or arbitrariness?

The problem has been obscured to a large extent by being identified with the controversy between the declaratory or constitutive character of recognition. The adherents of the constitutive theory are largely, although not exclusively, those who make recognition a matter of political discretion and bargaining; the adherents of the declaratory theory make it a matter of routine and of a purely administrative function. It is neither. It is constitutive in the meaning that it is not a formality: that it requires the active, deliberate, difficult and conscientious exercise of discretion in a matter which is frequently of extreme difficulty. It is declaratory in the meaning that, once given the requirements of statehood, the recognizing State is not free in law to refuse recognition for reasons connected with its own policy and convenience. Although it is a function per-

GENERAL RULES OF THE LAW OF PEACE

formed not by courts but by the executive department, recognition is an essentially judicial or quasi-judicial function of the administration of the law. This applies to all kinds of recognition—of States, Governments, and belligerency. The true division of opinion is, it will be suggested, not between the constitutive and declaratory, but between the political and legal view of the nature of the function of recognition.

56. *The constitutive theory of the recognition of States*

It was not unnatural that the question of recognition should become identified with the perennial controversy between the positivist school and its opponents. If, as the positivists maintain, the will of the State is the sole source of its obligations, then clearly it cannot be admitted either that the existing States can have new duties thrust upon them by the emergence of new States which they are henceforth bound to recognize, or that the new community can be compelled to abide by the established rules of international law with regard to the already existing States. The easiest—although, as will be seen, by no means easy—escape from the difficulty is to maintain that the new State does not exist as a subject of either international rights or duties so long as both the new and old States have not by express agreement assumed the reciprocal rights and obligations.

This view has recently been stated by Anzilotti with all requisite clarity.[1] It may be summarized as follows. Rules of international law are created by agreement. Accordingly, a subject of international law begins to exist as soon as, but not before, there comes into being the first agreement. That first agreement is the act of recognition. It is a treaty. It is reciprocal and constitutive. Like any other treaty it is binding ultimately by virtue of the fundamental rule *pacta sunt servanda*. (This last statement is a precaution calculated to meet the objection of those who point out that if the existence of a State is provided in a treaty, i.e. in the constitutive will of another State, then the recognized State can no longer be regarded as anything other than a delegated emanation of the recognizing State, and therefore as not truly sovereign.) It is an admitted consequence of the positivist view—and that admission is given clear expression by Anzilotti—that there are no legal relations with a non-recognized State and that recognition depends entirely and exclusively on the will of the States concerned parties to the contractual bargain of recognition.

---

[1] *Cours de droit international* (French trans. by Gidel, 1929), pp. 160–8.

RECOGNITION OF STATES

It is possible to attack that doctrine by criticism on the lines of that formulated by Kelsen, who points to the logical impossibility of a new State taking part in its own creation as an international person by means of a treaty which presupposes its very existence.[1] There must be the greatest disinclination to admit the existence of a gap if a system of law either fails to lay down what are the requirements of legal personality or, what is the same, if it lays down that legal personality shall be in the gift of the existing members of the community acting by reference to their own interests. We are not at liberty to assume, without overwhelming proof, the existence of such a fundamental gap. (Less convincing is the objection—adequately answered, it is believed, by Anzilotti—that recognition thus conceived denies the sovereignty of the recognized State by deriving it from the sovereignty of the recognizing State. The same applies to the criticism that, on the positivist view, a situation is created in which a new community exists as a State for those States which have recognized it, but not for the others. However, this objection applies also to the declaratory conception of recognition, unless one assumes that such declaration is a mere formality. It is only through recognition by an international organ, acting on behalf of all members of the community, that that particular anomaly can be removed.)

It is also doubtless possible to criticize from the ethical point of view the positivist 'grant' or 'bargain' theory of recognition the result of which deprives the new community, for no fault of its own, of the minimum of rights indispensable in international intercourse. However, the positivist would, rightly from his point of view, dismiss that criticism as a pathetic weapon taken from the armoury of national law.

57. *The practice of States. The 'delictual' aspect of recognition*

It is more profitable to test the political view of recognition by the professed standards of its adherents, namely, the practice of States. Does the practice of States suggest that the granting or refusing of recognition is a matter of political expediency or legal principle? Do States profess to act—and it is their disclosed profession that matters, not the surmised political motive and interest behind it—as if they were bound to act on broad considerations of legal principle or as if they were free to do as suits their political convenience?

There is no doubt that at least one aspect of the matter is governed by legal principle, and that is what may be called the tortious, delictual aspect. New communities claiming political independence

---

[1] In *Hague Recueil*, 42 (1932) (iv), 260–74.

GENERAL RULES OF THE LAW OF PEACE

arise, as a rule, by secession from the parent State. Now it is clear law that, so far as the parent State is concerned, recognition is governed by certain legal principles the disregard of which entails responsibility on the part of the recognizing State. Obviously, premature recognition is more than an unfriendly act; it is an act of intervention and an international delinquency. The new community must fulfil certain conditions of permanency and political cohesion; the parent State must in fact have ceased to make efforts, promising success, to re-assert its authority. Thus the question whether existing States are entitled, in relation to the parent State, to grant recognition is one of law, it being true that the application of the law requires in this case a judgment as to fact of a frequently controversial and political character.

But have the legal principles governing the tortious aspect of recognition any bearing on the seemingly different question as to the right of the new community to recognition by third States and as to their duty to grant recognition? They cannot be altogether irrelevant—unless one adopts a rigid, formal view that as the new community does not exist it has no rights. For after all those principles embody the objective requirements making legally possible the grant of recognition; they embody the objective conditions making the grant of recognition a step which is in accordance with the requirements of international justice, stability, and intercourse so as to justify what is after all an interference with established legal rights of the old State. This being so, the insistence on the difference between the right to recognize (in relation to the parent State) and the duty to recognize (in relation to the new community) may be formally correct, but it is not as convincing as appears at first sight. It is not easy to concede that in substance the objective conditions of recognition are different when looked at from the points of view, respectively, of the duty to the parent State and of the obligation to the new community.

58. *Governmental pronouncements*

Governmental pronouncements in the matter of the right to recognize are frequent; those in the matter of the duty to recognize are naturally rare. They are so for the simple reason that established States have as a rule no reason or inclination to expatiate on their duty to the new community; on the other hand, they have had occasion to defend, as against the complaints of the parent State, their right to grant recognition. It is this last aspect of the matter

RECOGNITION OF STATES

which has loomed large in diplomatic correspondence. The indirect result of this fact has been to create the impression that the question of recognition in relation to the community claiming it is not governed by rules of law at all.

And yet, although conditions have not been propitious, there exists a series of governmental pronouncements bearing on this question. Their cumulative effect is to make one wonder how it happened that, apart from the explanation given above, the doctrine here analysed has succeeded in becoming so predominant. These pronouncements are of two kinds. Some admit the right of the new community to recognition or the corresponding duty of established States to grant recognition; others lay down, in effect, the same principle by maintaining that the existence of a State is a question of fact. It is useful to survey some of these pronouncements of American and British statesmen—with an apology for italicizing the crucial passages or expressions.

In a significant message addressed on 24 August 1818 to President Monroe, the United States Secretary of State Mr Adams said:

There is a stage in such contests when the parties struggling for independence *have . . . a right to demand its acknowledgment by neutral parties* and when the acknowledgment may be granted without departure from the obligations of neutrality. It is the stage when independence is established as a matter of fact so as to leave the chance of the opposite party to recover their dominion utterly desperate.[1]

In the important Presidential Message of 30 January 1822 announcing the intention to recognize the independence of some of the South American Republics, the President referred as a matter for serious consideration to the question whether '*their right to the rank of independent nations . . . is not complete*'.[2]

In a communication of 10 April 1861, by Secretary Seward to Mr Adams, there occurs the following passage: 'We freely admit that a nation may, and even ought, to recognize a new State which has absolutely and beyond question effected its independence . . .' And he added:

Seen in the light of this principle, the several nations of the earth constitute one great federal republic. When one of them casts its suffrages for the admission of a new member into that republic, it ought to act under a profound sense of moral obligation, and be governed by considerations as pure, disinterested and elevated as the general interest of society and the advancement of human nature.[3]

[1] Moore, 1, 78.   [3] *Ibid.* p. 85.   [2] *U.S. Foreign Relations* (1861), pp. 76–9.

313

GENERAL RULES OF THE LAW OF PEACE

Even more explicit is the passage in the reply of the United States to the Spanish protest following upon the announcement of the intention to recognize the independence of the revolted provinces. It is there laid down that the Government of the United States, far from consulting the dictates of a policy questionable in its morality, yielded *to an obligation of duty of the highest order by recognizing* as independent States nations which, after deliberately asserting their right to that character, have maintained and established it against all the resistance which had been or could be brought to oppose it.[1]

The recognition, the Note continued, was 'the mere acknowledgment of existing facts'.[2]

59. *The existence of a State as a question of fact*

This insistence that the independence of a new community is a question of fact is a persistent feature of governmental declarations. Thus in reply to the Mexican protest against the recognition of the independence of Texas, Mr Forsyth, the Secretary of State, said in 1837:

The independence of other nations has always been regarded by the United States as question of fact merely, and that of every people has been invariably recognized by them whenever the actual enjoyment of it was accompanied by satisfactory evidence of their power and determination permanently and effectually to maintain it.[3]

In 1875, in his message concerning the question of the recognition of Cuba, President Grant said:

In such cases [of recognition of new States] other nations simply deal with an actually existing condition of things, and recognize as one of the powers of the earth that body politic which, possessing the necessary elements, has, in fact, become a new power. In a word, the creation of a new State is a fact.[4]

What, it must be asked, is the meaning of the statement that the question whether a new State exists is a question of fact? Does it not mean that it is not a question of a voluntary grant, of contractual bargain, of political expediency, of selfish consideration of the interests of the recognizing State? Undoubtedly, the latter has still to judge whether the fact exists, and it has to exercise its discretion in arriving at that judgment. But it is a judicial discretion aiming at ascertaining whether the fact exists or not. When the Declaration of London laid down that the effectiveness of a blockade is a question of fact, the intention was obviously to say that the requirement of

---

[1] Moore, I, 88.   [2] *Ibid.*   [3] *Ibid.* p. 102.   [4] *Ibid.* p. 107.

RECOGNITION OF STATES

effectiveness is an undoubted rule of law, but that it is impossible to lay down in advance the precise factual conditions of its operation. This is in general the meaning of the jurisprudential distinction between questions of fact and of law. It is submitted that the emphasis—and that emphasis is a constant feature of diplomatic correspondence—that the independence of the new State is a question of fact means simply that the granting of recognition is a legal duty, not a political act of grace.

The British practice in the matter has been well summarized by Hall. It is, in his view, governed by 'the principle that recognition cannot be withheld when it has been earned'[1] and that 'theoretically a politically organized community enters as of right into the family of states, and must be treated according to law, as soon as it is able to show that it possesses the marks of a state'.[1] He quotes Lord Liverpool's declaration, as coinciding in this matter with the views of Canning, Lord Lansdowne and Sir James Mackintosh, that 'there was no right [to recognition] while the contest was actually going on'. The question of the right was not in dispute; what was controversial was whether the contest was still going on. The actual, and not merely verbal, continuation of the struggle was necessary in order, to quote Hall once more, 'to prevent foreign countries from falling under an obligation to recognize as a state the community claiming to have become one'.[2]

In 1862 we find Lord Russell telling Mr Mason that 'In order to be entitled to a place among the independent nations of the earth, a State ought to have not only strength and resources for a time, but afford promise of stability and permanence.'[3]

There is probably no pronouncement of a responsible Government on record in which the granting or refusal of recognition of statehood is claimed to be a matter of grace or political expediency. It is only writers who from time to time go to the length of generalizing a non-existent practice. There is probably no State document in existence which professes to be based on the rule laid down by Fauchille who, surprisingly enough, was an adherent of the declaratory conception of recognition. He said: 'Les États sont libres de reconnaître ou de ne pas reconnaître un État récemment formé, de se déterminer selon les convenances de leur politique.'[4] Even in the course of the controversy with Colombia concerning the undoubtedly premature recognition of Panama, the Government of the United

---

[1] *International Law*, 4th ed. (1895), § 26. [2] *Ibid.* pp. 90–3.
[3] *Fontes Juris Gentium*, Series B, Section 1, Vol. 1, Part 1, 142. [4] 1, § 204.

315

GENERAL RULES OF THE LAW OF PEACE

States did not, although the temptation was considerable, have recourse to the argument that in granting recognition it was entitled to take into account its own interests only. In rejecting the Colombian claim for arbitration in the matter it confined itself to declaring that 'questions of foreign policy and of the recognition and non-recognition of foreign States are of a purely political nature, and do not fall within the domain of judicial decision'.[1]

60. *The criteria of recognition*

The pronouncements quoted show at the same time what are the legal conditions for recognition of statehood. They coincide with the conditions permitting a third State to recognize a new community without committing an illegality in relation to the parent State; they coincide with the requirements of statehood as laid down by international law and as uniformly expressed in text books. They are a reasonably well-defined territory, a population, and the existence of an independent Government enjoying a reasonable degree of stability. As will be seen, the existence of these requirements may on occasions be controversial. But on the whole these conditions are clear, easily ascertainable, and of an almost formal character. But they are formally definite and exhaustive. They have nothing to do with the quality of the State, with the legitimacy of its origin, with its religion, or with its political system. Once considerations of that nature are introduced as a condition of recognition, the clear path of law is abandoned and the door wide open to arbitrariness, to attempts at extortion and to intervention, at the very threshold of statehood.

Lorimer's treatment of the subject offers a good example of the danger of going beyond the normal requirements of recognition. He begins his exposition by emphasizing the fundamental importance of the subject in the system of international law. It is recognition, he says, which makes of international law a science. He lays down—in a manner strikingly reminiscent of Kelsen's teaching of the law-creating results of actual fact—that rights and duties have their origin in, and are limited by, the facts of natural life: 'Any doctrine which professes to regard it [recognition] as an act of courtesy, comity, or the like, exercise of which may be jurally withheld—deprives international law of a primitive basis and fails to bring it within the sphere of jurisprudence.'[2] The question, he says, is one

---

[1] Mr Hay, Secretary of State, to the Colombian Minister, 5 January 1904, as cited in Moore, III, 105. [2] Lorimer, I, 104.

316

of ascertaining whether there exist the necessary requirements of international law. With all this we must agree. But it is difficult to agree with his contention that, in the present state of international law, it is for each State to lay down what these conditions are. As he considers that it is the business of the science of international law to assist States in determining these conditions, he then proceeds to suggest what the proper tests are. With great respect for that distinguished and original writer, it must be said that the suggested tests are arbitrary, sweeping, and impracticable to the point of being ridiculous. In the first instance he divides humanity into three concentric spheres: into civilized, barbarous, and savage peoples. The last two are excluded from recognition. They are excluded because they cannot fulfil the fundamental condition of being able to have what Lorimer calls a 'reciprocating will'.[1] But that requirement excludes not only savage or barbarous peoples. It eliminates religious creeds whose doctrine excludes the presumption of reciprocating will, e.g. the Moḥammedan religion. It eliminates, further, secular creeds which are devoid of the 'reciprocating will', such as intolerant monarchies ('the very name of monarchy savours of exclusiveness'), intolerant republics (like that of the French Convention of 1793), intolerant anarchies, communities wedded to communism or nihilism (which are 'prohibited by the law of nations'), communities under personal or class Governments (on the ground that their form of government renders them incapable of expressing or reaching a reciprocating will). A very select and limited company of States could now successfully emerge from this rigorous test!

Some will think, perhaps not altogether without justification, that undue space has been devoted to an exposition of Lorimer's view. But possibly the example will prove of some usefulness as showing the wisdom of avoiding conditions of recognition other than those embodied in the three usual requirements of statehood. The practice of States in the last hundred years does not show any signs of such additional requirements with regard to recognition of States.

61. *The rôle of recognition*

On the other hand, it would be a mistake to assume that these tests are automatic and that recognition is therefore as a rule a purely ministerial function. The question whether the independent Government of the new community has asserted itself successfully against

[1] *Ibid.* p. 127.

GENERAL RULES OF THE LAW OF PEACE

the challenge of the mother country is not always easy to answer. The fact that the mother country does not, for the time being, make an effort to regain sovereignty may not always be decisive. The very independence of the new community may be controversial apart from the attitude of the mother country. Thus, with regard to the State of Manchukuo created in 1933 subsequent to the invasion of the province of Manchuria by Japan, the question of its recognition, quite apart from the so-called doctrine of non-recognition, has been dependent upon the answer to the question whether that State in fact possesses a Government independent of any other State. The international personality of the Vatican City as established as the result of the Lateran Treaty of 1929 has been doubted by some on the ground that the normal requirements of statehood are reduced to a minimum. The territory of the Vatican City does not exceed forty hectares. Its population, which does not exceed seven hundred, is composed almost exclusively of persons residing therein by virtue of their office and of their descent. It is of a radically different nature from the population of any other State. And its independence both of the Italian State and of the Holy See has been a matter of discussion. In cases like these, the ascertainment of the existence of conditions of statehood may well be a matter of some difficulty.

For these reasons it is not easy to accept the view that recognition is purely declaratory and that a State exists as soon as there exist the requirements of statehood. For this may often be the question at issue. In municipal law the beginning of the existence of physical or juridical persons is as a rule determinable by external tests. With regard to physical persons there has, in various systems of law, both private and criminal, been some discussion as to the precise moment of the beginning of life, but the question on the whole does not give rise to undue difficulties. With regard to juristic persons the nature of the various requirements of registration, minimum capital and articles of association, is such as to render their ascertainment comparatively easy. As has been shown, this is not the case in the matter of the existence of States. It is therefore not very helpful to rely on the Resolution of the Institute of International Law of April 1936, which lays down that 'recognition of a new State is the free [sic] act by which one or more States acknowledge the existence' of certain facts creative of statehood: that 'recognition has a declaratory effect'; and that 'the existence of a new State, with all the juridical effects which are attached to that existence, is not

RECOGNITION OF STATES

affected by the refusal of recognition by one or more States'. What is meant by the statement that the act is 'free'? Does it mean that although it has only a 'declaratory effect' it can be withheld without legally relevant reasons? Nor is it clear what the last mentioned paragraph means. Does it mean that non-recognizing States are bound to recognize all the juridical consequences of the new State as soon as it exists? But the question still remains whether the new community *exists*. It is not helpful to say that Manchukuo exists as a State independently of recognition; for the prior question must be answered, whether it exists. Not every community claiming existence as a State exists as such. It may not in fact be independent, although it claims to be; it may not in fact possess an organized Government, although it may claim to possess one. Sir John Fischer Williams, with many of whose conclusions we venture to agree, quotes as applying to recognition the Greek poet's saying: 'This is alone beyond the power of Heaven, to make what has been not to have been.'[1] But the question is whether the thing 'has been'. Sir John himself in another place[2] deplores as unfortunate the premature grant of recognition of statehood to some communities after the World War. Did these communities 'exist' or did they not? It is only recognition, given in good faith in pursuance of legal principle, that can decide this. The question whether the United States 'existed' in 1778 as an independent State so as to make the French recognition purely declaratory of an existing fact was not one capable of an automatic answer.

62. *Recognition as an international function*

Recognition is a substantial function of great moment. It is declaratory in the sense that it ascertains, as a fact, the existence of the requirements of statehood and the consequent right of the new community to be treated as a normal subject of international law; it is declaratory in the sense that in the contemplation of the law the new community is entitled to it as a matter of right and that one may safely disregard the objection that, not being recognized, it cannot be 'legally entitled'; it is declaratory in the sense that, once given, its effect dates back to the commencement of the existence of the new State as an independent community; it is declaratory in the sense that the recognizing State does not part with any of its rights by way of grant, concession, or act of grace. On the other hand, it is constitutive in the sense that, so long as discretion in

---

[1] *Harvard Law Review* (1934), p. 785.   [2] *Hague Recueil*, 44 (1933) (ii), 40.

GENERAL RULES OF THE LAW OF PEACE

ascertaining the existence of the conditions of statehood is exercised in good faith, it is decisive for the creation of the international personality of the new community and its rights as such; it is constitutive in the sense that, provided again that the State acts in good faith in the exercise of the discretion left to it by international law, it is not bound to apply to the new community the rules of international law.

These are the reasons why it may be considered in the future to be more conducive to the understanding of the problem of recognition to present the difference between the two opposing conceptions not as the difference between the declaratory and constitutive character of recognition, but between the legal and political, or juridical and diplomatic, view of its function.

The view which is here put forward as being in accordance with the bulk of the practice of States and with legal principle—the principle, that is to say, which denies to States the right to commence or terminate the existence of other States according to their political convenience—that view postulates that States in granting or refusing recognition are the trustees of the international legal order. There is no international judge or international central registrar or similar authority to determine whether the requirements of statehood exist. Individual States fulfil that function.

It is clear that in the existing circumstances they cannot always fulfil that function with absolute judicial detachment. This is so because their own interests are often directly involved. They are involved for the reason that although the granting of recognition is the fulfilment of a legal function, it is at the same time a highly political function. The manner of its exercise may bring upon the recognizing State the wrath of the parent State or the lasting enmity of the new community. When in 1777 France recognized the independence of the United States she adduced general reasons of legal principle and of necessities of peace in support of her action. She was answered by a declaration of war. It is owing to these political implications of recognition that the exercise of that function is entrusted to the political department of the State. Secondly, circumstances will often arise in which a State may see in the manner of the exercise of the function of recognition an opportunity for securing for itself benefits from the parent State or from the community claiming recognition. The consideration of such benefits cannot be regarded as legitimate, but obviously they cannot always be alien to the final decision of the recognizing State. The existing

320

RECOGNITION OF STATES

process of recognition is one of those deficiencies of international law which ensue from the fact that States combine the functions of an organ of international law and of the guardians of their own interests. This combination is apt to blur the disinterestedness of judicial detachment.

However, these imperfections of method do not destroy the essential nature of recognition. Governments do not invoke considerations of national policy as a factor in granting or refusing recognition except when they refer to the danger of being embroiled with the parent State on account of premature recognition. But then the duty not to grant premature recognition is merely another expression of the duty owed by the State as an organ of international law not to grant recognition except when the conditions of statehood are indisputably in existence.

63. *Possible developments towards recognition as a collective act*

But while States are as a rule conscious of the true nature of the function of recognition, it is impossible to deny the anomaly of that duality of function. The solution of the difficulty lies obviously in transferring that function to an international organ not labouring under the conflict between interest and duty. That innovation would also abolish the anomaly of a community existing as a State in relation to some but not to other States. The practical possibilities of such a development are not chimerical even in the present stage of international organization. If, as some maintain, admission to the League by the requisite majority implies the recognition of the new State even by those who voted against the admission, then we are in the presence of a collective act of recognition. The Resolution of the Assembly of March 1932 concerning the non-recognition of treaties and situations brought about in a way contrary to the Covenant and the General Treaty for the Renunciation of War must also be regarded as a step in the direction of collectivization of recognition. Neither is it inconceivable, even in the present state of the world, that in order to free themselves from the necessity of having to take embarrassing decisions States might agree to confer upon the Permanent Court of International Justice jurisdiction to ascertain whether a new community fulfils the requirements of statehood. The formal difficulty arising from the fact that the new community has not, prior to recognition, any status before the Court might be obviated by laying down that any of the existing States is entitled to bring the matter before the Court.

GENERAL RULES OF THE LAW OF PEACE

These are the possible lines of development. In the meantime, however, the bulk of practice makes it possible for the science of international law to comprehend facts of international life in this matter by reference to legal principle. There are obvious advantages in relating the fundamental features of international relations—and the rise of new States is one of them—to an objective rule of law rather than to the shifting arbitrariness of national expediency.

CHAPTER 7

RECOGNITION OF GOVERNMENTS AND OF BELLIGERENCY

64. *The nature of the function of recognition of Governments*

Although, for obvious reasons, the controversy as to the declarative or constitutive effect of recognition is not relevant to the question of recognition of Governments, the essential problems and the principles governing this matter are the same as in the recognition of States. The question whether recognition is governed by law or politics is essentially the same in both spheres; and the same applies to the conditions of recognition.

A State whose Government is refused recognition is to a large extent deprived of the ordinary rights of international personality. To admit therefore that the grant or refusal of such recognition is a matter of politics and not of legal rule is to admit that a vital aspect of international relations is subject to the vicissitudes of arbitrariness and changing circumstances of expediency. It is to admit a state of affairs in which the function of recognition is used to promote national interests of the recognizing State. To admit that is, finally, to throw open yet another avenue for the illegal act of intervention. For if a State can proceed in this matter regardless of legal principle, then, in case of a civil war in a foreign country, or even before hostilities have taken place on a large scale, there is nothing to prevent it from withdrawing recognition from the established Government and transferring it to the rebellious party with all the formidable consequences of the change thus effected in the legal position. It would mean that following upon that change in recognition the established Government is reduced to the status of a rebellious group, and the newly recognized authority raised to the position of the legitimate Government to which support and encouragement may be lawfully given. Nothing short of clear evidence in the practice of States could justify such a method of approach.

Actually, there is little, if anything, in the practice of States to support that view of recognition. It is true that statesmen and courts insist that recognition of Governments is a political function of the

GENERAL RULES OF THE LAW OF PEACE

executive department of government. In this—but not in any other sense—recognition of Governments, as well as of States, is a 'political' question. It is not, according to the existing division of powers within the State, a matter falling within the competence of courts. Recognition is a branch of international law administered not by the Judiciary but by the Executive. But it is international law that is administered. The difference is only in the nature of the organ applying international law. As in the matter of recognition of States, so also with regard to recognition of Governments there is no evidence to show that Governments deem themselves entitled to proceed regardless of principle, and to grant or refuse recognition of foreign Governments as a matter of bargain, grace, or expediency.

65. *The criteria of recognition. The principle of legitimacy*

On the other hand, with regard to the conditions and requirements of recognition of Governments, the practice of States has been less uniform and less constant than in the case of recognition of States. Undoubtedly, notwithstanding that absence of uniformity and notwithstanding the introduction of tests extraneous to the purpose of recognition, the matter may be regarded, on the whole, as governed by one clear principle, which is: A Government enjoying the habitual—although not necessarily willing—obedience of the bulk of the population must be regarded as representing the State in question and as such to be entitled to recognition. International law shows signs of definitely adopting that test as a working principle.

It is, in the first instance, finally abandoning the principle of legitimacy which refuses recognition to Governments originating in revolution. That principle was for a time adopted by the Holy Alliance. What is at first sight more surprising is that for a time it was acted upon by the United States, which was by tradition and inclination wedded to the principle of effectiveness. That principle was repeatedly voiced by American statesmen. 'It accords with our principles', wrote Jefferson to Pinckney, 'to acknowledge any government to be rightful which is formed by the will of the nation substantially declared.'[1] 'It is sufficient for us to know', wrote President Buchanan in 1848 in connection with the French Revolution, 'that a government exists capable of maintaining itself; and then its recognition on our part inevitably follows ...'[2] He was emphatic in laying down that 'we do not go beyond the existing

---

[1] *Works*, III, 500.   [2] Moore, I, 124.

324

Government to involve ourselves in the question of legitimacy'.[1] With isolated exceptions that principle was acted upon by the United States until the second decade of the twentieth century. It was abandoned by President Wilson in 1913 in favour of the doctrine of constitutionalism, as expressed in the Treaty concluded in 1907 by the five Central American Republics and reviewed by them in 1923 in the following terms:

> The Governments of the high contracting parties shall not recognize any other government which may come into power in any of the five republics as a consequence of a *coup d'état*, or of a revolution against the recognized government, so long as the freely elected representatives of the people thereof have not constitutionally reorganized the country.

There were various reasons explaining that departure from accepted practice. One was the relation of actual tutelage which by treaty, interest and intervention the United States exercised over some Latin American countries. It seemed desirable to discourage revolutions and to promote stability in these countries by refusing recognition to revolutionary Governments. The other explanation was that there is in fact some relation between the principle of effectiveness and that of legitimacy. Recognition was refused to a revolutionary Government so long as it did not secure confirmation by a free popular vote in accordance with the existing constitution. The object of the principle of legitimacy thus expressed is apparently to ensure that the titular Government should in fact represent the bulk of the population. Thirdly, it is not surprising that a nation wedded to principles of democracy should for a time have attempted to foster those principles by a specific policy of recognition.

There are still remnants of the principle of legitimacy as a test of recognition in the relations of some American States and in some conventions concluded by them. Thus in the Convention of 1928 concerning the Rights and Duties of States in Case of Civil Strife the principle of preferential treatment for the lawful Government, so long as belligerency is not recognized, still plays a part. When in 1930 a revolution broke out in Brazil the United States, apparently in pursuance of that Treaty, prohibited the export of arms to that country with the exception of arms for the lawful Government. The Secretary of State justified that action as a matter of elementary international duty. 'Until belligerency is recognized', he said, 'and the duty of neutrality arises, all the humane predispositions towards stability of government, the preservation of international amity, and

[1] *Ibid.*

GENERAL RULES OF THE LAW OF PEACE

the protection of established intercourse between nations are in favor of the existing government.'[1]

But on the whole the principle of legitimacy and constitutionality is now being abandoned over the whole of the American continent. It is no longer held even by the Central American States, which were most prominent in championing it. In December 1932 Costa Rica and Salvador denounced the Convention of 1923.[2] In 1930 Mexico expressly condemned it in the so-called Estrada doctrine, which is based on the view that diplomatic representatives are accredited not to the Government, but to the State. Apart from the special case of the Central American Republics, the United States has been withdrawing from it slowly, mainly on the ground that its maintenance may in fact require continued intervention.

As a matter of principle the requirement of both legitimacy and constitutionality is indefensible in the present stage of international organization. International society would be entitled to discourage revolutions with the assistance of the weapon of non-recognition if it afforded at the same time a way of ensuring, by means of effective review by international courts and institutions, the proper and just administration and development of the law within the individual States. Actively to champion stability without assuming the other duty may often result in becoming instrumental in perpetuating injustice. Similarly, to penalize revolution brought about and perpetuated through disregard of the democratic principle is to assume a world in which that principle is part of international law and enforced by international machinery. The practice of making recognition dependent on the results of a popular vote following upon the revolution is to assume that a genuine free vote is always possible under a régime established by force. It is possible—as it is ultimately desirable—that in the future the international order will effectively prevent not only international wars but also civil wars by means of a guarantee, review and enforcement of individual rights within the independent and autonomous component parts of the Federation of the World. In that case it will suppress and penalize revolutions as offences against the constitution of the

---

[1] Mr Stimson's address before the Council on Foreign Relations, 6 February 1931: *Publications of the Department of State* (1931), Latin American Series, no. 4. See also *A.J.* 25 (1931), 125. In 1869, Hoar, the United States Attorney General, expressed the opinion that the United States Neutrality Act of 1818 would extend to the fitting-out and arming of vessels for a colony in revolt whose belligerency had not been recognized, but would not apply to vessels for the parent State against such a colony whose independence (or, probably, belligerency) had not been recognized by the United States (Moore, VII, 1079). [2] *A.J.* 28 (1934), 320.

326

RECOGNITION OF GOVERNMENTS AND OF BELLIGERENCY

international commonwealth. But before this has come to pass, international law must be satisfied with a quite different function, namely, of ensuring continuity—otherwise radically broken—between the revolutionary and the old order.

66. *Other extrinsic criteria of recognition*

Partly connected with the principle of legitimacy but not entirely identical with it is the manner of the revolutionary change, as distinguished from its illegitimate source. The cruelty, inhumanity and ruthlessness accompanying the change may well arouse in foreign countries a volume of indignation and disapproval which expresses itself in the refusal to grant recognition to the new authority. The attitude of Great Britain to the Government of the French Convention of 1793 and to the Serbian Government in 1903, or the attitude of a number of countries to Soviet Russia after 1917, may be mentioned as examples.[1] It is difficult to apply abstract legal principles to cases of this nature; it is probably undesirable to do so. They must be left to the natural reaction of the moral judgment of foreign nations tempered with the realization that respect for human life has not been an invariable feature of revolutions in most countries. Also, even in such cases suspension or reduction of normal diplomatic intercourse is a better method than the much more comprehensive measure of refusal of recognition.[2]

The second principal departure from the test of effectiveness has been the refusal to grant recognition to a new Government on account of its alleged unwillingness to fulfil its international obligations. The refusal of a number of States to recognize the Soviet Government after 1917 on account of its unwillingness to give guarantees in respect of the fulfilment of the contractual obligations of the former Government as well as to refrain from hostile propaganda against foreign States affords a good illustration of this aspect of recognition. The Government of Soviet Russia has

---

[1] See, e.g., the outspoken declaration of Colby, United States Secretary of State, in *Russian Socialist Federated Soviet Republics* v. *Cibrario*: 235 N.Y. 256, 264; 139 N.E. 259, 262.

[2] A weighty justification of both these tests will be found in the treatise of Professor Hyde who suggests that 'in the interest of the society of nations the members thereof should habitually manifest extreme reluctance in recognizing as a new government one which acquires power in the teeth of popular opposition and by inhuman methods' (1 (1922), § 43), and who explains the practice of the United States, at that time, as based on the view that 'normally a government, which by force has won the ascendancy in opposition to the will of the people and with contempt for rights created under a local constitution, is internationally a menace because its very supremacy sows seeds of discord bound to ripen into a conflict which, however localized, may fairly be deemed hurtful to the maintenance of the general peace' (*ibid.* § 73).

GENERAL RULES OF THE LAW OF PEACE

now been recognized by most of these States without being obliged to give assurances not given reciprocally by the recognizing State, but it would not be safe to assume on that account that that particular test has been definitely abandoned. However, there are nevertheless formidable objections to its application. It involves the —by no means only theoretical—danger of its being used as a means of exacting promises in return for recognition. Whenever this is done the faculty of recognition is being abused for purposes alien to it. As a means of inducing conduct in conformity with international law, the refusal to recognize a Government may be effective only in exceptional cases, e.g. in the relations of a powerful State and a weak neighbour. The proper course is to grant recognition and then, by such means as international law permits, to insist on the fulfilment by the new Government of its international obligations. Above all, this particular reason for non-recognition is objectionable, inasmuch as it runs counter to the view which the practice of the overwhelming majority of States has accepted as just and in conformity with the law, namely, that recognition is not a means of pursuing objects of national policy but the fulfilment of a function with which a State is entrusted by international law.

67. *Recognition of Governments and the principle of effectiveness*
This function is the ascertainment of certain conditions of fact. That ascertainment may on occasions give rise to difficulties. But then as a rule third States are under no imperative necessity to arrive at a quick decision. For this reason the expedient of establishing some kind of international authority able and competent to assist States in deciding when and to whom recognition as a Government shall be granted may be an interesting development in theory; but it is hardly a necessary one. In the case of a civil war still raging they are helped by the presumption, which is now clearly established by international law, that, so long as the lawful Government maintains a scintilla of resistance on national territory, recognition of the insurgents is unlawful. They are assisted by the rule that they may without impropriety establish such relations with the insurgent authorities as are necessary for the protection of their interests and the maintenance of ordinary commercial intercourse—a relationship which in many material aspects is indistinguishable from recognition. But once the new authority has definitely established itself and utterly supplanted or defeated the former Government beyond any reasonable prospect of its re-establishing itself, the

RECOGNITION OF GOVERNMENTS AND OF BELLIGERENCY

course of other States is clear. They must follow the fact in the exercise of the small margin of legal discretion left by events. They are bound to accord recognition, without regard to real or supposed exigencies of national policy but as fulfilling an international duty of not withdrawing the benefits of international personality from a State represented by a Government enjoying the willing or imposed —but tolerated—acquiescence of the people. But for the departure from this right principle and the introduction of extraneous tests, the question of recognition of Governments would never have had the prominence which it has acquired in the literature and practice. For after all, the right to possess a Government chosen or tolerated by the people is a clear prerogative of State independence. And it is largely the introduction of these extraneous tests which has been responsible for obscuring the fact that recognition of Governments —like recognition of statehood and belligerency—although performed by the political department, is a legal and quasi-judicial function consisting in the application of international law to specific facts.

68. *Recognition of belligerency. The legal and political concepts*

As in the matter of recognition of States and Governments so also in the matter of recognition of belligerency the accurate view, it is believed, is that its grant is not a matter of political convenience, interest or grace, but a duty following from an impartial consideration of the facts of the situation. Once given the objective conditions of a state of belligerency, as laid down by international law, the contesting parties[1] are legally entitled to be recognized as such and third States are, in normal circumstances, under a duty to grant recognition. This is not a view supported by the majority of writers.[2] But it is a view which, it is submitted, has been repeatedly acted upon by Governments and which is supported by considerations of principle.

As in the case of recognition of States, the problem has been somewhat obscured by what may be called the 'tortious' aspect of

---

[1] Possibly it might be more accurate to say 'rebellious' parties seeing that it is not clear whether third States are legally entitled to deny to the lawful Government the right to bring about a formal state of belligerency. It is doubtful, for instance, whether during the American Civil War Great Britain was at liberty to deny to the United States the right to proclaim an internationally valid blockade of the coast of the Southern States. During the Carlist revolution in 1874 the British Government was advised, and acted on the advice, that, assuming that the blockade proclaimed by the Spanish Government was effective, Great Britain was bound to recognize the blockade *de facto* and *de jure* (Smith, I, 321). [2] See, for example, McNair in *L.Q.R.* 53 (1937), 471–500.

329

the matter. The recognition of the belligerency of the Southern States by Great Britain in 1861 has been the most widely discussed case of recognition of belligerency; but it has been discussed almost exclusively from the point of view of the right of Great Britain to recognize the belligerency without committing a breach of international law as against the United States. On the part of writers in the United States there was naturally no tendency to stress the right of insurgents to recognition; on the part of English writers there has been a tendency to emphasize the element of absolute discretion in the matter as a justification for the British refusal to agree to the arbitration of the American claim for damages on account of alleged premature recognition of belligerency. But while the emphasis on the tortious aspect of recognition tended to obscure the more fundamental question of the true nature of the function of recognition it had the merit, at the same time, of clearly defining the objective conditions justifying the grant of recognition. As generally stated, these conditions are the existence of an actual state of hostilities between the lawful Government and a body of men occupying and administering a portion of the territory of the State with some prospect of permanence and conducting operations under the direction of a responsible authority in accordance with the rules of warfare. As in the analogous case of recognition of States, these requirements, formulating as they do the objective conditions of belligerency, are not irrelevant for determining the question of right and duty as between the insurgent community and third States.

69. *The practice of States. Belligerency as a question of fact*

Among writers who discuss the question, the preponderance of opinion is clearly but not overwhelmingly against assuming a legal right to recognition on the part of the insurgents. The reasons for that attitude on the part of most Anglo-American writers have been explained; on the Continent the supremacy of the positivist-constitutive school in the matter of recognition of States had its repercussions also in this sphere. The pronouncements of Governments tell a different story. As far back as 1824 the British Government justified its recognition of the belligerency of the Greek insurgents on the ground that 'a certain degree of force and consistency, acquired by any mass of population engaged in war, entitled that population to be treated as belligerent'.[1] That view was endorsed in 1861 by Lord

---

[1] Wheaton, *International Law* (ed. by Lawrence, 1863), p. 43.

RECOGNITION OF GOVERNMENTS AND OF BELLIGERENCY

Russell in connection with the recognition of the belligerency of the Confederated States.[1] There is in existence an opinion of the British Law Officers in the matter which is even more emphatic. In 1864 they gave an opinion with regard to the revolt of San Domingo against Spanish rule. They said:

the question, whether a state of war does or does not exist between insurgents holding possession of a particular territory, and a Government claiming their allegiance and attempting to subdue them, is one of fact, quite as much as of law: and, if the facts are such, as really to constitute a state of war between the contending parties, according to the law of nations, it is not, we think, competent, by law, to any neutral Power, to withdraw its ships and subjects, upon the high seas, from the operation of the ordinary laws incident to that state of things, merely by declining to acknowledge its existence.[2]

In a further opinion they pointed out that once the British Government had granted to the Spanish Government the rights of a belligerent power, they could not, consistently with the principles and practice of international law, refuse to recognize the Dominican insurgents as belligerents.[3] The Government fully acted on that advice. That case, it is true, is an instance of recognition of the belligerency of insurgents following upon the granting of belligerent rights to the lawful Government, but it is at the same time instructive as showing the admission of the legal right of insurgents to recognition. Similarly, during the Carlist revolution in Spain in 1874 the British Government, acting on the advice of the Law Officers, took the view that while they were bound to recognize the blockade proclaimed by the Spanish Government, the automatic result of such recognition would be the conferment of belligerent status on the insurgents.[4]

As in the case of recognition of statehood and of Governments so also here the correct view, which is in the long run being adopted in practice, is that the question is one of fact—which means that it is a question not of policy but of legal obligation, to be fulfilled in accordance with an appreciation of facts freely arrived at in good faith. The American governmental declarations show this to be the correct test. They insist repeatedly on the principle that the existence of belligerency is a question of fact.[5] While regarding the ascertain-

---

[1] *Hansard*, 3rd ser. 162, cols. 1563, 1566. [2] Smith, I, p. 314.
[3] *Ibid.* p. 318. [4] *Ibid.* p. 321.
[5] See, e.g., the Note of Mr Cass, Secretary of State, to the Peruvian Minister, 22 May 1858 (Moore, I, 183), and President Grant's Annual Message, 7 December 1875 (*ibid.* p. 196).

331

GENERAL RULES OF THE LAW OF PEACE

ment of these facts as a matter of free appreciation by each State concerned, they take pains to show in individual cases that the conditions justifying the grant of belligerent status are not fulfilled. A series of President Grant's Annual Messages to Congress are a good example of the meticulous care with which these facts are scrutinized.[1]

In one important instance the insurgents' right to recognition was expressly admitted. In his Message of 8 March 1822, President Monroe said: 'As soon as the [revolutionary] movement assumed such a steady and consistent form as to make the success of the Spanish provinces probable, the rights to which they were entitled by the law of nations, as equal parties to a civil war, were extended to them.'[2]

Woolsey, in his *International Law* (appendix III, note 19), criticized this passage on the ground that the insurgents have *no right* under the law of nations and that 'the concession of belligerency is not made on their account, but on account of considerations of policy on the part of the State itself which declares them such, or on grounds of humanity', but then, as has been shown, the practice of States seems to be more consistent with right principle than with the opinions of writers.

70. *The right to recognition as belligerents*

There are no instances of States having put forward claims on account of refusal of recognition of statehood, but with regard to recognition of belligerency there are some interesting examples of claims put forward or admitted by States to enjoyment of belligerent rights prior to recognition of belligerency. Thus the United States for a time pressed against Denmark a claim for compensation on account of the latter's action in denying to the United States belligerent rights at a time when, during the War of Independence, Denmark had not recognized them as belligerents. That action consisted in the restoration to Great Britain of some prizes captured by the United States and brought into the Danish port of Bergen. Denmark at one time pleaded that she acted under the threat of compulsion on the part of Great Britain; at another time she offered to pay compensation which the United States rejected as inadequate. Eventually Denmark denied legal liability altogether.[3] But the

---

[1] See Moore, I, 194 *et seq.* See also *ibid.* p. 202, for the refusal of the request by the Brazilian insurgents in 1893 for recognition on the ground that they had not 'up to date established and maintained a political organization which would justify such recognition on the part of the United States'.   [2] Moore, I, 174.   [3] *Ibid.* p. 169.

332

RECOGNITION OF GOVERNMENTS AND OF BELLIGERENCY

United States insisted to the end on the juridical correctness of its claim. In the case of *The Macedonian,* decided in May 1863, the United States seems to have adopted a different view. It challenged the validity of the capture by Chilean forces in 1819 of American goods as contraband on the ground, *inter alia,* that at that time Chile had not been recognized by the United States either as a State or as a belligerent.[1]

But in the cases of *The Georgiana* and *The Lizzie Thompson,* decided in 1864, the United States again advocated the view that insurgents are entitled to exercise certain belligerent rights as against third States even without express recognition as belligerents.[2] In his Opinion bearing on the matter Attorney General Black expressed the view that while the right of insurgents to exercise, prior to recognition, belligerent rights against third States on the high seas was controversial, there was no doubt as to the right of parties to a civil war 'to conduct it, with all the incidents of lawful war, within the territory to which they both belong'.[3]

Undoubtedly, in the case of recognition of belligerency, the legal or juridical view—as distinguished from the political or diplomatic —of the nature of recognition is put to the most difficult test. To say that, given the necessary requirements of fact, insurgents are entitled to recognition as of right means to compel third States to acquiesce in far-reaching restrictions upon their commerce and shipping. These considerations are necessarily present in the minds of Governments, and they have often been adduced, not indeed as a factor of independent importance, but as an additional circumstance counselling caution when the objective requirements of belligerency appeared to be in doubt. Neither can they be ruled out as an inarticulate factor in determining the decision. Similarly, for the same reason and also having regard to the consideration due to the lawful Government, emphasis has been placed on the rule that recognition ought not to be accorded so long as the interests of third States are not directly involved so as to necessitate a definition of their attitude. But, in general, there is nothing unreasonable about third States having to submit to inconveniences resulting

---

[1] The Arbitrator did not pronounce on this aspect of the matter as he found that the seizure was in any case contrary to international law. This aspect of the dispute is discussed with great clarity by A. Rolin in Lapradelle–Politis, II, 215–17. He disapproves of the American contention and asserts that insurgents have a right to recognition as belligerents.

[2] See the *note doctrinale* in Lapradelle–Politis, p. 401, affirming that while recognition of belligerency must be regarded as a governmental function, it must be determined by the actual situation of fact, and not by arbitrary considerations, interest, or sympathy. And see Moore, *International Arbitrations,* II, pp. 1593–1614.   [3] *Ibid.* p. 1604.

333

GENERAL RULES OF THE LAW OF PEACE

from incidents over which they have no control. They must obviously submit to such inconveniences in case of a war between two independent States. The argument that this is no reason why they should be expected to submit to them in consequence of a civil war conducted by unrecognized rebels begs the whole question. In so far as it implies a disapprobation of the conduct of the party responsible for initiating the civil war, it cannot—as has been pointed out in the matter of the principle of legitimacy with regard to Governments—be regarded as a permissible principle in the present stage of international organization. There is a further disadvantage attaching to the refusal to grant recognition of belligerency in disregard of the actual situation. So long as no recognition is given the lawful Government may—and in the view of some ought—according to international law be given support and facilities the grant of which to the insurgents would constitute a breach of the law. The resulting situation must in the long run constitute actual interference—although not technical 'intervention'—in the affairs of a State so as to prevent its population from deciding for itself the fate of the country. Such result could only be justified by the view that there is a presumption—and more than a presumption—in international law in favour of the established Government. There cannot be such a presumption so long as international law has no control over independent Governments; there cannot be such a presumption at a time when a great number of 'lawful' Governments owe their origin to revolutions which took place in the not distant past. It must also be borne in mind that the burdens of recognition of belligerency are to some extent counterbalanced by the advantages accruing from the resulting regularization of intercourse and removal of causes of friction.

As a matter of possible development *de lege ferenda* there is no reason why, in order to avoid the necessity of making invidious decisions open to challenge on the ground of partiality, States should not by agreement confer upon an international—preferably judicial—authority the right to determine, on the application of any interested State, whether the objective requirements for recognition of belligerency exist in any particular case. Such a development would constitute the logical consummation of what, as has been submitted here, is the correct legal position. This may be summarized as follows: As a matter of preponderance of practice and of principle it appears that recognition of belligerency does not constitute an exception to the rule obtaining with regard to recognition of States

RECOGNITION OF GOVERNMENTS AND OF BELLIGERENCY

and Governments. That rule is that the existence of certain requirements of fact, as determined by international law, entitles a group of persons to recognition as a State, a Government or a belligerent; that third States in fulfilling the function of ascertaining the existence of these facts act as organs of international law and not as ministering to their own interests; that, in a word, this fundamental aspect of international relations is a matter governed by international law not only in its incidental, 'tortious', aspects in relation to the lawful Government, but also with regard to the rebellious community.[1]

71. *The recognition of insurgents*

The general considerations discussed above with regard to the recognition of States, Governments and belligerents do not apply to the question of recognition of insurgency. They do not so apply for the reason that the term 'recognition of insurgency' is in a sense a misnomer. Insurgency is not a status resulting from an express declaration in the form of recognition; it results from the absence of recognition, on the one hand, and the unwillingness, on the other hand, of third States to treat the rebels as law-breakers and pirates so long as they do not interfere unduly with the subjects of third States and their property. Insurgency is a frequent and well-recognized although not well-defined status. If, as often happens, the rebel party has not advanced so far as to be in possession of territory with an organized administration fulfilling the normal functions of government; if, although fulfilling that requirement, its success appears to be highly precarious and transient; or if there is reasonable doubt as to their ability or willingness to conduct hostilities in accordance with the accepted rules of warfare[2]—in all

---

[1] The lecturers at the Hague Academy of International Law are expressly enjoined to refrain from expressions of opinion likely to have a direct bearing on too controversial matters of current international politics. This being so, it is not intended to discuss in this connection what will probably prove to be the most important case of recognition of belligerency in the first four decades of the twentieth century, namely, the question of belligerency in the Spanish Civil War. But it is clear that students of international law will for a long time be busy trying to answer the question whether the refusal on the part of certain countries—such as Great Britain and France—to recognize a state of belligerency was in accordance with international law. Many will doubtless point out that the objective requirements of belligerency existed in the present case. This may well be so. On the other hand, the view will doubtless be put forward that the circumstances of the situation were abnormal at a time when the operation of rules of international law was suspended as the result of the conduct of a number of States, and that it would have been neither possible nor just rigidly to apply a principle of international law to some aspects of the situation while tolerating its violation with regard to others.

[2] The position is different here from the case of the inability or unwillingness of a Government to fulfil its international obligations. For as the conduct of war is the principal and primary object of belligerents, failure to comply with the rules of war must be regarded as decisive.

335

GENERAL RULES OF THE LAW OF PEACE

such cases third States without granting to them belligerent rights may enter into normal communications with them with a view to protecting the interests of their subjects and maintaining commercial relations. It is a *de facto* relationship which does not entail legal consequences. In particular, contrary to the common view, it has no effect in the field of State responsibility so as to free the lawful Government from responsibility for the acts of the insurgents. There is, as a rule, no such responsibility in any case. As said, the status of insurgency is not a legal status. It is a concession of humanity and convenience; it is essentially temporary and subject to withdrawal. It is for these reasons that, unlike recognition of belligerency, it is fundamentally a matter of political convenience and arrangement.

CHAPTER 8

RECOGNITION OF NEW TERRITORIAL TITLES AND INTER-NATIONAL SITUATIONS

72. *The practice of States before 1932*

The problem of recognition of new territorial titles, treaties and international situations generally was not, until recently, a topic of importance in the practice and doctrine of international law. It is of modern growth, and must be regarded as the logical and indirect result of the development of international law in other fields. Prior to these developments the question of recognition of new territorial titles and situations arose under three different heads.

It arose in the first instance in connection with the doctrine of the balance of power. Having regard to that doctrine, recognition of colonial acquisitions was on occasions sought and given but, like the doctrine of the balance of power itself, that act was of political and not legal significance. The general rule was that no recognition was deemed necessary for the validity of the acquisition of territorial title by conquest, occupation, etc. With regard to the latter the Congo Conference of 1885 established, as between the contracting parties, the duty of notification, but its purpose was not germane to the question of recognition. Its object was to prevent competing claims and to regularize this mode of acquisition of territory by stipulating for a certain amount of publicity.

More frequent and of obvious legal relevance was the practice of recognition in cases when the title was doubtful or controversial. Recognition in such cases was a combination of waiver of the competing claim and of an undertaking not to challenge the title in question in the future. For this reason recognition of this type often contains qualifications expressly limiting its scope. Thus when Great Britain recognized, in November 1930, Norwegian sovereignty over Jan Mayen Island, she stated that as she had no information concerning the reasons for the Danish decree extending Danish sovereignty to the island in question, the recognition was given 'independently of and with all due reserves in regard to the actual

GENERAL RULES OF THE LAW OF PEACE

grounds on which the annexation may be based.'[1] When in August 1930 Norway informed the Canadian Government that she recognized the sovereignty of His Britannic Majesty over the Otto Sverdrup Islands, she expressly stated that the recognition in no way implied consent to the so-called 'sector principle'.[2] When given by States not directly interested in the object of the transaction, as, for instance, was the case with regard to the recognition in 1920 by Great Britain, France, Italy and Japan of Roumanian sovereignty over Bessarabia, recognition amounted to a promise on their part to treat the State in question as the lawful owner. The function of recognition as a waiver of rights and confirmation of title appears clearly from the recognition by various Powers of Danish sovereignty over Eastern Greenland and the persistent attempts of Denmark, as surveyed in the Judgment of the Permanent Court of International Justice in that case, to secure such recognition from as many States as possible.[3]

Thirdly, practice shows instances of refusal of recognition—or the announcement of the intention of such refusal—on the ground that the treaty establishing the new title was not in conformity with previous treaty obligations. Thus when in 1890 Great Britain and Germany concluded a treaty regulating, *inter alia*, the British Protectorate over Zanzibar, France refused to recognize it on the ground that the arrangement was contrary to the Treaty of 1862 between France and Great Britain. In 1846 Great Britain refused to recognize the Treaty between Russia, Prussia and Austria providing for the annexation of Cracow, on the ground that the Treaty was contrary to the provisions of the General Act of Vienna of 1815. In 1908 Great Britain refused to recognize the acquisition of the Congo by Belgium on the ground that certain provisions of the Treaty of 1887 had not been complied with.

It is this last aspect of non-recognition which comes nearest to the doctrine of non-recognition as enunciated in 1932 and 1933. It is convenient to refer here to the three principal instruments bearing on the matter.

73. *The doctrine of non-recognition formulated in 1932*

The first is the identic Note of 7 January 1932, addressed by Mr Stimson, the American Secretary of State, to China and Japan. In that Note the United States informed the two countries that the

---

[1] Treaty Series, no. 13 (1931), Cmd. 3192. [2] *Ibid.* no. 25 (1931), Cmd. 3815.
[3] *P.C.I.J.* Series A/B, no. 53 (*Legal Status of Eastern Greenland*).

American Government 'does not intend to recognize any situation, treaty or agreement which may be brought about by means contrary to the covenants and obligations of the Pact of Paris of August 27, 1928'.[1] The second is the Resolution of the Assembly of the League of Nations of 11 March 1932, in which the Assembly declared that 'it is incumbent upon the Members of the League of Nations not to recognize any situation, treaty, or agreement which may be brought about by means contrary to the Covenant of the League of Nations or to the Pact of Paris'.[2] The third is Article 2 of the Anti-War Pact of Non-Aggression and Conciliation of 10 October 1933, concluded between a number of American States including the United States. In that Article the contracting Parties declared that 'they shall recognize no territorial arrangement not obtained through pacific means, nor the validity of an occupation or acquisition of territory brought about by armed force'.

Generally speaking, the refusal of recognition referred to in these instruments can have no bearing on the question of recognition of States. A State cannot come into existence contrary to a treaty. A new State is not bound by any international obligation; it is certainly not bound by an international obligation not to secede. If, to give a concrete example, Manchuria had voluntarily seceded from China and formed a new State, there would have been no question of non-recognition as intended by these instruments. The legal basis of non-recognition of Manchukuo as a State is apparently that it is not a State inasmuch as, in view of its relations with Japan, it lacks actual independence. In so far as the doctrine of non-recognition applies in this case it is an announcement of the intention of non-recognition of any future situation amounting to formal incorporation of Manchuria as part of Japan. Neither does the rule of non-recognition properly conceived extend to recognition of Governments. A new Government cannot as such be the result of a violation of international law—except perhaps when a State is under an international duty to possess a certain form of government or constitution. Non-recognition as announced in these instruments would therefore appear to refer to international situations other than recognition of States and Governments.

74. Criticisms of the doctrine of non-recognition

The new 'doctrine of non-recognition', as it has been called, has met with much criticism from apparently opposed quarters. Inas-

[1] *A.J.* 26 (1932), 342.   [2] *L.N.O.J.* Suppl. 101, p. 8.

GENERAL RULES OF THE LAW OF PEACE

much as it implied a measure of sanction for and repression of breaches of international law it was assailed by those who believe that real progress in international affairs lies in the abandonment of any effort of collective enforcement of international law and in the return, in this respect, to conditions obtaining before the establishment of the League. From this point of view it has found most uncompromising critics in the country of its origin. Mr Moore, a former Judge of the Permanent Court of International Justice, has criticized it in the following scathing terms:

> Its chief weakness lies in the fact that those who employ it often must content themselves with futile words or must fight, while the adoption of the latter alternative would necessarily be a confession of failure. All systems of law recognize, by the doctrine of prescription and otherwise, that the recognition of accomplished facts plays, as a principle of certainty and peace, a large part in human affairs; and nations are but aggregations of human beings, who may not relish daily reminders of their shortcomings by others whom they may not deem above reproach, or wholly disinterested or unprejudiced.[1]

On the other hand, the doctrine of non-recognition has been exposed to criticism on the part of those who have seen in it a regrettable device for avoiding the fulfilment of substantial obligations, accepted in the Covenant, by the proclamation of a verbal declaration faulty in law and ineffective in practice. In particular, it has been maintained that, in so far as that doctrine postulates the necessity of recognition for the acquisition of title, it is not supported by international law which, as we have seen, does not as a rule require such recognition; that, in so far as it asserts the objective invalidity of treaties and situations contrary to international law, it cannot be admitted as a sound legal doctrine; and that the doctrine cannot be admitted in so far as it usurps for one State or group of States the right to invalidate international acts.

75. *The legal effect of the doctrine of non-recognition*

Although it has now become a subject of controversy, the principle of non-recognition must be deemed to be of fundamental importance for two reasons. In the first instance, it is of general jurisprudential interest inasmuch as it raises the issue of the validity and effect in the international sphere of acts contrary to international law. Secondly, it claims to be, and probably is, a factor of unusual significance as an instrument for maintaining and, indirectly, for en-

[1] *Harvard Law Review*, 50 (1937), 436.

RECOGNITION OF NEW TERRITORIAL TITLES

forcing international law and morality. Both these aspects will now be considered.

Neither the declaration of the United States, nor the Resolution of the Assembly, nor the Anti-War Treaty of 1933 was intended to have or could have the effect of invalidating any purported legal act or the results thereof which but for the declaration of non-recognition would be valid. Their effect and, probably, intention, is of a quite different nature. They constitute, in the case of the United States, either a unilateral announcement or, in the other two cases, an assumption of the obligation not to contribute by a positive act of a quasi-legislative character to rendering valid the results of an act which is in itself devoid of legal validity. The following examples will illustrate the position.

As is submitted in another part of these lectures,[1] a treaty which to the knowledge of both contracting parties is contrary to pre-existing treaty obligations binding upon one or both of the parties is, in general, illegal, invalid and unenforceable, and unable to produce legal results between them. The doctrine of non-recognition does not invalidate such a treaty. The treaty is invalid *ipso facto*, by reason of the circumstances of its creation. States subscribing to the principle of non-recognition merely say that they will do nothing to cure the treaty of its invalidity. Similarly, as again pointed out elsewhere,[2] a treaty imposed by the victor upon the vanquished as a consequence of a war undertaken by the former is void in all cases in which he had resorted to war contrary to his obligations under the Covenant of the League or the General Treaty for the Renunciation of War. It is void on the ground that the established rule disregarding the vitiating effect of duress does not apply to treaties concluded under compulsion following upon wars undertaken by the victor in breach of these general undertakings. And it is void on the independent ground of being the result of a violation of the provisions of former treaties. Finally, as suggested below,[3] title by conquest can no longer be regarded as valid in international law if it follows upon a war undertaken in violation of the Covenant or the General Treaty for the Renunciation of War.

76. *Illegality as a source of rights*

In all these cases international law is confronted with acts, engagements and situations which claim to be but are not in fact productive of rights. They are invalid as a source and instrument of legal rights.

---

[1] See below, p. 359.   [2] See below, p. 354.   [3] See below, p. 380.

341

GENERAL RULES OF THE LAW OF PEACE

They are invalid, as had been pointed out, for reasons which are peculiar to the particular situations. They are invalid, secondly, on the general ground that, having their origin in an unlawful act, they cannot produce results beneficial to the law-breaker. *Ex injuria jus non oritur* is a general principle of law. Probably international law, being a weak law, is fully exposed to the impact of the phenomenon to which some jurists have referred as 'the law-creating influence of facts'. *Ex factis jus oritur*. Law must correspond to fact. But, obviously, unless law is to become a convenient code for malefactors, it must establish a balance between 'the law-creating influence of facts' and what is the essence of law, namely, the fact that the legal effectiveness and validity of its obligations are unaffected by individual acts of lawlessness. It is one thing to say that law is ultimately based on the facts of life and that it is a body of rules established by a system of force; it is another thing to say that breaches of the law, if they are repeated and remain unpunished, become part of the legal order.

It is of interest to note the way in which the Permanent Court has on a number of occasions given expression to the principle that no rights can be derived from an illegality. Thus in the *Free Zones* dispute between Switzerland and France the Court pointed out in its Order of 6 December 1930 that France could not invoke against Switzerland any changes resulting from the unilateral transfer, which the Court held to be illegal, of the French customs line.[1] In the Advisory Opinion of 3 March 1928 the Court held that Poland was not entitled to invoke the fact that, contrary to her international obligations, she had failed to incorporate the relevant treaty into Polish municipal law.[2] In the Judgment of 26 July 1927 in the case concerning the *Factory at Chorzów*, the Court disposed of one aspect of the Polish objection to its jurisdiction by stating that it is

a principle generally accepted in the jurisprudence of international arbitration, as well as by municipal courts, that one Party cannot avail himself of the fact that the other has not fulfilled some obligation or has not had recourse to some means of redress, if the former Party has, by some illegal act, prevented the latter from fulfilling the obligation in question, or from having recourse to the tribunal which would have been open to him.[3]

In refusing, in August 1932, the Norwegian request for interim measures of protection against certain acts of Denmark with regard to the South Eastern territory of Greenland, the Court drew attention

[1] *P.C.I.J.* Series A, no. 24.   [2] *P.C.I.J.* Series A/B, no. 53, p. 75.
[3] *P.C.I.J.* Series A, no. 9, p. 31.

to the fact that the acts in question could not in any event, or to any degree, affect the sovereign rights of Norway over the territory in question if such rights were otherwise valid.[1] In the final Judgment in that case, given on 5 April 1933,[2] the Court held that the Norwegian declaration of occupation and other measures taken by Norway in that connection constituted a violation of the existing legal situation and were accordingly 'unlawful and invalid'. This finding, given by a practically unanimous Court, is the more significant if we consider that, as may be seen from the Dissenting Opinion of Judge Anzilotti, the Court probably had the opportunity to consider this aspect of the question. In his Dissenting Opinion Judge Anzilotti maintained: 'the Court could not have declared the occupation invalid, if the term "invalid" signifies "null and void". A legal act is only non-existent if it lacks certain elements which are essential to its existence.'[3]

It may be of interest to refer to two instances illustrating the same principle on a minor scale. The first refers to the right of municipal courts to exercise jurisdiction over vessels and persons seized in violation of international law. Can the wrongful act of seizure be a source of the State's right of jurisdiction? In the recent case of *Cook* v. *United States*, the Supreme Court of the United States gave an emphatically negative answer to that question.[4] In a previous case —*United States* v. *Ferris*[5]—where members of the crew of a foreign ship seized 270 miles off the west coast of the United States were indicted for conspiracy to violate the Prohibition and Tariffs Acts, the United States District Court with equal emphasis rejected jurisdiction. The Court said: '... As the instant seizure was far outside the limit [established by treaty] it is sheer aggression and trespass ..., contrary to the treaty, not to be sanctioned by any court, and cannot be the basis of any proceeding adverse to the defendants.' The principal reason for the decisions in these cases is the view that as the United States has by international law no jurisdiction in such cases, the United States courts cannot exercise such jurisdiction. They are at the same time an illustration of the principle that a

---

[1] *P.C.I.J.* Series A/B, no. 48, p. 285. [2] *P.C.I.J.* Series A/B, no. 53, p. 75.

[3] *Ibid.* p. 95. The Judgment of 24 June 1932, concerning the *Interpretation of the Statute of the Memel Territory* (Series A/B, no. 47) and affirming the validity *in municipal law* of a measure declared to be contrary to an international obligation, does not in fact deny the general principle of the invalidity of acts which are contrary to international law. In that case the Court, as it itself pointed out, was asked to give a ruling for the future guidance of the Parties.

[4] (1933) 288 U.S. 102. And see, for comment thereon, Dickinson in *A.J.* 28 (1934), 231–45, and *Harvard Research: Jurisdiction with respect to Crime* (1935), p. 625.

[5] *Annual Digest*, 4 (1927–8), Case no. 127.

wrongful act cannot be a source of jurisdictional rights. But, in the sphere of municipal law, courts as a rule distinguish between the claim of the individual and those of the State whose interests have been injured by the wrongful seizure, and they have not therefore, in general, declined jurisdiction in cases in which a person has been brought before them in violation of customary international law.[1] Similarly with regard to the so-called 'claim of territory' in time of war, in cases where a seizure has taken place in neutral territorial waters, English and American (but not other) courts follow the practice of releasing the prize only at the instance of the neutral State in question and not of the owners of the seized ship.

However, there is a danger that these illustrations, bearing on subjects of limited importance, may obscure rather than clarify the principle which is fundamental to international as indeed to any other law—the principle that an illegality cannot, as a rule, become a source of legal right to the wrongdoer. This does not mean that it cannot produce any legal results at all. For it may naturally entail a legal sanction against the wrongdoer; it may in the interests of commerce and general security be a source of rights for third persons acting in good faith. But to admit the possibility of the unlawful act, or its immediate consequences and manifestations, becoming a source of legal right for the wrongdoer is to introduce into the legal system a contradiction which cannot be solved except by a denial of its legal character.[2]

77. Methods of validating illegality

If, as is here submitted, the legal position is that acts accomplished in violation of international law cannot result in benefit to the law-breaker, then the further question arises whether the results of such acts can ever be incorporated as part of international law. Can the illegality be cured? This might happen in a number of ways.

[1] For a survey of cases see *Harvard Research, op. cit.* pp. 628–30.

[2] The principle that unlawful acts cannot produce legal results beneficial to the law-breaker is subject to an important exception relating to the rules of war and neutrality. In principle it would follow that a war undertaken in violation of the Covenant of the League and, in particular, of the General Treaty for the Renunciation of War, cannot produce any legal results beneficial to the aggressor, including the operation of the rules of war and neutrality. Reasons of humanity and, to some extent, the absence of an authoritative organ charged with the duty to determine the fact of aggression, make it necessary to uphold the operation, in relation to both sides, of the ordinary rules of warfare. This being so, the continued application of the law of neutrality follows as a matter of course—unless the contracting parties deem it their right and duty to penalize the aggressor for the wrong committed against them through the withdrawal of the benefits of neutrality as a measure of reprisals.

RECOGNITION OF NEW TERRITORIAL TITLES

(i) In the first instance, there is the operation of the rule of prescription. The limits and conditions of the operation of acquisitive prescription in international law are not above controversy. The requirements of prescription in international law may not be as stringent as in municipal law, but it would seem that the patent illegality of the purported acquisition combined with continued protests on the part of the dispossessed State are sufficient to rule out the legalization in that manner of the original act. But assuming that it is admissible in the circumstances of the case, prescription must comply at least with the requirement of the lapse of a substantial period of time. To invoke the institution of prescription in municipal law as a reason for the immediate recognition or validity of internationally unlawful acts is to use the term 'prescription' in a peculiar sense unknown to any system of law. Also, even when admissible, prescription does not in law amount to a validation of the unlawful title. It constitutes an original acquisition of a new title.

(ii) Secondly, the question arises whether the objection of illegality may be waived and the title thus validated by the consent of the State whose interests are primarily affected. It would seem that such consent might as a rule cure the invalidity only when the right violated is grounded in a bilateral treaty or customary rule operating exclusively for the benefit of the wronged State. In case of a violation of a multilateral treaty laying down rules of conduct whose observance is in the interest of all the contracting parties, it is difficult to see how waiver on the part of one of them—even if such waiver is juridically possible in the circumstances, e.g. in case of duress—can free the act of the stigma of unlawfulness and its results of the taint of invalidity. If the invalidity is due, for instance, to the breach of the General Treaty for the Renunciation of War, how can the consent of the defeated State conceivably influence the legal situation?

(iii) There remains therefore the possibility of removing the invalidity of the act in question by a free act of other contracting parties and, generally, of other members of the international community. They may, by a quasi-legislative act, give legal force to something which does not exist in law. Probably it does not matter much whether we call that act one of recognition. States adhering to the 'doctrine of non-recognition' announce or undertake that they will not perform that quasi-legislative act of recognition. This, it is believed, is the true meaning of the doctrine.

We are now in a position to appreciate the juridical nature of the various declarations of 'non-recognition' cited above.

345

GENERAL RULES OF THE LAW OF PEACE

78. The effect of the declaration of the United States—the so-called Stimson Doctrine

That declaration is nothing more than an announcement of future policy. It is an announcement of the intention not to do anything in the future which might validate an illegal act. But it is a unilateral declaration not implying the assumption of any duty which did not exist before. Whether any such duty existed before is an interesting and controversial question which it is not proposed to answer here. It is undoubtedly a question of jurisprudential interest. Is a party to a treaty bound not to recognize in the future a legal situation brought about by the violation of the treaty by a third contracting party? In the Resolution of the International Law Association of 1934 interpreting the General Treaty for the Renunciation of War it was laid down that it is the duty of the signatories of the Treaty not to recognize titles and situations brought about as the result of violation of the Treaty. But it is controversial whether this is an interpretation which does not add to the obligations of the Treaty.

79. The effect of the Declaration of the League Assembly of 1932 and the American Treaty of 1933

The Resolution of the Assembly of March 1932 is in quite a different category. In the first instance, as pointed out by the Council of the League, it is to a large extent declaratory of the existing obligations under Article 10 of the Covenant. The refusal to recognize a conquest accomplished in violation of the Covenant constitutes the very minimum of the obligation to respect and preserve the territorial integrity of other members of the League.[1] Secondly, the Resolution, in addition to being declaratory of existing obligations, is in itself a source of obligation. The legal nature of that obligation as embodied in the Resolution is controversial and has been doubted by many. On the one hand, there seems to be no reason why, as a rule, a Resolution of the Assembly or the Council should not be binding upon the States assenting to it. A ratified treaty is not the only means of undertaking international obligations. At least in one case —in the Advisory Opinion concerning the *Lithuanian Railway Traffic*[2] —the Permanent Court of International Justice has treated a Resolution of the Council assented to by the two parties to the dispute as an engagement binding upon them. On the other hand,

---

[1] No such duty is stipulated in the General Treaty for the Renunciation of War.
[2] *P.C.I.J.* Series A/B, no. 42.

346

it may be argued that if resolutions interpreting the Covenant were binding on the States voting for them, the procedure might, in certain circumstances, amount to amending the Covenant in a way different from that prescribed in Article 26. A more persuasive, although not necessarily decisive, argument is that, in actual practice, interpretative resolutions like that of 1921 relating to Article 16 have not been regarded as formally binding.

The Anti-War Treaty of 1933 probably amounts to acceptance of a new obligation not hitherto unequivocally binding upon the contracting parties. This applies even to those signatories of the Treaty who are members of the League, seeing that such duty of non-recognition as there exists under the Covenant applies only to situations brought about contrary to its provisions, while the obligations of the Anti-War Treaty are more comprehensive.

80. *The rôle of the doctrine of non-recognition in international law*

The reasons why the so-called doctrine of non-recognition has acquired prominence in recent years are not difficult to understand. They are due to the fact that the Covenant of the League and the General Treaty for the Renunciation of War contain prohibitions upon the right of war and conquest which did not exist before. These instruments accordingly tainted with illegality a wide and significant area of State action which hitherto was entitled to claim full validity in the international sphere. From the jurisprudential point of view the acceptance of the policy or of the obligation of non-recognition is of interest as a vindication of the legal character of international law against 'the law-creating effect of fact'. In a society in which the enforcement of the law is in a rudimentary stage there is a natural tendency for breaches of the law to be regarded, for the sole reason of their successful assertion, as a source of legal right. Non-recognition obviates that danger to a large extent.

The value of the argument that the authority of international law and morality may in the long run be weakened in consequence of the doctrine of non-recognition is more apparent than real. There is undoubtedly a possibility that non-recognition may be used as an easy device for avoiding more substantial international obligations for actively enforcing the law. But these obligations are in some cases, as in the General Treaty for the Renunciation of War, non-existent; in others, such as the Covenant of the League, they are less rigid and comprehensive than is commonly assumed. To that extent non-recognition is an addition to the forces making for the

GENERAL RULES OF THE LAW OF PEACE

reality of international law. And even when there exists a duty to defend the rights of the injured State by means more substantial than a verbal declaration, such advantages as that declaration possesses are preferable to total inaction. Half a loaf is better than no bread. It is not reasonable to assume that if only we succeed in disclosing the actual ineffectiveness of the policy of non-recognition, States will thereupon embark upon the fulfilment of their obligations.

On the other hand, there is nothing in the policy of non-recognition which need necessarily constitute an obstacle in the way of normal international intercourse—so long as the State against which it is directed does not insist on formal recognition of the results of its illegal act. Thus, in the case of conquest, the recognition of the *de facto* authority of the annexing State provides a sufficient basis for ordinary intercourse and for the recognition of the legislative, administrative and judicial acts of the annexing State within the territory under its sway.[1] The results of non-recognition manifest themselves in such cases mainly in the sphere of the formalities of diplomatic intercourse in the relations with the annexing State and in the continued recognition *de jure* of the sovereignty and Government of the dispossessed State, with the resulting concession of jurisdictional immunities to its diplomatic representatives, the right, necessarily nominal, of representation in international institutions and conferences, and, probably, the ownership of such property of the annexed State as is situate abroad.[2]

Like any other policy, the obligation of non-recognition need not last for ever. It may, after a prolonged period of time, be adjusted to the requirements of international peace and stability. It may merge in a general international settlement. But there is a difference between this procedure and the automatic incorporation of any breach of international law as part of the law of nations.

---

[1] See *Bank of Ethiopia* v. *National Bank of Egypt*, (1937) 53 T.L.R. 751.

[2] In the abnormal event of the invalid situation taking the form of a separate political unit claiming to be an independent State—as in the case of Manchukuo—the consequences of non-recognition are more far-reaching but, as said, such cases must be regarded as exceptional.

PART III

SUBSTANTIVE LAW
AND ITS CHANGE

CHAPTER 9

CONTRACTUAL RELATIONS BETWEEN STATES. TREATIES

81. *Treaties and contracts. General principles of law*

Lawyers, and particularly English lawyers, are familiar with the much-quoted saying of Sir Henry Maine that the legal development of civilized societies coincides with the development from status to contract. In fact contract, and not the general body of the law, constitutes the bulk of obligations which determine the daily life of the individual. His family life is based on the contract of marriage; his employment is based on contract; the services which he receives are due to a contract. The law favours this extension of the domain of agreement by permitting it to alter, within limits, the general provisions of the law. *Modus et conventio vincunt legem.*

In the relations of States, the part played by contract is incomparably wider; it is so wide that it is to a large extent a sign of legal backwardness rather than legal progress. In the absence of other corresponding agencies, it fulfils there, imperfectly and metaphorically, some of the functions of legislation. While contract within the State creates as a rule particular obligations only, among States it is used, in the absence of an overriding Legislature, for the purpose of bringing about general obligations. In this, but in no other, sense does it fulfil a legislative activity. But whatever may be the significance of that function, it does not affect its contractual nature. The rules as to conclusion, validity, termination and interpretation are the same in the case of the 'legislative' or 'law-making' treaties as in the case of ordinary treaties. This is now no longer denied, and the contractual character of all treaties is now no longer seriously challenged. The once fashionable disinclination to adopt, in this as in many other subjects, the analogy of the corresponding general principles of the law of contract as the basis of scientific investigation, is now an exception rather than the rule.

It is not easy to see why this essential analogy of contracts and treaties—all treaties—should ever have been challenged. It obviously accords with the practice of States. The fact that the bulk of international obligations, general and particular, is based on treaty

351

GENERAL RULES OF THE LAW OF PEACE

does not derogate from their dignity. On the other hand, the circumstance that so much of the substance of international life is vitally dependent upon a consensual element makes it necessary and beneficent to comprehend it from the point of view of a legal institution almost as old as the law itself, and to try to infuse into it, in case of doubt, that wealth of legal principle and morality which ages of legal development have infused into the law of contract.

Undoubtedly, treaty relations of States show various situations which, on the face of it, are not to be found in the law of contract, like the question of reservations, ratification, constitutional limitations upon the treaty-making power. But some of the principal aspects even of these questions—unless they assume the complexion of mere technicalities—can, and have been, most conveniently and successfully treated with the help of general principles of law as developed in the law of contract. They are technical and specific in their formulation and in their normal operation, but, once they become the subject of analysis or dispute, the categories of agency or mandate become of obvious relevance and usefulness.

On the other hand, whenever positive international law has in the matter of treaties admitted a clear departure from general principles of law, such departure has admittedly been the result of a deficiency of international law *qua* law and was bound to disappear as soon as international law succeeded in this matter in ridding itself of doctrines and practices which were in utter contradiction with its claim to be a system of law. This may well be seen from the consideration of two rules of traditional international law—one pertaining to the conditions of the conclusion of a valid treaty, the other to those of its termination. The first is the rule that a treaty concluded under physical compulsion upon the State (as distinguished from its representatives) is valid; the other is the right unilaterally to terminate a treaty obligation by invoking the so-called doctrine of *rebus sic stantibus*. It is useful to survey from this point of view both these rules of orthodox international law.

82. *The effect of duress*

Freedom of consent is not only a necessary consequence of the conception of a contractual agreement; it is of the very essence of the notion of contract. Freedom of will is, of course, a relative notion. A person or group making a contract may be compelled by inescapable economic or other considerations to make an agreement which is distasteful or hateful. The law cannot attach decisive

CONTRACTUAL RELATIONS BETWEEN STATES

importance to this kind of compulsion. But at least it protects freedom of contract to the extent of refusing to recognize the law-creating effect of a will formed under direct physical compulsion. This any modern system of law has invariably done. International law, for reasons intimated below,[1] has disregarded this obvious general principle of law. It was assisted in that juridical heresy by the interposition of the impersonal State, as represented by one or more individuals, between the actual threat of overwhelming physical compulsion and the generality of persons actually composing the State. These representatives, it was said, were free to act as they liked; any direct compulsion against their person vitiated the treaty. The device is clearly a very unconvincing one, and is made possible only by the current personification of the State. But it was a fiction clearly accepted by international law.

The rule that duress does not invalidate a treaty has been occasionally denied or qualified by writers. Some, like Heffter,[2] G. F. de Martens,[3] and Klüber,[4] or, more recently, Professor Scelle,[5] distinguished between just and unjust compulsion. Others, like Pradier-Fodéré,[6] denied all validity to treaties signed under compulsion. Occasionally, Governments pleaded duress as a reason for challenging the validity of a treaty. This was the case, for instance, with China in regard to the so-called twenty-one Japanese demands which she was compelled to accept in 1915, or with Peru in regard to the Treaty with Chile in 1884. But on the whole, the traditional rule was not seriously challenged. It was not, in effect, challenged by those who permitted compulsion only when it was 'just' or 'legitimate'. Hall, for instance, was in favour of legalizing compulsion so long as no more was exacted than 'compensation for past wrongs and security against the future commission of wrongs'.[7] This is a very comprehensive exception indeed. But it is difficult to see how, with the law as it then stood, any other solution could have been adopted. Force is not illegitimate if it is authorized by law. If war was a process authorized by law for the purpose both of enforcing and of changing the law, then it is difficult to see how a treaty enforced by war could be held invalid on that account. This consideration is more decisive than the other, dialectical but not easily defeated, argument that, in the absence of a rule disregarding the vitiating influence of duress, no valid treaty could be concluded and war would as the result be perpetual.

[1] See below, p. 411.   [2] § 85.   [3] I, § 50, p. 165.   [4] § 143.
[5] II, 338.   [6] § 1076.   [7] P. 381.

GENERAL RULES OF THE LAW OF PEACE

The complacent logic and the resulting denial of a general principle of law inherent in both these arguments were possible only so long as States were willing to acquiesce in the major juridical monstrosity of admitting war as an instrument for the enforcement of rights and as capable of creating rights. This is no longer the case. Customary international law has in this respect undergone a fundamental change as the result of the limitation of the right of war in the Covenant of the League and of its total elimination in the General Treaty for the Renunciation of War as an instrument of national policy, i.e. as an instrument for enforcing and changing rights. A State which has resorted to war in violation of its obligations under these instruments is not applying force in a process authorized by law. In such cases duress renders the treaty invalid. The victor must, if he can, seek other means of regularizing the fruits of unlawful resort to force. The defeated State, confronted with the threat of occupation or annihilation by the victor, cannot validly give its consent to the treaty terminating the war. If the conditions of peace are such as would commend themselves to the generality of States, the situation may be regularized by a quasi-legislative act of third States expressly recognizing the position created by the treaty. This might best be done by the terms of the treaty being embodied in a general convention in the nature of an international settlement, in which the concurrence of a considerable number of third States might to some extent offer the assurance that the terms of the treaty thus concluded are not unreasonable or unjust. On the other hand, the traditional rule continues to obtain whenever resort to war on the part of the victorious State was not in violation of its international obligations.

It is probable that the majority of international lawyers have not as yet adjusted the traditional rule in the matter of freedom of consent as a condition of validity of treaties to the fundamental change brought about by the General Treaty for the Renunciation of War; it is probable that in their caution they are guided by the fact that the obligation of renunciation of war has been disregarded on several occasions since the conclusion of the Treaty. While that restraint can be explained psychologically, there is no justification for it from the juridical point of view. International law cannot scientifically be treated as a disjointed collection of rules; as a science it must be treated as a system whose rules are interdependent so that a major change in one of them is inevitably followed by a modification of the relevant aspects of others.

354

83. *The doctrine of* rebus sic stantibus

The second weak link in the law of treaties, namely, the traditional doctrine of *rebus sic stantibus*, stands in a different category. As occasionally formulated by law-breaking Governments or by writers intent upon supplying a legal justification for past or impending breaches of the law, it had actually no place in international law. It was a political maxim; it supplied convenient and impressive juridical terminology denying the legal nature of international law. It has seldom been invoked by Governments. In those rare cases in which treaties have been broken on account of a change of circumstances, the doctrine has only exceptionally been invoked *eo nomine*. Moreover, when a breach of a treaty has been unilaterally committed by reference to the plea of changed circumstances, the States affected have invariably protested and challenged the right of unilateral denunciation. The principle affirmed in 1871 by the European Powers subsequently to the Russian violation of the provisions of the Treaty of Paris of 1856 relating to the neutralization of the Black Sea was reaffirmed in identical terms in 1935 and 1936 when Germany unilaterally denounced her obligations under the Treaty of Versailles with regard to disarmament and the demilitarization of the Rhineland.

This being so, recent developments in international law could not, unlike duress, remove from it something which had never attained the dignity of a rule of law. These recent developments are in particular the provisions of Article 19 of the Covenant providing machinery for the investigation of claims for revision of treaties and international conditions on account of changed circumstances and for other reasons, and the existence of the Permanent Court of International Justice as an authoritative organ for deciding on claims for termination of treaties on account of supervening impossibility of performance or, what is essentially the same, frustration of the original purpose of a treaty. These developments have helped to deprive the political doctrine of *rebus sic stantibus* of its last shred of practical justification. Article 19 has shown the possibility of dealing with claims for revision not based on legally relevant grounds. The establishment of the Permanent Court of International Justice has supplied authoritative machinery—whose rudiments existed before in the form of international arbitration—for judicial elucidation and determination of those legal elements which the political doctrine of *rebus sic stantibus* undoubtedly possessed when

GENERAL RULES OF THE LAW OF PEACE

shorn of its extreme and anarchical assertions. These juridical elements, namely, the effect of changed circumstances on the continued legal validity of a treaty, are not only capable of further elucidation and study. They are badly in need of it.

The student surveying the cases of judicial determination of the doctrine of *rebus sic stantibus*, either *eo nomine* or in the form of the plea of *force majeure*, as a reason for liberation from an engagement will note that, without exception, in all of them the tribunals have refused to apply the doctrine. The award of the Permanent Court of Arbitration in 1912 in the *Indemnity* case between Russia and Turkey, the decision of the German Staatsgerichtshof in 1925 in the dispute between Prussia and Bremen,[1] the judgment of the Swiss Federal Court in 1928 in the dispute between the Cantons of Thurgau and St Gallen,[2] the Judgments of the Permanent Court of International Justice in 1929 in the cases of the *Serbian and Brazilian Loans* in France, and, last but not least, the Judgment of the same Court in 1932 in the case of the *Free Zones of Upper Savoy and the District of Gex*—in all these cases the Courts, while not denying that the doctrine had a place in international law, refused to admit that it applied in the case before it. There is no case on record in which an international or quasi-international tribunal admitted the plea based on the doctrine of *rebus sic stantibus* or its equivalent. This is significant. It shows not only the lure of that doctrine on the one hand but also, on the other hand, the importance which tribunals attach to the element of stability and continuity in international law as compared with the rival and no less fundamental consideration of change. It shows the vitality of the principle *pacta sunt servanda* not only as a formal norm of jurisprudence or political slogan of Governments benefiting from existing treaties, but as a working postulate of international law and justice. At the same time, these decisions, and in particular the decision of the Permanent Court of International Justice in the case of the *Free Zones*, suggest that there is room for reflection as to whether the conditions of application of the doctrine ought not to be less stringent. In the *Free Zones* case the Court refused to take into account the various changes in conditions invoked by France because, as it said, these changes had no reference to 'the whole body of circumstances—circumstances essentially governed by the geographical configuration of the Canton of Geneva and of the surrounding region—which the High Contracting Parties had in mind at the

---

[1] *Annual Digest*, 3 (1925–26), Case no. 266. [2] *Ibid.* 4 (1927–8), Case no. 280.

356

CONTRACTUAL RELATIONS BETWEEN STATES

time the Free Zones were created.'[1] There still remains the question whether there is not room for the application of the doctrine with regard to changes in circumstances which the parties did not have and could not possibly have had in mind when concluding the treaty. The political and destructive element of the traditional doctrine of *rebus sic stantibus* will disappear as soon as there is a disposition to apply its legal possibilities in a generous manner.

The disregard of the vitiating effect of compulsion and the pseudo-legal doctrine of *rebus sic stantibus*, as frequently preached by many writers and some Governments, shows the disintegrative effect of any radical departure from the solid basis of the contractual construction of treaties and the general principles of law connected therewith. At the same time, the consideration of some typical problems of the law of treaties shows both the possibility and the necessity of taking these general principles as a starting point. Three of these problems will be considered here as throwing light, from a different angle, upon the central problems of the contractual relations of States. They are the validity of immoral obligations, the validity of treaties inconsistent with former treaty obligations, and the interpretation of treaties.

84. *The validity of immoral obligations*

On the face of it, the question is of small practical importance. There is no pronouncement of an international tribunal declaring a treaty to be void because of the immoral nature of its provisions. There is perhaps no case on record of a Government having recourse to the argument that a contested treaty provision is invalid because of its immorality. To mention the most recent possible example, the validity of the Treaty of Versailles has not officially—as distinguished from private views of writers[2]—been challenged on the ground of being immoral as the result of the severe restrictions imposed upon Germany. And yet the perseverance of the reference, in the works of nearly all writers, to this ground of invalidity is significant; avowed positivist writers form no exception to the rule. It is in fact difficult to see how international law could disregard what is an inescapable general principle of law, namely, that the law must decline to be an instrument of immorality. But it is sufficient merely to state this rule in its general form in order to realize its far-reaching

---

[1] *P.C.I.J.* Series A/B, no. 46, p. 158.

[2] See, e.g., Verdross in *Z.ö.R.* 15 (1935), 289 *et seq.* and 16 (1936), 79 *et seq.*; Hold-Ferneck, *Lehrbuch des Völkerrechts*, II (1932), 261.

GENERAL RULES OF THE LAW OF PEACE

implications. Taken literally, it amounts to a re-introduction into the system of international law of natural law pure and simple; it signifies that law has no validity unless it can justify itself and be approved by the tribunal of morality. From the practical point of view, so long as there is no authoritative body endowed with obligatory jurisdiction to determine the morality or otherwise of a treaty obligation, the supposed invalidity of immoral treaties is a standing invitation to the law-breaker to disengage himself unilaterally—in a heroic manner—from an inconvenient duty.

Upon analysis, the statement that the law will not enforce obligations of which ethics disapproves is not as simple as it seems. It is common ground that law is not identical with morality. Law will often enforce duties which from the point of view of ethics it would be unconscionable and unpardonable to enforce. Immorality, in order to incur active disapproval by law to the point of unenforceability, must go a step further; it must be such as to render its enforcement contrary to public policy and to socially imperative dictates of justice. Thus, for instance, courts will not enforce contracts in restraint of trade and, generally, contracts interfering palpably with the freedom of human personality. But even in these cases it is well known that it is impossible to lay down any general rules enabling one to forecast with certainty what will be the decision of a court. Moreover, what may be a glaring injustice from the point of view of the individual concerned may assume a different complexion when viewed from the wider perspective of social needs. Thus, to give an example in the domain of international treaties, it is agreed by most writers that there is a vitiating stigma of immorality attaching to treaties which substantially interfere with a nation's right of self-development and self-preservation. But the same writers agree that these considerations do not wholly apply to a nation which has been guilty of a criminal attack against its neighbours; they all agree that it is just to exact from such a State adequate compensation and security against future wrongs by depriving it of means of offence. This is in fact the classical doctrine; it is expressive of a measure of social justice overriding the individual needs of the State directly affected. Within the State the fundamental rights of the individual to life and freedom may be taken away or invaded for similar reasons. These examples show how dangerous may be the attempts to introduce into international law general principles of law without at the same time adopting the safeguards which municipal jurisprudence has adopted for their operation. The general

CONTRACTUAL RELATIONS BETWEEN STATES

principle of law invalidating immoral treaties is a necessary and salutary corrective when applied by an impartial agency. It may become an abuse and a negation of law when determined unilaterally by Governments supported by writers anxious to supply a cloak of juridical decency for cynical breaches of the law.

85. *Treaties incompatible with the obligations of a previous treaty*

Of much greater importance from the point of view of its legal interest and practical applicability is the problem of the validity of treaties inconsistent with former treaty obligations. The literature and the practice[1] of international law are gradually recognizing that treaties which, to the knowledge of both contracting parties, are inconsistent with their former treaty obligations are not valid or enforceable by international courts; that international law cannot recognize and must discourage situations in which the law-creating faculty of States is abused for the purpose of throwing overboard the law as laid down in still-binding agreements; and that States cannot be permitted to discredit international law and to render it unreal by filling it with mutually exclusive obligations. It is incompatible with the unity of the law for the courts to enforce mutually exclusive rules of conduct, whether such rules are laid down in treaties, statutes or contracts. With regard to treaties, such inconsistency is more obvious and therefore more objectionable for the reason that treaties are relatively few and a matter of general knowledge, while contracts are infinite in variety and number. Accordingly, in the matter of treaties the shock to the unity of law resulting from the recognition of the subsequent inconsistent agreement is greater than in the case of contracts. The provision of Article 20 of the Covenant in which members of the League undertake not to conclude in the future engagements inconsistent with the terms of the Covenant is merely declaratory of an existing duty; non-compliance with that duty merely adds emphasis to what would in any case be the effect of the subsequent inconsistent engagement, namely, its invalidity.

But is there, it will be asked, a general principle of law postulating the invalidity of the second, inconsistent, contract? Lawyers of most countries would, when confronted with this question, deny that their system of law recognizes any principle of this nature. On

---

[1] For a survey of that practice, see Lauterpacht in *B.Y.* 17 (1936), 54–65. See also Rousseau in *R.G.* 39 (1932), 140–62; *Harvard Research: Treaties* (1935), pp. 1016–129. See in particular the Dissenting Opinion of Judges van Eysinga and Schücking in the *Oscar Chinn* case (*P.C.I.J.* Series A/B, no. 63).

GENERAL RULES OF THE LAW OF PEACE

further examination, however, it appears that—to refer only to English,[1] French,[2] and German[3] law—the invalidity of the second, inconsistent, contract is actually recognized by the law. The main reason for the uncertainty of the law on this question and for the absence of direct authority is the fact that, within the State, the law has found other means of discouraging the second, inconsistent, contract, namely, an action for damages against the party inducing the breach of the first contract ('inducing' being largely tantamount to knowledge of the first contract) or an injunction restraining the fulfilment of the second contract. Where these means of minimizing the mischief of the second contract fail, the law does not hesitate to declare the invalidity and the unenforceability of the second contract. In international law there are no regular means of making the third State accountable for inducing the breach of the former treaty or of restraining the fulfilment of the new one. This being so, the occasion for treating the second, inconsistent, treaty as invalid is in international law more imperative than in the relations of individuals.

However, as elsewhere, that general principle of law must be applied subject to modifications necessitated by the peculiarities of international intercourse and so as to make impossible the abuse of an otherwise beneficent rule of law. These modifications are necessary mainly on account of the existence of important multilateral conventions. Does invalidity attach to every treaty modifying a previous multilateral convention even if agreed to by most of the signatories of that convention? Does it lie with a single State or with a small minority of the signatories of the old convention to make impossible the conclusion of valid subsequent treaties modifying the provisions of the former? It is impossible to accept the view that the provisions of a multilateral treaty cannot be validly modified except with the concurrence of all its signatories, and that petty legalism or mere obstructionism may prevent improvements in the

---

[1] See the recent case of *British Homophone Co.* v. *Kunz* (1935) 152 L.T. 589. And see, for a discussion of English law on the subject, Lauterpacht, 'Contracts to break a contract', in *L.Q.R.* 52 (1936), 494–524.

[2] As the combined result of Articles 1131 and 1133 of the Code Civil. And see the decisions of the Court of Cassation in *Deutsche Celluloid Fabrik* v. *Schmerber* (*Sirey*, 1913, I, 259) and *Doeuillet* v. *Randnitz* (*ibid.* 1910, I, 118). See also *Josserand* v. *Leclère* (*ibid.* 1906, II, 242) (as the result of the combined effect of Articles 1167 and 1382 of the Code Civil). See Planiol and Ripert, *Traité pratique de droit civil français* (1930), VI, 809, 810; and Aubry and Rau, *Cours de droit civil français* (1920), VI, 338, 339.

[3] As the result of the operation of Articles 138 and 826 of the Bürgerliches Gesetzbuch. See *S.R.* v. *Bayerische Bierbrauerei zum Karlsberg* (*Decisions of the Reichsgericht in Civil Matters*, 79 (1912), 279; see also *ibid.* 108 (1924), 58). And see, for a clear statement on the matter, Staudinger, *Kommentar zum Bürgerlichen Gesetzbuch* (9th ed. by Loewenfeld and Riezler), I (1925), 576.

CONTRACTUAL RELATIONS BETWEEN STATES

law. The test, necessarily to be applied by an impartial agency, is whether the signatory of the original convention has a real and justifiable interest in opposing the new treaty. It must be within the competence of a tribunal to determine whether the new treaty has substantially interfered with the interests of one or more of the original co-signatories and whether it is on that ground invalid. In this and in other cases, a subsequent inconsistent treaty is invalid quite independently of any declaration or policy of non-recognition. The latter is merely the acceptance of an obligation or the announcement of a policy not to legalize, by an individual or collective law-creating act, an international instrument which is in itself invalid.

86. *Interpretation of treaties. Technical rules of interpretation and various categories of treaties*

This insistence on the fact that international treaties—of any kind —are only a species of the comprehensive genus of contracts, governed by the relevant general principles of law, is of considerable importance in the matter of interpretation of treaties. If treaties are contracts made by human beings acting as representatives of groups of human beings called States, then the only consideration that matters in the process of interpretation is to discover the intention of the parties thereto. The discovery of that intention may be hampered, instead of facilitated, by rules of interpretation. No rule of interpretation purports, of course, to serve a purpose other than the revealing of the intention of the parties. What it does is to suggest that certain factors, peculiar either to the persons of the contracting parties or to the circumstances in which the treaty was concluded, deserve special attention as a means of discovering the intention of the parties. This is not altogether illegitimate. In fact it is through private law that most of the technical rules found their way into international law. Vattel's and Pothier's rules of interpretation, both remarkably similar, can each be traced in a striking manner to the Digest.[1] But both in municipal and in international law, by a process not unknown elsewhere, the means has a tendency to overshadow the end, and rules of interpretation instead of becoming an aid to discovering the intention of the parties acquire a rigidity and artificiality which hinder the task of interpretation. As the law develops, rules of interpretation are being put in their proper place and are relegated from their position as substantive rules of law to purely persuasive maxims. The problem which confronts the work

[1] For an analysis, see Fairman in *Grotius Society*, 20 (1934), 129, 130.

GENERAL RULES OF THE LAW OF PEACE

of interpretation of treaties is therefore, it would seem, of a double nature: in one case it arises out of the general difficulty presented by the existence of rules of interpretation; in the other, it lies in the attempt to frame special rules of interpretation in international law because of the peculiar nature of international agreements and of the parties who conclude them.

To begin with the latter, there is the ever-present danger that we may forget that treaties are contracts if we attach undue importance to the fact that they emanate from sovereign entities called States. If we do that we fall into the trap of using interpretation for the purpose of disintegrating rather than implementing treaties. Thus the view is often expressed that so-called political treaties cannot be measured by the same standards as ordinary treaties. Treaties like the Covenant of the League or treaties of guarantee or alliance, it is often said, cannot be ruled by the same canons of interpretation as ordinary treaties. They involve, it is said, political interests of States and it would therefore be inappropriate and in the highest degree pedantic to interpret such instruments in the manner generally applied to the interpretation of consensual agreements. How, for instance—it has been said—could the existence of the *casus foederis* in the Austro-Italian Treaty of Alliance before the World War be decided by reference to ordinary canons of interpretation? But if such treaties cannot be interpreted by the ordinary tests of construction of contractual agreements, they cannot be interpreted at all. There is therefore some consistency, from this point of view, in the refusal to include the interpretation of treaties involving 'vital interests' of States within the purview of obligatory judicial settlement. But this means that the only valid ground for refusing to apply to such treaties the ordinary principles of interpretation is the assumption that they are not legal documents, creating legal rights and obligations, but political declarations.

Any attempt to base the function of interpretation not on the intention of the parties but on the fact that the treaty has been concluded by sovereign States, is bound to hamper in the last resort the work of interpretation. It is therefore necessary, notwithstanding the high authority of judicial dicta, to treat with caution such interpretative maxims as 'restrictions upon sovereignty cannot be presumed' or 'limitations upon sovereignty must be interpreted restrictively'. The primary effect, if not the very object, of legal instruments is to limit the freedom of the contracting parties. This explains why the Permanent Court of International Justice, although

362

CONTRACTUAL RELATIONS BETWEEN STATES

from time to time it has used expressions showing some respect for the doctrine of restrictive interpretation, has in fact reduced it to a mere shadow by laying down repeatedly that it can be validly resorted to only when all other means of interpretation have failed. Undoubtedly the rule as to restrictive interpretation of limitations of sovereignty finds its corresponding expression in the maxim '*in dubio mitius*', which is not unknown in municipal jurisprudence. But, for the reasons stated, it is very seldom that municipal tribunals rely on that rule. In general, technical rules of interpretation are not easily reconcilable with the existence of adequate and authoritative tribunals which may be trusted to discover the intention of the parties by means more effective than ready-made formulae. Moreover, such usefulness as technical rules possess must diminish when confronted with contractual arrangements like international treaties, the preparation and making of which is prolonged, deliberate, formal and recorded, with the result that there are ample means of ascertaining the intention of the parties.

87. *Preparatory work in the interpretation of treaties*

It is this circumstance which is highly relevant to another much-discussed question, namely, the use of preparatory work in the interpretation of treaties. It may now be regarded as a settled principle of interpretation of treaties that tribunals, international and national, will have recourse, in order to elucidate the intention of the parties, to the records of the negotiations preceding the conclusion of the treaty, the minutes of the conference which adopted the treaty, its successive drafts, and so on. This is the so-called preparatory work of the treaty. For a time its admissibility was questioned on the ground that the use of such evidence extraneous to the treaty is contrary to the principles of interpretation obtaining in Great Britain and the United States. Like other alleged differences between the so-called Anglo-American and Continental schools of thought, so also this particular distinction is without foundation. The Permanent Court of International Justice, probably in deference to the doubts raised under this head, has circumscribed with some caution the admissibility of preparatory work by limiting it to cases in which the treaty 'is not clear'. This limitation is, and has in fact proved to be, a purely nominal one. Whether the treaty is or is not clear is a question which can be answered only after all the available means, including preparatory work, of disclosing the intention of the parties have been exhausted. The finding whether the treaty is

GENERAL RULES OF THE LAW OF PEACE

clear is the result, not the starting point, of the work of interpretation. The alleged non-admissibility of preparatory work is in itself a technical rule of a negative character; its value is no greater than that of other technical rules.

88. *The rules of strict and liberal interpretation*

The sterility of the attempt to frame special rules for the interpretation of treaties may be well appreciated by the barrenness of the results of the rule that treaties ought to be given a liberal interpretation. Unless this means that the parties intended what they said, namely, that they intended the treaty to be effective rather than ineffective, that rule means little. Its artificiality is particularly apparent when it is put side by side with the contrary rule, that treaties imposing limitations upon sovereignty ought to be interpreted restrictively. To interpret a treaty liberally is to extend its scope instead of limiting it; but this means at the same time limiting the freedom of regulation enjoyed by the State in question; it means restricting the sovereignty of that State. Thus, for instance, to interpret a commercial treaty liberally is to increase the scope of liberties and exemptions granted to the subjects of the other party. The result is necessarily a limitation of the freedom of action of the State bound by the treaty.

Moreover, quite apart from its being irreconcilable with the rule as to restrictive interpretation, the liberal interpretation rule raises other difficulties. Thus, for instance, the question arises: what is meant by a 'liberal' interpretation of an extradition treaty? 'Liberally' for whom—the State requesting extradition, or the accused claiming exemption from extradition? For, contrary to the view which is too readily accepted, extradition treaties are concluded not only for the purpose of mutual aid in combating criminality. Their other purpose is the protection of the accused from the danger of being handed over to a foreign jurisdiction without good reason and without proper safeguards. The rule of double criminality and, to a smaller extent, the so-called specialty rule, belong to this category. When, in the case of *Factor* v. *Laubenheimer*,[1] the Supreme Court of the United States interpreted the extradition treaty with Great Britain 'liberally' to the requesting State, it was severely criticized on the ground that it disregarded the safeguards embodied in the rule—adopted not without regard to the interests of the accused individual—prohibiting extradition except when the act in

[1] (1933) 290 U.S. 276.

364

CONTRACTUAL RELATIONS BETWEEN STATES

question is criminal in both States.[1] Two years later, after its decision in the *Neidecker* case,[2] the Supreme Court was criticized[3] for a different and opposite reason, namely, for refusing to give a 'liberal' interpretation to the request for the extradition of a national and for insisting on interpreting the treaty 'liberally' by reference to the general principle that at least part of the law of extradition has been adopted for the sake of safeguarding the rights of individuals. Thus the Supreme Court, in refusing extradition, attached importance to the principle that 'the laws of the United States, like those of England, receive every fugitive, and no authority has been given to their executives to deliver them up'; it pointed out that that principle rested 'upon the fundamental consideration that the Constitution creates no executive prerogative to dispose of the liberty of the subject'.

These examples show the undesirability of adopting special canons and even special terminology for the interpretation of treaties because of their political character, because of the necessity of a restrictive interpretation of limitations of sovereignty, or for other reasons. The safest course is to disregard not only the differences between various categories of treaties but, more generally, the supposed difference between treaties and contracts. The same applies, as is pointed out elsewhere,[4] to the assumed fundamental difference between so-called law-making and other treaties—a difference which, while of some practical usefulness as a matter of exposition and classification, is irrelevant so far as substantive rules of law are concerned, for instance with regard to the conditions of validity of treaties or the principles of their interpretation.

This conclusion in regard to the interpretation of treaties is merely another illustration of the essential identity of consensual agreements in municipal and international law. There is no reason to regret it. As has been said above, there is no derogation from the dignity of international law on that account. It may be unsatisfactory that so much in the international sphere depends on agreement as distinguished from the overriding authority of the law. But while this drawback is admitted, two factors must be borne in mind. The first is that the consent once given, the treaty no longer depends

[1] See Hudson in *A.J.* 28 (1934), 274–306. But see Borchard, *ibid.* pp. 742–6.
[2] (1936) 299 U.S. 5.
[3] See Garner in *A.J.* 30 (1936), 481–6 (with reference to the decision of the United States Circuit Court of Appeals in this case: 81 F. (2d) 32); and Preuss in *R.I.F.* 3 (1937), 159–73, 244–59. See, on the other hand, two other recent American decisions in *United States* v. *Milligan* (1934) 74 F. (2d) 220 and (1935) 76 F. (2d) 511.
[4] See below, p. 414.

365

GENERAL RULES OF THE LAW OF PEACE

for its validity on the continued renewal of such consent; so long as the treaty has not been lawfully terminated, it remains the imperative law binding upon the parties. Secondly, although it may be a pity that so much depends on contract only, we may minimize the inconvenience—and are justified by the practice of States in doing so—by at least putting such agreement within the firm orbit of the general principles of the law of contract which the legal history of mankind has abundantly developed through the ages.

CHAPTER 10

PROPERTY RELATIONS BETWEEN STATES. STATE TERRITORY

89. *Territory as subject to a proprietary right of the State*

The problem of State territory and the nature of territorial sovereignty illustrates well the implications of the attempt to comprehend international law by reference not to what is called its specific character, but to general principles of law in the corresponding sphere of property relations among individuals. To many it seems pedantic or absurd to try to cast the modern relations of territorial sovereignty in the mould of the antiquated patrimonial conception and to look upon the relation of the State to its territory as that of the individual to the land or other property which he owns. For this is in effect the result of what has been called the 'object' theory of the nature of State territory. There is something almost blasphemous in that method for those who think of that relation in terms inspired by the metaphysical conception of the State. That attitude is eloquently expressed by Professor Kaufmann who asserts that 'chaque État a, à coté de sa mission ethnique, la mission spatiale d'utiliser son espace vital, de la développer, d'y accomplir toutes les fonctions nationales et sociales'.[1] The opponents of the 'object' theory point out that the territory is not owned by the State, but that it *is* the State, just as the individual, far from owning his body, constitutes an inseparable unity with it and is inconceivable without it.

The practice of States contradicts this view. It offers repeated examples of territory being treated as the object of a right external to the State. This was so not only in the days of the patrimonial conception of the State, when territory was parted with by way of marriage settlements or testamentary disposition. Exchange and sale of territory—not to speak of the ordinary method of cession— have occurred in the nineteenth and twentieth centuries. When in 1917 Denmark sold the West Indies to the United States, the Danish flag in the West Indies was removed and that of the United States hoisted at the moment when the Secretary of State handed over to the Danish Ambassador treasury bonds to the value of

[1] In *Hague Recueil*, 54 (1935) (iv), 379.

367

GENERAL RULES OF THE LAW OF PEACE

25,000,000 dollars—a significant practical application of the 'object' theory.

To maintain that territory is an objective right external to the State does not mean that it is as external to it as ownership is to the individual. Undoubtedly, territory, however small, is essential to the existence of a State, whereas an individual can be conceived as having no property at all—unless, with Hobbes and Locke, one regards his body as property. Thus Hobbes says: 'Of things held in propriety, those that are dearest to a man are his own life and limbs . . .'[1] Similarly, Locke tells us that 'every man has a property in his own person'.[2] However, most will prefer Ulpian's saying: *Dominus membrorum suorum nemo videtur*.[3] It will be noted that it is easier for a State to part with some of its territory with impunity—and, in some cases, with beneficent results—than for an individual to part with his body. But it is not necessary to deny the indispensability of territory for the State in order to maintain at the same time that it is the object of the proprietary right of the State. It is indispensable in the sense that for a State to exist some territory there must be, however small (the Vatican City reminds us that the requirements in this matter are not very exacting), although some legal theories and isolated instances in practice suggest the possibility of the existence of a State without territory. If we think of the State not in terms of an absolute and mystical entity but as the totality of the individuals organized as a State, then there is nothing artificial in regarding the State as the owner of territory. The individuals, in their collective capacity as a State, own the territory of the State. The State owns its territory. For certain purposes it is ownership not only analogous to, but identical with, that of property, namely, in regard to land owned by the State. In other respects that ownership, although in strict law identical with property over the territory of the State, actually amounts to a merely nominal ownership only. Thus in English law the fee simple absolute in possession, the most complete species of ownership, is in legal theory held of the King. But even that merely formal ownership on occasions asserts its supremacy in the form of expropriation, with or without compensation. In the external sphere that right of ownership manifests itself in the competence of the State to cede parts of its territory and, generally, as will be seen, to dispose of it in various ways.

[1] *Leviathan*, ch. xxx.   [2] *Treatise on Civil Government*, ii, ch. v, section 27.
[3] D. 9.12.13.pr.

368

90. *The consequences of the 'object' theory*

The fact that the relation of the State to its territory is to a substantial degree analogous to or identical with that of a proprietary right of an owner over his land does not, of course, exhaust the relationship between the State and its territory. In addition to being the object of its proprietary rights, the territory is the basis upon which and the area wherein the State exercises jurisdiction in conformity with its own law and international law. The State exercises its jurisdiction over persons and things upon its territory and within the air space above it. This is the gist of what has been called the 'space' theory. But much of the discussion bearing on this matter has been rendered sterile by the extreme and exclusive assertions of what may be called the 'object' and 'space' theories. The fact is that it is both. The territory is both the object of the State's right and the space within which its sovereignty and jurisdiction are exercised. They are both subject to limitations in accordance with customary international law and obligations of treaties.

As usual, behind seemingly theoretical differences there lurk also on the question of the nature of State territory not only conflicts of fundamental notions of international law but also of more tangible political interests. Practical consequences of significance follow upon the adoption of the one or the other view. A relation of the State to its territory conceived as a proprietary relation in terms of the general principles of the law of property renders that relation susceptible of modifications and limitations in the interest of other States and of international intercourse generally. Property is a bundle of rights, some or most of which may belong to or be exercised by others than the nominal owner; in this sense there is nothing about ownership that is indivisible or absolute. A conception of State territory as an essential, absolute and indivisible element of the State—and nothing else—has not only the disadvantage of leaving the radical and clumsy expedient of cession as the only means of settling difficulties resulting from the territorial divisions of the world. For, in the eyes of those who hold this view, territory is sacrosanct and therefore not to be parted with except under absolute necessity of compelling force, and even the clumsy expedient of cession is likely to be resorted to not as a normal instrument of peaceful adjustment but as an inescapable consequence of war. Secondly, as international practice has refused to follow the rigid conception of the absolute and indivisible relation of the State to its

GENERAL RULES OF THE LAW OF PEACE

territory, any attempt to apply that conception to relevant international situations must have, and often has had, the effect of giving to it a purely political interpretation rendering it difficult to understand that practice. Some examples will illustrate that aspect of the matter.

91. *Divisibility of territorial sovereignty.* Condominium

A territory under a *condominium* is a clear example of division of sovereignty or of joint exercise of it in respect of a given territory, or of both. It is a denial of the view of the indivisibility of territorial sovereignty. This is the reason why the traditional doctrine was able to comprehend juridically the institution of *condominium* by the clumsy device of explaining it as a temporary arrangement pending the final allocation of the territory. This may have been true of some *condominia*. Thus, for instance, after the World War certain territories detached by the Peace Treaties from the Central Powers and ceded to the Allied and Associated Powers, were held by them in *condominium* pending final allocation. But this does not apply to all *condominia*. Some of them are intended to constitute a permanent arrangement, e.g. the British–French *condominium* over the New Hebrides, which combines in an instructive manner the various aspects of the régime of a *condominium*. There is in the New Hebrides not only a joint sovereignty over the territory in general. That joint sovereignty manifests itself in a joint jurisdiction over the native population and in separate administrations with regard to the French and the British inhabitants. International law cannot, without admitting a condition of anarchy, contemplate any territory as not being subject to some ultimate authority capable of taking final decisions. But that authority need not be a single State. If two States jointly exercise territorial sovereignty, the ultimate authority is provided by the existence between them of special or general machinery for reaching a decision on disputed points. When there are two States, such power of decision can be given to an arbitral or judicial authority. When there are more States, the power of decision can be given to a majority of them. This is to a large extent the position with regard to that curious mixture of a protectorate and a *condominium* shown by the administration of the International City of Tangier.

The legal nature of a *condominium* may be obscured by the circumstance that on the plane of political facts the partnership is one-sided owing to the political preponderance of one party. This was

370

the case for a time with regard to the *condominium* of Great Britain and Egypt over the Sudan, established in 1899. Although the question of sovereignty was and is at present left in abeyance, in theory the *condominium* was almost complete. We say 'almost complete' for there was, and is, lacking an organ competent to give a decision in case of a dispute in matters in which joint action is necessary. The Governor-General is nominated by the King of Great Britain and appointed by the King of Egypt. The flags of Egypt and Great Britain have been flown side by side from the principal official buildings. This theoretical equality of rights subsisted even at periods when, owing to political events, the juridical equality of partnership was rendered largely theoretical. However, with the recent re-establishment of a substantial degree of political equality between the parties, the joint sovereignty as established by law gains in prominence. Article 11 of the Treaty of 1936 and its Annex, which put the relationship between the two parties on a new basis, give to some extent expression to this change by laying down details for the stationing of Egyptian troops in Sudan and for the joint action of Great Britain and Egypt in the conclusion and termination of international agreements in which Sudan participates. As a matter of existing law the question of sovereignty is now expressly reserved (in Article 11(1) of the Treaty of 1936). There is nothing in legal theory or in the nature of sovereignty to render impossible a permanent and agreed division of sovereignty as suggested by the very nature of a *condominium*. A recent decision of the German Supreme Administrative Court, given on 24 November 1932, illustrates on a smaller scale the same proposition. According to the Frontier Agreement between Prussia and Holland of 26 June 1816, watercourses running between the two countries shall be owned by them jointly. It was held that as the result of that Agreement there was created a joint ownership in the nature of a *condominium*, according to which both States exercised joint jurisdiction over frontier streams with the further result that the jurisdiction of each State was limited by that of the other State. The jurisdiction over these portions of the stream was joint and undivided, and Prussia could not, by unilateral action, legislate for them.[1]

A *condominium* may be a cumbersome method of reconciling territorial pretensions. It may be practicable only between States between which there exists an atmosphere of understanding or co-operation—in which case solutions more simple than a *condomi-*

---

[1] *Reichs- und preussisches Verwaltungsblatt*, 55 (1934), 253.

GENERAL RULES OF THE LAW OF PEACE

nium will be found in the first instance. Its importance lies in the fact that it reveals the possibility of a thoroughgoing modification of supposedly indivisible territorial rights to the point of a formal division or joint exercise of territorial sovereignty.

92. *Sovereignty and the exercise of sovereignty. Leases and grants in perpetuity*
Undue concentration on a political interpretation of legal phenomena has had the effect of obscuring another significant example of division of territorial sovereignty, namely, the division between the exercise of sovereignty and sovereignty proper. Of these, international leases of substantial pieces of territory, like the Chinese leases to Russia, France, Great Britain and Germany, offer an instructive example. The intrusion of political interpretations led some to describe these leases as disguised cessions. But they were—and are —very far from being disguised cessions. They would not have constituted cessions even if the sovereignty of the lessor had remained purely nominal. But that sovereignty was often more than nominal. It found expression, in some cases, in the continued exercise by the lessor of some jurisdictional rights or, in other cases, in the recognized necessity of the lessor's consent to transfer of the lease. And finally, the accurate legal position showed itself in the fact that a termination of the relation was claimed, and in some cases obtained, more easily than would have been the case in regard to a demand for retrocession of ceded territory. The position is the same with regard to grants in perpetuity. Witness, for instance, the persistence with which the courts of Panama have emphasized the sovereignty of Panama over the Canal Zone—a persistence occasionally rewarded by the pronouncements of the courts of the United States notwithstanding the almost complete measure of jurisdictional rights exercised by the United States in that territory.

The *Lighthouses in Crete and Samos* case, decided by the Permanent Court of International Justice on 8 October 1937, illustrates in a different way the same question. By virtue of the Cretan Constitutions of 1899 and 1907, imposed by the European Powers upon the Ottoman Empire, the latter renounced in fact a substantial portion of its sovereignty over the island to the point of conferring upon Crete a thoroughgoing autonomy in her internal and external affairs. In the picturesque periods of Judge Hudson's Dissenting Opinion, the residuary sovereignty of the Sultan was 'a sovereignty shorn of the last vestige of power'; he urged that 'a juridical concept must not be stretched to the breaking-point', and that 'a ghost

372

PROPERTY RELATIONS BETWEEN STATES

of hollow sovereignty cannot be permitted to obscure the realities of this situation'.[1] But the ten Judges composing the majority of the Court considered that although the Sultan had been obliged to accept 'important restrictions on the exercise of his rights of sovereignty in Crete, that sovereignty had not ceased to belong to him, however it might be qualified from a juridical point of view'.[2] The Court accordingly held that a contract made by the Ottoman Government with a French Company with regard to a certain lighthouse in Crete was 'duly entered into' and was binding upon Greece, the successor of Turkey. This insistence by the Court on the distinction between the exercise of rights of sovereignty and residuary sovereignty proper is significant and, it is submitted, correct in principle. There is always a danger in the attempt to comprehend the realities of a situation at the expense of the realities of the law. It is not the business of the law to give a political interpretation, however closely approximating to the facts, of the legal situation. The gap between the two is a creature of the parties and must not be bridged by attempts at realism. The administration of Bosnia and Herzegovina by Austria–Hungary was a clear example of a full separation of the exercise of sovereignty from the *nudum jus* of sovereignty of Turkey. But the violation of the 'hollow sovereignty' of Turkey through the annexation of Bosnia and Herzegovina was generally regarded as a major breach of international law.

93. *Mandates*

On a much larger and more significant scale, the separation of sovereignty from its normal exercise has manifested itself in the case of mandates. The theories in the matter of sovereignty over mandates are legion. The scope of these lectures does not permit me to do more than urge the accuracy of the view which I put forward some years ago,[3] namely, that normally the exercise of sovereignty is in this case vested in one person, i.e. the Mandatory, and its titular ownership in another person, i.e. the League. The principal rival view, which vests sovereignty and its exercise in the Mandatory, is contradicted not only by legal principle but also by practice. It would be difficult to point to a deliberate claim of a mandatory State asserting sovereignty over the mandated territory; it would be equally difficult to adduce any judicial pronouncement affirming that the mandated territory forms part of the territory of the Mandatory. But there are judicial decisions affirming the contrary. Moreover,

[1] *P.C.I.J.* Series A/B, no. 71, p. 127. [2] *Ibid.* p. 103. [3] *Analogies*, pp. 191–202.

GENERAL RULES OF THE LAW OF PEACE

the same legal experience shows that on crucial occasions the sovereignty of the League is by no means as nominal as the supposed realistic and political interpretation has made it appear. The supervision, on the part of the League, of the exercise of the mandate is by no means a nominal function. Neither can the termination or transfer of a mandate take place without its consent. But with the normal course of the exercise of governmental functions the League has no concern. It is a supervisory and residuary sovereignty, but one which nevertheless represents a real division of sovereign rights.

94. *International servitudes*

The much-criticized name and institution of servitudes illustrates from the same angle the general implications of the problem here discussed. Servitudes are rights of jurisdiction, rights of sovereignty, within the territory of another State; they constitute so far as they go a division of sovereignty between the two interested States. It is this aspect of servitudes which, together with their continuity in face of changes of sovereignty, distinguished them from other limitations of sovereignty. It is not the fact that, as is often said, they have reference to the territory as such. Every limitation of sovereignty—e.g. in the matter of tariffs or of treatment of aliens—has reference to territory in the sense that the acts or omissions in question take place on or with regard to the territory or in regard to persons or property on the territory. What distinguishes servitudes from any other limitation of territorial sovereignty is the fact that they imply the grant of a separate sovereign jurisdictional right; it is that they imply a division of sovereignty. This was clearly recognized in the often-quoted decision of the Cologne Court of Appeal in 1914, which laid down that with regard to the mining concession which constituted the servitude granted by Germany to Holland, part of the territorial sovereignty remained with Holland, that Holland was entitled to exercise there 'its own legislative authority and police supervision', and that it had 'real sovereign rights with respect to the object situated within the territory of the foreign State'.[1] This was the view urged by the United States—and in no way rejected by the Tribunal—in the case of the *North Atlantic Coast Fisheries*. It was the view according to which, in Senator Elihu Root's words, the Treaty of 1818 which was said to have created the servitude 'would be deemed to take out from Great Britain a fragment

[1] *A.J.* 8 (1914), 907.

374

PROPERTY RELATIONS BETWEEN STATES

of her sovereignty itself, and from that it would follow as a logical conclusion that Great Britain could not order, regulate, control, limit, or restrict the right that has passed to us, because it was not hers'.[1] The same view was adopted by a German Labour Court in 1928 with regard to the administration of the German section of the railway station at Basle.[2] The 'running with the land', i.e. the continuity of servitudes irrespective of changes of sovereignty, must be regarded as the consequence of this 'real' character of servitudes and not as the principal manifestation and result of the existence of a servitude. It is because of this character of servitudes as conferring a sovereign right *per se*, and not because of the unpleasant connotations of its name, that the opposition to servitudes has been so pronounced. But this is not necessarily the reason why that opposition should be regarded as representing a sound and progressive tendency. The difficulties resulting from the territorial apportionment of the world cannot be solved by the expedient of territorial changes. But they may be alleviated by more or less far-reaching modifications of rights enjoyed by a State within its territory. Servitudes are one of the various possible expressions of such modifications.

95. *Territorial waters and the contiguous zones*

The difficulties surrounding the question of territorial waters shows, in a different way, that *prima facie* full sovereign ownership need not be accompanied by the exclusive and undivided exercise of rights pertaining thereto. As to the question of sovereignty over territorial waters, the controversy seems now to have been settled in favour of the view that the littoral State has, subject to restrictions imposed by international law, full sovereignty over the littoral sea. In fact, one of the few questions with regard to territorial waters on which there was agreement in the course of the Hague Codification Conference was that the territorial waters are part of the territory of the State and that, subject to limitations imposed by international law, a State exercises over them sovereignty which is 'in no way different from the power which the State exercises over its domain on land'. But it is significant that, this notwithstanding, territorial waters are even today not invariably regarded as part of national territory. Thus we find in 1935 the French Court of Cassation laying down in the *Thireaut* case that territorial waters do not form part of French territory.[3] There are other judicial decisions to this effect. This

[1] *Argument* of Senator Root (*ibid.* p. 227).
[2] *Annual Digest*, 4 (1927–8), Case no. 90.   [3] *R.I.* (*Paris*) (1936), pp. 303–10.

375

denial, by authoritative courts, that territorial waters form part of the territory of the State is largely due to the realization of the character and the wide scope of the restrictions which international law places upon the sovereignty of States in this matter. But the difficulties and the hesitation disappear as soon as we realize that there is nothing about territorial sovereignty that is indivisible and impenetrable; that territorial sovereignty can and ought to be conceived as a highly modifiable and separable bundle of rights and competencies; and that restrictions, however wide, do not affect the essential nature of the relationship. Like sovereignty over the land, sovereignty over territorial waters can be exercised only subject to conditions laid down by customary or conventional international law.

It is also only by keeping apart full territorial ownership from exercise of jurisdictional rights that a way can be found out of the difficulty besetting that aspect of the question of territorial waters which was responsible for the failure of the Hague Codification Conference. These were the differences of view on the matter of the breadth of the maritime belt and, in particular, on the question of the so-called contiguous zones. The latter is in itself an interesting example of a claim to exercise of sovereign rights within an area which admittedly is not under the territorial sovereignty of the State asking for extended rights of this nature. Once it is realized that the exercise of sovereign rights can be divested from territorial sovereignty proper—which means either that the exercise of such rights in no way connotes either the fact of or even pretensions to territorial sovereignty or, conversely, that formal sovereignty does not imply unrestricted use of rights of sovereignty—once this is realized, there disappear many of the obstacles blocking the way to agreement and to reasonable adjustments in accordance with economic needs and technical developments. The possibilities of division of sovereignty in this direction are shown in the judgment of the German Staatsgerichtshof of 7 July 1928, in the dispute between Lübeck and Mecklenburg-Schwerin concerning the sovereignty over the Bay of Lübeck.[1] The Court rejected the view favouring either the territorial division of the bay or a joint and indivisible sovereignty over it. It based its judgment on the view that the historical development and the actual needs of the two States were of decisive importance and that the sovereignty over the same part of the bay ought to be divided functionally in the sense that one State should exercise

[1] *Annual Digest*, 4 (1927–8), Case no. 80.

PROPERTY RELATIONS BETWEEN STATES

sovereignty in regard to some matters and the other State with regard to others.

The examples given so far suggest the possibility of approaching the question of the nature of the territorial relations of States from an angle different from that of the identification of exercise of sovereign rights over and within a territory with the notion of an absolute and indivisible territorial ownership. This aspect of the matter is of wider significance than the question as to how far the law relating to State territory, i.e. to the property relations of States, is analogous to that of the property relations of individuals—although, as has been pointed out, the question of divisibility and exclusiveness of territorial sovereignty is one to which a broad answer can be found in the assumption that territory is the object of the proprietary right of the State and in the fact that, in general, property, far from being an absolute right, is a bundle of rights capable of modification, division and adjustment. This in itself is the primary and, it is believed, beneficent expression of the essential similarity of the property relations of individuals and the territorial relations of States.

96. *Acquisition of territorial title. Prescription*

Apart from the general consequences of that fundamental similarity, practically the entire branch of international law relating to territory bears the impress of that similarity. It is enough to survey the various modes of original acquisition of territory, from discovery and prescription to the minor instances of alluvion and accretion (the apparent but not real exception of conquest is referred to below). The prevalence of Roman law or of the patrimonial conception of the State is not a sufficient explanation of that phenomenon; the law in question has remained applicable long after the patrimonial conception or the compelling authority of the *ratio scripta* had gone. The fact of the close correspondence of the law in the two domains was not a matter of choice or of historical accident. It was due, as has been said, to the essential similarity of the relation. It was an historical necessity if that aspect of international relations was to be governed by international law. In the matter of the treaty relations of States, the acceptance of the established prototype of contract has been instrumental in infusing into that part of international law the decisive elements of order and legality. Equally with regard to State territory, the acceptance of the property relationship among individuals has contributed a juridical element of order and peaceful

377

settlement in a sphere of the international activity of States which, by reason of the availability of undiscovered territory and by reason of the passionate interest in this particular object of possession, offered powerful inducements to settlement by mere force.

These general principles of law in the matter had on occasions to be adapted to the requirements of State intercourse. Thus, in the matter of prescription, the requirement of good faith in the original acquisition is exacted less rigidly than in the municipal sphere. It is a requirement which is certainly not dispensed with altogether. Thus in a recent important decision given in 1933 by a Tribunal under the presidency of Chief Justice Hughes in a dispute between Guatemala and Honduras, we find the Tribunal laying down as one of the factors determining the boundary to be fixed by it 'the question whether possession by one Party has been acquired in good faith, and without invading the right of the other Party'.[1] In fact, without the requirement of good faith, prescription constitutes the negation of its first major juridical premise, namely, the assumption of lawful origin. (This, it will be seen, did not exclude altogether acquisition by force; but the title in such cases was conquest, not prescription.) But the second major premise of presumption is the social requirement of stability, and in deference to that requirement the necessity of good faith will on occasions be tested by standards of some elasticity. That on occasions municipal law may dispense altogether with the requirement of good faith may be seen, for instance, in the English Prescription Act of 1832, according to which it is not necessary, with regard to the easement of light, to prove that it has been exercised 'as of right'; mere enjoyment is enough. In international relations, where the claims of stability and peace are of greater immediate urgency, there is special reason for subordinating on occasions the stringency of the proof of the requirement of good faith to considerations underlying the maxim *quieta non movere*. This may on occasions be done by special agreement, as in the case of the *British Guiana Arbitration* in 1897, where the parties agreed that 'adverse holding or prescription during a period of fifty years shall make good title' and that 'the arbitrators may deem exclusive political control of a district, as well as actual settlement thereof, sufficient to constitute adverse holding or to make title by prescription'. The contention of the United States that that provision did not exclude good faith as an element of prescription was not, it appears, accepted by the Tribunal. On other occasions international

---

[1] Opinion and Award (Washington, 1933), p. 70.

PROPERTY RELATIONS BETWEEN STATES

tribunals have themselves subordinated the condition of good faith to the more pressing requirements of stability and order. The Award in the *Island of Palmas Arbitration* in 1928 is a good illustration of this aspect of the question.[1]

97. *Occupation and effectiveness of possession*

The history of the double requirement of *animus* and *corpus* in the matter of acquisition of territorial sovereignty by occupation illustrates the same aspect of the problem. The law on this question can be accurately conceived in terms of the gradual assertion of the principle of effectiveness over the pretensions of discovery either pure and simple or in its modified expressions like the doctrines of the watershed or of contiguity. This is, of course, consonant with a general principle of law governing original acquisition of property. But it is clear that, as in the case of prescription, the analogy of effective occupation must be adapted to the special requirements of international order and stability. A series of recent decisions, which cannot otherwise be easily reconciled with the doctrine of effectiveness, shows the necessity of reasonable departures from the general principles of law in the matter of thoroughgoing effectiveness of possession. Thus, for instance, in the dispute between Denmark and Norway concerning the *Status of Eastern Greenland*, decided by the Permanent Court of International Justice on 5 April 1933, the Court attached considerable importance to the fact that up to 1931 there had been no claim by any Power other than Denmark to sovereignty over Greenland.[2] As the Court pointed out, in many cases international tribunals have been satisfied with very little in the way of actual exercise of sovereign rights provided that the opponent could not make out a superior title. Effective occupation being thus a relative matter, it is not improbable that a modern arbitrator may attach decisive importance to what is nothing more than symbolic discovery. Thus in the dispute between France and Mexico concerning *Clipperton Island*, decided on 28 January 1931, the Arbitrator, the King of Italy, awarded the sovereignty over the island to France on the strength of acts of occupation no more tangible than a short landing, lasting two days, by several members of the crew of a vessel, the taking of geographical notes, a second, unsuccessful, attempt to reach the shore, and the publication in an English journal at Honolulu of a declaration of French sovereignty. The Arbitrator regarded the actual political organization of the

[1] *Annual Digest*, 4 (1927–8), Case no. 68.   [2] *P.C.I.J.* Series A/B, no. 53, pp. 45, 46.

GENERAL RULES OF THE LAW OF PEACE

territory merely as evidence of taking possession, but not as identical with it. He pointed out that there may be cases in which it is unnecessary to have recourse to this method. Thus, he said, if completely uninhabited territory is, from the first moment when the occupying Power makes its appearance there, at the absolute and undisputed disposal of that State, the possession must be regarded as accomplished and the occupation completed.[1] On the other hand, the same considerations of stability led the Arbitrator in the *Island of Palmas Arbitration*, decided on 4 April 1928, to disregard effective occupation in a case where, after it had taken place, it had been discontinued and displaced by an effective and undisputed occupation.[2]

98. *Conquest*

We have seen that the principle of effectiveness may be modified and made more elastic or more stringent as international conditions may require. This is merely a manifestation of the necessity of adapting the general principles of law to the requirements of international order and stability. Such modifications do not affect the fundamental analogy in the processes of acquisition of territorial title and of private proprietary rights. There is one point, however, on which that analogy definitely breaks down, namely, in the matter of acquisition of title by conquest and subjugation. There is no such mode of acquisition in general jurisprudence. It does not —and cannot—recognize private force as creative of title. Traditional international law undoubtedly recognized acquisition by conquest. But in so far as it did that it not only disregarded a general principle of law; it denied its own legal character. This defect was correlative to and the consequence of a more fundamental shortcoming, namely, the admissibility of war as an instrument for both changing and enforcing rights. With the elimination of war as a legally recognized process fulfilling either of these functions, conquest has now ceased to give a legal title. It is in itself an illegal act; and an illegality confers no title. An unlawful act is unable to produce a result beneficent to the law-breaker. As has been pointed out above,[3] in announcing their intention not to recognize conquest accomplished in violation of the Covenant of the League or of the General Treaty for the Renunciation of War, Governments do not render conquest null and void as a means of acquiring territorial

---

[1] The award is printed in *A.J.* 26 (1932), 390.
[2] See *Annual Digest*, 4 (1927–8), Case no. 68.   [3] See above, p. 341.

380

PROPERTY RELATIONS BETWEEN STATES

title. Such conquest is *per se* null and void, without any additional declaration. The declaration of non-recognition serves another purpose; it is the express adoption of a policy or the undertaking of an obligation not to impart, by an act of recognition, the character of a legal title to an otherwise illegal state of affairs. Thus, as the result of recent developments, there disappears from this part of international law a rule which constitutes both a departure from a general principle of law and a serious inroad on the legal nature of international law. It is a development analogous to that which we have noticed in the law of treaties with regard to the influence of duress.[1] However, in both cases the exercise of force may still produce results permitted by traditional international law in cases in which the party applying force is either not bound by the Covenant of the League or the General Treaty for the Renunciation of War, or in which it is applied against a party which itself has been guilty of a violation of these instruments.

99. *High seas and air space*

General principles of law have left their mark not only on questions of State territory proper. They have influenced substantially the development of the idea of the freedom of the sea by bringing to bear upon the subject the proposition that objects incapable of permanent occupation or effective exercise of jurisdiction are not a fit subject-matter for ownership. The rule as to the three-mile limit of territorial waters as determined by the range of gun batteries stationed on the shore is governed by the same consideration. In both cases, technical developments have made the original *rationale* of the rule to a large extent—but not altogether—obsolete. The rules on these matters now stand on their own feet as clear rules of customary international law necessitated by international inter-course and grounded in the will of States. But their influence has been beneficial and it may still exert itself as a useful corrective in other spheres. This applies in particular to the question of the sovereignty over the air conceived in terms of effectiveness of possession. The general principle of law on this matter was originally adequately expressed in the maxim *cujus est solum ejus est usque ad coelum.* This was so at a time when the use of the air for the purpose of communication and transmission of sound and light was unknown. With the advent of new technical developments that general principle has become modified so as to exclude abstract rights

[1] See above, p. 354.

GENERAL RULES OF THE LAW OF PEACE

unrelated to the real needs of the owner. To mention some examples, Article 9 of the British Air Navigation Act of 1920, Article 905 of the German Civil Code, and Article 667 of the Swiss Civil Code of 1907 express this idea. International law has adopted the *usque ad coelum* principle without having adopted as yet its modifications as accepted in the principal systems of municipal law. As in the case of the establishment of the principle of the freedom of the sea, the consideration of effectiveness of jurisdiction may not be entirely irrelevant or without usefulness. The analogy between the high seas and the open air in relation to State territory is admittedly incomplete, but the choice is not between the total exclusion of the sovereignty of the territorial State and its full assertion. The solution lies here also in the direction of treating sovereignty as divisible and modifiable. This is, in fact, the principal problem of territorial relations of States in general. It is from this angle that we have discussed these questions in the present lecture. It is here that the essential identity of State territory and ownership—in fact the 'object' theory—reveals itself as the secular and progressive principle most in keeping with the practice of States and the requirements of international intercourse.

CHAPTER II

DELICTUAL RELATIONS BETWEEN
STATES. STATE RESPONSIBILITY

100. *The principal problems of State responsibility*

It is obviously inadvisable to try to exhaust the subject of State responsibility in one lecture. But it is feasible to attempt to survey the general principles of that topic from the point of view of some typical problems of international law like the doctrines of State sovereignty and the position of individuals as subjects of international duties. The combination of these two doctrines has for a long time imparted to the treatment of the principal questions of State responsibility a degree of rigidity which has hindered the development of international law in this matter and from which it is slowly beginning to emancipate itself under the influence of increased judicial and arbitral activity. That rigidity has manifested itself in a limitation of the sources of State responsibility to a definite category of delicts defined in advance; in the tendency to adopt clear-cut and extreme solutions without an attempt to solve problems of State responsibility by a reasonable adjustment of conflicting considerations; in a limitation of the consequences of responsibility; and in a multitude of restrictions upon the admissibility of international claims. All these may be described as being, in some form or other, restrictions upon liability in deference to the sovereignty of States. The other two limitations which it is intended to discuss here are due to a large extent to the current separation of the individual from the State. They are, first, the opposition to basing responsibility on the mental attitude of the human beings directly concerned with the event said to give rise to liability, and secondly, some aspects of the limitation of the responsibility of the State for the acts of individuals within its borders. It is proposed to examine here from this angle the principal questions of State responsibility.

101. *The limitation of the sources of State responsibility. The prohibition of abuse of rights*

International law recognizes liability for a series of—on the whole —well-defined delicts such as breaches of treaty obligations, denial

383

GENERAL RULES OF THE LAW OF PEACE

of justice, violations of territorial sovereignty, denial of diplomatic immunity, etc. It is consonant with State sovereignty to refuse to recognize any source of liability other than that grounded in consent given by treaty or in a rule of law evidenced as binding by custom. But that limitation of liability to defined categories may not be consistent with justice and with the requirements of the law in a progressive society. Conduct which has hitherto been in accordance with the purpose of the law may cease to be so owing to developments which the law has not yet had time to take into account; behaviour which the law is as a rule content to regard as not in contradiction with social needs ceases to be so when the advantage accruing to one party from the exercise of an otherwise legal right results in disproportionately grave injury to others; action which is described as lawful may cease to be so if pursued in an unsocial manner or in a manner contrary to the purpose for which it has been allowed. In all these cases such conduct, while *prima facie* lawful, amounts to an abuse of a right conferred by the law. The term 'abuse of rights' has not yet become generally accepted, but most systems of law must necessarily cope with situations of this nature. Thus Article 226 of the German Civil Code lays down that the exercise of a right is not permitted when its only object can be to cause damage to another. The Swiss Code of Obligations lays down expressly that 'the law does not sanction the evident abuse of rights'. Here the doctrine of abuse of rights is adopted *eo nomine*. But such express incorporation of the doctrine is not an essential condition of its applicability. In England it underlies much of the law of nuisance. And it is probably one of the bases of the law of tort as a whole. There are still some English lawyers who maintain that the law of tort is a body of rules exhaustively establishing specific injuries so that it is for the plaintiff to prove that the act complained of falls within an established rule of liability. But the preponderant body of legal opinion and judicial authority seems now to be that any intentional infliction of damage is *prima facie* a cause of action.

To deny the existence in international law of the prohibition of abuse of rights or of any other analogous legal principle is to assert, in the name of State sovereignty and resulting presumptive liberty of action, a degree of formalism and rigidity which must be inimical to justice and progress. On occasions, international tribunals have gone far towards asserting complete freedom of action regardless of the interests of other States. The *Behring Sea Arbitration*, in which the State's right to claim all the advantages resulting from the principle of the freedom of the seas was upheld by the Tribunal, is an instructive example. In the case between Argentina and Great Britain concerning the closure of the port of Buenos Aires, the arbitrator went to the extreme length of upholding the principle *neminem laedit qui jure suo utitur*. But these cases are offset by others acting on the maxim *sic utere tuo ut alienum non laedas*—a maxim of which Westlake says that 'no principle is more firmly established in the science of law'.[1] And there are more recent signs that the doctrine is gaining increasing recognition in the international sphere. The Permanent Court of International Justice, notwithstanding its customary caution, has on a number of occasions expressed its willingness to act on it.[2] It is one of those 'general principles of law recognized by civilized nations' by which the Permanent Court is bound and which other international tribunals have declared as binding upon them. It is the basis of the now generally recognized prohibition of diverting or interfering with the flow of an international river to the detriment of the other riparian States. There is no good reason why the same principle should not be applied to the use of the air with regard to both aerial traffic and radiotelegraphy. No doubt considerable caution is required in applying the principle of abuse of rights as a source of State responsibility. Its injudicious or rash application may result in interference with rights conferred by law and meriting its protection. It is not every injury that the law prohibits. A person or a State may, when exercising a legal right, legitimately and justifiably injure another person or State. Law is not an ethical code of mutual sacrifice and forbearance. But it must step in when the injury arising from the exercise of a right is disproportionately grave, and especially when it is obvious that the particular right is used for a purpose different from or opposed to that for which it has been granted.

The existence of authoritative judicial tribunals is a guarantee that the doctrine of abuse of rights will not be extended too far to the extent of saddling States with liability for making proper use of rights given by treaty or custom. But, like any other general principle of law, it must be constantly in the background of the law of State responsibility. This is so in particular in cases in which international law entrusts States with the duty of acting as trustees of international law and of the international community at large. A State using the discretion which international law gives to it in the matter of

---

[1] *International Law* (1st ed. 1907), II, 322.
[2] *P.C.I.J.* Series A, no. 24, p. 12; Series A/B, no. 46, p. 167; Series A. no. 1, p. 30.

GENERAL RULES OF THE LAW OF PEACE

recognition of States and Governments for furthering its own political purposes is abusing its right and incurs international liability.[1] In general, the satisfactory development of the law of State responsibility is to a large extent conditioned by definitely abandoning the view that owing to the sovereignty of States the causes of international liability are rigidly and exhaustively defined in clearly accepted categories. It will be better for the development of that branch of international law if the *dictum*—which was unnecessary for the decision—in the *Lotus* case to the effect that 'international law governs relations between independent States' and that 'restrictions upon independence of States cannot therefore be presumed'[2] is not pushed too far. When used as a justification of ruthless although formally correct action, it represents a point of view appropriate to the relations of primitive societies and not of civilized States.

102. *State sovereignty and the exceptions to responsibility. The plea of non-discrimination in the treatment of aliens*

Another source of rigidity in the law of State responsibility—equally due to an uncompromising assertion of State sovereignty—arises when a rigid claim to exemption from liability is confronted by an equally uncompromising insistence on rights said to be guaranteed by international law. This is well exemplified in the so-called 'plea of non-discrimination' in the treatment of aliens. On the one hand, we are here confronted with the claim of the State to insist that the personal rights and property of its subjects abroad shall be respected; on the other hand, there is the plea that sovereignty implies full freedom of legislation and administration so long as the State, far from discriminating against aliens, treats them on the same footing as its own subjects. This is largely a question of substantive law relating to the treatment of aliens. At the same time, inasmuch as it raises a general and formal ground of exemption from liability, it is properly discussed as a problem of State responsibility. There is no difficulty with regard to the treatment of the persons of aliens. International tribunals have in this matter laid down with emphasis that a State incurs liability if it fails to treat aliens in accordance with a minimum standard of civilization. It is irrelevant how it treats its own subjects. A national may not be able to enforce against his own State what by civilized standards are now regarded as fundamental international rights; an alien may do so as against the State of residence with the assistance of diplomatic protection by

[1] See above, pp. 319 *et seq.*   [2] *P.C.I.J.* Series A, no. 10, at p. 18.

DELICTUAL RELATIONS BETWEEN STATES

his own State. This is a rule so clearly established that even States which in theory and practice deny the existence of such fundamental rights so far as their own subjects are concerned, have not seriously attempted to claim such freedom of action with regard to aliens.

103. *The property of aliens and the plea of non-discrimination*

The position is different with regard to interference with the property rights of aliens. The awards are conflicting. Some reject the plea of non-discrimination; others are content to agree that the alien is not entitled to claim treatment more favourable than that meted out to nationals.[1] The well-known *Hungarian Optants* dispute, which turned on this question and which produced an embarrassingly abundant crop of opinions of jurists, showed how deeply and uncompromisingly scientific opinion was and is divided on this matter. The official attitude of States at large is equally sharply divided. At the Hague Codification Conference of 1930 it was this aspect of the plea of non-discrimination which more than anything else was responsible for the failure of the proceedings.

And yet this very sharp divergence, not only in the attitude of Governments and writings of international lawyers but also in the practice of tribunals, suggests a reflection of a general character on the matter of State responsibility as a whole. Liability cannot be avoided by reference to external and formal tests of equality of treatment. A test of this nature constitutes an extreme assertion of freedom of action for the sovereign State irrespective of the obligations of international law. With regard to interference with property it would also mean that aliens who otherwise do not participate in

[1] Compare, for instance, the decision in the *George W. Hopkins* case, decided in March 1926 by the General Claims Commission between the United States and Mexico (*Annual Digest*, 3 (1925–6), Case no. 167) with that in the *Standard Oil Company Tankers* case between the Reparation Commission and the United States, decided in August 1926 (*ibid.* Case no. 169). In the first case the Tribunal held that the Mexican Government was liable for certain decrees annulling postal orders held by Mexican and other nationals alike. The Tribunal pointed out that under the rules of international law a State may often be required to afford to aliens more liberal treatment than it affords to its nationals and that the apparent equality of treatment cannot affect vested rights of aliens. In the second case, arising out of the handing over of certain ships by Germany to the Allied Powers under the Treaty of Versailles, the Tribunal held that vessels of companies registered in Germany were liable to be handed over irrespective of beneficial ownership vested in aliens on the ground that any person taking up residence or investing capital in a foreign State must submit to the laws and measures of that country so long as there is no discrimination between the alien and the national. See also *ibid.* Case no. 168, for an observation by the British–American Claims Tribunal in the *Canadian Claims for Refund of Duties* case, decided in March 1925, that it is doubtful whether the unreasonable and arbitrary nature of the means of redress against erroneous customs exactions open equally to nationals and aliens constituted a valid basis for an international claim.

GENERAL RULES OF THE LAW OF PEACE

the political rights and benefits of the régime would be called upon to contribute to it on the same footing as nationals. On the other hand, it is clear that absolute respect for the property of aliens, irrespective of the treatment accorded to the property of nationals, has never been a rule of international law and cannot rationally be postulated as such. The State constantly interferes with property rights of its subjects to the extent of taking them away without compensation. Ordinary taxation, death duties, destruction of property for reasons of public health or safety, depreciation of currency—all these are instances of the taking of property without compensation. States do not protest against interference, in this form, with the property of their nationals when abroad. This being so, it is difficult to maintain that expropriation of property for the purposes of fundamental social reforms must stop short of the property of aliens. To maintain this would mean to attempt to impose upon States a prohibition to regulate their social and political life as they are entitled to do by virtue of the independence and autonomy recognized by international law. For the duty of full compensation might in effect mean the frustration of the contemplated reform. It must also be noted that there is no duty of compensation in the case of destruction of neutral private property in the course of military operations in time of war.[1] Both these sets of considerations are entitled to be taken into account.

In view of this the question is essentially one of compensation for property taken away—for no one denies the right to take away property if fair compensation is paid and no discrimination adopted against aliens. It would appear therefore that the problem ought not to be put in terms of a rigid affirmative or negative, but in the more flexible terms of 'how much?'. How much compensation ought to be paid? Unfortunately international lawyers, who as a rule have been called upon to cope with this problem by reference to a definite controversy, have been inclined to favour either the one or the other alternative. In the *Hungarian Optants* dispute it does not seem to have been suggested that if the matter had come before the Permanent Court of International Justice that Court was certainly not restricted either to refusing compensation altogether or to awarding full compensation. It could legitimately have chosen a middle course. Unlike a conference of States, a judicial tribunal

---

[1] See the *Luzon Sugar Refining Co.* case, decided in November 1926 by the British–American Claims Tribunal (*Annual Digest*, 3 (1925–6), Case no. 164), where this rule was extended to cover losses suffered by British subjects in the course of the suppression of the insurrection in the Philippines in 1899.

388

DELICTUAL RELATIONS BETWEEN STATES

would not and could not regard itself as helpless when confronted with extreme and conflicting claims of sovereignty of this nature. It could not conveniently hide itself behind the absence of agreed law. The decision must be given somehow. With regard to the plea of non-discrimination it must be given, on the one hand, on the basis of the superiority of international law over national legislation (even if it applies to aliens and nationals alike); on the other hand, it cannot disregard the consideration which we have mentioned as possibly justifying interference with private property in the exercise of the powers of independence and autonomy which it is the object of international law to safeguard. It is the principal function of international law to secure to States the measure of freedom of action necessary for the development of their institutions and their national life in accordance with the ideas which determine the political life of the State at any given time. The rules of State responsibility—no less than substantive international law in general—cannot be framed or developed by the method of choosing between one or another uncompromising claim. This is possible—or necessary—in an anarchical system of unreasoning sovereignties settling a controversy by force. The rational way of developing the law is by way of balancing and adjusting conflicting claims by reference not only to such law as is already generally accepted but also by reference to justice and to the needs of the international community. As Huber, Arbitrator, said in the case of *Réclamations Britanniques dans la Zone Espagnole du Maroc* (Accord Anglo-Espagnol du 29 Mai 1923):

Il est acquis que tout droit a pour but d'assurer la coexistence d'intérêts dignes de protection légale. Cela est sans doute vrai aussi en ce qui concerne le droit international. Les intérêts contradictoires en présence pour ce qui est du problème de l'indemnisation des étrangers sont, d'une part, l'intérêt de l'Etat d'exercer sa puissance publique dans son propre territoire sans ingérence et contrôle aucun des Etats étrangers, et d'autre part, l'intérêt de l'Etat de voir respecter et protéger effectivement les droits de ses ressortissants établis en pays étranger.[1]

The decisions of the Permanent Court of International Justice on this matter, while apparently divergent, show nevertheless the possibility of a compromise between the two opposing views. On the one hand, the Court has repeatedly rejected the plea of non-discrimination. In the case concerning *Certain German Interests in Polish Upper Silesia*, the Court pointed out that 'a measure prohibited by the Convention cannot become lawful under this instrument by

[1] *Rapport*, p. 52, and *Annual Digest*, 2 (1923–4), Case no. 85.

389

GENERAL RULES OF THE LAW OF PEACE

reason of the fact that the State applies it to its own nationals'.[1] In a series of cases relating to rights of minorities the Court, in answering the plea that the law did not discriminate against minorities, affirmed the same principle in the form of the statement that there must be equality both in fact and in law.[2] On the other hand, it appears to have recognized the right to expropriate alien property for reasons of public utility.[3]

The question of the plea of non-discrimination has been selected here as typical of the problems raised in the law of State responsibility by extreme assertions of rights of sovereignty. But it is submitted that the method of approach here suggested applies to similar cases. Difficulties of this nature can be removed less by express codification than by sustained activity of international tribunals exercising in an impartial spirit one of the principal tasks of the judicial function, namely, the filling of gaps in the existing law by reconciling extreme claims of sovereignty in accordance with principles capable of general application.

104. *Limitations of the consequences of liability. Punishment of States*

On no other aspect of State responsibility has the regard for State sovereignty engrafted itself more persistently than in the matter of consequences of liability. The theory has become widely accepted that liability is limited to reparation for the damage only—material reparation in the form of damages, moral reparation in the various forms of apology. The view underlying that theory is that States, being sovereign, cannot be punished; they may be under a duty to repair the wrong, but beyond that their liability does not go. In the Dissenting Opinion of Judge Anzilotti in the recent case of the *Diversion of Water from the Meuse*, between Belgium and Holland, decided in June 1937, we find the learned Judge brushing aside the terminology in the Belgian application which asked the Court to enjoin Belgium 'to discontinue any supplying of water held to be contrary to the [relevant] Treaty, and to refrain from creating new facilities for supplying water contrary to the Treaty'. Judge Anzilotti pointed out that the word 'enjoin' 'is not entirely appropriate in international proceedings'.[4] It was not 'entirely appropriate' because it savoured of punishment—a possibility which many writers

---

[1] *P.C.I.J.* Series A, no. 7, p. 33. The same view was expressed in the case of *The Peter Pázmány University* v. *The State of Czechoslovakia* (Series A/B, no. 61, p. 243).

[2] *P.C.I.J.* Series B, no. 6, p. 24 (*German Settlers in Poland*); Series A/B, no. 44, p. 28 (*Treatment of Polish Nationals in Danzig*).

[3] *P.C.I.J.* Series A, no. 7, p. 22.   [4] *P.C.I.J.* Series A/B, no. 70, p. 49.

DELICTUAL RELATIONS BETWEEN STATES

reject as almost blasphemous.[1] The view that sovereign States cannot, in law, be punished seems to have been recognized to some extent in the practice of arbitral tribunals in so far as they have often rejected demands for vindictive damages. Indirectly, the same view has found expression in the tendency, now overcome, to restrict the consequences of State responsibility even in such details as the award of damages for indirect losses and the payment of interest. And it has even been suggested that the provision of Article 64 of the Statute of the Permanent Court of International Justice, according to which each party pays its own costs unless the Court directs otherwise, is grounded in the view that payment of the adversary's costs implies an element of punishment.

As will be seen presently,[2] there is much less support in arbitral practice than is commonly assumed for the view that no punishment can be meted out to sovereign States. But there is even less support for that view in legal principle. It might be possible to argue that sovereign States are not and cannot be subject to law and are therefore not subject to the consequences of its breach. Such a view would amount to a denial of international law, but it would be a consistent view. But to say that a community, because of assumed attributes of sovereignty and of the dignity attaching to it, is immune from certain consequences of breaches of the law is to put forward a wholly arbitrary statement. It is to limit arbitrarily the operation of justice in the international sphere. *Restitutio in integrum* may not always be possible; it is in fact not possible in many delicts giving rise to State responsibility. Even when *restitutio in integrum* is possible so far as the injured State is concerned, the offence against international law as a whole may be such as to necessitate in the interests of justice a form of disapproval going beyond material reparation. To limit responsibility within the State to *restitutio in integrum* would mean to abolish criminal law and a substantial part of the law of tort. To abolish these aspects of responsibility among States would mean to adopt, because of their sovereignty and dignity, a principle which is not only repulsive to justice but is in itself an inducement to injustice and lawlessness. It would mean that individuals, when grouped in the form of a State, acquire a degree of immunity in respect of criminal

[1] 'L'application de la justice vindictive aux États serait contraire à l'idée du droit international', says Professor Kaufmann in *Hague Recueil*, 54 (1935) (iv), 471. He does not explain why, unless one attaches importance to his statement that there is no relation of subordination in international law or that 'ce qui doit être compensé par la justice punitive, c'est le dommage causé à l'ordre moral, qui exige comme contre-partie un mal qui doit frapper le malfacteur' (p. 470).   [2] See below, pp. 393 *et seq.*

391

acts against the life and safety of their neighbours which they do not possess when acting in isolation; it is an immunity covering acts which, because they are collective and assisted by the almost infinite power of the modern State, are potentially of an unlimited destructiveness.

It is the current personification of the State, which artificially distinguishes between the association and the members composing it, that has been a contributory factor in suggesting that anarchical principle of moral and legal irresponsibility. 'You cannot indict a whole nation', said Burke. But the danger of such collective indictment is smaller than the danger resulting from collective irresponsibility. That danger has been well expressed by Westlake in terms which merit quotation. He said, in relation to the attempt to sever the responsibility of the State from that of the individuals composing it: 'It may weaken the sense that the action of the State is the action of those within it who help to guide it . . .; nay, that in a lesser degree it is also the action of those who suffer the other to guide it.'[1] The nation as a whole may gain enormous advantages from criminal acts perpetrated collectively. If successful, such acts enure to the benefit of all. When unsuccessful, appeal is made to the injustice of collective punishment. It is not the principle of collective liability to punishment that requires modification. What may be necessary is the adaptation of punishment in a way which removes the principal disadvantages of collective punishment. It must, so far as possible, avoid the infliction of physical suffering on the guilty and innocent alike. This means, in the first instance, the avoidance so far as possible of measures of physical force in which no discrimination is possible. This point of view found expression in 1921 when the Assembly of the League discussed the measures of economic blockade in pursuance of Article 16 and in the Resolution adopted on that matter which stressed the necessity of conducting the blockade in a manner minimizing the sufferings of the population. But it also means the adoption of the principle of international criminal responsibility of the individuals to whom liability for the criminal act can feasibly be traced. In this connection it may be pointed out that the idea of an International Criminal Court, one of the objects of which would be the ascertainment and punishment of individuals responsible for criminal acts of State, has not yet received the serious consideration which it merits. It has, so far, been discussed from the point of view of a court adjudicating on war crimes after the termination of a war. As such, it has been exposed to the easy

[1] *Papers*, p. 411.

DELICTUAL RELATIONS BETWEEN STATES

but not decisive objections based on the uncertainty of the laws of war and on the undesirability of making the war a subject of legal battles after the soldiers have made peace. But the idea of an international criminal court is much wider than the punishment of war crimes. It vitally affects the problem of individual responsibility for criminal violations of international law. There cannot be much hope for international law or morality if the individual acting as the organ of the State can, in violating international law, screen himself effectively behind the impersonal, metaphysical State; and if the State as such can avoid punitive responsibility by invoking the injustice of collective punishment.

Finally, the principle of punishment as distinct from reparation must, in a comparatively merciful form, find expression in the exaction of security against further breaches of the law. This is a constant theme with writers on international law, from Vattel to modern authors. Says Vattel:

> Enfin l'offensé est en droit de pourvoir à sa sûreté pour l'avenir, de punir l'offenseur, en lui infligeant une peine capable de la détourner dans la suite de pareils attentats et d'intimider ceux qui seroient tentés de l'imiter. Il peut même, suivant le besoin, mettre l'aggresseur hors d'état de nuire. Il use de son droit dans toutes ces mesures, qu'il prend avec raison; et s'il en résulte du mal pour celui qui l'a mis dans la nécessité d'en agir ainsi, celui-ci ne peut en accuser que sa propre injustice.[1]

Hall puts 'granting of security against the future commission of wrongful acts' on the same level as compensation for past wrongs; he approves of both.[2]

105. *The practice of tribunals*

When we look at international law as taught, practised and adjudicated we see clearly that the talk about the immunity of sovereign States from punishment is an empty gesture after all, covering very superficially a clear denial of international law and morality. International law, before and after the Covenant of the League and the General Treaty for the Renunciation of War, does recognize the liability of States to punishment. War was a weapon for changing and enforcing the law; its object was certainly not limited to reparation for a wrong committed. After 1928 it is still a weapon of punishment against the State which by breaking the Treaty has, in the terms of the Preamble, forfeited its benefits. The use of reprisals is limited by the requirement of proportionality. But this does not

---

[1] Book II, ch. IV, § 52.   [2] P. 381.

GENERAL RULES OF THE LAW OF PEACE

limit the admissibility of punishment as an element of reprisals; it merely limits its extent. The provisions of Article 16 of the Covenant of the League in the matter of so-called sanctions are a radical innovation inasmuch as they expressly lay down the right and obligation of repressive action against the Covenant-breaking State. Much energy has been spent in discussing whether these measures are merely intended as pressure applied in order to cause the delinquent State to desist from the unlawful conduct, or whether they are punishment proper. The discussion is somewhat academic. The views expressed by some of the draftsmen of the Covenant at the Peace Conference, e.g. by General Smuts, leave no doubt that sanctions were intended as an instrument of drastic retribution. Others are of a different opinion. It might be difficult to accept the view that the Covenant-breaker may escape all further liability and cause the cessation of the measures applied against him by terminating hostilities and withdrawing his troops regardless of the injury and expense caused by his action to the State directly affected and to other members of the League. The view that sanctions are merely preventive has also been used in support of the striking argument that, being no more than a means of rendering impossible or difficult a successful violation of the Covenant, they must be withdrawn as soon as the aggressor has temporarily achieved his unlawful purpose; for, it is maintained, to continue them after the unlawful object has been accomplished is to give them the character of punishment. This view, which in effect sets a premium on the energy and the ruthlessness of the aggressor, shows to what consequences that interpretation of the Covenant leads.

An analysis of the awards of international tribunals shows that there is in fact little authority for the view either, generally, that the State cannot be punished or, in particular, that punitive damages cannot be awarded against it. The case of *The Carthage*, in which the Permanent Court of Arbitration refused the demand of France that Italy should be condemned to pay a fine of one franc, is often cited in support of that view. But the award hardly justifies that conclusion. The Tribunal pointed out that

pour le cas où une Puissance aurait manqué à remplir ses obligations . . . vis-à-vis d'une autre Puissance, la constation de ce fait, surtout dans une sentence arbitrale, constitue déjà une sanction sérieuse

and that

cette sanction est renforcée, le cas échéant, par le paiement de dommages intérêts pour les pertes matérielles.

DELICTUAL RELATIONS BETWEEN STATES

And although the Tribunal was of the opinion that

l'introduction d'une autre sanction pécuniaire paraît être superflue et dépasser le but de la juridiction internationale

it qualified that statement by saying that this was so 'en thése générale' and that 'les circonstances de la cause présente ne sauraient motiver une telle sanction supplémentaire'.[1] A survey of awards in which the tribunals have refused punitive damages shows that in most of them the tribunal relied on the special terms of the convention conferring jurisdiction upon it for the assessment of damages for losses to private individuals. The Opinion of the Mixed Claims Commission between Germany and the United States in the *Lusitania* case, decided on 1 November 1923, brings out this point very clearly.[2] In fact, practically all tribunals concerned with claims for damages derive their jurisdiction from an arbitral convention which limits their activity to adjudicating upon claims for compensation. Compensation does not, as a rule, include punitive damages. In a system in which the jurisdiction of international tribunals is essentially voluntary, it can hardly be expected that they will interpret these clauses extensively.

Moreover, there are instances in the practice of States and tribunals in which there is a recognition of the right to moral reparation as distinguished from material restitution. But moral reparation contains a distinct element of punishment, the only difference being that with regard to punishment proper the reparation accrues for the benefit of the community and not of the injured party. As instances of such reparation for moral damage there may be mentioned the decision of the Council of the League in December 1925 consequent upon the frontier incident between Greece and Bulgaria. In that decision the Council awarded to Bulgaria the payment of ten million levas by Greece as reparation for material and moral damage, in addition to compensation for damage to moveable property. Again, in the Opinion of the Commissioners in the *I'm Alone* case, on 5 January 1935, the Commissioners recom-

[1] Scott, *Hague Reports*, 1, 560.

[2] *Annual Digest*, 2 (1923–4), Case no. 113. This aspect of the matter and the particular circumstances of the Treaty of Berlin, to which the Commission referred at length, would have been sufficient to justify an award of punitive damages. But the Commission obviously went too far in observing that 'it would be repugnant to the fundamental principles of international law that the Commission should treat as justiciable the question as to what penalty should be assessed against Germany as a punishment for her alleged wrong-doing'. See also the award of 30 June 1930 in the arbitration between Germany and Portugal, where the Tribunal refused to award punitive damages on the ground that, having regard to the Treaty of Versailles, it had jurisdiction to grant an indemnity only (*ibid.* 5 (1929–30), Case no. 126).

GENERAL RULES OF THE LAW OF PEACE

mended that the United States, in addition to formally acknow-ledging the illegality of its conduct and offering an apology to the Canadian Government, should pay to Canada the sum of $25,000 'as a material award in respect of the wrong'.[1]

The purely artificial character of the view denying the liability of sovereign States to punishment is shown by the long series of cases in which damages were awarded not as compensation for the injury received but as retribution for the inaction of the State in failing to punish the authors of the injurious act. Thus, for instance, damages have often been awarded to relatives of persons killed by criminals whom the State has failed to apprehend or to punish after they have been apprehended. It has been justly pointed out that in these cases no damage accrues to the relatives because of the failure to prosecute the criminal or to punish him effectively. Thus, in the *Janes* case decided on 16 November 1926 by the United States–Mexican Claims Commission, where damages were awarded for the failure of Mexico to apprehend the murderer of the husband of the claimant, the award stated that 'not only the individual grief of the claimants should be taken into account, but a *reasonable and sub-stantial redress should be made for the mistrust and lack of safety resulting from the government's attitude*'. As the last-mentioned consequences of non-apprehension do not in fact cause any damage to the claimants, it is clear that the award is in this respect of a general character. The position is identical in those numerous cases in which damages are awarded for denial of justice through the granting of an amnesty[2] or even the remission of a fine.[3]

It thus appears that there is no warrant for the assertion that international law does not admit punishment—as distinguished from reparation—of sovereign States. It would not be surprising if sove-reign States, after having taken a long time before submitting themselves to the rule of law, should be at pains to limit the effects of that submission. But it is doubtful whether Governments have put forward any such assertion before international tribunals. There is in any case no good reason why international lawyers should attempt to supply legal arguments in support of such an attitude. It is only by reference to a quasi-divine and mystical authority of a metaphysical State superior to both law and morals that any such

---

[1] *A.J.* 29 (1935), p. 331.

[2] See, e.g., the *West* case, decided on 21 July 1927 by the United States–Mexican Claims Commission (*Annual Digest*, 4 (1927–8), Case no. 143).

[3] See, e.g., the *Mallén* case, decided by the same Commission on 27 April 1927 (*ibid.* Case no. 144).

396

DELICTUAL RELATIONS BETWEEN STATES

claim to immunity can be supported. It can have no place in any system of law. It is of fundamental importance that the science of international law should clearly recognize this—not indeed in connection with the minor question of admissibility of punitive damages, but as a condition of the development of the law of State responsibility in accordance with legal and moral principles as generally accepted.

106. *Restrictions upon the admissibility of claims. Exhaustion of local remedies*

The inclination to limit the scope of State responsibility has manifested itself in the various restrictions upon the admissibility of international claims. It is proposed to illustrate this problem here in connection with the rule as to exhaustion of local remedies. It is a rule, often embodied in general arbitration agreements, which limits the admissibility of claims put forward by a State on behalf of its nationals. The injury complained of in such claims must previously have been the subject of adjudication not simply by one authority of the State, but by the final competent authority. The advantages of the rule are obvious. It prevents rash or abusive recourse to diplomatic or arbitral procedure in cases in which recourse to a higher competent authority might possibly have resulted in a reversal or punishment of the injurious act; it prevents the substitution of an international for the ordinary process of appeal; it makes it possible for the State to redress wrongs which are not the necessary result either of its legislation or of governmental acts. On the other hand, rigid insistence on the observance of the local remedies rule must often have the result of unduly postponing effective redress and of exposing the claimant to the considerable expense, which he may not be able to bear, of exhausting the best available remedy. These inconveniences are unavoidable and justifiable so long as the process of exhaustion of local remedies is not a mere formality offering to the plaintiff no chance of success. International arbitral activity has now circumscribed in a practical way the operation of the local remedies rule by laying down the principle that it is unnecessary to exhaust the legal remedies where there are no remedies to be exhausted. They have done this in a variety of ways. In the *Brown* case, decided in 1923 by the British–American Claims Tribunal, it was held that it was unnecessary to exhaust the legal remedies in cases in which the highest judicial organs were entirely subordinated to executive and legislative action

GENERAL RULES OF THE LAW OF PEACE

violative of international law.[1] In the award of Undén, Arbitrator, of 29 March 1933, in the arbitration between Greece and Bulgaria in the matter of Article 18 of the Treaty of Neuilly, another limitation of the rule of exhaustion of legal remedies was referred to. The Arbitrator stated there that the rule does not apply generally when the act complained of consists of measures taken by the Government or by a member of the Government in the performance of his official duties; the reason being that there are no real legal remedies against acts of that nature.[2] In the important arbitration between Great Britain and Finland decided on 9 May 1934, the question of the exhaustion of legal remedies constituted the sole issue. The decision goes a long way towards establishing the principle that the rule of exhaustion of local remedies does not apply, and that no appeal to a higher judicial authority is required, where, having regard to the law of the country, statutory or as established by decisions, substantive or adjective, there is no prospect of the appeal being successful. These examples show how arbitral activity succeeds in disregarding, in appropriate cases and in the interest of justice, a formal condition of admissibility of claims clearly established by conventions and practice. These exceptions engrafted upon the local remedies rule are an instructive example of judicial legislation. Its justification has never been seriously questioned by States. These exceptions to the local remedies rule gain in importance when we consider that, as the result of recent decisions, the so-called Calvo Clause—i.e. the clause in private contracts with foreign Governments containing a renunciation of diplomatic protection in matters arising out of the contract—has been in fact reduced to an undertaking to exhaust legal remedies. The rule as to exhaustion of legal remedies is a procedural limitation of State responsibility in deference both to reasons of convenience and to claims of sovereignty. Arbitral practice has consistently acted in the direction of not allowing the latter consideration to monopolize that procedural limitation in a manner which is obstructive of justice.

107. *Requirements of international liability. The requirement of fault*

We have been concerned so far with the limitations of State responsibility resulting from the claims of State sovereignty. It is now proposed to consider some of the limitations of State responsibility following upon the separation of the individual from the State and, in particular, upon the insistence on treating the State as a meta-

---

[1] *Annual Digest*, 2 (1923–4), Case no. 35.   [2] *A.J.* 28 (1934), 789.

DELICTUAL RELATIONS BETWEEN STATES

physical person divorced from the individuals who compose it and who act on its behalf. This latter aspect has expressed itself in the theory separating liability from fault and proclaiming the principle of absolute responsibility in international relations. It may be doubted whether that theory is in accordance with actual practice or with the requirements of international intercourse. Municipal law, it is true, recognizes in some cases the principle of absolute liability when justice requires that the loss should not lie where it falls. In English law, for instance, the owner of an animal *ferae naturae* is responsible, without further proof of guilt or of negligence, for damage caused by the animal even if he had no knowledge of its vicious propensities. This is only a specific application of the general rule of absolute responsibility as laid down in the well-known case of *Rylands* v. *Fletcher* to the effect that the person who brings on his land and keeps there anything likely to do damage if it escapes is bound at his peril to prevent its escape and is liable, even without negligence, for the damage which is the material and probable consequence of the escape.[1] Other systems of law recognize the same doctrine in a different form. But there is all the difference between occasionally admitting the principle of absolute liability and making it a rule. Moreover, even in cases in which the law imposes absolute liability, the responsibility is not entirely divorced from some act of volition of the person held liable. Liability is not imposed arbitrarily; it is imposed upon the person who has contributed to the harm in some way, however innocently. Similarly, the liability of the master for the acts of his servants arising out of their employment and in the course of it is an example of absolute liability. The master may be responsible even if he expressly forbade his servant to act in a certain way. But even here he forms a link, however remote and presumptive, in the chain of causation.

It is useful to turn to the example of the relation between master and servant for the reason that that analogy helps us in many ways to understand the responsibility of the State for the acts of its organs. This is, of course, the central aspect of the problem of State responsibility. The State acts in relation to other States through its servants —its Government, its officials, its courts, its armed forces. It bears therefore full responsibility for breaches of international law com-

---

[1] It is interesting to note the combination of the principle of absolute liability with the prohibition of abuse of rights. Thus Fletcher Moulton L.J. in *Wing* v. *L.G.O.* [1909] 2 K.B. 652, said that the principle of *Rylands* v. *Fletcher* applied in all cases 'where by excessive use of some private right a person has exposed his neighbour's property or person to danger'.

399

GENERAL RULES OF THE LAW OF PEACE

mitted by any of these. It does not matter whether the act or omission in question emanates from the Prime Minister or from a humble official in a remote village—except that in the former case the injury will be greater, more deliberate, and therefore entailing a higher and more pronounced degree of responsibility. But whoever may be connected with the injury, it is essential as a rule that there should be fault in these organs, that there should be intention to inflict an injury or negligence in preventing it. There is as a rule no absolute liability. It is only if this is clearly conceived that one may hope to understand the mass of judicial and arbitral decisions bearing on the matter.

If a claim is put forward on account of damage caused by rioters or bandits, the mere fact that effective protection has not been afforded is not enough to establish liability. The tribunal will enquire—and it has enquired in innumerable cases—whether the protection was adequate *having regard to the circumstances* so that its absence may be imputed to the guilty intention or negligence of the authorities. Thus, for instance, in the *Home Missionary Society* case[1] decided on 18 December 1920 by the British–American Claims Arbitral Tribunal, where the claimant Society suffered loss of property and life among its members as the result of a riot of the natives, the Tribunal held that the authorities showed no breach of good faith or negligence in suppressing the insurrection. Neither, in the view of the Tribunal, could responsibility be attached to the authorities on account of their having imposed a tax which led to the rebellion; there was no reason to assume that the imposition of the tax would be followed by a widespread revolt. The Tribunal refused to admit that it was for the State to bear the risk of such individuals. The Home Missionary Society took the risk involved in its work in a savage region.

---

[1] *Annual Digest*, 1 (1919–22), Case no. 118. And see the *Mead* case, decided on 29 October 1930 by the United States–Mexican Claims Commission (*ibid.* 5 (1929–30), Case no. 168) and other cases referred to in the Note thereto for an exposition of the principles relating to responsibility for failure to afford protection. And see *ibid.* Case no. 101, the *Laura A. Mecham* case, decided on 2 April 1929 by the same Commission, with regard to failure to apprehend a criminal. It was held that 'even though more efficacious measures might perhaps have been employed to apprehend the murderers . . . that is not the question, but rather whether what was done shows such a degree of negligence, defective administration of justice, or bad faith, that the procedure falls below the standards of international law'. This passage is worth recalling as showing clearly the element of fault as a prerequisite of State responsibility.

DELICTUAL RELATIONS BETWEEN STATES

108. *Absolute liability*

On the other hand, once there is proof forthcoming of fault on the part of the State organ—be it negligence or *dolus malus*—the State is responsible so long as the organ in question acts within the scope or in the course of its employment. The terms used are reminiscent of the law of master and servant but they express adequately the legal position. They show—and here enters a measure (but a measure only) of absolute responsibility—that, as in the law of master and servant, the State may be responsible if the injurious act in question is a wanton act in breach of the law of the State and not attributable to the State, but if that act is connected with the employment as an organ of the State and if it has been rendered possible only because the person in question was able to inflict the injury on account of his position as the organ of the State. Thus in the *Youmans* case[1] the Mexican Government was held liable for injurious acts of soldiers who had been called out to quell a riot but who actually joined the rioters and fired at the victims. The Tribunal held that a Government is responsible for wrongful acts of soldiers even when they are acting in disobedience of rules laid down by a superior authority, when it is clear that at the time of the commission of these acts the soldiers were on duty and under the immediate supervision of the commanding officer and in his presence. This responsibility of the State for the acts of its soldiers has even been extended so as to cover unlawful acts of soldiers when on leave[2] or, in special circumstances, when ashore in a foreign port which is temporarily not subject to a régime of civil or military control.[3] We have spoken of cases of this description as implying a measure—but only a measure—of absolute liability. It would not be accurate to regard them—as did the President of the French–Mexican Claims Commission in the *Jean-Baptiste Caire* case[4]—as a confirmation of the doctrine of 'responsabilité objective' as a general principle of international law in the matter of State responsiblity. That general principle is fault, not absolute or objective responsibility. It is true that in cases like unlawful acts of soldiers the unlawful intention cannot be attributed to the State directly, but there *is* unlawful

[1] Decided on 23 November 1926 by the United States–Mexican Claims Commission (*Annual Digest*, 3 (1925–6), Case no. 162).

[2] The *Bellon* case, decided by the French–Mexican Claims Commission on 18 June 1929 (*Annual Digest*, 5 (1929–30), Case no. 104).

[3] *The Zafiro*, decided by the British–American (1910) Claims Tribunal on 30 November 1925 (*Annual Digest*, 3 (1925–6), Case no. 161).

[4] *Annual Digest*, 5 (1929–30), Case no. 91, decided on 7 June 1929.

GENERAL RULES OF THE LAW OF PEACE

conduct on the part of its organs acting in the course of their employment and enabled so to act because of their employment. As the President himself said, in order to justify 'absolute responsibility' on the part of the State for the acts of its organs outside the scope of their competence 'it is necessary either that they should have acted, at least apparently, as authorised officers or that, in acting, they should have exercised powers or measures connected with their official character'. The State is, for instance, not responsible for damage done by its officers engaged in private target practice; purely personal acts of officials, not within the scope of their authority, do not engage the responsibility of the State.[1] Where the State is liable for unlawful acts of soldiers committed in violation of the law of the State, its responsibility is to a large extent absolute and independent of fault; but only 'to a large extent'. There must be fault with these organs; and there is some constructive fault of the State in having unreliable organs.

In any case this is not the typical phenomenon in the law of State responsibility; the typical phenomenon is that of organs acting (or failing to act) within the scope of their competence. Here fault is the decisive test. It is a rigid and exacting condition of responsibility in cases of alleged failure to act. But it is a workable test even in cases where there is a question of responsibility for the failure to enact legislation in conformity with international law. It is less rigid in cases of active, positive, interference with the established legal situation, e.g. with the person or property of aliens. Here the fault consists in the fact of interference not accompanied by the greatest possible care. Municipal law knows of many cases where persons act at their peril—to mention only, in English law, the acts of libel, or conversion, or trespass. No proof of negligence or intention to injure is required in such cases. There are exceptions—more apparent than real—to the basic requirement of fault as a condition of responsibility. That condition must remain the basis of State responsibility. It is certainly the foundation of the vast arbitral activity in the last twenty years. It imparts to this branch of the law not only a degree of reasonableness and elasticity but a distinct ethical element. The elimination of the element of fault is obnoxious because it fosters the conception of the State as an entity divorced from the state of mind of the individuals who compose it and the organs which act on its behalf. This, for reasons which have been adduced elsewere, must be regarded as a retrograde conception.

---

[1] The *L.B. Gordon* case, decided by the United States–Mexican Claims Commission on 8 October 1930 (*Annual Digest*, 5 (1929–30), Case no. 103).

DELICTUAL RELATIONS BETWEEN STATES

109. *Limitations upon responsibility for the acts of individuals. Subversive propaganda against foreign States*

We have now reached the stage where it is necessary to answer the question which may have crossed the minds of some who have attended these lectures. If, as suggested here, international duties are ultimately imposed upon individuals, then how is it possible that in many branches of international law there is a clear separation, in the matter of responsibility, between the duties of the State as such and those of individuals? There are clearly such branches of international law. Much of the law of neutrality is based on that principle. The neutral State may not sell to either belligerent munitions or men-of-war; it may not grant loans to the belligerents; and, generally, it may not withhold from one of them advantages which it grants to the other. But neutral individuals apparently may do all these things, subject, in some cases, to the consequences of a breach of the law of contraband and blockade. The same applies to the question—which is bound to remain topical for some time—of subversive activities and propaganda against foreign States.

The answer is that these branches of international law are really not in conflict with the view which has here been put forward on the ultimate destination of international duties. These duties are in all cases duties of individual human beings. But in the great majority of cases the duties are thus imposed upon individuals in their capacity as the organs of the State; it is only in exceptional cases that they are imposed upon individuals as such. In both categories of cases it is upon individuals that the duty rests; but it rests upon them in different capacities.

The important question of responsibility for subversive activity against foreign States illustrates this matter very lucidly. It is an established principle that it is a clear breach of international law for a Government to indulge in any such activity. Such conduct is in many ways indistinguishable from war; and it is aggravated by the fact that it takes place in time of peace. It approaches illegal intervention in its most crude, although indirect, form; it is a disguised interference with the internal relations of a foreign State; it is a denial of its independence.[1] It is a form of intervention so

---

[1] After the World War a number of treaties were concluded expressly stipulating for reciprocal duties of non-interference. Thus, e.g., the Trade Agreement between Great Britain and Soviet Russia of 6 March 1921 provided in its first article that 'each party refrains from hostile action or undertakings against the other and from conducting

GENERAL RULES OF THE LAW OF PEACE

obnoxious that many have doubted whether it is permissible even in time of war;[1] where practised in time of peace by diplomatic envoys it has been resented to the extent of making even a semblance of interference a reason for summarily terminating the diplomatic mission. The principle forbidding interference with internal relations has been interpreted, quite justly, so strictly as to make it highly improper for a Government to express criticism of the constitution or political régime of a foreign State. These restraints have, it is true, been abandoned to a large extent in Europe since the World War when heads of Governments and foreign ministers have become mouthpieces of wars of ideologies. But this phenomenon, far from seriously affecting the accepted principle of international law, merely shows the disquieting suspension, in this as in many other matters, of the normal operation of international law.

On the other hand, it is equally clearly established that such activities, when emanating from individuals in their private capacity, are lawful in the sense that international law does not prohibit them, and that they do not engage the responsibility of the State so long as it merely tolerates them without conniving at them and so long as it does not permit them to develop into organized hostile expeditions against foreign States or into preparation of common crimes like assassination, arson, or forgery. But apart from this, there is no duty to secure foreign Governments against hostile criticism or subversive propaganda and activities generally. The society of States is not a society for the mutual insurance of established Governments. Treason is not an international crime. An active enemy of the Government of his country is not an enemy of mankind. The principles of legitimacy as introduced by the Holy Alliance do not form part of international law although there exists a small number of treaties and municipal statutes which render unlawful subversive activities of private persons against foreign States. But, in general, the enlightened practice of States has rejected any such

outside its borders any official propaganda, direct or indirect, against the institutions of the British-Empire or the Russian Republics respectively' (Hertslet's *Commercial Treaties,* 30, p. 977). The Supreme Allied Council at Cannes in 1922 found it necessary to adopt the following resolution as one of the bases of the proposed Genoa Conference: 'Nations can claim no right to dictate to each other regarding the principles on which they are to regulate their system of ownership, internal economy and government': Cmd. 1821 (1922). It is obvious that such treaties and declarations are merely declaratory of existing rules of international law.

[1] When in 1803 and 1804 Great Britain engaged the services of several thousand French royalist refugees, France vigorously protested. In its answer the British Government merely asserted that belligerents have the right to take advantage of discontent already existing in countries with which they happen to be at war.

404

DELICTUAL RELATIONS BETWEEN STATES

conception of international duty. Writers at times use very general language in this matter, but there is really no rule of international law obliging a State to prevent within its territory all injury to a foreign State. Subject to the qualification referred to above, international law cannot reasonably impose upon States the duty to afford within their territory protection to a foreign constitutional régime which may be a matter of indifference to or clear disapproval by the overwhelming majority of their nationals.

The question of subversive activities and propaganda against foreign Governments is thus an instructive instance of the different scope of duties of individuals when acting in their private capacity and when acting as an organ of the State. As pointed out, there is in this phenomenon nothing contrary to the principle which underlies much of what is said in these lectures as to the ultimate subjects of international duties. But it is a phenomenon which may give rise to difficulties when the individuals acting on behalf of the State adopt the device of sheltering themselves behind private individuals and associations in order to act in a way in which international law prohibits them to act. This situation is likely to arise in cases in which the Government of a State becomes identified with a political ideology wedded to missionary zeal. This happened, for instance, in 1792 when the French National Convention passed, amidst scenes of enthusiasm, a decree promising assistance to all peoples struggling for their freedom.[1] It would be improper in these lectures to adduce instances taken from more modern history. It is for international law to devise means calculated to prevent Governments from abusing the immunity justly enjoyed by individuals in their private or even corporate capacity. The test must. to a large extent be artificial, but this does not mean that it is altogether useless and unworkable. The test is whether the private association in question is so closely associated with the Government and the State as to become indistinguishable from it. Most Governments rely for their support on political parties and associations. The majority in the legislative bodies supporting the Government is in fact determined by a decision of the party, as in practice the policy of the Government may be determined by a vote of the political organization supporting it. Is then the responsibility of the State engaged whenever such political associations indulge in subversive propaganda or

---

[1] It may be noted that a year later the Convention solemnly declared on behalf of the people of France that henceforth it would not interfere in any way with the Governments of other Powers.

GENERAL RULES OF THE LAW OF PEACE

activities against foreign Governments? The answer must be in the negative. Individuals when acting in association cannot be deprived of rights which they enjoy individually. On the other hand, it is clear that Governments cannot be permitted to use associations of individuals as instruments of action prohibited by international law. But there are three external tests which determine the responsibility of the Government for such acts of private associations: (1) The responsibility of the State is engaged if by the very Constitution of the State the political association in question forms part of its legislative or executive machinery. In such cases the association becomes part of the State. (2) Secondly, the State is liable if its organs—or, perhaps, only its leading organs—are at the same time members of the political association in question. This is not a case in which the law can properly distinguish between individual action in a public and in a private capacity. (3) Thirdly, the responsibility of the State is engaged if such political association is in receipt of financial or other assistance from the State. This is clearly a case in which, at least partially, the State, by making its own resources available, indirectly participates in action in which it is unlawful for it to engage directly.

110. *International boycott*

The same distinction between the duties of the individual and the duties of the State, as well as the tests of responsibility here suggested, apply to another aspect of State responsibility recently discussed, namely, the responsibility of the State for so-called boycott of goods from another State. The question was discussed in particular in connection with the dispute between China and Japan in 1931, when Japan put forward as one of the reasons for her action the alleged international delinquency of China consisting in tolerating or inciting the boycott of her goods. In dealing with that matter the Lytton Commission appointed by the Council of the League to enquire into the dispute observed that it was controversial from the point of view of international law whether 'the organized application of the boycott to the trade of one particular country is consistent with friendly relations or in conformity with treaty obligations'. The Commission thought it desirable that 'in the interest of all States, this problem should be considered at an early date and regulated by international agreement'. More urgent international questions intervened, and the matter has not so far come up for international discussion. Actually, the problem is not a difficult one if we rely on

406

DELICTUAL RELATIONS BETWEEN STATES

the principles suggested above. International law does not impose —and cannot effectively impose—upon a State the duty to compel its subjects to buy the goods of a foreign country. The proverb applies here that you can bring a horse to the water but you cannot make it drink. This being so, the State is under no duty to prevent its subjects from conducting boycott propaganda. On the other hand, the State as such may be under a duty to admit foreign merchandise on a footing of equality and not to place any obstacle in the way of its free entry. This is a duty usually stipulated in commercial treaties. In such case the State must not do *per alium* what it is not permitted to do *per se*. While it is not responsible for acts of private associations in general, its responsibility is engaged in the same circumstances in which it arises in the case of subversive propaganda. There is also an additional ground of responsibility, namely, when the State fails to enforce the criminal law of the country with regard to such acts of boycott as amount to a common crime, like acts of violence against persons disregarding the boycott or the burning of boycotted goods, even if the persons directly affected are its own nationals. However, so long as it is not so assisted by the State directly or indirectly, the conduct of individuals in the matter of boycott of goods does not become a source of State responsibility on account of the absence of prevention or repression. It is often the kind of weapon used by the population of politically weak States unable to protest effectively in a different way against conduct of foreign States deemed to be contrary to law or morality or both. It may be difficult to say that this is a case in which the separation of the duties of the organs of the State from those of other individuals within the State works in an unjust and reprehensible manner.

CHAPTER 12*

THE ORGANIZATION OF PEACE AND THE REVISION OF THE 'STATUS QUO'

111. *Revision of the* status quo *as a general problem of the international society*
The problem of the revision of customary and conventional international law is and is likely to remain for some time one of the outstanding problems in the sphere of international relations. It is one of the fundamental questions of international law in general. It is justly regarded by many as one of the crucial problems of the legal organization of peace. It has now irrevocably joined the trilogy of arbitration, disarmament, and collective security. This, we believe, justifies the, on the face of it, disproportionate amount of space which we propose to devote to what has been called 'the international problem of peaceful change'.[1]

This term covers a wide variety of subjects. In its natural, and we believe scientific, meaning, it seems to refer to the question of the existence in international society of institutions established to change the law, institutions analogous to or identical with those to be found in this field within the State. But the same term can be and is used as a term of generalization for changes and requests for changes of rights established by international law, such as are fixed by custom or by treaties. In particular, it is used most commonly as a convenient expression for the question of the revision of the Peace Treaties which put an end to the World War. This question cannot form the subject of these lectures. In so far as it raises legal issues of a permanent character the international problem of peaceful change must be treated separately from the topical subject of the revision of the Peace Treaties. In fact, it is the legal aspect—in its broadest sense—of the problem of peaceful change which best expresses the constant political importance of this problem. The question of peaceful change is much broader and more fundamental than the

---

* Only fragments of the original English version of this and the following chapter of this work have been found. Miss Maureen MacGlashan has, therefore, retranslated the whole of these two chapters from the French text which appears in the *Hague Recueil* and the surviving fragments of the original have been inserted at the appropriate places.

[1] The English expression 'peaceful change' has now almost been naturalized in the French language, but probably the term 'revision pacifique' includes the essential elements of that conception.

PEACE AND THE REVISION OF THE STATUS QUO

revision of the Peace Treaties terminating the War of 1914–1918. It will continue after these Treaties have been revised to the satisfaction of all the interested parties. Even if it should happen that this event comes about, one will still feel the same urgent need for a system of peaceful change, which the world did not possess in 1914, and the absence of which made change by war a legal and legitimate process.

It would be no more accurate to say that the problem of peaceful change affects only the territorial division of the world. Even if, to cite a more than improbable event, statesmen should succeed in sharing out the world in accordance with justice and reason, and if—to give only some examples—the present international legal situation concerning migration, customs tariffs and raw materials, were left intact, the problem of peaceful change would still remain important. For it is a problem which forms one of the fundamental questions of international law and probably of every legal system. Before 1928 (the date of the General Treaty for the Renunciation of War) the principal reason for which international law was denied the quality of law was not the absence of an international executive or judicial power, but the legal admissibility of war as a means of changing the law. The law was obliged to recognize war as an instrument of change because there was no institution permitting the peaceful adaptation of the law to new conditions. An institution of this nature is indispensable in relations between human beings and groups of human beings supposed to be governed by law. A legal system which does not include such institutions carries in itself the seed of its own destruction. It itself encourages violence. It becomes, in the long run, unjust and inapplicable in practice. These are obvious truths, proclaimed with eloquence in recent years by the protagonists of peaceful change.

Two other reasons add urgency to the problem of peaceful change and prevent us from identifying it with any specific request for particular change. The first is that after the World War the question of peaceful change constituted an obstacle to the recognition of the rule of law by the acceptance of duties of binding judicial settlement. When, in 1920, the Council of the League of Nations rejected the part of the draft for the Statute of the Permanent Court of International Justice giving the tribunal compulsory jurisdiction, Lord Balfour gave as one of the principal reasons for this attitude the fact that the Covenant contained no effective provision for peaceful change.[1] The following years saw in this

---

[1] *First Assembly, Plenary Session*, p. 148.

409

GENERAL RULES OF THE LAW OF PEACE

respect the new phenomenon of the virtual identification of international law with the Peace Treaties. The latter have been thought of as unjust and temporary, and all progress in the sphere of international judicial settlement has been considered with mistrust because, in the absence of any machinery for peaceful change, compulsory judicial settlement involves the perpetuation of the *status quo*. In the absence of effective machinery for securing modification of the existing legal situation, the rule of law has become synonymous with injustice.

The opponents of international progress found in this a powerful argument: they became the champions of justice against the oppression of the law. At the same time, they energetically rejected the suggestion that the solution of the difficulty should consist not in repudiating the rule of law, but in creating an effective machine permitting peaceful change. The only lesson which they have been prepared to draw from the dilemma was that a just war is preferable to an unjust peace, that we must grant others the right to make war to defend justice against a harmful *status quo*, and that we must be strong enough to overcome the defiance which may follow. When the question of the acceptance of the obligations of the Optional Clause was discussed in Great Britain, well-known international lawyers uttered warnings against too rapid an advance towards international progress in one direction while remaining stationary in others—that is to say, in the development of institutions for peaceful change. They feared lest, under a régime of compulsory judicial settlement and in the absence of organs of revision, international tribunals should find themselves in a situation where they would be forced to pronounce judgments rendered in conformity with the law but contrary to justice and inimical to international peace and progress. This attitude must be considered in part responsible for the fact that when, in 1930, the British Government signed the Optional Clause it did so only with various reservations which quite altered the avowed goal of the undertaking. Faced with the same problem, the draftsmen of the General Act for the Pacific Settlement of International Disputes tried, in 1928, to achieve the impossible by making the instrument a means both of applying and of changing the existing law. The result was a document deplorable from the point of view of both drafting and application.[1] At the same time,

---

[1] In Article 28 of the General Act, the Arbitral Tribunal on which is conferred compulsory jurisdiction to settle disputes other than those concerning 'their respective rights' (commonly called 'political' or 'non-justiciable' disputes), is empowered to settle these suits in accordance with the same rules of law that the Permanent Court of International

410

PEACE AND THE REVISION OF THE STATUS QUO

while there was no tendency to accept peaceful change as an institution with all that that implies, the determination to slow down the development of institutions applying the existing law has been much more pronounced. It is thus that there has come about an event quite frequent in a little-developed society, namely, the reduction of the general standard of behaviour to the lowest level of the acceptable minimum.

In the second place, a revolutionary event in the history of international law has emphasized the importance of the problem of peaceful change. This event was the signature, in 1928, of the General Treaty for the Renunciation of War. Prior to this Treaty, the system of international law, manifestly inconsistent on many questions, was at least coherent from one point of view: since it provided no institution for peaceful change, it authorized war as a means of changing the existing legal situation. Every State had the right, by entering formally into war and thereby risking its own existence, to change the *status quo* either by annihilating the defeated adversary or by dictating to him the terms of peace. The Treaty of 1928 prohibited war as a means either of applying the law or of modifying it. But it is clear that unless the institution of war, proscribed as a means of changing the law, is replaced by another instrument, the Treaty, far from becoming the point of departure for progress, may become a cause of illegality, by necessarily increasing the occasions for infringing the law.

Such are the reasons why it is not desirable to see the question of peaceful change reduced to the level of a particularly important but essentially transitory controversy about the revision of the Treaty of Versailles and the other Peace Treaties terminating the War of 1914–1918.

112. *The meaning of peaceful change as a legal institution*

What is revision of international law as an effective institution of international society? It is the acceptance by States of a legal duty

Justice is bound to apply by the terms of its Statute. Thus it comes about that a tribunal charged with the settlement of disputes which cannot be decided by law because, *ex hypothesi*, they are not disputes concerning legal rights, is eventually called upon to apply international law in pronouncing upon these disputes. The situation is rendered even more confused by the final provision of this Article, which provides that if there is no rule of law applicable to the case, the Tribunal can decide *ex aequo et bono*, that is to say, as a legislator. For it is fundamental that every dispute should be capable of being settled by a tribunal applying rules of law. It is not surprising that while some German authors interpreted this Article as empowering the Tribunal to act as a factor in the revision of the law, French jurists have considered it as expressly prohibiting the Tribunal from acting in this way.

to acquiesce in changes in the law decreed by a competent international organ. It is the existence of a legislature imposing, if necessary, its fiat upon the dissenting State. This, it is submitted, is the only correct meaning of peaceful change as an effective legal institution of the international society. Undoubtedly, peaceful change may be brought about, in individual cases, in various ways. Territorial changes have often been brought about by marriage settlement, testamentary disposition, gift, exchange, or sale. While the former modes of transfer have become obsolete with the disappearance of the patrimonial conception of the State, exchange or sale has been resorted to on occasion in the nineteenth and twentieth centuries.

With regard to treaties, the change may take place as the result of the denunciation of a treaty agreed to or tolerated by the other contracting party. It may be the product of agreement following upon negotiations, or mediation of a third party, or a recommendation of a commission of conciliation, or the efforts of the Council of the League. The Peace Treaties of 1919 have already been substantially revised by some of these methods. But all these are not instances of the working of a system of peaceful change as a legal institution. They are isolated instances of modification of the law. It is nothing short of a confusion of thought to speak of the institutional problem of peaceful change and to point to the isolated instances of international changes by agreement which have occurred in history. The real and abiding problem is: What can international law do in order to deal with a situation in which there is no such agreement? This and nothing else is the real problem of international peaceful change.

However, the definition here suggested is not the only possible meaning of the conception of peaceful revision of international law as a legal institution. It may be said that international law, so long as it is based on State sovereignty, cannot hope to provide for effective peaceful change by international legislation; that it may nevertheless provide machinery calculated to facilitate peaceful change by agreement as distinguished from overriding legislation; and that such machinery merits the name of an institution of peaceful change. It is not profitable to devote too much time to terminology, and there is nothing to prevent anyone from giving the name of an institution of peaceful change to machinery of conciliation, of negotiation or of conferences intended to help States to arrive at an agreement—just as there is nothing to prevent anyone from

PEACE AND THE REVISION OF THE STATUS QUO

referring to negotiation, conciliation and conferences as institutions for the pacific settlement of international disputes. But it must be realized that institutions in that form already exist, and that the real problem with which international society is confronted—the problem of peaceful change—is the fact that the existing institutions are, and within their scope must remain, inadequate. It is their very insufficiency which has created the problem of peaceful change. There is no likelihood of progress in this matter unless international lawyers and public opinion at large realize that fully and until the discussion bearing on this problem has been freed from irrelevant reference to cases in which change has been accomplished peacefully and by agreement. Neither is it profitable to insist that there is no absolutely effective means of ensuring peaceful change seeing that, after all, States may refuse to accept the binding pronouncement of the competent authority although they have previously agreed to accept it. By parity of reasoning one might oppose obligatory judicial settlement on the ground that after all States may break the arbitration treaty or disregard the arbitral award. On that line of reasoning all law is unnecessary, and anarchy is the preferable method.

The real problem—at least the legal problem—of peaceful change is not how to induce States by moral persuasion or by appeal to political expediency to give up existing rights with respect to a particular State. No more does it lie in the search for machinery designed to allow States to achieve more easily this frame of mind. It is to be found in the search for regular and constitutional means of achieving peaceful change, if need be without the consent of the State which does not wish to relinquish its rights. Here is the real question. This can only come about by means of binding legislation overriding the will of interested States. It is essential in these matters to use unambiguous language. Questions which touch on the international aspects of the sovereignty of the State and, in a general way, on international relations, easily lend themselves to artificially solemn language, in which the words serve rather to conceal than to reveal intention. Those who are familiar with the formulae of and the reservations to treaties of compulsory arbitration will appreciate this point. The same danger threatens the discussion of peaceful change. There are statesmen and lawyers who speak with eloquence of the absurdity of a legal system which contains no organic provision for the revision of the law: indeed, the situation is so utterly unsatisfactory that it makes eloquence easy. But, when

GENERAL RULES OF THE LAW OF PEACE

they find themselves faced with the inevitable consequences which the establishment of a system of peaceful change involves they recoil from them with horror and impatience. They realize, and with reason, that peaceful change, as an effective element of the constitution of international society, requires international legislation, not in the rather vague sense of multilateral treaties of a general character but in the sense of an external and imperative will. It is important, for reasons far more serious than mere pedantry, that we should be aware of the true implications of the demand for peaceful change as an effective international institution.

To appreciate this, it is necessary in turn to be fully conscious of the meaning of legislation in international society. In recent years the terminology used in this respect by some international lawyers has fallen prey to the confusion inherent in every use of metaphor. They have spoken of general international conventions as acts creative of law and as fulfilling in this quality the function of international legislation. However, it is possible and desirable to distinguish law-making treaties, treaties creative of law, from other treaties only on condition that we do not lose sight of the fact that this distinction is scientifically inaccurate. All treaties are creative of law in that they set down rules of conduct regulating the mutual relations of the parties.[1] But they are so in a way which is not fundamentally different from that in which a private contract fixes the law which the parties undertake to observe. In describing these treaties as international legislation, we must be aware of the fact that we are using this term in a specific and metaphoric sense, different from that generally accepted by legal usage. Nothing in the history or theory of legislation as a general conception of law justifies the view that it would be anything other than an attempt on the part of society to control the conduct of its members, without taking account of the dissent of any individual member.[2] There are obvious inconveniences in using a terminology which tends to create the impression that international society has reached an advanced stage of true legislation. It may be more exact to say that a political society, in its rudimentary form, can exist without legislation; but in the long run it is harmful to the cause of progress

---

[1] The remarkable monograph of Professor Scelle, entitled *Théorie juridique de la revision des traités* (1936), arrives indirectly at the same result. The learned author begins by regretting that the distinction between law-creating treaties and others has not been used in practice, but consideration of the question leads him to conclude that this distinction 'is a little oversimplified' (p. 41), that in practice every treaty creates law, and that this distinction can be disregarded from practically every point of view.

[2] See Akzin in *Iowa Law Review*, 21 (1936), 713–50.

PEACE AND THE REVISION OF THE STATUS QUO

to describe as legislation certain aspects of the creation of law which depend for their validity on the consent of the interested parties.[1]

113. *Peaceful change by agreement*

An effective legal institution of peaceful change may be said to exist when members of the community are bound to accept changes in the law decreed by a competent organ. But there is an intermediate stage between an effective institution of peaceful change in the form of international legislation and the entire absence of any such institution. That intermediate stage exists when States agree, as a matter of binding obligation, to a procedure offering a peaceful change, without promising to comply with the results of this procedure. They may undertake not to refuse to negotiate on a request for a revision of the law, either directly with the State which makes it, or with the assistance of a mediator or a commission of conciliation (including an organ empowered to conciliate, such as the Council of the League of Nations). They thus agree not to reject in advance every claim for change; they bind themselves to permit an enquiry as to the justice of the law on which existing rights are founded; and they agree to allow an impartial opinion, in the form of a non-binding recommendation, to be given on the substance of the case. Definitions being a matter of discretion, one can consider these obligations to engage in a procedure of peaceful change without being bound by the results as meriting the name of a legal institution for peaceful change. It may be more difficult to consider it as an effective legal institution for peaceful change. States can contract these obligations in several different ways.

(*a*) *The obligation to negotiate.* In the first place, the parties may, in a treaty dealing with some particular question, accept the obligation to consider requests for revision of that treaty. They may go further and agree that, if a party fails to respond to a request for negotiation leading to revision, or in the absence of agreement, the party which considers itself injured by the change of circumstances will have the right to denounce the treaty. In practice, all recent multilateral treaties of a technical or administrative character contain clauses providing for revision as well as details of the procedure for arriving at it. A growing number of bilateral treaties contain similar

[1] See however Hudson, *Legislation*, 1, xiii, and 5, viii, for a defence of the term 'international legislation' in this sense. See also Brierly, 'The Legislative Function in International Relations', in *Problems of Peace*, 5th series (1930), pp. 205–9. But see McNair in *Iowa Law Review*, 19 (1934), 178.

415

clauses.[1] In exceptional cases, e.g. in the Anglo-Egyptian Treaty of 1936, Governments have gone to the length of authorizing a third party, such as the Council of the League of Nations or an arbitral body, to effect the revision should they be unable to reach agreement.[2] Once they have done this, they have set up, for that particular purpose, an effective machine of peace through international legislation. The International Sugar Convention of May 1937 provides an interesting example of a combination of these methods.[3] It provides, in the first instance, for the obligation to negotiate in all cases of claims for the revision of the Convention; in the event of the failure of the negotiations, it provides for an award of arbitrators on the merits of the dispute; and in the event of the award not being accepted by the other parties, it grants to the State claiming revision the right to withdraw from the Convention.

(*b*) *Conciliation commissions.* In the second place, every State which is party to a treaty providing for conciliation procedure—and there are today several hundreds of these treaties—has the duty, in the absence of any contrary reservations, to submit to the enquiry, report and recommendation of the Conciliation Commission every claim for change, territorial or otherwise, of conventional or customary international law. As long as the Locarno Agreements of 1 December 1923 between Germany and France, Belgium, Poland and Czechoslovakia continued to exist in an indisputable manner, Germany could have submitted to a conciliation commission her demand against any one of these States for revision of the Treaty of Versailles. She would have been in a position to obtain a full public consideration of her claim in all its aspects; and she would have been able to obtain from the Conciliation Commission a reasoned decision on the justice—as opposed to the legal merits—of her demands. For it is the principal function of conciliation commissions to settle so-called political disputes, that is to say, those which do not concern respective legal rights. Disputes arising out of a claim for a revision of the law are a typical, if not the only, example of disputes of this kind.

(*c*) *Conciliation by the League of Nations.* Finally, in the Covenant of the League of Nations, the Members of the League have undertaken

---

[1] See Wilson in *American Political Science Review*, 28 (1934), 901; Engel, *Les Clauses de revision dans les traités internationaux multilatéraux* (1937). See also Oppenheim, 1 (5th ed. 1937), 742, 743. [2] Treaty Series, no. 6 (1937), Cmd. 5360, Art. 15. [3] Misc. no. 3 (1937), Cmd. 5461.

PEACE AND THE REVISION OF THE STATUS QUO

to allow the Council or the Assembly to examine all questions within the competence of the League or which concern international peace. These questions include requests for the revision of existing international law. The League may be seised of these requests under several articles of the Covenant: primarily under Article 19, but also under Articles 3, 4 and 11, in so far as these requests concern world peace or constitute a threat of war. It may also act under Article 15 in relation to the settlement of disputes likely to lead to a rupture. In the dispute between China and Japan on the subject of Manchuria, the Assembly, in adopting the Lytton Report, recommended, in fact, a solution which involved profound changes in the legal *status quo*. The Council was about to make such recommendations in the Italo-Abyssinian dispute, but events rendered that function superfluous.

114. *The effectiveness of peaceful change by agreement*

It appears from the foregoing survey that there is an abundance of machinery for peaceful change by agreement through negotiation and conciliation. There is practically no State which is not bound by some obligation or other to agree to such machinery being set in motion. Accordingly, those who dwell at length on this particular form of peaceful change render themselves open to the criticism that they either ask for something which already exists or that they do not appreciate the essential inadequacy of that machinery. It is that inadequacy which constitutes the problem of peaceful change. For, lest we fail to see the wood for the trees, it must be remembered that no such recommendation either of a conciliation commission or of the Council or Assembly of the League is, subject to the obligations of Article 15, in any way binding. Whatever may be its moral force, one can brush such a recommendation aside without violating any legal duty. Conciliation is a procedure designed to help States to achieve peaceful change—*if they desire it*. It is not a legally effective institution for peaceful change, in the same way that it is not, in general, a legally effective institution for the settlement of disputes. This last circumstance helps to explain why, despite the existence of several hundreds of treaties requiring the setting up in advance of commissions of conciliation, one cannot quote a single example of States invoking this procedure.[1] It would be a mistake to exaggerate

---

[1] It is almost pathetic to find a note, inserted by the translator of Van Vollenhoven (*The Law of Peace* (1936), p. 196), which points out that there has been a case of settlement by conciliation by a Belgo-Luxembourg commission. The translator gives no reference to this exceptional case.

GENERAL RULES OF THE LAW OF PEACE

the possibilities of the Council of the League of Nations in this direction. The Council is a useful organ for achieving agreement when the interested parties wish to reach one, or at least when they understand that their intransigence would be of little advantage to them. But there is no driving power of extraordinary value, moral or otherwise, in the functioning or atmosphere of the Council. Indeed, the movement for the establishment of a non-political machine for conciliation, which was born in 1919 and which was responsible for the decision of the Third Assembly in 1922 recommending in effect the decentralization of the machinery of conciliation,[1] stemmed largely from the opinion that the political atmosphere of the Council was not always suitable for the impartial consideration of complaints. The Council was justly praised for its rôle in the settlement of international disputes. But, save in the case of a weak State, confronted by one of the powerful Members of the League there has been no example of the Council managing to persuade one of the adversaries to renounce its rights. This being so, it is a step backwards for lawyers to begin by insisting on the fundamental need for institutions for peaceful change and to conclude by pointing to the Council of the League as the principal instrument for achieving change.[2]

It is equally unconvincing to exaggerate the influence of public opinion in this matter. History has shown that public opinion may be insufficient as an effective force, even in cases where the law, ethics and humanity have been jointly and indisputably outraged. It is possible that, in relations between States, the practically unanimous disapproval of the other Members of the Community has not the same influence as in relations between individuals. The individual who finds himself without a defender feels isolated and disposed to admit that after all there must be something morally defective in his conduct or in his insistence upon formal rights. It is not necessarily the same for nations. Their delegates may feel themselves isolated in a conference, but the nation as such does not. Its solidarity is strengthened and its appreciation of the justice of its cause, far from being weakened by outside disapproval, draws increased strength from its reaction against persecution and outside hypocrisy. So it is when outside public opinion pronounces its verdict against a State which claims rights lawfully enjoyed by

[1] *Third Assembly, Plenary Session*, 1, 196, 201.
[2] See, for example, Fischer Williams, *International Peace and International Change* (1932), pp. 1–3, 64–74.

418

PEACE AND THE REVISION OF THE STATUS QUO

another. It is even more so when the decision is taken against a State which is asked to renounce its own valid legal right.

The limitations of conferences, negotiation and conciliation in the scheme of peaceful change are obvious when one compares these techniques with the more comprehensive remedy in the shape of international legislation. This does not mean that the student of international law or international relations is at liberty to neglect them. The limited possibilities inherent in their persuasive action must be studied and used. It would, in particular, be advantageous to examine the methods both by which the Council of the League can profit from the vast Secretariat machinery for research and collation, and by which revision clauses in treaties, or the procedure of revision, can be perfected. But, in doing this, care must be taken not to treat the imperfect palliative as constituting a solution of the problem. In so far as the existence of means for peaceful change—and the discussions of which they are the subject—has the effect of masking their fundamental insufficiency, they constitute a danger. For they hide the fact that the true problem of international law and of international society is to provide means of peaceful change in default of agreement. The situation is, from many points of view, analogous to the question of pacific settlement of international disputes in general. There again, the existence of a considerable number of treaties of conciliation has obscured the fact that while conciliation is, in theory, useful and desirable, the numerous existing instruments often reveal themselves as a source of confusion by creating the impression—not only amongst laymen, but also amongst lawyers—that States are already bound by effective obligations of pacific settlement.

115. *International tribunals and peaceful change*

Courts are primarily and fundamentally instruments for applying the law and not for changing it. But they may become instruments of change in two ways. In the first instance, there are occasions on which courts may and must, consistently with their judicial functions, take account of a change of circumstances, as much affecting the parties as society in general. Secondly, the parties may expressly confer on tribunals the power to change the law.

Consideration of changed conditions as an element of the judicial function

(a) *Jurisprudence and judicial legislation.* In the first place, the question arises of the possibility of adapting the law to new conditions by

419

GENERAL RULES OF THE LAW OF PEACE

the continuous, though scarcely perceptible, action of judicial organs. Within the State, tribunals not only apply the law, but discreetly develop it by moulding the existing principles to meet social needs. One might therefore expect that these possibilities could play a useful rôle in international relations. However, in considering the analogy of judicial legislation within the State, the fact must be constantly borne in mind that radical changes in the law—changes involving a profound interference with existing rights —have only rarely, if ever, been achieved by means of judicial legislation. In addition to express judicial legislation the law finds itself in a constant state of development, in a manner amounting to change or extension, by the less visible process of judicial creation of the law in the course of deciding cases. This process is a feature generally to be found in all legal systems, whether or not they formally recognize the doctrine of judicial precedent. It differs from judicial legislation properly so-called both in form and in substance. It completes the law without modifying the existing rules in a formal and deliberate manner (though such may be in many cases the real effect of the decided cases).

In the international sphere, the possibilities of these two aspects of judicial activity are clearly limited, because their intensity—of judicial legislation and continuous jurisprudence—is in direct proportion to the powers of jurisdiction of judicial tribunals. Within the State, these are practically unlimited; in the international sphere, they are narrowly circumscribed. International tribunals have, in principle, no compulsory jurisdiction; in general all international jurisdiction is voluntary, although it is given the name of compulsory jurisdiction when it has been accepted in advance. Even in this case, it follows from the multiplicity of reservations that it remains precarious and subject to controversy. (Indeed, one of the first objects in peaceful international change would be to modify the existing rule of international law according to which, in the absence of agreement, no State is obliged to settle by judicial means its disputes with other States.) The Permanent Court of International Justice has often given bold decisions approaching judicial legislation, as, for example, in the Advisory Opinion concerning the *Danzig Railway Officials*, which asserted the principle that individuals can, if the parties wish, acquire rights directly under the terms of a treaty;[1] or as in the Advisory Opinion concerning the *Interpretation of the Treaty of Lausanne (Frontier between Turkey and Iraq)*, where the

[1] *P.C.I.J.* Series B, no. 15.

PEACE AND THE REVISION OF THE STATUS QUO

Court went so far as to introduce the principle *nemo judex in re sua* as an element in the interpretation of the Covenant.[1] But judicial courage cannot effectively attack the sort of established rights which are a source of friction and, as such, a proper object for normal legislative change. The very precariousness of the powers of jurisdiction of international tribunals imposes on the latter a special duty and an obligation of restraint in this respect. Legislation cannot be made to enter by the back door, by transforming the nature of the judicial function. On the other hand, the relative rarity of arbitral and judicial decisions prevents international tribunals from bringing about slow and imperceptible changes in the law by filling the lacunae which arise from divergencies of practice and the absence of express rules.[2]

(*b*) *The doctrine of* rebus sic stantibus. The powers of tribunals to modify the law by the application of the doctrine of *rebus sic stantibus* are similarly limited. According to this doctrine, a vital change of circumstances fundamentally affecting the intention of the treaty as it had been understood by the two parties is a valid ground for liberation from or nullification of the treaty. There are several reasons for the limited application of this doctrine as an instrument of peaceful change. First, it applies only to treaties: it does not touch those danger points of international life which are not based on the express provisions of treaties. Secondly, there can be no doubt that it is not applicable to so-called 'executed' treaties, such as those providing for a transfer of territory which has effectively taken place, in such a way that there no longer remains anything to be done by one or other of the parties (unless, of course, we accept the audacious theory according to which a transfer of territory is, in fact, a transfer of rights of jurisdiction which operates *de die ad diem*, that is to say, an agreement by which the ceding State binds itself no longer to exercise the powers of jurisdiction which it previously had exercised—in which case there is no difficulty in conceiving of a transfer of territory as an executory treaty). Thirdly, as long as the doctrine of *rebus sic stantibus* is considered, not as an excuse for affirming the independence of the State vis-à-vis international law, but as a legal doctrine functioning in a manner analogous to the doctrine of frustration, or of impossibility of

[1] *P.C.I.J.* Series B, no. 12, pp. 29–31.
[2] See Lauterpacht, *The Function of Law*, pp. 70–135, for a study of the way in which international tribunals in practice fill lacunae in international law.

421

GENERAL RULES OF THE LAW OF PEACE

execution, the limits of its operation are severely circumscribed, even as far as executory treaties are concerned. This explains why, in practice, in every case in which they have found themselves faced with an appeal to the doctrine of *rebus sic stantibus*, international and quasi-international tribunals have refused to apply it, not because they declined to recognize the doctrine as a principle of law, but because they considered that the case was not in fact covered by the legal principle invoked by one of the parties.[1] Fourthly, the majority of executory treaties concluded in recent years contain denunciation clauses which allow Contracting Parties to put an end to them at relatively short notice. Moreover, this broad power of denunciation finds itself still further enlarged, in a growing number of treaties, as a consequence of the right given to the parties to suspend the execution of the treaty or to put an end to it in certain specified cases, including that of a change of conditions. Finally, the fact that the compulsory jurisdiction of international tribunals has not yet become a generally accepted rule of international law makes it difficult in practice to apply the principle of *rebus sic stantibus* as a legal doctrine. It would seem, in consequence, that its influence as a means of change is severely limited. This is so because, in addition to the reasons which we have just given, this doctrine is not a means for changing the law. Its aim is to give effect to the true goal of the law, as it was agreed by the parties at the time of the conclusion of the treaty.

(c) *The prohibition of abuse of rights.* It would not be right to place too much emphasis on the possibility of judicial application of the principle forbidding the abuse of rights as an element of peaceful change. This principle constitutes, in a large measure, the basis of the law in the matter of civil responsibility, particularly that relating to 'nuisance' in England, in America, and in the corresponding branches of the law of other systems. It renders illegal the exercise of rights in a manner incompatible with the object for which the rights have been conferred or the social needs of a developing community.[2] It gives legal sanction to the principle *sic utere tuo ut alienum non laedas*, and rejects the view contained in the contrary maxim: *qui utitur jure suo alterum non laedit*. In international arbitration, the arbitrators have relied on this principle to discourage the arbitrary expulsion of aliens or the closure of ports to foreign ships without reasonable notice. The Permanent Court of International

---

[1] See above, p. 356.   [2] See above, p. 383.

422

PEACE AND THE REVISION OF THE STATUS QUO

Justice has given expression to it, in *obiter dicta*, in a number of cases.[1] One might legitimately refer to it to prevent a State granting (or withdrawing) nationality in a way incompatible with the rights of other States.[2] In general, it could render useful service in every case where international law gives discretionary powers to States who act as trustees of the international community, as, for example, on the question of recognition of States and Governments.[3] States who exercise this power in an arbitrary manner, as an exclusive instrument of a selfish national policy, are obviously guilty of an abuse of right. If there existed an international judicial power functioning regularly and endowed with a full jurisdiction, it would likewise be possible legitimately to apply the doctrine of abuse of rights to questions such as those of damage emanating from the territory of a State, of an arbitrary application of freedom of action on the high seas, or of sovereignty in the air.[4] It would be possible, perhaps, to brand as illegal the insistence of a State on the principle of the freedom of the seas in the neighbourhood of the territorial waters of another State and in circumstances harmful to that State, or, perhaps more doubtfully, it might treat as an abuse of right the inflexible assertion by a State of its absolute sovereignty over the column of air which rises above its territory. This last example brings out strongly the possible rôle of the prohibition of abuse of rights in the field of peaceful change through the channel of judicial activity. This rôle consists in treating as illegal the assertion of rights the exercise of which was in origin purely theoretical and not inconvenient, but which has since become harmful as being opposed to new social developments. However, there are limits to the doctrine of abuse of rights. It is not a normal means of peaceful change. For example, it could not, contrary to the opinion persuasively expressed by an Italian writer in 1934, be applied to a State which 'abuses its rights' by neglecting to develop territory placed under its sovereignty.[5] In any case its application, even in its limited sphere, depends on the good will of States to confer

---

[1] *Certain German Interests in Polish Upper Silesia* (*P.C.I.J.* Series A, no. 7, p. 30); *The Free Zones of Gex and Geneva* (Series A, no. 24, p. 12, and Series A/B, no. 46, p. 167).

[2] See Article 1 of the Hague Convention of 1930 on Certain Questions relating to the Conflict of Laws of Nationality and the *procès-verbal* of the First Committee of the Conference, relating to this article (pp. 20 and 197). See also Rundstein in *Z.V.* 16 (1931), 41–5.

[3] In these cases, international law confers on States the discretionary power to decide whether or not certain conditions of independence exist in a body claiming recognition. There is an abuse of rights every time that this power is exercised in an arbitrary manner and not by reference to principle. See above, p. 320.   [4] See above, p. 381.

[5] See Salvioli in *Hague Recueil*, 46 (1933) (iv), 56–69.

423

GENERAL RULES OF THE LAW OF PEACE

upon international tribunals powers of jurisdiction more permanent and less restricted than those which they enjoy today.

It would seem, from our examination of the topics of judicial legislation, the doctrine of *rebus sic stantibus* and the prohibition of abuse of rights, that international judicial and arbitral organs cannot legitimately play a decisive rôle in the process of peaceful change. Their principal aim is to apply the law, not to modify it. On the other hand, there are some cases in which they may act in this sense both legitimately and usefully. If their rôle in this capacity is almost insignificant when one compares it with the effectiveness of the solution contained in compulsory international legislation, it is not quite the same if one looks at it in the perspective of existing international organization. For these reasons the possible use of arbitral and judicial bodies as instruments of peaceful change is a worthy subject for research and more detailed study.

116. *Grant of legislative powers to judicial tribunals*

In delivering decisions involving judicial legislation or applying the doctrine of *rebus sic stantibus* or the prohibition of abuse of rights, international tribunals do not change the law, they apply it, while taking account of new conditions. 'Peaceful change' on their part is, in these cases, indirect and almost fortuitous. But there are cases in which they may openly modify the law by a decision which binds the parties; there are occasions when they are able, properly speaking, to act as legislators. They may do so when the States expressly invite them to fulfil this function. This can come about in two ways:

(*a*) *Grant of legislative powers for a given dispute.* States may, by a special agreement, give a tribunal the power to settle a dispute in accordance, not with the existing law, but with what the tribunal thinks that law ought to be. In a few cases, States have asked a tribunal to act in this way. They may ask it to determine their mutual relations on a new basis by taking into account a change of circumstances which has come about. The last paragraph of Article 38 of the Statute of the Permanent Court of International Justice empowers that Court to decide cases *ex aequo et bono* if the parties agree. We have here a function which, although coming within the competence of the Court by virtue of its Statute, does not come within the framework of its normal competence. For this reason, only a clear and indisputable authorization will suffice to induce the Tribunal

424

PEACE AND THE REVISION OF THE STATUS QUO

to fulfil this function. This was not the case in the *Free Zones* dispute between France and Switzerland,[1] where the *compromis*, while apparently giving the Court competence to settle the dispute in all its aspects, left it in doubt whether the parties really had the intention of empowering the Court not to take account of the legal situation as it found it. But there is no reason to suppose, as some do, that the Tribunal considers itself free to refuse to exercise a jurisdiction which the parties have clearly conferred on it, and which it is empowered to exercise by virtue of its Statute. However, the exercise of legislative functions at the request of the parties to a given dispute does not constitute, on analysis, an example of peaceful change as a legal institution. It comes rather within the framework, studied above, of peaceful change by consent, the only difference being that the parties, instead of themselves fixing the details of the new system, charge the Court with that task.

No more is there 'peaceful change' as the result of the effective functioning of a legal institution when the parties ask the tribunal, after it has laid down the legal principles, to recommend a future system more appropriate, in its opinion, to the objective needs of the situation. This is what Great Britain and the United States did in 1893, when they submitted to arbitration the *Behring Sea Fur Seals* dispute. They adopted the same procedure in 1910 in the case of the *North Atlantic Coast Fisheries* arbitration. These are not, as we have said, examples of peaceful change by means of international legislation as a matter of legal obligation, but they are interesting in that they show how international tribunals can help the parties, provided that the latter have agreed in a particular case to ask the forum to act in this way.

(*b*) *Grant of legislative powers in general.* The situation is quite different when States agree in advance, for their future disputes, to confer on a tribunal legislative powers in respect of every request for revision of the existing law. It is thus that a certain number of treaties, modelled on the Italo-Swiss Treaty of 19 September 1924, provide for the compulsory jurisdiction of the Permanent Court of International Justice in disputes which are not of a 'legal nature'. The exact nature of such disputes is not, and doubtless cannot be, clearly indicated, but they probably include disputes which arise on the subject of requests for revision of the existing law. The Court has power to settle these differences *ex aequo et bono*, that is to say, without

[1] *P.C.I.J.* Series A/B, no. 46.

425

GENERAL RULES OF THE LAW OF PEACE

taking into account existing law. Other treaties stipulate that the function of settling in a compulsory manner disputes of this nature shall be exercised *ex aequo et bono* but by an arbitral tribunal. The principal treaty in this developing category is the Treaty concluded in 1926 between Belgium and Sweden. Finally, other treaties contain identical provisions, with the sole difference that the arbitral tribunal is expressly required to act as *amiable compositeur* in settling the case. All these treaties confer on the Permanent Court of International Justice or on an arbitral tribunal compulsory competence to act as legislator, without taking account of existing law. The consequences of such a compulsory jurisdiction are truly formidable. There is not, as in the case of the sovereign legislature, any limit to its powers of creating or revising the law. Such a jurisdiction implies: the grant to a tribunal of the right to remove territories from one State in order to give them to another; the right to impose on a State a defined policy on the subject of customs tariffs or migration—in fact, the competence to settle and to limit every one of the undisputed rights which a State possesses in international law. There is here an immeasurably greater risk than in the case of the grant to a tribunal of competence to apply the existing law. In this last case, a State, without any doubt, hands over its interests to a tribunal from whose decisions there is in general no appeal. But there is an enormous difference between the powers of a tribunal applying the existing law and bound to observe it, and the powers of a body which is not bound by any rule beyond its own notions of the law, of justice and of equity. Indeed, these treaties correspond so closely with a possible renunciation of rights that one wonders if they mean exactly what they say.[1] One will notice equally that these treaties have not once been invoked or applied as a means of peaceful change. They have been concluded, moreover, only by States between whom no serious conflicts of interests have arisen or are likely to arise. Following these reflections one may wonder if peaceful international change by the grant of compulsory legislative powers to international tribunals is a means of progress both desirable and of practicable application. The question is not of knowing if the judges are capable and competent to act in this

---

[1] See, for example, Habicht, *Le Pouvoir du juge international de rendre une décision* 'ex aequo et bono' (1935), pp. 29–43. Dr Habicht cites, amongst others, the judgment—mentioned above—of the Permanent Court of International Justice in the *Free Zones* case, as an argument in favour of the thesis that in the case of a controversy over the question of jurisdiction, the Court will undertake not to change existing rights. However, the judgment of the Court must be interpreted in the light of the circumstances of that case; it does not apply to cases where there is an undisputed right of jurisdiction.

PEACE AND THE REVISION OF THE STATUS QUO

way. They are certainly as competent to fulfil this function as ordinary legislators. They can, if necessary, have the assistance of experts. Judges within the State are often called upon to settle the interests and to lay down the administrative details of future relations between the parties. But in the international sphere it cannot be good for the administration of international justice that tribunals should be given a regular competence in this matter. *De legende ferenda*, it is difficult to advise Governments (or to expect them to follow such advice) to entrust to a majority within a judicial or arbitral body composed of a small number of members the burden of taking decisions outside the control of the law on questions of vital interests. Until now States have not been willing to grant to tribunals the right to exercise so unlimited a jurisdiction within the framework of the existing law.

However, that said, there remains the problem of the procedure which ought regularly to be followed by States which wish—as long as there is no international legislative organ—to provide between themselves for the compulsory settlement of requests for revision of the law. The situation would be less difficult if there were a larger number of States in this category. They would then be able to form among themselves a sort of international legislature on a regional basis. But as far as bilateral agreements are concerned the choice of a compulsory machine of peaceful change must be exercised between the judicial or political organs of the State—with all the disadvantages which must follow—and the general political organs, such as the Council of the League of Nations.

CHAPTER 13

THE ORGANIZATION OF PEACE AND THE REVISION OF THE 'STATUS QUO'
(concluded)

117. Article 19 of the Covenant and international legislation

What we have said above provides us with some guidelines in the study of the question of the place and the possibilities of Article 19 of the Covenant in the revision of international law. In its present form, this Article relates to the institution of peaceful change by agreement. At the same time it contains, as a result of the position which it occupies in the Covenant, distinct possibilities which lead towards the only effective solution of the problem of the revision of international law, to wit, compulsory international legislation. It is as well to recall the terms of Article 19: 'The Assembly may from time to time advise the reconsideration by Members of the League of treaties which have become inapplicable and the consideration of international conditions whose continuance might endanger the peace of the world.'

Although it has sometimes been doubted,[1] this Article is sufficiently broad to cover all requests for revision of a *status quo* existing by virtue of a treaty or any other situation. The 'reconsideration of treaties' includes all executory treaties which a State claims have become inapplicable by reason of the doctrine of *rebus sic stantibus* or in any other way. (The application of the doctrine of *rebus sic stantibus*, being a question of law, relates above all to the competence of a judicial or arbitral tribunal, but since, according to the Covenant, such tribunals have no compulsory jurisdiction, there is no reason for excluding the doctrine of *rebus sic stantibus* from the textually unlimited scope of Article 19. Above all, the function of the Assembly, in the words of Article 19, is not judicial but political. The principal aim of Article 19 is to modify the law, not to apply it.)

'Inapplicable' does not mean only 'physically impossible', which would in any case be a ground for automatic extinction of the treaty, in accordance with the general principles of law relating to physical impossibility of execution. The term applies to treaties

---

[1] See, for example, the article by Mr Gathorne Hardy in *International Affairs*, 14 (1935), 813 *et seq.* See also Wright in *A.S. Proc.* (1936), pp. 65–73.

PEACE AND THE REVISION OF THE STATUS QUO

whose continued execution ceases to be possible for reasons of equity as distinct from law, or whose execution either is incompatible with supervening changes in the law and in international relations or is even objectively[1] considered dangerous for the peace of the world. There should be no particular obstacles to the inclusion of territorial clauses in this description, especially if we think of the cession of territory in terms of acts of continued jurisdiction, positive or negative or, as is more convincing, if we remember—as the history of the drafting of Article 19 shows—that authors had in view above all questions of territorial change. Be that as it may, requests for territorial modification enter clearly into the second part of Article 19, which relates to the consideration of situations whose continuance might endanger the peace of the world. Situations created by the existing territorial *status quo* enter into this category.

118. *The possibilities of Article 19*

It is somewhat difficult to understand the narrowness of the interpretation of the formal scope of Article 19 reflected in the attempts made to withdraw certain categories from its field of application. For, after all, the Assembly, acting in accordance with this Article, has no compulsory powers. It can only recommend consideration or reconsideration, and even its recommendation seems to cover in law less the contents of the new agreement than the merits of the old. Is this why Article 19 has not been invoked in practice? It is generally believed that its application has been 'sabotaged' by States with vested interests. That is only partially true. The fact is that—with the sole exception of the request presented in 1921 by Peru and Bolivia for the revision of their treaties of peace with Chile dated 1883 and 1904, a request which was properly found to be out of order in the form in which it was made—that Article has never been relied upon by the Assembly. China invoked it in 1925 with regard to her request for the revision of her treaties—on extraterritoriality and similar matters. The Assembly, without pronouncing on the substance of the claim, drew attention to the fact that a conference of the interested Powers was about to take place in China, and expressed the hope that a satisfactory solution of the problem might be found. In 1929 China proposed the appointment of a committee to examine the means of making Article 19 more effective than it had theretofore been. The Assembly did not consider it necessary

---

[1] This means that a simple threat of violence on the part of the State asking for revision cannot by itself justify the application of Article 19.

429

GENERAL RULES OF THE LAW OF PEACE

to appoint such a committee but instead recorded a vote which, in fact, constituted a general invitation to every interested Member of the League to initiate—on the responsibility of the Council—the procedure provided by Article 19. Neither China nor any other State took advantage of the opportunity thus afforded to them. Again, we may ask, for what reason did States refrain from making use of the available procedures?

It is true that statesmen of several nations have from time to time given discouraging warnings on the subject of requests for territorial change. The representatives of the Little Entente used to speak of requests for territorial change as artificially creating danger points, all consideration of which was foreign to the spirit of Article 19.[1] After the Four Power Agreement of 1933, France gave her allies the formal assurance that in her view absolute unanimity, including the votes of the interested Parties, was necessary to give legal force to a vote expressed in accordance with Article 19. But in opposition to these discouraging declarations one might cite frequent professions of governmental faith, beginning with the official British Commentary on the Covenant. The present scope of this Article is obviously limited, but the fact of having had recourse to it ought not in any way to have weakened the position of States asking for a revision of the law. Such recourse should have helped to develop the procedure provided for and to make a reality of it within the institution of the League of Nations. An affirmative opinion, given by a substantial majority, whatever its legal effect, could only have strengthened the moral and political situation of the State seeking change. Quite apart from the content of the recommendation and the problem of its binding character, every interested State could, by invoking Article 19, raise before the Assembly for discussion a claim for revision. And no one could have prevented it from doing so. Nor is there any doubt that a simple majority of the Assembly would suffice, in terms of Article 5 of the Covenant, for the appointment of a committee charged with an investigation and the production of a report. In fact, all the usefulness which one might legitimately have hoped for from Article 19 disappeared as soon as it was shown that force and unilateral change were possible within the League framework and that their reward was neither punishment nor repression, but success—which proves the close link that exists between peaceful change and collective security. Of this we will speak later.[2]

[1] See the Declaration of the Permanent Council of the Little Entente of 30 May 1933; *Documents*, 1933, p. 262.   [2] See below, pp. 440 *et seq.*

430

PEACE AND THE REVISION OF THE STATUS QUO

Despite its shortcomings as an effective instrument of peaceful change, Article 19 constitutes the first deliberate attempt to create an institution for peaceful change within the framework of a general system of legal organization of the world. It is the first act which provides for the periodic revision of the international *status quo* as one of the tasks of the organized international community: 'The Assembly may from time to time advise . . .'[1] Revision of the law thus becomes a duty and a legitimate aim of the League as a whole, independently even of the initiative of the States directly interested. According to other articles of the Covenant, the League may legally consider the merits of claims for revision, particularly when these form the subject of disputes endangering the peace of the world. In terms of Article 19, the process of revision of the law constitutes as such one of the functions of the League of Nations. There would have been nothing incompatible with the Covenant in the League of Nations setting up permanent bodies for consultation and study to help it in its task. It is instructive to notice that as yet there does not exist in the complicated organization of the Secretariat, any administrative or departmental machine intended to concern itself with requests, actual or potential, for the application of Article 19. When we contrast this fact with the abundance and the detail of the studies and enquiries of which other aspects of the activity of the League of Nations have the benefit, it is difficult to understand why no similar apparatus has been set up in respect of one of the vital needs of international society.

Further, although a recommendation of the Assembly is not binding, there is in it an element of particular importance. It contains a clear opinion to the effect that the existing situation is not satisfactory; that it is possible and necessary to remedy it; and that legal measures are objectively justifiable. It would be unwise to say that this opinion is completely without legal effect—although it is difficult to say in what this effect consists. If the opinion is expressed on the question of an executory treaty and if the interested State refuses to comply with it, it is possible for the other interested Party to invoke it in law as objective and irrefutable proof of the existence of good grounds for unilateral denunciation of the treaty, on the basis of the doctrine *rebus sic stantibus*, provided that the other legal conditions permitting the invocation of this doctrine are present. As far as other treaties and situations are concerned, the opinion does not

---

[1] The English version probably expresses in a more precise manner the desired regularity of the revision than the French words 'de temps à autre'.

431

GENERAL RULES OF THE LAW OF PEACE

affect in law the guarantee of the territorial integrity of the State against which it has been given and which refuses to comply with it. But it is a case where one can truly say that the formal validity of an obligation is stretched until it is made to give way before a moral impossibility.[1]

To what extent has the incorporation in the Covenant of Article 19 in its present form been able to promote the cause of international progress? That must remain a matter of opinion. One can argue that Article 19 has not been relied upon because legal recourse to this article offers only a doubtful chance of success; that it does not correspond with the needs of a society whose principal object is to achieve peace and international security; and that its very existence in the Covenant has tended to obscure the need for the only real solution, which lies in the creation of compulsory and legally effective machinery for peaceful change by way of international legislation. On the other hand, it is impossible to reject the point of view that, if it were suitably invoked, this Article would reveal itself as a means of adjustment and change; that it may still fulfil this function in the future; and that it constitutes a necessary transition towards a more advanced stage (assuming that such a stage is desirable). There is much to be said in favour of this point of view. There is certainly room for a more detailed study of the possibilities of the procedure of Article 19 and its connection with other articles of the Covenant than has yet been undertaken. But, if the efforts made in this direction are one day to bear fruit, it can only be on condition that they are closely linked with the only real solution, which is international legislation properly so called.

119. *Peaceful change. International legislation and the world State*

Whatever may be the merits or defects of Article 19, this article cannot, if one wishes to give the words their true meaning, be considered as that legal institution for effective peaceful change which in recent years has been added to the trinity of disarmament, arbitration and security as an indispensable condition of international progress. Such an institution is equivalent to international legislation,

---

[1] See below, p. 440, on the proposals which were made in 1919. The goal aimed at in refusing the guarantee would probably not be achieved by incorporating the opinion expressed pursuant to Article 19 in a subsequent recommendation made under Article 15, with the result that the State which accepts the recommendation might legally have the right to undertake hostilities against the State which refused to accept it. There is nothing in the Covenant which suspends or weakens the guarantee in such a case. It is noteworthy that Article 15 of the unratified Protocol of Geneva of September 1924 provided that 'having regard to Article 10 of the Covenant, neither the territorial integrity nor the political independence of an aggressor State will in any case be affected as a result of the application of the sanctions mentioned in the present protocol'.

432

PEACE AND THE REVISION OF THE STATUS QUO

that is to say, to a process of peaceful change of the law for which the consent of the interested State is not indispensable. But international legislation, in its primary and non-metaphorical sense, is the work of an international legislature. An international legislature is the organ of a supra-national authority, which can be described variously and with sufficient exactitude as a world State, a super-State, or a world federation. These words and their consequences can be sufficiently frightening or unpopular to induce the rejection of the solution implied by peaceful change as a dynamic and effective organ of international law. If we think that, then we must put a brake on our praise of peaceful change as an institution of international society without which there can be no lasting rational attempt to construct security and international peace on a durable basis. But the consequences of the rejection of peaceful change as an effective legal institution are so serious that it is as well to make sure that we are rejecting it for scientific reasons, that is to say, for reasons other than those usually advanced against the idea of a so-called world State. An alternative—more scientific—method consists in firmly adopting the view that no progress is possible in relations between States without an organic arrangement providing for the revision of the law; in taking, therefore, the principle of supra-national legislation as the point of departure in the consideration of this question and in seeking to discover on what conditions and within what limits this principle can reasonably claim a chance of being accepted by States.

We must understand clearly the profoundly radical character of such a solution. We can admit that international legislation established with a view to securing peace is not the same, either in fact or in intention, as an international government or an administration replacing the normal activities of the independent national State. We can admit that the function of this international legislation would be mainly preventive and corrective and that one would not be able to ask it to assume responsibility for the general progress of peoples and individuals. In short, we can console ourselves by realizing that, as a result of the great diversity of peoples who make up international society, international legislation, like international law in general, is necessarily limited to the narrow category of matters of common interest. It is so because law, in general, must normally limit its effect to matters capable of general regulation.[1]

[1] One can mention here the interesting observations of Professor Brierly in *N.T.* (1936), p. 9, where he seems to have arrived at the same conclusion but apparently by

GENERAL RULES OF THE LAW OF PEACE

120. *The competence of an international legislature*

But, despite all, it none the less remains clear that international legislation, thus circumscribed, would still be almost broad enough to escape the definition. For it would be wrong to suppose that its competence would be limited to territorial questions, a competence by itself of formidable extent when we consider that the territory of the Member States of the American Union cannot be ceded without their consent. It is possible that in order to reduce the need for this jurisdiction concerning territory, the most extensive of all and the object of a mysterious attachment, the competence of the international legislature should extend to questions such as migration, customs tariffs and raw materials—questions in which, for example, the members of that other league of nations, the British Commonwealth, enjoy complete freedom of action in their mutual relations. And as these questions are intimately tied to conditions of work and wages, the régime—at present voluntary—resulting from various conventions concluded under the auspices of the International Labour Organisation would become an integral part of the machinery of international legislation. The close link between these questions and international peace emerges clearly from the first lines of the Preamble to Part XIII of the Treaty of Versailles, concerning the International Labour Organisation: 'Whereas the League of Nations has for its object the establishment of universal peace, and such a peace can be established only if it is based upon social justice'.

In order to escape or reduce the need for territorial change—a remedy which often creates as many problems as it solves[1]—international legislation, as an instrument for peaceful change, must necessarily make provision for the rights of minorities, economic servitudes, rights of passage, the use of ports, etc. From all these points of view international legislation can, instead of being a means of peace, become a fertile source of wars, in the same way that within a State draconian legislation can, and occasionally does, lead to civil war.

the opposite reasoning. He points out that, since the number of persons of international law, that is to say, States, is very small, and that since the individuality of each such person plays, as a result, a more important rôle than is the case within the State, international legislation, by adopting general principles equally applicable to all, is strictly limited. See also Schindler in *Hague Recueil*, 46 (1933) (iv), 265.

[1] See, for a lucid account of this aspect of the question, Professor Mitrany's article in *International Affairs*, 14 (1935), 831–5.

434

PEACE AND THE REVISION OF THE STATUS QUO

121. *Gradual development towards an international legislature. The principle of unanimity*

But once we have candidly faced all that is implied by a corrective and preventive international legislation, we may observe ways of progress and adjustment which make this radical reform less revolutionary and more acceptable than the first reaction of surprise would suggest. Indeed, it is an essential condition for the scientific examination of the question of the State known as the 'super-State' —that ultimate and inevitable problem of peaceful change and international relations in general—that it should not be dealt with under the influence of the mental image of its logical and final transformation into a centralized State, endowed with and making use of all the attributes of sovereignty as a result of the total abolition of the sovereignty and independence of its component States. We have here a mental image conjured up by those who think it their duty to defend the historical and cultural values of the national State against the international and cosmopolitan Leviathan. We have here also the point of view of those who, taking as a basis what they believe to be the brutal facts of reality, are tempted, as an advantage in argument, to compare this ultimate result in all its rigid perfection with the degenerate state of the world as it is today. It is doubtful whether this apparently realistic and logical point of view can claim any scientific value. In strict logic, the abyss is deep which separates the sovereignty of the national State from the sovereignty of the international legislature. In actual fact, it is not difficult to conceive the difference which separates them as a matter of degree and of gradual transition. From many points of view there already exist the rudiments of a supra-national power. In pure legal theory, the super-State in law exists in a large degree, even today, by virtue of the fact of the binding character of international law independently of the will of States. With regard to the apparently revolutionary innovation of international legislation overruling the sovereignty of States, the transition and compromise may consist in making the exercise of those binding powers depend upon certain defined conditions and certain guarantees. The science of law and international relations, instead of associating itself with the superficially realistic condemnation of 'utopian plans', can legitimately contribute to the elaboration of such conditions and guarantees. Of what will they consist?

In the first place it is at the same time in keeping with both the

435

GENERAL RULES OF THE LAW OF PEACE

principle and the realities of the sovereignty of the State that the essential rights of States give way only before the overwhelming impact of justice and necessity such as is expressed in the practically unanimous vote of the other members of the community. The question of the degree of this unanimity alone is a subject for study and discussion. Excellent reasons might be advanced in support of the thesis that one sort of qualified majority (for example, of four-fifths) would answer the needs of the situation better than another (for example, three-quarters). Or, as Sir Arthur Salter has recently suggested,[1] it might be advantageous to combine the unanimous vote of the Council with a qualified majority of the Assembly. As the Assembly can, at any time, modify the composition of the Council, this plan would be sufficient to avoid the possibility of obstruction by one or several Members of the Council. (This plan, as we shall notice, follows in several details the one actually adopted in Article 26 relating to the amendment of the Covenant. This Article contains some elements of binding legislation, given that non-assenting States are bound by the amendments if they decide to remain within the League.) The sovereignty of States would thus continue to be a factor of considerable reality, since a State would be constrained to abandon a right only by an overwhelming majority of the other States. But it would cease to be the absolutely decisive force, obstructive and elementary, entrenching itself within a sovereign irresponsibility against the judgment of organized humanity.

122. *The doctrine of State equality*

It is sufficient to mention the method of voting to reveal the cloven hoof of the doctrine of the equality of States. It should be clear that no progress such as we have just been considering is possible while the abstract principle of the equality of States continues to apply. An organized international society striving to resolve the problem of peaceful change by true legislation, will have to lower the political and legal standards of the degree of representation in the vote, in the same way that it has reduced the size of the share of the financial contributions to the International Postal Union and the League of Nations. To cite an example, when the Covenant was drafted Switzerland proposed that the decisions of the Assembly should be taken by a majority of three-quarters of the Members, representing at least three-quarters of the total population of the

---

[1] *The Future of the League of Nations* (1936), p. 20. (Reprint from a series of discussions which took place at the Royal Institute of International Affairs, Chatham House, London.)

PEACE AND THE REVISION OF THE STATUS QUO

Members of the League of Nations, a solution which would have taken account, if not of all the relevant factors, at least of the most important of them. Abstract equality is possible—and perhaps desirable—so long as there exists no international organization in which the small States see, in exchange for the abandonment of a formal right, a substantial increase in their security and their real independence.[1] This consideration forms the basis of the formal renunciation of the principle of equality in the composition of the Council of the League of Nations. What remains in the Covenant of the doctrine of equality has revealed itself in practice as less embarrassing than might otherwise have been the case. This is due, in large part, to the sense of responsibility which the small States have shown. But the principal reason why the doctrine of equality, as incorporated in the Constitution of the League, has shown itself relatively unembarrassing stems from the fact that the League has not, by its Constitution, been in a position to give binding decisions on important points. If one gave the League wider powers, their exercise, in the long run, would be incompatible with the existing equality of representation and vote. It is for politics, the science of ethics and international policy to draw up generally applicable rules of representation to replace the mechanical and fundamentally immoral principle of equality. It is doubtless a difficult task—though not more difficult than that which confronts philosophers, experts in political science and economists in the corresponding domain of the science of individual rights, needs and values. But it is a task whose solution as a political and scientific duty must be attempted; it must not be evaded by the simple method of insisting on the absurd practical results of equality based on the area of territory or the sum of population.

Every serious study of peaceful change as an institution of international society must, in a large measure, consist in a detailed and systematic study of the possibilities, the methods and the procedure of compulsory international legislation, and in particular in an

[1] This has been clearly recognized by Professor Huber, the distinguished Swiss international jurist, who wrote, before the World War, that 'an association of States empowered to command and to compel must possess a form of organization corresponding to the relative strength of its Members', and that 'in entering into such an association the weakest members of the community will be compensated for the loss of equality by an increase of security in the enjoyment of their rights' (quoted by Rappard in *American Political Science Quarterly*, 1934, p. 544). It is in this sense that President Wilson refers to the Covenant 'as the first serious and systematic attempt to place the nations of the world on a footing of equality amongst themselves in their international relations', while insisting at the same time on the fact 'that the principal physical burden of the League rests upon the Great Powers' (Hunter Miller, *The Drafting of the Covenant*, 1, 463).

GENERAL RULES OF THE LAW OF PEACE

examination of the question of unanimity and equality. Such a study can be usefully assisted by an investigation into the functioning of the rule of unanimity and equality of States, not only in the League of Nations but in other institutions of international government, such as international river commissions and administrative bodies of international technical unions.

123. *An international legislature and international realism*

The practical and enduring nature of the solutions implied by an effective international legislature should not be calculated by reference to the immediate past or to what one believes to be the prospects of the immediate future. These offer no permanent standard for rational thought or action. The distance which separates the Covenant as drafted from the creation of a real international legislature is smaller than the gulf which separates the political reality of 1919 from that of 1937. In the draft for the Covenant prepared by Colonel House on 16 July 1918 it was in fact proposed to give the League power to decide territorial changes by a three-quarters majority. President Wilson adopted this proposal in his own draft for the Covenant. The same provision appeared again in substance in President Wilson's two subsequent drafts dated 10 and 20 January 1919. In the so-called 'Cecil-Miller' draft of 27 January 1919 the refusal to comply with a territorial change was to be followed by a withdrawal of the guarantee of territorial integrity. This series of drafts is significant in that it shows that the idea characterizing these consecutive proposals was not the sudden inspiration of an idealist, but represented the well-established opinion of practical men of affairs. When in February and March 1930 a Committee of the League of Nations, composed of representatives of States, discussed the proposal to modify the Covenant in order to make it harmonize with the Kellogg-Briand Pact, the suggestion was put forward of giving binding force to recommendations made under Article 15. But as the Council, in making its recommendation, is not bound by existing law, the adoption of the proposal would have given it legislative powers. The Committee considered 'that a report which was unanimously adopted had so great an authority that it ought to prevail over the individual will of States'. Similar possibilities are inherent in the proposals made in 1936 by a certain number of States tending towards the abandonment of the rule of unanimity imposed by Article 11.[1]

---

[1] Doc. A.31, 1936, VII; Doc. C.376, M.247, 1936, VII, pp. 17, 18.

438

PEACE AND THE REVISION OF THE STATUS QUO

It is in this indirect and somewhat inconspicuous manner that a binding international legislature, if it ever sees the light of day, will become an institution of positive international law. It will not appear by the direct adoption, *eo nomine*, of the Constitution of a world State. This emerges from the way in which Professor Oppenheim, a well-known international jurist, arrived at what is, in fact, a super-State. He insisted constantly, in his treatise, that there was not and never would be an international authority overruling sovereign States. But, in discussing the merits and demerits of the League of Nations, he considered that the fact that participation in the League was voluntary and that the Members have the right to leave the League was a real defect, but one capable of being overcome. He insisted on the fact that 'a recalcitrant Member ought, in case of need, to be forced to submit to the decisions of the League'. A society endowed with such an authority would clearly constitute a world State.

Likewise, questions whose consideration was at one time regarded by States as an intolerable intrusion on their sovereignty have been later considered, by those same States, as a propitious subject for international discussion. The attitude of Canada in this respect is particularly instructive. When in 1920 the Council of the League of Nations adopted a resolution asking the economic section of the Economic and Financial Committee to study the difficulties experienced by certain countries in obtaining necessary raw materials the Canadian delegates at the Assembly criticized this decision on the ground that the question of raw materials was one of 'domestic jurisdiction'. One of them expressed the opinion that the Council's resolution created a new doctrine which permitted international interference in the free disposal of the natural wealth of various nations. But in June 1936 the Canadian Prime Minister declared to the Canadian House of Commons that the League of Nations could constitute an appropriate tribunal for the discussion of economic grievances. 'We should', he said, 'examine closely and seriously what common international action could do to eliminate the sources of political conflict, of the economic insecurity, which are largely responsible for national rivalries and the threat of war.'[1]

Similarly, scholars and statesmen who approach these problems in a constructive spirit have no need to be frightened by the argument or the reproach that an international legislature, as a means of peaceful change, implies a world State. They are not obliged to

[1] *Debates of the House of Commons*, 1936, col. 3872.

439

GENERAL RULES OF THE LAW OF PEACE

employ a term so badly interpreted and misused; they may prefer, and with reason, to confine themselves to the immediate problem. But, if they are attacked on the real logical consequences of an international legislature, they must recognize that, in so far as the term 'super-State' has a scientific meaning, an international legislature is a constituent part of it. If they are jurists they need not attach excessive importance to the banal argument that a world federation would put an end to international law, by transforming it into the constitutional law of the world State. It would not necessarily be so: the change which would result would be above all a question of terminology. In any case, if that result is desirable from other points of view, the formal disappearance of the science of international law would be a matter of indifference.

124. *An international legislature and the sovereignty of States*

On the other hand, one must not underestimate the difficulties presented by international legislation as a solution of the problem of peaceful change. We have already cited several examples of these above. In addition to the wide, almost unlimited, power of an international legislature over questions constituting enormous encroachments on the sovereignty of States, an international legislature, an institution of peaceful change, raises even graver problems. But for peaceful change, carried out by means of international legislation, to be effective, it must be accompanied by a sanction, whether in the form of direct compulsion or, as was proposed in 1919, of indirect pressure by the withdrawal of the guarantee of territorial integrity. Thus an international legislature, as an instrument of change, implies either an international executive power or—in the case of withdrawal of the guarantee—an indirect encouragement to war or the licence to make war, a licence of which in fact only a powerful State can make use.[1]

All things considered, peaceful change, even by means of international legislation, must necessarily remain precarious and artificial unless it is incorporated in a system of collective repression of illegal war. In its absence, States wishing to bring about modifications in the law will naturally prefer to run the risk of a vast, implacable

[1] These results of the withdrawal of the guarantee cannot be considered as a decisive objection; see the discussion by Sir Arthur Salter, *loc. cit.* The fact that a reasonable and beneficial rule cannot be used equally by all members of the community is not a sufficient reason for condemning it or for passing it by. In any case, the guarantee would be weakened actually and morally, if not legally, as a result of the refusal to comply with the decision ordering the change.

440

PEACE AND THE REVISION OF THE STATUS QUO

change of which they themselves are the authors, rather than to entrust to the international community the task of modifying the *status quo* on an equitable basis. An international system of peaceful change thus runs the risk of being impracticable if it is not made an integral part of a comprehensive political organization of humanity.

These links between collective security and peaceful change are so close that, while some recommend the postponement of the establishment of a system of collective security and arbitration until there has been real progress on the question of peaceful change, others think that even the existing provisions for peaceful change, such as Article 19 of the Covenant, cannot be applied as long as no effective system of security has been organized. Thus, what can be called the problem of parallelism in international organization finds itself posed anew in an acute form. Must the different factors of international progress advance *pari passu* in order to be effective? Or is it permissible, and preferable, to advance in the directions offering the least resistance? If the view prevails that progress must be simultaneous and parallel in all directions, it will have the effect of retarding indefinitely all progress. For parallelism presupposes a show of initiative and a real and deliberate authority; but that is the crown of progress, and not the point of departure. The process must be founded rather on generosity and political courage, allied to foresight, preparing the way for progressive developments in other fields. There are matters in which progress can be made by accepting obligations which do not involve immediate risks for the vital interests of a State, even if the other contracting parties render themselves guilty of a breach of their obligations. Life is often less logically interdependent than dialectic would have us believe.

It is possible—some say probable—that the obstacles which beset the way towards an institution for peaceful change worthy of that name in international relations are insurmountable. Were we obliged to conclude that it is so, or if we thought that such progress were not desirable, we might still hope to see States from time to time changing the law and renouncing their rights out of respect for principles of ethics and moral wisdom. We could continue to study and to develop international procedures in order to help them to cultivate that state of mind. But—and this is not the least of the lessons which will be drawn from their course—we ought not in this case to continue to speak of peaceful change as a legal institution necessary and indispensable to the international community. Otherwise, we risk acquiring the habit, which some may consider pharisaic

441

GENERAL RULES OF THE LAW OF PEACE

and which certainly leads to confusion, of commending certain measures of international progress as desirable and practical, while making them depend on conditions which we maintain to be impossible of achievement. It is not sufficient, to overcome the difficulty, to use *ad hoc* legal terminology or a legal theory subject to controversy, which create the impression or are intended to support the view that international legislation is already a fact.[1] We do not advance matters further by underestimating the disadvantages of this lack of real international legislation or by having pointed out the limits and even the dangers of legislation within the State.[2] For these limits and dangers, recognized and real though they are, are negligible when compared with the benefits and the indispensable nature of legislation functioning in a normal way.

It is not our function as jurists to reply to the question whether the obstacles outlined above are insurmountable, and whether or not the conditions necessary for the establishment of international legislation as an effective institution for peaceful change can be achieved. From the point of view of ethics and politics, we are not at liberty to regard international legislation in its true sense as a solution impossible of achievement. It may not be compatible with the dignity of human life to act on any other assumption than that reason and order will triumph, not only in the end, but in the course of our own lifetime. As far as international law is concerned, we believe that effective machinery for peaceful change by binding legislation is an essential element for its transformation from a rudimentary law existing between primitive communities into a real law such as men in civilized society adopt. Meanwhile, international law can assist the cause of the scientific study of the problem of peaceful change—by drawing attention to its paramount importance in the plan of international organization, in contrast to the transitory political controversies of the moment, by trying to clarify the meaning of the terms used and to secure appreciation of their implications; by studying the operation and possibilities of the existing machinery of international justice, such as customary or conventional international law, as an agent of change of the *status quo*; and by relating these factors to what we believe to be the true

[1] See above, p. 414, on the use of 'international legislation' to designate international conventions of a general character. See also Scelle, *La théorie juridique de la revision des traités* (1936), for an account of the view that, since an international society exists, and since it is impossible to conceive of an international society without legislation, the existence of international legislation must be assumed as a fact.

[2] See Brierly in *Problems of Peace*, 5th series (1930), pp. 205–9.

442

PEACE AND THE REVISION OF THE STATUS QUO

—and with time inevitable—solution of the problem of peaceful change.

This solution, as we have not ceased to point out, is international legislation in its proper sense as opposed to its metaphorical sense. Such legislation corresponds with the restriction of the sovereignty of the State in one of its vital aspects. In fact, the right of States to reject any change brought about in international law without reference to their own consent forms the principal example of their sovereignty. So far as the latter shows itself in the doctrine of the equality of States, it has already been modified by the pre-eminence of the Great Powers, provided for in the Covenant of the League of Nations, and by similar developments. Another manifestation of the sovereignty of the State still remains, namely, the principle that States, in the absence of any contrary agreement, are not bound to confer jurisdiction upon a tribunal to settle their conflicts with other States. However, in practice this principle finds itself modified to a certain extent by the acceptance of various obligations of judicial settlement. But in the domain of absolute freedom from all binding legislation the sovereignty of the State still has the status of an absolute legal rule.

In recent years criticism of the sovereignty of the State as a characteristic trait of international law has abated. In the years which followed the World War, this criticism spread to the point of becoming almost popular, and of being applied without discrimination. To a certain extent that has sapped its strength. Secondly, it has produced in international institutions, which one thinks of as potential brakes on the sovereignty of the State, a continuous and visible retrogression. Thirdly, there has arisen the development of the omnipotent power of the State, directly as a political ideology in certain countries, indirectly and by necessity in others. All these factors have contributed to the restoration of the power, if not the prestige, of the sovereignty of the State as a source and creator of law.

These, however, are not reasons why the science of international law should cease to emphasize the essential incompatibility which exists between international law, conceived as a true system of law, and the assertion of the sovereignty of the State in its traditional manifestations. The transformation of international law into a system meriting its place in jurisprudence is not a matter of pure form. It is a conscious and deliberate development, tending to submit the sovereignty of States not only to the binding force of obligations

GENERAL RULES OF THE LAW OF PEACE

which they have voluntarily assumed, but to the larger and even more fundamental social duty of accepting and observing the law as it has been modified by the will of the community, expressed objectively and in conformity with justice and progress. Certainly, international law is, and must remain, a law of independent, autonomous States. But the international lawyer can presume to know enough of the essence of international life to affirm that it is on the reality of this progress towards the submission of the State to a moral and legal force superior to itself that the independence and the very existence of the sovereign State finally depends.

III

SURVEY OF INTERNATIONAL LAW IN RELATION TO THE WORK OF CODIFICATION OF THE INTERNATIONAL LAW COMMISSION

EDITOR'S NOTE

This Survey is reprinted from United Nations document A/CN.4/1/Rev. 1, 10 February 1949 (United Nations Publication, 1948.V.1 (1)). It was prepared in 1948 at the request of Mr Yuen-li Liang, the Director of the Codification Division of the Office of Legal Affairs of the United Nations, as part of the preparatory work within the purview of Article 18, paragraph 1, of the Statute of the International Law Commission. Although the document does not bear Lauterpacht's name as author the fact that it was his work was soon recognized, and it was later publicly attributed to him by Mr Liang at the 535th meeting of the International Law Commission on 9 May 1960 (see *Yearbook of the International Law Commission*, 1960, I, p. 52).

The permission given on behalf of the Secretary-General of the United Nations to reprint this memorandum is gratefully acknowledged.

CONTENTS

	page
INTRODUCTION	449
PART I. THE FUNCTION OF THE COMMISSION AND THE SELECTION OF TOPICS FOR CODIFICATION	450
PART 2. A SURVEY OF INTERNATIONAL LAW IN RELATION TO CODIFICATION	469

1 The General Part of International Law 469

(*a*) Subjects of international law; (*b*) Sources of international law; (*c*) The obligations of international law in relation to the law of the State

2 States in International Law 475

(*a*) Fundamental rights and duties of States; (*b*) Recognition of States; (*c*) Succession of States and Governments

3 Jurisdiction of States 481

(*a*) Recognition of acts of foreign States; (*b*) Jurisdiction over foreign States; (*c*) Obligations of territorial jurisdiction; (*d*) Jurisdiction with regard to crimes committed outside national territory; (*e*) The territorial domain of States; (*f*) The régime of the high seas; (*g*) The régime of territorial waters

4 The Individual in International Law 498

(*a*) The law of nationality; (*b*) The treatment of aliens; (*c*) Extradition; (*d*) The right of asylum

5 The Law of Treaties 507

6 The Law of Diplomatic Intercourse and Immunities 509

7 The Law of Consular Intercourse and Immunities 511

8 The Law of State Responsibility 512

9 The Law of Arbitral Procedure 514

CONTENTS

page

PART 3. THE METHOD OF SELECTION AND THE
WORK OF THE INTERNATIONAL LAW COMMISSION 516

1 The Method of Selection 516

2 The Character of the Work of the Commission 521

3 The Procedure of Codification 527

INTRODUCTION

1. Article 18 of the Statute of the International Law Commission provides that 'the Commission shall survey the whole field of international law with a view to selecting topics for codification, having in mind existing drafts whether governmental or not'. The same article lays down that 'when the Commission considers that the codification of a particular topic is necessary or desirable, it shall submit its recommendations to the General Assembly'.

The second session of the General Assembly by Resolution 175 (II) instructed the Secretary-General to do the necessary preparatory work for the beginning of the activity of the International Law Commission. The Resolution reads as follows:

175 (II). PREPARATION BY THE SECRETARIAT OF THE WORK OF THE INTERNATIONAL LAW COMMISSION

The General Assembly,

Considering that, in accordance with Article 98 of the Charter, the Secretary-General performs all such functions as are entrusted to him by the organs of the United Nations;

Considering that, in the interval between the first and the second session of the General Assembly, the Secretariat of the United Nations contributed to the study of problems concerning the progressive development of international law and its codification,

Instructs the Secretary-General to do the necessary preparatory work for the beginning of the activity of the International Law Commission, particularly with regard to the questions referred to it by the second session of the General Assembly, such as the draft declaration on the rights and duties of States.

Hundred and twenty-third plenary meeting,
21 November 1947.

The object of this memorandum is to present considerations and to put before the Commission the data which may facilitate the accomplishment of its preliminary task as envisaged in Article 18 of its Statute.

PART I

THE FUNCTION OF THE COMMISSION AND THE SELECTION OF TOPICS FOR CODIFICATION

2. The selection of topics for codification must depend to a large extent upon the meaning which the Commission will attach to the term 'codification' having regard to its Statute, to the discussions which preceded it, and to the experience of the previous efforts at codification. In Article 15 of the Statute of the Commission it is stated that 'the expression "codification of international law" is used for convenience as meaning the more precise formulation and systematization of rules of international law in fields where there already has been extensive State practice, precedent and doctrine'. This is so as distinguished from the expression 'progressive development of international law' which, in the words of the same article, 'is used for convenience as meaning the preparation of draft conventions on subjects which have not yet been regulated by international law or in regard to which the law has not yet been sufficiently developed in the practice of States'.

3. These definitions of what constituted 'progressive development' and 'codification' were adopted for the sake of convenience. In particular it may be assumed that there was no intention that the Commission should limit itself, in the matter of codification, to mere recording, in a systematized form, of the existing law, i.e., of the law as to which there exists an agreed body of rules. The discussions of the Committee on the Progressive Development of International Law and its Codification of 12 May–17 June 1947 revealed general agreement on this aspect of the subject. In the statement made on 20 May 1947, the Rapporteur of the Committee. Professor Brierly, expressed full approval of the view that codification cannot be limited to declaring existing law. He said:

As soon as you set out do to this, you discover that the existing law is often uncertain, that for one reason or another there are gaps in it which are not covered. If you were to disregard these uncertainties and these gaps and simply include in your code rules of existing law which are absolutely certain and clear, the work would have little value. Hence, the

450

FUNCTION OF THE COMMISSION

codifier, if he is competent for his work, will make suggestions of his own; where the rule is uncertain, he will suggest which is the better view; where a gap exists, he will suggest how it can best be filled. If he makes it clear what he is doing, tabulates the existing authorities, fairly examines the arguments pro and con, he will be doing his work properly. But it is true that in this aspect of his work he will be suggesting legislation—he will be working on the *lex ferenda*, not the *lex lata*—he will be extending the law and not merely stating the law that already exists.[1]

Similarly, in his final report, as approved by the Codification Committee, the Rapporteur said:

For the codification of international law, the Committee recognized that no clear-cut distinction between the formulation of the law as it is and the law as it ought to be could be rigidly maintained in practice. It was pointed out that in any work of codification, the codifier inevitably has to fill in gaps in, and amend, the law in the light of new developments.[2]

In the final report the Committee recognized that 'the terms employed ["progressive development" and "codification"] are not mutually exclusive, as, for example, in cases where the formulation and systematization of the existing law may lead to the conclusion that some new rule should be suggested for adoption by States'.[3]

4. The same interpretation of the task of the Commission was given expression in the course of the deliberations of the General Assembly and of its Legal Committee which in November 1947 adopted the Statute of the Commission.[4] It will be noted that the definition adopted in Article 15 of the Statute of the Commission does not refer to the more precise formulation and systematization of rules of international law as to which there is substantial agreement. The Statute refers to fields 'where there already has been extensive State practice, precedent and doctrine'.

---

[1] A/AC.10/30, pp. 2–3.   [2] A/AC.10/50, p. 7.

[3] A/AC.10/51, p. 4. The merely relative and provisional value of definitions adopted in this matter may be gauged by the fact that in its communication addressed in 1931 to the Council of the League of Nations in connection with the future work of codification the British Government used the term 'codification' in the sense in which 'development' is used in the Statute of the Commission. It described codification as 'free acceptance, by means of law-making conventions, of certain rules by which the parties to such conventions agree to abide in their mutual relations'. The process defined in the Statute of the Commission as 'codification' was described in the British memorandum as 'consolidation', i.e. 'the ascertainment and establishment in precise and accurate legal phraseology of rules of international law which have already come into existence' (*L.N.O.J.* Special Supplement no. 94), pp. 101–14, at p. 102).

[4] Thus M. Castberg (Norway) was of the opinion that no sharp distinction should be made between codification and progressive development. In his view, the International Law Commission should be free to explore the field of international law without being necessarily bound by international precedent: Sixth Committee, 25 September 1947 (A/C.6/SR.37, p. 2).

SURVEY OF INTERNATIONAL LAW: CODIFICATION

5. In adopting that view of the task of the Commission in the matter of codification as not confined to a mere restatement of the existing law, the Codification Committee and the Legal Committee were following the experience of the work of codification under the League of Nations. The problem confronted the Committee of Experts at the very outset of its activity. At the first session of the Committee held from 1 to 8 April 1925, most of its members emphasized that its task went beyond that of registration of existing law. The considerations adduced by the members of the Committee in support of that view are persuasive, and it may be useful to cite some of them. Thus Dr Suarez said:

The task of the Committee should not be limited to a systematic cataloguing of questions of an international administrative character, but should endeavour to reach solutions and to prepare agreements on disputed questions. Many questions were in dispute, not because they were insoluble, but because hitherto there had been no impartial legal authority which was above suspicion and in a position to suggest conclusions or arrive at a general *modus vivendi*. In his view, the task of the Committee was not merely passive and confined to codifying points on which the States seemed to be in agreement. The Committee had also an active mission in the sense of drawing attention to general principles and seeking general conclusions, and of settling questions in regard to which the modern international community of interests made it necessary to secure legal uniformity.[1]

Professor Diena reiterated that view. He expressed the hope that the members of the Committee would 'probably consider that they should not content themselves with registering results already obtained, but that they ought to contribute as far as possible to the progress of international law'.[2] Dr Rundstein, a Polish jurist of distinction and experience, expressed himself in terms even more emphatic:

The codification of international law was an act of legislation. It was a legislative process in the broad sense of the term. It was necessary to distinguish from codification a process which in Anglo-Saxon law was known as 'consolidation'. Consolidation would be equivalent to a mere act of registration—that was to say, the arrangement and classification of rules already existing.

He regarded 'codification as a creative process. By unifying existing rules, it discovered new rules which were inherent in them, and crystallised the principles which emerged from legal and customary practice.'[3]

[1] *Minutes of the First Session*, 1925, p. 7.   [2] *Ibid.* p. 8.   [3] *Ibid.* p. 14.

452

FUNCTION OF THE COMMISSION

Professor Brierly insisted that

the Committee should endeavour to find those subjects of international law which were of practical, not of theoretical, interest and, if possible, to choose questions which, in the present condition of international law, were causing difficulties to Governments at the moment and which would, as a result of the Committee's work, be capable of settlement by international agreement.[1]

Professor De Visscher pointed out that 'codification, even in its strictest sense, always implied a certain legislative element, as it aimed at achieving a certain uniformity and at reducing to a minimum the differences which existed between the various schools'.[2]

6. This insistence on the legislative aspect of the work of the Committee was not due to the absence of suggestions outlining the possibilities of a mere restatement. Thus Mr Wickersham drew attention to the work, in the United States, of the Commissioners of Uniform State Legislation and, in particular, of the American Law Institute, with regard to so-called restatements of various topics of customary law which, after full discussion and adoption by the Institute, would be treated by the courts as reliable statements of the existing law.[3]

7. In fact, the terms of reference of the Committee indicated with some clarity that its work was not to be confined to a passive registration of the existing law. The preamble of the Resolution adopted by the Assembly in September 1924 and requesting the Council to convene the Committee of Experts referred to the 'legislative needs of international relations'. At the first session of the Committee, Dr Mastny put on record the view that 'it was difficult to believe that the League of Nations, in setting up the Committee of Experts, desired to limit the activity of the Committee to a codification which was nothing more than a process of registration'.[4] Subsequently, the Resolution of the Assembly of 27 September 1927 declared that codification 'should not confine itself to the mere registration of the existing rules, but should aim at adapting them as far as possible to the contemporary conditions of international life'.

8. In so far as the Hague Codification Conference of 1930 achieved positive results, in particular in the field of the law of nationality, it was generally recognized that its work was largely legislative in character. The true position in the matter was put with some clarity by one of the United States delegates to the Conference. He said:

Early in the discussions at the recent Hague Conference it was realized that there was little international law on the subject of nationality which

[1] *Minutes of the First Session*, 1925, p. 17.　[2] *Ibid.* p. 25.　[3] *Ibid.* p. 7.　[4] *Ibid.* p. 15.

453

could be codified, if 'codification' is to be limited to the reduction to writing of rules of law already agreed upon by States. The idea of such a declaration of existing law was, therefore, early discarded at the Conference, and all efforts were directed toward the formulation of a convention to embody rules governing conflicts of nationality laws, regardless of whether such rules declared old law or made new law.[1]

In fact, it was pointed out that Article 18 of the Convention on Certain Questions relating to the Conflict of Nationality Laws declared that 'the inclusion of the above-mentioned principles and rules in the convention should in no way be deemed to prejudice the question whether they do or do not already form a part of international law'. The two principal protocols adopted at the Conference—that relating to the obligations of military service of persons of double nationality and that referring to the deportation of persons deprived of their nationality while abroad—were distinctly legislative in character. Governments represented at the Conference shared in that interpretation of its work. In fact, when the Assembly of the League of Nations laid down in 1927 the broad principles of the Conference to be convened, it adopted the recommendation of its First Committee to the effect that 'the Governments which might be invited to the Conference should be informed that the codification effort to be undertaken by the First Codification Conference must aim at adapting existing rules to contemporary conditions'.[2] It may be added that the experience of the Hague Codification Conference was, in this respect, a repetition of the history of some previous international instruments—such as the Declaration of London of 1909—which, although described at the outset as merely aiming at codifying existing international law, were in fact to a large extent of a legislative character.[3]

9. The experience of the Hague Codification Conference of 1930 and of the entire work of codification under the auspices of the

[1] Flournoy in *A.J.* 24 (1930), 468.   [2] *L.N.O.J.* 1927, Special Supplement no. 55.
[3] Thus, with regard to the Declaration of London, Great Britain as the convening State informed the participating Powers that the main task of the Conference would not be 'to deliberate *de lege ferenda*' but 'to crystallize, in the shape of a few simple propositions, the questions on which it seems possible to lay down a guiding principle generally accepted'. The Declaration itself stated that 'the Signatory Powers are agreed that the rules contained in the following Chapters correspond in substance with the generally recognized principles of international law'. Actually, in vital matters—such as the application of the doctrine of continuous voyage to conditional and absolute contraband —the Declaration created new law by way of compromise. For that reason Article 65 provided that the Declaration must be accepted as a whole or not at all. When in 1916 the British and French Governments announced that they would no longer act upon the provisions of the Declaration, they did so in order, as stated in the announcement, that they might revert to the rules of customary international law as they existed prior to the Declaration.

FUNCTION OF THE COMMISSION

League of Nations led most Governments to a firm rejection of the view that codification can—or ought properly to—be confined to those branches of international law with regard to which there exists a full and clear agreement as ascertained by a uniform governmental practice, judicial precedent and doctrine. Some of the reasons underlying this attitude have been stated by Governments; others, no less cogent, are closely related to the question of the standards of selection of topics for codification. It is therefore necessary to set them out in some detail.

10. In the first instance, there are only very few branches of international law with regard to which it can be said that they exhibit such a pronounced measure of agreement in the practice of States as to call for no more than what has been called consolidating codification. The survey undertaken in Part 2 of this memorandum shows that while in most branches of international law there is a common basis of agreement on principle, there is a wide divergence of practice in the matter of its detailed application. This applies even to questions with regard to which, because of the vast amount of existing practice, it has been customary to assume an almost universal measure of agreement—as, for instance, on the subject of the law relating to consuls or to jurisdictional immunities of States. Thus, with regard to the former subject, we find the following observation on the part of the authors of the Harvard Research Draft Convention: 'A perusal of the material indicates that comparatively few of the functions and privileges of consuls are established by universal international law. Thus a code on the subject will be to a large extent legislation.'[1] The authors of the Draft Convention on the Competence of Courts in regard to Foreign States thought it necessary to append the following caveat: 'The present draft convention is an endeavour to offer a set of rules on this subject which may prove acceptable to the States of the world. The convention does not purport to be merely a declaration of existing international law.'[2] In the matter of piracy—another subject abundantly covered by international practice—the discussions before the Committee of Experts revealed disagreement not only on matters of detail, but also with respect to the broad principle governing the subject. Thus M. Fromageot denied emphatically the right of a State to try a piratical ship flying the flag of a foreign State. He insisted repeatedly that the French Government had never recognized the right of jurisdiction by another country over a ship flying

[1] *A.J.* 26 (1932), Suppl. p. 214.   [2] *Ibid.* p. 474.

455

SURVEY OF INTERNATIONAL LAW: CODIFICATION

the French flag, and that a crime committed on the high seas was justiciable only by the country whose flag the incriminated vessel flew.[1]

11. It is clear that if the task of the International Law Commission were confined to fields with regard to which there is a full measure of agreement among States, the scope of its task would be reduced to a bare minimum. It would be reduced to matters of small compass the exclusive preoccupation with which would impair from the very inception the stature and authority of the International Law Commission. The League of Nations Committee of Experts, the resources of which were distinctly limited when compared with those available to the International Law Commission, consistently refused to become a party to any such interpretation of the scope of its function. It did not consider, for instance, that the subject of the revision of the classification of diplomatic agents merited its continued attention.

12. The view may be put forward—and it has been put forward by jurists of high authority—that codification of international law ought not to be concerned with the detailed regulations of its various branches, but that it ought to be confined to laying down their general principles—'les grandes lignes'.[2] If that view were adopted, the task of codification would undoubtedly be simplified and rendered easy. However, both the necessity for and the usefulness of such a course are open to question. The task, thus conceived, would hardly appear to be necessary. For there is no lack of wide agreement on general principles in most branches of international law. Neither would any appreciable measure of usefulness attach to the task of the Commission thus interpreted. What is required—for the sake of the authority of international law, the alleviation of the task of international tribunals, and the removal of one of the traditional causes of the unwillingness of States to submit disputes to the compulsory jurisdiction of international tribunals—is the introduction of certainty, precision and uniformity in matters of detail. That task is in fact comprised within the terms of reference of the International Law Commission.

It will also be noted that, with regard to many matters, codification, if limited to the ascertainment of the existing legal position, would amount to a mere registration of existing disagreements.

---

[1] *Minutes of the Third Session*, 1927, p. 45.

[2] See, for instance, the observations of Judge Alvarez in *Annuaire* (1947), pp. 53, 54, 60, 61.

456

FUNCTION OF THE COMMISSION

13. The second main objection to codification conceived as a mere registration—in a systematized form—of the existing law is that it may crystallize the law in matters in which the existing rules are obsolete and unsatisfactory. Codification which constitutes a record of the past rather than a creative use of the existing materials—legal and others—for the purpose of regulating the life of the community is a brake upon progress. This factor was one of the reasons why some Members of the United Nations have expressed doubts as to the method of mere restatement by experts of the existing law. In the statement of the Dutch representative a warning was uttered against such restatement by experts as being a 'purely static function'. It was alleged that 'it can only "freeze" international law in the shape in which it is at a certain moment'.[1] There is probably no reason for such apprehension. For restatement—properly conce ed and as, in fact, interpreted in the Statute of the International Law Commission —is not confined to a mere registration of the existing law. But the apprehension thus voiced is significant. It draws attention to the drawbacks and dangers of codification when regarded as confined to a statement of the existing law. There is no compelling reason why the International Law Commission should be exposed to that danger and why it should attach a restrictive meaning to the term 'codification'. This is not a question of creating new law on subjects which fall within the category of 'progressive development of international law' for the reason that they have not yet been regulated by international law or that there is not as yet a sufficiently developed practice of States in regard to them. For there are subjects which have been regulated by international law, but the regulation of which is unsatisfactory and fragmentary. The law with regard to these subjects has sufficiently developed, but it has not developed in a manner compatible with the requirements of a peaceful and neighbourly intercourse of States. These subjects fall within the category of codification of international law as envisaged in Article 15 of the Statute.

14. Finally, codification conceived as confined to a mere registration, in a systematized form, of existing law would be open to the objection, often voiced by Governments in regard to conventions codifying international law, that it would be interpreted as a replacement of customary international law by what is in effect a treaty. The disadvantages of any such consummation have often

[1] Committee on the Progressive Development of International Law and its Codification, statement by the Netherlands respresentative (A/AC.10/23).

457

SURVEY OF INTERNATIONAL LAW: CODIFICATION

been stated. It would expose what has hitherto enjoyed the unchallenged and secure authority of a customary rule to the uncertainties and vicissitudes of treaties in all phases of their creation and operation. It might be interpreted as doing away with those parts of customary law which it has failed to include within the orbit of the codifying instrument. It is true that some international codifying conventions—such as the Fourth Hague Convention on the Rules and Customs of War on Land and the Hague Convention on Certain Questions relating to the Conflict of Nationality Laws—provide expressly that they do not derogate from customary international law; but the possibility of written codification being interpreted as laying down the existing law and no more has led some Governments to draw attention, in emphatic terms, to the drawbacks of that conception of codification. Some Governments have, because of these apprehended drawbacks, gone to the length of suggesting that codification should refrain from registering existing international law and that it should 'lay down rules which it would appear desirable to introduce into international relations in regard to the subjects dealt with'.[1] It is not believed that such suggestions are likely to

[1] Statement of the Swiss Government in 1931 in connection with the discussion of the future work of codification (League Doc. A. 12 (b) 1931.V, p. 3). Part of that statement may usefully be quoted: 'It is not the task of codification conferences to register existing international law, but to lay down rules which it would appear desirable to introduce into international relations in regard to the subjects dealt with. Their work should, therefore, mark an advance on the present state of international law. In certain cases, indeed, it would be extremely difficult to say what the existing law really is, as it is not clearly known or is a matter of controversy. It would be most unfortunate if the attempt to discover an adequate solution of an important problem were abandoned on the ground that no such solution is to be found in the existing positive law. One of the fundamental tasks of codification conferences should be to choose between disputed rules and, within the limits of their agenda, to fill up the gaps in a law where deficiencies and obscurities are obvious.' The relevant part of the statement of the French Government ran as follows: 'It is necessary to bear in mind that to attempt to negotiate and conclude conventions with the object of setting out the rules of customary law in the form of written law would involve a danger of creating unnecessary difficulties and, *inter alia*, of throwing doubt upon the existence of particular rules which an international judge, as for example the Permanent Court of International Justice, would have been in a position to recognize. It appears, therefore, that codification by way of conventions ought not to be directed towards the laying down of rules which would be declared to be already part of existing international law' (League Doc. A. 12 (a) 1931.V, p. 2). The statement made in May 1947 by the Swedish representative before the Codification Committee followed similar lines (A/AC. 10/24). It recalled, with approval, the following statement made in 1931 by the Swiss Government to the League of Nations: 'The Government of Switzerland, being in agreement with the three-fold consultation of Governments recommended in the Resolution adopted at The Hague, asked in its reply whether the codification conventions should be declaratory or enactory, whether they should supplant or supplement customary law. The Federal Council of Switzerland declared that "such new law cannot have the effect of merely supplanting the old. The old law, which is derived from international practice or the decisions of international tribunals, or from both combined, remains in force in its entirety. Otherwise we should be forced to the conclusion that

secure general approval. They are not in accordance with the task of the International Law Commission as understood by the Codification Committee which in May and June 1947 framed its terms of reference, or by the General Assembly. Neither are they in accordance with the terms of the Statute of the Commission. But they are helpful inasmuch as they emphasize the drawbacks of considering the registration or systematization of existing international law to be the only task of the International Law Commission or the only or main criterion for the selection of topics for codification.[1] An International Law Commission which limits its function to that of a research institute for the collection of material and for registering either existing agreement or, perhaps, more frequently, the absence of agreement, would not be fulfilling the purpose assigned to it by its Statute. Neither would it be fulfilling the urgent need of international society which has prompted the codification movement from its inception and which has found an expression in the provisions of the Charter of the United Nations.

15. It follows from what has been said in the preceding sections of this memorandum that the existence of agreement—or the measure of such agreement—on any particular topic cannot be regarded as an adequate criterion for the selection of topics for codification. The experience of the work of codification under the auspices of the League of Nations denies the validity or usefulness of any such

States not bound by the new conventions are free from all obligations. International law would be shaken to its very foundations, and codification accepted in this sense would cause irreparable harm."' The same view was given expression in the resolution of the Institute of International Law adopted in 1947: 'L'Institut de Droit international, Reconnaissant combien est désirable une codification du Droit des Gens, de nature à dissiper certaines de ses incertitudes et favoriser son observation: Souligne les dangers que présenterait actuellement toute codification officielle suivant la méthode de la Conférence de Codification de La Haye de 1930, dans la mesure où elle fondait la force obligatoire des règles codifiées sur l'acceptation expresse des Etats. Une telle méthode aboutit à fournir à chaque gouvernement l'occasion de remettre en question, par son refus d'acceptation, des règles de droit que la doctrine et la jurisprudence considéraient, d'une manière générale, jusqu'à cette date, comme établies; il existe de ce fait un risque d'affaiblir et d'ébranler le droit que la codification avait pour objet de préciser et de consolider' (*Annuaire* (1947), p. 261).

[1] For the same reasons it is doubtful whether the resolution of the Institute of International Law on the subject of codification adopted in August 1947 adequately expresses the objects of codification. The relevant part of the resolution runs as follows: 'L'Institut, sans écarter la possibilité de conventions et de déclarations internationales sur les objets pour lesquels elles seraient jugées réalisables, estime que, pour le moment, la contribution la plus importante à l'œuvre de codification consisterait à effectuer, sur le plan national et international, des recherches de caractère scientifique en vue d'arriver à la constatation exacte de l'état actuel du droit international. Cet inventaire servirait de base tant à un effort doctrinal qu'à un effort officiel entrepris suivant des méthodes jugées mieux appropriées, en vue de combler les lacunes du droit international et de parer à ses imperfections' (*Annuaire* (1947), p. 262).

459

SURVEY OF INTERNATIONAL LAW: CODIFICATION

standard. This being so, what is the standard of selection to be adopted by the Commission? The Statute of the Commission provides—in Article 18 (2)—that 'when the Commission considers that the codification of a particular topic is *necessary or desirable* it shall submit its recommendations to the General Assembly'. However, the expression 'necessary or desirable' is not self-explanatory. It still leaves the Commission with the substantive responsibility for the task of selection. When is a subject ripe for codification in the sense that its codification is 'necessary or desirable'? There is room for the view that a topic is ripe for codification in this sense if the importance of the subject-matter—from the point of view of the necessities of international intercourse, of the wider needs of the international community, and of the authority of international law —requires that, notwithstanding any existing disagreements, an attempt should be made to reduce it to the form of a systematized and precise branch of international law. This was the interpretation given to that term by the Committee of Experts and by the Assembly of the League of Nations in connection with the work of codification.

16. It is significant that the topics eventually selected by the Committee of Experts and the Assembly for codification were not 'ripe' for it in the ordinary sense of the word (i.e. in the sense of having behind them a substantial body of agreement). They were topics with regard to which practice had previously registered a distinct measure of disagreement; with regard to which the divergencies had reference to political and economic interests of apparent importance; and in relation to which divergent traditions of national law and jurisprudence had indicated from the outset the difficulties of codification. The statement may sound paradoxical, but the affirmative criterion of 'ripeness' as eventually acted upon seemed to have been not the ease with which the subject could be codified, but the difficulty, as expressed in existing divergencies and in the need for regulation, of regulating it by way of codification. This applied to all three topics eventually chosen as the subject-matter of the Hague Codification Conference in 1930. The difficulties besetting the codification of these topics were discussed in full by the Committee of Experts. The objections, of a political and legal nature, to codifying any of these subjects were put before them fully and forcibly.[1] They were not discarded without thorough discussion.

---

[1] Thus with regard to nationality, M. Fromageot pointed out that these questions were closely connected with the constitutional, social, economic and racial interests of each country, and would undoubtedly raise obstacles of a political kind. He was doubtful whether it was possible to settle by means of a general convention matters with regard to

460

FUNCTION OF THE COMMISSION

Moreover, the eventual choice of subjects ripe for the Codification Conference or for codification generally was not due exclusively to a decision of the Committee of Experts or even the Council and the Assembly of the League. It was made, in the first instance, by Governments the overwhelming majority of which answered in the affirmative the question whether they regarded these subjects as a suitable topic for codification. Thus, with regard to State responsibility, twenty-two Governments expressed themselves in favour of codification, while only five dissented and two made reservations.[1] At the same time, a number of topics were discarded or postponed although with regard to them the measure of existing agreement and the prospects of achieving success were considerable. Thus with regard to diplomatic immunities the replies of Governments were almost unanimously in favour of codification.[2] Matters of a limited compass and technical character were discarded for the ostensible reason that they were not urgent. This was clearly revealed in the discussions concerning the revision of the classification of diplomatic agents.[3] This view was put forcibly by Mr Wickersham:

The Committee would be making a mistake if it were to choose a subject of secondary importance at a moment when the world was calling for the establishment of the Rule of Law in the place of the Rule of Force. The

which the interests of various States were so different, if not contradictory (*Minutes of the Committee of Experts, First Session*, 1925, p. 29). On the other hand, Mr Wickersham urged that members of the Committee should not restrict themselves to certain questions because they feared that others might possess a political character. He said: 'There was a great difference between political questions and questions raising political obstacles. It was, for instance, quite possible to examine in a purely scientific manner the legislation regarding the status of married women. He did not believe that the Government of his own country, for instance, whose legislation on the subject was very recent, would in any way object to such an investigation. Were the Committee to set aside all questions which might possibly raise political considerations, its work would be very greatly reduced' (*ibid.* pp. 29–30). But it is significant that the Committee appointed a sub-committee to enquire: '(1) Whether there are conflicts of laws regarding nationality the solution of which by way of international conventions could be envisaged without encountering political obstacles; (2) If so, what these problems are and what solution should be given to them' (*ibid.*). With regard to the question of the responsibility of States, M. Fromageot thought that 'it was not sufficiently ripe for it affected too closely the internal or external policy of States, their social life and the stability of their institutions' (*Minutes of the Committee of Experts, Third Session*, 1927, p. 14). On the other hand, Dr McNair, while admitting the existence of wide divergencies, drew attention to a considerable consensus of opinion in favour of the desirability of attempting to reconcile the divergencies of view on this thorny subject. He feared that if the Committee were not satisfied with the degree of unanimity manifested on this question, it would find very few questions indeed which it could consider ripe for international treatment (*ibid.*). Similarly, with regard to territorial waters, M. Fromageot urged that 'it was impossible to contemplate an open convention on a question regarding which the contracting States possessed interests which were quite unequal' (*ibid.* p. 31).

[1] *Committee of Experts, Third Session*, 1927, p. 13.
[2] *Ibid.* pp. 32–3.   [3] *Ibid.* pp. 17–19.

461

SURVEY OF INTERNATIONAL LAW: CODIFICATION

Committee would expose itself to the criticism of having been superficial, and of having wasted its time, when its chief object should have been to solve certain major problems of international law.[1]

It seems almost as if the decisive criterion of ripeness and desirability of codification was not the existence of agreement, but the fact of the existence of discrepancies and divergencies rendering international regulation necessary. 'One would perhaps not be accused of extravagance of expression if he suggested that a more difficult subject could hardly have been selected for the first Codification Conference'—this observation, with regard to the question of State responsibility, by one of the delegates of the United States,[2] is indicative of what may perhaps be regarded as one of the principal factors determining the choice of subjects of codification.

17. The experience of codification under the League of Nations and of the work of its Committee of Experts cannot be without instruction for the future work of the International Law Commission. That experience shows that the decisive criterion must be not the ease with which the task of codifying any particular branch of international law can be accomplished, but the need for codifying it. A subject of small dimensions with regard to which general agreement could be taken for granted would not be a 'necessary or desirable' subject of codification. On the other hand—and in this respect the task of the International Law Commission in the matter of codification differs from that of the Committee of Experts—the test of such desirability and necessity need not be sought in the immediate urgency of some new topic requiring regulation. For any such need is covered by the other major task of the Commission, namely, the development of international law.

18. It will thus be seen that the standard of selection of topics for codification cannot be found by reference to any single test, such as the degree of agreement or disagreement on the subject or the urgency of its formulation. In a substantial sense the existence of a high degree of agreement in the field of customary international law would be irrelevant in this connection—for if there is a conspicuous measure of agreement then codification might appear neither necessary nor, according to many, particularly desirable in view of the disadvantages attaching to the transformation of custom into treaty. If, on the other hand, the absence of agreement and the existence of disagreement is a recommendation for codification, then the latter would approach a

---

[1] *Committee of Experts, Third Session,* 1927, p. 18.
[2] Mr Hackworth in *A.J.* 24 (1930), 516.

462

FUNCTION OF THE COMMISSION

legislative process for the success of which there is no warrant in international society as at present constituted. For the more urgent the regulation of a subject appears to be having regard to the continued adherence of States to divergent practices, the more difficult it may be to remove effectively such divergencies by means of codification expressed in binding conventions and not falling within the purview of 'development of international law'. For this reason it is not likely that, apart from novel subjects falling within the category of development of international law, it is feasible to assign any obvious priority to certain subjects, as distinguished from others, from the point of view of urgency in the field of codification.

19. While it is thus clear that the test for the selection of topics is neither easy nor automatic, the difficulty surrounding the question can be solved to a large extent when it is borne in mind that the selection of topics is part of the major task of the Commission, which may extend over a generation, of codifying, in the various forms contemplated by the Statute, the entire body of international law. Selection there must be because, obviously, the Commission cannot codify the whole of international law at once. But provided it is realized (a) that the regulation of urgent and *novel* questions requiring a legislative effort is covered by that part of the work of the Commission which is described as development of international law, and (b) that the eventual codification of the entirety of international law must properly be regarded as the ultimate object of the International Law Commission—then the question of selection of topics no longer presents an insoluble or perplexing problem. If we bear that in mind, then the question of selection of topics is no longer one of haphazard and, possibly, arbitrary choice, but one of fitting the work of the Commission at any particular time into the orbit of a comprehensive plan. The selection then becomes a question to be determined by considerations of convenience, of available means and personnel, of classification, and of scientific symmetry. From this point of view the Statute of the Commission provides one standard of selection which, upon analysis, is of greater usefulness than may appear at first sight—namely, that codification is, in the language of Article 15 of the Statute of the Commission, to cover fields 'where there already has been extensive State practice, precedent and doctrine'. This may comprise the entire field of international law as traditionally expounded in text-books and treatises. There is nothing in the Statute of the Commission which prevents it from envisaging its task of selection and of execution of individual projects

of codification as forming part of the eventual codification of international law as a whole. It is probably within the framework of some such comprehensive undertaking that the otherwise perplexing and intractable problem of selection of topics may be brought nearer solution. In fact, the Statute of the Commission contemplates the process of selection of topics as being the result of a survey of the whole field of international law. In this connection the deliberations of the Committee of Experts, at its fourth session in 1928, in the matter of the Paraguayan proposal for the preparation of a general and comprehensive plan of codification of international law will be found to be of interest. The Committee pointed to the possibility of drawing up 'a systematic outline of a more complete codification, on the understanding always that what was contemplated was not immediate and simultaneous realization of a plan thus formed'.[1] The Committee itself felt that it could not undertake that task seeing that its original mandate appeared 'more than sufficient to occupy its efforts during the infrequent and short sessions which circumstances permitted it to hold'. The character and status of the International Law Commission, as envisaged by its Statute and by the General Assembly, in no way preclude it from interpreting the scope of its function by reference to a wide and comprehensive task in keeping with the place which the codification of international law occupies in the Charter of the United Nations.

20. The task of the Commission in deciding upon its plan of work is simplified by the deliberate elasticity of its Statute. The character of the work of the Commission is no longer determined by the necessity of producing such drafts only as are intended to materialize as conventions to be adopted by a considerable number of States. The Statute provides for possibilities of various kinds with regard to action which may be taken by the General Assembly in the matter of the drafts produced by the Commission. The Commission may submit a complete draft on a subject which, because of the existing divergencies and uncertainties, or for other reasons, is not likely to secure the acceptance of the majority of States. Nevertheless the draft thus adopted may be a model piece of codification. It may state accurately the existing law on matters on which there is agreement. It may clarify the position in other respects. It may provide for solutions of conflicting views and practices. And it may even go

---

[1] *Minutes of the Committee of Experts, Fourth Session*, 1928, p. 51. See also the *Minutes of the First Session*, 1925, p. 18, for the suggestion that the Committee should draw up 'a kind of a balance sheet of international law' as a preliminary step for the selection of topics.

FUNCTION AND THE SELECTION OF TOPICS

to the length of proposing changes in what it considers to be agreed law if it arrives at the conclusion that the existing law is unsatisfactory or obsolete. Such a draft, accepted by the Commission, may, because of the absence of likelihood of its securing a sufficiently wide measure of support, be considered a proper subject for a recommendation to the General Assembly under (a) or (b) of Article 23 of its Statute, but not under (c) or (d). This means that the Commission may be of the view that a draft, however sound and desirable in itself, would best serve its purpose in the scheme of codification if it remained in the form of a draft either merely submitted to the General Assembly or of which the General Assembly has taken note or which it has approved by resolution without going to the length of recommending it to the Members of the United Nations with a view to the conclusion of a convention or without proceeding to convene a conference for the purpose of concluding a convention. Drafts which are permitted to retain that preliminary status—under (a) and (b) of Article 23 of the Statute of the Commission—would be contributions to the eventual codification of international law in the form of conventions. They would exercise influence partly as statements of the existing law and partly as pronouncements of what is a rational and desirable development of the law on the subject. They would be at least in the category of writings of the most qualified publicists, referred to in Article 38 of the Statute of the International Court of Justice as a subsidiary source of law to be applied by the Court. Most probably their authority would be considerably higher. For they will be the product not only of scholarly research, individual and collective, aided by the active co-operation of Governments, of national and international scientific bodies, and the resources of the United Nations. They will be the result of the deliberations and of the approval of the International Law Commission. Outside the sphere of international judicial settlement they will be of considerable potency in shaping scientific opinion and the practice of Governments.

21. If this picture represents an adequate account of the possibilities opened up by the procedure envisaged in Article 23 of the Statute of the Commission then it is probable that, after a time, practically the entire field of international law may be covered—codified—by the products of the work of the Commission in various forms and of varying degrees of authority. There will be drafts which the Commission has considered to be sufficiently satisfactory to warrant publication as a Commission document, but with regard to which no other action will, for the time being, be regarded as necessary.

Drafts will be in existence of which the General Assembly has taken note or which it has approved by resolution. There will be drafts which the General Assembly has recommended to Members with the view to the conclusion of a convention. Even if the suggested convention does not materialize, the drafts thus dealt with by the General Assembly will be of considerable authority. The same will apply, to an even higher degree, to drafts with regard to which the General Assembly has recommended the convening of a conference for the purpose of concluding a convention. This will be so even if the conference or convention—or both—do not materialize. Finally, there will be drafts which have in fact ripened into conventions. And the conventions themselves will differ in authority having regard to the numbers and the importance of the States which effectively become parties to them. Experience has shown that the quest for unanimity in conventions of this kind is both futile and, in effect, retrogressive.[1]

22. There is thus no reason why in two decades or so of such activity the results of the work of the International Law Commission should not cover practically the entire field of international law. Such results would not constitute a single comprehensive piece of codification, but they would provide the basis of some such ultimate achievement. They would show that the compromise represented in the present Statute between the views of those who would confine the work of the International Law Commission to unofficial statements and restatements of the existing law and those who would limit it to preparing drafts of formal conventions, is a workable instrument of beneficent potentialities. From this point of view the survey of the whole field of international law which the Commission is instructed to undertake appears to be in keeping with the ultimate task of the International Law Commission as the principal instrument for the codification of international law.

23. The view underlying this part of the present memorandum is that urgent and novel questions demanding international regulation are covered by that aspect of the function of the Commission which

---

[1] The Assembly of the League adopted in 1927 a resolution relating to the future Codification Conference and stating that 'although it is desirable that the Conference's decisions should be unanimous, and every effort should be made to obtain this result, it must be clearly understood that, where unanimity is impossible, the majority of the participating States, if disposed to accept as among themselves a rule to which some other States are not prepared to consent, cannot be prevented from doing so by the mere opposition of the minority' (*L.N.O.J.* Special Supplement no. 55, p. 53). See also the observations on the question of unanimity at the third session of the Committee of Experts (*Minutes*, 1927, pp. 11, 12).

FUNCTION OF THE COMMISSION

relates to 'development of international law', and that 'codification' embraces, in principle, the entire field of international law. If that view is accepted the question of selection of topics in the matter of codification becomes simpler and less perplexing than may otherwise be the case. The selection will no longer be determined exclusively by the necessity of producing drafts likely to secure immediate acceptance in the form of conventions. Neither will the work be confined to a mere passive registration of agreement or disagreement. It may be expected that the Commission will be guided by the desire that ultimately its drafts should be accepted as law and that therefore they should be of such a nature and quality as to qualify them for a place on the international statute book within the framework of the comprehensive task of codification. The 'statements' and 'restatements' of the law are but a necessary and preliminary step in the process of eventual codification in the form of conventions. This was the view not only of the various Governments, such as the Soviet Union[1] and Brazil,[2] represented on the Codification Committee of 1947. The British representative, who also acted as Rapporteur of the Committee, expressed himself with all requisite clarity:

I am not, as a matter of principle, opposed to codifying conventions. I think they are the ideal toward which we have to work. I merely think that at present codifying conventions which are worth having are impracticable. I think a concluded convention would be better and more satisfactory than a mere scientific restatement of the law which has no actual authority ... Restatements are only a stage in the process, they are a way for preparing the ground for what we all hope we shall eventually reach—a comprehensive statement, an eventual codification of international law by international agreement.[3]

24. At the same time, the fact that the function of the Commission

---

[1] See the statement of the representative of the Union of Soviet Socialist Republics of 22 May 1947: Doc. A/AC.10/32, p. 6. He warned against the danger of misleading 'public opinion by inspiring an unjustified confidence that codification in the form of informal compilations is adequate, and that there therefore remains nothing more to be done'. He added: 'The nations await the consolidation of legality in international relations. Legality demands precise legal forms.'

[2] Statement of the representative of Brazil, on 15 May 1947 (Doc. A/AC.10/28). He said: 'Neither the codification nor the development of international law can be achieved merely by submission of learned opinions. They must take the form of resolutions by the General Assembly or of multilateral conventions.'

[3] Doc. A/AC.10/35, pp. 3–4. In view of this it is not considered necessary in this memorandum to discuss the question whether, as occasionally maintained, codification of international law by means of conventions is derogatory to the authority of customary international law and ought to be discouraged. For a recent statement of this view see the observations of M. Basdevant before the Institute of International Law in 1947 (*Annuaire*, 1947, pp. 227–30).

SURVEY OF INTERNATIONAL LAW: CODIFICATION

is not, in the first instance, synonymous with drafting instruments intended for immediate adoption as conventions, brings into relief the comprehensive character of its function both with regard to the method to be pursued and with regard to the field to be covered. The question of method, which—as already stated—cannot be confined to a mere registration of the existing law, is discussed in Part 3 of this memorandum. The question of the field to be covered can best be approached by a survey of the entire field of international law as suggested in Article 18 of the Statute of the Commission. Within that framework the selection of topics is no longer a matter of assigning decisive priority to some at the permanent expense of others. It is a question of evolving a long-range plan, on a systematic basis, for a scientific and legislative undertaking of a magnitude commensurate with the task of the United Nations as one of the principal agencies for the development of international law.

PART 2

A SURVEY OF INTERNATIONAL LAW
IN RELATION TO CODIFICATION

25. It is proposed to survey here in general outline 'the whole field of international law' referred to in Article 18 of the Statute of the International Law Commission, having regard to the task of the Commission as outlined in Part 1 of this memorandum, to the previous efforts at codification, and to existing drafts, governmental and other. The list of topics which will be surveyed in this part is not intended to be exhaustive. Thus this memorandum does not attempt to cover fields already covered by existing international conventions such as those in the fields of air law or of international postal communications. Likewise, no attempt is made to survey subjects of private international law.

I. THE GENERAL PART OF INTERNATIONAL LAW

26. In so far as the function of the Commission embraces the eventual codification of international law as a whole, it will be necessary for it to consider whether it may not be incumbent upon it to attempt a formulation, in the form of draft articles, of what may be described as the general part of international law. Some of the great municipal codes contain introductory and general articles of this nature formulating the bases and the principles of the legal system as a whole—in particular with regard to the subjects of the law, its sources, and its relation to the various branches of the law. It is probable that, for both practical and doctrinal reasons, an authoritative statement of the law of this nature would be of considerable usefulness in the sphere of international law. This applies in particular to the following three questions: (1) the subjects of international law; (2) the sources of international law; (3) the relation of the law of nations to the municipal law of States. It is now proposed to consider these three questions in turn.

(a) Subjects of international law

27. The question of the subjects of international law has, in particular in the last twenty-five years, ceased to be one of purely theoretical

469

SURVEY OF INTERNATIONAL LAW: CODIFICATION

importance, and it is now probable that in some respects it requires authoritative international regulation. Practice has abandoned the doctrine that States are the exclusive subjects of international rights and duties. Although the Statute of the International Court of Justice adheres to the traditional view that only States can be parties to international proceedings, a number of other international instruments have recognized the procedural capacity of the individual. This was the case not only in the provisions of the Treaty of Versailles relating to the jurisdiction of the Mixed Arbitral Tribunals, but also in other treaties such as the Polish–German Convention of 1922 relating to Upper Silesia, in which—as was subsequently held by the Upper Silesian Mixed Tribunal—the independent procedural status of individuals as claimants before an international agency was recognized even as against the State of which they were nationals.

28. In the sphere of substantive law, the Permanent Court of International Justice recognized, in the Advisory Opinion relating to the postal service in Danzig, that there is nothing in international law to prevent individuals from acquiring directly rights under a treaty provided that this is the intention of the contracting parties. A considerable number of decisions of municipal courts rendered subsequently to that Advisory Opinion of the Permanent Court expressly affirmed that possibility.

29. In the field of customary international law the enjoyment of benefits of international law by individuals as a matter of right followed from the doctrine, accepted by a growing number of countries, that generally recognized rules of the law of nations form part of the law of the land. In the sphere of duties imposed by international law the principle that the obligations of international law bind individuals directly regardless of the law of their State and of any contrary order received from their superiors was proclaimed in the Charter annexed to the Agreement of 8 August 1945 providing for the setting up of the International Military Tribunal at Nürnberg, as well as in the Charter of the International Military Tribunal at Tokyo of 19 January 1946. That principle was fully affirmed in the judgment of the Nürnberg Tribunal as flowing from the imperative necessity of making international law effective. The Tribunal said: 'Crimes against international law are committed by men, not by abstract entities, and only by punishing individuals who commit such crimes can the provisions of international law be enforced.' It was reaffirmed in the Resolution of the General Assembly of 11 December 1946 expressing adherence to the principles

THE GENERAL PART

of the Nürnberg Charter and Judgment. It has loomed large in the discussions and statements bearing upon the resolution of the General Assembly in the matter of the codification of the law applied in the Judgment of the International Military Tribunal. The General Assembly directed the Committee on Codification of International Law 'to treat as a matter of primary importance plans for the formulation, in the context of a general codification of offences against the peace and security of mankind, or of an International Criminal Code, of the principles recognized in the Charter of the Nürnberg Tribunal and in the judgment of the Tribunal'. In a memorandum submitted by the representative of France to the Codification Committee in 1947 it was proposed that the general principle enunciated by the Tribunal and cited above should be confirmed as part of the codification of this aspect of the law: 'The individual is subject to international penal law. Without thereby excluding the penal responsibility of the criminal State, international penal law can inflict penalties on the authors of international offences and their accomplices.'[1]

30. On a different plane, the Charter of the Nürnberg Tribunal— and the Judgment which followed it—proclaimed the criminality of offences against humanity, i.e. of such offences against the fundamental rights of man to life and liberty, even if committed in obedience to the law of the State. To that extent, in a different sphere, positive law has recognized the individual as endowed, under international law, with rights the violation of which is a criminal act. The repeated provisions of the Charter of the United Nations in the matter of human rights and fundamental freedoms are directly relevant in this connection.

31. Finally, account must be taken of the developments in modern international law amounting to a recognition of the international personality of public bodies other than States. The international legal personality of the United Nations, of the specialized agencies established under its aegis, and of other international organizations, calls for a re-definition of the traditional rule of international law in the matter of its subjects. That legal personality is no longer a postulate of scientific doctrine. It is accompanied by a recognized contractual capacity in the international sphere and, as with regard to the right to request an advisory opinion of the International Court of Justice, by a distinct measure of international procedural capacity.

32. All these developments may be considered as rendering

[1] A/AC.10/34.

471

SURVEY OF INTERNATIONAL LAW: CODIFICATION

necessary, within the orbit of the codification of the general part of international law, the clarification and revision of some of the traditional notions. Such clarification and revision would do no more than give expression both to actual changes in the law and to the changing conditions of international society which no longer permit the maintenance of what, in the view of many, is becoming a fiction obstructive of progress. Previous efforts at codification have touched only the fringe of the question. Thus the League of Nations Committee of Experts for the Progressive Codification of International Law discussed in some detail draft rules for formulating, by way of an international convention, international provisions concerning the nationality of commercial corporations and for the recognition of the legal personality of foreign commercial corporations.[1] At its fourth session in 1928 the Committee had before it a report on the legal position of private non-profit-making international associations and of private international foundations.[2] In the Project of the American Institute of International Law on Fundamental Bases of International Law, Article 2 provided, somewhat tentatively, as follows:

In addition to those matters which heretofore have come within the domain of international law, there belong other new matters arising out of the exigencies of modern social life, as well as the international rights of individuals, namely, the rights which natural or juridical persons can invoke in each nation in the cases expressly provided for in the convention on this subject.[3]

(b) Sources of international law

33. The codification of this aspect of international law has been successfully accomplished by the definition of the sources of international law as given in Article 38 of the Statute of the International Court of Justice. That definition has been repeatedly treated as authoritative by international arbitral tribunals. It is doubtful whether any useful purpose would be served by attempts to make it more specific, as, for instance, by defining the conditions of the creation and of the continued validity of international custom or by enumerating, by way of example, some of the general principles of law which Article 38 of the Statute recognizes as one of the three principal sources of the law to be applied by the Court. The inclusion of a definition of sources of international law within any general

---

[1] *Minutes of the Third Session*, 1927, pp. 57–63, 64–7.
[2] *Minutes of the Fourth Session*, 1928, p. 49.
[3] Project No. 4; see *A.J.* Special Number 20 (1926), p. 304.

THE GENERAL PART

scheme of codification would serve the requirements of systematic symmetry as distinguished from any pressing practical need. A distinct element of usefulness might, however, attach to any commentary accompanying the definition and assembling the experience of the International Court of Justice and other international tribunals in the application of the various sources of international law. It may be noted that Project No. 4, prepared by the American Institute of International Law, on 'Fundamental Bases of International Law', is devoted almost exclusively to the various aspects of sources of international law.[1]

(c) *The obligations of international law in relation to the law of the State*

34. It must be a matter for consideration to what extent and in what detail the obligation of States to give effect, through their national law, to their duties arising out of international law should find a place in any general scheme of codification. The problem is one which is closely related to the authority and the effectiveness of international law. To a large extent it is a question of the reaffirmation of what has now become a prominent feature of the law and of the practice of many States. The doctrine of incorporation, according to which the rules of international law form part of the municipal law of States, originated in England and in the United States. However, this is not now a doctrine confined to those countries. It has been adopted by other States, for instance in the German Constitution of 1919 and in the Constitutions of Argentina and Venezuela. The preamble to the French Constitution of 1946 contains a general declaration to the effect that France conforms to the principles of public international law. The courts of many other countries, the Constitution of which does not expressly include the principle of incorporation, have acted upon it. The time would therefore appear ripe for the incorporation of the principle, suitably elaborated and defined, that treaties validly concluded by the State and generally recognized rules of customary international law form part of the domestic law of the State; that courts and other national agencies are obliged to give effect to them; that they cannot be unilaterally abrogated by purely national action; and that a State cannot invoke the absence of the requisite national laws and organs as a reason for the non-fulfilment of its international obligations.

35. Admittedly a codification, on these lines, of this fundamental aspect of international law will raise difficult questions of constitu-

[1] See *A. J.* Special Number 20 (1926), pp. 304–7.

473

SURVEY OF INTERNATIONAL LAW: CODIFICATION

tional law in various States, and the question will arise whether this is a suitable subject within the general scheme of codification. Thus in England treaties ratified by the Crown but affecting private rights are not enforced by the courts unless they are followed by an enabling Act of Parliament (though this difficulty has tended to disappear in view of the recent practice of submitting treaties for parliamentary approval, coupled with an enabling Act, prior to the ratification of the treaty). Similarly, in the United States though treaties ratified with the consent and advice of the Senate constitute the supreme law of the land, abrogating any law inconsistent with the terms of the treaties, a subsequent Act of Congress will be acted upon by the courts though its provisions may be inconsistent with the terms of a treaty binding upon the United States. These and similar problems bring to mind the difficulties of this aspect of codification. However, it is significant that it has formed the subject-matter of some previous efforts in this direction. Thus, for instance, Article 3 of Project No. 4 adopted in 1925 by the American Institute of International Law—one of the series of 'projects of conventions for the preparation of a code of public international law'—on Fundamental Bases of International Law provides that 'international law forms a part of the national law of every country' and that 'in matters which pertain to it, it should therefore be applied by the national authorities as the law of the land'.[1] Article 4 laid down that 'national laws should not contain provisions contrary to international law'. Similar provisions were incorporated in Articles 2 and 3 of Project No. 1 (Fundamental Bases of International Law) submitted in 1927 by the International Commission of Jurists for the consideration of the Sixth International Conference of American States.[2] In the jurisprudence of international tribunals the principle of the supremacy of international obligations over national law has found repeated expression—as, for instance, in Advisory Opinion no. 17 (Greece and Bulgaria, 'Communities' case) where the Permanent Court of International Justice laid down that 'it is a generally accepted principle of international law that in the relations between Powers who are contracting Parties to a treaty, the provisions of municipal law cannot prevail over those of the treaty' (Series B, no. 17, at p. 32).

36. In this connection attention may be directed towards international regulation, in the general scheme of codification, of the application of international law in Federal States. A great—and

---

[1] *Loc. cit.* p. 304.   [2] *A.J.* 22, No. 1 (1928), Special Supplement, p. 238.

STATES IN INTERNATIONAL LAW

probably growing—part of the world is organized on a federal basis. The growth of the scope of multilateral treaties has revealed the complexities of the situations arising out of the fact that the effective treaty-making power of Federal States—and, as the result, the efficacy of international treaties—may be reduced by the fact that questions forming the subject-matter of these treaties fall within the province of the member States of Federal States. The constitution, recently revised, of the International Labour Organisation has accommodated the functioning of the Organisation to that fact. The courts of various countries have, by reference to the peculiarities of the constitutions of the countries concerned, adopted divergent attitudes on the subject—as may be seen, for instance, from the decisions of the Judicial Committee of the Privy Council with regard to certain international labour conventions concluded by Canada and the decisions of the Supreme Court of Canada in the matter of the International Air Navigation Convention of 1919. Some decisions of the Supreme Court of the United States—such as *Missouri* v. *Holland* (1920), 252 U.S. 416, *U.S.* v. *Pink* (1942), 315 U.S. 203, and *Hines* v. *Davidowitz* (1941), 312 U.S. 52—have drawn attention to the impact of the federal structure of States on their capacity to fulfil the obligations of international law. The time may be ripe for considering this question within the framework of the codification of the general principles, the 'fundamental bases', of international law. It will be noted that the French representative on the Codification Committee in 1947 proposed, in connection with the codification of the principles of the Nürnberg Charter and Judgment, 'confirming the supremacy of international law over municipal law in the international penal sphere'.[1]

2. STATES IN INTERNATIONAL LAW

37. Sovereign and independent States are the principal—though not exclusive—subjects of international law. A systematic exposition of international law, whether in the form of a code or otherwise, must therefore be concerned, in the first instance, with three aspects of independent statehood. The first is a general formulation of the principal—the 'fundamental'—rights and duties of States; the second refers to the rules and principles governing the formal or substantive commencement of statehood—the subject of recognition; the third refers to questions arising out of changes in the personality

[1] A/AC.10/34, p. 3.

475

SURVEY OF INTERNATIONAL LAW: CODIFICATION

and territorial composition of States—the subject usually referred to as State succession. While the question of fundamental rights and duties of States has loomed large in the official efforts at codification, this has not been the case with regard to recognition and succession of States and Governments.

(a) Fundamental rights and duties of States

38. This subject will be under special consideration by the International Law Commission by virtue of a separate resolution cf the General Assembly, and it is therefore not considered necessary to comment upon it in this context except in two respects. In the first instance, it is assumed that the Declaration—or some similar instrument—would be drafted and adopted as part of what may in the future become a comprehensive codification of international law and that, therefore, the Declaration would not cover, except by way of a general statement of principle, other branches of international law such as the law of treaties or of State responsibility. Secondly, the Declaration on Fundamental Rights and Duties of States will necessarily include rules and principles which would not normally be covered by any specific topic of international law, such as the prohibition of intervention or the affirmation of the right of self-preservation and self-defence.

39. With regard to these questions, it is probable that the codification of the relevant principles of international law will not reach the required degree of usefulness unless it goes beyond a general enunciation of principles. Thus the principle of prohibition of intervention may have to be accompanied, if it is to be complete and authoritative, by an elaboration of the exceptions which are generally considered as rendering intervention legal and permissible. Similarly, with regard to the prohibition of that category of intervention which, as occasionally asserted, assumes the form of revolutionary propaganda, a codification, properly conceived, of the relevant rules of international law would have to take into consideration the difference between revolutionary propaganda by governmental agencies and by private persons and bodies. With regard to the latter, rules would have to be considered for defining the responsibility of the State for such revolutionary activities and propaganda against foreign States as emanate from non-governmental bodies in receipt of governmental support or actually directed by persons in governmental service. With regard to the enunciation of the right of self-preservation and self-defence, a purely general rule would be lacking in authority

STATES IN INTERNATIONAL LAW

unless it were coupled with clear recognition of the principle that while the State concerned is, in the first instance, the sole judge of its right to have recourse to action in self-preservation or self-defence, the ultimate determination of the legal justification of such action must be within the competence of an impartial international authority. Codification, like written law in general, cannot envisage and deal with all the possible contingencies which may arise. A proper degree of generality is of the essence of the law. But its purpose is defeated when the general statement of a legal principle assumes the form of an abstract pronouncement disregarding possibilities and situations which experience has shown to be typical. For this reason, instruments such as the Convention on Rights and Duties of States adopted in 1933 by the Seventh Conference of American States, while providing a useful contribution to any future codification of this aspect of international law, must probably be regarded as a starting point rather than a consummation of the work of codification in this respect.

(b) Recognition of States

40. The question of recognition of States—alongside that of recognition of Governments and belligerency—is, from the practical point of view, one of the most important questions of international law. Yet no attempt has so far been made to include it, on an adequate scale, as part of the work of codification. The League of Nations Committee of Experts devoted a brief discussion to the subject in so far as it is connected with the form of recognition of Governments and the international position of Governments which have not been formally recognized. The great majority of the Committee experienced little hesitation in removing the question from its agenda. Professor Brierly urged that the Committee should

refuse to discuss this question of all others, since the regulation of it by means of international conventions was neither realizable nor desirable. The difficulties arising from it and the delicacy of the question were well known, and, from a purely legal point of view, it was a subject which neither could nor ought to be treated juridically. To take an analogy, it was as though a State passed a law regulating the choice of friends to be adopted by its citizens. Such a law, if passed, would be null and void at the outset, and the same was true of a regulation of international relations.[1]

M. Fromageot fully concurred in that view: 'The recognition of a Government was not a matter which could be legally regulated. It

[1] *Minutes of the First Session*, 1925, pp. 39–40.

477

SURVEY OF INTERNATIONAL LAW: CODIFICATION

was entirely a political question.'[1] This was also the view of most of the members of the Committee. On the other hand, Dr Suarez stated 'definitely that the question was an urgent one, that it had been put aside for political reasons, and that he personally would have desired to see it investigated'. He urged that 'if international relations were to be subordinated to political interests and not to sound legal principles, progress would be too slow'.[2] The Committee did not consider other aspects of recognition.

41. In the projects prepared in 1927 by the International Commission of Jurists in America, the question of recognition appeared, in a somewhat general way, in five articles of Project No. 2 entitled 'States. Existence–Equality–Recognition'. It figured also in two articles of the Convention on Rights and Duties of States adopted in 1933 by the Seventh International Conference of American States. The question of recognition was also the subject of a resolution of the Institute of International Law in 1936[3]—a fact suggesting that the matter is not as incapable of legal regulation as the Committee of Experts tended to assume. It is understood that the Harvard Research had under consideration the subject of recognition with the view to including it among the research Drafts; that valuable preparatory work was done; but that it was not possible to register sufficient progress for the production of a Draft Convention.

42. The main reason for the inability—or reluctance—to extend the attempts at codification to what is one of the central and most frequently recurring aspects of international law and relations has been the widely held view that questions of recognition pertain to the province of politics rather than of law. There are many who believe that that view is contrary to the evidence of international practice—governmental and judicial—and that, if acted upon, it is probably inconsistent with the authority of international law and its effectiveness in one of the most crucial manifestations of the international relations of States. It would seem inconsistent with the authority of international law that the question of the rise of statehood and the capacity of States to participate in international intercourse should be regarded as a matter of arbitrary discretion rather than legal duty. It must therefore be a matter for consideration whether that vast problem ought to remain outside the codifying task of the International Law Commission. There is an imposing body of practice and doctrine making feasible the attempt at

---

[1] *Minutes of the First Session*, 1925, p. 40. [2] *Ibid.* p. 40.
[3] *A.J.* 30 (1936), Suppl. p. 185.

STATES IN INTERNATIONAL LAW

formulating and answering, as a matter of international law, such questions as the requirements of statehood entitling a community to recognition; the legal effects of recognition (or of non-recognition) with regard to such matters as jurisdictional immunity, State succession, diplomatic intercourse; the admissibility and effect, if any, of conditional recognition; the question of the retroactive effect of recognition; the modes of implied recognition; the differing legal effects of recognition *de facto* and *de jure*; the legal consequences of the doctrine and practice of non-recognition; and last—but not least—the province of collective recognition.

43. Most of these problems are also germane to the question of recognition of Governments which, from the practical point of view, seems to be even more urgent than that of recognition of States. In relation to codification the position in this respect would seem to be more favourable than in the matter of recognition of States, for, unlike the latter case, the majority of writers consider that the question of recognition of Governments is regulated by rules of international law. Similar considerations apply to the question of recognition of belligerency.

(c) Succession of States and Governments

44. The question of State succession—even more than that of recognition—has so far remained outside the work of codification. One possible explanation of this fact is that State succession has often been regarded as a problem arising primarily as the result of war and that as such it ought, like the law of war itself, to remain outside the field of codification. This view is open to question. Experience has demonstrated that changes of sovereignty may take place in ways other than the liquidation of the aftermath of war—as has been shown, for instance, by the questions of State succession which have arisen as the result of the emergence of the independent States of India and Pakistan.

45. However that may be, it would seem desirable, in the first instance, to consider the possibility of giving a precise formulation to what has now become a generally recognized principle of law on the subject, namely, that of respect for acquired private rights. That principle has never been seriously challenged. It has been given frequent and authoritative judicial recognition. The Permanent Court of International Justice affirmed it emphatically with regard to what many considered as the borderline case of private rights of political origin created with a view to destroying cultural and

479

SURVEY OF INTERNATIONAL LAW: CODIFICATION

economic values identified with the very being of the successor State. Yet, while the principle of respect for private rights forms part of international law, there is no adequate measure of certainty with regard to its application to the various categories of private rights such as those grounded in the public debt, in concessionary contracts, in relations of government service, and the like. Arbitral practice has occasionally affirmed exceptions to the general principle, as, for instance, with regard to the obligations of the predecessor State in the matter of tort. But these exceptions do not necessarily follow a general principle of law, and their validity has been challenged. Similarly, the exception with regard to the public debt contracted for purposes inimical to the successor State may require clarification.

46. While there has been agreement as to the general principle of respect for private rights, the position with regard to rights and obligations arising out of the treaties concluded by the predecessor State is in many respects obscure. There may be room for the view that, with regard to situations in the matter both of private rights and of treaty obligations, the regulation of the questions involved can more conveniently take place by agreement between the States concerned. On the other hand, international arbitral practice has shown that problems of State succession may arise even when there exist treaties bearing on the subject; that it cannot reasonably be expected that treaties will deal with the whole range of problems which may arise in this connection; and that provision must be made for the contingency of there being no treaty at all. Considerations of justice and of economic stability in the modern world probably require that in any system of general codification of international law the question of State succession should not be left out of account. The law of State succession prevents the events accompanying changes of sovereignty from becoming mere manifestations of power. As such it would seem to deserve more attention in the scheme of codification than has been the case hitherto. The League of Nations Committee of Experts left the question on one side. One member of the Committee did not think that 'it would be practical or desirable and realizable to regulate questions of private, fiscal or administrative law connected with the succession of States. These were problems in which political considerations took precedence of legal considerations.'[1]

47. In connection with State succession it may also be considered to what extent that aspect of codification ought to concern itself (a)

---

[1] M. Rundstein at the first session, 1925: *Minutes*, p. 14.

480

JURISDICTION

with so-called succession of Governments, i.e. of the rights and obligations of a Government which has been successful in a civil war with respect to rights and obligations of the defeated *de facto* Government; and (*b*) with the affirmation of the principle, which is well recognized, that the obligations of the State continue notwithstanding any changes of Government or of the form of Government of the State in question. Any attempt to codify the rules governing the latter principle would not be feasible without a parallel attempt to qualify some such rules as that the obligations in question must have been validly contracted or that their continuation cannot be inconsistent with any fundamental changes in the structure of the State accompanying the revolutionary change of Government. It is clear that any attempt to formulate the principles—and their qualifications—in question would raise problems of great legal and political complexity. However, this need not necessarily constitute a decisive argument against including it within the scheme of codification.

3. JURISDICTION OF STATES

(*a*) *Recognition of acts of foreign States*

48. The obligation of States to give effect to—to recognize—through their courts and other organs the legislative, judicial and, to some extent, administrative acts of foreign States, and private rights acquired thereunder, is occasionally described as following from the principles of independence or equality, or both. It is said that it would be inconsistent with the independence—or equality—of States if the organs of one State were to constitute themselves judges of the legal validity of the legislative, judicial or administrative acts of another State and if they were to refuse to recognize private rights grounded in such acts. Thus conceived, the question of the recognition of acts of foreign States is one of public international law. On the other hand, it is generally acknowledged that the extent to which private rights acquired under foreign law must be recognized is one of private international law. It must also be borne in mind that the question has seldom formed the subject-matter of protests or representations, as a matter of international law, by one State against another.[1] Courts have often referred to it as one of

---

[1] For an example of such representations see the British complaint to Peru, in 1862, with regard to the refusal of Peruvian courts to recognize the right of the courts of the place of domicile to try the question of the validity of a will, at least so far as personal property is concerned (*State Papers*, 1864, vol. 64, no. 31, p. 80). And see Niboyet in *Hague Recueil*, 40 (1932) (ii), 153-77.

international 'comity'—though it is not always clear whether such terminology is due to a somewhat lax use of language or to a considered view that these are not matters within the province of public international law. In this connection it may be a matter for consideration whether the question of judicial assistance ought to be examined by the International Law Commission as a subject for codification in the context of the present section or whether it ought not to come, more suitably, within the orbit of 'development' of international law. That question was among the topics discussed by the League of Nations Committee of Experts; it formed the subject-matter of a draft convention and a scholarly commentary prepared by the Harvard Research.

49. These conflicting considerations are relevant to the question whether the problem of recognition of legislative, judicial and administrative acts of foreign States should form part of the codifying effort of the International Law Commission. There may be weighty reasons of international economic stability and orderly intercourse counselling an international regulation of the subject. Account would also have to be taken of the fact that, quite apart from considerations of *ordre public* of various States setting a limit to the recognition of foreign laws and judgments, international practice has evolved other limitations upon the duty, if any, of giving effect to emanations of foreign sovereignty. Thus the right of a State to recognition of the effects of its jurisdiction is rigidly limited by the right of other States not to permit the exercise of foreign jurisdiction within their territory. This explains the refusal of most States to give effect to foreign penal or confiscatory laws and decrees or to enforce foreign revenue laws. The problem involves the intricate question of the recognition of foreign decrees intended to have extraterritorial effect. It is also germane to the limits of the duty of a State to recognize the nationality laws of other States. While that duty is generally admitted, it does not, as may be seen from the Hague Convention of 1930 on Certain Questions of Conflict of Nationality Laws, extend to nationality conferred in disregard of international law or of general principles of law.

(b) *Jurisdiction over foreign States*

50. This is a subject with regard to which the municipal jurisprudence of States has produced material more abundant than in any other branch of international law. It covers the entire field of jurisdictional immunities of States and their property, of their public

JURISDICTION

vessels, of their sovereigns, and of their armed forces. Its importance in the sphere of international relations is only inadequately reflected in the fact that it has seldom given rise to representations made by one State to another or, as in the *Casablanca* case decided in 1909 under the aegis of the Permanent Court of Arbitration, to international arbitral pronouncement. The same applies to the circumstance that occasionally judges describe the obligation to grant jurisdictional immunity as flowing from international 'comity'. The principle that these obligations of States are grounded in the overriding legal duty to respect the independence and equal status of States is generally recognized. This underlying general agreement explains why, notwithstanding the divergencies in detail, the Committee of Experts was of the view that some of the aspects of this subject were ripe for codification and would be considered by an international conference convened for that purpose.[1] In reply to the questionnaire sent out by the Committee, twenty-one Governments had previously expressed themselves in favour of the codification of this subject; only three States answered in the negative.

51. The Draft Convention of the Harvard Research on the Competence of Courts in regard to Foreign States constitutes a comprehensive attempt at the codification of this branch of the law in most of its aspects—substantive and procedural—including the position of foreign States as plaintiffs. It contains, in addition, a detailed discussion, against the background of an instructive documentation, of the methods of asserting immunity and of the question of enforcement of judgments given in proceedings conducted with the assent of the foreign States concerned. It does not include a treatment of the position of warships and of armed forces in foreign territory. The Brussels Convention of 1926 on the Immunity of State-owned Ships and Cargoes in Time of Peace provides an instructive example of the regulation of a limited portion of the subject.

52. There would appear to be little doubt that the question—in all its aspects—of jurisdictional immunities of foreign States is capable and in need of codification. It is a question which, more than any other aspect of international law, figures in the administration of justice before municipal courts. The increased economic activities of States in the foreign sphere and the assumption by the State in many countries of the responsibility for the management of the principal industries and of transport have added to the urgency of a compre-

[1] For a discussion of the subject by the Committee of Experts see *Minutes of the Fourth Session*, 1928, pp. 22, 23.

483

SURVEY OF INTERNATIONAL LAW: CODIFICATION

hensive regulation of the subject. While there exists a large measure of agreement on the general principle of immunity, the divergencies and uncertainties in its application are conspicuous not only as between various States but also in the internal jurisprudence of States. This applies in particular to that aspect of jurisdictional immunities which arises out of the increase in the economic activities of the State. Thus while in 1926 the Supreme Court of the United States held—in *Berizzi Brothers* v. *Steamship Pesaro* (271 U.S. 562)— that a vessel owned by a foreign State and engaged in ordinary commercial activities is entitled to jurisdictional immunities, much authoritative doubt as to the meaning and effect of that decision was expressed in a case decided in 1945 where Mr Justice Frankfurter, in a concurring opinion, expressed the view that the result in *Berizzi Brothers* v. *Steamship Pesaro* 'was reached without submission by the Department of State of its relevant policies in the conduct of our foreign relations and largely on the basis of considerations which have steadily lost whatever validity they may then have had' (*Republic of Mexico* v. *Hoffman* (1945), 324 U.S. 30).[1] Similarly, while in Great Britain it had been assumed for a long time that the nature of the activity of a foreign governmental vessel is irrelevant for the question of jurisdictional immunity—a principle emphatically though regretfully reaffirmed in 1920[2]—in a more recent decision members of the highest English tribunal expressed doubts whether, having regard to the changed character of international economic activities, the established rule could continue to be applicable.[3] The divergencies of view on the subject as between various countries may be gauged from the fact that while Italian courts have held that a contract for the purchase of shoes for the army is an act of a private law nature and as such outside the principle of immunity,[4] in the United States the same transaction was held to constitute the 'highest sovereign function of protecting itself against the enemies'.[5] In the course of the discussion of the subject before the League of Nations Committee of Experts, M. Fromageot pointed out that the 'situation became rather more doubtful when it was a question of dealing with commercial operations affecting the very existence of the State. A State which engaged in commercial operations would

---

[1] In the internal sphere the Supreme Court, in *State of New York and Saratoga Springs Commission* v. *The United States of America* (1946, U.S. Law Week 4089), followed the same tendency in holding that a State which sells liquor, even in the exercise of the police power, is amenable to the Federal taxing power.

[2] In *The Porto Alexandre* [1920] P. 30.   [3] *The Cristina* [1938] A.C. 845.

[4] *Governo Rumeno* v. *Trutta: Giurisprudenza Italiana*, 1926, 1 (i), 774.

[5] *Kingdom of Roumania* v. *Guaranty Trust Co. of New York*, 250 Fed. 341, 343.

JURISDICTION

of course be regarded as a private individual, but when that State was engaged in transactions affecting the very existence of the nation the situation was not quite the same.'[1]

53. It is doubtful whether considerations of any national interest of decisive importance stand in the way of a codified statement of the law commanding the agreement of a vast majority of nations on this matter. This applies not only to questions of detail on such matters as counter-claim, set-off and various forms of waiver—on all these questions there are occasional divergencies of practice—but also with regard to what is perhaps the central issue in this connection, namely, immunity with regard to State transactions and activities of a commercial and similar character as well as with regard to such transactions and activities of bodies possessing a personality separate from that of the State but in fact acting as an agency of the State. The indications of a change of attitude in the highest tribunals of countries such as the United States and Great Britain show that the obtaining divergencies are not grounded in such fundamental conceptions of national jurisprudence as to preclude a statement of the law commanding general agreement. Reference may also be made in this connection to the changing conceptions of legislative practice in the matter of the immunities of the State's own organs before its courts, as shown by the British Crown Proceedings Act, 1947, and the United States Tort Claims Act, 1946. States may be less inclined to grant jurisdictional immunity to other States at a time when they submit their own agencies to the incidence of legal liability. This factor may act as a reminder of the tendency, which will unavoidably confront those engaged in the task of codifying this aspect of international law, to limit jurisdictional immunities of States not only with regard to activities *jure gestionis* but also in general.

54. While, for various reasons, the question of diplomatic and consular immunities will probably require separate treatment, it may be found convenient to include in the effort to codify this branch of the law the immunities of the Head of the State as well as those of men-of-war and of the armed forces of the State. With regard to the latter, recent decisions of national tribunals have shown that the wide acceptance of the general principle of immunity covers divergencies of practice which amount to a large extent to a denial of the principle of immunity as such. This was clearly shown by the decision, rendered in 1943, of the Canadian Supreme Court,[2] in

---

[1] *Minutes of the Fourth Session*, 1928, p. 23.   [2] [1943] 4 D.L.R. 11; S.C.R. 483.

SURVEY OF INTERNATIONAL LAW: CODIFICATION

which various judges expressed diametrically opposed views on the subject, and in the series of decisions given during the Second World War by Egyptian courts. These decisions suggest also that a bilateral regulation of a subject by the States concerned does not necessarily do away with the necessity of interpreting it against the background of customary international law and of general international treaties of a legislative and codifying character.

55. In this connection reference may also be made to the necessity of making precise and uniform the rules relating to the jurisdictional immunities of not fully sovereign States such as protectorates or member States of Federal States. Here, too, practice has not tended to uniformity.

56. Finally, consideration will probably have to be given to the desirability and feasibility of removing a source of uncertainty and occasional friction resulting from the divergencies of method by which municipal courts take cognizance of the existence of the right to jurisdictional immunity. In many, but not all, countries the courts have relied for that purpose on the statement of the executive branch of the Government, which they have treated as conclusive. So long as such statements of the Executive—given in the form of a certificate, or 'suggestion', or in other ways—are based on an impartial ascertainment, by expert officials, of the legal position and of the status of the foreign Governments or persons concerned, they probably do not amount to an undue interference with the function of the judiciary applying international law as part of the law of the land. The same applies, to some extent, to the question of the weight attached by courts to the statements and declarations of the representatives of the foreign State concerned with regard to the issues of fact and law raised by actions brought before courts. However, in this field, too, the practice has not been uniform and consideration may be given to the necessity of clarifying the existing practice.

(c) Obligations of territorial jurisdiction

57. A general statement of the duties of States arising out of the fact that they exercise jurisdiction within their territory—their territorial sovereignty—can suitably find a place in the Declaration of Rights and Duties of States (which, it may be hoped, will eventually be incorporated within the general scheme of codification as the introductory and basic exposition of the part of international law relating to States). However, in addition to a general statement of that nature, it must be a matter for consideration whether there is not

JURISDICTION

required a 'formulation and systematization' of rules of international law bearing upon the obligations of territorial sovereignty in the interest of orderly neighbourly intercourse and relations. There has been general recognition of the rule that a State must not permit the use of its territory for purposes injurious to the interests of other States in a manner contrary to international law. This rule has been applied, in particular, with regard to the duty of States to prevent hostile expeditions against the territory of their neighbours. The relevant rules of law have found frequent expression in the Foreign Enlistment Acts of the United States and Great Britain; they have also been embodied in the criminal legislation of a number of other States. Some of the main aspects of this part of international law have found expression in the Convention on Duties and Rights of States in the Event of Civil Strife incorporated in 1928 in the Final Act of the Sixth International Conference of American States and subsequently ratified by a number of countries.

58. In the same category of duties grounded in the exclusive jurisdiction of States over their territory may be considered the obligation of the State to prevent its territory from causing economic injury to neighbouring territory in a manner not permitted by international law. The award in the *Trail Smelter Arbitration*—in which it was held that a State is responsible for injury done to the neighbouring territory by noxious fumes emanating from works operated within the State—provides an instructive example of this category of duties. They include a great deal of what is known in the common law countries as the law of nuisance. They comprise the obligation to take measures both of a preventive nature and of active co-operation with other States against the spread of disease and epidemics. They cover the duties of States with regard to the use of the flow of international and non-national rivers in such matters as the pollution of and interference with the flow of rivers. A substantial body of diplomatic correspondence, judicial practice and doctrine has grown around this subject, which is of considerable economic importance and urgency. Unless the law relating thereto is codified in connection with the law bearing upon international rivers as such, its proper place would appear to be in connection with the codification of the law arising from the obligations of territorial jurisdiction.

59. That branch of the codified law would also suitably regulate the following two other matters: The first refers to the obligation of States to refrain from performing jurisdictional acts within the territory of other States except by virtue of a general or special

SURVEY OF INTERNATIONAL LAW: CODIFICATION

permission. Such acts include, for instance, the sending of agents for the purpose of apprehending within foreign territory persons accused of having committed a crime. The second bears upon the question of the duty of courts to refrain from exercising jurisdiction over persons apprehended in violation of the territorial sovereignty of other States or, generally, in violation of international law. The existence of any such duty has been denied by the courts of some States, e.g. of the United States; it has been affirmed by the courts of other States, e.g. of France. In the *Savarkar* case between Great Britain and France decided in 1911, a Tribunal of the Permanent Court of Arbitration did not accede to the view that a country which has irregularly apprehended a suspected criminal in a foreign country is under an obligation to return the fugitive to the country where he had been apprehended in a manner inconsistent with existing treaties.

60. The questions enumerated in this section—the law of hostile expeditions, obligation in case of a civil war, injurious economic use of territory, the law of nuisance, improper interference with the flow of rivers, exercise of jurisdictional acts within foreign territory, and jurisdiction of courts with regard to persons apprehended in violation of foreign sovereignty—seem to represent an unconnected series of questions. In reality, they form part of one aspect of international law as to which there exists already a substantial body of practice and which is probably in need of clarification in the interest of peace and of neighbourly intercourse of States.

(d) Jurisdiction with regard to crimes committed outside national territory

61. The typical question of the jurisdiction of States with regard to offences committed outside their territory is that associated with their jurisdiction over offences committed abroad by aliens. The right of a State to try its own nationals for offences committed abroad is not at issue. It has received authoritative confirmation on the part of national tribunals of many countries. With regard to offences committed or alleged to have been committed by aliens, the subject, though of limited compass, is one which by general admission requires clarification and authoritative solution. It is doubtful whether such final solution has been achieved—or perhaps attempted —by the Judgment of the Permanent Court of International Justice in the case of *The Lotus*. In that case the Court by a bare majority— by the casting vote of its President—held that there was no rule of international law to prevent a State from exercising jurisdiction over

JURISDICTION

aliens with regard to crimes committed abroad. It is possible that, to some extent, the decision of the Court must be read in the light of the special circumstances of the case, namely, of the fact that in one part of its Judgment the Court treated the offence as having in fact been committed on the territory of the State which had assumed jurisdiction. In so far as the Judgment of the Court purports to express a general and unqualified proposition of international law, it has been subjected to criticism and is unlikely to secure general acceptance. In 1937 a Convention concluded in Paris under the auspices of the International Maritime Committee provided, for the case of collision, that the master, or any other person in the service of the ship, can be prosecuted only before the courts of the flag of the vessel, and that no arrest or detention of the vessel can be ordered by any other authority. The League of Nations Committee of Experts considered this question and, after receiving a learned report on the subject, decided, in accordance with the recommendations of the report, that the subject was not 'ripe' for codification. The reason underlying the recommendations of the Rapporteur and the decision of the Committee was that, in view of the diversity of national systems on the subject, 'the international regulation of this question by way of a general convention, although desirable, would encounter grave political and other obstacles' (report of 26 January 1926).

62. It is not certain to what extent the reasons which moved the Committee of Experts to abandon this subject as not being ripe for codification are relevant to the function of the International Law Commission in the matter. Unlike the Committee of Experts, the Commission is not under an obligation to consider the matter from the point of view of its suitability to form the subject-matter of a convention to be adopted by a conference to be convened in the immediate future. The Commission may, in the circumstances of the case, be satisfied with the adoption of a draft stating the more generally accepted and the most acceptable rule of law; it may be content with publishing it or with mere submission of it to the General Assembly for the purpose of being noted or approved without the taking of further action. Neither is it certain to what extent the Commission would feel impelled to attach decisive importance to the existence of any fundamental differences of national jurisprudence on the subject. It may attach greater importance to the fact that such differences as there exist do not disclose an underlying clash of national interests of significance. It may note the fact that

SURVEY OF INTERNATIONAL LAW: CODIFICATION

such national differences may be of a transient character. Thus, for instance, the British House of Lords in the case of *Joyce* v. *Director of Public Prosecutions* declined to recognize the unqualified validity of the rule that in no case can a State assume jurisdiction over an alien for an offence committed abroad. The House of Lords pointed out that having regard to modern developments in the field of communications, adherence to the strict rules of territoriality may lead to results of some absurdity. The Lord Chancellor, in giving judgment, said:

> It would, I think, be strangely inconsistent with the robust and vigorous common-sense of the common law to suppose that an alien quitting his residence in this country and temporarily on the high seas beyond territorial waters or at some even [more] distant spot now brought within speedy reach and there adhering and giving aid to the King's enemies could do so with impunity.[1]

But English law has often been regarded as firmly wedded to the doctrine of territoriality. In dealing with this subject the Commission may wish to attach importance to the fact that, in a world in which distances have shrunk so considerably, the doctrine of territoriality has become capable of modification in many directions.

63. As stated above, the question of the jurisdiction of States in the matter of offences committed by aliens abroad is of limited compass, and it is arguable that, in any scheme of codification, it ought to figure merely as a subdivision of a larger topic such as 'Obligations and Limitations of Territorial Jurisdiction'. At the same time it would appear to be a question of considerable practical importance. States have shown themselves particularly sensitive to other States assuming jurisdiction over their nationals for crimes committed abroad. The subject was regulated in the Havana Convention of 1928 (the so-called Bustamante Code) and in some previous American treaties; it was covered by the resolutions of the Institute of International Law of 1883 and 1931; and it was studied at a series of international congresses of comparative and penal law. It was among the topics dealt with by the Harvard Research which resulted in a Draft Convention of great value. The controversial nature of the principal article in the Draft Convention[2] serves as a

---

[1] [1946] A.C. at p. 369.

[2] Article 7 of the Convention provides that 'A State has jurisdiction with respect to any crime committed outside its territory by an alien against the security, territorial integrity or political independence of that State, provided that the act or omission which constitutes the crime was not committed in exercise of a liberty guaranteed the alien by the law of the place where it was committed.' Yet States are not in the habit of penalizing acts prejudicial to the safety of other States except in the case of active participation in

JURISDICTION

reminder that the subject is not free from difficulty, but the following passage from the Introduction to this Convention of the Harvard Research may usefully be quoted as being relevant not only to the particular question dealt with in the Convention, but—probably—to many other potential topics of codification:

> The investigation indicates that States have much more in common with respect to penal jurisdiction than is generally 'appreciated, that the gulf between those States which stress traditionally the territorial principle and the States which make an extensive use of other principles is by no means so wide as has been generally assumed, that there are other practicable bases of compromise, without sacrifice of any essential State interest, on most if not all of the controverted questions, and that it is feasible to attempt a definition of penal jurisdiction in a carefully integrated instrument which combines recognition of the jurisdiction asserted by most States in their national legislation and jurisprudence with such limitations and safeguards as may be calculated to make broad definitions of competence acceptable to all.[1]

(e) The territorial domain of States

64. The law relating to State territory has remained almost entirely outside the efforts at codification. There have been occasional multilateral declarations and instruments relating to boundaries and to acquisition of territorial sovereignty, such as the General Act of the Berlin Congo Conference of 1885 on notification of future occupations on the African coast; the repeated affirmation by the American States relating to the non-recognition of acquisition of territorial sovereignty by force; the declarations bearing on the Latin-American doctrine of *post-liminii*; and, more important, Projects nos. 10 and 11 of the American Institute of International Law which cover, respectively, the question of territorial boundaries and 'rights and duties of nations in territories in dispute on the question of boundaries'.[2] But, otherwise, the subject has remained untouched by the codification movement. The reasons for that fact are perhaps not difficult to explain. The salient aspect of this part of international law lies in the rules relating to the original acquisition of territorial sovereignty by discovery, occupation, conquest and prescription. Rights and claims to territory have been traditionally regarded as synonymous with the most vital interests of States, and

hostile expeditions. Probably the more satisfactory test is whether such acts constitute an injury to the State or its citizens sufficiently serious to be so treated by an impartial judicial agency.   [1] *A.J.* 29 (1935), Suppl. pp. 446–7.

[2] *A.J.* 20 (1926), Special Number, pp. 318–22.

491

it is perhaps not surprising that there has been a reluctance to cast the applicable rules of law in the form of codified principles which might be invoked immediately, with some eagerness, by parties to pending disputes. This has been so in particular in view of the fact that throughout the last century a number of territorial disputes, still unresolved, have been pending and that the adoption of any rules would, in many cases, have run counter to the interests or views propounded by the parties to existing controversies. The reservation, in connection with the acceptance of the optional clause of Article 36 of the Statute of the Court, relating to so-called past disputes has been largely due to the disinclination to submit territorial disputes to compulsory judicial settlement. Yet, next to claims in respect of the treatment of aliens, territorial disputes have figured most prominently before international arbitrators and tribunals, and there has been as a result an accumulation of a substantial amount of law on the subject. International awards and decisions—as shown, for instance, in the practically unanimous Judgment of the Permanent Court of International Justice in the case of *Eastern Greenland*—have demonstrated that situations of great complexity going back into the distant past and affecting considerable territories can be solved by the application of legal rules. With regard to conflicting claims resulting from discovery and disputed degrees of effectiveness of occupation, these rules, while admitting of a pronounced measure of elasticity in their application, are clear in principle. The obstacle to their being made a subject-matter of codification is political, not legal. The negative importance of the political obstacle may decrease in proportion as it is realized that only an authoritative formulation of the law on the subject may be able to remove the existing unedifying accumulation of conflicting and mutually inconsistent claims with regard to the sovereignty over Arctic and Antarctic regions. Within the framework of some general statement of the law—in one of the forms envisaged in Article 23 of the Statute of the Commission —its work may prove a factor in overcoming what may otherwise be an insoluble deadlock.

65. In this connection consideration may be given to the question to what extent it is feasible, through an authoritative statement of the required period of limitation, to formulate a rule of international law with regard to prescription. The experience of the British Guiana–Venezuelan Arbitration showed that, within a general scheme of codification, the formulation of some other requirements of acquisitive prescription might usefully be attempted. The numerous

JURISDICTION

decisions of high tribunals, such as the Supreme Court of the United States, which have applied the doctrine of prescription to territorial disputes between members of Federal States, would provide instructive material on the subject. It is possible that the majority of the members of the League of Nations Committee of Experts, in denying the existence—and, indeed, the propriety of the existence—of prescription in international law,[1] did not fully take into account both established doctrine and judicial and arbitral practice. Numerous decisions of national courts may also act as a reminder that there are questions of a technical character related to the territorial domain of States which are capable of systematization and clarification through any one of the methods open to the International Law Commission. These include some technical questions of determination of boundaries, the rule of the thalweg, accession and alluvion, and the like.[2]

66. Thirdly, with the prohibition of the right of war—either as the result of the Charter of the United Nations or of the General Treaty for the Renunciation of War—the time would appear ripe for a revaluation of the rôle of conquest as conferring a legal title. There is room for the view that, within the framework of a codification of international law, the principle of non-recognition of acquisition of territory by force may find a place as a legal rule denying the title of conquest to States resorting to war in violation of their fundamental obligations.

67. In addition to the modes of original acquisition of territory, a number of other questions would seem to require clarification in connection with acquisition of and changes in sovereignty. These include the question of the effect of changes of sovereignty—through conquest or cession—upon the nationality of the residents of the territories concerned, in particular of persons not resident in the territory at the time of the transfer of sovereignty. Secondly, experience has shown that the regulation by treaty of the right of option frequently raises problems for the solution of which a general formulation of the applicable law would be both feasible and useful.

(f) The régime of the high seas

68. The question of the codification of the law of the sea presents itself under two aspects, both of which are well illustrated by the two subjects which fall within this branch of international law and

---

[1] *Minutes of the First Session*, 1925, p. 39.

[2] Some of these questions were covered by Project no. 10, referred to above, of the American Institute of International Law.

SURVEY OF INTERNATIONAL LAW: CODIFICATION

which were considered by the League of Nations Committee of Experts. The first was one which may perhaps more properly be considered as falling within what the Statute of the International Law Commission describes as development of international law, namely, the introduction of predominantly new rules of law aiming at regulating some common international interest. This was to some extent the question of the exploitation of the products of the sea. The League of Nations Committee of Experts, after receiving the replies of the Governments and the report of Dr Suarez, one of its members, came to the conclusion, at its second session, that the report submitted to it indicated the problems which a conference including experts of various kinds might be called upon to solve, and emphasized the urgent need for action. At their third session, in 1927, the Committee decided that the international regulation of that branch of the law of the sea can best take place by means of a special procedure involving the co-operation of experts, in particular of the Permanent International Council for the Exploitation of the Sea located at Copenhagen.

69. It will be noted that even in respect of subjects such as the exploitation of the products of the sea, the borderline between 'development' and 'codification' of international law is necessarily elastic—inasmuch as these subjects, too, are covered by a considerable body of progress. Thus the Rapporteur of the Committee, in a report drafted in 1925, submitted a list of sixteen international treaties on the regulation of maritime industries. Since then, further important conventions on the subject have been concluded, such as the Halibut Conventions of 1930 and 1937 between Canada and the United States of America; the Sockeye Salmon Fisheries Convention of 1930 between the same countries; the Regulation of Meshes Agreement of 1937; the London Fisheries Convention of 1943; and the series of Conventions and Protocols concerning the regulation of Whaling of 1931, 1937, 1938 and 1944. Primarily, however, this would appear to be a subject to be covered by the procedure appropriate for the 'development' of international law within the meaning of the Statute of the International Law Commission. The proposals, submitted in this connection by the International Law Association[1] and the Institute of International Law,[2] for an International Sea Commission emphasize this aspect of the problem.

70. On the other hand, by far the greater part of the law of the sea

[1] Report of the International Law Association of 1926, p. 104.
[2] *Annuaire*, 39 (1934), pp. 711–13.

494

would more suitably fall within the framework of 'codification'. For the law of the sea, perhaps more than any other branch of international law, would seem to call for a comprehensive codification in the light of the existing considerable practice intent upon preventing the principle of the freedom of the sea from being transformed into a régime of anarchy. That practice has produced a number of conventions regulating transport by and safety at sea, such as the Conventions concluded under the auspices of the International Maritime Committee on the Unification of the Law in regard to Collisions, of the Law respecting Assistance and Salvage at Sea (a Convention amplified by the Treaty of Montevideo relating to Salvage by Aircraft at Sea), on the Limitation of Shipowner's Liability, and on the Carriage of Goods by Sea (the York–Antwerp Rules adopted by the International Law Association in 1890 and repeatedly revised); the Hague Rules of 1921; the Brussels Convention of 1924 on the Unification of Rules relating to Certain Bills of Lading); and on Maritime Liens and Mortgages (the Brussels Convention of 1926). There is, in addition, a considerable amount of State practice in the form of instruments for securing the safety of traffic on the high seas, such as the Convention for the Safety of Life at Sea concluded in 1914 and revised in 1929, the International Load Line Convention of 1930, and the Convention of 1930 concerning Manned Lightships not on their Stations. The International Code of Signals has now acquired a recognized international character. Various other conventions, such as the International Radiotelegraph Convention, the International Convention for the Protection of Submarine Cables, the numerous Conventions relating to slavery and the slave trade, and treaties aiming at curbing abuses such as illicit liquor traffic, have regulated other aspects of the law of the sea.

71. Alongside that conventional regulation of a substantial part of the law of the sea there exist rules of customary law, some of them of long standing and of a great generality of acceptance. They include the principle of the freedom of the sea in its various applications, the law relating to navigation through straits, to ship's papers, to the powers of visit and search of ships in time of peace, to hot pursuit, to the régime of the surface and subsoil of the bed of the sea, and to piracy. The last-named was the only subject of the customary law of the sea which the League of Nations Committee of Experts considered ripe for codification, but which the Council and the Assembly of the League did not regard as being of sufficient impor-

SURVEY OF INTERNATIONAL LAW: CODIFICATION

tance to warrant the convening of an international conference for the purpose of codifying it. Recent experience has shown that that particular subject, which is one of the oldest branches of customary international law and on the general principles of which there is a substantial measure of agreement—though not as universal as is widely assumed (see above, paragraph 10)—is in need of clarification. This applies not only to such, apparently novel, questions of detail as piracy in territorial waters or the criminality of attempts at piracy, but also to the more fundamental question whether piracy is limited to acts committed by private individuals *animo furandi*.

72. The law of the sea offers an inducement which is of some urgency for a co-ordinated effort at codification. For, in the absence of international regulation aiming at introducing clarity and a reconciliation of conflicting interests, the régime of the freedom of the sea often threatens to assume a complexion of waste and disorder calling for unilateral measures of self-help. While in some matters the principle of the freedom of the sea provides a sufficient and rational basis for a régime of order and co-operation, in others it is productive of gaps which are inimical to peaceful relations between States and to the general international interest. The award in the *Behring Sea Arbitration* affirming the principle of the freedom of the sea disclosed the unsatisfactory nature of the position created by exclusive reliance upon it. The arbitrators, in compliance with the authorization of the parties, recommended a régime based upon a more rational application of the rule. Numerous treaties have been concluded relating to the proper exploitation and preservation of the resources of the sea. But they have not fully met the situation, and the conclusions of the League of Nations Committee of Experts emphasized the urgent need for international regulation. Failing such regulation, nations will have recourse to unilateral action which, while unimpeachable as a matter of equity and justice, is a reflection upon the regulative force of international law. The action of the United States, Mexico, Argentina and Chile in 1945, 1946 and 1947 with regard to the conservation of the natural resources of the sea adjoining their territories provides an instructive example of the drawbacks of the existing situation.

73. In view of the already available substantial body of practice, in the form of conventions and otherwise, in these matters it would appear that they would more properly fall within the framework of codification rather than 'development'—although it would be

496

JURISDICTION

codification with a considerable element of 'development' in it. As mentioned, there is in existence an imposing body of non-controversial rules and principles on other aspects of the international law of the sea. This being so, it must be a matter for consideration whether, of all the branches of international law, that of the law of the sea does not lend itself to comprehensive treatment by way of codifying the entire branch of the law. A codification—in its widest sense—of the entire field of the law of the sea in a unified and integrated 'restatement' or similar, more ambitious, instrument, would go far towards enhancing the authority both of the work of codification and of international law as a whole.

(g) *The régime of territorial waters*

74. In this branch of international law the task of codification will probably proceed on the basis of the achievements of the Hague Codification Conference of 1930 and of the preparatory work which preceded it. No expression of opinion is called for here on the question whether the results of that Conference may legitimately be called a failure. It will be noted that the Conference produced some agreed instruments in the form of Articles on the Legal Status of the Territorial Sea—a detailed and valuable document—and on the base line, both in general and with regard to the particular cases of bays, islands, groups of islands, and straits. There is general agreement that the Bases of Discussion, the documentation on which they were based and the discussions in the relevant Committees provide material of the utmost usefulness. However that may be, in attempting the codification of this part of international law the Commission will be in a different position from that of the Committee of Experts and the Hague Conference. Its task will not be limited to adopting articles and producing a draft intended to be accepted as a convention requiring the agreement of all or most States. On the crucial question of the extent of territorial waters it will be in the position to state the existing law in terms not only of agreement, but also, in an analytical and critical manner, of the absence of agreement; it will be able to disregard extravagant demands; it will possess the authority to put unorthodox but justified claims in terms of principle rather than of mileages. It will be in the position to attach significance to prescriptive rights, to important economic and strategic interests, to changes resulting from modern conditions. By reference to these factors it will be in the position to approach the no less crucial question of the contiguous zone and protective jurisdiction.

SURVEY OF INTERNATIONAL LAW: CODIFICATION

75. The fact that the International Law Commission is by its Statute enabled to adopt methods and pursue objects somewhat different from those which the League of Nations prescribed for the Committee of Experts suggests that it may be possible to achieve a distinct measure of continuity in relation to past efforts at codification. There need be no disposition to discard subjects with regard to which previous efforts are deemed to have failed. For the failure which attended one method and one object need not be decisive with regard to different methods and objects. Moreover, it would be unfortunate if the regulation of questions of obvious importance in the sphere of international transport and international economic intercourse generally—such as the position of foreign merchantmen in territorial and in national waters—were to suffer from the inability to achieve uniformity with regard to the breadth of territorial waters.

4. THE INDIVIDUAL IN INTERNATIONAL LAW

(a) The law of nationality

76. As in the matter of the two other subjects covered by the work of the Hague Codification Conference, so also with regard to the question of nationality, the International Law Commission will be able to draw upon instructive lessons of past experience. Both in the formal and in the substantive sense the achievement of the Conference in the matter of nationality was a promising one. It produced a Convention and a number of protocols on subjects which had previously shown a conspicuous divergency of practice and of doctrine and which, because of the importance of nationality, were considered to be highly political. Moreover, the adoption of these instruments was followed in some countries by legislative changes with regard to matters which had been considered as constituting characteristic and permanent features of national jurisprudence. But it would probably be a mistake to exaggerate the significance of the achievement of the Hague Conference in the matter of nationality and to assume that that subject need no longer be considered for the purpose of codification. In particular, it may not be fully accurate to gauge the achievement of the Conference from the fact that it produced a Convention—an instrument which has not secured many ratifications in excess of the minimum number often required for its entry into force. While the Convention embodied

498

THE INDIVIDUAL IN INTERNATION LAW

agreement on such questions as the general principles governing conferment of nationality and the diplomatic protection of persons of dual nationality, no agreement proved possible on important questions of substance such as the removal of the principal causes of double nationality and of statelessness and the right of expatriation. Mainly owing to the solution—or semblance of solution—adopted by the Conference on the latter subject, the United States declined to sign the Convention. No serious attempt was made to investigate the possibility of a single criterion for acquisition of nationality by birth. While the Convention recognized the right of persons of dual nationality to renounce one of them, it made such renunciation conditional upon the authorization of the State whose nationality was being surrendered. With regard to nationality of married women, the subsequent legislation of some countries has gone further than the hesitating provisions of the Convention, which in this respect lags behind recent developments. Of the protocols adopted by the Conference—they all referred to matters of detail—two have entered into force.

77. It may thus be said that while revealing the potentialities of the international regulation of the subject, the work of the Hague Codification Conference on the question of nationality touched only the fringes of the problem. In an era of economic nationalism and isolation, when freedom of movement across the frontiers tends to become nominal, the urgency of an international regulation of conflicts of nationality laws and statelessness is less apparent. But, it is to be hoped, the position in this respect may undergo a change. Moreover, in an international system in which the fundamental rights and freedoms of the individual are bound to gain increasingly effective recognition, the law of nationality is likely to become once more the subject of remedial codification aiming both at systematizing existing agreement and at removing anomalies which are a cause of inconvenience and are derogatory to the dignity of man. With regard to the right of expatriation, the Convention on Nationality adopted in 1933 by the Seventh International Conference of American States may provide a promising starting-point for further efforts at codification.[1] This applies also to some other questions regulated in that Convention.

[1] Articles 1 and 2 of the Convention provide, in simple language, as follows:
'Article 1. Naturalization of an individual before the competent authority of any of the signatory States carries with it the loss of the nationality of origin.'
'Article 2. The State bestowing naturalization shall communicate this fact through diplomatic channels to the State of which the naturalized individual was a national.'

SURVEY OF INTERNATIONAL LAW: CODIFICATION

78. With regard to the abolition of statelessness—a status, or the absence thereof, which is both derogatory to the dignity of the individual human being and a reflection upon the logic of traditional international law which makes the possession of nationality the only link between the individual and the benefits and duties of the law of nations—the Hague Conference made little, if any, progress. The Protocol which it adopted with regard to the deportation of persons denationalized while abroad was based on the assumption of the continuance of statelessness in international law rather than on its abolition. However, it is probable that in this respect the proper sphere of international regulation through the efforts of the International Law Commission will be not through codification but through 'development' aiming at introducing a departure from the existing practice.[1] That practice still continues to multiply the potential causes of statelessness. In particular, many countries have recently adopted or are on the eve of adopting legislation which provides for the deprivation of certain classes of their citizens of their nationality by way of punishment for disloyalty or otherwise.

(b) The treatment of aliens

79. The reasons which have been adduced in the previous section as militating in favour of a renewed effort at codifying the law of nationality and of conflicts of nationality—the growing movement across frontiers in an age in which barriers of distance have dwindled, and the enhanced status of the individual as the subject of fundamental rights and freedoms—apply even more cogently to the question of the treatment and the legal position of aliens. Apart from the somewhat general provisions of the Convention on the Status of Aliens adopted in 1928 by the Sixth International Conference of American States, and apart from individual references to the civil equality of aliens in resolutions adopted by the Pan-American Conferences (e.g. in Article 2 of the Resolution of the Seventh Conference in 1933 on the International Responsibility of the State), this subject has so far remained outside the orbit of the codifying movement. Some aspects of it were discussed indirectly in connection with the question of the responsibility of the State for

---

[1] The Economic and Social Council in its Resolution no. 116 (VI) D, adopted in March 1948, recognized that the problem of stateless persons 'demands ... the taking of joint and separate action by Member nations in co-operation with the United Nations to ensure that everyone shall have an effective right to a nationality', and requested that the Secretary-General undertake a study relative to statelessness and submit recommendations to the Council as to the desirability of concluding a further convention on this subject. The Secretariat study is contained in United Nations document E/1112.

500

THE INDIVIDUAL IN INTERNATIONAL LAW

damage done to the persons and property of aliens, within the framework of the Hague Conference of 1930. The matter was examined in detail by the Economic Committee of the League of Nations, as one aspect of the 'equitable treatment for the commerce of all members of the League' which members undertook to observe in Article 23 of the Covenant. It includes such questions as the taxation of aliens; their right to exercise any particular profession, industry, or occupation; the treatment of aliens in respect of residence, travel, and the right to hold and bequeath property; the extent of the obligation to perform public services of local and national importance. There is on this subject a substantial body of State practice which, however, is only imperfectly related to principle. In some cases that practice is due to particular economic or strategic considerations, and it may be difficult to put it within the framework of a generally applicable rule. The League Committee formulated a draft convention which, in most matters, constituted not so much an attempt to state the rule of law on the basis of existing practice as an expression of desirable rules of equitable treatment.[1] The draft was submitted in 1929 to a Conference but the results of its deliberations proved inconclusive.

80. The International Law Commission may have to give detailed consideration to the question whether these and similar aspects of the treatment of aliens ought to be brought within a uniform rule of international law or whether they ought to be left to the discretion of States and to bilateral agreements. The question would also have to be considered to what extent it is feasible to provide for equality of treatment as between alien and alien and to prohibit discrimination against certain categories of aliens with regard to both economic benefits and eligibility for legal assimilation to the majority population.

81. In one definite respect the law relating to the treatment of aliens would seem to require authoritative statement or restatement, namely, with regard to (a) the full equal protection of such rights as they possess by the law of the State and (b) absolute recognition and protection of what the Charter of the United Nations describes as human rights and fundamental freedoms. So long as the equality of the rights of the alien and of the national has not become part of international or domestic law, the rule—which is an undoubted

---

[1] See League Docs. A.11, 1923.II; A.52, 1924.II; A.46, 1925.II. See also, for a useful survey, Norman MacKenzie (ed.), *The Legal Status of Aliens in Pacific Countries* (1937).

SURVEY OF INTERNATIONAL LAW: CODIFICATION

part of international law—must be authoritatively affirmed that the position of an alien before courts and administrative authorities is the same as that of a national for the purpose of asserting rights granted to him by the law of the State. That duty is already recognized in the form of the obligation of the State to prevent a denial of justice. But there would appear to be room for an expansion of that principle, for instance, by generalizing the rule, adopted in numerous treaties, to the effect that aliens, like nationals, are exempted from the requirement to deposit security for costs.

82. Secondly, the effective recognition of the provisions of the Charter of the United Nations relating to human rights and fundamental freedoms—applicable by definition to nationals and aliens alike—would naturally find a place in any codification of the law relating to the treatment of aliens. The controversy, which was largely responsible for the negative result of the Hague Codification Conference, on the subject of whether a State can adduce the fact of non-discrimination as a reason for relieving it of responsibility for the treatment of aliens has now been resolved so far as fundamental human rights and freedoms are concerned. The principle authoritatively asserted by arbitral tribunals, that the plea of non-discrimination cannot be validly relied upon if the State does not measure up to a minimum standard of civilization, has now found expression in the provision of the Charter relating to human rights and fundamental freedoms. These must be deemed to be co-extensive with the minimum standard of civilization. Thus some courts in the United States have held that the enjoyment of certain fundamental rights guaranteed by the Constitution must be conceded even to those aliens who have entered the country illegally; this applied, in particular, to the right of access to courts. It is possible that the adoption of an international Bill of Human Rights may be of assistance in defining what constitutes the minimum standard of civilization. Even after an effective Bill of Rights has materialized there will still remain the question of the relevance of the plea of non-discrimination in matters others than those pertaining to the 'minimum standard of civilization', such as the limits of the respect for property of aliens. It will be a matter for consideration whether the answer to that question can be attempted within the framework of a codification of the law relating to aliens. It is possible that in the recent experience of various controversies on the subject there may be discernible a solution which would act both as an inducement to and as a basis of codification.

THE INDIVIDUAL IN INTERNATIONAL LAW

83. In connection with the codification of that part of the law relating to the treatment of aliens which bears upon human rights and fundamental freedoms, there may also be considered the desirability of formulating as part of this branch of the law the rules relating to the treatment of stateless or similarly situated persons. In general conventions concluded before the Second World War—such as the Convention of 1936 concerning the Status of Refugees from Germany —the refugees, stateless and other, were in most respects assimilated to aliens with regard to residence and access to courts. So long as international law has not eliminated the possibility of a category of stateless persons it ought to make provision for making operative with respect to them those human rights and fundamental freedoms which pertain to the human being as such regardless of the possession of any nationality.[1]

84. Finally, in connection with the codification of the law relating to the treatment of aliens it will probably be necessary—and feasible—to formulate the law relating to the expulsion of aliens and stateless persons. Arbitral practice has clarified the law sufficiently to make such an attempt practicable. The principle that aliens lawfully admitted and permanently established must not be arbitrarily expelled has tended to receive general recognition. It will still be necessary to define, in connection with a general codification of the law on the subject, the details and conditions of its application.

(c) Extradition

85. The codification of the law of extradition—largely in the direction of evolving a general treaty of extradition—has been the subject of numerous, and in many cases successful, attempts on the part of private individuals, scientific bodies, and Governments.[2] Of the latter efforts, the Treaty of 1911 between Argentina, Paraguay, Uruguay, Bolivia and Peru, the Bustamante Code of 1928, the Convention on Extradition signed in 1933 at the Seventh International Conference of American States, and the Central American Convention of 1934 are in force and have received frequent judicial application. The subject of extradition received detailed attention on the part of the League of Nations Committee of Experts. In 1926 the Committee, in reliance upon the conclusions of a sub-committee, adopted a report according to which only the following five questions could

---

[1] See United Nations document E/1112 prepared pursuant to Economic and Social Council Resolution no. 116 (VI) D, adopted in March 1948.

[2] These attempts are enumerated on p. 47 of the introductory comment of the Harvard Research Draft Convention on Extradition (*A.J.* 29 (1935), Suppl.).

503

SURVEY OF INTERNATIONAL LAW: CODIFICATION

properly be made the subject-matter of codification by way of a general international convention:

1. The question whether and in what conditions a third State ought to allow a person who is being extradited to be transported across its territory.

2. The question which of two States both seeking extradition of the same person from a third State ought to have priority over the other.

3. The questions which arise as to the extent of the restrictions on the right to try an extradited person for an offence other than that for which he was extradited and on a State's right to extradite to a third State a person who has been delivered to it by way of extradition.

4. The question as to the right of adjourning extradition when the person in question has been charged or convicted, in the country where he is, for another crime.

5. The question of confirming the generally recognized rule by which the expenses of extradition should be borne entirely by the claimant State.

With regard to other, more substantial, questions—such as extradition of nationals, the evidence of guilt required in support of a request for extradition, and the relative positions of the Executive and the Judiciary in connection with extradition proceedings—the divergencies in the practice of States were, in the view of the Committee, such as to make impracticable any attempt to codify the law of extradition in the form of a general international convention. For these reasons the Committee refrained from including extradition in the list of subjects which were ripe for codification. These reasons were subsequently re-examined by the authors of the Harvard Research Draft Convention on Extradition. They were not considered sufficient to justify abandoning the efforts to codify the law on the subject. The resulting Draft Convention of the Harvard Research will doubtless provide a most convenient and useful starting-point for any future efforts in this connection. In addition, the Draft Convention is accompanied by a schedule containing draft articles of reservations on such subjects as capital punishment, fiscal offences, non-extradition of nationals coupled with the duty of prosecution by the requested State, and requirement of proof of a *prima facie* case either generally or in relation to nationals of the requested State.

86. It will be for the International Law Commission to consider

THE INDIVIDUAL IN INTERNATIONAL LAW

whether the reasons which prompted the League Committee of Experts not to include the law of extradition in the list of subjects ripe for codification are sufficiently persuasive in the light of the general nature of the task confronting the Commission. As already stated in other parts of this survey, the function of the Commission is not limited to drafting instruments offering an immediate prospect of acceptance by way of a general international convention. In this, as well as in other matters, it will be within the province of the Commission to consider to what extent the divergencies in national practice—especially in matters not reflecting an underlying conflict of important political or economic interests—can legitimately be regarded as an obstacle to codification rather than as an incentive to it. (It will be noted that because of the differences in national laws and procedure the Committee decided not to proceed with another subject of codification closely related to extradition, namely, communication of judicial and extra-judicial acts in penal matters and letters rogatory in penal matters.[1])

87. There would seem to exist persuasive reasons counselling a unification and clarification of the law of extradition within the general task of codification. The law of extradition has traditionally served two purposes the importance and urgency of which have tended to increase rather than diminish. In the first instance, the law of extradition is an instrument of international co-operation for the suppression of crime. Its increased importance is obvious at a time of rapid development of communications enabling offenders to leave the country where the crime was committed. Secondly, some aspects of the law of extradition have served to afford a measure of protection to persons accused of crime. This applies, for instance, to the rule that the extradited person must not be tried for a crime other than that in respect of which extradition has been granted (though the purpose of this rule is also, to some extent, to safeguard

[1] See the discussion at the fourth session of the Committee, 1928, pp. 11–16. The Committee attached decisive importance to the fact that, according to what was believed to be a fundamental rule of procedure in Anglo-Saxon countries, witnesses could be heard only in the presence of the accused. However, at its fourth session, held in 1928, the Committee of Experts, in connection with the consideration of a report of the Mixed Committee for the Suppression of Counterfeiting Currency, decided that 'it is desirable and it would seem to be realizable that, in multilateral conventions dealing with crimes and offences the prosecution and repression of which are recognized to be of international interest, collaboration between States in the preliminary judicial investigation of such crimes and offences should be ensured to the extent compatible with the municipal laws of the Contracting Parties' (*Minutes*, p. 28). 'In these circumstances and with these restrictions' the Committee felt able to recommend the formulation of international rules concerning the communication of judicial and extra-judicial acts in penal matters and letters rogatory in penal matters.

505

SURVEY OF INTERNATIONAL LAW: CODIFICATION

the sovereignty of the extraditing State). Above all, this function of the law of extradition covers one of its central aspects, namely, the principle of non-extradition of political offenders. While that principle has been recognized almost universally, there has been a considerable divergence in the practice of the courts and in municipal legislation as to the manner of its application. Thus, for instance, according to the Finnish Law of 1922 a political offence was extraditable if the act was in the nature of an atrocity. The French Law of 1927 adopted a similar test. Both English and French courts have declined to extend the principle of non-extradition of political offenders to crimes committed in furtherance of anarchism on the ground, which is controversial, that anarchism, which does not aim at the substitution of one Government (or form of government) for another, is not a political faith at all. In general, it is possible that the International Law Commission may find it difficult to act on the view that the differences of national laws and jurisprudence on the subject of extradition are so fundamental and decisive[1] as to render impracticable any attempt to include it within the general scheme of codification.

(d) The right of asylum

88. The question of the right of asylum, although closely connected with that of non-extradition of political offenders, is considerably wider in scope. In the first instance, it refers not only to the obligation not to extradite political offenders. It implies a positive duty to receive them. Secondly, it not only covers political offenders; it embraces victims of persecution fleeing from the country of oppression. Thirdly, it has acquired prominence in connection with asylum in legations, warships, and military camps. It is this latter category of cases which forms the main subject-matter of the Pan-American Convention on Asylum concluded in 1928, as distinguished from the more general Convention on Political Asylum adopted in 1933 by the Seventh International Conference of American States. At a time when revolutions in democratic States have not as yet become a matter of the past and when in other States the nature of the political régime produces a climate favourable to rebellion and persecution alike,

---

[1] Thus, for instance, during the discussion of the subject in the course of the first session of the Committee of Experts in 1925 Professor Brierly adduced as a main reason for the unsuitability of extradition as a subject of codification the fact that the criminal law of some countries was distinctly territorial (*Minutes*, p. 32). But see the above section of this survey [paras. 61–63] for the suggestion that the principle of territoriality of criminal law may not be as immutable as is occasionally believed.

TREATIES

the subject cannot be regarded as obsolete or as restricted to the principle of non-extradition of political offenders. In the Constitution of 1946 France reaffirmed its attachment to the principle of asylum for victims of persecution.

89. On the other hand, recent developments have not been uniformly in the direction of the vindication of the principle of asylum. This applies to such instruments as the Convention for the International Prevention and Punishment of Terrorism and the Convention for the Creation of an International Criminal Court. These Conventions, signed by a small number of States in 1937, have not entered into force. Under the stress of the circumstances produced by the Second World War, exceptions have been made with regard to traitors, 'quislings', and persons acting contrary to the principles of the United Nations. In the Paris Peace Treaties of 1947 provision was made for extradition by the defeated States not only of war criminals but also of traitors accused of collaboration with the Axis Powers. It·will be for the Commission to take stock of the situation. It is possible that in a world in which the observance of human rights and fundamental freedoms has become a reality there will be no room for revolutions which purport to vindicate the rights of man or for persecutions which assault them. It will be for the International Law Commission to decide whether that possibility is so distinct as to render unnecessary the more precise formulation, in modern conditions, of what has been regarded by many as a significant principle of international law and practice.

5. THE LAW OF TREATIES

90. The law of treaties has figured prominently, in various ways, in connection with codification. It constituted what was perhaps the most ambitious and detailed effort in the work of the Harvard Research. It was considered in 1925 by the American Institute of International Law, the project of which was submitted in 1927 by the Governing Body of the Pan-American Union to the International Commission of American Jurists and eventually adopted in 1928 by the Sixth International Conference of American States as a 'Convention on Treaties'—a document somewhat general in character. Some aspects of the subject were considered by the League of Nations Committee of Experts in connection with the question 'whether it is possible to formulate rules to be recommended for the procedure of international conferences and the conclusion and drafting of treaties,

507

SURVEY OF INTERNATIONAL LAW: CODIFICATION

and what such rules should be'. Although the Committee, after having received the replies òf Governments, came to the conclusion that the subject was ripe for codification,[1] the Council of the League decided that the subject was 'in no sense urgent' and recommended that it be further studied by the Secretariat.

91. Persuasive reasons may be adduced in support of the view that it is desirable to include the entire subject of treaties within the orbit of codification. Their place in the system of international law needs no emphasis. The majority of cases which came before the Permanent Court of International Justice were concerned with the interpretation of treaties. Yet there is hardly a branch of the law of treaties which is free from doubt and, in some cases, from confusion. This applies not only to the question of the terminology applied to the conception of treaties, to the legal consequences of the distinction between treaties proper and inter-governmental agreements, and to the designation of the parties to treaties. There is uncertainty as to the necessity of ratification with regard to treaties which have no provision for ratification; in the matter of the important subject of the relevance of the constitutional limitations upon the treaty-making power; and in respect of conferment of benefits upon third parties. The field of interpretation of treaties continues to be overgrown with the weed of technical rules of construction which can be used—and are frequently used—in support of opposing contentions. The Permanent Court of International Justice did a great deal to reduce to proper proportions the rule that treaties ought to be applied so as to involve a minimum of restriction of sovereignty. Experience has shown the doubtful usefulness of the 'liberal' interpretation of treaties. Thus, in the matter of extradition, in some cases the rule as to 'liberal' interpretation has been invoked with a view to benefiting the accused; in others, in order to make the treaty more effective to the disadvantage of the accused. The rule that treaties must be interpreted so as to make them effective rather than ineffective has often been relied upon in disregard of the fact that the parties intended to limit the effectiveness of the treaty in a manner involving a minimum of obligation. Although the activity of international tribunals has now evolved a substantial body of practice with regard to the use of *travaux préparatoires*, that subject continues to be a matter of uncertainty and discussion in international proceedings. The

---

[1] There was, however, a difference of opinion in the Committee of Experts as to the methods best calculated to achieve that object. While the majority favoured an international conference, others preferred to entrust the subject to a limited body of experts. For a discussion of the subject see *Minutes of the Third Session*, 1927, pp. 42–4.

DIPLOMATIC INTERCOURSE AND IMMUNITIES

divergent interpretations of the most-favoured-nation clause continue to cause difficulties, and it may be necessary to reconsider the view expressed by the League of Nations Committee of Experts that the subject, which it discussed in detail on the basis of a thorough report, can be best dealt with by way of bilateral agreements.

92. Above all, there is room for a further scientific effort to clarify and make more precise the conditions of the operation of the doctrine *rebus sic stantibus*. Thus the Harvard Research Convention, following closely the decision of the Permanent Court of International Justice in the *Free Zones* case between Switzerland and France, adopted a formulation of the *clausula rebus sic stantibus* which many may find unduly restrictive (Article 28). But if the principle of fidelity to treaties is to be maintained and strengthened, then a more searching enquiry than has been made hitherto is necessary as to the effect of changed conditions upon the continued obligation to perform a treaty. To say, as suggested in the Harvard Draft, that the change must refer to a 'state of facts the continued existence of which was envisaged by the parties as a determining factor moving them to undertake the obligations stipulated' may mean attaching too rigid a condition upon the operation of the clause which, in the general interest, ought not to be reduced to a mere formula. There is reason to believe that this is the kind of subject which, both because of its importance and because of its political implications, can be suitably treated by a highly authoritative body such as the International Law Commission in connection with the codification of the law of treaties.

6. THE LAW OF DIPLOMATIC INTERCOURSE AND IMMUNITIES

93. The subject of the law of diplomatic intercourse and immunities requires but brief comment in the present survey. The question of diplomatic privileges and immunities was among those which the Committee of Experts of the League of Nations, after studying the replies of the Governments, considered without much hesitation as ripe for codification. The Assembly of the League, while deciding in September 1927 that a conference should be convened for the purpose of codifying the laws of nationality, of responsibility of States, and of territorial waters, was of the opinion that no action should be taken with regard to diplomatic privileges and immunities.[1] What were believed to be the discouraging results of the First Hague

---

[1] This was also the decision with regard to the law of piracy.

509

Codification Conference and the political conditions of the world in the last decade of the existence of the League of Nations were responsible for the fact that no further attempt was made to proceed with the codification of a subject as to which there exists a very substantial measure of agreement on matters of principle, which forms one of the oldest and most firmly established parts of international law, and the application of which is a constant occurrence. In 1927 and 1928 the Committee of Experts considered also the question of the revision of the classification of diplomatic agents. However, in the light of the answers received from Governments the Committee found that the matter was not of sufficient urgency and importance to warrant its retention as one of the topics of codification. In 1928 the Sixth International Conference of American States concluded at Havana a Convention on Diplomatic Officers —an instrument which is of a more detailed character than most of the other Pan-American Conventions of this type and which is not confined to the question of diplomatic immunities. For it is also concerned with the organization of the diplomatic mission, the duties of diplomatic representatives, and the commencement and termination of the diplomatic mission. In 1932 the Harvard Research in International Law published a Draft Convention, accompanied by scholarly comment and abundant material, on Diplomatic Privileges and Immunities.

94. The work of the League of Nations Committee of Experts, of the Havana Convention of 1928, and of the Harvard Research, the documentation on which that work was based, as well as the rich sources of judicial practice, of diplomatic correspondence, and of doctrinal writing and exposition, provide sufficient material for a comprehensive effort at codifying this part of international law. The wealth of the available practice need not necessarily mean that such codification would be merely in the nature of systematization and imparting precision to a body of law with regard to which there is otherwise agreement on all details. This is not the case. Practice has shown divergencies, some of them persistent, on such questions as the limits of immunity with regard to acts of a private law nature, the categories of the diplomatic staff which are entitled to full jurisdictional immunities, the immunities of the subordinate staff, the immunities of nationals of the receiving State, the extent of the immunities from various forms of taxation, conditions of waiver of immunities, and the nature of acts from which such waiver will be implied. There may also have to be considered the consequences of

CONSULAR INTERCOURSE AND IMMUNITIES

the partial amalgamation, in some countries, of the diplomatic and consular services. For the task confronting the International Law Commission in this matter is not only one of diplomatic immunities and privileges, but also of the various aspects of diplomatic intercourse in general.

7. THE LAW OF CONSULAR INTERCOURSE AND IMMUNITIES

95. Some of the considerations referred to in the preceding section on the codification of the law of diplomatic intercourse and immunities apply also to the law relating to consuls. Both constitute one of the oldest branches of international law; both loom large in the daily relations of States. In 1928 the League of Nations Committee of Experts reported to the Council of the League that the question of the 'legal position and functions of consuls' was 'sufficiently ripe for codification'. In the same year the Assembly decided to reserve this question 'with a view to subsequent conferences'. For reasons already stated, no conference on this subject took place. Important aspects of the law of consular intercourse had been previously codified in the Caracas Agreement between some South American States in 1911. The Sixth International Conference of American States adopted in 1928 a comprehensive Convention on Consular Agents the principal sections of which are concerned with the appointment and functions of consuls, their prerogatives and immunities, and the suspension and termination of consular functions. The Harvard Research produced in 1932 a detailed Draft Convention on the Legal Position and Functions of Consuls. Any subsequent effort to codify this aspect of international law will, in addition, be able to rely on unusually extensive material in the form of regulations issued by almost all States to their consular representatives abroad and on a great number of treaties which cover the subject either within the framework of general treaties of commerce and navigation or in instruments devoted entirely to the legal position and functions of consuls.

96. While the law on the subject is based on the general recognition of the principle that consuls do not enjoy diplomatic character,[1] the

---

[1] The cautious wording of Article 12 of the Havana Convention of 1928 may be noted in this connection. It lays down that 'in case of the absence of a diplomatic representative of the consul's State, the consul may undertake such diplomatic actions as the Government of the State in which he functions may permit in such cases'. An express reservation to this article was entered by Venezuela on the ground that 'it is totally opposed to our tradition, maintained since it was established until the present time in a way that admits of no change'.

511

SURVEY OF INTERNATIONAL LAW: CODIFICATION

existing practice, however abundant, does not show such a degree of uniformity as to make the work of codification one of mere co-ordination and systematization. It is of interest to note that the authors of the Harvard Research Draft, after drawing attention to the voluminous material on the subject, state that 'a perusal of this material indicates that comparatively few of the functions and privileges of consuls are established by universal international law' and that 'thus a code on the subject will be to a considerable extent legislation'.[1] However, it is probable that in the field of consular functions and immunities the work of the International Law Commission will be less in the nature of legislation than in other fields. Thus in the matter of immunities of consuls from the civil and criminal jurisdiction of the receiving State with respect to their official acts, the existing practice, which is fairly uniform, will be found to be one of the application of the general rule of international law with regard to the jurisdictional immunities of foreign States. On the other hand, the International Law Commission will probably have to consider afresh the objections raised in the Committee of Experts to the codification of this branch of the law on the ground that, in view of the wide diversity in the economic and political conditions of various States, this was a subject more suitable for regulation by way of bilateral treaties.[2] Eventually the opinion prevailed that, in view of the continual expansion of international trade, the legal position and functions of consuls should be regulated on as universal a basis as possible.

8. THE LAW OF STATE RESPONSIBILITY

97. A substantial portion of international law relating to State responsibility has received attention and considerable study in connection with the work of codification under the auspices of the League of Nations. The bases of discussion drafted in preparation for the Codification Conference of 1930; the replies of the Governments on which its draftsmen relied; the preliminary discussions of the Committee of Experts; and the work, however inconclusive, of the Conference of 1930—have all made a notable contribution to

---

[1] *A.J.* 26 (1932), Suppl. p. 214.

[2] See the observations of Dr McNair at the third session of the Committee in 1927, *Minutes of the Third Session*, p. 25, and of M. Fromageot at the first session, 1925, *Minutes of the First Session*, p. 31. The replies of Governments were less favourable to codification than in the case of diplomatic immunities. While eighteen were in favour of codification, eight were against it. See *Minutes of the Fourth Session*. 1928, p. 16.

STATE RESPONSIBILITY

the further study of the subject. The same applies to the Draft Convention prepared in 1929 under the auspices of the Harvard Research. It was only natural that the preparatory work of a codification conference on the subject of the responsibility of States for damage to the person and property of aliens should cover what is perhaps the major part of the law of State responsibility. This is so for two reasons. In the first instance, treatment of aliens and injuries to aliens have constituted in practice the most conspicuous application of the law of responsibility of States. In the jurisprudence of international tribunals claims arising out of injuries to the person and property of aliens have constituted the bulk of the cases decided by them. Secondly, whatever may be the occasion for charging a State with responsibility under international law—whether it be the treatment of aliens, or the violation of a treaty, or failure to prevent the use of national territory as a base for acts noxious to the legitimate interests of. neighbouring States—these questions are connected, in most cases, with the central problems of State responsibility and call for elucidation of the conditions under which a State is liable. Thus, questions of the responsibility of the State for acts of officials acting outside the scope of their competence; its responsibility for acts of private persons; the degree, if any, to which national law may be invoked as a reason for the non-fulfilment of international obligations; the requirement of fault as a condition of liability—these questions are common to all aspects of State responsibility. Some of these questions were discussed in connection with the topic which was the subject-matter of the Hague Conference. Others, referred to in the Bases of Discussion, were not considered by the Conference. These included: concessions and public debts, extent of liability for deprivation of liberty, losses incurred by foreigners as the result of insurrections and riots, liability of the State for the acts of its political subdivisions and protected States, the measure of damages, nationality of claims, and the factors excluding or limiting liability such as self-defence, reprisals and the Calvo clause. As mentioned, some of these problems are common to other aspects of the law of State responsibility.

98. However, it is clear that that branch of international law transcends the question of responsibility for the treatment of aliens. Its codification must take into account the problems which have arisen in connection with recent developments such as the question of the criminal responsibility of States as well as that of individuals acting on behalf of the State. These, together with the question of

SURVEY OF INTERNATIONAL LAW: CODIFICATION

superior orders, may be considered in conjunction with the codification of the principles of the Nürnberg Charter and Judgment as envisaged in the resolution of the Assembly. There are other questions which will require consideration in connection with a codification of the law of State responsibility. These include the problem of the prohibition of abuse of rights—a subject of increasing importance in the growing and interdependent international society; the forms of reparation; the question of penal damages; and the various forms and occasions of responsibility resulting from the increasing activities of the State in the commercial and economic fields. Probably the Commission will also be confronted with the necessity of reconsidering the decision of the League of Nations Committee of Experts, reached by a majority vote at its fourth session, that extinctive prescription does not form part of international law and need not therefore be considered as a subject for codification.[1] Apart from the controversial nature of the reasons adduced by the Committee in support of its decision, the question of suitability for codification in respect of extinctive prescription—as, indeed, in respect of some other questions of limited compass—will assume a different complexion when considered as part of a codification of a wider branch of international law. It will be noted that the Eighth International Conference of American States decided in 1938 to proceed with the codification of various aspects of pecuniary claims, including the question of 'prescription as extinguishing international obligations in the matter of pecuniary claims' (Resolution no. XIX). Previously, the Seventh Conference had decided to recommend the study, in connection with the work of codification under the League of Nations, of the entire problem relating to the international responsibility of States (Resolution no. LXXIV).

9. THE LAW OF ARBITRAL PROCEDURE

99. It may be a matter for consideration whether the formulation of a code of arbitral procedure could usefully be included among the tasks of the International Law Commission. No such task was contemplated in connection with the work of the League of Nations

---

[1] See *Minutes of the Fourth Session*, 1928, pp. 18–22, and *ibid.* pp. 47, 48, for the report of Professor Ch. de Visscher on the subject. It is of interest to note that in the previous year the Greco–Bulgarian Mixed Arbitral Tribunal, in the case of *Sarropoulos* v. *Bulgarian State*, affirmed emphatically that 'prescription being an integral part of every system of law must be admitted in international law' and that 'it was the duty of an arbitral tribunal . . . to consider the principles of international law in regard to prescription and to apply it in the specific case submitted to it' (*Annual Digest* 4 (1927–8), Case no. 173).

ARBITRAL PROCEDURE

Committee of Experts. A number of cases and incidents which took place mainly after the First World War and which arose out of the activities of the Mixed Arbitral Tribunals and other organs of arbitration raised the question of an authoritative formulation of some of the principles of arbitral procedure. This was so in particular with regard to the effects of excess of jurisdiction or alleged excess of jurisdiction on the part of the Tribunal, and to such matters as the consequences of essential error in the award as well as rehearing and revision and interpretation of arbitral awards. By way of what may be clearly a legislative step, such codification might include provision for the appellate jurisdiction of the International Court of Justice, on the lines, for instance, of the proposal put forward by Finland in 1929 before the Assembly of the League of Nations and discussed in some detail by a representative Committee appointed by the Council. In general, the Draft Code of Arbitral Procedure submitted in 1875 to the Institute of International Law, the relevant provisions of the Hague Convention on the Pacific Settlement of International Disputes, and Chapter IV of the Peace Code adopted in 1933 by the Seventh International Conference of American States might be resorted to as a starting-point for any codification of the subject. The entire absence of any activity of arbitral bodies in the period immediately following the Second World War may suggest that the codification of that subject is a matter of purely academic interest. However, there may be a disadvantage in generalizing the negative experience of what may be no more than a passing period of transition.[1]

[1] In a resolution adopted in 1927 at Lausanne, the Institute of International Law decided to continue the work begun on the subject in 1875 and to undertake the preparation of a Code of Arbitral Procedure.

PART 3

THE METHOD OF SELECTION AND THE WORK OF THE INTERNATIONAL LAW COMMISSION

I. THE METHOD OF SELECTION

100. The Survey of International Law undertaken in the preceding part of this memorandum, the conclusion of its first part, and what is there suggested to be the correct interpretation of Article 18 of the Statute of the Commission may be of assistance in supplying part of the answer to what otherwise appears to be the difficult and intractable problem of the selection of topics for codification. The problem is of some obvious difficulty, for there is no ready and practicable test of the 'necessity' or 'desirability', in the sense of Article 18 (2) of the Statute, of codifying a particular topic. It is not easy, from this point of view, to assign any clear priority to any of the topics here surveyed. If the term 'desirable' is intended to cover subjects the codification of which is comparatively easy on the ground that there exists concerning them a substantial measure of agreement offering a prospect of success in the proposed international regulation, and if that test is acted upon, then there is some danger that the stature of codification through the International Law Commission may be reduced at the outset to matters—and even these are very few in number—which are of little importance. It may be reduced to those subjects which the League of Nations Committee of Experts and the Assembly of the League discarded for the very reason that they were not important and therefore in no sense urgent. However, it is possible that the Commission may regard the term 'desirable' as not differing substantially from 'necessary'—as indeed seems to be indicated by the natural meaning of these words. In this case, the Commission will tend to select topics the codification of which is considered 'necessary or desirable' because of the importance of their subject-matter having regard to international interest, the requirement of peaceful international intercourse, and the authority of international law. From this point of view it may be found, as already suggested, that there is no criterion of selection which is capable of general formulation and

516

METHOD OF SELECTION AND WORK

that all subjects are important and their codification 'necessary or desirable'. In fact, should the Commission approach the question of selection from the point of view of relative urgency—assuming that any such relation can be established—it may feel compelled to select the topics which the Committee of Experts and the Assembly of the League chose as ripe for codification by international conference and which it has proved impossible to regulate through that procedure.

101. The question of continuity of the task of codification in relation to the efforts of the organs of the League of Nations in and prior to 1930 will thus present itself for early consideration by the Commission. Such consideration may, it is believed, have to be guided to a large extent by the fact that, because of the entirely novel character of the task of the Commission (which is not confined to the choice of subjects fit for immediate codification through an international conference), its standard of selection must differ from that adopted by the organs of the League. For while the test referred to in Article 18 (2) of the Statute of the Commission is whether the codification of a topic is 'necessary or desirable', the resolution of the Assembly of the League of 22 September 1924, laying down the terms of reference of the Committee of Experts, instructed them 'to prepare a provisional list of the subjects of international law the regulation of which by international agreement would seem to be the most desirable *and realizable* at the present moment'. This latter condition— that the codification of the topics selected must be realizable—was often referred to in the deliberations of the Committee of Experts although, in the event, the codification of the three topics actually chosen for codification through an international conference proved to be not 'realizable'. However, in a considerable number of cases the Committee, while admitting that the codification of the proposed topic was desirable, discarded it for the reason that owing to the divergencies of national laws and jurisprudence the codification was not realizable. This took place with regard to such subjects as extradition, judicial assistance in penal matters, and jurisdiction of States with regard to crimes committed outside their territory. The International Law Commission is not confined to these narrow limits. There is no reference in its Statute to the necessity of any topic selected being 'realizable' as a subject of codification. As already mentioned, the reason for that difference is not difficult to surmise. The International Law Commission is not limited to the selection of such subjects as can be codified in the form of an inter-

517

SURVEY OF INTERNATIONAL LAW: CODIFICATION

national convention by an international conference of Governments or experts. It may, and is expected to, produce drafts of varying degrees of formal authority. A subject the codification of which may not be realizable by way of a convention adopted by an international conference, may still be a 'necessary or desirable' subject of codification in any other of the various forms envisaged in Articles 20–23 of the Statute. For this reason the scope of selection open to the International Law Commission is much broader than in the case of the League of Nations Committee of Experts. That scope is not only wider. In a substantial sense it is almost unlimited, inasmuch as the Commission is instructed to select subjects the codification of which is necessary or desirable.

102. It is in this latter respect that the work of the Committee of Experts is highly instructive as showing that the codification of *most* subjects of international law is necessary or desirable. This applies not only to the seven subjects which the Committee reported to the Council as ripe for codification. It applies also to those numerous topics, already mentioned, where codification was considered necessary but, owing to the divergencies in national practice, not realizable (a consideration which, as pointed out below, is of very limited relevance in relation to the International Law Commission). Moreover, the hall-mark of 'necessity' is applicable also to those few subjects which the Committee discarded for other—controversial— reasons, namely, that they were political in nature, as in the case of recognition of Governments and State succession, or that they were not yet covered by a sufficient practice of States, as in the matter of prescription. In fact, it is believed that the Commission will be faced with the task of considering, at the very outset of its activity, whether, in the light of principle and of previous experience, it cannot rightly be said that the codification of probably every subject of international law is necessary and desirable—'necessary and desirable' not in the sense of overwhelming and immediate urgency, but in the sense of appropriateness for international regulation made desirable by the necessity of removing uncertainty productive of confusion and friction, by the necessity of preventing waste of international resources, by the necessity of filling gaps and meeting the new conditions of international life, and, generally, by the necessity of enhancing the authority of international law. From this point of view there is room for the opinion that every subject discussed in the preceding Survey is a necessary and desirable subject of codification. This applies—perhaps with greater urgency

METHOD OF SELECTION AND WORK

than in other matters—to such seemingly theoretical questions as those referred to in the General Part of International Law, for instance, with regard to a codification of the principles governing the international rights and duties of individuals or the relation of international law to the law of the land. In general, however, there is no intrinsic priority and no corresponding standard of selection from the point of view of necessity or desirability of codification between such subjects as diplomatic immunities, extradition, obligations of territorial jurisdiction, State responsibility, the law of treaties, acquisition of territorial sovereignty, problems of the law of the sea, and so on.

103. If we bear in mind that most questions of international law are generally of equal importance as objects of codification, that it may be found difficult to discover a working test of preference for the purpose of deciding whether it is necessary or desirable to codify a particular subject, and that the Commission must nevertheless proceed to some selection for the reasons both that it is instructed to do so by the Statute and that it cannot possibly codify all subjects at once—if we bear these factors in mind then the problem of selection no longer appears as one of perplexing and arbitrary choice. On the contrary, it resolves itself into a question of priority in point of time, within the framework of a comprehensive scheme embracing potentially the entirety of international law and by reference to such factors as the amount and accessibility of material on any given subject, the availability of the appropriate personnel, and the continuity with the work already performed under the auspices of the League of Nations. Thus the Commission may wish to consider whether, in the first instance, it ought to continue the work on subjects which the League Committee of Experts declared to be ripe for codification or which, after ample investigation, it discarded for the reason that owing to divergencies of national laws and jurisprudence no codification through international conference was feasible (a reason which, once more, does not apply to the International Law Commission, since its function is not limited to producing drafts to be accepted forthwith as conventions). On the other hand, it may be hoped that the selection of topics will be made by reference to a comprehensive and long-range plan, which could be the product of mature and prolonged deliberation, of codifying international law as a whole over a period which may cover a generation. The following three questions may have to be considered in this connection.

519

SURVEY OF INTERNATIONAL LAW: CODIFICATION

104. In the first instance, a decision will have to be made whether the topics selected shall cover limited and isolated branches of the law or whether the work of the Commission at any given period shall be devoted to a wider subject. By way of example, shall the work of the Commission at any given time embrace isolated and disconnected questions such as prescription, jurisdiction over aliens for crimes committed abroad, piracy, and extradition, or shall the policy be to limit the work of the Commission in one period to specific aspects of one integrated subject such as the law of the sea, the law of treaties, the law of jurisdictional immunities of States (i.e. States as such, their property, their ships, their armed forces, and so on)? Each of these general subjects could be divided and studied *pari passu* by a number of co-ordinated bodies. It is possible that in order to obviate the necessity of a selection of topics by reference to tests which at best are controversial and subjective, the Commission may decide to choose the broad fields of study in accordance with— and, possibly, in the order of—a systematic classification of international law on some such lines as suggested in the survey undertaken in Part 2 of this memorandum. Thus it is possible that in any given period various Rapporteurs of the International Law Commission will be devoting themselves each to a specific problem within the wider division. A procedure on these lines might have the double merit of (*a*) giving an element of cohesion and integration to the work of the Commission and (*b*) preventing the impression, which would be detrimental to the authority of the Commission and to the usefulness of its work, that it is concerned with matters of minor importance selected at random.

105. Secondly—and this is a matter connected with the selection of topics—the Commission may have to consider at an early stage whether its drafts shall be in the form of a general statement of principle (as is the case in some of the codification conventions concluded by the American States) or whether they should follow the lines of the Bases of Discussion prepared for the Hague Codification Conference of 1930 on the subjects of Territorial Waters and State Responsibility or, apart from its occasional deliberate obscurity and evasiveness, the Hague Convention on Certain Questions relating to the Conflict of Nationality Laws. The problem of the degree of the requisite generality of the law is, of course, not confined to codification of international law. In approaching it the Commission will probably have to take into account the fact that, in so far as one of the principal incentives for the codification movement in the

METHOD OF SELECTION AND WORK

international sphere is the removal of uncertainties in the law, that object cannot be achieved by instruments of a general character. Similarly, in so far as the object of codification is to reconcile divergencies and remove causes of friction, that object can be achieved only imperfectly by drafts and conventions which may conceal continued disagreement behind the cloak of a vague and elastic statement of general principle. There may be a disadvantage in weakening the authority of customary law by pronouncements of studied generality and incompleteness which are of limited usefulness for the settlement of disputes. International practice shows examples of such pronouncements in the form of conventions and otherwise.

106. Finally, it will probably be necessary to clarify the import of Article 18, paragraph 2, which lays down that 'when the Commission considers that the codification of a particular topic is necessary or desirable, *it shall submit its recommendations to the General Assembly*'. Does the italicized part of this provision mean that decisions of the International Law Commission relating to the selection of every individual topic are subject to confirmation by the General Assembly? Such a result does not follow from the terminology of Article 18. The records of Sub-Committee 2 of the Sixth Committee suggest that the question of the proper meaning of the word 'recommendations' as used in Article 18, paragraph 2, was left open for interpretation by the International Law Commission.[1]

2. THE CHARACTER OF THE WORK OF THE COMMISSION

107. Before enquiring into the question of the method of the work of the International Law Commission, in particular with reference to Article 20 of its Statute, it is necessary to consider the nature of the task of the Commission. The principal aspects of this problem were discussed in Part 1 of the present memorandum, where it was submitted that the function of the Commission is not limited to a statement of the existing law by way of ascertaining the exact measure of existing agreement or disagreement. On the face of it,

---

[1] Proposals made in Sub-Committee 2 to define more specifically the word 'recommendations' were defeated. Mr Beckett (United Kingdom) proposed at the eleventh meeting of Sub-Committee 2 that this paragraph should be amended to read: '. . . it should present its recommendations to the General Assembly in the form of draft articles or otherwise'. This proposed addition was not carried, there being 7 votes in favour and 7 against. The representative of Australia then proposed that the paragraph be amended to read: '. . . should present its recommendations to that effect'. This proposed addition was rejected by 7 votes against 5.

SURVEY OF INTERNATIONAL LAW: CODIFICATION

Article 20 would not seem to limit the task of the Commission in any such way. It lays down that:

The Commission shall prepare its drafts in the form of articles and shall submit them to the General Assembly together with a commentary containing:

(a) Adequate presentation of precedents and other relevant data, including treaties, judicial decisions and doctrine;

(b) Conclusions relevant to: (1) The extent of agreement on each point in the practice of States and in doctrine; (2) Divergencies and disagreements which exist, as well as arguments invoked in favour of one or another solution.

These terms of Article 20 suggest that it deliberately avoids any limitation of the function of the Commission to a mere registration of the existing law. In the first instance, it does not provide that the Commission shall confine itself to ascertaining the extent of the agreement and of the divergencies. On the contrary, it lays down that in the commentary to its draft the Commission shall present its *conclusions relevant* to the extent of agreement or divergencies. This implies a critical task of appreciation and of weighing the causes of the existing discrepancies. Moreover, the Statute expressly instructs the Commission to present its conclusions 'relevant to . . . arguments invoked in favour of one or another solution'. Secondly, the task of the Commission to arrive at a conclusion and judgment of its own is clearly indicated by its duty to prepare drafts in the form of articles. In the nature of things these cannot be hesitating, inconclusive and purely informative statements of detached compilation. They imply an expression of decisive judgment as to what is the proper rule of law. What is the proper rule of law in this context? It is, in the first instance, the rule based on existing law as evidenced, in the terminology of Article 38 of the Statute of the International Court of Justice, by international treaties, international custom, general principles of law and the subsidiary sources of law enumerated therein. In the absence of guidance from these sources of law—in particular, in the absence of agreement—the proper rule of law is that which in the view of the Commission ought to be the law. As already stated, in the case of the International Law Commission the possible combination of functions follows naturally from the varying degrees of formal authority which its drafts and comments may possess at any given time. Accordingly, much of the product of its work may follow the lines of some of the past great achievements of codification in the municipal sphere. They will not only be acts of

522

METHOD OF SELECTION AND WORK

international law finding, but also, if necessary, acts of international legislation and of international statesmanship.

108. The above considerations do not imply that the Commission will be absolved from stating, in the first instance, what the law is. To do that is its primary task, and it is probable that the Commission will wish to adhere to it wherever possible. In the sphere of codification—as distinguished from that of development of international law—the main purpose of the Commission is not that of an international legislator. Its function is essentially and in the first instance that of a judge. It has to find what the law is and to present it in a form which is precise, systematic and as detailed as the overriding principle of the necessary generality of the law allows.

109. However, that principal function of ascertaining the existing law does not exhaust the task of the Commission. In two respects it must go outside the province normally—but not invariably—reserved for the judge. In the first instance, when there is a divergence of practice or views it cannot be limited to purely formal solutions on which courts have occasionally relied—as they did, for instance, in the *Savarkar* case between Great Britain and France and in the *Behring Sea Arbitration* between Great Britain and the United States of America. In both cases the Tribunals solved the difficulty occasioned by the absence of a rule of international law directly applicable to the distinctly novel situation before them by relying on the fact that international law, in the particular case, did not impose upon the State in question any obligation to act in such a way as to renounce its freedom of action apparently grounded in a general rule of international law. It is controversial whether a formal test of that nature is sound even in relation to an international tribunal. Thus in other cases—as, for instance, in the *Trail Smelter* case between the United States and Canada—the Arbitrators held that the presumptive freedom of action of the State within its territory must yield to higher legal considerations which had previously received no *imprimatur* of an international convention or of international judicial precedent. It is doubly controversial whether such purely formal finding of the existing law is appropriate in relation to the task of codification. On the other hand, the International Law Commission will be in the same position as an international tribunal which, in cases where there is a clear discrepancy of practice, cannot solve the difficulty by pronouncing that there is no law at all for the reason that there is no agreed law. On the contrary, like an international tribunal, the Commission,

523

SURVEY OF INTERNATIONAL LAW: CODIFICATION

entrusted with the task of codifying the law, must either choose among conflicting contentions or, more reasonably, formulate a solution which is in the nature of a compromise—a compromise not of a diplomatic character but one reached by reference to requirements of justice, of general interest of the international community, of international progress, and of the neighbourly adjustment of international relations, as well as to such established rules of international law in other spheres as are not inconsistent with these factors. In some cases, as in the case of the breadth of territorial waters, a solution of this nature may take into consideration, in terms of general principle, the legitimate interests of individual States and acquired and prescriptive rights. Or, as in the case of the plea of non-discrimination with regard to the responsibility of the State to respect the property of aliens, it may be found in what appears at first sight to be a mechanical compromise but which would in effect be a recognition of the fact that neither the absoluteness of the rights of property nor freedom from responsibility postulated by reference to the equality of treatment of aliens and nationals are, without qualification, a principle of international law.

110. There is, secondly, no reason why the independent creative function of the Commission should be limited to cases in which it has ascertained disagreement in the existing practice. For even in cases in which practice has not revealed marked divergencies, it will be within the province of the Commission, after it has laid down what is the indisputable rule of law, to examine that rule in the light of modern developments and requirements and to suggest such improvements in the law and such modifications of the existing law as may be required in the interest of justice and of international social progress. There is no objection to the fulfilment of that duty—for a duty it probably is in terms both of the provisions of the Statute of the International Law Commission and of the task of codification in general—so long as the Commission contrives to preserve a clear distinction between what it finds to be the law and what it considers to constitute the necessary improvement of the law. The Statute lays down expressly, in Article 20, that the task of the Commission embraces the presentation of conclusions, by way of a commentary, relevant not only to 'divergencies and disagreements which exist' but also 'to the extent of *agreement* in the practice of States and in doctrine'. The performance of a task thus conceived is not inconsistent even with the function of a judge. International arbitrators have exercised it either in pursuance of a special authorization by

METHOD OF SELECTION AND WORK

the parties—as in the case of the *North Atlantic Fisheries Arbitration* between Great Britain and the United States—or independently of it. The last paragraph of Article 38 of the Statute of the International Court of Justice envisages the possibility of such an authorization. So long, it may be repeated, as the International Law Commission distinguishes clearly between what it finds *de lege lata* and what it proposes as the proper rule of law *de lege ferenda*, there is no objection—there is every inducement—to its acting in that capacity and to giving expression to a constructive, and what is currently referred to as the sociological, approach to international law.

111. In thus acting—with regard to cases both of agreement and of disagreement in existing law and practice—the Commission will be in a position to reduce to their legitimate proportions the divergencies and peculiarities of national laws and judicial and other practice. In the context of an international conference aiming at decisions which are unanimous or which approach unanimity, such divergencies assume a complexion of rigidity and permanency which is often out of all proportion to the national interest involved or even to the truly fundamental principles of international jurisprudence. Such divergencies are frequently a matter of form. As in the case of the alleged fundamental differences between the so-called Anglo-American and Continental conceptions of international law, they have proved, upon analysis, to be grossly exaggerated. There have been cases where divergencies which at an international conference were elevated to the dignity of an immutable principle of national law and tradition have been subsequently changed by normal and inconspicuous processes of international legislation. The changes effected in some countries in the law of nationality and of exemption of governmental agencies from civil liability may be quoted as an instructive example. However that may be, the International Law Commission is not in the same position as an international conference aiming at unanimity or quasi-unanimity. Its province and its terms of reference are of sufficient breadth and elasticity to enable it to consider national divergencies of various kinds in the framework of a function of international legislation and of statesmanship in their wider sense. In accomplishing this task the International Law Commission may be aided by a compilation—a synopsis—showing the divergencies in governmental practice, in national law, and in the jurisprudence of courts in the entire field of international law. A compilation of that nature would form a useful

525

SURVEY OF INTERNATIONAL LAW: CODIFICATION

supplement to a Survey of International Law, in conformity with Article 18 of the Statute, which the Commission may eventually adopt as the basis of its work. The usefulness of such a survey of divergencies—a work of some magnitude—would be enhanced if it were accompanied by a critical examination of the causes which underlie them.

112. These, then, are the two principal aspects of the task of the Commission: (1) the ascertainment, in a systematic form, of the existing law; (2) the development of the law, in the wider sense, 'in the fields where there has already been extensive State practice, precedent and doctrine' (Article 15), by filling the gaps, reconciling divergencies and the formulation of improvements in cases in which the situation calls for a combination of the consolidating and legislative aspects of codification. In addition, it must be a matter for consideration to what extent the Commission ought to combine with these tasks another function which is largely political in nature, namely, that of initiative and active assistance in the transformation of the products of its work into international conventions proper. This aspect of its task would involve constant consultation with Governments. The possibility of such consultation was suggested to the Codification Committee of 1947. Thus we find the following observation in the statement submitted by the representative of 'Brazil: 'Neither the codification nor the development of law can be achieved merely by submission of learned opinions. They must take the form of resolutions by the General Assembly or of multilateral conventions. But these resolutions and conventions must not be submitted under "take it or leave it" conditions.'[1]

113. Finally, apart from the possibility of contributing directly to the development of positive international law by way of conventions and of influencing governmental and judicial practice by the products of its work which have not yet materialized into conventions, there will offer itself to the Commission an opportunity of a scientific achievement of unusual magnitude in the field of international law. If the Commission contrives to avail itself to the full of the avenues offered by Article 19 of its Statute[2]—a task which requires a considerable amount of direction and centralization—then, in the course of time,

---

[1] Document A/AC.10/28.

[2] Article 19 provides as follows: 'The Commission shall adopt a plan of work appropriate to each case. The Commission shall, through the Secretary-General, address to Governments a detailed request to furnish the texts of laws, decrees, judicial decisions, treaties, diplomatic correspondence and other documents relevant to the topic being studied and which the Commission deems necessary.'

METHOD OF SELECTION AND WORK

it will assemble an abundance of material which has not been available in the past to other official or private organs of codification. That material when woven into the fabric of the drafts and commentaries of the Commission will represent a most valuable scientific result covering, in the fullness of time, the entire *corpus juris gentium*. Valuable as have been in the past the efforts of private initiative in this field, the cumulative product of the work of the International Law Commission, aided by the resources of the United Nations as a whole, ought—regardless of how much of it will materialize in the form of conventions—to represent a correspondingly higher achievement of lasting value, usefulness, and authority.

3. THE PROCEDURE OF CODIFICATION

114. In view of the observations of the preceding chapters concerning the character and the method of the function of the International Law Commission, only brief comment is required with regard to the procedure which may be followed in the matter of codification. Unlike the case of 'development of international law', the Statute of the Commission does not prescribe in detail the procedure to be followed in the matter of codification. It merely lays down, in Article 19, that 'the Commission shall adopt a plan of work appropriate to each case'. In general, it would appear that with regard to codification the volume of research, discussion and other preparatory work will be distinctly more considerable than in the case of 'development'. For in the former case the scope of the subject in relation to each particular topic will be both wider and covered by abundant material which will have to be collected, examined, and analysed. The Commission may consider the possibility of the following procedure.

115. The main part of the preparatory work on a given subject, when not entrusted to the Secretariat,[1] might be performed by a Rapporteur under the general guidance of and in constant consultation with a sub-committee of the Commission. In his work, which would have to extend in the first instance over a period of one year to eighteen months, he would have the professional collaboration of the regular members of the Secretariat in the Division for the Development and Codification of International Law, and of such

[1] The Commission may desire to entrust much of the preparatory work to the Division for the Development and Codification of International Law in the United Nations Secretariat, as was done by the General Assembly in resolution 175 (II) of 21 November 1947.

SURVEY OF INTERNATIONAL LAW: CODIFICATION

special research assistants and consultants as necessary. One of the members of the Division for the Development and Codification of International Law would assume, at the request of the Rapporteur concerned, the responsibility for the collection, in the language of Article 19 of the Statute, of 'the texts of laws, decrees, judicial decisions, treaties, diplomatic correspondence and other documents relevant to the topic being studied and which the Commission deems necessary'.

116. The Commission would appoint, with regard to each particular topic, a sub-committee of three or four of its members to guide and to assist the Rapporteur in the preparation of the preliminary version of the draft and the commentary. Arrangements would be made, with that object in view, for frequent meeting—three or four times a year—between the sub-committee and the Rapporteur. The Commission and the sub-committee may have to lay down, from the very outset, the guiding principle that the actual preparation of the drafts and commentaries must be the responsibility of one person, and that it would be inconsistent with the scientific character and the importance of the work of codification to encourage any system of collective drafting.

117. After the Rapporteur, in co-operation with the sub-committee, has prepared the preliminary draft of the articles and of the commentary, the draft might be submitted to the International Law Commission. Comments might also be invited from bodies concerned with the scientific study of international law, in particular from the Institute of International Law. With regard to the latter it may be a matter for consideration to what extent the authority and resources of that highly qualified body of experts should be utilized in connection with the work of codification. It might be possible to agree that, at least with regard to some topics, the Institute of International Law should appoint commissions the work of which would cover subjects studied by the Rapporteur and the sub-committee and that these commissions should comment and express an opinion on the drafts and commentaries. Similarly, the preliminary drafts of the articles and of the commentary covering the individual topics could be published for study and discussion by other scientific bodies, in particular the International Law Association—a committee of which, under the chairmanship of Judge McNair, produced a valuable report on the subject—and in legal periodicals. Thus the work of the Commission would be accompanied and aided by—as it would be a stimulus to—fruitful and invigorating scientific activity

METHOD OF SELECTION AND WORK

in the field of international law in various countries. The Commission may also find it desirable to maintain close contact with and to benefit from the experience of the organs of the Pan-American Union charged with the codification of international law. The detailed resolutions on the methods of codification of international law adopted by the Seventh International Conference of American States in 1933, by the Inter-American Conference for the Maintenance of Peace in 1936, and by the Eighth International Conference of American States in 1938, may be found of considerable assistance in this connection.[1]

118. After a suitable interval—perhaps of one year or so—the Rapporteur and sub-committee would reconsider the preliminary draft of the articles and the commentary in the light of the criticism and observations of Governments, of the members of the International Law Commission, of scientific bodies and of private scholars. The revised draft would then be submitted for discussion by the International Law Commission as a whole and for such action as the Commission might consider appropriate by reference to Articles 21–23 of its Statute. Such action would include, in the terms of Article 22, the preparation of 'a final draft and explanatory report' for submission, with recommendations, to the General Assembly. Even at this stage, in order to ensure continuity and to minimize the drawbacks inherent in collective drafting, the Commission, while retaining full responsibility for the final draft, might usefully consider the advisability of availing itself of the services of the Rapporteur and of the sub-committee concerned.

119. It may be assumed that at any given period a number of Rapporteurs and sub-committees of the Commission will be engaged in studying and proposing drafts and commentaries on a series of topics—probably within an integrated wider field in the sense suggested above. Thus, in the scheme as contemplated, the Commission—sitting either as a body or through its sub-committees co-operating with the Rapporteurs—would conduct its activity in semi-permanent session. In this respect it would differ from some other commissions, especially those set up by the Economic and Social Council. A development of this nature would be in accordance with the importance of the task entrusted to the Commission. Its Statute, which in its principal aspect is the result of a statesmanlike

---

[1] These resolutions are conveniently reproduced in *The International Conferences of American States*, First Supplement, 1933–40; published by the Carnegie Endowment for International Peace (1940), pp. 84, 145 and 246, respectively.

SURVEY OF INTERNATIONAL LAW: CODIFICATION

and beneficent compromise between the codification of international law through formal conventions and codification through non-governmental scientific statement and restatement of the law, affords the United Nations the opportunity, long awaited, of removing a grave defect in international law and of enhancing its usefulness and authority as a true system of law. It may properly be claimed that the scope and intensity of the work of the International Law Commission should be commensurate with the significance and the potentialities of the task with which its Statute and the United Nations have entrusted it.

INDEX

abuse of rights, 202, 383–6, 399 n., 422–4, 514

acquiescence, 64, 67 n., 238

acquired rights, respect for, 38, 131, 479

Act of State, 84

acts of foreign States, recognition of, 38–40, 42, 44, 163

adoption of international law: *see* incorporation of international law

aggressive war, punishment for, German Federal Constitution, 175–6

air space, 381–2, 423

aliens, crimes committed abroad, jurisdiction over, 272, 488–91

aliens, treatment of, 386–90, 500–3, 513
  access to courts, 502
  expulsion, 503
  minimum standard of civilization, 296–8, 386, 502
  non-discrimination, 386–90, 501, 502
  property rights, 387–90

American Civil War
  blockade, 329 n.
  Instructions for Armies in the Field, 99 n.
  recognition of belligerency, 330, 331

American international law, 122–4, 269–70

American States, Anti-War Pact (1933), 339, 347

angary, right of, 167 n., 220

Anglo-American school of international law, 124–6, 218, 271–5, 363

Anglo-Egyptian *condominium* over Sudan, 371

Anti-War Pact of Non-Aggression (1933), 339, 347

Anzilotti, theory of international law, 210, 216, 310

arbitral procedure, codification of, 514–15

arbitration, 'law and equity', on basis of, 85

Argentina, Constitution, international law provision, 473

asylum, 506–7
  constitutional provisions, 176
  Pan-American Convention, 124, 506

Austinian conception of law, 11–12, 32, 55, 209

balance of power, recognition of title and, 337

basis of international law, 51, 89–94, 231–3

belligerency, recognition of, 329–35
  American Civil War, 330, 331

belligerent rights of Crown, treaties concerning, 160

Bentham and international law, 99

Bessarabia, recognition of Roumanian sovereignty 338

Blackstone, on adoption of international law, 154, 166 n., 218, 222

blockade
  civil war in, 329 n., 331
  effectiveness, requirement of, 314
  Southern States, American Civil War, 329 n.

Bluntschli, draft code, 99 n.

Bosnia and Herzegovina, annexation of, 373

boycott, international, 406

Brussels Convention, Immunity of State-owned Ships (1926), 483

Burma, Constitution, 1947, international law provision, 174 n.

Bustamante Code on Private International law (1928), 41 n., 490

Calvo Clause, 297, 398, 513

Canada, title to Sverdrup Islands, 338

capitulations, régime of, 119

Cavaglieri, theory of international law, 210, 216, 240

Central American Court of Justice, 145
  suits between States and aliens, 287

Central American Treaty, 1907, recognition provision, 325, 326

Charter of the United Nations
  amendment of, 13
  human rights provisions, 142- 4, 471, 502
  non-members, effect on, 116 ,
  prohibition of use of force, 18

China, request for revision of treaties, 429

Christian foundation of modern international law, 118–22

Civil Strife, Convention on (1928), 325, 487

civil war: *see also* American Civil War *and* Spanish Civil War
  aid to lawful Government, 334

codification, 26, 98–112, 258–60, 445–530
  development of international law and, 110, 258, 445, 463, 467
  League of Nations, under, 102–4, 452–3, 462, 516–17: *see also* Hague Codification Conference (1930)
  meaning, 98, 450–3
  non-governmental projects, 99–100
  private international law of, 41 n.
  procedure of, 527–30

531

INDEX

codification (*cont.*)
  regional, 104–5 n., 529
  registration of existing law, 452, 455–9
  selection of topics, 459–68
codification treaties, effect on customary law, 457–8, 467 n.
collective enforcement of law, 19
collective security, 264–7, 440–1
Colombia, recognition of Panama, dispute with U.S.A., 315–16
comity, international law and, 43–6, 239 n.
  recognition as act of, 316
  recognition of foreign acts of State, 482
commercial relations between Governments, 72–4
comparative law and international law, 74
completeness of international law, 57, 68, 75, 94–8, 242–3, 246, 450
conciliation, 416–17
conclusiveness of statements of Executive, 162–3, 170–1, 229 n., 486
condominium, 370–2
confiscation of property, 388
Conflict of Nationality Laws, Convention on (1930), 104, 260, 301, 454, 458, 482
Congo, acquisition by Belgium, 338
Congo Conference, 1885, notification of acquisition of territory, 337, 491
conquest
  recognition of *de facto* sovereignty, 348
  title to territory, as, 202, 241, 252
consent as source of international law, 9, 32, 52, 56–8, 66, 196, 208–13, 242–4, 267, 309, 443
consuls, Harvard Draft Convention, 455, 511, 512
consular intercourse and immunities, 511–12
  Havana Convention on Consular Agents (1928), 511
contiguous zone, 64, 375–7, 497–8
Continental school of international law, 124–6, 218, 271–5, 363
continental shelf, 64, 98
  Continental Shelf Convention, 98
contracts, inconsistent obligations, 359–60
corporations, nationality of, 472
courtesy, international, 63
Cracow, annexation by Austria, 338
Crete, Turkish sovereignty over, 372
crimes against humanity, 143, 471
criminal responsibility of individuals, war crimes, 19
cujus est solum ejus est usque ad coelum, 381
customary international law, 14–15, 43, 51, 53, 61–8, 237–41
  abolition of customary rules, 241
  codification treaties and, 457–8, 467 n.
  new States, 57, 238

opinio necessitatis, 62–4, 66 n., 67, 238, 240
  practice, 61–2, 238, 255
  time element, 130–2

damages, measure of, 202, 391
  punitive, 394–5
Declaration of London (1909), 454
definitions of international law, 9
delicts, international, 383–6
  see also State responsibility
Denmark
  Eastern Greenland, title to, 338, 342
  U.S.A., refusal to recognize belligerent rights, 332 ,
dependent territories, participation in organizations, 141
diplomatic intercourse and immunities, 509–11
  Harvard Draft Convention, 510
  Harvard Convention on Diplomatic Officers (1928), 510
disputes, legal and political, 242
domestic jurisdiction, matters of, 22, 68, 133 n., 303, 439
Dominions, treatment as States, 138
dualistic or pluralistic theory, 152, 168
Duguit, 55
duress, effect on treaties, 47, 54, 87, 203, 241, 341, 352–4

Eastern Greenland, recognition of Danish sovereignty, 338
Egypt, *condominium* over Sudan, 371
English law, incorporation of international law, 154–69
equality of States, 128, 217, 436–8, 443
equity
  continuance of treaties, 429
  source of international law, 85–6, 256–7
estoppel or preclusion, 67 n., 70, 83, 203, 257
Estrada doctrine on recognition, 325
European Convention on Human Rights (1950), 144
European Economic Community, legislative powers, 176
evidence, rules of, international tribunals, 272
ex factis jus oritur, 342
ex injuria jus non oritur, 342
Executive determination of international questions, 162–3, 170–1, 229 n.
exhaustion of local remedies, 397–8
expropriation, property of aliens, 388–90
extinctive prescription, 514
extradition, 503–6
  American treaties on, 503
  Harvard Research Draft, 504
  political offenders, 301 n., 506

532

INDEX

extradition treaties, liberal interpretation, 364

extraterritorial jurisdiction, 38

Fauchille, on recognition, 315

Federal Republic of Germany, Constitution, international law provisions, 173–4

federal States
decisions of courts, international law, applying, 82–3, 171 n.
treaty-making power, 475

First World War, doctrine of international law and, 10 n.

fisheries, conventions on, 494

Fishing and Conservation of Living Resources, Convention (1958), 98

foreign acts of State, recognition of, 481–2

foreign armed forces, jurisdictional immunities, 485–6

France
Constitution, 1946, provision on international law, 174 n., 473
treaties, 173
recognition of Unites States, 320

freedom of the seas, 385, 423

frontier streams, *condominium*, 371

fundamental norm, 90 n.

gaps in international law, 57, 68, 75, 94–7, 243, 246, 450

General Act for Pacific Settlement of International Disputes (1928), 102, 410

general principles of law, 28, 34, 47, 52, 54, 57, 61, 68–77, 87–8, 91, 114, 125, 147, 201, 204, 236, 241–9, 268, 273, 360, 367, 379, 381, 385
basis of validity, 75–7
equitable principles, 257
treaties and, 236

General Treaty for the Renunciation of War (1928), 17–18, 22, 102, 116, 198, 229 n., 354, 380, 393, 411, 493
customary international law and, 241, 253
League Resolution on non-recognition (1932), 321, 339, 346
neutrality and, 241, 254 n., 344 n.
non-recognition, Stimson Doctrine, 338–341, 346, 380

Geneva Conference on the Law of the Sea (1958), 108–9

Geneva Conventions (1929), 102

Geneva Conventions (1949), 115

Geneva Conventions Act, 1957, object of, 160 n.

Geneva Conventions, private international law, 40 n.

Genocide Convention, 142

German law
international law and, 223

Germany: *see also* Federal Republic of Germany
Constitution, 1919, international law provision, 172, 224, 473
good faith, 47, 257, 268, 378
prescription, acquisitive, 378
recognition, in grant of, 319, 320
third persons and illegal acts, 344

grants in perpetuity, 372

Grotius, 75, 251, 265

Hague Codification Conference (1930), 26, 103–6, 258, 375, 387, 453, 460–2

Hague Conferences on Private International Law (1902, 1905), 40 n.

Hague Conventions (1907), 101–2, 458

Hague Peace Conferences, 101–2, 120

Hall, on recognition, 315

high seas, 381–2, 493–7: *see also* fisheries
transport and safety, conventions on, 495

High Seas Convention (1958), 98

Hobbes, Leviathan, 55

Holy See, status of, 138, 306

hostile expeditions, 487

human dignity, object of law, 149

human rights, 22, 48
European Convention (1950), 144
German Federal Constitution, 176
U.N. Charter provisions, 142–4, 471, 502

humanitarian intervention, 302–4

illegal acts, validity and effect, 340–5

inadimplenti non est adimplentum, 245

incorporation of international law
constitutional provisions, 172–7, 229
English law, 154–69, 218–22
European legal systems, 171, 222–4
primacy of international law, 227–8
significance of, 165–6, 222, 225

individual responsibility, war crimes, 19, 141

individuals
claims against national State, 289
fundamental rights, 295–304
injury to foreign State by, 294
international protection of rights of, 298–302
law-creating process, participation in, 305
petition to organizations, right of, 147
procedural capacity, 143–7, 470
subjects of international law, 31, 47, 81, 114, 127, 136, 141–3, 166, 193–4, 279–304, 470
transformation, doctrine of, 285–6

Institute of International law, 100 n., 528
Codification, Resolution (1947), 459 n.
Recognition, resolution on (1936), 478
Rights of Man, Declaration of (1929), 295

533

INDEX

insurgents
  recognition of, 328, 332, 335–6
  subjects of international law, 138
interdependence of States, 51
interest, award of, 202, 391
international administrative law, 74
international boycott, 406
international claims
  extinctive prescription, 514
  local remedies, 397–8
  nationality of claims, 145
  State control over, 143–4, 291–3, 295
international community, existence of, 9,
  16, 28–31, 52, 58, 76, 92, 128, 232,
  261–7
International Court of Justice
  acceptance of jurisdiction, reservations,
  25
  advisory jurisdiction, 24
  decision *ex aequo et bono*, 86, 256
  jurisdiction limited to States, 146
  Statute, Art. 38…55–6, 61, 75, 231, 233
international crimes, individual responsibility, 148
International Criminal Court, proposals
  for, 392, 507
International Labour Conventions, 102
International Labour Organisation, 434
  complaints procedures, 290
  law-making, employers and employees,
  by, 305
international law
  ascertainment of, 197–8
  binding character, 16, 196–7, 222
  codification, *q.v.*
  common will of States, 209–10
  completeness of, 57, 68, 75, 94–8, 242–3,
  246, 450
  concept of, 193–5
  creation of new rules, 196
  enforcement of, 9, 16–20, 34, 198–9, 264,
  340
  indefiniteness of rules of, 25–8
  jurisprudence, place of, in, 193–215, 242,
  443
  jus inter gentes, 194
  law of co-ordination, as, 36, 196, 208–13,
  270
  matters regulated by, 21–3
  morality and, 46–9, 205–7
  national concepts of, 126–9, 270
  non-external character, 198
  partial observance of, 20–1
  permanently weak character of, 207–8
  primacy of, 227–8, 474
  proof of, in English courts, 158, 221 n.
  shortcomings, effects of, 31–3, 199, 308
  transient nature of 33, 35, 200, 208, 214
  sources: *see* Sources of international law

specific character, 27, 208–9
  subjects of, 31, 47, 81, 114, 127, 136–50,
  166, 193–4, 279–304, 470
  ultimate foundation of, 89–94, 200, 231–3
international law and municipal law, 151–
  78, 214, 216–30, 473–5
  municipal law as defence to claim, 230
  transformation, doctrine of, 285–6
international law as law, 9, 11–36, 193,
  194–200, 265, 347
International Law Association, 100 n.,
  528
  Resolution on Pact of Paris (1934),
  346
International Law Commission, 26, 107–8,
  110, 445–530
  character of work, 521–7
  consultation with Governments, 526
  creative function, 524
  drafts, status of, 465
  method of work, 521–30
  Rapporteurs, role of, 528
  selection of topics, 516–21
  Statute, adoption of, 451
  Statute: Art. 18. 468, 516, 521, 526;
    Art. 19. 526, 527, 528;
    Art. 20. 521, 522, 524;
    Art. 22. 529;
    Art. 23. 464–6;
international lawyer, function of, 252–6
international legislation, 13–14, 59, 111,
  115, 196, 412–15, 432–44
  European Economic Community, 176
international organizations
  subjects of international law, 136, 138,
  471
  treaty-making power, 138–9, 471
international penal law, 471, 475
International Prize Court, proposed, 145,
  287, 289
international society, 51, 193, 210, 232
  structure of, 27, 30 n.
international tribunals
  access by individuals, 145, 286–95
  compulsory jurisdiction, absence of, 23–5,
  197, 409, 443
  decision *ex aequo et bono*, 424–6
  evidence, rules of, 272
  individual and foreign State, suits
  between, 290
  peaceful change and, 419–25
international tribunals, decisions of, as
  source, 78–80, 246–7
inter-temporal international law, 129–34
intervention
  humanitarian, 302–4
  premature recognition, 312
  prohibition of, 476
  recognition of Governments, 323

534

INDEX

intervention (*cont.*)
    subversive activity, 403–6
Ireland
    Constitution, 1937, international law provision, 174 n.
Islamic international relations, 121
Italy, Constitution, 1948, international law provision, 174 n.

Japan, relations with Western Powers, 119
Jellinek, theory of international law, 210
judgments, international, enforcement of, 18
judicial acts, communication of, 505
judicial legislation, 419–21
judicial precedent, 274
jurisdiction
    aliens, crimes committed abroad, 272, 488–91
    aliens, crime committed in territorial waters, 155 n.
    exercise of, in foreign territory, 487–8
    foreign acts of State, recognition of, 481–2
    foreign ships in port, 272
    limits of State competence, 217, 487–8
    person arrested contrary to international law, 344, 488
    ship seized contrary to international law, 343
    territorial basis, 369
    territorial, obligations of, 486
    wrongful seizure as basis, 343, 488
jurisdictional immunities of States, 64, 455, 482–6
jurisprudence, international law in, 193–215, 242, 443
jus cogens, 87, 113–14, 234
jus gentium and *jus inter gentes*, 194
jus gentium, modern, 74, 304

Kaufmann, on law of co-ordination, 211–13
Kellogg Pact (1928), 17–18, 22, 102, 116, 198, 229 n., 354, 380, 393, 411, 493
    customary international law and, 241, 253
    League Resolution on non-recognition (1932), 321, 339, 346
    neutrality and, 241, 254 n., 344 n.
    non-recognition, Stimson Doctrine, 338–41, 346, 380
Kelsen, theory of international law, 55, 90 n., 214, 217, 311

law
    Anglo-American and Continental concepts of, 274
    command, as, 208–9
    concept of, 55, 195
    external nature, 194, 197–8
    growth of community and, 263
    morality and, 13, 46, 194, 198, 205

law merchant, 167, 169
law of nature, 28, 33, 46
law-making treaties, 59, 102 n.
laws of war
    individual responsibility for violation of, 141
Laws and Customs of War on Land, Hague Convention (1899), 101
League of Nations
    Assembly, powers under Art. 19. 429
    Assembly, recommendation of, effect, 431
    codification under, 102–4, 452–3, 462, 516–17: *see also* Hague Codification Conference (1930)
    conciliation by, 416–18
    Council, composition of, 437
    non-recognition, Resolution on (1932), 321, 339, 346, 380
    resolutions, legal effect, 346
    subject of international law, as, 140
League of Nations Covenant
    amendment of, 436
    Art. 10. 346, 392;
    Art. 11. 438;
    Art. 15. 432 n., 438;
    Art. 16. 198, 199, 254 n., 347, 394;
    Art. 19. 355, 428–32;
    Art. 20. 359;
    Art. 23. 501
    drafting, 438
    sanctions provision, 198, 199, 254 n., 347, 394
leases, international, 372
legal system, requirements of, 12
legislation, international, 13–14, 59, 111, 115, 196, 412–15, 432–44
    European Economic Community, 176
legislative function, 13, 15
litispendance, principles of, 245
Lorimer, on recognition, 316

Manchukuo, State of, 318, 339, 348 n.
Mandated territory, petitions of inhabitants, 290
Mandates
    jurisdiction of P.C.I.J. in respect of, 299
    sovereignty and, 373–4
maritime collisions, criminal jurisdiction, 489
maritime law, 167, 169
Mexico, Estrada doctrine on recognition, 326
Military Obligations in Cases of Double Nationality, Protocol (1930), 104
minorities treaties, 145, 290, 299
Mixed Arbitral Tribunals, individual access, 287, 470
Mixed Claims Commission, U.S.A.–Germany, general principles of law, use of, 244

535

INDEX

modern international law, 117–22

modus et conventio vincunt legem, 234, 351

monism, as basis of international law, 213–15

monist and dualist theories, 152, 216–17, 228

Montevideo Conventions, private international law, 41 n.

moral reparation, 395

morality and international law, 46–9, 281–2, 358

morality and law, 13, 46, 194, 198, 205, 268

municipal courts, decisions of, as source, 80–5, 239–40, 247–9

enforcement of international law in, 20

municipal law and international law: *see* international law and municipal law

Nansen passports, 302

national conceptions of international law, 126–9, 270

National-Socialist conception of international law, 127 n., 270

nationality

cession of territory and, 493

Convention and Protocols (1930), 104, 260, 301, 454, 458, 482, 498

denationalization, 300, 423

expatriation, right of, 499

grant of, 423

loss of, German Federal Constitution, 176

nationality of claims, 513

international protection of individual rights, 299–300, 302

natural law, 28, 33, 46, 52, 74, 76–7, 121, 236, 246, 358

natural right, *potentia*, 206

negotiation, obligation to undertake, 415

neminem laedit qui jure suo utitur, 385

nemo judex in re sua, 236, 245, 252

Netherlands Constitution, 1956, provision on treaties, 173, 177

neutral nationals, freedom of action, 403

neutral private property, destruction of, 388

neutral territorial waters, ship seized in, 344

neutrality, Kellogg Pact and, 241, 254 n., 344 n.

neutrality rules, Scandinavian States, 99

New Hebrides *condominium*, 370

new States, 57, 238

non liquet, 57, 68, 75, 94–97, 243, 246, 450

non-recognition, doctrine of, 338–41, 346–8

non-nationals, protection of, 145

non-retroactivity, principle of, 133–4

non-State entities, as subjects of international law, 138

Norway, title to Jan Mayen Island, 337

Nuremberg, International Military Tribunal, 134 n., 141, 148, 470, 514

Agreement establishing, 143

Charter of, 470, 471, 475, 514

General Assembly resolution (1946), 470–1

observance, validity of legal rules and, 20

occupation, acquisition of territory by, 379–80, 492

offences against the law of nations, 142, 166 n., 169 n.

Pacific Settlement of Disputes, Hague Convention (1899), 101

General Act (1928), 102

Pact of Paris (1928): *see* General Treaty for the Renunciation of War

pacta sunt servanda, 210, 233, 310, 356

Panama Canal Zone, sovereignty over, 372

Panama, recognition of, 315–16

Pan-American Conferences, codification, 104–5 n.

particular international law, 112

peaceful change, 408–44

Permanent Court of International Justice

costs, 391

decision *ex aequo et bono*, 424–5

Optional Clause, British acceptance (1930), 410

Statute, 102, 204, 233, 241–2, 244, 409

personality of groups, concept of, 47 n., 282

personality, international, 136, 138–41

Peru, request for revision of treaties, 429

piracy, 141, 250, 284, 455, 495–6

ports, jurisdiction over foreign ships in, 272

positivist theories, 82 n., 207–13, 238, 240, 242–4, 268, 310

preclusion: *see* Estoppel

prescription, 70, 201

acquisitive, 345, 377–9, 491

extinctive, 514

primitive communities, law in, 10, 11–12, 199

private international law

public international law and, 31, 36–43

treaties on, 40–2

prize courts, international character, 165 n., 221

prize, ship in neutral territorial waters, 344

propaganda, subversive, 403–6, 476

public opinion, as means of law enforcement, 18, 199

public ships, jurisdictional immunities, 484

publicists, teachings of: *see* Writers

quieta non movere, 378

INDEX

reason and justice as source of international law, 32

rebels, as subjects of international law, 137–8

recognition
legal duty of, 23
legal principle, matter of, 197, 229 n., 478

recognition of belligerency, 138, 329–335
American Civil War, 330, 331

recognition of Governments, 309, 323–9, 479
criteria of, 324–8
effectiveness, principle of, 328–9
Executive function, 324
international obligations, fulfilment of, 327
legitimacy, test of, 324–7
nature of, 323–4
non-recognition clauses in treaties, 339
non-recognition, effects, 309

recognition of insurgents, 328, 332, 335–6

recognition of States, 308 -22, 477–9
collective act, as, 321–2
declaratory or constitutive, 309–11, 318–20
discretionary character, 308, 314, 423
duty to recognize, 312–14
existing international law and, 57
non-recognition clauses in treaties, 339
premature recognition, 312, 315, 319, 321
retroactive effect, 319
rôle of, 317–21

recognition of territorial titles, 337–48
qualified, 337–8

Refugees
Convention on International Status (1933), 302 .
from Germany, Convention (1936), 302

regional arrangements, 113

regional international law, 27, 113, 124

Renunciation of War, General Treaty for (1928), 17–18, 22, 102, 116, 198, 229 n., 354, 380, 393, 411, 493
customary international law and, 241, 253
League resolution on non-recognition (1932), 321, 339, 346
neutrality and, 241, 254 n., 344 n.
non-recognition, Stimson Doctrine, 338–341, 346, 380

reprisals, 18, 198, 393

res judicata, 203

restitutio in integrum, 391

revision of status quo, 408–44

revision of the law, 431

rivers, international, 27, 487
diversion of, 385

Roman law, 78 n.

Rousseau, general will, 55

sanctions, League Covenant provisions, 19, 254 n.
U.N. Charter provisions, 19

Scandinavian States, codification among, 99

Scelle, law of symbiosis, 55

Second World War, doctrine of international law and, 10 n.

self-defence, 17, 202, 476–7

self-help, 16, 198, 200

self-preservation, 23, 197, 202, 211

servitudes, 201, 374–5

sic utere tuo ut alienum non laedas, 385, 422

sources of international law, 51–135, 231–60, 472
basis and causes, 51–3
completeness of, 94–8
consent of States, 9, 32, 52, 56–8, 66, 196, 208–13, 242–4, 267, 309, 443
customary international law: q.v.
evidence of law and, 51, 53, 79, 237–41, 247
general principles of law: q.v.
hierarchy of, 55, 86–94, 234, 244
international tribunals, decisions of, 78–80, 246–7
municipal courts, decisions of, 80–5, 239–40, 247–9
scope of validity of, 112–34
treaties, 51, 53, 58–61, 234–7
writers, 249–56, 465

sovereign immunity, 64, 455, 482–6

sovereignty
criticism of, 443
renunciation of, constitutional provisions, 176–7

Soviet Government, non-recognition of, 327

Soviet views on international law, 126, 128 n., 270

Spain, Constitution, 1931, international law provision, 174 n.

Spanish Civil War, recognition of belligerency, 335 n.

Spinoza, on inter-State relations, 205–7, 265

State and individual, analogy between, 205–7

State practice, decisions of courts, 82

State responsibility, 383–407, 512–14
absolute liability, 399, 401–2
Codification Conference (1930), 104, 512
consequences of liability, 390–7
criminal responsibility, 513
fault, requirement of, 398–402, 513
Harvard Draft Convention, 513

537

INDEX

State responsibility (*cont.*)
 imputability, 399–402, 513
 individuals, acts of, propaganda, 403–6
 insurgents, acts of, 336
 inter-temporal law, 133–4
 judgments of municipal courts, for, 230
 municipal law, relevance of, 151–2, 161
 non-discrimination, plea of, 386–90
 private associations, for acts of, 406
 private law principles, 202
 rioters, acts of, 400, 513
 sources of, 383–6
State succession, 479–81
 private law analogies, 202
 treaties, legislative, 116
Statehood, requirements of, 316, 368
stateless persons, rights of, 145, 503
 international protection of, 300–2
statelessness
 abolition of, 500
 avoidance of, German Federal Constitution, 176
 Protocol on (1930), 104, 260, 301, 500
States
 creation of international law rules, 305
 equality of, 128, 217, 436–8, 443
 existence of, question of fact, 313, 314–16. 319
 fundamental rights and duties, 475–7
 normal subjects of international law, 194, 279
 personality of, 282–4, 392
 punishment of, 390–7
 rights and duties, as individual rights and duties, 147–9, 225, 283–5, 392, 402, 403
statutes
 presumption of conformity with international law, 157, 170, 228
 supremacy of: in English law, 163–5, 221; in general, 227
Stimson Doctrine of non-recognition, 338–41, 346, 380
subjects of international law, 31, 47, 81, 114, 127, 136–50, 166, 193–4, 279–307, 469–72
subversive acts and propaganda, 403–6
succession of Governments, 481
succession of States: *see* State succession
Sudan, Anglo-Egyptian *condominium*, 371
Switzerland, statement on codification (1931), 458 n.

Tangier, International City, 370
territorial change, 429, 430
Territorial Sea and Contiguous Zone, Convention (1958), 98
territorial sovereignty, 367–82, 491–3
 cession, effect of, 421, 493

condominium, 370–2
 nature of, 376
 'object' theory, 367–70, 382
 private law concepts, 201, 367–8, 377, 380
 residual, 372–3
 territorial sovereignty, acquisition of, 491
 conquest, 202, 241, 252, 380–1, 492
 occupation, 379–80, 492
 prescription, 70, 201, 345, 377–9, 491
 recognition, 337–48
 Roman law concepts, 377
 time element, 130
territorial waters
 Codification Conference (1930), 104, 376, 377, 497
 contiguous zone and, 375–7, 497–8
territory, use for injurious purposes, 487, 513
Terrorism, Convention on (1937), 507
title, acquisition of: *see* Territorial sovereignty, acquisition of
treaties, 351–6, 507–9
 binding force, 89
 codification, customary law and, 457–8, 467 n.
 codification of law of, 507–9
 conclusion of, majority vote, by, 13
 contractual character, 351, 361, 365
 customary law, as evidence of, 60, 237
 derogating from customary law, 87, 234
 duress and, 47, 54, 87, 203, 241, 341, 352–4
 English law and, 158–61, 225–7, 474
 federal States, 475
 force majeure, plea of, 356
 frustration, 355, 428
 immoral obligations, 357
 inconsistent obligations, 203, 234, 338, 341, 359–61
 individuals, rights and duties under, 142, 288–90, 470
 interpretation of, 88, 203, 361–6; constitutional treaties, 133; customary international law and, 235; effective interpretation, 95, 253, 364, 508; Executive, by, 174–5; general principles of law and, 236; intention of parties, 203, 253, 361; inter-temporal law, 132–3; liberal, 364, 508; 'political' treaties, 362; private law terms, 204; restrictive, 362, 364; subsequent conduct, 133; *travaux préparatoires*, 272, 363–4, 508
 invalid, 341, 357, 359–60
 'law-making', 14, 236–7, 351, 365, 414
 legal content, 252–3
 legislative effect, 236–7, 351
 multilateral, modification of, 360
 non-parties, position of, 60, 88, 234

538

INDEX

treaties (*cont.*)
  private international law, on, 40–2
  private law concepts, 202–3
  rebus sic stantibus doctrine, 197, 203, 206, 355–7, 421–2, 428, 431, 509
  reconsideration of, League Covenant, under, 428–32
  registration of, 139, 147
  revision clauses, 415
  rights and duties of individuals under, 142, 288–90, 470
  source of international law, as, 51, 53, 58–61, 234–7
  State succession, 480
  U.S.A., law of, 159, 170, 474
  unilateral denunciation, 355, 431
  universal international law, comprising, 115
tribal communities, international law and, 122
Triepel, theory of international law, 209, 216, 219, 226
Turkey, admission to Concert of Europe, 118

ubi societas ibi jus, 28
unanimity, rule of, 88, 109, 111, 127, 236, 259, 436, 438, 466 n.
unification of law, treaties for, 40–1 n.
unilateral declaration, effect of, 346
United Kingdom, statements on recognition, 315, 330
United Nations: *see also* Charter of the United Nations
  international personality of, 140
  specialized agencies, capacity before International Court, 139
United States of America
  Act of Congress, supremacy of, 170
  adoption of international law, 169–71, 218
  Civil War: blockade, 329 n.; Instructions for Armies in the Field, 99 n.; recognition of belligerency, 330, 331
  Constitution, proposed Bricker amendment, 159 n.
  Denmark, refusal to recognize belligerent rights, 332
  executive agreements, status of, 171
  Naval War Code (1900), 101 n.
  Neutrality Act, 1818, ships for revolting colony, 326 n.

Panama, recognition of, 315–16
recognition of, by France, 320
reservation to acceptance of jurisdiction of I.C.J., 25
statements on recognition, 313–14, 324–5
Stimson Doctrine, non-recognition, 338–41, 346
'suggestion' of State Department on immunity, 163
treaties and internal law, 159, 170, 474
universal international law, 113–17, 120–1, 166, 261, 267–75
Upper Silesian Convention (1922), 145–6
Upper Silesian Mixed Tribunal, 470
uti possidetis doctrine, 123 n., 269

Vatican City, international personality, 306, 318
Vattel
  on punishment of States, 393
  on treaty interpretation, 361
Venezuela, Constitution, international law provision, 473
Versailles, Treaty of
  individual claims against Germany, 145
  political inequality, 128, 224 n.
voluntas civitatis maximae est servanda, 233

waiver of illegality, title and, 345
war
  as means of changing law, 409, 411
  as sanction of international law, 17, 393
  constitutional provisions prohibiting, 175–6
  General Treaty for Renunciation of (1928), 17–18, 22, 102, 116, 198, 229 n., 354, 380, 393, 411, 493
  illegal, application of laws of war, 344
  right to resort to, 22–3, 197, 203, 206, 207, 211, 212, 308, 353–4, 229 n.
war, laws of
  Anglo-American and Continental practices, 272
  individual responsibility for violation, 141
war crimes, 19, 141, 284
  superior orders, plea of, 284–5
will of states as source of law, 52
writers, source of international law, 249–56, 465

Zanzibar, British Protectorate, 338

539

For EU product safety concerns, contact us at Calle de José Abascal, 56–1°,
28003 Madrid, Spain or eugpsr@cambridge.org.

 www.ingramcontent.com/pod-product-compliance
Ingram Content Group UK Ltd.
Pitfield, Milton Keynes, MK11 3LW, UK
UKHW010855060825
461487UK00012B/1144